The Making of the Slavs

This book offers a new approach to the problem of Slavic ethnicity in south-eastern Europe between *c.* 500 and *c.* 700, from the perspective of current anthropological theories.

The conceptual emphasis here is on the relation between material culture and ethnicity. The author demonstrates that the history of the Sclavenes and the Antes begins only at around AD 500. He also points to the significance of the archaeological evidence, which suggests that specific artifacts may have been used as identity markers. This evidence also indicates the role of local leaders in building group boundaries and in leading successful raids across the Danube. The names of many powerful leaders appear in written sources, some being styled "kings." Because of these military and political developments, Byzantine authors began employing names such as Sclavenes and Antes in order to make sense of the process of group identification that was taking place north of the Danube frontier. Slavic ethnicity is therefore shown to be a Byzantine invention.

FLORIN CURTA is Assistant Professor of Medieval History, University of Florida

D1481551

Cambridge Studies in Medieval Life and Thought

THE MAKING OF THE SLAVS

Cambridge Studies in Medieval Life and Thought
Fourth Series

General Editor:

D. E. LUSCOMBE
Research Professor of Medieval History, University of Sheffield

Advisory Editors:

CHRISTINE CARPENTER
Reader in Medieval English History, University of Cambridge, and Fellow of New Hall

ROSAMOND McKITTERICK
Professor of Medieval History, University of Cambridge, and Fellow of Newnham College

The series Cambridge Studies in Medieval Life and Thought was inaugurated by G. G. Coulton in 1921; Professor D. E. Luscombe now acts as General Editor of the Fourth Series, with Dr Christine Carpenter and Professor Rosamond McKitterick as Advisory Editors. The series brings together outstanding work by medieval scholars over a wide range of human endeavour extending from political economy to the history of ideas.

For a list of titles in the series, see end of book.

THE MAKING OF THE SLAVS

History and Archaeology of the Lower Danube Region,
c. 500–700

FLORIN CURTA

CAMBRIDGE
UNIVERSITY PRESS

PUBLISHED BY THE PRESS SYNDICATE OF THE UNIVERSITY OF CAMBRIDGE
The Pitt Building, Trumpington Street, Cambridge, United Kingdom

CAMBRIDGE UNIVERSITY PRESS
The Edinburgh Building, Cambridge CB2 2RU, UK
40 West 20th Street, New York, NY 10011–4211, USA
10 Stamford Road, Oakleigh, VIC 3166, Australia
Ruiz de Alarcón 13, 28014 Madrid, Spain
Dock House, The Waterfront, Cape Town 8001, South Africa

http://www.cambridge.org

First published 2001

Printed in the United Kingdom at the University Press, Cambridge

Typeface Monotype Bembo 11/12pt   *System* QuarkXPress™   [SE]

A catalogue record for this book is available from the British Library

Library of Congress cataloguing in publication data
Curta, Florin.
The making of the slavs: history and archaeology of the Lower Danube Region,
c. 500–700 / by Florin Curta.
p.   cm. – (Cambridge Studies in Medieval Life and Thought)
Includes bibliographical references and index.
ISBN 0 521 80202 4
1. Slavs – Danube River Region – History.   2. Slavs – Balkan Peninsula – History.   3.
Danube River Region. – Antiquities, Slavic.   4. Slavs – Ethnicity.   5. Slavs – History.   6.
Excavations (Archaeology) – Danube River Region.   I. Title.   II. Series.
DR49.26.C87 2001
949.6′01–dc21   00–052915

ISBN 0 521 80202 4 hardback

CONTENTS

FIGURES

List of figures

TABLES

ACKNOWLEDGMENTS

In the process of researching and writing this book, I have benefited from the help and advice of many individuals. The following are just a few who contributed in the completion of this book. My deepest academic debt is to Radu Harhoiu from the Archaeological Institute in Bucharest, who guided my training as an archaeologist and encouraged me to think historically about artifacts. It is he who gave me the idea of studying the Slavs in the context of the sixth-century Barbaricum and called my attention to parallel developments in the Carpathian basin and the steppes north of the Black Sea. I am also grateful to Alan Stahl for his interesting criticism and excellent advice on the interpretation of hoards.

I wish to thank Deborah Deliyannis, Lucian Rosu, Allen Zagarell, and Speros Vryonis for their guidance and support. Among the individuals to whom I also owe personal debts of gratitude, I would like to acknowledge Igor Corman, Alexandru Popa, and Ioan Tentiuc from Chişinău, Anna Kharalambieva from Varna, Ioan Stanciu from Cluj-Napoca, Mihailo Milinković from Belgrade, Vasile Dupoi and Adrian Canache from Bucharest. They all generously gave me encouragement, suggestions, and access to unpublished material. I am also indebted to the American Numismatic Society for its financial assistance during the Summer Seminar of 1995 in New York. I also wish to acknowledge Genevra Kornbluth, Patrick Geary, Larry Wolff, Robert Hayden, and the participants in the University of Michigan conference on vocabularies of identity in Eastern Europe (1998), who expressed their interest in and encouraged me to continue research on the Slavic archaeology and its political use.

Finally, I am immeasurably indebted to my wife Lucia and my daughter Ana, who never let me give up. Without them, this book would not have existed.

ABBREVIATIONS

AAC	*Acta Archaeologica Carpathica* (Cracow, 1958–).
AAnt	*American Antiquity* (Menasha, 1935–).
AAnth	*American Anthropologist* (Washington, 1888–).
AClass	*Acta Classica* (Kaapstad, 1958–).
AClassDebrecen	*Acta Classica Universitatis Scientiarum Debreceniensis* (Debrecen, 1965–).
ActaAntHung	*Acta Antiqua Academiae Scientiarum Hungaricae* (Budapest, 1951–).
ActaArchHung	*Acta Archaeologica Academiae Scientiarum Hungaricae* (Budapest, 1951–).
Actes IX	*Actes du IX-e Congrès international d'études sur les frontières romaines, Mamaia 6–13 septembre 1972.* Ed. Dionisie M. Pippidi. Bucharest and Cologne: Editura Academiei RSR and Böhlau, 1974.
Actes X	*Actes du X-e Congrès international d'archéologie chrétienne. Thessalonique, 28 septembre – 4 octobre 1980.* 2 vols. Vatican and Thessaloniki: Pontificio Istituto di Archeologia Cristiana and Hetaireia Makedonikon Spoudon, 1984.
Actes XI	*Actes du XI-e Congrès international d'archéologie chrétienne. Lyon, Vienne, Grenoble, Genève et Aoste (21–28 septembre 1986).* Ed. Noël Duval. 3 vols. Rome: Ecole Française de Rome, 1989.
Actes XIIa	*Actes du XII-e Congrès international d'études byzantines (Ochride, 10–16 septembre 1961).* 2 vols. Belgrade: Comité Yougoslave des Etudes Byzantines, 1963.
Actes XIIb	*Actes du XII-e Congrès international des sciences préhistoriques et protohistoriques, Bratislava, 1–7 septembre 1991.* Ed. Juraj Pavuj. 4 vols. Bratislava: VEDA, 1993.

List of abbreviations

Actes XIV	*Actes du XIV-e Congrès international des études byzantines, Bucarest, 6–12 septembre 1971.* Ed. Mihai Berza and Eugen Stănescu. 3 vols. Bucharest: Editura Academiei RSR, 1974–6.
AE	*American Ethnologist* (Washington, 1974–).
AEMA	*Archivum Eurasiae Medii Aevi* (Wiesbaden, 1975–).
AJA	*American Journal of Archaeology* (New York, 1885–).
Akten 11	*Limes. Akten des 11. internationalen Limeskongresses Székesfehérvár 30.8–6.9. 1976.* Ed. Jenő Fitz. Budapest: Akadémiai kiadó, 1977.
Akten 13	*Studien zu den Militärgrenzen Roms III. 13. internationaler Limeskongreß Aalen 1983. Vorträge.* Stuttgart: Konrad Theiss, 1986.
Akten 14	*Akten des 14. internationalen Limeskongresses 1986 in Carnuntum.* Ed. Hermann Vetters and Manfred Kandler. Vienna: Verlag der Österreichische Akademie der Wissenschaften, 1990.
AM	*Arheologia Moldovei* (Bucharest, 1961–).
AMN	*Acta Musei Napocensis* (Cluj, 1964–).
AMT	*Archaeological Method and Theory* (Tucson, 1989–93).
Anthropology	*The Anthropology of Ethnicity. Beyond "Ethnic Groups and Boundaries."* Ed. Hans Vermeulen and Cora Govers. The Hague: Het Spinhuis, 1994.
Approaches	*Archaeological Approaches to Cultural Identity.* Ed. Stephen Shennan. London, Boston, and Sydney: Unwin Hyman, 1989.
ARA	*Annual Review of Anthropology* (Palo Alto, 1972–).
ArchBulg	*Archaeologia Bulgarica* (Sofia, 1997–).
ArchÉrt	*Archaeologiai Értesitö* (Budapest, 1881–).
ArchIug	*Archaeologia Iugoslavica* (Belgrade, 1954–).
ArchMéd	*Archeologie Médiévale* (Paris, 1971–).
ArchPol	*Archaeologia Polona* (Wrocław, 1958–).
ArchRoz	*Archeologické Rozhledy* (Prague, 1949–).
Argenterie	*Argenterie romaine et byzantine. Actes de la table ronde, Paris 11–13 octobre 1983.* Ed. Noël Duval, François Baratte, and Ernest Will. Paris: De Boccard, 1988.
ASGE	*Arkheologicheskii Sbornik Gosudarstvennogo Ermitazha* (Leningrad, 1959–).
ASSAH	*Anglo-Saxon Studies in Archaeology and History* (Oxford, 1979–).
AT	*Antiquité Tardive* (Paris, 1993–).
AV	*Arheološki Vestnik* (Ljubljana, 1950–).

Avari	*Gli Avari. Un popolo d'Europa.* Ed. Giàn Carlo Menis. Udine: Arti Grafiche Friulane, 1995.
Awarenforschungen	*Awarenforschungen.* Ed. Falko Daim. 2 vols. Vienna: Institut für Ur- und Frühgeschichte der Universität Wien, 1992.
Balcanica	*Balcanica Posnaniensia* (Poznań, 1984–).
Baltic	*From the Baltic to the Black Sea. Studies in Medieval Archaeology.* Ed. David Austin and Leslie Alcock. London: Unwin Hyman, 1990.
Barbaren	*Das Reich und die Barbaren.* Ed. Evangelos Chrysos and Andreas Schwarcz. Vienna and Cologne: Böhlau, 1989.
BCH	*Bulletin de Correspondance Hellénique* (Athens and Paris, 1877–).
BE	*Balkansko ezikoznanie* (Sofia, 1959–).
Berichte	*Berichte über den II. internationalen Kongreß für slawische Archäologie. Berlin, 24.-28. August 1970.* Ed. Joachim Herrmann and Karl-Heinz Otto. 2 vols. Berlin: Akademie-Verlag, 1973.
BHR	*Bulgarian Historical Review* (Sofia, 1973–).
BJ	*Bonner Jahrbücher des Rheinischen Landesmuseums in Bonn und des Vereins von Altertumsfreunden im Rheinlande* (Bonn, 1842–).
BMGS	*Byzantine and Modern Greek Studies* (Oxford, 1975–).
BMIM	*Bucureşti. Materiale de istorie şi muzeografie* (Bucharest, 1964–).
BS	*Balkan Studies* (Thessaloniki, 1960–).
BSAF	*Bulletin de la Société Nationale des Antiquaires de France* (Paris, 1871–).
BSNR	*Buletinul Societăţii Numismatice Române* (Bucharest, 1904–).
Bucureşti	*Bucureştii de odinioară în lumina săpăturilor arheologice.* Ed. I. Ionaşcu. Bucharest: Editura Ştiinţifică, 1959.
Bulgaria	*Ancient Bulgaria. Papers Presented to the International Symposium on the Ancient History and Archaeology of Bulgaria, University of Nottingham, 1981.* Ed. Andrew G. Poulter. Nottingham: University of Nottingham, 1983.
BV	*Bayerische Vorgeschichtsblätter* (Munich, 1921–).
ByzF	*Byzantinische Forschungen* (Amsterdam, 1966–).
ByzZ	*Byzantinische Zeitschrift* (Munich, 1892–).

CAB	*Cercetări Arheologice în Bucureşti* (Bucharest, 1963–).
CAH	*Communicationes Archaeologicae Hungariae* (Budapest, 1981–).
CAnth	*Current Anthropology* (Chicago, 1960–).
CCARB	*Corso di Cultura sull'Arte Ravennate e Bizantina* (Ravenna, 1955–).
Christentum	*Das Christentum in Bulgarien und auf der übrigen Balkanhalbinsel in der Spätantike und im frühen Mittelalter.* Ed. Vasil Giuzelev and Renate Pillinger. Vienna: Verein "Freunde des Hauses Wittgenstein," 1987.
CIG	*Corpus Inscriptionum Graecarum*
CIL	*Corpus Inscriptionum Latinarum*
City	*City, Towns, and Countryside in the Early Byzantine Era.* Ed. Robert L. Hohlfelder. New York: Columbia University Press, 1982.
Conference 18	*Ethnicity and Culture. Proceedings of the Eighteenth Annual Conference of the Archaeological Association of the University of Calgary.* Ed. Réginald Auger et al. Calgary: University of Calgary Archaeological Association, 1987.
Congress 8	*Roman Frontier Studies 1969. Eighth International Congress of Limesforschung.* Ed. Eric Birley, Brian Dobson, and Michael Jarrett. Cardiff: University of Wales Press, 1974.
Constantinople	*Constantinople and its Hinterland. Papers from the Twenty-Seventh Spring Symposium of Byzantine Studies, Oxford, April 1993.* Ed. Cyril Mango and Gilbert Dagron. Aldershot: Variorum, 1995.
Corinthia	*The Corinthia in the Roman Period Including the Papers Given at a Symposium Held at the Ohio State University on 7–9 March, 1991.* Ed. Timothy E. Gregory. Ann Arbor: Journal of Roman Archaeology Supplementary Series, 1993.
CPh	*Classical Philology* (Chicago, 1906–).
CRAI	*Comptes Rendus de l'Académie des Inscriptions et Belles-Lettres* (Paris, 1857–).
CSSH	*Comparative Studies in Society and History* (London and New York, 1958–).
Development	*Development and Decline. The Evolution of Sociopolitical Organization.* Ed. Henri J. M. Claessen, Pieter van de Velde, and M. Estellie Smith. South

List of abbreviations

Hadley: Bergin and Garvey, 1985.

Dnestr   *Slaviane na Dnestre i Dunae. Sbornik nauchnykh trudov.* Ed. V. D. Baran, R. V. Terpilovskii, and A. T. Smilenko. Kiev: Naukova Dumka, 1983.

Dokladi   *Vtori mezhdunaroden kongres po bălgaristika, Sofiia, 23 mai–3 iuni 1986 g. Dokladi 6: Bălgarskite zemi v drevnostta. Bălgariia prez srednovekovieto.* Ed. Khristo Khristov et al. Sofia: BAN, 1987.

Donau   *Die Völker an der mittleren und unteren Donau im fünften und sechsten Jahrhundert.* Ed. Herwig Wolfram and Falko Daim. Vienna: Verlag der Österreichischen Akademie der Wissenschaften, 1980.

DOP   *Dumbarton Oaks Papers* (Washington, 1941–).

Drevnosti   *Rannesrednevekovye vostochnoslavianskie drevnosti. Sbornik statei.* Ed. P. N. Tret'iakov. Leningrad: Nauka, 1974.

DS   *Đerdapske Sveske* (Belgrade, 1980–).

EAZ   *Ethnographisch-archäologische Zeitschrift* (Berlin, 1960–).

EB   *Etudes Balkaniques* (Sofia, 1964–).

EH   *Etudes Historiques* (Sofia, 1960–).

Eirene   *From Late Antiquity to Early Byzantium. Proceedings of the Byzantinological Symposium in the 16th International Eirene Conference.* Ed. Vladimír Vavřínek. Prague: Academia, 1985.

EME   *Early Medieval Europe* (Harlow, 1992–).

ERS   *Ethnic and Racial Studies* (London and New York, 1978–).

FA   *Folia Archaeologica* (Budapest, 1939–).

Familie   *Familie, Staat und Gesellschaftsformation. Grundprobleme vorkapitalistischer Epochen einhundert Jahren nach Friedrich Engels' Werk, "Der Ursprung der Familie, des Privateigentums und des Staates".* Ed. Joachim Herrmann and Jens Köhn. Berlin: Akademie Verlag, 1988.

Festschrift   *Studien zur vor- und frühgeschichtlichen Archäologie. Festschrift für Joachim Werner zum 65. Geburtstag.* Ed. Georg Kossack and Günter Ulbert. 2 vols. Munich: C. H. Beck, 1974.

FO   *Folia orientalia* (Cracow, 1959–).

FS   *Frühmittelalterliche Studien* (Berlin, 1967–).

List of abbreviations

Germanen	*Germanen, Hunnen und Awaren. Schätze der Völkerwanderungszeit.* Ed. Gerhard Bott and Walter Meier-Arendt. Nuremberg: Germanisches Nationalmuseum, 1987.
GMSB	*Godishnik na muzeite ot Severna Bălgariia* (Varna, 1975–).
Gosudarstva	*Rannefeodal′nye gosudarstva i narodnosti (iuzhnye i zapadnye slaviane VI–XII vv.).* Ed. G. G. Litavrin Moscow: Nauka, 1991.
GOTR	*Greek Orthodox Theological Review* (Brookline, 1954–).
GZMBH	*Glasnik Zemaljskog Muzeja Bosne i Hercegovine u Sarajevu* (Sarajevo, 1967–).
Historiographie	*Historiographie im frühen Mittelalter.* Ed. Anton Scharer and Georg Scheibelreiter. Vienna and Munich: R. Oldenbourg, 1994.
Hommes	*Hommes et richesses dans l'Empire byzantin.* Ed. Gilbert Dagron et al. 2 vols. Paris: P. Lethielleux, 1989–91.
Iatrus	*Iatrus-Krivina. Spätantike Befestigung und frühmittelalterliche Siedlung an der unteren Donau.* 5 vols. Berlin: Akademie Verlag, 1979–95.
IBAI	*Izvestiia na Bălgarskiia Arkheologicheskiia Institut* (after 1950: *Izvestiia na Arkheologicheskiia Institut*) (Sofia, 1921–).
IBID	*Izvestiia na Bălgarskoto Istorichesko Druzhestvo* (Sofia, 1905–).
Identity	*Cultural Identity and Archaeology. The Construction of European Communities.* Ed. Paul Graves-Brown et al. London and New York: Routledge, 1996.
IIAK	*Izvestiia Imperatorskoi Arkheologicheskoi Kommissii* (St. Petersburg, 1901–14).
IIBI	*Izvestiia na Instituta za Bălgarska Istoriia* (after 1957: *Izvestiia na Instituta za Istoriia*)(Sofia, 1951–).
INMV	*Izvestiia na Narodniia Muzei Varna* (Varna, 1965–).
Interaktionen	*Interaktionen der mitteleuropäischen Slawen und anderen Ethnika im 6.–10. Jahrhundert. Symposium Nové Vozokany, 3.–7. Oktober 1983.* Ed. Bohuslav Chropovský. Nitra: Archäologisches Institut der Slowakischen Akademie der Wissenschaften, 1984.
Issledovaniia	*Arkheologicheskie issledovaniia srednevekovykh pamiatnikov v Dnestrovsko-Prutskom mezhdurech′e.* Ed. P. P. Byrnia. Kishinew: Shtiinca, 1985.

xx

List of abbreviations

Istoriia	*Problemi na prabălgarska istoriia i kultura.* Ed. Rasho Rashev. Sofia: BAN, 1989.
IZ	*Istoricheskii zhurnal* (Moscow, 1931–45).
JAA	*Journal of Anthropological Archaeology* (New York, 1982–).
JGO	*Jahrbücher für Geschichte Osteuropas* (Breslau and Wiesbaden, 1936–).
JIES	*Journal of Indo-European Studies* (Washington, 1973–).
JMV	*Jahresschrift für mitteldeutsche Vorgeschichte* (Berlin, 1902–).
JÖB	*Jahrbuch der Österreichischen Byzantinistik* (Vienna, 1969–).
JRA	*Journal of Roman Archaeology* (Ann Arbor, 1988–).
JRGZ	*Jahrbuch des Römisch-Germanischen Zentralmuseums* (Mainz, 1954–).
Karta	*Etnokul'turnaia karta territorii Ukrainskoi SSR v I tys. n. e..* Ed. V. D. Baran, R. V. Terpilovskii, and E. V. Maksimov. Kiev: Naukova Dumka, 1985.
KJVF	*Kölner Jahrbuch für Vor- und Frühgeschichte* (Berlin, 1955–).
KSIA	*Kratkie Soobshcheniia Instituta Arkheologii AN SSSR* (Moscow, 1952–).
Kul'tura	*Slavianskie drevnosti. Etnogenez. Material'naia kul'tura drevnei Rusi. Sbornik nauchnykh trudov.* Ed. V. D. Koroliuk. Kiev: Naukova Dumka, 1980.
Limes	*Der Limes an der unteren Donau von Diokletian bis Heraklios. Vorträge der internationalen Konferenz, Svištov, Bulgarien (1.–5. September 1998).* Ed. Gerda von Bülow and Alexandra Milcheva. Sofia: NOUS, 1999.
MAA	*Macedoniae Acta Archaeologica* (Prilep, 1975–).
MAIET	*Materialy po Arkheologii, Istorii i Etnografii Tavrii* (Simferopol, 1990–).
MAIUAW	*Mitteilungen des Archäologischen Instituts der Ungarischen Akademie der Wissenschaften* (Budapest, 1972–).
Mathematics	*Mathematics and Information Science in Archaeology: A Flexible Framework.* Ed. Albertus Voorrips. Bonn: Holos, 1990.
MCA	*Materiale şi Cercetări de Arheologie* (Bucharest, 1955–).

MEFRA	*Mélanges d'Archéologie et d'Histoire de l'Ecole Française de Rome* (Paris, 1881–).
Mélange	*Zbornik posveten na Boško Babić. Mélange Boško Babić 1924–1984.* ed. Mihailo Apostolski. Prilep: Institut des recherches scientifiques de la culture des anciens Slaves, 1986.
MemAnt	*Memoria Antiquitatis* (Piatra Neamţ, 1969–).
MGH: AA	*Monumenta Germaniae Historica: Auctores Antiquissimi*
MGH: Epistolae	*Monumenta Germaniae Historica: Epistolae*
MGH: SRM	*Monumenta Germaniae Historica: Scriptores Rerum Merovingicarum*
MGH: SS	*Monumenta Germaniae Historica: Scriptores Rerum Germanicarum in Usum Scholarum Separatim Editi*
Nikopolis	*Nikopolis I. Proceedings of the First International Symposium on Nikopolis (23–29 September 1984).* Ed. Evangelos Chrysos. 2 vols. Preveza: Demos Prevezas, 1987.
Noblesse	*La noblesse romaine et les chefs barbares du IIIe au VIIe siècle.* Ed. Françoise Vallet and Michel Kazanski. Saint-Germain-en-Laye: Association Française d'Archéologie Mérovingienne and Musée des Antiquités Nationales, 1995.
NZ	*Novopazarski Zbornik* (Novi Pazar, 1971–).
Obrazovaniia	*Slaviane nakanune obrazovaniia Kievskoi Rusi.* Ed. Boris A. Rybakov. Moscow: Izdatel'stvo Akademii Nauk SSSR, 1963.
P&P	*Past and Present* (Oxford, 1952–).
PA	*Památky Archeologické* (Prague, 1914–).
Palast	*Palast und Hütte. Beiträge zum Bauen und Wohnen im Altertum von Archäologen, Vor- und Frühgeschichtlern.* Ed. Dietrich Papenfuss and Volker Michael Strocka. Mainz: Philipp von Zabern, 1982.
PG	*Patrologiae cursus completus. Series Graeca*
Pliska	*Pliska-Preslav. Prouchvaniia i materiali.* Ed. Zhivka Văzharova. 3 vols. Sofia: BAN, 1979–81.
Praveké	*Praveké a slovanské osídlení Moravy. Sborník k 80. narozeninám Josefa Poulíka.* Ed. Vladimír Nekuda. Brno: Muzejní a vlastivedná společnost v Brne and Archeologický ústav Československé Akademie Ved v Brne, 1990.
Prilozi	*Prilozi Instituta za Arheologiju u Zagrebu* (Zagreb, 1983–).

List of abbreviations

Probleme	*Ausgewählte Probleme europäischer Landnahmen des Früh- und Hochmittelalters.* Ed. Michael Müller-Wille and Reinhard Schneider. 2 vols. Sigmaringen: Jan Thorbecke, 1993.
Problemi	*Problemi seobe naroda u Karpatskoj kotlini. Saopštenja sa naučkog skupa 13.-16. decembre 1976.* Ed. Danica Dimitrijević, Jovan Kovačević, and Zdenko Vinski. Belgrade: Matica Srpska, 1978.
Problemy	*Problemy etnogeneza slavian. Sbornik nauchnykh trudov.* Ed. V. D. Baran. Kiev: Naukova Dumka, 1978.
RA	*Rossiiskaia Arkheologiia* (Moscow, 1992–).
Rapports	*Rapports du III-e Congrès international d'archéologie slave. Bratislava 7–14 septembre 1975.* Ed. Bohuslav Chropovský. 2 vols. Bratislava: VEDA, 1979–81.
RBPH	*Revue Belge de Philologie et d'Histoire* (Brussels, 1922–).
Recherches	*Recherches sur la céramique byzantine.* Ed. V. Déroche and J.-M. Spieser. Athens and Paris: Ecole Française d'Athènes and De Boccard, 1989.
RESEE	*Revue des Etudes Sud-Est Européennes* (Bucharest, 1963–).
RM	*Revista Muzeelor* (after 1974: *Revista Muzeelor şi Monumentelor)*(Bucharest, 1964–).
RP	*Razkopki i Prouchvaniia* (Sofia, 1948–).
RRH	*Revue Roumaine d'Histoire* (Bucharest, 1962–).
Rus'	*Drevniaia Rus' i slaviane.* Ed. T. V. Nikolaeva. Moscow: Nauka, 1978.
RVM	*Rad Vojvodanskih Muzeja* (Novi Sad, 1952–93).
SA	*Sovetskaia Arkheologiia* (Moscow, 1933–).
Sbornik	*Sbornik v chest na akad. Dimităr Angelov.* Ed. Velizar Velkov et al. Sofia: BAN, 1994.
SBS	*Studies in Byzantine Sigillography* (Washington, 1987–).
Schwarzmeerküste	*Die Schwarzmeerküste in der Spätantike und im frühen Mittelalter.* Ed. Renate Pillinger, Anton Pülz, and Hans Vetters. Vienna: Verlag der österreichischen Akademie der Wissenschaften, 1992.
SCIV	*Studii şi Cercetări de Istorie Veche* (after 1974: *Studii şi Cercetări de Istorie Veche şi Arheologie*) (Bucharest, 1950–).
SCN	*Studii şi Cercetări de Numismatică* (Bucharest, 1957–).
SF	*Südost-Forschungen* (Leipzig, 1936–).

List of abbreviations

Simpozijum	*Simpozijum "Predslavenski etnički elementi na Balkanu u etnogenezi južnih Slovena", održan 24–26. oktobra 1968 u Mostaru.* Ed. Alojz Benac. Sarajevo: Akademija Nauka i Umjetnosti Bosne i Hercegovine, 1969.
Sitzungsberichte	*Sitzungsberichte der Kaiserlichen Akademie der Wissenschaften. Philosophisch-historische Klasse (Vienna, 1848–1918).*
SlA	*Slavia Antiqua* (Warsaw, 1948–).
Slavi	*Gli Slavi occidentali e meridionali nell'alto medioevo.* Spoleto: Presso la Sede del Centro, 1983.
Slavianite	*Slavianite i sredizemnomorskiiat sviat VI-XI vek. Mezhdunaroden simpozium po slavianska arkheologiia. Sofiia, 23–29 april 1970.* Ed. Stamen Mikhailov, Sonia Georgieva, and Penka Gakeva. Sofia: BAN, 1973.
SlovArch	*Slovenská Archeológia* (Bratislava, 1952–).
Sosedi	*Drevnie slaviane i ikh sosedi.* Ed. Iu. V. Kukharenko. Moscow: Nauka, 1970.
Soviet	*Soviet Ethnology and Anthropology Today.* Ed. Julian V. Bromley. The Hague and Paris: Mouton, 1974.
SovS	*Sovetskoe Slavianovedenie* (after 1992: *Slavianovedenie*)(Moscow, 1960–).
SP	*Starohrvatska Prosvjeta* (Zagreb, 1949–).
Starozhitnosti	*Slov'iano-rus'ki starozhitnosti.* Ed. V. I. Bydzylia. Kiev: Naukova Dumka, 1969.
Stepi	*Stepi Evrazii v epokhu srednevekov'ia.* Ed. Svetlana A. Pletneva. Moscow: Nauka, 1981.
Struktura	*Etnosocial'naia i politicheskaia struktura rannefeodal'nykh slavianskikh gosudarstv i narodnostei.* Ed. G. G. Litavrin. Moscow: Nauka, 1987.
Studien	*Studien zum 7. Jahrhundert in Byzanz. Probleme der Herausbildung des Feudalismus.* Ed. Helga Köpstein and Friedhelm Winckelmann. Berlin: Akademie Verlag, 1976.
Svod	*Svod drevneishikh pis'mennykh izvestii o slavianakh.* Ed. L. A. Gindin et al. 2 vols. Moscow: Nauka and "Vostochnaia literatura" RAN, 1991/5.
T&MByz	*Travaux et Mémoires du Centre de Recherches d'Histoire et Civilisation Byzantines* (Paris, 1965–).
Trudy	*Trudy V Mezhdunarodnogo Kongressa arkheologov-slavistov, Kiev 18–25 sentiabria 1985.* Ed. Vladimir D. Baran. 4 vols. Kiev: Naukova Dumka, 1988.
Typology	*Essays in Archaeological Typology.* Ed. Robert

	Whallon and James A. Brown. Evanston: Center for American Archaeological Press, 1982.
Uses	*The Uses of Style in Archaeology.* Ed. Margaret W. Conkey and Christine A. Hastorf. Cambridge: Cambridge University Press, 1990.
VAHD	*Vjesnik za Arheologiju i Historiju Dalmatinsku* (Split, 1878–).
VAMZ	*Vjesnik Arheološkog Muzeja u Zagrebu* (Zagreb, 1958–).
VDI	*Vestnik Drevnei Istorii* (Moscow, 1937–).
Verhältnisse	*Ethnische und kulturelle Verhältnisse an der mittleren Donau vom 6. bis zum 11. Jahrhundert.* Ed. Darina Bialeková and Jozef Zábojník. Bratislava: VEDA, 1996.
Villes	*Villes et peuplement dans l'Illyricum protobyzantin. Actes du colloque organisé par l'Ecole française de Rome (Rome, 12–14 mai 1982).* Rome: Ecole Française de Rome, 1984.
Vizantii	*Iz istorii Vizantii i vizantino-vedeniia. Mezhvuzovskii sbornik.* Ed. G. L. Kurbatov. Leningrad: Izdatel'stvo Leningradskogo Universiteta, 1991.
Völker	*Die Völker Südosteuropas im 6. bis 8. Jahrhundert.* Ed. Bernhard Hänsel. Berlin: Südosteuropa-Gesellschaft, 1987.
Voprosy	*Voprosy etnogeneza i etnicheskoi istorii slavian i vostochnykh romancev.* Ed. V. D. Koroliuk. Moscow: Nauka, 1976.
VPS	*Vznik a Počátky Slovanů* (Prague, 1956–72).
VV	*Vizantiiskii Vremennik* (Moscow, 1947–).
WA	*World Archaeology* (London, 1968–).
WMBHL	*Wissenschaftliche Mitteilungen des bosnich-herzegowinischen Landesmuseum* (Sarajevo, 1971–).
WZRostock	*Wissenschaftliche Zeitschrift der Universität Rostock* (Rostock, 1950–75).
Zbirnyk	*Starozhytnosti Rusi-Ukrainy. Zbirnyk naukovykh prac'.* Ed. P. P. Tolochko et al. Kiev: Kiivs'ka Akademyia Evrobyznesu, 1994.
ZC	*Zgodovinski Časopis* (Ljubljana, 1947–).
ZfA	*Zeitschrift für Archäologie* (Berlin, 1967–).
ZfS	*Zeitschrift für Slawistik* (Berlin, 1956–).
ZNM	*Zbornik Narodnog Muzeja* (Belgrade, 1964–).
ZRVI	*Zbornik Radova Vizantološkog Instituta* (Belgrade, 1961–).

INTRODUCTION

Mein Freund, das ist Asien! Es sollte mich wundern, es sollte mich höch-
lichst wundern, wenn da nicht Wendisch-Slawisch-Sarmatisches im Spiele
gewesen wäre.

(Thomas Mann, *Der Zauberberg*)

To many, Eastern Europe is nearly synonymous with *Slavic* Europe. The
equation is certainly not new. To Hegel, the "East of Europe" was the
house of the "great Sclavonic nation," a body of peoples which "has not
appeared as an independent element in the series of phases that Reason
has assumed in the World".[1] If necessary, Europe may be divided into
western and eastern zones along a number of lines, according to numerous criteria. Historians, however, often work with more than one set of
criteria. The debate about the nature of Eastern Europe sprang up in
Western historiography in the days of the Cold War, but despite Oskar
Halecki's efforts explicitly to address the question of a specific chronology and history of Eastern Europe, many preferred to write the history
of Slavic Europe, rather than that of Eastern Europe.[2] Today, scholarly
interest in Eastern Europe focuses especially on the nineteenth and twen-
tieth centuries, the period of nationalism. The medieval history of the
area is given comparatively less attention, which often amounts to slightly
more than total neglect. For most students in medieval studies, Eastern
Europe is marginal and East European topics simply *exotica*. One reason
for this historiographical reticence may be the uneasiness to treat the
medieval history of the Slavs as (Western) European history. Like
Settembrini, the Italian humanist of Thomas Mann's *Magic Mountain*,
many still point to the ambiguity of those Slavs, whom the eighteenth-
century *philosophes* already viewed as "Oriental" barbarians.[3] When Slavs

[1] Hegel 1902:363.
[2] Halecki 1950. Slavic Europe: Dvornik 1949 and 1956. Eastern Europe as historiographical construct: Okey 1992.   [3] Wolff 1994.

I

come up in works on the medieval history of Europe, they are usually the marginalized, the victims, or the stubborn pagans. In a recent and brilliant book on the "making of Europe," the Slavs, like the Irish, appear only as the object of conquest and colonization, which shaped medieval Europe. Like many others in more recent times, the episodic role of the Slavs in the history of Europe is restricted to that of victims of the "occidentation," the shift towards the ways and norms of Romano-Germanic civilization.[4] The conceptual division of Europe leaves the Slavs out of the main "core" of European history, though not too far from its advancing frontiers of "progress" and "civilization."

Who were those enigmatic Slavs? What made them so difficult to represent by the traditional means of Western historiography? If Europe itself was "made" by its conquerors and settlers, who made the Slavs? What were the historical conditions in which this ethnic name was first used and for what purpose? How was a Slavic ethnicity formed and under what circumstances did the Slavs come into being? Above all, this book aims to answer some of these questions. What binds together its many individual arguments is an attempt to explore the nature and construction of the Slavic ethnic identity in the light of the current anthropological research on ethnicity. Two kinds of sources are considered for this approach: written and archaeological. This book is in fact a combined product of archaeological experience, mostly gained during field work in Romania, Moldova, Hungary, and Germany, and work with written sources, particularly with those in Greek. I have conducted exhaustive research on most of the topics surveyed in those chapters which deal with the archaeological evidence. Field work in Sighişoara (1985–91) and Târgşor (1986–8) greatly contributed to the stance taken in this book. A study on the Romanian archaeological literature on the subject and two studies of "Slavic" bow fibulae published separately.[5] A third line of research grew out of a project developed for the American Numismatic Society Summer Seminar in New York (1995).[6] With this variety of sources, I was able to observe the history of the area during the sixth and seventh centuries from a diversity of viewpoints. Defining this area proved, however, more difficult. Instead of the traditional approach, that of opposing the barbarian Slavs to the civilization of the early Byzantine Empire, I preferred to look at the Danube *limes* as a complex interface. Understanding transformation on the Danube frontier required understanding of almost everything happening both north and south of that frontier. Geographically, the scope of inquiry is limited to the area comprised between the Carpathian basin, to the west, and the Middle

---

[4] Bartlett 1993:295.   [5] Curta 1994a and 1994b; Curta and Dupoi 1994–5.   [6] Curta 1996.

Dnieper region, to the east. To the south, the entire Balkan peninsula is taken into consideration in the discussion of the sixth-century Danube *limes* and of the Slavic migration. The northern limit was the most difficult to establish, because of both the lack of written sources and a very complicated network of dissemination of "Slavic" brooch patterns, which required familiarity with the archaeological material of sixth- and seventh-century cemeteries in Mazuria. The lens of my research, however, was set both south and east of the Carpathian mountains, in the Lower Danube region, an area now divided between Romania, Moldova, and Ukraine.

My intention with this book is to fashion a plausible synthesis out of quite heterogeneous materials. Its conclusion is in sharp contradiction with most other works on this topic and may appear therefore as argumentative, if not outright revisionist. Instead of a great flood of Slavs coming out of the Pripet marshes, I envisage a form of group identity, which could arguably be called ethnicity and emerged in response to Justinian's implementation of a building project on the Danube frontier and in the Balkans. The Slavs, in other words, did not come from the north, but became Slavs only in contact with the Roman frontier. Contemporary sources mentioning Sclavenes and Antes, probably in an attempt to make sense of the process of group identification taking place north of the Danube *limes*, stressed the role of "kings" and chiefs, which may have played an important role in this process.

The first chapter presents the *Forschungsstand*. The historiography of the subject is vast and its survey shows why and how a particular approach to the history of the early Slavs was favored by linguistically minded historians and archaeologists. This chapter also explores the impact on the historical research of the "politics of culture," in particular of those used for the construction of nations as "imagined communities." The historiography of the early Slavs is also the story of how the academic discourse used the past to shape the national present. The chapter is also intended to familiarize the reader with the anthropological model of ethnicity. The relation between material culture and ethnicity is examined, with a particular emphasis on the notion of style.

Chapters 2 and 3 deal with written sources. Chapter 2 examines issues of chronology and origin of the data transmitted by these sources, while Chapter 3 focuses on the chronology of Slavic raids. Chapter 4 considers the archaeological evidence pertaining to the sixth-century Danube *limes* as well as to its Balkan hinterland. Special attention is paid to the implementation of Justinian's building program and to its role in the subsequent history of the Balkans, particularly the withdrawal of the Roman armies in the seventh century. A separate section of this chapter deals with the evidence of sixth- and seventh-century hoards of Byzantine coins in Eastern Europe, which were often used to map the migration of the Slavs. A new interpretation is advanced, which is based on the examination of the age-structure of hoards. Chapter 5 presents the archaeological evidence pertaining to the presence of Gepids, Lombards, Avars, and Cutrigurs in the region north of the Danube river. Special emphasis is laid on the role of specific artifacts, such as bow fibulae, in the construction of group identity and the signification of social differentiation. The archaeological evidence examined in Chapter 6 refers, by contrast, to assemblages found in the region where sixth- and seventh-century sources locate the Sclavenes and the Antes. Issues of dating and use of material culture for marking ethnic boundaries are stressed in this chapter. The forms of political power present in the contemporary Slavic society and described by contemporary sources are discussed in Chapter 7. Various strands of evidence emphasized in individual chapters are then brought into a final conclusion in the last chapter.

As apparent from this brief presentation of the contents, there is more than one meaning associated with the word 'Slav.' Most often, it denotes two, arguably separate, groups mentioned in sixth-century sources, the Sclavenes and the Antes. At the origin of the English ethnic name 'Slav' is an abbreviated form of 'Sclavene,' Latin *Sclavus*. When Slavs appear instead of Sclavenes and Antes, it is usually, but not always, in reference to the traditional historiographical interpretation, which tended to lump these two groups under one single denomination, on the often implicit assumption that the Slavs were the initial root from which sprung all Slavic-speaking nations of later times. Single quotation marks are employed to set off a specific, technical, or, sometimes, specious use of ethnic names (e.g., Slavs, Sclavenes, or Antes) or of their derivatives, either by medieval authors or by modern scholars. Where necessary, the particular use of these names is followed by the original Greek or Latin. With the exception of cases in which the common English spelling was preferred, the transliteration of personal and place names follows a modified version of the Library of Congress system. The geographical terminology, particularly in the case of archaeological sites, closely follows the language in use today in a given area. Again, commonly accepted English equivalents are excepted from this rule. For example, "Chernivtsi" and "Chişinău" are always favored over "Cernăuţi" or "Kishinew," but "Kiev" and "Bucharest" are preferred to "Kyïv" and "Bucureşti." Since most dates are from the medieval period, "AD" is not used unless necessary in context. In cases where assigned dates are imprecise, as with the numismatic evidence examined in Chapter 4, they are given in the form 545/6 to indicate either one year or the other.

4

Introduction

The statistical analyses presented in Chapters 4, 5, and 6 were produced using three different softwares. For the simple "descriptive" statistics used in Chapter 4, I employed graphed tables written in Borland Paradox, version 7 for Windows 3.1. More complex analyses, such as cluster, correspondence analysis, or seriation, were tested on a multivariate analysis package called MV-NUTSHELL, which was developed by Richard Wright, Emeritus Professor at the University of Sydney (Australia). The actual scattergrams and histograms in this book were, however, produced using the Bonn Archaeological Statistics package (BASP), version 5.2 for Windows, written in Borland Object Pascal 7 for Windows by Irwin Scollar from the Unkelbach Valley Software Works in Remagen (Germany). Although the final results were eventually not included in the book for various technical reasons, the study of pottery shape described in Chapter 6 enormously benefited from estimations of vessel volume from profile illustrations using the Senior-Birnie Pot Volume Program developed by Louise M. Senior and Dunbar P. Birnie from the University of Arizona, Tucson.[7]

---

[7] Senior and Birnie 1995.

Chapter 1

SLAVIC ETHNICITY AND THE *ETHNIE* OF THE SLAVS: CONCEPTS AND APPROACHES

Our present knowledge of the origin of the Slavs is, to a large extent, a legacy of the nineteenth century. A scholarly endeavor inextricably linked with forging national identities, the study of the early Slavs remains a major, if not the most important, topic in East European historiography. Today, the history of the Slavs is written mainly by historians and archaeologists, but fifty or sixty years ago the authoritative discourse was that of scholars trained in comparative linguistics. The interaction between approaches originating in those different disciplines made the concept of (Slavic) ethnicity a very powerful tool for the "politics of culture." That there exists a relationship between nationalism, on one hand, and historiography and archaeology, on the other, is not a novel idea.[1] What remains unclear, however, is the meaning given to (Slavic) ethnicity (although the word itself was rarely, if ever, used) by scholars engaged in the "politics of culture." The overview of the recent literature on ethnicity and the role of material culture shows how far the historiographical discourse on the early Slavs was from contemporary research in anthropology and, in some cases, even archaeology.

THE HISTORIOGRAPHY OF SLAVIC ETHNICITY

Slavic studies began as an almost exclusively linguistic and philological enterprise. As early as 1833, Slavic languages were recognized as Indo-European.[2] Herder's concept of national character (*Volksgeist*), unalterably set in language during its early "root" period, made language the perfect instrument for exploring the history of the Slavs.[3] Pavel Josef

---

[1] See, more recently, Kohl and Fawcett 1995; Díaz-Andreu and Champion 1996.
[2] Bopp 1833. See also Niederle 1923:4; Sedov 1976:69.
[3] Herder 1994a:58. Herder first described the Slavs as victims of German warriors since the times of Charlemagne. He prophesied that the wheel of history would inexorably turn and some day, the industrious, peaceful, and happy Slavs would awaken from their submission and torpor to reinvigorate the great area from the Adriatic to the Carpathians and from the Don to the Moldau rivers (Herder 1994b:277–80). For Herder's view of the Slavs, see Wolff 1994:310–15; Meyer 1996:31.

Šafařik (1795– 1861) derived from Herder the inspiration and orientation that would influence subsequent generations of scholars. To Šafařik, the "Slavic tribe" was part of the Indo-European family. As a consequence, the antiquity of the Slavs went beyond the time of their first mention by historical sources, for "all modern nations must have had ancestors in the ancient world."[4] The key element of his theory was the work of Jordanes, *Getica*. Jordanes had equated the Sclavenes and the Antes to the Venethi (or Venedi) also known from much earlier sources, such as Pliny the Elder, Tacitus, and Ptolemy. On the basis of this equivalence, Šafařik claimed the Venedi for the Slavic history. He incriminated Tacitus for having wrongly listed them among groups inhabiting Germania. The Venedi, Šafařik argued, spoke Slavic, a language which Tacitus most obviously could not understand.[5] The early Slavs were agriculturists and their migration was not a violent conquest by warriors, but a peaceful colonization by peasants. The Slavs succeeded in expanding all over Europe, because of their democratic way of life described by Procopius.[6]

Šafařik bequeathed to posterity not only his vision of a Slavic history, but also a powerful methodology for exploring its Dark Ages: language. It demanded that, in the absence of written sources, historians use linguistic data to reconstruct the earliest stages of Slavic history. Since language, according to Herder and his followers, was the defining factor in the formation of a particular culture type and world view, reconstructing Common Slavic (not attested in written documents before the mid-ninth century) on the basis of modern Slavic languages meant reconstructing the social and cultural life of the early Slavs, before the earliest documents written in their language. A Polish scholar, Tadeusz Wojciechowski (1839–1919), first used place names to write Slavic history.[7] Using river names, A. L. Pogodin attempted to identify the *Urheimat* of the Slavs and put forward the influential suggestion that the appropriate homeland for the Slavs was Podolia and Volhynia, the two

---

[4] Schafarik 1844:1, 40. Šafařik, who opened the All-Slavic Congress in Prague in June 1848, shared such views with his friend, František Palacký. See Palacký 1868:74–89. For the Manifesto to European nations from Palacký's pen, which was adopted by the Slavic Congress, see Pech 1969:133. For Palacký's image of the early Slavs, see Zacek 1970:84–5.

[5] Schafarik 1844:1, 75 and 78. There is still no comprehensive study on the influence of Šafařik's ideas on modern linguistic theories of Common Slavic. These ideas were not completely original. Before Šafařik, the Polish historian Wawrzyniec Surowiecki (1769–1827) used Pliny's *Natural History*, Tacitus' *Germania*, and Ptolemy's *Geography* as sources for Slavic history. See Surowiecki 1964 (first published in 1824). On Surowiecki's life and work, see Szafran-Szadkowska 1983:74–7. Surowiecki's ideas were shared by his celebrated contemporary, Adam Mickiewicz (1798–1855), and his theory of the Slavic Venethi inspired at least one important work of Polish Romantic literature, namely Julius Słowacki's famous tragedy, *Lilla Weneda* (1840).

[6] Schafarik 1844:1, 42 (see also II, 17). These ideas were not new. The "dove-like Slavs," in sharp contrast with the rude Germans, was a common stereotype in early nineteenth-century Bohemia. See Sklenář 1983:95.   [7] Wojciechowski 1873. See Szafran-Szadkowska 1983:115.

regions with the oldest river names of Slavic origin.[8] A Polish botanist, J. Rostafiński, pushed the linguistic evidence even further. He argued that the homeland of the Slavs was a region devoid of beech, larch, and yew, because in all Slavic languages the words for those trees were of foreign (i.e., Germanic) origin. By contrast, all had an old Slavic word for hornbeam, which suggested that the *Urheimat* was within that tree's zone. On the basis of the modern distribution of those trees, Rostafiński located the *Urheimat* in the marshes along the Pripet river, in Polesie.[9] Jan Peisker (1851– 1933) took Rostafiński's theory to its extreme. To him, "the Slav was the son and the product of the marsh."[10]

Despite heavy criticism, such theories were very popular and can still be found in recent accounts of the early history of the Slavs.[11] The rise of the national archaeological schools shortly before and, to a greater extent, after World War II, added an enormous amount of information, but did not alter the main directions set for the discipline of Slavic studies by its nineteenth-century founders. Lubor Niederle (1865–1944), who first introduced archaeological data into the scholarly discourse about the early Slavs, endorsed Rostafiński's theory. His multi-volume work is significantly entitled *The Antiquities of the Slavs*, like that of Šafařík.[12] Niederle believed that climate and soil shape civilization. Since the natural conditions in the Slavic *Urheimat* in Polesie were unfavorable, the Slavs developed forms of social organization based on cooperation between large families (of a type known as *zadruga*), social equality, and

---

[8] Pogodin 1901:85–111. For Pogodin's theories, see Sedov 1976:70. A recent variant of these theories is Jürgen Udolph's attempt to locate the Slavic *Urheimat* on the basis of river-, lake-, and moor-names. According to Udolph, Galicia was the area in which the Indo-Europeans first became proto-Slavs. See Udolph 1979:619–20.

[9] Rostafiński 1908. For Rostafiński's "beech argument," see Kostrzewski 1969:11; Sedov 1976:71; Szafran-Szadkowska 1983:105; Gołab 1992:273–80. Pogodin's and Rostafiński's arguments were couched in the theory of Indo-European studies. A growing field in the early 1900s, this theory attempted to reconstruct the original language (*Ursprache*) of the original people (*Urvolk*) in their homeland (*Urheimat*), using the method of the "linguistic paleontology" founded by Adalbert Kuhn. See Mallory 1973; Anthony 1995:90.

[10] Peisker 1926:426; see Peisker 1905. For Peisker's life and work, see Šimák 1933. Peisker's ideas are still recognizable in the work of Omeljan Pritsak, who recently argued that the Sclavenes were not an ethnic group, but amphibious units for guerilla warfare both on water and on land. See Pritsak 1983:411.

[11] Many scholars took Rostafiński's argument at its face value. See Dvornik 1956:59; Gimbutas 1971:23; see also Baran 1991; Dolukhanov 1996. For good surveys of the most recent developments in Slavic linguistics, in which the "Indo-European argument" refuses to die, see Birnbaum 1986 and 1993.

[12] Niederle 1911:37–47, 1923:21, and 1925:iii. A student of Jaroslav Goll, the founder of the Czech positivist school, Niederle was a professor of history at the Charles University in Prague. His interest in archaeology derived from the idea that ethnography was a historical discipline, capable of producing evidence for historical constructions based on the retrogressive method. For Niederle's life and work, see Eisner 1948; Zasterová 1967; Tomás 1984:39; Gojda 1991:4. For Niederle's use of the linguistic evidence, see Dostál 1966:7–31 and 1967:147–53.

the democracy described by Procopius, which curtailed any attempts at centralization of economic or political power.[13] This hostile environment forced the early Slavs to migrate, a historical phenomenon Niederle dated to the second and third century AD. The harsh climate of the Pripet marshes also forced the Slavs, whom Niederle viewed as *enfants de la nature*, into a poor level of civilization. Only the contact with the more advanced Roman civilization made it possible for the Slavs to give up their original culture entirely based on wood and to start producing their own pottery.[14]

Others took the archaeological evidence much further. Vykentyi V. Khvoika (1850–1914), a Ukrainian archaeologist of Czech origin, who had just "discovered" the Slavs behind the Neolithic Tripolye culture, was encouraged by Niederle's theory to ascribe to them finds of the fourth-century cemetery at Chernyakhov (Ukraine), an idea of considerable influence on Slavic archaeology after World War II.[15] A Russian archaeologist, A. A. Spicyn (1858–1931), assigned to the Antes mentioned by Jordanes the finds of silver and bronze in central and southern Ukraine.[16] More than any other artifact category, however, pottery became the focus of all archaeological studies of the early Slavic culture. During the inter-war years, Czech archaeologists postulated the existence of an intermediary stage between medieval and Roman pottery, a ceramic category Ivan Borkovský (1897–1976) first called the "Prague type" on the basis of finds from several residential areas of the Czechoslovak capital. According to Borkovský, the "Prague type" was a national, exclusively Slavic, pottery.[17] After World War II, despite Borkovský's political agenda (or, perhaps, because of it), the idea that the "Prague type" signalized the presence of the Slavs was rapidly embraced by many archaeologists in Czechoslovakia, as well as elsewhere.[18]

---

[13] Niederle 1923:26 and 1926:173.

[14] Niederle 1923:49, 1925:513, and 1926:1–2 and 5. For Niederle's concept of Slavic homeland, see Zasterová 1966:33–41.

[15] Baran, Gorokhovskii, and Magomedov 1990:33; Dolukhanov 1996:4. On Khvoika's life and work, see Bakhmat 1964; Lebedev 1992:260–2.

[16] Spicyn 1928:492–5. See also Prikhodniuk 1989:65. On Spicyn, see Lebedev 1992:247–52.

[17] Borkovský 1940:25 and 34–5. Emanuel Šimek (1923) first called this pottery the "Veleslavín type." Niederle's successor at the Charles University in Prague, Josef Schraníl, suggested that this type derived from the Celtic pottery, an idea further developed by Ivan Borkovský. Borkovský argued that when migrating to Bohemia and Moravia, the Slavs found remnants of the Celtic population still living in the area and borrowed their techniques of pottery production. For the history of the "Prague type," see Preidel 1954:56; Zeman 1966:170.

[18] Borkovský's book was published shortly after the anti-German demonstrations in the protectorate of Bohemia and Moravia under Nazi rule (October 1939). The idea that the earliest Slavic pottery derived from a local variant of the Celtic, not Germanic, pottery was quickly interpreted as an attempt to claim that the Czechs (and not the Germans) were natives to Bohemia and Moravia. Borkovský's work was thus viewed as a reaction to Nazi claims that the Slavs were racially

Following Stalin's policies of fostering a Soviet identity with a Russian cultural makeup, the Slavic ethnogenesis became the major, if not the only, research topic of Soviet archaeology and historiography, gradually turning into a symbol of national identity.[19] As the Red Army was launching its massive offensive to the heart of the Third Reich, Soviet historians and archaeologists imagined an enormous Slavic homeland stretching from the Oka and the Volga rivers, to the east, to the Elbe and the Saale rivers to the west, and from the Aegean and Black Seas to the south to the Baltic Sea to the north.[20] A professor of history at the University of Moscow, Boris Rybakov, first suggested that both Spicyn's "Antian antiquities" and the remains excavated by Khvoika at Chernyakhov should be attributed to the Slavs, an idea enthusiastically embraced after the war by both Russian and Ukrainian archaeologists.[21] The 1950s witnessed massive state investments in archaeology and many large-scale horizontal excavations of settlements and cemeteries were carried out by a younger generation of archaeologists. They shifted the emphasis from the Chernyakhov culture to the remains of sixth- and seventh-century settlements in Ukraine, particularly to pottery. Initially just a local variant of Borkovský's Prague type, this pottery became the ceramic archetype of all Slavic cultures. The origins of the early Slavs thus moved from Czechoslovakia to Ukraine.[22] The interpretation favored by Soviet scholars became the norm in all countries in Eastern Europe with Communist-dominated governments under Moscow's

Footnote 18 (*cont.*)

and culturally inferior. As a consequence, the book was immediately withdrawn from bookstores and Borkovský became a sort of local hero of the Czech archaeology. Nevertheless, the concept of Prague-type pottery was quickly picked up and used even by German archaeologists working under the Nazi regime. See Brachmann 1983:23. For the circumstances of Borkovský's book publication, see Preidel 1954:57; Sklenář 1983:162–3. For the "politics of archaeology" in the protectorate of Bohemia and Moravia under Nazi rule, see Mastny 1971:130–1.

[19] For the political and cultural circumstances in which the academic discourse in the Soviet Union adopted the Slavic ethnogenesis as its primary subject matter, see Velychenko 1992; Aksenova and Vasil'ev 1993; Shnirel'man 1993 and 1995.

[20] E.g., Derzhavin 1944:46; Mavrodin 1945:15.

[21] Rybakov 1939 and 1943. For the influence of Rybakov's theories, see Liapushkin 1965:121; Shchukin 1980:399; Baran, Gorokhovskii, and Magomedov 1990:35–6. Despite heavy criticism in recent years, these theories remain popular. See Sedov 1972:116–30; Dolukhanov 1996:158 ("indisputable archaeological evidence proving that the peoples who made up the bulk of the agricultural population of the east Gothic 'state' were Slavs"). For Rybakov's political activity after the war, see Novosel'cev 1993; Hösler 1995:25–6.

[22] For excavations in Polesie in the 1950s, see Rusanova 1976:12–13; Baran 1985:76 and 1990:59–60; Baran, Maksimov, and Magomedov 1990:202. During the 1960s and 1970s, the center of archaeological activities shifted from Polesie to the basins of the Dniester and Prut rivers, not far from the Ukrainian–Romanian border. See Baran 1968. For the "Zhitomir type," a local variant of the Prague type, and its further development into the archetype of all Slavic cultures, see Kukharenko 1955:36–8 and 1960:112; Rusanova 1958:33–46; Petrov 1963a:38; Rusanova 1970:93.

protection.[23] The "Prague-Korchak type," as this pottery came to be known, became a sort of symbol, the main and only indicator of Slavic ethnicity in material culture terms. Soviet archaeologists now delineated on distribution maps two separate, though related, cultures. The "Prague zone" was an archaeological equivalent of Jordanes' Sclavenes, while the "Pen'kovka zone" was ascribed to the Antes, fall-out curves neatly coinciding with the borders of the Soviet republics.[24]

The new archaeological discourse did not supersede the old search for the prehistoric roots of Slavic ethnicity. In the late 1970s, Valentin V. Sedov revived Šafařík's old theories, when suggesting that the ethnic and linguistic community of the first century BC to the first century AD in the Vistula basin was that of Tacitus' Venedi. According to him, the Venedi began to move into the Upper Dniester region during the first two centuries AD. By the fourth century, as the Chernyakhov culture emerged in western and central Ukraine, the Venedi formed the majority of the population in the area. As bearers of the Przeworsk culture, they assimilated all neighboring cultures, such as Zarubinec and Kiev. By 300 AD, the Antes separated themselves from the Przeworsk block, followed, some two centuries later, by the Sclavenes. The new ethnic groups were bearers of the Pen'kovka and Prague-Korchak cultures, respectively. Sedov's theory was used by others to push the Slavic ethnogenesis back in time, to the "Proto-Slavo-Balts" of the early Iron Age, thus "adjusting" the results of linguistic research to archaeological theories. The impression one gets from recent accounts of the Slavic ethnogenesis is that one remote generation that spoke Indo-European produced children who spoke Slavic.[25]

---

[23] For Czechoslovakia, see Poulík 1948:15–9; Klanica 1986:11. In the 1960s, Borkovský's idea that the Slavs were native to the territory of Czechoslovakia surfaced again. See Budinský-Krička 1963; Bialeková 1968; Chropovský and Ruttkay 1988:19. For a different approach, see Zeman 1968 and 1979; Jelínková 1990. For Poland, see Lehr-Spławinski 1946; Hensel 1988. In the late 1960s, Jozef Kostrzewski, the founder of the Polish archaeological school, was still speaking of the Slavic character of the Bronze-Age Lusatian culture; see Kostrzewski 1969. Kostrzewski's ideas die hard; see Sulimirski 1973; Hensel 1994. For the final blow to traditional views that the Slavs were native to the Polish territory, see more recently Parczewski 1991 and 1993. For a survey of the Romanian literature on the early Slavs, see Curta 1994a. For Yugoslavia, see Karaman 1956; Korošec 1958a; Ćorović-Ljubinković 1972; Kalić 1985. For Bulgaria, see Văzharova 1964; Milchev 1970; Vasilev 1979.

[24] Fedorov 1960:190; Rafalovich 1972a; Prikhodniuk 1983:60–1. For an attempt to identify the Slavic tribes mentioned in the *Russian Primary Chronicle* with sixth- and seventh-century archaeological cultures, see Smilenko 1980.

[25] Lunt 1992:468. For Sedov's theory, see Sedov 1979, 1994, and 1996. For the Zarubinec, Kiev, and other related cultures of the first to fourth centuries AD, see Baran, Maksimov, and Magomedov 1990:10–97; Terpilovskii 1992 and 1994. For the association between the respective results of the linguistic and archaeological research, see Lebedev 1989. Russian linguists still speak of Slavs as "the sons and products of the marsh." See Mokienko 1996.

More often than not, archaeology was merely used to illustrate conclusions already drawn from the analysis of the linguistic material. The exceptional vigor of the linguistic approach originated in the fact that, after Herder, language was viewed as the quintessential aspect of ethnicity. As depository of human experiences, languages could thus be used to identify various "historical layers" in "fossilized" sounds, words, or phrases. In this ahistorical approach, human life and society was viewed as a palimpsest, the proper task for historians being that of ascribing various "fossils" to their respective age. It was an approach remarkably compatible with that of the culture-historical archaeologists, described further in this chapter. This may also explain why so many archaeologists working in the field of Slavic studies were eager to adopt the views of the linguists, and rarely challenged them. The current discourse about the Slavic homeland has its roots in this attitude. Though the issue at stake seems to be a historical one, historians were often left the task of combing the existing evidence drawn from historical sources, so that it would fit the linguistic-archaeological model. Some recently pointed out the danger of neglecting the historical dimension, but the response to this criticism illustrates how powerful the Herderian equation between language and *Volk* still is.[26] Ironically, historians became beset by doubts about their ability to give answers, because of the considerable time dimension attributed to linguistic and archaeological artifacts. With no Tacitus at hand, archaeologists proved able to explore the origins of the Slavs far beyond the horizon of the first written sources.

Together with language, the search for a respectable antiquity for the history of the Slavs showed two principal thrusts: one relied on the interpretation of the historical sources as closely as possible to the linguistic-archaeological argument; the other located the Slavic homeland in the epicenter of the modern distribution of Slavic languages. The former began with the affirmation of trustworthiness for Jordanes' account of the Slavic Venethi, an approach which ultimately led to the claim of Tacitus', Pliny's, and Ptolemy's Venedi for the history of the Slavs. The cornerstone of this theory is Šafářik's reading of Jordanes as an accurate description of a contemporary ethnic configuration. Šafářik's interpretation is still widely accepted, despite considerable revision, in the last few decades, of traditional views of Jordanes and his *Getica*. The explanation

---

[26] Ivanov 1991c and 1993. For the vehement response to Ivanov's claim that the ethnic history of the Slavs begins only in the 500s, see Vasil'ev 1992; Cheshko 1993. Though both Ivanov and his critics made extensive use of archaeological arguments, no archaeologist responded to Ivanov's challenge in the pages of *Slavianovedenie*. Before Ivanov, however, a Czech archaeologist advocated the idea that "as a cultural and ethnic unit, in the form known from the sixth century AD on, [the Slavs] did not exist in antiquity." See Váňa 1983:25.

of this extraordinary continuity is neither ignorance, nor language barriers. Jordanes' Venethi have become the key argument in all constructions of the Slavic past primarily based on linguistic arguments. Like Šafařik, many would show condescension for Tacitus' "mistake" of listing Venethi among groups living in Germania, but would never doubt that Jordanes' account is genuine. Archaeological research has already provided an enormous amount of evidence in support of the idea that the Venethi were Slavs. To accept this, however, involves more than a new interpretation of *Getica*. Jordanes built his image of the Slavs on the basis of earlier accounts and maps, without any concern for accurate description. It also means to give up evolutionary models created for explaining how the early Slavic culture derived from earlier archaeological cultures identified in the area in which Tacitus, Pliny, and Ptolemy apparently set their Venedi. A considerable amount of intellectual energy was invested in this direction between the two world wars and after 1945, and to question the theoretical premises of this approach is often perceived as denying its utility or, worse, as a bluntly revisionist coup. It is not without interest that claims that the Slavic ethnicity is a sixth-century phenomenon were met with the reaffirmation of Sedov's theory of Slavic culture originating from the Przeworsk culture, which is often identified with the Venethi.

The more radical the reaffirmation of Slavic antiquity becomes, the more writing about the history of the Slavs takes on the character of a mere description of the history of humans living since time immemorial in territories later inhabited by the Slavs. Pavel Dolukhanov opens his recent book on the early Slavs by observing that "the succeeding generations of people who lived in the vast spaces of the Russian Plain" without being noticed and recorded in any written documents cannot be ascribed to any ethnic group. "They had no common name, whether it was 'Slavs' or anything else." Yet, like the Soviet historians of the 1940s, Dolukhanov believes that "the origins and early development of peoples known as Slavs could be rightly understood only if viewed from a wide temporal perspective." This, in his description of Slavic history, means that the proper beginning is the Palaeolithic.[27]

But the diagnosis comes easier than the remedy. Historians and archaeologists dealing with the progress of the migration of the Slavs outside their established *Urheimat* have, at times, correctly perceived the contradictions and biases ingrained in the current discourse about the origins of the Slavs. But they still work within a framework defined by the concept of migration. The discrepancy between the efforts of Romanian

---

[27] Dolukhanov 1996:ix–x; see Derzhavin 1944:3–4; Mavrodin 1945:15.

archaeologists, who argue that the Slavs reached the Danube by the end of the sixth century and did not wait too long for crossing it *en masse*, and those of Bulgarian and Yugoslav archaeologists, who strive to demonstrate an early sixth-century presence of the Slavs in the Balkans, has prompted some to voice reservations and objections to both the dominance and the perceived accuracy of the archaeological view of Slavic history. Yet focusing on numismatic, rather than archaeological, data did not banish the concept of migration outright. Just as with pots, the invasions of the Slavs could nevertheless be traced by plotting finds of coins and coin hoards on the map.[28]

Modifying the linguistic-archaeological view of Slavic history seems a better alternative than negating it. Even in America, where this view was most seriously challenged, scholars speak of the Slavs at the Roman frontiers as "the first row of countless and contiguous rows of Slavic, Venedic, and Antic peoples who spread from the Danube to the Dnieper and to the Elbe" and of Proto-Slavs as forerunners of the Zhitomir or Prague cultures. Indeed, in their work of historiographical revision, historians still acknowledge the link between ethnicity and language. Either as "cumulative mutual Slavicity" or as Sclavene military units organized and controlled by steppe nomads, the idea that the Slavs became Slavs by speaking Slavic is pervasive.[29]

WHAT IS ETHNICITY?

No other term in the whole field of social studies is more ambiguous, yet more potent, than ethnicity. In English, the term "ethnic" has long been used in its New Testament sense, as a synonym for "gentile," "pagan," or "non-Christian," a meaning prevailing until the nineteenth century. The current usage of "ethnicity" goes back to 1953, as the word was first used to refer to ethnic character or peculiarity. We now speak of ethnicity as a mode of action and of representation. Some twenty years ago, however, no definition seemed acceptable. Ethnicity was "neither culture, nor society, but a specific mixture, in a more or less stable equilibrium, of both culture and society." As a consequence, attempts to define ethnicity were remarkably few.[30]

Today, ethnicity is used to refer to a decision people make to depict

---

[28] Romanian archaeologists: Nestor 1973:30; Teodor 1972:34; Diaconu 1979:167. Bulgarian and Yugoslav archaeologists: Milchev 1975:388; Angelova 1980:4; Čremošnik 1970:58–9 and 61; Ljubinković 1973:182. See also Barišić 1969:25–6. Numismatic evidence for the invasions of the Slavs: Kovačević 1969; Popović 1980:246.

[29] Bačić 1983:201; Milich 1995:49 and 204; see Pritsak 1983:423–4.

[30] The term "ethnicity": Fortier 1994. Ethnicity as both culture and society: Nicolas 1973:107. Definitions of ethnicity: Isajiw 1974:111; Parsons 1975:53.

themselves or others symbolically as bearers of a certain cultural identity. It has become the politicization of culture. Ethnicity is not innate, but individuals are born with it; it is not biologically reproduced, but individuals are linked to it through cultural constructions of biology; it is not simply cultural difference, but ethnicity cannot be sustained without reference to an inventory of cultural traits. One anthropologist defined ethnicity as the "collective enaction of socially differentiating signs." Others argue that ethnicity is a relatively recent phenomenon, resulting from dramatic historical experiences, notably escape from or resistance to slavery. According to such views, ethnic groups grow out of "bits and pieces, human and cultural, that nestle in the interstices" between established societies. Diasporas of exiles in borderlands coalesce around charismatic entrepreneurs, who gather adherents by using familiar amalgamative metaphors (kinship, clientelism, etc.), and also spiritual symbolism, such as ancestral aboriginality or other legitimizing events.[31]

Ethnicity may therefore be seen as an essential orientation to the past, to collective origin, a "social construction of primordiality." Some scholars believe that ethnicity is just a modern construct, not a contemporary category, and that examinations of "ethnic identity" risk anachronism when the origins of contemporary concerns and antagonisms are sought in the past. Although ethnic groups constantly change in membership, ethnic names used in early medieval sources, such as *Gothi* or *Romani*, cannot usefully be described as ethnic groups, because the chief forces of group cohesion were not ethnicity, but region and profession. Others claim that ethnicity is only the analytical tool academics devise and utilize in order to make sense of or explain the actions and feelings of the people studied.[32] But ethnicity is just as likely to have been embedded in sociopolitical relations in the past as in the present. What have changed are the historical conditions and the idiomatic concepts in which ethnicity is embedded.

In Eastern Europe, particularly in the Soviet Union, the study of ethnicity (especially of Slavic ethnicity) was dominated until recently by the views of the Soviet ethnographer Julian Bromley. According to him, ethnicity was based on a stable core, called *ethnos* or *ethnikos*, which persisted through all social formations, despite being affected by the prevailing economic and political conditions. Soviet scholars laid a strong emphasis

[31] Cohen 1993:197; see also Verdery 1994:42. Ethnicity and the inventory of "cultural traits": Williams 1992. Ethnicity and collective enaction: Eriksen 1991:141. Ethnicities as recent phenomena: Chappell 1993:272.

[32] Ethnicity and primordiality: Alverson 1979:15. The orientation to the past, however, may also be associated with other forms of group identity, such as class; see Ganzer 1990. Ethnicity as a modern construct: Geary 1983:16; Amory 1994:5 and 1997:317. Ethnicity as a scholarly construct: Banks 1996:186.

on language. As the "precondition for the rise of many kinds of social organisms, including ethnic communities," the language "received and developed in early childhood, is capable of expressing the finest shades of the inner life of people," while enabling them to communicate.[33] The association between language and ethnicity, so tightly bound in the Soviet concept of ethnicity, is no accident. For a long period, the literature concerning ethnic phenomena was completely dominated by Stalin's definition of nation and by N. Ia. Marr's ideas. Marr (1864–1934) was a well-trained Orientalist who had made valuable contributions to Armenian and Georgian philology, and became interested in comparative linguistics and prehistory. He adopted the view that language was part of the ideological superstructure depending upon the socioeconomic basis and therefore developing in stages like Marx's socioeconomic formations. Marr treated ethnicity as something of a non-permanent nature, as ephemeral, and discounted "homelands" and "proto-languages." Instead, he argued that cultural and linguistic changes were brought by socioeconomic shifts. Marr's theories were a reaction to the nineteenth-century approach of the culture-historical school based on Herderian ideas that specific ways of thought were implanted in people as a result of being descended from an ancestral stock, the *Volksgeist*.[34]

Despite its revolutionary character, Marrism was gradually abandoned, as Stalin adopted policies to force assimilation of non-Russians into a supranational, Soviet nation. He called for a "national history" that would minimize, obfuscate, and even omit reference to conflict, differences, oppression, and rebellion in relations between Russians and non-Russians. Instead, historians were urged to combat actively the fascist falsifications of history, to unmask predatory politics toward the Slavs, and to demonstrate the "real" nature of Germans and their culture. By 1950, Soviet anthropologists completely abandoned the stadial theory, as Stalin

[33] Bromley and Kozlov 1989:431–2; Kozlov 1974:79. To be sure, all ethnic identity is often associated with the use of a particular language. But language itself is only one of the elements by which access to an ethnic identity is legitimized in a culturally specific way. It is by means of an "associated language" that language and ethnicity are related to each other; see Eastman and Reese 1981:115. It is also true that much of what constitutes identity, including its ethnic dimension, takes form during the individual's early years of life. Recent studies insist that the family contributes in a fundamental way to the formation of ethnic identity and recommend that family-based studies become the methodological strategy of future research on ethnic identity. See Keefe 1992:43.

[34] Bruche-Schulz 1993:460; Slezkine 1996. According to Marr's ideas, meaning was attached to thought processes which were characteristic for a given social formation. The lesser or lower production stages produced lower or "primitive" forms of thought and language. Bruche-Schulz 1993:462. While denying the permanency of ethnicity, Marr viewed class as a structure inherent to human nature, an idea well attuned to the Bolshevik ideology of the 1920s and to the policies of the Comintern. See Szynkiewicz 1990:3; Taylor 1993:725; Shnirel'man 1995:122.

himself was now inflicting the final blow when denouncing Marrism as "vulgar Marxism."[35]

In the late 1960s, a "small revolution" (as Ernest Gellner called it) was taking place in Soviet anthropology. The tendency was now to treat ethnic identity as a self-evident aspect of ethnicity, though, like all other forms of consciousness, ethnic identity was still viewed as a derivative of objective factors. Soviet anthropologists now endeavored to find a place for ethnicity among specifically *cultural* phenomena, as opposed to social structure. To them, ethnic specificity was the objective justification for a subjective awareness of affiliation to a given *ethnos*. Despite considerable divergence as to what exactly constituted the "objective factors" of ethnicity (for some, language and culture; for others, territory or common origin), Soviet anthropologists viewed ethnicity as neither eternal, nor genetic, but as socially real and not a mystified expression of something else.[36]

To many Soviet scholars of the 1960s and 1970s, ethnicity appeared as a culturally self-reproducing set of behavioral patterns linked to collective self-identity, which continued through different modes of production. Issues of continuity and discontinuity among ethnic entities and of their transformation were thus given theoretical and empirical attention as ethnic-related patterns of collective behavior. Ethnohistory became a major field of study and ethnogenesis, the process of formation of ethnic identity, replaced social formation as the main focus. This new concept of ethnicity was closely tied in to the ideology of ethno-nationalism, a politics in which ethnic groups legitimized their borders and status by forming administrative units or republics. The classification of "ethnic types" (tribe, *narodnost'*, and nation) involving Bromley's conceptual categorizations justified the administrative statehood granted to "titular nationalities," those which gave titles to republics.[37] Paradoxically, the Soviet approach to ethnicity could be best defined as primordialistic, despite its admixture of Marxist–Leninist theory. By claiming that ethnicities, once formed through ethnogeneses, remained essentially unchanged through history, Soviet anthropologists suggested that ethnic groups were formulated in a social and political vacuum. According to them, ethnicity was thus a given, requiring description, not explanation. To contemporary eyes, the academic discourse of ethno-nationalism in Eastern Europe in general and in the former Soviet Union, in particular,

---

[35] Stalin's concept of national history: Velychenko 1993:20; Shnirel'man 1995:130. Abandonment of Marrist theories: Klejn 1977:13; Dolukhanov 1996:5; Slezkine 1996:852–3.

[36] Gellner 1988:135; Bromley and Kozlov 1989:427; Dragadze 1980:164.

[37] Shanin 1989:413; Klejn 1981:13; Sellnow 1990; Tishkov 1994:444.

appears as strikingly tied to political rather than intellectual considerations. This may well be a consequence of the romanticization and mystification of ethnic identity, which is viewed as rooted in the ineffable coerciveness of primordial attachments.[38]

The *communis opinio* is that the emergence of an instrumentalist approach to ethnicity is largely due to Fredrik Barth's influential book,[39] which ironically coincides in time with Bromley's "small revolution" in the Soviet Union. Ethnicity, however, emerged as a key problem with Edmund Leach's idea that social units are produced by subjective processes of categorical ascription that have no necessary relationship to observers' perceptions of cultural discontinuities. Before Barth, Western anthropologists had limited their investigation to processes taking place within groups, rather than between groups. All anthropological reasoning has been based on the premise that cultural variation is discontinuous and that there were aggregates of people who essentially shared a common culture, and interconnected differences that distinguish each such discrete culture from all others. Barth shed a new light on subjective criteria (ethnic boundaries) around which the feeling of ethnic identity of the member of a group is framed. Barth emphasized the *transactional* nature of ethnicity, for in the practical accomplishment of identity, two mutually interdependent social processes were at work, that of internal and that of external definition (categorization). By focusing on inter-ethnic, rather than intragroup social relations, Barth laid a stronger emphasis on social and psychological, rather than cultural-ideological and material factors. His approach embraced a predominantly social interactionist perspective, derived from the work of the social psychologist Erving Goffman. Objective cultural difference was now viewed as epiphenomenal, subordinate to, and largely to be explained with reference to, social interaction. Barth's followers thus built on concepts of the self and social role behavior typified by a dyadic transactional (the "we vs. them" perspective) or social exchange theory.[40]

Because it was a variant of the general social psychological theory of self and social interaction, Barth's approach led to a high degree of predictability and extensibility to new contexts and situations, which, no doubt, was a primary determinant of its popularity. To be sure, the subjective approach to ethnicity, which is so often and almost exclusively attributed to Barth, long precedes him. Both Weber and Leach were aware of its significance. Another important, but notably ignored, scholar is the German historian Reinhard Wenskus. Eight years prior to the

---

[38] Banks 1996:186; Jones 1994:48.   [39] Barth 1969.
[40] Barth 1994:12. For the process of categorization, see also Jenkins 1994:198–9. For the relation between Barth's and Goffman's works, Buchignani 1987:16.

publication of Barth's book, Wenskus published a study of ethnic identity in the early Middle Ages, which would become the crucial breakthrough for studies of ethnicities in historiography. Wenskus' approach was based on the ideas of the Austrian anthropologist Wilhelm Mühlmann, himself inspired by the Russian ethnographer S. M. Shirogorov, the first to have used the concept of "subjective ethnicity." In a Weberian stance, Wenskus claimed that early medieval *Stämme* were not based on a biologically common origin, but on a strong *belief* in a biologically common origin. His approach, much like Barth's, focused on the subjective side of ethnic belonging and he specifically attacked the concept of ethnogenesis (as understood at that time by Soviet anthropologists) and the model of the family-tree in ethnohistory. He pointed out that "kernels of tradition" were much more important factors in making early medieval ethnic groups, for tradition also played an important political role, as suggested by the conceptual pair *lex* and *origo gentis,* so dear to medieval chroniclers.[41] Wenskus' approach is congenial with the more recent studies of the British sociologist Anthony Smith and was followed by some major contemporary medievalists.[42] Though never clearly delineating its theoretical positions in regards to anthropology (though Wenskus himself has been more open to contemporary debates in the field), this current trend in medieval history quickly incorporated concepts readily available in sociological and anthropological literature. Patrick Geary, for instance, used the concept of "situational ethnicity" coined by Jonathan Okamura. He might have found it extremely useful that the structural dimension of situational ethnicity pointed to the essentially *variable* significance of ethnicity as an organizing principle of social relations. More recently, Walter Pohl cited Smith's concept of *mythomoteur* as equivalent to Wenskus' "kernel of tradition."[43]

Both Barth and Wenskus tried to show that ethnic groups were socially constructed. According to both, it was not so much the group which

---

[41] Wenskus 1961:14–18, etc. See also Jarnut 1985; Pohl 1994:11.
[42] Smith 1984; 1986; 1995. See also Wolfram 1988; Pohl 1988; Heather 1996.
[43] Okamura 1981; Geary 1983; Pohl 1991a:41. For the *mythomoteur* as the constitutive myth of the ethnic polity, see Smith 1986:15. Smith typically views ethnicity as "a matter of myths, symbols, memories, and values. They are 'carried' by forms and genres of artifacts and activities which change very slowly. Therefore, an *ethnie*, once formed, tends to be exceptionally durable under 'normal' vicissitudes" (1986:16 and 28). Smith also argues that "without a *mythomoteur* a group cannot define itself to itself or to others, and cannot inspire or guide effective action" (1986:25). There is, however, no attempt to explain the association between a particular "myth-symbol" complex and an *ethnie*, for Smith characteristically lists among the latter's components, "a distinctive shared culture" (1986:32). He thus seems to reproduce the general fallacy of identifying ethnic groups with discrete cultural units. More important, though recognizing that artifacts could provide a rich evidence of cultural identity, Smith argues that they "cannot tell anything [about] how far a community felt itself to be unique and cohesive" (1986:46).

endured as the *idea* of group. They both argued that ethnic groups existed not in isolation, but in contrast to other groups. Unlike Wenskus, however, Barth does not seem to have paid too much attention to self-consciousness and the symbolic expression of ethnic identity. Enthusiasm for a transactional model of social life and for viewing ethnicity as process was accompanied in both cases by an interpretation of social relations as rooted in reciprocation, exchange and relatively equitable negotiation. In most cases, activation of ethnic identity was used to explain contextual ethnic phenomena, but this very ethnic identity, since it was not directly observable, had to be derived from the actor's "ethnic behavior." Barth's model of social interaction is so general that there is virtually nothing theoretically unique about ethnic phenomena explained through reference to it, for the model could be as well applied to other forms of social identity, such as gender. Despite its strong emphasis on ethnic boundary processes, Barth's approach does not, in fact, address issues concerning objective cultural difference (subsistence patterns, language, political structure, or kinship).

The instrumentalist approach received its new impetus from Abner Cohen, one of the important figures of the Manchester School, who published his *Custom and Politics in Urban Africa* in 1969 (the same year in which Barth's book was published). Cohen's approach was more pragmatic. His main point was that political ethnicity (such as defined by Wenskus' students) was goal-directed ethnicity, formed by internal organization and stimulated by external pressures, and held not for its own sake but to defend an economic or political interest. To him, such ethnicity needed to be built upon some preexisting form of cultural identity rather than be conjured up out of thin air. Cohen's approach thus came very close to Wenskus' idea of ethnicity as constructed on the basis of a "kernel of tradition," or to Smith's concept of *mythomoteur*. Unlike them, however, Cohen concentrated on changes in corporate identification (not individual identification) and on the politicization of cultural differences in the context of social action. He paid attention to ethnicity as a social liability and thus opened the path for modern studies of ethnicity as a function of power relations.[44] Many students of ethnicity now concentrate on ethnicity as an "artifact," created by individuals or groups to bring together a group of people for some common purpose. They are increasingly concerned with the implications of ethnic boundary construction and the meaning of boundary permeability for when, how, and, especially, why groups selectively fashion "distinctive trait inventories,"

---

[44] Cohen 1969. For the study of ethnicity as a function of power relations, see McGuire 1982:171 and 173; Roosens 1989:158; Eriksen 1991:129.

symbolize group unity and mobilize members to act for economic or political gain, and "invent" traditions. Scholars now struggle with the counterfactual qualities of cultural logics that have made *ethnic* the label of self- and other-ascription in modern nation-states.[45]

The emphasis of the post-Barthian anthropology of ethnicity has tended to fall on processes of group identification rather than social categorization.[46] Ethnicity as ascription of basic group identity on the basis of cognitive categories of cultural differentiation, is, however, very difficult to separate from other forms of group identity, such as gender or class. Moreover, both primordialist and instrumentalist perspectives tend to be based on conflicting notions of human agency manifested in an unproductive opposition between rationality and irrationality, between economic and symbolic dimensions of social practice. It has been noted that cultural traits by which an ethnic group defines itself never comprise the totality of the observable culture but are only *a combination* of some characteristics that the actors ascribe to themselves and consider relevant. People identifying themselves as an ethnic group may in fact identify their group in a primarily prototypic manner. Recognizable members may thus share *some* but not all traits, and those traits may not be equally weighted in people's minds.[47] How is this specific configuration constructed and what mechanisms are responsible for its reproduction?

A relatively recent attempt to answer this question resurrected the idea that ethnic groups are bounded social entities internally generated with reference to commonality rather than difference.[48] Bentley dismisses instrumentality by arguing that people live out an unconscious pattern of life, not acting in a rational, goal-oriented fashion. His approach draws heavily from Pierre Bourdieu's theory of habitus. Habitus is produced by the structures constitutive of a particular type of environment. It is a system of durable, transposable dispositions, "structured structures predisposed to function as structuring structures."[49] Those durable dispositions are inculcated into an individual's sense of self at an early age and can be transposed from one context to another. Habitus involves a form of socialization whereby the dominant modes of behavior and representation are internalized, resulting in certain dispositions which operate largely at a pre-conscious level. Ethnicity is constituted at the intersection of habitual dispositions of the agents concerned and the social conditions existing in a particular historical context. The content of ethnic

---

[45] Banks 1996:39; Williams 1992:609.   [46] Horowitz 1975:114.
[47] Jones 1994:42 and 61; Roosens 1989:12; Mahmood and Armstrong 1992:8.
[48] Bentley 1987. For a critique of Bentley's approach, see Yelvington 1991. For an earlier suggestion that ethnic identity may be the result of a learning process, see also Horowitz 1975:119.
[49] Pierre Bourdieu, cited by Bentley 1987:28.

identity is therefore as important as the boundary around it. An important issue, resulting from this approach, is that of the reproduction of identity on the level of interaction. The praxis of ethnicity results in multiple transient realizations of ethnic difference in particular contexts. These realizations of ethnicity are both structured and structuring, involving, in many instances, the repeated production and consumption of distinctive styles of material culture. The very process of ethnic formation is coextensive with and shaped by the manipulation of material culture. Bentley suggested that the vector uniting culture and ethnicity ran through daily social practice. He emphasized the cultural character of the process of ethnic identity creation, which provided a key reason for the emotional power associated with it. On this basis, the creation of ethnic identities should have repercussions in terms of the self-conscious use of specific cultural features as diacritical markers, a process which might well be recorded in material culture. Bentley's thrust coincides in time with an independent line of research inspired by Edmund Husserl and stressing ethnicity as a phenomenon of everyday life (*Alltagsleben*). Routine action, rather than dramatic historical experiences, foodways, rather than political action, are now under scrutiny. As the idea of ethnicity turns into a mode of action in the modern world, it becomes more relevant to study the very process by which the ethnic boundary is created in a specific social and political configuration.[50]

WHAT IS *ETHNIE*?

"Ethnicity" derives from the Greek word ἔθνος, which survives as a fairly common intellectual word in French, as *ethnie*, with its correlate adjective *ethnique*. The possible noun expressing what it is you have to have in order to be *ethnique* is not common in modern French. In English, the adjective exists as "ethnic" with a suffix recently added to give "ethnicity." But the concrete noun from which "ethnicity" is apparently derived does not exist. There is no equivalent to the ἔθνος, to the Latin *gens*, or to the French *ethnie*. Until recently, such a term was not needed, for it was replaced in the intellectual discourse by "race," a concept which did not distinguish very clearly, as we do today, between social, cultural, linguistic, and biological classifications of people, and tended to make a unity of all these.[51] "Ethnicity," therefore, is an abstract noun, derived by non-vernacular morphological processes from a substantive

---

[50] Creation of ethnic identities: Jones 1996:72; Shennan 1989:16–7. Ethnicity and everyday life: Greverus 1978:97–8; Räsänen 1994:17–18; Tebbetts 1984:83 and 87; Tvengsberg 1991:17; Keefe 1992.

[51] Chapman, McDonald, and Tonkin 1989:12; Jones 1997:40– 51. See also Johnson 1995:12.

that does not exist. It makes sense only in a context of relativities, of *processes* of identification, though it also aspires, in modern studies, to concrete and positive status, as an attribute and an analytical concept. Ethnicity is conceptualized as something that inheres in every group that is self-identifying as "ethnic," but there is no specific word for the end product of the process of identification. When it comes to designate the human group created on the basis of ethnicity, "ethnic group" is the only phrase at hand.

More recently, in an attempt to find the origins of modern nations, Anthony Smith introduced into the scholarly discourse the French term *ethnie*, in order to provide an equivalent to "nation" for a period of history in which nations, arguably, did not yet exist. Smith argues that ethnicity, being a matter of myths and symbols, memories and values, is carried by "forms and genres of artifacts and activities."[52] The end product is what he calls an *ethnie*. The *ethnie* is a human group, a concrete reality generated by the meaning conferred by the members of that group over some generations, on certain cultural, spatial, and temporal properties of their interaction and shared experiences. Smith identifies six components of any *ethnie*: a collective name; a common myth of descent; a shared history; a distinctive shared culture; an association with a specific territory; and a sense of solidarity. He argues that in some cases, the sense of ethnic solidarity is shared only by the elite of a given *ethnie*, which he therefore calls a "lateral" or aristocratic *ethnie*. In other cases, the communal sense may be more widely diffused in the membership, such an *ethnie* being "vertical" or demotic. One can hardly fail to notice that to Smith, the *ethnie* is just the "traditional" form of the modern nation. His list of traits to be checked against the evidence is also an indication that, just as with Bromley's "ethnosocial organism," there is a tendency to reify ethnic groups and to treat ethnicity as an "it," a "thing" out there to be objectively measured and studied, albeit by means of ancestry myths rather than by language.[53]

No scholar followed Smith's attempt to find a concrete noun to be associated with the more abstract "ethnicity." Terminology, however, does matter; it shapes our perceptions, especially of controversial issues. The use of Smith's *ethnie* in this book is simply a way to avoid confusion between the ethnic group and the phenomenon it supposedly instantiates (ethnicity). More important, if viewed as a result of a process of differentiation and identity formation, the use of *ethnie* suggests that ethnic groups are not "born," but made.

[52] Smith 1986:16.
[53] Smith 1986:22, 32, 76–7, and 28, and 1984:29. For ethnic groups as "fiduciary associations," see Parsons 1975:61–2.

ETHNICITY, MATERIAL CULTURE AND ARCHAEOLOGY

It has become common knowledge that the foundations of the culture-historical school of archaeology were laid by the German archaeologist Gustaf Kossinna. Today, both archaeologists and historians attack Kossinna's tenets and, whenever possible, emphasize his association with Nazism and the political use of archaeology. No book on nationalism, politics, and the practice of archaeology could avoid talking about Kossinna as the archetypal incarnation of all vices associated with the culture-historical school. Kossinna's own work is rarely cited, except for his famous statement: "Sharply defined archaeological culture areas correspond unquestionably with the areas of particular peoples or tribes."[54] Kossinna linked this guiding principle to the retrospective method, by which he aimed at using the (ethnic) conditions of the present (or the historically documented past) to infer the situation in prehistory. The two together make up what he called the "settlement archaeological method" (*Siedlungsarchäologie*). It has only recently been noted that in doing so, Kossinna was simply using Oskar Montelius' typological method, which enabled him to establish time horizons for the chronological ordering of the material remains of the past.[55] Kossinna also stressed the use of maps for distinguishing between distribution patterns, which he typically viewed as highly homogeneous and sharply bounded cultural provinces. This method, however, was nothing new. Before Kossinna, the Russian archaeologist A. A. Spicyn had used the map to plot different types of earrings found in early medieval burial mounds in order to identify tribes mentioned in the *Russian Primary Chronicle*. Like Spicyn, Kossinna simply equated culture provinces with ethnic groups and further equated those groups with historically documented peoples or tribes. Attempts to identify ethnic groups in material culture date back to Romanticism, and represent correlates of linguistic concerns with finding *Ursprachen* and associating them to known ethnic groups. Many German archaeologists before Kossinna used the concept of culture province. Though not the first to attempt identifying archaeological cultures with ethnic groups, Kossinna was nevertheless the first to focus exclusively on this idea, which

---

[54] "Streng umrissene, scharf sich heraushebende, geschlossene archäologische Kulturprovinzen fallen unbedingt mit bestimmten Völker- und Stammesgebiete" (Kossinna 1911:3 and 1936:15). For the association between Gustaf Kossinna and the culture-historical approach in "Germanophone" archaeology, see Amory 1997:334 with n. 10. Amory deplores the influence of "Continental archaeologists" working in the ethnic ascription tradition. See Amory 1997:335–6.

[55] Klejn 1974:16; Veit 1989:39. To Kossinna, the concept of closed-find (introduced into the archaeological discourse by the Danish archaeologist Christian Jürgensen Thomsen and of crucial importance to Oskar Montelius) and the stratigraphic principle were less important than mere typology. See Trigger 1989:76, 78, and 157.

became his *Glaubenssatz*. He was directly inspired by the Romantic idea of culture as reflecting the national soul (*Volksgeist*) in every one of its elements.[56]

The Berlin school of archaeology established by Kossinna emerged in an intellectual climate dominated by the Austrian *Kulturkreis* school. The roots of biologizing human culture lie indeed not in Kossinna's original thought, but in the theory of migration developed by Fr. Ratzel and F. Graebner. According to Graebner, there are four means for determining whether migration (*Völkerwanderung*) caused the spread of cultural elements. First, one should look for somatic similarities possibly coinciding with cultural parallels. Second, one should check whether cultural and linguistic relationships coincide. Third, one should examine whether certain cultural elements are *schwerentlehnbar*, i.e., whether there are any obstacles to their transfer, in accord to Vierkandt's idea of readiness and need. If positive, the result may indicate that those cultural elements were carried by migrating groups. And finally, one should investigate whether two cultures occur entire (not fragmented or simplified) at two widely separated locations. This last argument gains strength with distance and also to the extent that the set of culture elements occurs in closed form. Wilhelm Schmidt, the founder of the journal *Antropos*, tended to speak of a *Kulturkreis* even when only one element was present, for this was to him a clue of the earlier presence of other elements.[57]

The concept of a philosophically derived nationalism, acquired in an intellectual context molded by Herder's and Fichte's ideas applies therefore to Graebner, as well as to Kossinna. It is, however, a mistake to speak of Kossinna's blatant nationalism as causing his *Herkunft der Germanen*, for the first signs of his nationalistic views postdate his famous work. Though often viewed as Kossinna's main opponent, Carl Schuchhardt shared many of his ideas, including that of identifying ethnic groups by means of archaeological cultures. Wenskus was certainly right in pointing out that Kossinna's mistake was not so much that he aimed at an ethnic interpretation of culture, than that he used a dubious concept of ethnicity, rooted in Romantic views of the *Volk*.[58] It is not the overhasty equation between archaeological cultures and ethnic groups that explains the extraordinary popularity the culture-historical paradigm enjoyed even among Marxist historians. Of much greater importance is the concept of *Volk* and its political potential. It is therefore no accident that after World

---

[56] For Spicyn, see Formozov 1993:71. For Romanticism, *Ursprachen*, and ethnic ascription, see Brachmann 1979:102. For the use of the concept of culture province before Kossinna, see Klejn 1974:13. For Kossinna's *Glaubenssatz*, see Eggers 1950:49.

[57] For the *Kulturkreis* school, see Lucas 1978:35–6.

[58] Wenskus 1961:137. Kossinna's political views: Smolla 1979–80:5.

War II, despite the grotesque abuses of Kossinna's theories under the Nazi regime, this concept remained untouched. It was Otto Menghin, one of the main representatives of the prehistoric branch of the *Kulturkreislehre*, who began replacing the term *Volk* by the presumably more neutral and less dubious term "culture." Kossinna's post-war followers passed over in silence the fundamental issue of equating *Völker* and cultures.

Like Kossinna, Vere Gordon Childe used the concept of culture to refer to an essence, something intrinsically natural that preceded the very existence of the group, provoked its creation, and defined its character. But he began using the phrase "archaeological culture" as a quasi-ideology-free substitute for "ethnic group," and the very problem of ethnic interpretation was removed from explicit discussion. The standard demand now was a strict division between the arguments used by various disciplines studying the past, in order to avoid "mixed arguments." This latter error derived, however, from considering culture as mirroring the national soul. Since all cultural elements were imbued with *Volksgeist*, this organicist concept of culture allowed one to use information about one cultural element to cover gaps in the knowledge of another. "March separately, strike together" became the slogan of this attempt at "purifying" science and keeping apart the disciplines studying ethnicity.[59] In order to understand why and how Kossinna's ideas continued to be extremely popular in post-war Europe, we need to examine briefly the situation in a completely different intellectual environment, that of Soviet Russia.

We have seen that a culture-historical approach was used by Spicyn some ten years before Kossinna. Much like in Germany, Spicyn and his colleagues' endeavors to unearth the national past had a great impact on pre-1917 Russian historiography.[60] Some of Spicyn's students became major figures of the Soviet school of archaeology. Marr's theories and the cultural revolution, however, drastically altered this intellectual configuration. In the early 1930s, such concepts as "migration" and "archaeological cultures" were literally banned, being replaced by a bizarre concept of ethnic history, in which stages of development were equated to certain historically attested ethnic groups. Marxism in its Stalinist version was brutally introduced in archaeology and the culture-historical paradigm

---

[59] For Vere Gordon Childe's concept of "archaeological culture," see Díaz-Andreu 1996:48. For the separation of disciplines, see Klejn 1981:20; Veit 1989:43.

[60] Some of Kliuchevskii's students (Iu. V. Got'e, S. K. Bogoiavlevskii, N. P. Miliukov) participated in excavations of burial mounds. Kliuchevskii's successor at the chair of Russian history at the University of Moscow opened his course not with Kievan Rus', but with the Palaeolithic (Formozov 1993:71). This approach is remarkably similar to Dolukhanov's recent book on the early Slavs (1996:ix–x).

was replaced with internationalism that required scholars to study only global universal regularities that confirmed the inevitability of socialist revolutions outside Russia. Closely following Marr, Soviet archaeologists now stressed the association between migrationist concepts and racism, imperialism, and territorial expansionism. But following the introduction of Stalinist nationalist policies of the late 1930s, this new paradigm quickly faded away. As Stalin had set historians the task to combat actively the fascist falsifications of history, the main focus of archaeological research now shifted to the prehistory of the Slavs. Archaeologists involved in tackling this problem have, however, been educated in the years of the cultural revolution and were still working within a Marrist paradigm. Mikhail I. Artamonov first attempted to combine Marrism and Kossinnism, thus recognizing the ethnic appearance of some archaeological assemblages, which rehabilitated the concept of "archaeological culture." The attitude toward migration and diffusion also changed from prejudice to gradual acceptance, though the general philosophical principles on which Soviet archaeology was based remained the same. As a consequence of this strange alliance, Soviet archaeologists tended to focus on two main issues: isolating archaeological cultures and interpreting them in ethnic terms; explaining the qualitative transformations in culture.[61]

The culture-ethnic concept was thus rehabilitated. A. Ia. Briusov believed that archaeological cultures reflected groups of related tribes in their specific historic development, while Iu. M. Zakharuk equated archaeological cultures not simply with ethnic groups, but also with linguistic entities. Finally, M. Iu. Braichevskii claimed that no assemblage could be identified as culture, if it did not correspond to a definite ethnic identity. After 1950, Soviet archaeologists completely abandoned Marrist concepts and Soviet archaeology became of a kind that would have been easily recognizable to Kossinna and which would have been amenable to the kind of culture-historical *Siedlungsarchäologie* he developed. Mikhail I. Artamonov, the main artisan of this change, claimed that ethnicity remained unchanged through historical change, which could not alter its specific qualities. Russians living under Peter the Great's rule were just those of Kievan Rus' in a different historical environment. One can hardly miss the striking parallel to Bromley's idea of *ethnikos*. Indeed, Bromley's theories made a great impression on Soviet archaeologists. On the basis of this alliance with the theory of *ethnos*, archaeology now became the "science about ethnogenesis." Indeed,

---

[61] Shnirel'man 1995:124; Ganzha 1987:142; Klejn 1977:14.

continuity of material culture patterning was now systematically interpreted as ethnic continuity.[62]

The culture-historical approach made extensive use of the concept of culture. This concept carried many assumptions which were central to nineteenth-century classifications of human groups, in particular an overriding concern with holism, homogeneity, and boundedness. Traditionally, the archaeological culture was defined in monothetic terms on the basis of the presence or absence of a list of traits or types, which had either been derived from the assemblages or a type site, or were intuitively considered to be most appropriate attributes in the definition of the culture. In practice, no group of cultural assemblages from a single culture ever contains all of the cultural artifacts, a problem first acknowledged by Vere Gordon Childe. Childe's response was to discard the untidy information by demoting types with discontinuous frequency from the rank of diagnostic types, thus preserving the ideal of an univariate cultural block. Culture-historical archaeologists regarded archaeological cultures as actors on the historical stage, playing the role for prehistory that known individuals or groups have in documentary history. Archaeological cultures were thus easily equated to ethnic groups, for they were viewed as legitimizing claims of modern groups to territory and influence. The first criticism against the equivalence of archaeological cultures and ethnic groups came from within the framework of culture-history, but critiques usually consisted of cautionary tales and attributed difficulties to the complexity and incompleteness of the artifactual record, without calling into question the assumption of an intrinsic link between artifacts and groups. The general response in the face of such problems was therefore a retreat into the study of chronology and typology as ends in themselves, and the emergence of debates concerning the meaning of archaeological types, in particular whether such types represent etic categories imposed by the archaeologist or emic categories of their producers.[63]

The processualist approach associated with the American-based school of thought known as the New Archaeology never seriously tackled this

[62] Briusov 1956; Artamonov 1971. See also Shennan 1989: 29; Klein 1993:43. To Wenskus (1961:113 with n. 1), these new trends in Soviet archaeology appeared in 1961 as "curiously" similar to Kossinna's approach. Bromley's theories are cited by Irina P. Rusanova in the introduction to a recent collection of studies dedicated to Proto-Slavic cultures. Rusanova (1993:5) believes that, since there are no two ethnic groups (*naroda*) with the same culture, it is worth trying to identify the Slavs by archaeological means.

[63] Klejn 1974:225 and 1981:18; Jones 1994:29 and 82; Hides 1996:26. For the earlier criticism of the idea that archaeological cultures were equivalent to ethnic groups, see Wahle 1941. For Childe's views, see Childe 1956:33 and 124. For similar views in the Soviet archaeology of the early 1960s, see Ganzha 1987:147–8.

problem.[64] Instead of answering the normative question "What do cultures relate to?", American archaeologists of the 1960s and the early 1970s simply took away the emphasis from such questions, as they now concentrated on the adaptive role of the components of cultural systems. According to the New Archaeology, culture is not shared; it is participated in. However, though criticizing the idea that all material culture distributions represent variation in the ideational norms of different ethnic groups, processualist archaeologists continued to accept the idea that some bounded archaeological distributions (if only in the domain of stylistic variation) correlate with past ethnic groups. Nor did Barth's ideas change this perspective too much, for the social interaction model rests on the assumption that stylistic characteristics will diffuse or be shared among social entities to an extent directly proportional to the frequency of interactions between these entities, such as intermarriage, trade, or other forms of face-to-face communication.[65]

In order to verify this assumption, the British archaeologist Ian Hodder chose East Africa as a suitable place for an ethnoarchaeological study of how spatial patterning of artifacts relates to ethnic boundaries. In his study of ethnic boundaries in the Baringo district of Kenya, Hodder found that, despite interaction across tribal boundaries, clear material culture distinctions were maintained in a wide range of artifact categories. He argued that distinct material culture boundaries were foci of interaction, not barriers. Hodder showed that material culture distinctions were in part maintained in order to justify between-group competition and negative reciprocity, and that such patterning increased in time of economic stress. However, not all cultural traits were involved in such differentiation, since, typically, interaction continued between competing groups. Boundaries did not restrict movement of all traits and the between-group interaction and the diffusion of cultural styles was sometimes used to disrupt the ethnic distinctions. Hodder thus suggested that the use of material culture in distinguishing between self-conscious ethnic groups would lead to discontinuities in material culture distributions which may enable the archaeologist to identify such groups. The form of intergroup relations is usually related to the internal organization of social relationships within the group. In the case of the Baringo, between-group differentiation and hostility was linked to the internal

---

[64] For the history and basic tenets of the New Archaeology school, see Trigger 1989:289–328; Flannery 1982. For the processualist approach to ethnicity, see Hodder 1982:5; Hegmon 1992:528; Jones 1994:83.
[65] The assumption that propinquity produces stylistic (cultural) homogeneity forms the basis of the so-called "Deetz-Longacre hypothesis." See Braun and Plog 1982:509; Roe 1995:51–2.

differentiation of age sets and the domination of women and young men by old men.[66]

Hodder provided another example of the way in which individuals may manipulate ethnic identity for their own goals. The Maasai sometimes "became" Dorobo in order to escape drought, raiding, or government persecution. But, though the Dorobo had a real separate existence in the conscious thoughts of those who called themselves by this name, there was no symbolic expression of any differences between Dorobo and Maasai. Different groups may manipulate material culture boundaries in different ways depending upon the social context, the economic strategies chosen, the particular history of the socioeconomic relations, and the particular history of the cultural traits which are actively articulated within the changing system.[67]

Hodder's study suggests that the symbolic status and cultural meaning of material items determine the morphology and distribution of those items within and beyond a single society. Though ethnicity may involve certain aspects of culture, the choice of distinctive cultural styles is not arbitrary, for the signification of self-conscious identity is linked to the generative structures which infuse all aspects of cultural practice and social relations characterizing a particular way of life. Hodder observed, for instance, that though there were no zooarchaeological indications of ethnicity *per se*, meat-eating, the division of the carcass, or the dispersal of bones always had a symbolic content behind which there was a conceptual order. This seems to come very close to Bentley's point that the cultural practices and representations which become objectified as symbols of ethnicity are derived from, and resonate with, the habitual practices and experiences of the agents involved, as well as reflect the instrumental contingencies of a particular situation. Thus, the ethnic differences are constituted in the mundane as well as in the decorative, for the "tribal" distinctions and negative reciprocity become acceptable and are "naturalized" by their continual repetition in both public and private.[68]

There is a problematic circularity in Hodder's definition of culture, as

---

[66] Hodder 1982:27, 31, 35, 85, 187, and 205; Jones 1994:90–1; Watson 1995:91. Roy Larick's more recent ethnoarchaeological research in Kenya corroborates Hodder's conclusions. In Loikop communities studied by Larick, spears, which play an important role in the construction of ethnicity, are constantly appropriated in the signification of age differentiation among the male population. See Larick 1986 and 1991.   [67] Hodder 1982:104. See also Lyons 1987:108.

[68] Hodder 1982:56 and 161; Jones 1994:98 and 104. For faunal remains and ethnicity, see Crabtree 1990:181; Hesse 1990:198. Recently, it has been argued that the roomsize pattern may be related to the proxemic values of the ethnic group that produced the space. On an individual level, this proxemic system is shaped to a great extent during enculturation as a child. Conformity to external social constraints brings in the role of the dwelling as a symbol. See Baldwin 1987:163 and 169; Kobyliński 1989:309.

artifacts actively manipulated in the negotiation of identities based on age, gender, or ethnicity. The meaning of the artifact is derived from its context, and its context is defined by those associated artifacts which give it meaning. Moreover, material culture is not primarily semiotic in character. Its structure is not essentially syntactical, but rather consists of "constellations" of knowledge, which inhere in the immanent relation between actor and material. The "meaning" of artifacts is not primarily semantic, in that artifacts do not communicate about anything. Their "meaning" inheres in and through their use and their design for use. Material objects instantiate cognition in that they embody practices. They record a now-extinct relationship between an actor and the material world. Material culture is therefore fundamentally social: an artifact embodies a transaction, its manufacture represents the transfer of action from its maker to its users or, in the case of the exchange of artifacts, the transfer of use between actors. Artifacts are thus rendered "appropriate" for use *only* in social context. Decisions about the use of artifacts are, however, embodied in artifacts themselves in terms of the conventions of culture. Artifacts are not properties of a society, but part of the life of that society. They cannot and should not be treated as "phenotypic" expressions of a preformed identity. Ethnic identity, therefore, represents a kind of polythesis. What should concern archaeologists is not so much what people do, what kind of pots they make, what shape of houses they build, but the "way they go about it."[69]

ETHNICITY AND STYLE

The common notion that style is primarily expressive assumes that the primary use of material culture is to reinforce ethnic boundaries. Style may indeed be used to express ethnic identity, but convention is effectively the vocabulary from which expressive style is drawn. This is why most archaeologists expect material correlates of ethnically specific behaviors to be better and more frequently represented in the archaeological record than the material symbols of ethnic identification.[70]

The basic point of contention in recent debates about style is the question whether style symbolizes ethnicity, because it is intended by artisans to do just that or because it just happens to do so for other, perhaps less purposeful, reasons. Another controversial issue is whether style resides

---

[69] Graves-Brown 1996:90–1; Graves 1995:165.

[70] McGuire 1982:163; Giardino 1985:17 and 22. It is therefore wrong to take *a priori* individual pottery types or decoration, ceramic design elements, design layout, surface treatment, etc., as ethnic indicators. See Kleppe 1977:39; Esse 1992:102–3; Kobyliński 1989:306–7; Cordell and Yannie 1991:98–9.

in particular sorts of artifacts which have a social rather than a practical function or in all sorts of artifacts, from ceramics to tools, along with other qualities such as function.

The traditional approach borrowed from art history held that each group had its own style, which it had preserved through history, for it was assumed that cultures were extremely conservative. In their criticism of this culture-historical approach, processualist archaeologists argued that style is a "residue," properties of material culture not accounted for in *prima facie* functional terms. They also argued that material mediation is primarily practical and only secondarily expressive. As a consequence, style must be treated as a form of social status communication, which reduces style to a particular form of practical mediation, since no matter what meaning style may have "said" or had for its producers, its "real" cause is founded on the adaptive advantage it granted to its users. Moreover, this function of style is realized over a long period of time, beyond the life experience of any particular generation. Thus, its consequences are outside the awareness of the actors and always work "behind their backs."[71]

But style and function are not distinct, self-contained, mutually exclusive realms of form in themselves, but instead complementary dimensions or aspects of variation that coexist within the same form. If both style and function are simultaneously present in the artifactual form, then the question is how can we tell when, and to what extent, the observed makeup of an assemblage reflects ethnicity and when, and to what extent, it reflects activity? James Sackett attempted to make a radical break with the residual view of style by invoking isochrestic variation, which he defined as the practical or utilitarian variation in objective properties of material culture things that makes no functional mediation difference. As a consequence, isochrestic variation grounds style and style is an intrinsic, rather than an added-on, or adjunct, function. In Sackett's view, style is thus a "built-in." Isochrestic variation permeates all aspects of social and cultural life and provides the means by which members of a group express their mutual identity, coordinate their actions, and bind themselves together. It could thus be viewed as idiomatic or diagnostic of ethnicity. Such views seem to be rooted in those assumptions of holism, homogeneity, and boundedness, which, as shown above, characterize the nineteenth-century concept of culture.[72]

In contrast, Polly Wiessner argued that style is a form of nonverbal communication through doing something in a certain way that

[71] Franklin 1989:278; Pasztory 1989:17; Byers 1991:3; David, Sterner, and Gavua 1988:365 and 378–9. [72] Sackett 1985, 1986, and 1990. See also Byers 1991:10: Hegmon 1994:172.

communicates about relative identity. Her approach is inspired by the information-exchange theory, which emphasizes that differences in stylistic behavior result more from social constraints on the choosing of alternative decorative options during the act of decoration than from the social context in which a person learned his/her decorative repertoire. Max Wobst first proposed the idea that style operates as an avenue of communication. Wobst was working within a functionalist, system-theory paradigm and he argued that since style is a relatively expensive form of communication, stylistic information exchange will only be used in certain contexts so as to maximize efficiency. Wiessner attacked this position by rightly pointing out that in identity displays efficiency of message is not a major concern. On the contrary, identity displays are often extravagant, the resources and effort expended being an index of ability and worth. Moreover, stylistic messages need not be clear or uniform, and in fact a certain amount of ambiguity may help achieve the desired effect.[73]

Wobst has raised another important problem. By stressing the communicative role of style he implied that not *all* material culture variation should be viewed as style. Rather style is only that part of material culture variation which conveys information about relative identity. Style is an *intentional*, structured system of selecting certain dimensions of form, process or principle, function, significance, and affect from among known, alternate, possibilities to create variability within a behavioral-artifactual corpus. Polly Wiessner even argued that one could differentiate between "emblemic style," which has a distinct referent and transmits a clear message to a defined target population about conscious affiliation or identity, and "assertive style," which is personally based and carries information supporting individual identity. Because emblemic style carries a distinct message, it should undergo strong selection for uniformity and clarity, and because it marks and maintains boundaries, it should be distinguished archaeologically by uniformity within its realm of function.[74]

Style may be viewed as the pattern we make around a particular event, recalling and creating similarities and differences. It only exists in these repetitions and contrasts. But variation expressed in material items is multireferential, as Wiessner suggested, which implies that style is likely to be heavily invested with multiple levels of symbolic coding. When used as a tool in social strategies, style provides the potential for the control of the meaning and thus for power. Recent studies demonstrate

---

[73] Wiessner 1983:257, 1985:161, and 1990:107. For style as a form of communication, see Wobst 1977. See also Braun and Plog 1982:510; Hegmon 1992:521.   [74] Wiessner 1983:257–8.

that emblemic style appears at critical junctures in the regional political economy, when changing social relations would impel displays of group identity. It has been argued, on the other hand, that with the initial evolution of social stratification and the rise of chiefdoms, considerable stylistic variability may exist between communities in clothing and display items. At the regional level, however, iconography and elite status become important to legitimize and "naturalize" the inherent inequality in these systems. Extensive interchiefdom trade and shared political ideology serve to deliver rare and foreign objects linked symbolically to universal forces.[75]

CONCLUSION

Understanding ethnicity in the past presents a particular challenge. The sweeping survey of the most relevant literature on ethnicity and material culture reveals that both topics have undergone considerable re-evaluation in recent years, with many older assumptions being questioned. The increased interest in ethnicity, in general, and in the use of material culture for its construction, in particular, means that the old questions can be now looked at in new ways. Early medieval ethnicities are one of the most lively areas of current research.[76] The large volume of new material generated analytical advances of the first importance. Clearly it is misleading, if not impossible, to generalize over so wide an area and so eventful a chronological span. But modern historiography abounds in confident value-judgments about early medieval *ethnies*, many of which still rest on unacknowledged assumptions about what ethnicity is and how it works.

As a conclusion to this chapter, therefore, it might be helpful to state clearly the assumptions on which this study is based. Its premise is that early medieval ethnicity was embedded in sociopolitical relations just as modern ethnicity is. Ethnicity was socially and culturally constructed, a form of social mobilization used in order to reach certain political goals. Then, just as now, an *ethnie* was built upon some preexisting cultural identity, in a prototypic manner. But ethnicity is also a matter of daily social practice and, as such, it involves manipulation of material culture. Since material culture embodies practices, "emblemic style" is a way of communicating by non-verbal means about relative identity. Because it carries a distinct message, it is theoretically possible that it was used to mark and maintain boundaries, including ethnic ones. But ethnicity is also a function of power relations. Both "emblemic style" and "tradition"

---

[75] Hodder 1990:45–6; Macdonald 1990:53; McLaughlin 1987; Earle 1990:74–5. See also Byers 1991:12; Pasztory 1989:36.   [76] Pohl 1988; Wood 1995; Heather 1996; Amory 1993 and 1997.

34

become relevant particularly in contexts of changing power relations, which impel displays of group identity. In most cases, both symbols and "tradition" will entail a discussion of the power configuration in the Slavic society, with an emphasis on the political forces which may have been responsible for the definition of symbols, their organization and hierarchization. In asking what developments in material culture accompanied the making of a Slavic *ethnie*, I will therefore alternate the focus between power and style.

Chapter 2

SOURCES FOR THE HISTORY OF THE EARLY
SLAVS (*c.* 500–700)

Much of what we know about sixth- and seventh-century Slavs comes from works of contemporary authors writing in Greek and, to a lesser extent, in Latin or Syriac. The majority did not pay special attention to the Slavs, but simply mentioned them and a few other things about them in connection to events relevant to the history of the Empire. Some were accounts of eyewitnesses, but most were written long after the event or at a considerable distance. Their coverage is patchy, and the basic narrative has to be reconstructed from a wide variety of standpoints and perspectives. This chapter will examine some of the issues concerning authorship, trustworthiness, and dating, which might be relevant for the image of the Slavs resulting from early medieval sources. The following chapter will take into consideration the image which is often derived from these accounts.

PROCOPIUS AND JORDANES

Procopius was often viewed as the voice of the senatorial opposition to Justinian's regime. He is believed to have addressed an audience still fond of Homer, Herodotus, and Thucydides. His description of the Slavic god as the "maker of lightning" (τὸν τῆς ἀστραπτῆς δημιουργόν) is indeed reminiscent of Sophocles. The episode of the "phoney Chilbudius" betrays the influence of the neo-Attic comedy and, possibly, of Plautus. There is also a weak echo of Thucydides where Procopius claims that he had written about buildings which he had seen himself, or heard described by others who had seen them.[1]

---

[1] Procopius, *Wars* VII 14.23 and VII 14.11–16; *Buildings* VI 7.18. See Sophocles, *Aias* 1035: ἐχάλκευσε ξίφος . . . Ἀΐδης δημιουργὸς ἄγριος. See also Ivanov, Gindin, and Cymburskii 1991:221 and 231–2. Procopius, the senatorial opposition, and classical models: Irmscher 1969:470; Benedicty 1965:52–3; Irmscher 1971:340. See also Cesa 1982:203. For Procopius' concept of God and gods, see Veh 1951:21 and 23; Elferink 1967.

Despite his credentials as an eyewitness reporter, however, his account could hardly be checked, for he usually does not mention his sources. But doubts are rarely, if ever, raised about the authenticity of his account. It is nevertheless very likely that, except the regions in the immediate vicinity of the Capital, Procopius hardly knew the Balkan area other than from maps.[2] He probably had contact with the Slavs in Italy, where he was at Belisarius' side as his legal advisor and secretary.[3] In 542, Procopius was back in Constantinople, where he certainly was an eyewitness to the plague. The writing of the *Wars* may have already started in the 540s, but Books I–VII containing material relevant to the Slavs were only completed in 550 or 551, probably at the same time as the *Secret History*.[4] As for the *Buildings*, with its controversial date, Procopius seems to have left it unfinished. Some have argued that parts of the *Buildings*, if not the entire work, must have been written in 559/60. There is, however, a reference to the recent strengthening of the fortifications of Topeiros, after the city has been sacked by Sclavene marauders in 550, as narrated in the *Wars*. There are several other indications that Procopius had formed the plan of writing the *Buildings* while he was still at work on the very different *Secret History*. If the two works were contemporary, we can date them with some exactitude before May 7, 558, the date of the collapse of the dome of Hagia Sophia (an event not mentioned in Procopius' *Buildings*). It is thus possible that the first books of the *Buildings* (including the reference to the Sclavenes in book IV) were written before 558 and remained unrevised, probably because of their author's untimely death.[5]

Procopius' view of the Slavs is a function of his general concept of *oikumene*. An analysis of his diplomatic terminology reveals his idea of an empire surrounded by "allies" (ἔνσπονδοι), such as the Saracens, the

---

[2] Procopius' description of the road between Strongylum and Rhegium, on the *via Egnatia*, leaves the impression that he has seen the coarse paving stones with his own eyes (*Buildings* IV 8). But the lack of coherence in the direction of the author's account of Illyricum and Thrace may reflect the lack of personal experience of the area. Other details, such as the use of Mysia for Moesia (Inferior), may be attributed to the influence of Homer, (*Buildings* IV 6; *Iliad* XIII 5). See Veh 1951:35 with n. 18; Cesa 1982:203; Cameron 1985:13 and 220 with n. 96; Litavrin 1986:25; Adshead 1990:108.

[3] After the first siege of Rome, Procopius was sent to Naples, in charge of supplies for the army, and then to Auximum, in 539/40, where Sclavene mercenaries were used by Belisarius to capture some Ostrogoths from the besieged city (*Wars* VI 26.16–22). See Evans 1970:219; Ivanov, Gindin, and Cymburskii 1991:171; Anfert'ev 1991:132.

[4] Veh 1951:9; Evans 1972:37; Cameron 1985:8; Greatrex 1994:102. For a different, but unconvincing, dating of the *Secret History*, see Scott 1987:217.

[5] Evans 1969:30. For Topeiros, see *Buildings* IV 11.14–17; *Wars* VII 38.9–19. In his *Buildings*, Procopius places the capture of the city οὐ πολλῷ ἔμπροσθεν. He also lists the Goths among the Empire's neighbors on the Danube frontier, which could only refer to the pre-555 situation (IV 1). See Veh 1951:9; Whitby 1985a:145; Scott 1987:220; Greatrex 1994:113 and 1995. See also Beshevliev 1967b:276.

Lombards, the Gepids, the Goths, the Cutrigurs, and the Antes. The Sclavenes do not belong to this group, most probably because Procopius viewed them as "new." Indeed, among all forty-one references to Sclavenes or Antes in Procopius' work, there is no use of the adverbs παλαιόν, πάλαι, ἀεί, ἐς ἐμέ, or ἀνέκαθεν, while all verbs used in reference to settlement (οἰκέω, ἱδρύομαι, νέμονται) appear in the present tense or in the medium voice. Procopius constantly referred to Sclavenes in relation to Antes and Huns or to other nomads. When talking about Slavic dwellings, he employed καλύβαι, a phrase he only used for military tents and for Moorish compounds. Both this phrase and the claim that the Slavs set up their dwellings far from one another betray the influence of military terminology.[6]

The Slavic ethnographic *excursus* is nevertheless the longest in all of his work. It includes a rich list of topics: political organization, religion, dwellings, warfare, language, physical appearance, ethnic name, and territory. It is thus the richest of all *excursus*, an indication of the special interest of both Procopius and his audience for things Slavic. Moreover, the Slavic *excursus* shows that, despite claims to the contrary, Procopius' attitude toward Sclavenes is altogether not hostile, for to him they are neither θηριώδης, nor ἀγριώτερος, as most other barbarians are described (e.g., the Herules).[7] Most of this *excursus* was probably written on the basis of the information Procopius obtained through interviews with Sclavene and Antian mercenaries in Italy. His knowledge of the Slavs in the period following his return to Constantinople seems, however, to have been primarily based on archival material and oral sources.[8] In the main narrative of the *Wars*, the accounts of Sclavene raids are often introduced by temporal clauses, as if Procopius is striving to synchronize events in the Balkans with those in Italy or on the eastern frontier. He even suggests that a certain Sclavene raid may have not been an accident, but a deliberate attempt by Totila to keep Roman armies occupied in the Balkans.[9]

---

[6] Sclavenes, Antes, and Huns: *Wars* v 27.2; vii 14.2; *Secret History* 18.20; Slavic dwellings: *Wars* vii 14.24. See Gindin 1988:180–1. See also Ivanov 1987:31; Gindin 1987:24–5; Ivanov, Gindin, and Cymburskii 1991:224.

[7] Cesa 1982:207 and 212. For a cautious approach to Procopius' digressions and "origins"-passages, see Cameron 1985:213.

[8] Veh 1951:11; Litavrin 1986:27. Procopius' Constantinopolitan perspective is betrayed by his account of the Sclavene invasion of 549 (*Wars* vii 38.21–3). Procopius tells us that after crossing the Danube river, the 3,000 Sclavene warriors split into two groups, operating independently. One group attacked the cities in Thrace, the other invaded Illyricum. But Procopius' account focuses only on those Sclavenes who approached the walls of Constantinople and completely ignores those raiding Illyricum. It is likely that Procopius used an oral source for the obviously exaggerated figure of 15,000 prisoners taken by the Sclavenes after capturing Topeiros, as well as for the report of their torture and execution (*Wars* vii 38.23). The latter is an accurate description of the torture known in Late Antiquity as κατωμισμός and specifically associated with Christian martyrdom; see Vergote 1972:118–19, 125, and 139–40.   [9] *Wars* vii 29.1, vii 38.1, vii 40. 31. See Cesa 1982:199.

If Procopius imagined the Slavs as newcomers and nomads, Jordanes viewed them totally different. In writing the *Getica*, Jordanes may have engaged in a polemic with Procopius over the issue of the Empire's attitude toward barbarians, particularly Goths. Their respective treatment of Sclavenes and Antes suggests that Jordanes' polemic with his contemporary may have been broader than that. In an attempt to establish a quasi-legendary origin for the Slavs, Jordanes points to Venethi, Procopius to Spori. Procopius classifies Sclavenes and Antes as nomads, Jordanes gives them swamps and forests for cities. Procopius locates the Sclavenes close to the Danube frontier of the Empire, while Jordanes moves them northward as far as the Vistula river. Procopius maintains that the Sclavenes and the Antes "are not ruled by one man, but they have lived from of old under a democracy"; Jordanes gives the Antes a king, Boz. The number of examples could easily be multiplied. The evidence is too compelling to rule out the possibility that Jordanes was responding to Procopius' account. The coincidence in time of their works also supports this idea.[10]

Jordanes ended his *Getica* shortly before the *Romana*, in 550 or 551. According to him, the Antes were the strongest among all Venethi, a possible allusion to their treaty with Justinian, in 545. Despite serving as *notarius* to a certain general of the Empire named Gunthigis or Baza, Jordanes wrote *Getica* in Constantinople. From his work he appears to have been familiar with the horizons and viewpoint of the military or court circles in the Capital.[11] The preface to *Getica* contains a long paragraph borrowed from the preface of Rufinus to his translation of Origen's commentary on *Romans*. This suggests that Jordanes was not only a devout Christian, but also familiar with serious theology at a time when Origen was a controversial author. Jordanes apparently wrote in a sort of semi-retirement after his *conversio*, as a devout elderly layman deeply mindful of the transience of earthly life but nonetheless possessed of strong views on the state of the Roman world, and the immediate directions that imperial policy should take.[12]

What was Jordanes' source of information about Sclavenes and Antes? The issue of Jordanes' sources for his *Getica* is one of the most controversial. Nineteenth-century scholars claimed that Jordanes did no

[10] Jordanes, *Getica* 35; Procopius, *Wars* VII 14.22. For the polemic between Jordanes and Procopius, see Goffart 1988:93–5 and 101.

[11] The Antes as the strongest of all Venethi: *Getica* 35; Jordanes as *notarius*: *Getica* 266. Date of *Getica*: Várady 1976:487; Croke 1987:126; Anfert'ev 1991:99. Walter Goffart (1988:106–7) proposed the *Getica* was written before 552, but his ideas were met with criticism: Heather 1991a:44 and 47–9; Anton 1994:280 and 283. For *Getica* as written in Constantinople, see Wagner 1967:27; Croke 1987:119–20; Goffart 1988:106–7; Anfert'ev 1991:98.

[12] Croke 1987:134; see also O'Donnell 1982:227 and 240. Justinian's advisor in matters regarding adherents and opponents of the council at Chalcedon was Bishop Theodore Ascidas of Caesarea, an enthusiastic supporter of Origen's doctrines. It is on Theodore's advice that Justinian issued the famous edict of the Three Chapters in 543/4. See Moorhead 1994:130.

more than copy, with slight alterations, the now-lost *Gothic History* of Cassiodorus. Others tend to give him credit for originality. In fact, there is little evidence to claim that Jordanes did more than use a cursory abridgement of Cassiodorus' work as the basis for a work of his own.[13] Could the information about the Slavs have come from Cassiodorus? For his digression on Scythia, Jordanes cites the "written records" of the Goths, which was often interpreted as an indication that Jordanes used Cassiodorus as a source. In fact, the passage looks more like an insertion by Jordanes. Jordanes calls one and the same river Viscla when referring to Sclavenes, and Vistula, when speaking of Venethi. This was interpreted as an indication of two different sources. In the case of the Venethi, the source may have been an ancient work similar to Ptolemy's geography. It is equally possible, however, that Jordanes was inspired here by Tacitus, for, like him, he constantly associates Venethi with Aesti. Some argued that the name Viscla indicates a Gothic oral source. However, the river is named Vistla three times by Pliny the Elder. Moreover, one of these references is associated with the Venedi. A citation from Pliny's work by Julius Solinus is rendered by some manuscripts as Vistla, by others as Viscla. That Jordanes used Solinus has long been demonstrated by Mommsen. It is therefore very likely that Jordanes borrowed Viscla not from an oral source, but from a manuscript of the third-century *Collection of Remarkable Facts.*[14]

Jordanes' sources seem to have been written, rather than oral. This is also true for the passage referring to the conquest of Venethi by Ermenaric. The king of the Ostrogoths had subdued many tribes, which Jordanes calls *thiudos*. It is possible that both this term and the list of tribal names were derived from a Gothic source, but there is no indication that this was an oral one. Jordanes' source for the subjugation of the Herules is Ablabius. Is it possible that his account of Ermenaric's victory over the Venethi originated in either the "Gothic source" or Ablabius? In my opinion, the answer must be negative for a variety of reasons. First, unlike the Herules, whom Jordanes describes as living near Lake Maeotis, the only thing he has to say about Venethi is that they were "a multitude of cowards of no avail." Second, the reference to God in this passage looks more like a commentary by Jordanes, with his idea of Divine Providence as the main force behind all events. Third, the passage contains a cross-reference, by which Jordanes, as if not willing to repeat himself, sends us back to the "catalogue of nations" for further information on Venethi.

[13] Bradley 1966:79; Croke 1987:121; see also Baldwin 1981:145. For the relation between Cassiodorus and Jordanes, see Anton 1994:275–6.

[14] The "written records" of the Goths: *Getica* 38; see Croke 1987:123; Barnish 1984:339. Viscla/Vistula: *Getica* 34–5; Pliny the Elder, *Naturalis Historia* IV 81, 97, and 100; Julius Solinus, *Collectanea Rerum Memorabilium* 20.2. See also Mommsen 1882:xxxi and 1895:xxvi; Anfert'ev 1991:131. For Venethi and Aesti, see *Getica* 35–6 and 119– 20; Tacitus, *Germania* 46. See also Anfert'ev 1986:10.

The reference is not exactly accurate. In the "catalogue of nations" (chapter 35), we were told that the Venethi were "chiefly called Sclaveni and Antes," which could only mean that Venethi were (later) subdivided into two subcategories, the Sclavenes and the Antes. By contrast, in chapter 119, Jordanes claims that Venethi is just one of the three current names (*tria nunc nomina ediderunt*). They are a subcategory, not the archetype. The word *nunc* appears again when Jordanes claims that they, the Venethi, are raging in war far and wide. His concern is more to evoke the sixth-century setting of his argument than to impress upon readers the very distant antiquity of King Ermenaric's victory over the peoples of Scythia. Jordanes wants his audience to believe that Venethi was a name still in use during his own lifetime. Procopius, Jordanes' contemporary, only knows of Sclavenes and Antes. In his *Romana*, Jordanes himself only speaks of Bulgars, Sclavenes, and Antes. In fact, his audience must have been familiar with attacks by Sclavenes and Antes, but might have never heard of Venethi. Jordanes' mention of the Venethi linked the narrative of the Gothic history to events taking place during his lifetime. This narrative strategy, however, was not very well thought out, for he clumsily superposed a vague geographical concept of contemporary invasions on the ethnic configuration described in his "catalogue of nations."[15]

When compared to Procopius, Jordanes' account of the Slavs is poorly informed. Besides locating them in Scythia, the only thing Jordanes knows about Sclavenes is that they have swamps and woods for cities, a passage that has a distant parallel in Tacitus' description of the wooded and mountainous country raided by Venedi. The only "hard" piece of evidence about Antes is the episode of Vinitharius' victory over King Boz. Could this episode have originated in the oral Gothic tradition? In order to substantiate this idea, some pointed to the narrative pattern of the story. As in *Romana*, Jordanes employs here an unusual spelling, *Anti* instead of *Antes*, which suggests his source was Greek, not Latin. The episode of Vinitharius did not originate in Cassiodorus, because there is no indication that Cassiodorus read Greek. Just as in the case of Ermenaric's episode, Jordanes filled the imaginary map of much earlier accounts with sixth-century ethnic names.[16]

[15] *Getica* 116–17 and 119; *Romana* 52. For *thiudos* as an indication of a Gothic (oral) source, see Wolfram 1988:87–8; Anfert'ev 1991:149–50; Kazanski 1991a:36. *Contra*: Heather 1996:55. There is additional evidence that the reference to Venethi in the account of Ermenaric's military deeds originated in the "catalogue of nations." Following his victory over the Venethi, Ermenaric subdued the Aesti, "who dwell on the farthest shore of the German Ocean" (*Getica* 120). Again, the Tacitean association between Venethi and Aesti betrays Jordanes' sources.

[16] *Getica* 247; *Romana* 52; see Tacitus, *Germania* 46. See also Pritsak 1983:381; Wolfram 1988:251–2; Anfert'ev 1991:159. For the spelling of Antes in both Greek and Latin, see Werner 1980:577. For Cassiodorus and Greek, see Croke 1987:121; O'Donnell 1982:229 and 235.

It has long been recognized that one of Jordanes' sources for his *Getica* was a map. His account of the Venethi, however, suggests that there was more than one. Though Jordanes usually conceptualizes the Vistula river with a south–north direction, the "abode of the Sclaveni extends . . . northward as far as the Vistula." This indicates a west–east direction for the river, which contradicts not only all other references to Vistula, but also the entire geographical system on which Jordanes' description of Scythia is based. In addition, the river named here is Viscla, not Vistula. Jordanes' source may have been Pliny, who set his Venedi, along with Sciri and Cimbri, between the river Vistla and Sarmatia, thus acknowledging a south–north direction for this river. No other source describes the Sclavenes as being bounded to the north by any river. The only exception is the Peutinger map. The twelfth- or early thirteenth-century copy of this road map, Codex Vindobonensis 324, reproduces an early fifth-century map, itself based on a third-century prototype. The Peutinger map shows the Venedi placed between the Danube and another river, named *Agalingus*, which is perhaps a corrupted form of Ptolemy's Axiaces river. In addition, the Venedi appear across the Danube, immediately beside a staging post named *Nouiodum. XLI.* This is, no doubt, the city of Noviodunum (present-day Isaccea), with the distance in Roman miles to the next staging post, Salsovia (present-day Mahmudia). Jordanes' *ciuitas Nouitunensis* is an equivalent of *Nouiodum* on the Peutinger map. His description is based on a map showing a route along the Danube, not on an oral source.[17]

Historians imagined Jordanes as a thorough observer of the ethnographic situation on the northern frontier of the Empire in the mid-500s. The purpose of his work, however, was not accurate description. *Getica* was probably meant to be a reply to Procopius in the current debate on the attitude towards barbarians. To support his arguments, Jordanes made extensive use of various, ancient sources. The description of Scythia is based on these sources for both the geographical framework and the tribal names used to fill the map.

Jordanes used at least three sources for his description of the Venethi. Tacitus may have served as the basis for the ethnographic material, but Jordanes used maps for his geographical orientation. One of them, based on a conical or coniclike projection, had the river Vistula with a south–north direction and was probably close to, if not inspired by,

---

[17] *Getica* 35; Pliny the Elder, *Naturalis Historia* IV 97; *Tabula Peutingeriana* Segment VII.4; see also Ptolemy, *Geographia* III 5.18. For Jordanes' use of maps, see Mommsen 1882:xxxi; Curta 1999. The traditional interpretation of *ciuitas Nouitunensis* was that it referred to Neviodunum in Pannonia. This was further interpreted as indicating that in the mid-sixth century, the Slavs inhabited a vast area along the eastern slopes of the Carpathian mountains, from the Vistula river to the Middle Danube. See Skrzhinskaia 1957:6–10.

Ptolemy. The other, however, had the same river with a west–east direction, so typical for Roman road maps with no real geographical projection, such as the Peutinger map. Jordanes seems to have been unable to solve the apparent contradictions between these sources, for he was not interested in matters geographical. The issue of history concerned him to a much higher degree. Jordanes interpreted his sources as evidence for contemporary concerns. The attacks of the Sclavenes and the Antes were an experience too familiar to his audience to be neglected, even in a history of the Goths. Through his research in ancient sources about the geography of Eastern Europe, Jordanes became convinced that the ethnic groups mentioned by second- or third-century authors were the same as those rampaging everywhere during his lifetime. Although in the mid-sixth century "their names were dispersed amid various clans and places," the Venethi were still recognizable to Jordanes' eyes. And although they were now known as Sclavenes and Antes, it was the same *natio* that both Ermenaric and Vinitharius had subdued to the Goths.

Jordanes' perspective thus proves to be the exact opposite of Procopius' standpoint. Instead of representing the Slavs as "new" and nomads, Jordanes calls them Venethi and thus makes them look ancient. This, however, is not a consequence of Jordanes' inability to cope with chronology, but derives from the specific purpose of his work. Like all Christian historians of the 500s and 600s, Jordanes had a high respect for the authority of the sources he used. He was aware that not to match account and source or to distort a document would damage the truthfulness of a writer. He fully embraced therefore the historical and geographical viewpoint of his predecessors, because he needed their authority as sources. This conclusion is in sharp contrast to traditional views, which held Jordanes for a better and more accurate source for the history of the early Slavs than Procopius, because of his alleged use of Gothic oral sources.[18]

THE SLAVS, THE THEORY OF CLIMATES, AND CONSTANTINOPLE

Revision is also needed for the old idea that the earliest reference to Sclavenes is that of the author of *Erotapokriseis*, known as Pseudo-Caesarius. He must have been a Monophysite monk, most probably from the Constantinopolitan monastery Akimiton. His work is a collection of 220 queries and answers on a variety of topics (hence its Greek title, usually translated into English as *Dialogues*). Paradoxically, the style of the work reminds one more of a rhetorician than of a theologian. Pseudo-Caesarius seems to have been familiar with court life and he had certainly

---

[18] *Getica* 35. For the historiography of Jordanes' Venethi, see Curta 1999:1–5. For Jordanes as accurate source for the history of the early Slavs, see Sedov 1978; Eeckaute, Garde, and Kazanski 1992.

visited Cappadocia, Palestine, and the region of the Danube frontier. This is suggested not so much by his use of a biblical name for the Danube (Physon), as by the phrase 'Ριπιανοί he uses in reference to the inhabitants of the Danube region. The term is a derivative of the Latin word *ripa* and most probably refers to inhabitants of the province Dacia Ripensis, located alongside the Danube frontier. A *terminus a quo* for the dating of Pseudo-Caesarius' work is the reference to Lombards as living beyond the Danube, which indicates a date after *c.* 530. Moreover, in a passage referring to the same region, Pseudo-Caesarius uses the example of the frozen Danube to illustrate an argument based on a biblical citation (Gen. 1.6). He argues that 10,000 horsemen were thus able to invade Illyricum and Thrace, a clear allusion to the invasion of the Cutrigurs in the winter of 558/9. *Eratopokriseis* was therefore composed less than ten years after Procopius' and Jordanes' accounts. Pseudo-Caesarius, nevertheless, shares the former's attitude toward Slavs. He claims that the Sclavenes are savage, living by their own law and without the rule of anyone (ανηγεμόνευτοι). This may be an echo of Procopius' report that they "are not ruled by one man, but they have lived from of old under a democracy."[19]

Pseudo-Caesarius' point of view is, however, radically different from that of Procopius. His purpose was to refute the so-called theory of climates (*Milieutheorie*), which claimed that the character of a given ethnic group was a direct consequence of the influence exerted by the geographical and climatic region in which that group lived. Pseudo-Caesarius made his point by showing that completely different peoples could in fact live within the same climatic zone. He chose, among other examples, the savage Sclavenes, on one hand, and the peaceful and mild inhabitants of the Danube region (the "Physonites"), on the other. Pseudo-Caesarius' most evident bias against Sclavenes has led some to believe that his appalling portrait of the Slavs is in its entirety a cliche, while others are more inclined to give him credit of veracity.[20]

---

[19] The Greek text of the passage cited after Riedinger 1969:302 and 305–6; for its English translation, see Bačić 1983:152. See also Procopius, *Wars* VII 14.22. In his narration of the invasion of 558/9, Agathias of Myrina refers to a multitude of horsemen, crossing the frozen river "as if it were land (καθάπερ χέρσου)" (v.11.6). This is very much like Pseudo-Caesarius' description: χείμωνος πηγνυμένου καὶ εἰς λιθώδη ἀντιτυπίαν μεθισταμένης τῆς μαλακῆς τοῦ 'ρείθρου φύσεως. See Bakalov 1974:48. For the literary cliche of barbarians crossing the frozen Danube, see Hornstein 1957:155–8. Pseudo-Caesarius and the earliest reference to Sclavenes: Gorianov 1939b:310; Skrzhinskaia 1957:13 and 35; Köpstein 1979:67. Pseudo-Caesarius' life: Ivanov 1991d:251–7. Date of *Eratopokriseis*: Duichev 1953:205.

[20] Duichev 1953:207–8; Malingoudis 1990. For the theory of the seven climates and its astrological underpinnings, see Honigman 1929:4–7, 9, and 92–4. Pseudo-Caesarius' attack on the theory of climates suggests that he endorsed the measures adopted by the fifth ecumenical council (553) against astrology; see Ivanov 1991d:253.

A date slightly later than, if not closer to, that of Pseudo-Caesarius' *Eratopokriseis* could also be assigned to Agathias of Myrina's *History*. He provides little information relevant to the history of the Slavs, except the names of an Antian officer and a Sclavene soldier in the Roman army operating in the Caucasus region. The importance of this source is rather that, together with John Malalas, Agathias is the first author to mention the Sclavenes under a new, shorter name (Σκλάβοι, instead of Σκλαβηνοί or Σκλαυηνοί). Since he obtained most of his information about Roman campaigns in Italy and Caucasus from written sources (military reports and campaign diaries), rather than from personal experience, the question is whether this change in ethnic naming should be attributed to Agathias himself or to his sources. Though born in Myrina, in Asia Minor, Agathias lived most of his life in Constantinople. He was one of the most prominent lawyers in the city and he died there in *c.* 582. He certainly was in Constantinople in 558/9, as Zabergan's Cutrigurs attacked the Long Walls, for the abundance of detailed information (names of participants, place names, consequences of the invasion) betrays an eyewitness.[21]

The same event is narrated by John Malalas on the basis of a now lost source, a Constantinopolitan city chronicle, later used by Theophanes for a version of the same invasion clearly not inspired by Malalas. Unlike Agathias, Malalas specifically refers to Sclavenes as participants in this invasion. It is difficult to explain why Agathias failed to notice this detail, but it is important to note that, like him, Malalas (or his source, the Constantinopolitan chronicle) employs the shorter ethnic name (Σκλάβοι). Historians, perhaps influenced by the tendency to view Malalas as Justinian's mouthpiece to the masses, tend to give credit to Malalas and believe that Sclavenes may have indeed taken part in Zabergan's raid. There are, however, insurmountable difficulties in assuming that Malalas' audience were *breite Volksmassen* or monastic circles. Malalas provides a summary of world history from a sixth-century point of view organized around a central chronographical framework and informed by an overriding chronographical argument. Whoever was responsible for the last part of Book XVIII, whether an aged Malalas living in Constantinople or someone else, appears to have been affected by the gloom of the later part of Justinian's reign and so to have produced a desultory list of unconnected events of a sort to be associated with a putative city chronicle. Malalas did not witness the attack of 558/9 and, like Theophanes, relied exclusively on the Constantinopolitan chronicle. If

---

[21] Agathias III 3.6.9, III 3.7.2, III 21.6, IV 18.1–3, IV 20.4. For Agathias' life and work, see Veh 1951:18; Cameron 1970:3; Bakalov 1974:207; Levinskaia and Tokhtas'ev 1991a:292.

Sclavene warriors participated in Zabergan's invasion, they probably had a subordinate role, for they were invisible to the otherwise trustworthy testimony of Agathias.[22]

An equally Constantinopolitan origin must be attributed to the reference to *Sclavus* in Bishop Martin of Braga's poem dedicated to St Martin of Tours, most likely written in the late 570s. Martin, who was born in Pannonia in the 510s, visited the Holy Land in 550 or 552, travelling via Constantinople. The short ethnic name given to the Slavs suggests a Constantinopolitan source. In writing his epitaph, Bishop Martin was inspired by two poems of Sidonius Apollinaris, in which, like Martin, he listed randomly selected ethnic, barbarian names, in order to create a purely rhetorical effect. Besides *Sclavus*, there are two other ethnic names not mentioned by Sidonius, but listed by Martin: *Nara* and *Datus*. The former is interpreted as referring to inhabitants of the former province of Noricum, the latter as designating Danes. In spite of the obvious lack of accuracy of these geographical indications, some have attempted to locate the Sclavenes on a sixth-century ethnic map of Europe. It is very unlikely, however, that the mention of *Sclavus* in Bishop Martin's poem is anything more than a rhetorical device in order to emphasize the rapid spread of Christianity among *inmanes variasque gentes* through the spiritual powers of St Martin. Besides simply mentioning the Slavs, among other, more or less contemporary, ethnic groups, Bishop Martin's poem has no historical value for the Slavs.[23]

No contemporary source refers to Sclavenes during the reigns of Justin II and Tiberius II. The next information about them comes from Menander the Guardsman's now lost *History*. Menander wrote, under Maurice, a work continuing that of Agathias. It survived in fragments incorporated into *De Legationibus* and *De Sententiis*, two collections compiled under Constantine VII Porphyrogenitus in the mid-tenth century.[24] Menander's *History* may have been commissioned by Emperor Maurice

---

[22] John Malalas XVIII 129. See Litavrin 1991a:269 and 272. The use of a Constantinopolitan city chronicle for Book XVIII of Malalas' chronicle is betrayed by his dating by indiction, which is rare before the middle of Book XVI and becomes frequent only from the beginning of XVIII. At this point, entries in Malalas' chronicle are brief and almost entirely focused on Constantinople. For Malalas' sources and style, see Jeffreys 1990a:166 and 1990b:214; Croke 1990:27 and 37; Scott 1990b:84. Malalas as Justinian's mouthpiece to the masses: Irmscher 1969:471 and 1971:342. That both Agathias and Malalas used Σκλάβοι instead of Σκλαβηνοί shows that, despite recent claims to the contrary, the shorter name originated in Constantinople, not from an allegedly Thracian or Illyrian intermediary. See Schramm 1995:197.

[23] Barlow 1950:282. For Martin's life, see Ivanov 1991b:357 and 359–60. See Sidonius, *Poems* 5.474–7 and 7.323, ed. W. B. Anderson (Cambridge, 1963), pp. 102 and 146. For Martin's poem as a source for the ethnic map of sixth-century Europe, see Zeman 1966:165–6; Pohl 1988:97; Třeštík 1996:258.

[24] Another fragment has been identified in a fourteenth-century manuscript at the Bibliothèque Nationale in Paris. See Halkin 1973.

or by a powerful minister, for it seems that he enjoyed ready access to imperial archives. The work probably had ten books covering the period from the end of Agathias' *History* (558/9) to the loss of Sirmium in 582. The core of the work was built around the careers of the two men who are in the center of the narration, Tiberius and Maurice. The outlook is Constantinopolitan and the city's concerns are paramount. Menander relied heavily, if not exclusively, on written sources, especially on material from the archives (minutes of proceedings, supporting documents and correspondence, reports from envoys of embassies and meetings). His views were traditional and his main interest was in Roman relations with foreign peoples, in particular Persians and Avars. The Slavs thus appear only in the context of relations with the Avars. Menander reworked the material he presumably found in his written sources. When talking about the devastation of the territory of the Antes by Avars, who "ravaged and plundered (their land) (πιεζόμενοι δ' οὖν ταῖς τῶν πολεμίων ἐπιδρομαῖς)," he strove to imitate Agathias' style. When Dauritas/Daurentius boastfully replies to the Avar envoy that "others do not conquer our land, we conquer theirs[; a]nd *so it shall always be for us* (ταῦτα ἡμῖν ἐν βεβαίῳ), as long as there are wars and weapons (emphasis added)," this is also a phrase Menander frequently employed, particularly in rendering speeches of Roman or Persian envoys.

Despite Menander's considerable contribution to the speeches, which served both to characterize the speakers and to explore the issues, it is likely that they were fairly close to the available records. It is not difficult to visualize the possible source for Daurentius' speech. The whole episode may have been based on a report by John, "who at this time was governor of the isles and in charge of the cities of Illyricum," for when referring to the Sclavene chiefs, Menander employs the phrase τοὺς ὅσοι ἐν τέλει τοῦ ἔθνους. This is a phrase commonly used in Byzantine administration in reference to imperial officials. As such, it indicates that Menander's source for this particular episode must have been an official document. The same might be true for the episode of Mezamer. Detailed knowledge of Mezamer's noble lineage or of the relations between "that Kutrigur who was a friend of the Avars" and the qagan suggests a written source, arguably a report of an envoy. Menander may have only added his very traditional view of barbarians: greedy, cunning, arrogant, lacking self-control, and untrustworthy. To him, the Sclavenes murdered the Avar emissaries specifically because they lost control.[25]

---

[25] Menander the Guardsman, frs. 3 and 21; see Agathias I 1.1. For Menander's sources and style, see Blockley 1985:1, 5, 11, 14, and 20; Baldwin 1978:118; Levinskaia and Tokhtas'ev 1991b:328 and 349–50. For the use of ὅσοι ἐν τέλει τοῦ ἔθνους in reference to imperial officials, see Benedicty 1965:53.

Unlike Menander, John of Ephesus personally witnessed the panic caused by Avar and Slav attacks during Tiberius' and Maurice's reigns. His *Ecclesiastical History*, now lost, contained three parts, the last of which had six books. Book VI was compiled at Constantinople over a period of years, as indicated by chronological references in the text. The last event recorded is the acquittal of Gregory of Antioch in 588. John first came to Constantinople in the 530s, where he enjoyed Emperor Justinian's favors. He was absent from the Capital between 542 and 571, as he was first nominated missionary bishop in Asia Minor and then elected bishop of Ephesus. He was back in Constantinople when Justin II launched his persecution of the Monophysites. Beginning in 571, John spent eight years in prison. Most of Book VI, if not the entire third part of the *History*, was written during this period of confinement. John must have died soon after the last event recorded in his work, for the surviving fragments leave the impression of a draft, which he may not have had the time to revamp. The concluding chapters of Book VI are lost, but significant parts could be reconstructed on the basis of later works, such as the eighth-century chronicle attributed to Dionysius of Tell Mahre, that of Elias Bar Shinaya (tenth to eleventh century), the twelfth-century chronicle of Michael the Syrian, the Jacobite patriarch of Antioch, and the thirteenth-century chronicle of Gregory Barhebraeus.[26]

John was no doubt influenced by the pessimistic atmosphere at Constantinople in the 580s to overstate the intensity of Slavic ravaging. His views of the Slavs, however, have a different source. John was a supporter of that *Milieutheorie* attacked by Pseudo-Caesarius. To him, the Slavs were *lyt'* (accursed, savage), for they were part of the seventh climate, in which the sun rarely shone over their heads. Hence, their blonde hair, their brutish character, and their rude ways of life. On the other hand, God was on their side, for in John's eyes, they were God's instrument for punishing the persecutors of the Monophysites. This may also explain why John insists that, beginning with 581 (just ten years after Justin II started persecuting the Monophysites), the Slavs began occupying Roman territory, "until now, that is up to the year 895 [i.e., 584] . . . [and] became rich and possessed gold and silver, herds of

---

[26] For John's life and work, see D'iakonov 1946:20 and 25; Allen 1979:254; Serikov 1991:276, 281, and 283; Ginkel 1995. For John writing in prison, see III 3.1 and III 2.50. Despite Michael the Syrian's claims to the contrary, he borrowed much of his chapter X 21 from John's *Historia Ecclesiastica*. He might have used John through an intermediary, possibly the chronicle attributed to Dionysius of Tell Mahre, who might have misled him over the precise conclusion of John's work. Certainly borrowed from John is the account of widespread Slav ravaging, including the sack of churches at Corinth, and the payments made by Maurice to the Antes for attacking the Sclavenes.

horses and a lot of weapons, and learned to make war better than the Romans."[27]

The echo of the panic caused by Slavic raids in the Balkans also reached Spain, where John of Biclar recorded their ravaging of Thrace and Illyricum.[28] Between 576/7 and 586/7, John was in Barcelona, where he may have received news from Constantinople, via Cartagena. The last part of his chronicle, written in 589/90, recorded only major events. For the year 575, there are thirteen entries concerning the East and ten referring to events in the West. The last entries, covering the period between 576 and 589/90, include only three events from the East, but twenty-two from the West. Two, if not all three, of the Eastern events mentioned are in relation to Slavic raids. Though John's chronology of Byzantine regnal years is unreliable, the raids were correctly dated to 576 and 581, respectively, because beginning with year 569, entries in the chronicle were also dated by King Leuvigild's and his son's regnal years. John of Biclar may thus have recorded events that, at the same time, in Constantinople, John of Ephesus interpreted as God's punishment for sinners.[29]

In a passage most probably borrowed from a now lost part of John of Ephesus' *History*, Michael the Syrian speaks of Slavs plundering churches, but calls their leader, who carried away the *ciborium* of the cathedral in Corinth, a qagan. John of Biclar also speaks of Avars occupying *partes Graeciae* in 579. Evagrius visited Constantinople in 588 to assist his employer, Gregory, patriarch of Antioch, to defend himself against accusations of incest. On this occasion, he recorded information about the capture, enslavement, and destruction by Avars of Singidunum, Anchialos, the whole of Greece, and other cities and forts, which could not be prevented because of the Empire's Eastern commitments. Both

---

[27] John of Ephesus III 6.25. This passage is one of the key arguments for the chronology of the Slavic *Landnahme* in the Balkans. See Nestor 1963:50–1; Popović 1975:450; Weithmann 1978:86; Ferjančić 1984:95; Pohl 1988:82. To John, "wars, battles, destruction, and carnage" proclaimed the return of Christ (III 6.1). The end of his *History* seems to have been specifically added as a warning that the end of the world was close. For the intensifying eschatological apprehension, which is evident in a number of contemporary texts, such as John Malalas and Romanos the Melodist's hymn *On the Ten Virgins*, see Magdalino 1993:5 and 7. For John's image of the Slavs, see also Whitby 1988:110. The seventh climate was the northernmost and traditionally placed at the mouth of the Borysthenes (Bug) river. See Honigman 1929:9.

[28] John of Biclar, *Chronicle*, ed. Th. Mommsen, *MGH: AA* 11:214 and 216. John also knew of Avar attacks in Thrace, Greece, and Pannonia (11:215). See Weithmann 1978:88; Yannopoulos 1980:333; Pohl 1988:76 with n. 40.

[29] It is possible that the first raid was misdated by two years (578 instead of 576); see Waldmüller 1976:106. For Slavs in John's chronicle, see also Cherniak 1991:395.

John of Ephesus and Evagrius must have learned about these events in the Capital and there are good reasons to believe that John of Biclar's ultimate source of information was also in Constantinople. It has been rightly pointed that Evagrius was undoubtedly referring to invasions by Avars, not Slavs, and that it is unfair to accuse him of muddling Avars and Slavs. If this is true, however, we should apply the same treatment to both John of Biclar and John of Ephesus. Unlike Evagrius, they both refer elsewhere to Slavs, in the context of otherwise well datable events. We may safely assume, therefore, that in the 580s, in Constantinople, devastations in Greece were attributed to Avars, not Slavs. The ethnic terminology of later sources, such as the *Chronicle of Monemvasia* or *Vita S. Pancratii*, may be a dim recollection of this interpretation of events.[30]

That the Slavs were considered the most important danger, however, is suggested by the analysis of a military treatise known as the *Strategikon*. Its author was an experienced officer, who had undoubtedly participated in Maurice's campaigns against Avars and Sclavenes, some ten years after the events narrated by John of Ephesus, John of Biclar, and Evagrius. He was accustomed to the life of military camps and knew a lot about different forms of warfare from his own experience of fighting on at least two different fronts. Unlike other military treatises, the author of *Strategikon* devotes a whole chapter to what might be called "exercise deception," describing a series of mock drills to be practiced so that enemy spies will not find out which one will be applied by Roman troops. He is also an enthusiastic proponent of misleading the enemy with "disinformation" and has a sophisticated appreciation of how to make defectors and deserters work against, instead of for, enemy interests. All this is strikingly similar to Theophylact Simocatta's later description of Priscus' and Peter's tactics during their campaigns against the Sclavenes and the Avars.

That the chapter in the *Strategikon* dedicated to Sclavenes and Antes is entirely based on the author's experience is shown by his own declaration at the end of Book XI: "Now then, we have reflected on these topics to the best of our ability, drawing on our own experience (ἔκ τε τῆς

---

[30] Michael the Syrian x 21; John of Biclar p. 215; Evagrius, *Historia Ecclesiastica*, VI 10. See Whitby 1988:110. That this selective memory ostensibly operated only in connection with *certain* Constantinopolitan sources is indirectly suggested by the letters of Pope Gregory the Great. Before being elected pope, he had spent some time between 579 and 585/6 in Constantinople as papal *apocrisiarius*. Gregory, however, was unaware of the importance of Avars in contemporary events relevant to the Balkans. Throughout his considerable correspondence (over 850 letters), there is no mention of the Avars. Two letters (IX 154 of May 599 and x 15 of July 600) specifically refer to Sclavene raids into Istria. See Ronin 1995a:351–2. Paul the Deacon, arguably relying on independent sources, would later claim that besides Slavs, both Lombards *and* Avars had invaded Istria (*Historia Langobardorum* IV 24). In the tradition established by Constantinopolitan sources that have inspired both Agathias and Malalas, Gregory speaks of *Sclavi*, instead of *Sclaveni* (IX 154: *de Sclavis victorias nuntiastis*; x 15: *Sclavorum gens*).

πείρας αὐτῆς) and on the authorities of the past, and we have written down these reflections for the benefit of whoever may read them."[31] Despite his reliance on the "authorities of the past," there can be no doubt that, when describing Slavic settlements, warfare, or society, the author of the *Strategikon* speaks of things he saw with his own eyes. By contrast, the chapters dedicated to the "blonde races" (Franks and Lombards) and to "Scythians" (Avars) are more conventional. Moreover, the chapter dedicated to Sclavenes and Antes, twice labelled ἔθνη (XI 4.1 and 4), is almost as long as all chapters on Franks, Lombards, and Avars taken together.[32]

In sharp contrast to all treatises written before him, the author of the *Strategikon* boldly introduced ethnographic data into a genre traditionally restricted to purely military topics. It is true, however, that ethnographic details appear only when relevant to the treatise's subject matter, namely to warfare. Indeed, like John of Ephesus, the author of the *Strategikon* was inspired by the theory of climates. He believed that the geographical location of a given ethnic group determined not only its lifestyle and laws, but also its type of warfare.[33] If the *Strategikon* pays attention to such things as to how Slavic settlements branch out in many directions or how Slavic women commit suicide at their husbands' death, it is because its author strongly believed that such details might be relevant to Slavic warfare.

Who was the author of the *Strategikon* and when was this work written? Both questions are obviously of great importance for the history of the early Slavs. The issue of authorship is still a controversial one. The oldest manuscript, Codex Mediceo-Laurentianus 55.4 from Florence, dated to *c.* 950, attributes the treatise to a certain Urbicius. Three other manuscripts dated to the first half of the eleventh century attribute the work to a certain Maurice, whom Richard Förster first identified with one of Emperor Maurice's contemporary namesakes. The most recent manuscript, Codex Ambrosianus gr. 139, reproducing the oldest version, explicitly attributes the treatise to Μαυρικίου . . . τοῦ ἐπὶ τοῦ βασιλέως Μαυρικίου γεγονότος. It is very likely that Emperor

---

[31] *Strategikon* XI 4.46. See Mihăescu 1974:20–1; Kuchma 1978:12; Dennis and Gamillscheg 1981:13; Petersen 1992:75.

[32] The importance attributed to Sclavenes also results from the reference to "Sclavene spears" (λογχίδια Σκλαβινίσκια; XII B5), which apparently were in use by Byzantine infantrymen. Their equipment also included "Gothic shoes," "Herulian swords," and "Bulgar cloaks" (XII B 1 and XII 8.4). See Dennis 1981. Some even claimed that the chapter on the Slavs was the only original part of the work: Cankova-Petkova 1987:73. It is interesting to note, however, that the *Strategikon* lists Antes among enemies of the Empire, despite their being its allies since 545. See Kuchma 1991:381. For army discipline, see Giuffrida 1985:846.

[33] For the theory that each climate was governed by a star or a planet that determined its "laws," see Honigman 1929:92–3.

Maurice had commissioned this treatise to an experienced high officer or general of the army. This seems to be supported by a few chronological markers in the text. There is a reference to the siege of Akbas in 583, as well as to stratagems applied by the qagan of the Avars during a battle near Heraclea, in 592. Some have argued, therefore, that the *Strategikon* may have been written during Maurice's last years (after 592) or during Phocas' first years. A long list of military commands in Latin used throughout the text also suggests a dating to the first three decades of the seventh century, at the latest, for it is known that after that date, Greek definitely replaced Latin in the administration, as well as in the army.[34] But it is difficult to believe that the recommendation of winter campaigning against the Slavs could have been given, without qualification or comment, after the mutiny of 602, for which this strategy was a central issue. The *Strategikon* should therefore be dated within Maurice's regnal years, most probably between 592 and 602. In any case, at the time the *Strategikon* was written, the Sclavenes were still north of the river Danube. Its author recommended that provisions taken from Sclavene villages by Roman troops should be transported south of the Danube frontier, using the river's northern tributaries.[35]

THE SAINT AND THE BARBARIANS

The next relevant information about Slavs is to be found in Book I of a collection known as the *Miracles of St Demetrius*, written in Thessalonica. The collection, which was offered as a hymn of thanksgiving to God for His gift to the city, is a didactic work, written by Archbishop John of Thessalonica in the first decade of Heraclius' reign. A clear indication of this date is a passage of the tenth miracle, in which John refers to events happening during Phocas' reign but avoids using his name, an indication of the *damnatio memoriae* imposed on Phocas during Heraclius' first regnal years.[36]

Book I contains fifteen miracles which the saint performed for the benefit of his city and its inhabitants. Most of them occurred during the

---

[34] Förster 1877. See Dennis and Gamillscheg 1981:18; Kuchma 1982:48–9. J. Wiita believed that the author of the *Strategikon* was Philippikos, Maurice's brother-in-law and general. According to Wiita, the treatise was calculated to facilitate Philippikos' return to power after Phocas' coup. See Wiita 1977:47–8. For Latin military commands, see Mihăescu 1974:203; Petersmann 1992:225–8.

[35] *Strategikon* XI 4.19 and 32; see Whitby 1988:131.

[36] *Miracles of St Demetrius* I 10.82. For the date of Book I, see Lemerle 1981:44 and 80; Whitby 1988:116; Macrides 1990:189. Paul Speck (1993:275, 512, and 528) has argued against the idea that Archbishop John was the author of Book I, which he believed was of a much later date. I find Speck's arguments totally unconvincing, for a variety of reasons. Most important, he claimed that John, who is mentioned in Book II as responsible for the collection in Book I, was an abbot, not a bishop. John, however, is specifically mentioned as πατὴρ καὶ ἐπίσκοπος (II 2.201).

episcopate of Eusebius, otherwise known from letters addressed to him by Pope Gregory the Great between 597 and 603. The purpose of this collection was to demonstrate to the Thessalonicans that Demetrius was their fellow citizen, their own saint, always present with them, watching over the city. The saint is therefore shown as working for the city as a whole, interceding on behalf of all its citizens in plague, famine, civil war, and war with external enemies. The fact that sometimes Archbishop John addresses an audience (οἱ ἀκούοντες), which he calls upon as witness to the events narrated, suggests that the accounts of these miracles were meant for delivery as sermons.[37]

Moreover, each miracle ends with a formulaic doxology. John also notes a certain rationale which he follows in the presentation of miracles. His aim is to recount St Demetrius' "compassion and untiring and unyielding protection" for the city of Thessalonica, but the structure of his narrative is not chronological. The episode of the repaired silver *ciborium* (1 6) is narrated *before* that of the fire which destroyed it (1 12). Following a strictly chronological principle, the plague (1 3), the one-week siege of the city by the qagan's army (1 13–15), and the subsequent famine (1 8) should have belonged to the same sequence of events. Archbishop John, however, wrote five self-contained episodes, each ending with a prayer and each possibly serving as a separate homily to be delivered on the saint's feast day. This warns us against taking the first book of the *Miracles of St Demetrius* too seriously. The detailed description of the progress of the two sieges should not be treated as completely trustworthy, but just as what it was meant to be, namely a collection of a few sensational incidents which could have enhanced St Demetrius' glory. John depicted himself on the city's wall, rubbing shoulders with the other defenders of Thessalonica during the attack of the 5,000 Sclavene warriors.[38] Should we believe him? Perhaps.[39] It may not be a mere coincidence, however, that, though never depicted as a warrior

[37] John's audience: *Miracles of St Demetrius* 1 12.101. In the prologue, John addresses the entire brotherhood (πᾶσαν τὴν ἀδελφότητα) and the pious assembly (ὦ φιλόθεος ἐκκλησία). He will not speak from his "hand" or "pen," but with his tongue (γλῶττα, διὰ μιᾶς γλώττης), and will employ a simple and accessible language (Prologue 6–7). See also Lemerle 1953:353 and 1981:36; Ivanova 1995a:182; Skedros 1996:141. St Demetrius as intercessor for Thessalonica: Macrides 1990:189–90. The fifteenth miracle even shows him disobeying God, who is explicitly compared to the emperor, by refusing to abandon the city to the enemy (1 15.166–75).

[38] Prologue 6; 1 12.107. John begins with miracles of bodily healing (1 1–3), moves on to a miracle of healing of the soul (1 4), then presents three miracles in which the saint appears to individuals (1 5–7), and ends his collection with miracles that directly affect Thessalonica and its citizens (1 8–15).

[39] The author of Book II explicitly states that Archbishop John led the resistance of the Thessalonicans during the thirty-three-day siege of the city by the qagan (*Miracles of St Demetrius* II 2.204).

saint, St Demetrius also appears on the city's walls ἐν ὁπλίτου σχήματι during the siege of Thessalonica by the armies of the qagan. Moreover, John would like us to believe that he had witnessed the attack of the 5,000 Sclavenes, which occurred on the same night that the *ciborium* of the basilica was destroyed by fire. He had that story, however, from his predecessor, Bishop Eusebius. On the other hand, John was well informed about the circumstances of the one-week siege. He knew that, at that time, the inhabitants of the city were harvesting outside the city walls, the city's eparch, together with the city's troops, were in Greece, and the notables of Thessalonica were in Constantinople, to carry a complaint against that same eparch. He also knew that the Sclavene warriors fighting under the qagan's command were his subjects, unlike those who attacked Thessalonica by night, whom John described as "the flower of the Sclavene nation" and as infantrymen.[40] My impression is that John may have been an eyewitness to the night attack, but he certainly exaggerated the importance of the one-week siege. Despite the qagan's impressive army of no less than 100,000 warriors and the numerous handicaps of the city's inhabitants, the enemy was repelled after only one week with apparently no significant losses for the besieged. To blame Archbishop John's contemporary, Theophylact Simocatta, for having failed to record any of the sieges of Thessalonica, is therefore to simply take the *Miracles of St Demetrius* at their face value and to overestimate the events narrated therein. That the sieges of Thessalonica were not recorded by any other source might well be an indication of their local, small-scale significance. As for Archbishop John, who was using history to educate his fellow citizens and glorify the city's most revered saint, he may have been well motivated when exaggerating the magnitude of the danger.[41]

THE SIEGE OF CONSTANTINOPLE, THE CAMPAIGN DIARY, AND THE WENDS

There are few Western sources that mention the Slavs after John of Biclar and Gregory the Great. By the end of his chronicle, Isidore of Seville refers to the occupation of Greece by Slavs, sometime during Heraclius'

[40] St Demetrius on the walls of Thessalonica: I 13.120; the episode of the *ciborium* related by Eusebius: I 6.55; circumstances of the one-week siege: I 13.127–9; Sclavene warriors in the army of the qagan: I 13.117; Sclavene warriors during the night attack: I 12.108 and 110. John never calls the Slavs Σκλάβοι, only Σκλαβίνοι or Σκλαβηνοί. Paul Lemerle (1981:41) suggested that St Demetrius became a military saint only after the attacks of the Avars and the Sclavenes. In Book II, St Demetrius already introduces himself as στρατιώτης to Bishop Kyprianos (II 6.309).
[41] The army of the qagan: I 13.118 and 126. See Tăpkova-Zaimova 1964:113–14. For the lack of information about Thessalonica, see Proudfoot 1974:382; Olajos 1981:422; Whitby 1988:49.

early regnal years. It is difficult to visualize Isidore's source for this brief notice, but his association of the Slavic occupation of Greece with the loss of Syria and Egypt to the Persians indicates that he was informed about the situation in the entire Mediterranean basin.[42]

Isidore's *Chronica Maiora* ends in 624 or 626 and there is no mention in it of the siege of Constantinople by Avars, Slavs, and Persians. We have good, though brief, descriptions of the role played by Slavs in the works of three eyewitnesses. George of Pisidia refers to them in both his *Bellum Avaricum*, written in 626, and his *Heraclias*, written in 629.[43] The author of the *Chronicon Paschale*, a work probably completed in 630 and certainly extending to 629, was also an eyewitness to the siege, despite his use of written sources, such as the city chronicle of Constantinople.[44] As for Theodore Syncellus, he is specifically mentioned by the author of the *Chronicon Paschale* as having been one of the envoys sent from the city to the qagan on August 2, 626. His name is derived from the office he held under Patriarch Sergius, the great figure behind the city's heroic resistance. Theodore Syncellus' mention of the Slavs is therefore important, particularly because he is the first author to refer to cremation as the burial rite favored by Slavs.[45] What all these three authors have in common is the awareness that there were at least two categories of Sclavene warriors. First, there were those fighting as allies of the Avars, the "Slavic wolves," as George of Pisidia calls them. On the other hand, those attacking Blachernae on canoes were the subjects of the Avars, as clearly indicated by the *Chronicon Paschale*.[46] We have seen that Archbishop John also recorded that Thessalonica was attacked at one time by the qagan's army, including his Sclavene subjects, at another by 5,000 warriors, "the flower of the Sclavene nation," with no interference from the Avars.

Was Theophylact Simocatta also a witness to the siege of 626? He certainly outlived the great victory, for the last events explicitly mentioned in his *History* are Heraclius' victory over Rhazates in 627, the death of Khusro II, and the conclusion of peace with Persia in the following year. It has also been argued that since the introductory *Dialogue* of his *History* alludes to the patriarch of Constantinople, Sergius, as the man who had encouraged the composition of the work, Theophylact must have pursued his legal career in the employment of the patriarch. It is therefore possible that he was in Constantinople in 626, but there is no evidence for

---

[42] Isidore of Seville, *History*, ed. Th. Mommsen, *MGH: AA* 11:479. See Szádeczky-Kardoss 1986b:52–3; Ivanova 1995b:356–7. The use of an official, perhaps Constantinopolitan, report is also betrayed by the use of *Sclavi* instead of *Sclavini*. The same event is recorded by *Continuatio Hispana*, written in 754 (*Sclavi Greciam occupant*). Its author derived this information not from Isidore, but from another, unknown source, which has been presumably used by Isidore himself (Szádeczky-Kardoss 1986b:54; Ivanova 1995b:355). [43] Ivanov 1995c:66–7.
[44] Scott 1990a:38; Ivanov 1995d:75. [45] Ivanov 1995d:80. [46] Ivanov 1995d:82.

that in his work. Theophylact has often been compared to George of Pisidia or the author of the *Chronicon Paschale*, for having composed substantial parts of his narrative in the optimistic mood of the late 620s, after Heraclius' triumph, or to Theodore Syncellus, for his style. His *History* only focuses on the Balkans and the eastern front, in other words only on Roman dealings with Avars (and Slavs) and Persians, the major enemies of 626. It is possible that Theophylact's *History* was an attempt to explain current events in the light of Maurice's policies in the Balkans and the East. If so, this could also explain Theophylact's choice of sources for Maurice's campaigns across the Danube, against Avars and Slavs.[47]

It has long been noted that, beginning with Book VI, Theophylact's narrative changes drastically. Although his chronology is most erratic, he suddenly pays attention to such minor details as succession of days and length of particular marches. The number and the length of speeches diminishes drastically, as well as the number of Theophylact's most typical stylistical marks. The reason for this change is Theophylact's use of an official report or bulletin, to which he could have had access either directly or through an intermediary source. Haussig rightfully called this official report a *Feldzugsjournal*, a campaign diary, which was completed after Phocas' accession of 602. Indeed, there is a consistency of bias throughout this part of Theophylact's *History*, for he obviously favors the general Priscus at the expense of Comentiolus and Peter. Peter's victories are extolled and his failures minimized, while his rivals appear lazy and incompetent. Any success they achieve is attributed to their subordinates, either Alexander, in 594, or Godwin, in 602, both winning victories against the Slavs for Peter. But Priscus was Phocas' son-in-law and it may be no accident that Theophylact (or, more probably, his source) laid emphasis on the army's dissatisfaction against Maurice on the question of winter campaigning against the Slavs, for this was at the very root of the 602 revolt. It has even been argued that for the chapters VIII 5.5 to VIII 7.7 narrating the events of 601 and 602, particularly Phocas' revolt of November 602, Theophylact may have used reports of surviving participants, such as Godwin himself, who is in the middle of all actions.[48]

The campaigns in the *Feldzugsjournal* were narrated in correct sequence, but without precise intervals between important events. The

---

[47] Last events mentioned: Theophylact Simocatta, *History* VIII 12.12–13. See Olajos 1981–2:41 and 1988:11; Whitby and Whitby 1986:xiv; Whitby 1988:39–40.

[48] Succession of days and length of marches: VI 4.3, VI 4.7, VI 4.12, VI 6.2–VI 11.21, etc. See Olajos 1982:158 and 1988:132 and 136; Whitby 1988:49–50, 93, and 96. For the *Feldzugsjournal*, see Haussig 1953:296. The complimentary reference to Bonosus, Phocas' hated henchman (VIII 5.10), is also an indication that the *Feldzugsjournal* was produced in the milieu of Phocas' court. For the extolling of Peter's victories, see Whitby and Whitby 1986:xxiii, Olajos 1988:131; Whitby 1988:99.

account tends therefore to disintegrate into a patchwork of detailed reports of individual incidents, deprived of an overall historical context. This caused Theophylact considerable trouble, leading him to overlook gaps of months or even years. He must have been aware of the fact that his source recorded annual campaigns (usually from spring to fall), without any information about intervals between them. He therefore filled in the gaps with information taken from other sources, in particular from the Constantinopolitan chronicle, without noticing his dating errors. The Constantinopolitan chronicle also provided Theophylact with information about some major military events in the vicinity of the Capital, such as Comentiolus' victories over the Slavs, in which there is no hint of the anti-Comentiolus bias of the *Feldzugsjournal*.[49]

But Theophylact's inability to cope with contrasting sources led him and modern historians into confusion. Theophylact places the beginning of the emperor's campaign against Avars and Slavs immediately after the peace with Persia, in 592. On the other hand he tells us that in that same year a Frankish embassy arrived in Constantinople, but the king allegedly sending it came to power only in 596. Without any military and geographical knowledge, Theophylact was unable to understand the events described in his sources and his narrative is therefore sometimes obscure and confusing. This is also a result of Theophylact's bombastic style. In Books VI–VIII, he uses the affected "parasang" instead of "mile," an element which could hardly be ascribed to his source. He describes the problem of Romans drinking from a stream under Slavic attack as a "choice between two alternatives . . ., either to refuse the water and relinquish life through thirst, or to draw up death too along with the river." Again, it is very hard to believe that these were the words of the *Feldzugsjournal*. It is true that Books VI–VIII contain no Homeric citations, but the stylistic variation introduced in order to attenuate the flat monotony of the military source amounts to nothing else but grandiloquent rhetoric. More often than not, the end result is a very confusing text.[50]

---

[49] Duket 1980:72; Olajos 1988:133–4. Theophylact's inability to understand his source may have also been responsible for some obscure passages, such as VII 4.8, where the river crossed by Peter's army against Peiragastus cannot be the Danube, because ποταμός only occurs singly when preceded by Ἴστρος. Theophylact may have omitted that paragraph from his source which dealt with the crossing of the Danube and only focused on the actual confrontation with Peiragastus' warriors. For the use of the Constantinopolitan chronicle for Comentiolus' victory over the Slavs, see I 7.1–6; Whitby and Whitby 1986:xxv. The Constantinopolitan chronicle, however, did not provide Theophylact with sufficient information to help him resolve the chronological uncertainties of his military source.

[50] In his account of the victory of the Romans against Musocius (VI 9.14), Theophylact tells us that "the Romans inclined toward high living" (πρὸς τρυφὴν κατεκλίνοντο), "were sewed up in liquor" (τῇ μέθῃ συρρήπτονται), and disregarded sentry-duty (τῆς διαφρουρᾶς κατημέλησαν).

In addition, Theophylact's view of history, as expressed in the introductory *Dialogue* between Philosophy and History, is that of a sequence of events that were fully intelligible to God alone. History is far superior to the individual historian whose role is to function as History's lyre, or even as her plectrum. Theophylact believed in the "extensive experience of history" as being "education for the souls," for the "common history of all mankind [is] a teacher." As a consequence, his heroes are not complex human beings, but repositories of moral principles.[51]

Far from being an eyewitness account of Roman campaigns against the Slavs, replete with personal observations, Theophylact's narrative is thus no more than a literary reworking of information from his military source. Like Diodorus' *Bibliotheca*, his work remains important for having preserved historical evidence from sources that are completely or partially lost. This is, in fact, what makes Theophylact's *History* an inestimable source for the history of the early Slavs. Despite his evident biases, Theophylact was unable to entirely absorb the *Feldzugsjournal* into his narrative and his intervention is relatively well visible. The episode of the three Sclavenes captured by Maurice's bodyguards at Heraclea, who wore no iron or military equipment, but only lyres, is certainly a cliche, for the same is said by Tacitus about the Aestii. This is in sharp contrast to the factual tone of Theophylact's account of Priscus' campaign against Ardagastus and Musocius or Peter's expedition against Peiragastus. Books VI and VII have little direct speech and flowery periphrases are comparatively fewer than in preceding books.[52]

Theophylact preserved not only the day-by-day chronology recorded in the campaign diary, but numerous other details, such as the names and the status of three Slavic leaders. Moreover, there are several instances in

Footnote 50 (*cont.*)

Although all three actions took place at the same definite time in the past, Theophylact's use of tenses is most inconsistent, for, in a bizarre combination, he employs imperfect, present, and aorist, respectively. For Theophylact's bombastic style, see Olajos 1982:160. For Homeric citations in Theophylact's *History*, see Leanza 1972:586. The Frankish embassy: VI 3.6–7; Romans drinking from a stream: VII 5.9. Theophylact was aware that a parasang was not the equivalent of a mile. The distance between Constantinople and Hebdomon is at one time given in parasangs (V 16.4), at another in miles (VIII 10.1), and Theophylact also uses miles separately (e.g., VII 4.3).

51 Krivushin 1991:54 and 1994:10. For Theophylact's concept of God's role in history, see Leanza 1971:560 and 565. For his concept of history, see *Dialogue* 15; *History* Proem 6 and 13.

52 Olajos 1982:158. For Theophylact and Diodorus, see Whitby 1988:312 and 350. For Theophylact and Tacitus, see VI 2.10; *Germania* 46; see also Ivanov 1995b:48. A literary influence may also explain Theophylact's use of Γετικὸν (ἔθνος) for the Slavs, a phrase more often applied to the Goths. It is interesting to note that he also called the Persians "Babylonians" and the Avars "Scythians." Despite claims to the contrary, the fact that the last part of the *History* is less stylish and organized does not support the idea that Theophylact's historical interest in Books VI–VIII was only limited and that he must have died before re-editing this part of his work. See Olajos 1988:135; Whitby 1988:49–50.

which the actions of Priscus or Peter seem to follow strictly the recommendations of the *Strategikon*.[53] It is possible, though not demonstrated, that the author of the *Feldzugsjournal* was a participant in those same campaigns in which the author of the *Strategikon* gained his rich field experience. If true, this would only make Theophylact's account more trustworthy, despite his literary reworking of the original source. We may well smile condescendingly when Theophylact tells us that the three Sclavenes encountered by Emperor Maurice did not carry any weapons, "because their country was ignorant of iron and thereby provided them with a peaceful and troublefree life."[54] But there is no reason to be suspicious about his account of Priscus' campaign in Slavic territory. He may have clothed the plain narrative of the *Feldzugsjournal* with rhetorical figures; but he neither altered the sequence of events, nor was he interested in modifying details.

Theophylact's approach is slightly different from that of his contemporary in Frankish Gaul, the seventh-century author known as Fredegar. Until recently, the prevailing view was that the *Chronicle of Fredegar* was the product of three different authors, the last of whom was responsible for the Wendish account, but new research rejuvenated Marcel Baudot's theory of single authorship. Judging from internal evidence, Fredegar's Book IV together with its Wendish account must have been written around 660. A partisan of the Austrasian aristocracy, in particular of the Pippinid family, Fredegar may have been close to or even involved in the activity of the chancery. The purpose of his chronicle seems to have been to entertain his audience, as suggested by the epic style of his stories about Aetius, Theodoric, Justinian, or Belisarius.[55]

Where did Fredegar find his information about Samo, the Wendish king? Some proposed that he had obtained it all from the mouth of Sicharius, Dagobert's envoy to Samo. Others believe that the entire episode is just a tale. Fredegar's criticism of Dagobert's envoy and his

---

[53] Ardagastus is attacked by surprise, in the middle of the night (VI 7.1; cf. *Strategikon* IX 2.7). The author of the *Strategikon* knows that provisions may be found in abundance in Sclavene territory, a fact confirmed by the booty taken by Priscus that caused disorder among his soldiers (VI 7.6; cf. *Strategikon* XI 4.32). As if following counsels in the *Strategikon*, Priscus ordered some of his men to move ahead on reconnaissance (VI 8.9 and VI 9.12; cf. *Strategikon* XI 4.41). Finally, Maurice's orders for his army to pass winter season in Sclavene territory (VI 10.1, VIII 6.2) resonate with strategic thoughts expressed in the *Strategikon* (XI 4.19).   [54] Theophylact Simocatta VI 2.15.

[55] Fredegar II 53, 57–9, and 62; see Kusternig 1982:7; Goffart 1988:427–8. His anti-Merovingian attitude and declared hostility toward Brunhild and her attempts at centralization of power also show Fredegar as a partisan of the Austrasian aristocracy. For the problem of authorship, see Krusch 1882; Baudot 1928; Kusternig 1982:12; Wood 1994a:359; Goffart 1963. For the date of Book IV, see Labuda 1949:90–2; Goffart 1963:239; Kusternig 1982:5 and 12. Fredegar's erratic chronology in Book IV has long been noted. See Gardiner 1978:40 and 44. For chronological aspects relevant to the Wendish account, see Curta 1997:144–55.

detailed knowledge of juridical and administrative formulaic language suggests a different solution.[56] According to Fredegar, the Slavs have long been subject to the Avars, "who used them as Befulci." The word is cognate with *fulcfree*, a term occurring in the Edict of the Lombard king Rothari. Both derive from the Old German *felhan, falh, fulgum* (hence the Middle German *bevelhen*), meaning "to entrust to, to give someone in guard." To Fredegar, therefore, Wends was a name for special military units of the Avar army. The term *befulci* and its usage further suggest, however, that Fredegar reinterpreted a "native," presumably Wendish, account. His purpose was to show how that Wendish *gens* emerged, which would later play an instrumental role in the decline of Dagobert's power.[57]

Fredegar had two apparently equivalent terms for the same *ethnie*: *Sclauos coinomento Winedos*. There are variants for both terms, such as *Sclavini* or *Venedi*. The 'Wends' appear only in political contexts: the Wends, not the Slavs, were *befulci* of the Avars; the Wends, and not the Slavs, made Samo their king. There is a Wendish *gens*, but not a Slavic one. After those chapters in which he explained how a Wendish polity had emerged, Fredegar refers exclusively to Wends. It is, therefore, possible that 'Wends' and 'Sclavenes' are meant to denote a specific social and political configuration, in which such concepts as state or ethnicity are relevant, while 'Slavs' is a more general term, used in a territorial rather than an ethnic sense.[58]

'Wends' and 'Slavs' were already in use when Fredegar wrote Book IV. They first appear in Jonas of Bobbio's *Life of St Columbanus*, written sometime between 639 and 643. According to Jonas, Columbanus had once thought of preaching to the Wends, who were also called Slavs (*Venetiorum qui et Sclavi dicuntur*). He gave up this mission of evangelization, because the eyes of the Slavs were not yet open for the light of the Scriptures. That Fredegar knew Jonas' work is indicated by a long passage cited from *Vita Columbani*. It has been argued that Jonas of Bobbio's source on Columbanus' missionary activity was his disciple, Eustasius, abbot of Luxeuil. Fredegar's Wendish account may have been inspired by

---

[56] Fredegar IV 68. See Baudot 1928:161; Goffart 1963:237–8.
[57] Fredegar IV 48. See Schütz 1991:410–11; Fritze 1980:498–505; Pritsak 1983:397 and 411. A dim recollection of the same story is preserved in the *Russian Primary Chronicle* and may have originated in the West. See Zasterová 1964; Swoboda 1970:76; Curta 1997:150. According to Fredegar, the Wendish *gens* was the outgrowth of a military conflict, but the *befulci* turned into a fully fledged *gens* only through the long-suffering *uxores Sclavorum et filias*. This suggests that the Wendish account operates as a counterpart to other equivalent stories, such as that of the Trojan origin of the Franks or that of chapter 65 of Book III, significantly entitled *De Langobardorum gente et eorum origine et nomine*. For the historiographic genre of *origo gentis*, see Wolfram 1981:311 and 1990; Anton 1994.   [58] Fredegar IV 48, 68, 72, 74, 75, and 77. See Curta 1997:152–3.

missionary reports. He may have used the perspective, if not the accounts, of the missionaries for explaining the extraordinary success of Samo against Dagobert and his Austrasian army. In Fredegar's eyes, the Wends were a *gens* primarily in the political sense of the term. To him, they were agents of secular history, though more of political dissolution, as indicated by their alliance with Radulf, whose victories "turned his head" to the extent that he rated himself King of Thuringia and denied Sigebert's overlordship. The use of missionary reports may also explain why Fredegar's image of the Slavs does not include any of the stereotypes encountered in older or contemporary Byzantine sources. No *Milieutheorie* and no blond Slavs emerge from his account. Despite Fredegar's contempt for Samo's haughtiness, he did not see Wends primarily as heathens. Samo's "kingdom'"may have not been the first Slavic state, but Fredegar was certainly the first political historian of the Slavs.[59]

THE SAINT AND THE BARBARIANS AGAIN

In contrast to Fredegar's attitude, to the unknown author of Book II of the *Miracles of St Demetrius* the Slavs were nothing else but savage, brutish, and, more important, heathen barbarians. Despite his ability to speak Greek and to dress like Constantinopolitan aristocrats, King Perbundos dreams only of slaughtering Christians. At any possible moment, the Slavs are to be impressed by St Demetrius' miracles. When an earthquake devastates the city, they are stopped from plundering the victims' destroyed houses by a miraculous vision. After yet another failure to conquer Thessalonica, the barbarians acknowledge God's intervention in favor of the city and St Demetrius' miraculous participation in battle. St Demetrius slaps in the face a dexterous Sclavene craftsman who builds a siege tower, driving him out of his mind and thus causing the failure of a dangerous attack on the city walls.[60]

On the other hand, however, one gets the impression that the Slavs were a familiar presence. They are repeatedly called "our Slavic neighbors." They lived so close to the city that, after the imperial troops chased them from the coastal region, the inhabitants of Thessalonica – men, women, and children – walked to their abandoned villages and carried home all provisions left behind. Moreover, while some were attacking the city, others were on good terms with its inhabitants, supplying them with grain. Still others were under the orders of the emperor in

---

[59] Fredegar I 27, IV 36, IV 77; *Vita Columbani* I 27. For the date of Jonas' work, see Wood 1994b:248–9; Ronin 1995b. For Fredegar's Wends as agents of secular history, see Fritze 1994:281. For Samo's 'kingdom' as the first Slavic state, see Labuda 1949.

[60] *Miracles of St Demetrius* II 4.241, II 3.219, II 2.214, II 4.274.

Constantinople, who required them to supply with food the refugees from the Avar qaganate under Kuver's commands. In contrast to Archbishop John's account, Book II also provides a more detailed image of the Slavs. Its author knew, for instance, that the army of the Sclavenes besieging Thessalonica comprised units of archers, warriors armed with slings, lancers, soldiers carrying shields, and warriors with swords. Unlike John who invariably called them either Σκλαβίνοι or Σκλαβηνοί, the author of Book II at times prefers Σκλάβοι. He also provided the names of no less than seven Slavic tribes living in the vicinity of Thessalonica.[61]

He also seems to have used oral sources, especially those of refugees from Balkan cities abandoned in the early 600s, such as Naissus or Serdica. It has been argued that he may have used written sources as well, probably the city's annals or chronicle. He specifically referred to some iconographic evidence (ἐν γραφῇ) in order to support a point that he made. Book II has fewer miracles and miraculous deeds than Book I and seems to have relied more heavily on documentary material.[62]

Unlike Archbishop John, who was using history to glorify St Demetrius and to educate his fellow citizens, the author of Book II, despite his obvious desire to imitate John's style, took a different approach. He wrote some seventy years later, shortly after the events narrated. His account is visibly better informed, his narration approaches the historiographic genre. Paradoxically, this is what would make Book II less popular than Book I, despite the growing influence of St Demetrius' cult in the course of the following centuries. There are numerous manuscripts containing miracles of Book I, but only one rendering Book II. In the late ninth century, Anastasius Bibliothecarius translated into Latin ten miracles from Book I, but only one from Book II. Unlike Archbishop John, the author of Book II was more concerned with facts supporting his arguments and often referred to contemporary events, known from other sources. His mention of "July 25 of the fifth indiction" and of the emperor's war with the Saracens makes it possible to date the siege of Thessalonica precisely to July 25, 677. Book II must have been written, therefore, at some point during the last two decades of the seventh century.[63]

---

[61] *Miracles of St Demetrius* II 3.219, 3.222, 4.231, 4.279–80, 4.254, 5.289, II 4.262. For a list of five tribes, see II 1.179; for other tribes, see II 4.232.

[62] *Miracles of St Demetrius* II 2.200, II 1.194; see Lemerle 1979:174 with n. 19. For the use of city annals or chronicles, see Lemerle 1981:84. For the use of administrative sources, see Beshevliev 1970a:287–8. For the attitude toward the central government, see Margetić 1988:760; Ditten 1991.

[63] *Miracles of St Demetrius* II 4.255. See Lemerle 1979:34 and 1981:172; Ivanova 1995a:203. Ivanova (1995a:200) argued that since its author refers to a numerous Slavic population living near Bizye, at a short distance from Constantinople (II 4. 238), Book II must have been written after Emperor Justinian II's campaign of 688 against the *Sklavinia*.

LATER SOURCES

With Book II of the *Miracles of St Demetrius* we come to the end of a long series of contemporary accounts on the early Slavs. None of the subsequent sources is based on autopsy and all could be referred to as "histories," relying entirely on written, older sources. First in this group is Patriarch Nicephorus. His *Breviarium* may have been designed as a continuation of Theophylact Simocatta, but Nicephorus did not have personal knowledge of any of the events described and it is very unlikely that he had recourse to living witnesses. The source of the first part of the *Breviarium*, covering the reigns of Phocas and Heraclius, was most probably the Constantinopolitan chronicle. In tone with such sources as George of Pisidia or the *Chronicon Paschale*, Nicephorus spoke of Slavs besieging the capital in 626 as the allies of the Avars, not as their subjects. When referring to Slavic canoes attacking Blachernae, Nicephorus spoke of μονόξυλοι ἀκατίοι, which suggests that at the time he wrote his *Breviarium*, a Slavic fleet of canoes was something exotic enough to require explanation. For their respective accounts of the settlement of the Bulgars, both Nicephorus and his contemporary, Theophanes Confessor, used a common source, probably written in the first quarter of the eighth century in Constantinople.[64]

But unlike Nicephorus, Theophanes' accounts of Maurice's campaigns are a combination of the Constantinopolitan chronicle and Theophylact Simocatta. At several places, Theophanes misunderstood Theophylact's text and confused his narrative. The most significant alterations of Theophylact's text result from Theophanes' efforts to adapt Theophylact's loose chronology, based on seasons of the year, to one that employed indictions and the world years of the Alexandrine chronological system. This makes the controversy over Theophanes' reliability a cul-de-sac, for any chronological accuracy that is present in Theophanes is merely accidental.

Theophanes spread some of Theophylact's campaigns over more than one year, and at one point he repeated some information which he had

---

[64] *Breviarium* 13; see Mango 1990:7. In 769, the terminal date of his *Breviarium*, Nicephorus was about eleven years old (he was born in or about 758, in the reign of Constantine V). The *Breviarium* was finished in or shortly after 828. See Litavrin 1995d:221–2. For the Constantinopolitan source used by both Nicephorus and Theophanes, see Mango 1990:16. It has been argued that the source was the Great Chronographer. None of the surviving fragments, however, refers to the settlement of the Bulgars. See Bozhilov 1975:29. On the other hand, for much of the seventh and eighth centuries, Theophanes was also dependent on a Syriac chronicle, not available to Nicephorus (Scott 1990a:41). It is possible that this source provided Theophanes with a description of the Black Sea northern coast and an *excursus* on the history of the Bulgars, which cannot be found in Nicephorus. See Chichurov 1980:107. For relations between the Great Chronographer and Theophanes, see also Whitby 1982a; Mango 1997:xci.

already used. He paraphrased the much longer and more grandiloquent account of Theophylact. Though Theophylact had no date for the Slavic raid ending with Comentiolus' victory over Ardagastus' hordes, Theophanes attached the year AM 6076 (583/4) to this event, on the basis of his own interpretation of Theophylact's text. He dated Priscus' campaign against the Sclavenes to AM 6085 (592/3), abbreviated Theophylact's account, and changed parasangs into miles. The end result is that Theophylact's originally confusing narrative becomes even more ambiguous. It is only by considering Theophanes' summary of Theophylact that we begin to appreciate the latter's account, based as it is on the *Feldzugsjournal*. If Theophylact's history had been lost, Theophanes' version of it would have been entirely misleading, if not altogether detrimental, to any attempts to reconstruct the chronology of Maurice's wars against Avars and Sclavenes. Since he had also incorporated bits of information from other sources, now lost, this caveat should warn us against taking Theophanes' text at its face value.[65]

Theophanes, together with Nicephorus, is the first to use the word Σκλαυινία to refer to a loosely defined Sclavene polity, arguably a chiefdom. There is no basis, however, for interpreting his use of the term in both singular and plural forms, as indicating the fragmentation of an originally unified union of tribes into smaller formations. Composed as it was in *c.* 812, the *Chronographia* of Theophanes is not the work of a historian in the modern sense of the word. He was certainly capable of skillful amalgamation of various sources, but his coverage of the seventh century is poor and it is very unlikely that his labor went beyond mere copying of now extinct sources.[66]

Modern approaches to the history of the Balkans during the first half of the seventh century have been considerably influenced by one particular text: *De Administrando Imperio*, a work associated with the emperor Constantine VII Porphyrogenitus. There is not too much material relevant to the history of the early Slavs in this tenth-century compilation, but chapters 29 to 36 represent a key source for the controversial issue of the migration of Croats and Serbs. It has long been recognized that all

---

[65] Theophylact Simocatta I 7.5; Mango 1997:376 and 394. Theophanes misunderstood Theophylact's reference to the city of Asemus (VII 3.1), and transformed it into the ἐπίσημοι (leading soldiers) of Novae (p. 399 with n. 3). There are also instances of innovative modification, as in the case of the episode of Peter's military confrontation with 1,000 Bulgar warriors (VII 4.1–7), which Theophanes enriched with a short reply of Peter to Bulgar offers of peace (p. 399), a detail absent from Theophylact's account. See Whitby 1982a:9 and 1983:333; Chichurov 1980:90; Litavrin 1995a:299. For Theophanes' chronological system, see also Duket 1980:85; Mango 1997:lxiv–lxvii. For Theophanes' narrative, see Liubarskii 1995.

[66] Mango 1997:484, 507–8, 595, and 667. For *Sklaviniai*, see Litavrin 1984:198. For the use of the word (*Sclavinia*) in contemporary Carolingian sources, see Bertels 1987:160–1. For the date of the *Chronographia*, see Whitby 1982a:9; for a slightly later date (815), see Mango 1997:lxii.

these chapters were written in 948 or 949, with the exception of chapter 30, which must be regarded as a much later interpolation, composed by another author, after 950, arguably after Constantine's death in 959. In any case, the book seems never to have received its final editing, for there are striking differences, as well as some repetition, between chapters 29, 31, and 32, on one hand, and 30, on the other. The problem of reliability and truth raised by this source derives primarily from the fact that it contains two significantly different accounts of the same event, the migration of the Croats. The one given in chapter 30 is a legendary account, which may well represent a "native" version of the Croat *origo gentis*, arguably collected in Dalmatia, in one of the Latin cities. The same is true about the story of the migration of the Serbs, which most probably originated in a Serbian account. By contrast, the narrative in chapter 31 betrays a Byzantine source, for Constantine rejects any Frankish claims of suzerainty over Croatia. He mentions a minor Bulgarian–Croatian skirmish almost a century earlier, but has no word for the major confrontation between King Symeon of Bulgaria and Prince Tomislav of Croatia, which happened in his own lifetime (926). This further suggests that the account in chapter 31 is biased against both Frankish claims and Croatian independent tendencies, in order to emphasize Byzantine rights to the lands of the Croats. As a consequence, some believe that chapter 30 is the only trustworthy source for early Croat history, for it reflects Croat native traditions. These scholars also reject the version given by chapter 31 as Constantine's figment.[67]

Indeed, the presumed Croat version in chapter 30 has no room for Emperor Heraclius helping Croats in settling in Dalmatia or ordering their conversion to Christianity. By contrast, the constant reference to Heraclius and the claim that Croatia was always under Byzantine overlordship were clearly aimed at furthering Byzantine claims of suzerainty. But the "Croat version" is not without problems. The motif of the five brothers, which also occurs in the account of the Bulgar migration to be found in Theophanes and Nicephorus, is a mythological projection of a ritual division of space which is most typical for nomadic societies. Moreover, in both chapter 30 and 31, the homeland of the Balkan Croats is located somewhere in Central Europe, near Bavaria, beyond Hungary, and next to the Frankish Empire. In both cases, Constantine makes it clear that Croats, "also called 'white'," are still living in that region. "White" Croatia is also mentioned by other, independent, sources, such as King Alfred the Great's translation of Orosius' *History of the World*, tenth-

---

[67] For chapter 30 as a later interpolation, see Bury 1906. For the migration of the Serbs, see Maksimović 1982; Lilie 1985:31–2. For the migration of the Croats, see Grafenauer 1952; Fine 1983:52.

century Arab geographers (Gaihani, Ibn-Rusta, and Mas'udi), the *Russian Primary Chronicle*, and the Emperor Henry IV's foundation charter for the bishopric of Prague. None of these sources could be dated earlier than the mid-ninth century and no source refers to Croats, in either Central Europe or the Balkans, before that date. Traditional historiographical views, however, maintain that the Serbs and the Croats referred to by Constantine were a second wave of migration, to be placed during Heraclius' reign.[68] There are other anachronisms and blatant errors that warn us against taking Emperor Constantine's account at its face value.[69] That *De Administrando Imperio* contains the first record of a "native" version of the past cannot be denied. There is, however, no reason to project this version on events occurring some two hundred years earlier.

The same is true about other late sources. Emperor Leo VI's treatise entitled *Tactica* borrows heavily from the *Strategikon*. But unlike the author of the *Strategikon*, Leo had few original things to say about the Slavs, in general, and those of the sixth and seventh centuries, in particular. To him, the Slavs were not a major threat, because they had already been converted to Christianity, though not fully subjugated. Leo placed the narrative taken from the *Strategikon* in the past and claimed that the purpose of Byzantine campaigns against the Sclavenes had been to force them to cross the Danube and "bend their necks under the yoke of Roman authority." Another late source, the eleventh-century chronicle of Cedrenus, contains a reference to Heraclius' reconstruction, in his fourteenth year, of the Heraios leper hospital at Galata, which had been burnt by Slavs. According to the *Vita Zotici*, written under Emperor Michael IV (1034–41), the hospital was, however, restored by Maurice, after being burnt by Avars. It is possible therefore that Cedrenus' reference to the Slavs at Galata is the product of some confusion.[70]

Highly controversial is the testimony of the so-called *Chronicle of Monemvasia*, the source on which Fallmerayer based his theories concern-

---

[68] Constantine found it necessary to explain why Croats lived in two different places so far from each other. His explanation, however, is an impossible and meaningless etymology: "'Croats' in the Slav tongue means 'those who occupy much territory'" (chapter 31). For earlier approaches, see Dümmler 1856:57–8; Jireček 1911:108; Mal 1939. Despite clear evidence that Constantine's account of early Croat history is an amalgamation of various sources freely interpreted in accordance to Byzantine political claims, the idea of migration is too powerful to be abandoned by modern historians. See Margetić 1977; Klaić 1984 and 1985; Fine 1983:53 and 59. For the Serbs, see also Schuster-Šewc 1985.

[69] The Serbs sent a request to Emperor Heraclius through the military governor of Belgrade (Βελέγραδον, instead of Σιγγιδών, as in chapter 25). They were first given land in the province (ἐν τῷ θέματι) of Thessalonica, but no such theme existed during Heraclius' reign. Emperor Constantine's explanation of the ethnic name of the Serbs as derived from *servi* is plainly wrong.

[70] Leo the Wise, *Tactica* 78 and 98; Cedrenus, *Compendium Historiarum*, ed. I. Bekker, 1 (Bonn, 1838), 698–9; Aubineau 1975:82. See Whitby 1988:124.

ing the extent of the Slav penetration into Greece. The chronicle survives in three late manuscripts. Only one of them, which is preserved at the Iberon monastery at Mount Athos and dates to the sixteenth century, deals exclusively with Avar invasions into Peloponnesus, the settlement of the Slavs, and Nicephorus I's campaigns against them. The *communis opinio* is that this manuscript should therefore be treated as the earliest version of the text. It also gives the impression of a more elaborate treatment which has led to a more "scholarly" style. But recent studies have shown that the Iberon manuscript uses the Byzantine system of dating, whereas the other two manuscripts use the older Alexandrine system. As a consequence, the Iberon cannot be the earliest of all three, for the Byzantine system of dating was introduced only after the Alexandrine one. The *Chronicle of Monemvasia* is not a chronicle properly speaking, but a compilation of sources concerning Avars and Slavs and referring to the foundation of the metropolitan see of Patras. Patras, and not Monemvasia, is at the center of the narrative. It has been argued therefore that this text may have been written in order to be used in negotiations with the metropolitan of Corinth over the status of the metropolitan of Patras.[71] Since the emperor Nicephorus I is referred to by the unknown author of the text as "the Old, who had Staurakios as son," it is often believed that he must have written after the reign of Nicephorus II Phocas (963–9). It has been noted, on the other hand, that the text explicitly refers to the death of Tarasius, the patriarch of Constantinople (784–806), which gives the first *terminus a quo*. Moreover, the author calls Sirmium Στρίαμος and locates the city in Bulgaria, an indication that the chronicle was written before the conquest of that city by Basil II, in 1018. Its composition must have taken place in the second half of the tenth century or in the early eleventh century.[72] The author of the chronicle drew his information from Menander the Guardsman, Evagrius, Theophylact Simocatta, and Theophanes. Descriptions of the attacks of the Avars in the *Chronicle* are modeled after the description of Hunnic attacks by Procopius. But the author of the *Chronicle* was completely ignorant of Balkan geography outside Peloponnesus. More important, his account of invasions into Peloponnesus refers exclusively

---

[71] Fallmerayer 1845:367–458. See Charanis 1950:142–3; Setton 1950:516; Kalligas 1990:13; Turlej 1997:410. For the style of the chronicle, see Koder 1976:76. For the ecclesiastical division in Peloponnesus, see Yannopoulos 1993. For the *Chronicle of Monemvasia* as a forgery of ecclesiastical origin, perpetrated by or on behalf of the metropolitan of Patras, see Setton 1950:517. For the *Chronicle* as an "exposé," an elaborate report on the circumstances leading to the establishment of the metropolis of Patras, see Turlej 1998:455 with n. 23.

[72] For the date of the chronicle, see Kougeas 1912:477–8; Barišić 1965; Duichev 1976:xliii and 1980. For less convincing attempts to attribute the *Chronicle* to Arethas of Caesarea and to date it to *c.* 900, see Koder 1976:77; Pohl 1988:99; Avramea 1997:69.

and explicitly to Avars, not Slavs. The Slavs only appear in the second part of the Iberon version of the text, which describes how Emperor Nicephorus I (802–11) conquered Peloponnesus and established the metropolis of Patras.[73]

This account comes very close to a scholium written by Arethas of Caesarea on the margin of a manuscript of Nicephorus' *Historia Syntomos* written in 932. The note is a comment made by Arethas, while reading Nicephorus' work and thus must be viewed as a text of private, not public nature. In some instances, the one repeats the other verbatim. Arethas, nevertheless, speaks only of Slavs. Though the *Chronicle of Monemvasia* was clearly composed much later, it is very unlikely that its author derived his information from Arethas. It has been argued, therefore, that both drew their information from an unknown source, but it is also possible that there was more than one hand at work in the earliest known version of the *Chronicle*. Others have argued that since Arethas only speaks of Slavs, the Avars are a later addition to the *Chronicle*. Still others attempted to solve the quagmire by pointing to a now-lost privilege of Emperor Nicephorus I for Patras as the possible source for the story of the Avar rule in the Peloponnesus. This, it has been argued, was a propaganda response to Charlemagne's claims to both the imperial title and victories over the Avars. But the evidence of the eighth-century *Life of St Pancratius*, as well as of sixth-century sources, such as Evagrius, John of Ephesus, or John of Biclar, contradicts this view. If the source for the *Chronicle*'s account of heavy destruction in Greece during Maurice's reign were oral traditions of Greek refugees in southern Italy and Sicily, then we must also admit that they remembered being expelled by Avars, not by Slavs. Arethas, who had been born at Patras in or around 850 to a rich family, may have well applied this tradition to a contemporary situation and therefore changed Avars into Slavs.[74] Family memories or stories may well have been the source for Arethas' knowledge about such things as

---

[73] The author of the chronicle confounds Anchialos with Messina in Macedonia; see *Chronicle of Monemvasia*, pp. 8 and 16. See also Charanis 1950:145; Duichev 1976:xlii; Kalligas 1990:25; Litavrin 1995c:338; Pohl 1988:100–1.

[74] For the scholium of Arethas, see Westerink 1972. The date and authenticity of the scholium have been disputed, mainly because it refers to both Thessalia prima and Thessalia secunda, an administrative division that took place in the eleventh century. See Karayannopoulos 1971:456–7. For a common source for Arethas and the *Chronicle of Monemvasia*, see Charanis 1950:152–3. For the Avars as a later addition, see Chrysanthopoulos 1957. For the privilege of Nicephorus and the story of Avar rule, see Turlej 1998:467. For oral traditions of Greek refugees as a source for the chronicle, see Setton 1950:517; Pohl 1988:101. For the *Life of St Pancratius*, see Vasil'ev 1898:416; Capaldo 1983:5–6 and 13; Olajos 1994:107–9. Arethas' knowledge of and interest in South Italy derives from the Greek refugees returning to Patras. See Falkenhausen 1995. For Arethas' life, see Litavrin 1995e:345.

the exact period (218 years) between the attacks of the Slavs and the settlement of Greeks in Peloponnesus by Emperor Nicephorus I, or the exact whereabouts in Italy of the population transferred to Greece by that emperor. But it is much more difficult to visualize how the emperor himself could have known that the successors of those expelled from Patras by the Slavs, more than two hundred years earlier, were still living in Reggio Calabria.[75] This warns us against pushing too far any kind of argument based on either the *Chronicle* or Arethas.

After 700, Slavs also appear in Western sources. Around 630, Bishop Amandus, one of St Columbanus' disciples, led the first known mission to the Slavs. His *Life*, written a century later, describes his journey across the Danube, to the *Sclavi*, who "sunk in great error, were caught in the devil's snares." Amandus' mission had no success but the association of the Slavs with the river Danube proved to be a lasting one. The Danube appears again in the Frankish Cosmography, written after 650, as providing grazing fields to the *Sclavi* and bringing *Winidi* together.[76]

Much of what we know about the early history of the Slavs in the West derives, however, from Paul the Deacon's *History of the Lombards*. The entries concerning the Slavs fall into two groups: those referring to conflicts between Slavs and Bavarians and those in which Slavs appear in a more or less direct relation to Lombards. These references are characteristically dated, sometimes even by month, a practice quite uncommon for the rest of Paul's *History*. This has been interpreted as an indication that, as this point, Paul closely followed the now-lost history of Secundus of Trento.[77]

The Slavs are described as allies or paying tribute to the dukes of Forum Julii, "up to the time of Duke Ratchis." Some of Paul's heroes are well accustomed to their presence. According to Paul, when Raduald, the duke of Beneventum, attempted to revenge the death of Aio by the hands of the invading Slavs, he "talked familiarly with these Slavs in their own language, and when in this way he had lulled them into greater

---

[75] In contrast to the richness of detail in the preceding paragraph, Arethas' text is very vague at this point. We are only told that the emperor "has been informed" (βασιλεὺς γὰρ ὁ εἰρημένος ἀναμαθών) where the "ancient inhabitants" (τοῖς ἀρχῆθεν οἰκήτορσιν) of Patras lived at that time. See the *Chronicle of Monemvasia*, p. 19.

[76] *Vita Amandi*, ed. Krusch, *MGH: SRM* 5:440; *Frankish Cosmography*, vv. 22–4, ed. G. H. Pertz (Berlin, 1847). Some sixty years after Bishop Amandus, St Marinus was burnt at the stake by *Uuandali* on the Bavarian frontier (*Vita Sancti Marini*, p. 170). By contrast, the bishop of Salzburg, St Hrodbert, successfully converted a *rex Carantanorum* in the late 600s, and also preached to the *Wandali* (*Vita Hrodberti*, p. 159). For 'Vandals' as Wends, see Steinberger 1920.

[77] *Historia Langobardorum* IV 7, 10, 28, and 40. For Secundus of Trento, see IV 10. See also Kos 1931:207; Gardiner 1983:147; Pohl 1988:9. For a detailed discussion of Paul's image of the Slavs, see Curta 1997:155–61.

indolence for war," he fell upon them and killed almost all of them. Friulan Lombards were annoyed by *latrunculi Sclavorum*, who "fell upon the flocks and upon the shepherd of the sheep that pastured in their neighborhoods and drove away the booty taken from them." The Slavs were a familiar neighbor: in times of trouble, both Arnefrit, Lupus' son, and Duke Pemmo fled to the Slavs. Knowing that his audience was familiar with the Slavs, Paul projects this familiarity into the past. He argues that, sometime after 663, when the invading Slavs saw Duke Wechtari coming from Forum Julii against them with only twenty-five men, "they laughed, saying that the patriarch was advancing against them with his clergy." This is pure anachronism, since according to Paul's own testimony, Calixtus, the patriarch of Aquileia, moved to Forum Julii only in 737 or shortly before that. Moreover, Wechtari raising his helmet and thus provoking panic among Slavs, is a stereotypical gesture, pointing to the style and ethos of an oral heroic model, and may be easily paralleled by a series of similar accounts.[78]

Paul's Slavs, particularly those from later references in Book v and vi, are lively beings, have "faces" and feelings, and are always active, not passive, elements. An old Slavic woman helped Paul's great-grandfather to escape from the Avars, gave him food and told him what direction he ought to go. One can speak with the Slavs in their own language or use their corruptly constructed place names. They can laugh, recognize a hero from his bald head, be alarmed or terrified, cry, or even fight manfully. However, although Paul's Slavs are a *gens* and even have a *patria*, they lack any political organization that would make them comparable to other *gentes*. Unlike Fredegar's Wends, they have no *rex* and no *regnum*, despite the fact that by the time Paul wrote his *History*, the *Carantani* were already organized as a polity under their *dux* Boruth and his successors. No Slavic leader whatsoever appears in Paul's account. He occasionally focused on individuals such as the old Slavic woman. If looking for more narrowly defined social groups, we are left only with the *latrunculi Sclavorum*. Despite its animation, Paul's picture is thus a stereotypical one, probably rooted in ethnic stereotypes developed along the Friulan border by successive generations of Lombards.[79]

---

[78] *Historia Langobardorum* IV 28, IV 38, IV 44, VI 24, V 22, VI 45, V 23, and VI 51. Aio's death is also mentioned in the *Chronica Sancti Benedicti Casinensis*, ed. G. H. Pertz, *MGH: Scriptores Rerum Langobardorum* (Berlin, 1878), p. 202; see also Borodin 1983:56. For the hero raising his helmet, see Pizarro 1989:153 with n. 51.

[79] *Historia Langobardorum* VI 24. See Curta 1997:160–1. Boruth ruled between *c.* 740 and *c.* 750, followed by his son Cacatius (*c.* 750 to 752) and his nephew Cheitmar (752 to *c.* 769), then by Waltunc (*c.* 772 to *c.* 788), and Priwizlauga (*c.* 788 to *c.* 799). See *Conversio Bagoariorum et Carantanorum* c. 4–5.

Table 1 *Sources of sources: origin of accounts*

Eyewitness	Possible contact	Second-hand information
Strategikon	Procopius	Jordanes
George of Pisidia	Pseudo-Caesarius	Agathias
Chronicon Paschale	*Miracles of St Demetrius*	John Malalas
Theodore Syncellus		Menander the Guardsman
Theophylact Simocatta		John of Ephesus
(*Feldzugsjournal*)		John of Biclar
		Gregory the Great
		Isidore of Seville
		Fredegar

CONCLUSION

There are at least three important conclusions to be drawn from this
survey of sources concerning the history of the early Slavs between *c.*
500 and 700. First, many contemporary accounts are based on second-
hand information (Table 1). Some authors, like Jordanes, Agathias, or
Menander the Guardsman, only used written sources of various origins.
There are, however, a number of sources that most certainly originated
in eyewitness accounts, such as the *Strategikon* or Theophylact
Simocatta's narrative of Maurice's campaigns against Avars and
Sclavenes. The analysis of other accounts reveals a possible contact of
some sort with the Slavs, as in the case of Procopius' *Wars*, arguably
based on interviews with Sclavene and Antian mercenaries in Italy.
Second, there is a substantial overlap in the time-spans covered by these
accounts (see Table 2), despite their divergent perspectives and aims.
This has encouraged historians to look for parallels, but also to fill in
the gaps of one source with material derived from another. It is clear,
however, that only a few, relatively short, periods witnessed an increasing interest with Slavs and things Slavic (Table 3). No source specifically
talks about Slavs before the reign of Justinian (527–65), despite Jordanes'
efforts to fabricate a venerable ancestry for them by linking Sclavenes
and Antes to Venethi.[80] It was the first half of Justinian's reign that witnessed the rise of a "Slavic problem." During the last half of Justinian's
reign and during the reigns of his successors, Justin II (565–78) and

---

[80] Marcellinus Comes, whose chronicle covered the period between 379 and 518, to which he later
added a sequel down to 534 (a supplement to 548 being added by another author), had no knowledge of Sclavenes.

Table 2 *Time-spans covered by sixth- and seventh-century sources*

Years	500	525	550	575	600	625	650
Source							
Jordanes		----------------					
Procopius		------------------					
Agathias				---			
John Malalas		------------------					
Menander the Guardsman				------			
John of Ephesus		-------------------------					
John of Biclar				-------			
Evagrius		---------------------------					
Theophylact Simocatta					------		
Miracles I					-------		
Isidore of Seville		----------------------------					
Chronicon Paschale		-------------------------------					
Fredegar				------------------			
Miracles II						---------	

Tiberius II (578–82), informations about Slavs were scarce. The "Slavic problem" resurfaced under Emperor Maurice (582–602). This is the period in which some of the most important sources were written, such as Menander the Guardsman's *History*, the *Strategikon*, and the campaign diary later used by Theophylact Simocatta for his *History*. Finally, the last period witnessing a considerable interest in Slavs is that of Heraclius' reign, most probably because of their participation in the siege of Constantinople in 626. The Slavs now appear in the works of those who had witnessed the combined attacks of Avars, Slavs, and Persians on the capital city (George of Pisidia, Theodore Syncellus, and the author of the *Chronicon Paschale*). Archbishop John of Thessalonica viewed them as a major threat to his city requiring the miraculous intervention of St Demetrius. Theophylact Simocatta incorporated the *Feldzugsjournal* written in the last few years of the sixth century into his narrative of Maurice's reign. The same period witnessed the first attempts to convert the Slavs to Christianity, which most likely stimulated Fredegar to write the first independent account in the West. After Heraclius' reign, there are no other sources referring to Slavs, except Book II of the *Miracles of St Demetrius*. Justinian (the mid-sixth century), Maurice (the late sixth century), and Heraclius (the second third of the seventh century) are thus the major chronological markers of the historiography of the early Slavs.

Sources

Table 3 *Chronology of sources*

Date	Source	Emperor
		Justinian
550/1	Jordanes, *Getica*	
	Jordanes, *Romana*	
	Procopius, *Wars* I–VII	
	Procopius, *Secret History*	
c. 554	Procopius, *Wars* VIII	
	Procopius, *Buildings* IV	
c. 560	Pseudo-Caesarius	
		Justin II
c. 560–80	Agathias	
c. 565–74	John Malalas	
c. 570–9	Martin of Braga	
		Tiberius II
		Maurice
582–602	Menander the Guardsman	
c. 590	John of Ephesus	
	John of Biclar	
c. 592–602	*Strategikon*	
c. 593	Evagrius	
599/600	Gregory the Great	
		Phocas
		Heraclius
610–20	*Miracles of St Demetrius* I	
626	George of Pisidia, *Bellum Avaricum*	
629	George of Pisidia, *Heraclias*	
630	*Chronicon Paschale*	
c. 630	Isidore of Seville, *Chronica Maiora*	
c. 630	Theophylact Simocatta	
c. 626–41	Theodore Syncellus	
		Constans II
639–42	Jonas of Bobbio, *Life of St Columbanus*	
c. 660	Fredegar	
		Constantine IV
		Justinian II
c. 690	*Miracles of St Demetrius* II	

Chapter 3

THE SLAVS IN EARLY MEDIEVAL SOURCES
(c. 500–700)

A major, still unresolved, problem of the modern historiography of the early Middle Ages remains that of defining the settlement of the Slavs in the Balkans. On the assumption that the Slavs originated in an *Urheimat* located far from the Danube river, nineteenth-century historians used the concept of migration (*Einwanderung, Auswanderung*). They were followed by modern historians under the influence of the concept and the historiography of the *Völkerwanderung*. More recently, a linguist searching for the original homeland of the Slavs even spoke of *reconquista*.[1] Palacký and Šafářik also insisted, a few years before the Slavic Congress in Prague (1848), that the migration of the Slavs was a peaceful one, quite unlike the brutal Germanic invasions. As a consequence, some modern historians and archaeologists prefer to write of colonization or of *Landnahme* and imagine the early Slavs as a people of farmers, travelling on foot, "entire families or even whole tribes," to the promised land.[2] Noting, however, that such a *Landnahme* was completely invisible to early medieval sources, Lucien Musset called it an *obscure progression*, a tag quickly adopted by others. After World War II, particularly in Communist countries, the acceptable terms were "infiltration" and "penetration" and the favorite metaphor, the wave. Others, more willing to use the perspective of contemporary sources, observed that more often than not, after successful raids, the Slavs returned to their homes north of the Danube. Current usage has therefore replaced "migration" and "infiltration" with "invasion" and "raid."[3]

---

[1] Trubachev 1985:204 and 1991:11. For the Slavic migration, see Schafarik 1844:111 and 42; Bogdan 1894:15. See also Lemerle 1980; Guillou 1973; Ditten 1978; Ivanova and Litavrin 1985; Pohl 1988:95. For *Völkerwanderung*, see Goffart 1989.

[2] Gimbutas 1971:14. Peaceful migration of the Slavs: Schafarik 1844:1, 42; Palacký 1868:74–89. Slavic *Landnahme*, see Evert-Kapessowa 1963; Zasterová 1976; Weithmann 1978:18; Braichevskii 1983:220. For the historiography of the *Landnahme*, see Schneider 1993.

[3] *Obscure progression*: Musset 1965:75, 81, and 85, and 1983:999. See also Pohl 1988:95. Infiltration: Comşa 1960:733; Cankova-Petkova 1968:44; Tăpkova-Zaimova 1974:201 and 205; Popović 1980:246; Velkov 1987. See also Cross 1948:7 and 28. Slavic "wave": Skrzhinskaia 1957:9; Váňa

It is often assumed that Jordanes' source for his account of the Slavs was Cassiodorus, who wrote in the late 520s or early 530s. Some argued therefore that the *Getica* is a genuine report of the earliest stages of the Slavic infiltration in Eastern Europe. In the eyes of Procopius, Jordanes' contemporary, the Slavs were, however, a quite recent problem, which he specifically linked to the beginnings of Justinian's reign. Since no other source referred to either Sclavenes or Antes before Justinian, some have rightly concluded that these two *ethnies* were purely (early) medieval phenomena.[4]

In this chapter, I intend to examine the historical sources regarding the Sclavenes and the Antes in the light of a strictly chronological concern. My purpose is not a full narrative of events, for which there are better and more informative guides at hand.[5] This chapter has a different scope. I devote particular attention to the broader picture in which Slavic raiding activity took place, partly in order to point up its relative impact in comparison to other problems of the Danube frontier. Discussion of interaction between Slavs, on one hand, Gepids, Cutrigurs, Avars, and Bulgars, on the other, occupies a large amount of space for similar reasons. The chapter's emphasis is on the Slavs rather than the Empire, and so it points to the territories north of the Danube, where transformations may have occurred that are reflected in our sources. Those transformations may provide a key to the problem of defining the Slavic settlement and to understand the mechanisms of Slavic raiding activities, two aspects discussed in detail in the following chapters.

SLAVIC RAIDING DURING JUSTINIAN'S REIGN

Procopius is the first author to speak of Slavic raiding across the Danube. According to his evidence, the first attack of the Antes, "who dwell close to the Sclaveni," may be dated to 518. The raid was intercepted by Germanus, *magister militum per Thraciam*, and the Antes were defeated. There is no record of any other Antian raid until Justinian's rise to power. It is possible therefore that this attack, like that of the *Getae equites* of 517, was related to Vitalianus' revolt.[6]

1983:39. The wave metaphor is still in use: Avramea 1997:79–80. For Slavic "invasions" and "raids," see Ensslin 1929; Fine 1983:29; Ferjančić 1984; Whitby 1988:85–6 and 175; Pohl 1988:68; Fiedler 1992:6; Stavridou-Zafraka 1992.

[4] Procopius, *Secret History* 18.20–1. For *Getica* as genuine report, see Waldmüller 1976:19; Sedov 1978:9; Anfert'ev 1991:134–5. For Sclavenes and Antes as medieval *ethnies*, see Bačić 1983:21; Godłowski 1983:257; Váňa 1983:16.

[5] See Ensslin 1929; Stein 1968; Waldmüller 1976; Ditten 1978.

[6] Procopius, *Wars* VII 40.5–6. *Getae equites*: Marcellinus Comes, trans. B. Croke (Sydney, 1995), pp. 39 and 120. See also Nestor 1965:148; Comşa 1973:197 and 1974:301; Ditten 1978:86; Irmscher 1980:158. For Vitalianus' revolt, see Waldmüller 1976:34; Weithmann 1978:64; Velkov 1987:157; Soustal 1991:697. For Vitalianus' barbarian allies, see Schwarcz 1992.

The Sclavenes first appear in the context of Justinian's new, aggressive policies on the Danube frontier. In the early 530s, Chilbudius, a member of the imperial household, replaced Germanus as *magister militum per Thraciam*.[7] He gave up defending the Balkan provinces behind the Danube line and boldly attacked barbarians on the left bank of the river.[8] This was the first time the Romans had launched campaigns north of the Danube frontier since Valens' Gothic wars of 367–9. Chilbudius' campaigns also indicate that the Sclavenes were not far from the frontier. Three years after his nomination, he was killed in one of his expeditions north of the river. Indirectly criticizing Justinian's subsequent policies in the Balkans, Procopius argues that thereafter, "the river became free for the barbarians to cross all times just as they wished." Elsewhere, he describes the territories between the Black Sea and the Danube as "impossible for the Romans to traverse," because of incessant raids.[9]

At the end of the episode of Chilbudius, Procopius claims that "the entire Roman empire found itself utterly incapable of matching the valor of one single man." This may well have been intended as a reproach for Justinian.[10] It is true, however, that the death of Chilbudius, which coincides in time with the beginning of Justinian's wars in the West, was followed by a radical change of policy in the Balkans. Besides the measures taken to fortify both the frontier and the provinces in the interior, to be discussed in the next chapter, Justinian now remodeled the administrative structure of the Balkans. In 536, he created the *quaestura exercitus*. The new administrative unit combined territories at a considerable distance from each other, such as Moesia Inferior, Scythia Minor, some islands in the Aegean Sea, Caria, and Cyprus, all of which were ruled from Odessos (present-day Varna) by the "prefect of Scythia." The prefect of the *quaestura* was given a special *forum* for a court of justice and an entire staff, both of them being "generated from the prefecture [of the East]." The only links between all these provinces were the sea and the navigable Danube. Since Cyprus, the Aegean islands, and Caria represented the most

---

[7] Procopius, *Wars* VII 14.1–6. For Procopius' confusion between Justinian and Justin, see Ensslin 1929:698; Rubin 1954:227; Ivanov, Gindin, and Cymburskii 1991:240–1. Misled by Procopius' story of Chilbudius' Antian namesake, many historians believe the *magister militum per Thraciam* was of Slavic origin. See Ditten 1978:78; Ferjančić 1984:88; Litavrin 1986; Whitby 1988:82; Soustal 1991:70; Moorhead 1994:150. See also Duichev 1960:34. For the origin of the name, see Strumins'kyj 1979–80:790.

[8] The terms used by Procopius to indicate that Chilbudius prevented barbarians from crossing the Danube (ὁ ποταμὸς διαβάτος, τὴν διάβασιν πολλάκις, διαβῆναι), but allowed Romans to cross over the opposite side (ἐς ἤπειρον τὴν ἀντιπέρας . . . ἰόντες ἐκτείνάν τε), show that, at least in his eyes, the Lower Danube was still an efficient barrier. See Chrysos 1987:27–8. For the date of Chilbudius' death, see Waldmüller 1976:36.

[9] Procopius, *Wars* VII 14.4–6, III 1.10. See Ivanov, Gindin, and Cymburskii 1991:217. Chilbudius' campaign north of the Danube may have taken advantage of the transfer of troops from the East following the 532 peace with Persia. See Duichev 1942.

[10] Procopius, *Wars* VII 14.5; Ivanov, Gindin, and Cymburskii 1991:217 and 232.

important naval bases of the Empire, but were also among the richest provinces, the rationale behind Justinian's measure may have been to secure both militarily and financially the efficient defense of the Danube frontier.[11] Important changes were also introduced at the other end of the Danube frontier. The novel 11 of 535, which created an archbishopric of Justiniana Prima, also intended to move the see of the Illyrian prefecture from Thessalonica to the northern provinces. The bishop of Aquis, a city in Dacia Ripensis, on the right bank of the Danube, was also given authority over the city and the neighboring forts, an indication that, instead of aggressive generals, Justinian's policies were now based on the new military responsibilities of bishops.[12]

But this adjustment of policy in the Balkans did not prevent Justinian from boasting about Chilbudius' victories. In November 533, a law was issued with a new intitulature, in which Justinian was described as *Anticus*, along with titles such as *Vandalicus* and *Africanus* relating to Belisarius' success against the Vandals. The title *Anticus* occurs in Justinian's intitulature until 542, then again between 552 and 565. It also appears in inscriptions. Despite Justinian's new defensive approach on the Danube frontier, Roman troops were still holding the left bank of the river. This is indicated by a law issued by Justinian in 538, which dealt with the collection of taxes in Egypt. Officers refusing to assist *augustales* in collecting taxes were facing the punishment of being transferred, together with their entire unit, to the region north of the river Danube, "in order to watch at the frontier of that place."[13]

But Justinian also adopted another way of dealing with the problems on the Danube frontier. In accordance with traditional Roman tactics, he sought to divide and rule. Shortly after the reconquest of Sirmium from the Ostrogoths (535/6), the Gepids took over the city and rapidly conquered "almost all of Dacia."[14] The capture of Sirmium by his old allies, the Gepids, and their subsequent hostile acts were hard for Justinian

---

[11] Novel 41 of May 18, 536 (*Corpus Iuris Civilis* III: 262); John Lydus, *On Powers* II 28. According to John, Justinian set aside for the prefect of Scythia "three provinces, which were almost the most prosperous of all" (II 29). For the *quaestura exercitus*, see also Stein 1968:474–5; Lemerle 1980:286; Hendy 1985:404; Szádeczky-Kardoss 1985; Whitby 1988:70. The *quaestor Iustinianus exercitus* was directly responsible for the *annona* of the army and also exercised supreme judiciary power. See Torbatov 1997.

[12] *Corpus Iuris Civilis* III: 94. It is unlikely that the see was ever transferred to Justiniana Prima. See Granić 1925:128; Maksimović 1984:149.

[13] *Codex Iustinianus*, edict 13 (*Corpus Iuris Civilis* I: 785). See Whitby 1988:166 with n. 34. For the epithet *Anticus*, see the introduction to *Institutiones* (*Corpus Iuris Civilis* II: xxiii) and novel 17 (*Corpus Iuris Civilis* III: 117). For inscriptions, see *CIG* IV 8636; *CIL* III 13673. See also Velkov 1987:159; Irmscher 1980:161; Ivanov 1991a:261; Günther 1992. Justinian's successors imitated his intitulature. The last emperor to do so was Heraclius (novel 22 of May 1, 612).

[14] Procopius, *Wars* V 3.15, V 11.5, and VII 33.8; *Secret History* 18.18. The first Gepid occupation of Sirmium dates back to 473. See Šašel 1979:750; Pohl 1980:299; Christou 1991:64–5. See also Wozniak 1979:144–7.

to take. In response to this, he settled the Herules in the neighboring region of Singidunum (present-day Belgrade). The same principle was applied to the situation on the Lower Danube frontier. Procopius tells us that, sometime between 533/4 and 545, probably before the devastating invasion of the Huns in 539/40, the Antes and the Sclavenes "became hostile to one another and engaged in battle," which ended with a victory of the Sclavenes over the Antes.[15] It is possible, though not demonstrable, that the conflict had been fueled by Justinian. In any case, as Antes and Sclavenes fought against each other, Romans recruited soldiers from both ethnic groups. In 537, 1,600 horsemen, most of whom were Sclavenes and Antes, "who were settled above the Ister river not far from its banks," were shipped to Italy, in order to rescue Belisarius, who was blocked in Rome by the Ostrogoths.[16]

But none of Justinian's attempts to solve the problems in the Danube area proved to be successful. In December 539, a numerous "Hunnic army" crossed the frozen Danube and fell as a scourge upon the eastern Balkan provinces. This, Procopius argued, "had happened many times before, but . . . never brought such a multitude of woes nor such dreadful ones to the people of that land."[17] According to Procopius, the Hunnic raid covered the entire Balkan peninsula from the Adriatic coast to the environs of Constantinople, and resulted in 32 forts taken in Illyricum and no less than 120,000 Roman prisoners. Since Procopius is our only source for this raid, there is no way of assessing the accuracy of his testimony. It is possible, however, that he had the same raid in mind when claiming that the Huns, the Sclavenes, and the Antes, in their daily inroads, wrought frightful havoc among the inhabitants of the Roman provinces.[18] As in the *Wars*, he argues that more than twenty myriads of

[15] Procopius, *Wars* VII 14.7–10; see Waldmüller 1976:36. On this occasion, according to Procopius, a young man of the Antes, named Chilbudius, was taken captive by a Sclavene. The namesake of the former *magister militum per Thraciam* proved to be a vigorous warrior, thus distinguishing himself by his deeds of valor, "through which he succeeded in winning great renown" (*Wars* VII 14.8–9). Procopius prepares his audience for the story of how the Antes would obtain a *foedus* from Justinian, a story in which the *quiproquo* created by "phoney Chilbudius" would play a major role. For Herules in Singidunum, see *Wars* VI 15.30–40, VII 33.13. Around 539, the Gepids formed an alliance with the Franks and the Lombards (Agathias I 4); see Pohl 1980:299. For Justinian's policy on the northern frontier, see Wozniak 1979:156; Patoura 1997.
[16] Procopius, *Wars* V 27.1: οἱ ὑπὲρ ποταμὸν Ἴστρον οὐ μακρὰν τῆς ἐκείνῃ ὄχθης ἵδρυνται. See also Teall 1965:302; Comşa 1973:197; Waldmüller 1976:60; Velkov 1987:154. The troop of 537 is remarkably numerous, especially when compared to Belisarius' entire army amounting to no more than 5,000 men. More important, this is a rare case of Procopius mentioning the place of origin for foreign mercenaries. Among thirteen ethnic groups in the Roman army, there are only two other cases (*Wars* I 15.1, VIII 14.7).
[17] Procopius, *Wars* II 4.1 and 4–7. The date of the raid was established on the basis of the reference to a comet, "at first long as a tall man, but later much larger." See Rubin 1954:108. It is often assumed, perhaps wrongly, that the Huns of 539/40 were Bulgars. See Beshevliev 1981:84.
[18] Procopius, *Secret History* 23.6: σχεδόν τι ἀνὰ πᾶν καταθέοντες ἔτος; 18.20–1: τὴν Σκυθῶν ἐρημίαν ἀμέλει ταύτης πανταχόσε τῆς ξυμβαίνειν. For the date of Procopius' reference, see

these inhabitants were killed or enslaved, so that a veritable "Scythian wilderness" came to exist everywhere in the Balkan provinces. In the same vein, Jordanes refers to regular invasions of Bulgars, Antes, and Sclavenes. A sixth-century Midrashic homilist also complains about havoc brought to Jewish communities by Berbers and Antes.[19] Mistakenly applying John Malalas' account of Zabergan's invasion of 559 to the events of 540, some argued that the Sclavenes may have also participated in the Hunnic invasion of 540. Taking into account that Procopius describes in his *Wars* similar invasions of the Sclavenes, with a similar development, and clearly refers to Sclavenes, along with Huns and Antes, in his *Secret History*, it is a likely possibility.[20] However, since Procopius is our only source for the raid of 540, there is no way to prove the point and the wisest solution is to accept that Procopius' reference to Sclavenes in his *Secret History* cannot be dated with any precision. He might have referred in general to the situation in the Balkans during the 530s. On the other hand, Procopius certainly had in mind a new raid when claiming that during their conflict with the Sclavenes between 533 and 545, the Antes invaded Thrace and plundered and enslaved many of the Roman inhabitants, leading the captives with them as they returned to their "native abode."[21]

At this point in his narrative, Procopius introduces a young Antian prisoner of war, named Chilbudius, like the former *magister militum per Thraciam*. The story is clearly influenced by plots most typical of neo-Attic comedy or of Plautus. Since Antes and Sclavenes were now on peaceful terms, "phoney Chilbudius" was redeemed from the Sclavenes by one of his fellow tribesmen, who also had a Roman prisoner with a Machiavellian mind. The latter persuaded his master that the man he had just purchased from the Sclavenes was Chilbudius, the Roman general, and that he would be richly recompensated by Justinian if he would bring

---

Ferjančić 1984:92. For the "Scythian wilderness" cliche, see Ivanov, Gindin, and Cymburskii 1991:247.

[19] Jordanes, *Romana* 388: *instantia cottidiana*; *Midrash Tehillim* 25.14, ed. S. Buber (Trier, 1892): *ʿAnatiim*. The reference to Berbers points to the Moorish revolts of 534 to 548, as Africa was raided by Berber tribes. See Sperber 1982:179–82; for Jordanes, see Pritsak 1983:367; Soustal 1991:70.

[20] John Malalas XVIII 129. See Angelov 1981:8; Bonev 1983:113; Pritsak 1983:367; Velkov 1987:154; *contra*: Nestor 1963:58. See also Weithmann 1978:66.

[21] Procopius, *Wars* VII 14.11: οἵπερ ἐπαγόμενοι ἀπεκομίσθησαν εἰς τὰ πατρία ἤθη. In this passage, "Thrace" is the diocese, not the province known by the same name. In his *Secret History* (23.6), Procopius speaks of Huns, Sclavenes, and Antes plundering "the whole of Europe," levelling cities to the ground, and stripping others of their wealth "in very thorough fashion through levied contributions." He also claims the invaders enslaved the population "with all their property, making each region destitute of inhabitants by their daily inroads (ταῖς καθ'ημέραν ἐπιδρομαῖς)." Procopius associates these events to Medes and Saracens plundering "the greater part of the land of Asia." This may refer to the reopening of hostilities on the eastern front in 540, but the text is too vague to permit any conclusion.

Chilbudius back to "the land of the Romans."[22] But as soon as he was brought back to his fellow tribesmen, "phoney Chilbudius" frankly revealed his true identity, for he now expected to join again his tribe as a freeman. The whole story was made public when "the report was carried about and reached the entire nation [of the Antes]." Under their pressure, "phoney Chilbudius" then agreed to claim that he really was the Roman general and the Antes sent him immediately to Constantinople. At about the same time, as if knowing what was going on, Justinian sent an embassy to the Antes, asking them all to move into "an ancient city, Turris by name, situated to the north of the river Ister." The city had been built by Trajan, but was left deserted, after it had been plundered by the barbarians of that region. Justinian promised to give them the city and the region around it, and to pay them great sums of money, on condition that they should become his allies (ἔνσπονδοι) and constantly block the way against the Huns, "when these wished to overrun the Roman domain."[23] The Antes accepted all conditions, provided that Chilbudius, the *magister militum per Thraciam*, would be restored to his office of general of the Roman army and would assist them in settling in Turris.[24] The rationale behind their request, Procopius argues, was that they wanted and stoutly maintained that the man there among them was Chilbudius, the Roman general. In the end, the whole plot was unmasked by Narses, who captured "phoney Chilbudius" on his way to Constantinople.[25]

It is difficult to visualize the source of this story. Some have argued that Procopius may have had access to the official forms of the cross-examination of "phoney Chilbudius" by Narses, others that he might

---

[22] Procopius, *Wars* VII 14.11–16. See Bonev 1983:109–12. For comic influences, see Ivanov, Gindin, and Cymburskii 1991:231–2.

[23] Procopius, *Wars* VII 14.21 and 32–3. It would make sense to locate Turris, the city transferred by Justinian to the Antes, in the region that could have blocked the access of steppe nomads to the Danube frontier. Procopius' description (ὑπὲρ ποταμὸν Ἴστρον) is very vague and he does not seem to have had a clear idea of the geography of the region. Since he uses neither ἐν τῇ ἀντιπέρας ἠπείρω nor ἐπὶ θάτερα, however, there is no reason to believe that Turris was located next to the Danube river. On the other hand, any land offered for settlement through the *foedus* had to be less populated, have no major cities, and be strategically isolated and controllable. See Chrysos 1989:17. For Turris, see also Bolşacov-Ghimpu 1969; Madgearu 1992.

[24] Dewing's unfortunate translation ("to give them all the assistance within his power while they were establishing themselves") stands for καὶ σφίσι ξυνοικεῖν μὲν δυνάμει τῇ πάσῃ. But συνοικέω literally means "to settle," as in *Wars* II 14.1: "Now Chosroes built a city in Assyria . . . and settled (ζυνῴκισεν) there all the captives from Antioch." Note that the use of the prefix ξυν- implies that Justinian intended to bring together at least two different groups. See Ivanov, Gindin, and Cymburskii 1991:229.

[25] Procopius *Wars* VII 14.32–5; see also VII 13.24–6. "Phoney Chilbudius" fluently spoke Latin (which greatly contributed to his successful impersonation of the Roman general). This is remarkable, given that Gilacius, an Armenian who had become a military commander in the Roman army, "did not know how to speak either Greek or Latin or Gothic or any other language except Armenian" (*Wars* VII 26.24).

have taken the whole story from the Antian envoys in Constantinople. Whatever its origin, Procopius surely re-worked the account and arranged it according to comic narrative patterns. He may have intended to stress a few important points. First, there is the ambition of the Antes, as a group, to be given a Roman official who would guide them into some more sophisticated organization. They all agreed to become Justinian's ἔνσπονδοι and would remain allies of the Empire until 602.[26] The fact that Justinian transferred to his new allies a Roman fort on the left bank of the Danube river shows that the Romans were still claiming rights to territories north of the frontier. Procopius' story is thus designed to adjust such claims to the actual situation. He also needed "phoney Chilbudius" in order to explain how Justinian could conceivably have allied himself with barbarians who "are not ruled by one man, but . . . lived from old under a democracy" and by whom "everything which involves their welfare, whether for good or for ill, is referred to the people." Barbarians ignorant of the benefits of monarchy may have understood "Chilbudius" not as a certain person, but as a military and political title of an official able to bolster their request. Narses unmasking the plot of the Antes did not, therefore, cause the invalidation of the *foedus*, for in the following years, Antes would constantly appear in historical sources as allies of the Romans.[27] Just two years after the treaty of 545, 300 Antes were fighting in Lucania (Italy) against the Ostrogoths. In the 580s, the Romans bribed the Antes to attack the settlements of the Sclavenes. In 602, the qagan dispatched Apsich, his general, to destroy the "nation of the Antes, which was in fact allied to the Romans."[28]

From a Roman perspective, the treaty of 545 was meant to eliminate the problem of Hunnic raids, against which one of its stipulations was

[26] Ensslin 1929:698–9; Ditten 1978:82; *contra*: Stein 1968:522. For the source of Procopius' account, see Rubin 1954:198; Litavrin 1986:27. For ἔνσπονδοι as *foederati* and σύμμαχοι as barbarian troops under their own commanders, see Christou 1991:32–5. Romans, too, could become ἔνσπονδοι, for example in relation to Persia (*Wars* VIII 11.24; *Secret History* 11.12). Unlike σύμμαχοι, ἔνσπονδοι were not only military allies, but also political partners. Other examples of ἔνσπονδοι: Lombards (*Wars* VII 33.12), Gepids (*Wars* VII 34.10), Saginae (*Wars* VIII 2.18), Goths (*Wars* VIII 5.13), Sabiri (*Wars* VIII 11.24), and Cutrigurs (*Wars* VIII 19.5). The majority were on the northern frontier of the Empire.

[27] Procopius, *Wars* VII 14.22: ἐν δημοκρατίᾳ ἐκ παλαιοῦ βιοτεύουσι. For the concept of "democracy" derisively applied to Slavic society, as the opposite of Byzantine monarchy, see Benedicty 1963:46–7; Havlík 1985:174. Patrick Amory (1997:287–8) sees this episode as an illustration of how uncertain (ethnic) identity was, since "the Slavs were unable to tell the difference" between Chilbudius, the Roman general, and his Antian namesake. This is a naive interpretation, for it takes Procopius' account at its face value.

[28] Theophylact Simocatta VIII 5.13. For the 300 Antes in Italy, see Procopius, *Wars* VII 22.3–6; for Antes attacking the Sclavenes, see John of Ephesus VI 45. Dabragezas, a Roman officer of Antian origin, led the Roman fleet during the siege of Phasis, in Crimea, and took part in the campaigns of 555 and 556 against Persia, in Lazike. See Agathias III 6.9 (Δαβραγέζας, Ἄντης ἀνήρ, ταξιάρχος), III 7.2, III 21.6.

clearly phrased. The rationale behind Justinian's offer may have been the devastating invasion of 540. But the respite was relatively short, for a still more destructive attack would follow in 558.

In response to the threat posed by the Frankish king Theudebert, who, according to Agathias, was preparing a large coalition of barbarians against the Empire, Justinian offered in 546 an alliance to the Lombard king Auduin. Like the Antes, the Lombards were settled on formerly Roman territory (Pannonia), and were paid great sums of money. Like Turris, Pannonia was only nominally under the control of the Romans. The Lombards were now very close to the Gepids and a conflict soon arose between the two groups. Since both recognized the Empire's nominal claims of suzerainty over their respective territories, embassies from both arrived in Constantinople. Justinian decided for the Lombards, because the Gepids were still controlling Sirmium. However, despite his victory over the Herules, who had meanwhile turned into the allies of the Gepids, and despite his permanent efforts to fuel the rivalry between Lombards and Gepids, both groups eventually agreed to a truce in 549.[29]

At this moment, a candidate to the Lombard throne, Hildigis, fled to the Sclavenes, who presumably lived somewhere near the Gepids and the Lombards. As Justinian offered the *foedus* to Auduin, Hildigis went to the Gepids, followed by a retinue of Lombards and Sclavenes. He later returned to the Sclavenes, together with his followers, but then moved to Italy, where he joined the army of King Totila, "having with him an army of not less than six thousand men." After brief skirmishes with Roman troops, Hildigis recrossed the Danube river and, once again, went to the Sclavenes. Meanwhile, in 549, the kings of the Lombards and the Gepids had agreed to a truce. But the attitude of the Gepids toward the Empire remained hostile, for they would later invite the Cutrigurs to a joint raid across the Danube.[30]

By 550, Justinian seems to have contained the threat on the Danube frontier by means of large payments. He allied himself with Lombards and Antes against Gepids and Huns, respectively. The Sclavenes were obviously not part of this system of alliances. It is no surprise, therefore, to see them starting their own, independent raids. In 545, a great throng of Sclavenes crossed the river Danube, plundered the adjoining country,

[29] Agathias I 4.1–3; Procopius, *Wars* VII 33.10–12, VIII 34.1–10, and VII 35.12–22; Paul the Deacon, *Historia Langobardorum* I 21–2 and II 27. See Christou 1991:78–9, 82, and 91. For the date of the truce, see Pohl 1996:31–2.

[30] Procopius, *Wars* VII 35.16, 19, and 21–2, VIII 18.16–18). The use of the word "army" (στράτευμα) indicates horsemen. The *communis opinio* is that the Sclavenes to whom Hildigis fled lived in present-day Slovakia or Moravia. See Zeman 1966:164; Godłowski 1979:434; Szydłowski 1980:234; Pohl 1988:96–7; Třeštík 1996. For Hildigis' route, see Margetić 1992:169. Hildigis resurfaced in Constantinople in 552 (*Wars* VIII 27).

and enslaved a great number of Romans. The Herulian mercenaries under Narses' command intercepted and defeated them and released the prisoners. According to Procopius, this is the moment when Narses discovered "a certain man who was pretending to bear the name of Chilbudius."[31] It would be difficult to believe that the recently appointed leader of the Antes, who wished so much to enter the Roman alliance, could have joined the plundering raid of the Sclavenes. Procopius has told us that "phoney Chilbudius" had spent some time with the Sclavenes, as a prisoner of war, and, according to the chronology of his narrative, the raid of the Sclavenes may have followed the assembly of the Antes, in which they had proclaimed their fellow tribesman as "Chilbudius."[32] It is very unlikely that the Antian envoys to Constantinople arrived there as Narses' prisoners. Did Procopius intend to minimize the importance of the *foedus* of 545 by implying that it had been agreed upon by an emperor dealing with a barbarian liar who had entered Roman territory as an enemy? In view of his criticism of Justinian, who "kept bringing all the barbarians into collision with one another," it may be a plausible hypothesis.[33] It is also possible that the entire story of "phoney Chilbudius" was made up by Procopius, as a narrative strategy in order to emphasize Justinian's weakness. The use of comic patterns may support this idea.

In any case, Procopius provides clear evidence that no attempts were made to approach the Sclavenes with similar offers of alliance. They always appear on the side of the Empire's enemies, as in the episode of Hildigis. To Procopius, the Sclavenes were unpredictable and disorderly barbarians. His attitude thus comes very close to that of the author of the *Strategikon* who, some decades later, describes the Sclavenes as completely faithless and having "no regard for treaties, which they agree to more out of fear than by gifts."[34] Here and there, individual Sclavenes may indeed appear as fighting for the Romans, as in the case of Souarounas, a Sclavene soldier in the Roman army operating in the Caucasus region.[35]

---

[31] Procopius, *Wars* VII 13.26. See also Waldmüller 1976: 39 and 56; Irmscher 1980:162; Velkov 1987:155. The word "throng" (ὅμιλος) appears seventy times in Procopius' *Wars*, always in reference to a group of warriors without either discipline or order. For Justinian's successful attempts to set one barbarian group against another, see Patoura 1997.

[32] Procopius, *Wars* VII 14.19–20. [33] *Secret History* 11.5–9.

[34] *Strategikon* XI 4.4. Unpredictable Sclavenes: Adshead 1990:104.

[35] Agathias IV 20.4. Agathias also mentions Dabragezas, the Antian officer who commanded the Roman fleet in Crimea (III 6.9, III 7.2, III 21.6). See Werner 1980:590; Strumins'kyj 1979–80:792. In the same context (III 21.6), he mentions another officer, Leontios, whom many believed to be Dabragezas' son. This is further viewed as a case of a successful assimilation of the Slavs. See Ditten 1978:80; Waldmüller 1976:64. However, Λεόντιος ὁ Δαβραγέζου refers to Dabragezas' *bucellarius*, not son, for the phrase is obviously a counterpart to Ζύπερ ὁ Μαρκελλίνου δορυφόρος in the first part of the sentence.

Another Sclavene mercenary proved himself useful to Belisarius during the siege of Auximum in 540. But unlike Antes, these soldiers seem to have been hired on an individual basis, due to their special skills.[36]

In 548, another army of Sclavenes crossed the Danube, probably via the Iron Gates fords. They raided deep into Roman territory, reaching Dyrrachium in Epirus Nova. Procopius even claims that they succeeded in capturing numerous strongholds, "which previously had been reputed to be strong places."[37] The military commanders of Illyricum followed them at a distance with an army of 15,000 men, without getting too close or engaging in any battle. The following year (549), another 3,000 Sclavene warriors crossed the Danube and immediately advanced to the Hebrus (present-day Maritsa) river, which they also crossed with no difficulty. They split into two groups, one with 1,800, the other with 1,200 men. The two sections separated from each other. One of them attacked the cities in Thrace, while the other invaded Illyricum. Both routed Roman armies sent against them, and both captured many fortresses, although, as Procopius argues, "they neither had any previous experience in attacking city walls, nor had they dared to come down to the open plain."[38] But Procopius' narrative focuses more on those Sclavenes who came closer to the capital city. He tells us that the commander of the cavalry cohorts stationed at Tzurullum (present-day Çorlu) was defeated, captured, and savagely executed. Procopius claims that the Sclavenes of 549 "had never in all time crossed the Ister river with an army before."[39] It is hardly conceivable that Procopius forgot what he had reported about the invasions following Chilbudius' death, particularly about that of 545. Could he have implied that the Sclavenes of 549 were not those of 545?[40]

[36] Procopius, *Wars* VI 26.16–22. At Auximum, Belisarius is told that the Sclavenes "are accustomed to conceal themselves behind a rock or any bush which may happen to be near and pounce upon an enemy" and that "they are constantly practicing this in their native haunts along the river Ister, both on the Romans and on the [other] barbarians as well." This reminds one of what the *Strategikon* has to say about Sclavenes: "They make effective use of ambushes, sudden attacks, and raids, devising many different methods by night and by day" (XI 4.9).

[37] Procopius, *Wars* VII 29.2. The Sclavenes of 548 were most probably horsemen, for Procopius calls them an "army" (στράτευμα), a word he commonly uses for cavalry troops (e.g., *Wars* I 12.6, I 21.15, II 4.4, III 18.13; see also Ivanov, Gindin and Cymburskii 1991:234). This is also indicated by the fact that they raided deep into Roman territory, moving rapidly. Iron Gates fords: Maksimović 1980:33–4. Date: Ensslin 1929:221; Waldmüller 1976:39; Irmscher 1980:162; Bonev 1983:114; Velkov 1987:155.

[38] Procopius, *Wars* VII 38.7. For the commanders of Illyricum, see *Wars* VII 29.3. Sclavenes of 549 as horsemen: Ivanov, Gindin, and Cymburskii 1991:236.

[39] *Wars* VII 38.10. See also Braichevskii 1953:24. Only Berthold Rubin (1954:226) seems to have noticed this difficulty. According to Rubin, Procopius' narrative of events taking place after Chilbudius' death is often contradictory.

[40] Procopius, *Wars* VII 13.24–6. Note also the difference in terms applied by Procopius to these two groups. The Sclavenes of 545 were a "throng" (ὅμιλος), those of 549, an "army" (στράτευμα).

84

Theoretically, it is not impossible that the marauders of 549 were just a different group from those of 545. However, there are two reasons for not favoring this interpretation. First, Procopius' source for this raid seems to have been a combination of archival material (as suggested by such indications as the number of Sclavenes, the direction of their attacks, or the mention of Asbadus, Justinian's bodyguard, who commanded the cavalry troops stationed at Tzurullum) and oral reports (as indicated by the obviously exaggerated number of prisoners taken after the capture of Topeiros and by the description of their torture and execution). Second, what Procopius has to say about these "newcomers" ("they [never] dared to come down to the open plain") is strikingly similar to what John of Ephesus would write about the Sclavenes of the 580s: they "had never dared to leave the woods and the inaccessible areas."[41] The details of the account of the 549 raid look suspiciously like stereotypes. Procopius was certainly not an alert observer of the Sclavenes and it is unlikely that he was able to distinguish between the two raids in minute details. He might, however, have had access to more material on the raid of 549 than on those of 545 or 548, which allowed him to make comments on the margins. He reports that, for the first time, the Sclavenes succeeded in conquering a city (Topeiros, near Abdera, in Rhodope). In a long passage, he also describes in detail how the Sclavenes captured the city and what happened to the Roman captives. Procopius' description of the atrocities committed by Sclavenes after conquering Topeiros matches not only contemporary historiographical cliches about barbarians, but also the appalling portrait of the Sclavenes by Pseudo-Caesarius.[42] But Procopius' argument is consistent: the Slavs were indeed an unpredictable enemy. Until conquering Topeiros, they "had spared no age . . ., so that the whole land inhabited by the Illyrians and Thracians came to be everywhere filled with unburied corpses."[43] After the bloodshed at Topeiros, as if they "were drunk with the great quantity of blood they had shed,"[44] the Sclavenes suddenly decided to spare some prisoners, whom they took with them when departing on their homeward way. Again, Procopius seems to have forgotten what he himself told us,

---

[41] John of Ephesus VI 25. For the execution of the Roman prisoners by κατωμισμός, see Vergote 1972:139–40.

[42] Procopius, *Wars* VII 38.11–23. For Pseudo-Caesarius, see Riedinger 1969:302. Topeiros captured by Sclavenes is also mentioned in the *Buildings* (IV 11). For the location, see Soustal 1991:71 and 480–1; Kasapides 1991:2. According to Procopius, the Sclavenes of 549 imprisoned their victims in their huts (ἐν τοῖς δωματίοις) together with their cattle and sheep, and then "set fire to the huts without mercy." This is remarkably similar to the episode of the *Getae equites* of 517, who burnt their prisoners alive, locked in their own houses (*inclusi suis cum domunculis captivi Romani incensi sunt*; Marcellinus Comes, pp. 39 and 120). For a comparable treatment of prisoners by Vidini and Gelones, see Ammianus Marcellinus 31.2.13–16.   [43] *Wars* VII 38.19.

[44] *Wars* VII 38.23.

namely that in 545, the Sclavenes had also taken a great number of prisoners, later to be released by the Herulian mercenaries of Narses.

In the summer of the year 550, as Roman troops were gathering in Serdica under the command of Germanus in order to be sent to Italy against Totila, a great throng of Sclavenes, "such as never before was known," crossed the Danube and easily came close to Naissus (present-day Niš).[45] The attack of the Sclavenes occurred at a time when Narses, who was also preparing to embark on a campaign to Italy, was forced to postpone his departure by Cutrigur attacks on Philippopolis (present-day Plovdiv).[46] According to Procopius, the Sclavenes were bent on capturing Thessalonica and the surrounding cities. The threat must have been truly serious, for Justinian ordered Germanus to defer his expedition to Italy and to defend Thessalonica and the other cities. This measure proved to be efficient, for the Sclavenes gave up their plans to capture Thessalonica. Instead, they crossed the mountain ranges to the west and entered Dalmatia, at that time still disputed between Ostrogoths and Romans. Germanus did not follow them, both because of his other commitments and because once in Dalmatia, the Sclavenes did not represent any major threat to southern Macedonia. He would soon die, before being able to advance on Italy. As for the Sclavenes, the Romans did nothing to make them leave Dalmatia. Despite their great number, therefore, the Sclavenes of 550 did not pose any major problem to the Roman defense. But the raid is significant for a different reason. Procopius tells us that the Sclavenes spent the winter of 550 and most of the following year in Dalmatia, "as if in their own land."[47] They had no fear of any possible Roman attack, an indication of the confused situation in Dalmatia on the eve of Narses' campaign of 552, which put an end to the Ostrogothic war and kingdom. This is the first case of a two-year Sclavene raid, but there is no reason to believe that the Sclavene marauders intended to settle. They seem to have recrossed the mountains to the east in the spring of 551 and joined another group of Sclavene warriors

---

[45] *Wars* VII 40.4–5 and 7–8. It is possible that the Sclavenes of 550, like those of 549, crossed the river by the Iron Gates fords. See Popović 1978:608; Maksimović 1980:35; Janković 1981:197. For the date of this raid, see Teall 1965:311.

[46] Procopius, *Wars* VIII 21.20–1. Some interpreted this coincidence as an indication that the Sclavene attack had been instigated by Totila. See Ensslin 1929:699; Weithmann 1978:68; Ditten 1978:87; Irmscher 1980:162. According to Procopius, however, Justinian ordered his military commanders in Thrace and Illyricum to avoid any confrontation with the invading Huns, for they were his allies against the Ostrogoths (*Secret History* 21.26).

[47] Procopius, *Wars* VII 40.31–2: ὥσπερ ἐν χώρᾳ οἰκείᾳ διαχειμάζοντες. For the Ostrogothic–Byzantine war in Dalmatia, see Basler 1993:17. Indulf led a raid on the Dalmatian coast in 548, but Totila was unable to regain Dalmatia. On the other hand, by 535, only parts of the former province of Dalmatia had been reoccupied by Roman troops. Parts of northern Bosnia may have been already controlled by the Lombards.

who had just crossed the Danube. Just as in 549, they all divided themselves into three groups operating separately. Procopius' narrative, however, focuses only on the group approaching Constantinople.[48]

Annoyed by their devastations, the emperor now sent an army commanded by several generals, but headed by an imperial eunuch, Scholastikos. At only five days' journey from Constantinople, near Adrianople, the Roman army came upon one of the three groups mentioned by Procopius. The Sclavenes were carrying with them a great deal of booty. In the ensuing battle, most of the Roman army was destroyed, and, according to Procopius, "the generals came within a little of falling into the hands of the enemy, succeeding only with difficulty in making their escape with the remnant of the army." The Sclavenes savagely plundered the region in the vicinity of the capital, up to the Long Walls. With some of the troops saved from the debacle at Adrianople, the Romans intercepted the Sclavene marauders, rescued a vast number of Roman captives, and recovered a standard, which has been captured during the battle of Adrianople. The rest of the Sclavenes, however, "departed on the homeward way with the other booty."[49]

The year 551 was not yet over, when a great throng of Sclavenes (Σκλαβηνῶν δὲ πολὺς ὅμιλος) descended upon Illyricum and "inflicted sufferings there not easily described." The army sent by Justinian under the command of Germanus' sons cautiously followed the raiders, without engaging into any confrontation. The raid continued and the Sclavenes were able to return home with all their plunder. The Romans did nothing to stop them at the crossing of the Danube river, for the Gepids took the Sclavenes "under their protection and ferried them across," receiving one solidus per head as payment for their labor.[50]

In response, Justinian started negotiations with the Gepids, but at the same time supported the Lombards against them. An army sent by Justinian under the command of Amalafridas, King Alboin's brother-in-law, sided with the Lombards, defeated the Gepids, and killed their king Turismod. The "eternal peace" agreed upon by King Alboin and Turisind, the new king of the Gepids, would last another ten years.[51]

But the key to Justinian's new policy in the Balkans was not playing off Lombards and Gepids against each other. Shortly before 558, most likely

---

[48] See Procopius, *Wars* VII 40.31: "But the Slavs reappeared, both those who had previously come into the emperor's land, as I have recounted above, and others who had crossed the Ister not long afterwards and joined the first, and they began to overrun the Roman domain with complete freedom." First two-year raid: Nestor 1963:47–8; Cankova-Petkova 1970:221; Waldmüller 1976:44; Velkov 1987:161. The Slavs of 550/1 as settlers: Ditten 1978:87.

[49] Procopius, *Wars* VII 40.31–45. See also Ensslin 1929:699.   [50] Procopius, *Wars* VIII 25.1–6.

[51] Jordanes, *Romana* 386–7; Procopius, *Wars* VIII 25.1–10 and 13–15, VIII 27.1–5 and 7–29; Paul the Deacon, *Historia Langobardorum* I 23–4.

in 554, as Procopius was finishing Book IV of his *Buildings*, the building program on the Danube frontier was completed. According to Procopius, Justinian built or renewed more than 600 forts in the Balkans, eight times more than in the entire Asian part of the Empire. There is a tendency among scholars to downplay the significance of this major building program or to treat Procopius' evidence with extreme suspicion. The archaeological evidence will be examined in detail in the following chapter. It is worth mentioning for the moment that, just because the *Buildings* is a panegyric, it does not mean that we should expect a heightening of the evidence. It is not true that Procopius, in accordance with the convention of the time, credited Justinian with achievements which were not his. Two recently discovered inscriptions from Albania corroborate Book IV. One of them clearly attests that the forts in Moesia, Scythia Minor, Illyricum, and Thrace were built for Justinian by his architect, Viktorinos. We have all reasons to believe that Justinian's strategy described in Book IV *was* realized in practice and that Procopius' description of it is, in its essentials, sound. The ending phase of this building program may have been sped up by the devastating Sclavene raids of 549–51, for the Sclavenes are the only barbarians to whom Procopius specifically refers in relation to Justinian's building program. He tells us that the fort at Ulmetum (present-day Pantelimonu de Sus, in Dobrudja) had come to be wholly deserted and "nothing of it was left except the name," for the Sclavenes had been making their ambuscades there for a great length of time and had been tarrying there very long (διατρίβην τε αὐτόθι ἐπὶ μακρότατον ἐσχηκότων). The fort was built all up from the foundations.[52] Justinian also built a new fort named Adina, because the "barbarian Sclaveni were constantly laying concealed ambuscades there against travellers, thus making the whole district impassable."[53]

The evidence of the *Buildings* gives one the impression that Procopius perceived the challenge of the Sclavenes as the great military problem of his day and, at the same time, saw himself challenged to describe it. Procopius explains that the entire strategy underlying the building program in the Balkans was centered upon the Danube frontier and that the forts built by Justinian responded to a particular kind of warfare, being designed to resist sudden attacks from the north.[54] The defense system was also designed to protect the countryside rather than the urban

---

[52] Procopius, *Buildings* IV 7. See Nestor 1961:429 and 1963:45; Shuvalov 1991:40. Albanian inscription: Feissel 1988.   [53] Procopius, *Buildings* IV 7.

[54] Procopius, *Buildings* IV 1: "Indeed it was the custom of these peoples [barbarians, in general] to rise and make war upon their enemies [the Romans] for no particular cause, and open hostilities without sending an embassy, and they did not bring their struggle to an end through any treaty, or cease operations for any specified period, but they made their attacks without provocation and reached a decision by the sword alone." See Adshead 1990:107.

centers, for, according to Procopius, the first target of the barbarian raids was fields, not cities. According to Procopius, Justinian's strategy was therefore not to close the frontier, but to build three successive lines, one along the Danube, the other along the Stara Planina range, and a third one along the Istranca Dağlar range, in the vicinity of Constantinople. All three were expected to slow down, if not stop, any barbarian raids. Book IV has therefore been viewed as a "codified" map of barbarian invasions into the Balkans, of their direction and impact. In any case, despite claims to the contrary, Procopius' *Buildings* provides solid evidence that in the mid-500s, the Danube frontier together with the provinces in the interior received a level of fortification the Balkans had never witnessed before.[55]

Justinian's concept of defense proved its efficiency, for no Sclavene raid is known for a long period between 552 and 577. With the exception of Zabergan's invasion of 558/9 and the Cutrigur raid into Dalmatia in 568, there is no mention of raiding activity of any kind in the Balkans until the last quarter of the sixth century.[56] It has been argued that this may be an indirect result of Justinian's decisive victory against the Goths in Italy. However, Zabergan's devastating invasion of 558/9 does not support this argument. According to Agathias of Myrina, Zabergan crossed the frozen river "as if it were land," with a great number of horsemen. Victor of Tunnunna, writing in 565 in Constantinople, reported that the Huns captured and killed a *magister militum* named Sergios, the son of a certain priest named Bacchus. The same details appear in John Malalas, who also claimed that the invaders found parts of the Long Walls collapsed, as they indeed were after the earthquake of 557. Theophanes gave a slightly different account of the same attack. Sclavenes among Zabergan's hordes appear in both John Malalas' and Theophanes' accounts, but are not mentioned by either Agathias or Victor of Tunnunna. If groups of Sclavene warriors participated in Zabergan's invasion, they certainly played a subordinate role. No independent raid of the Sclavenes is known for the entire period until 578, despite the fact that the period is covered by more than one source.[57]

---

[55] Procopius, *Buildings* IV 1. See also Velkov 1987:155. "Codified" map of barbarian invasions: Ivanov 1984. For the defense system in the Balkans, see Ovcharov 1977:468 and 1982:19.

[56] Whitby 1988:88; Soustal 1991:71. For the Cutrigur raid of 562, see Menander the Guardsman 12.5. See also Blockley 1985:268 with n. 160.

[57] Agathias v 11.6; Victor of Tunnunna, *Chronica*, ed. Mommsen, *MGH: AA* 11:205; John Malalas XVIII 129; Mango 1997:341. Justinian's victory over the Goths: Shuvalov 1989. Cutrigur invasion: Bakalov 1974:206; Waldmüller 1976:48 and 50; Irmscher 1980:163; Pohl 1988:19; Fiedler 1992:8. I am not persuaded by Vladislav Popović's attempt to reconstruct a Sclavene raid not recorded by historical sources on the basis of the numismatic evidence. See Popović 1978:617 and 1981.

THE AVARS AND THE SLAVS: RAIDING ACTIVITY IN THE 580S

As a consequence of the calamitous invasion of Zabergan's Cutrigurs, the Avars became Justinian's new allies. The newcomers were remarkably successful in establishing their suzerainty in the steppes north of the Black Sea. One by one, all nomadic tribes were forced to acknowledge their supremacy. Among them were also the Antes, for the Avars, in about 560, "ravaged and plundered the[ir] land". Mezamer, the envoy sent by the Antes to ransom some of their tribesmen taken prisoner by the Avars, was killed at the orders of the qagan. Menander the Guardsman claims that the qagan's decision was taken under the influence of "that Kutrigur who was a friend of the Avars and had very hostile designs against the Antae." It is very likely that, in order to subdue the world of the steppe, the Avars took advantage of dissensions between various nomadic groups. In this case, Menander's reference to the leaders of the Antes, who "had failed miserably and had been thwarted in their hopes," may imply that, before the arrival of the Avars, the Antes had experienced some serious defeat at the hands of their Cutrigur neighbors.[58] Following the defeat of the Antes, the Avars became the masters of the steppe, with no other rivals except the Gök Türk Empire to the east.[59] They felt indeed strong enough to send an embassy to Justinian asking for land south of the Danube, in Scythia Minor. Their request was rejected, although a later source, the *Chronicle of Monemvasia*, claims that Justinian granted the Avars the city of Durostorum.[60] A few years, later, however, the Avars, in alliance with the Lombards, destroyed the Gepids in Pannonia and soon remained the only masters of the Hungarian plain.

The direct consequences of this conquest were immediately visible. The Avars attacked Sirmium, and negotiations with the Romans failed

---

[58] Menander the Guardsman, fr. 3. Avars as Justinian's allies: Szádeczky-Kardoss 1986a:267–8; Soustal 1991:71. Location of the Antian polity: Ditten 1978:89 and 93. Date of the Avar attack: Litavrin 1991b:8; Levinskaia and Tokhtas'ev 1991b:327–8. For Mezamer's name, see Wiita 1977:262; Werner 1980:590; Strumins'kyj 1979–80:792–3.

[59] The confederation of tribes known as the Gök Türk Empire had formed in 552 when the Ashina clan had seized power from their Juan-Juan overlords in Mongolia. The Empire was divided into a senior eastern and a junior western qaganate. Envoys of the western qaganate came to Constantinople in 562 or 563 to complain about Justinian's alliance with the Avars. See Mango 1997:351; Pohl 1988:40–1; Whittow 1996:220–2. The Byzantine response was to send an embassy to Qagan Sizabul, in 569 (Menander the Guardsman, fr. 10,2). By 565, Justin II was already using the Gök Türk as a threat against the Avars (Pohl 1988:49). In 576/7, Turxanthos, the qagan of the western division, conquered Bosporus (Panticapaeum). Chersonesus fell in 579. See Menander the Guardsman, fr. 19,2 and 25,2; see also Gajdukević 1971:518; Szádeczky-Kardoss 1986a:269–70; Pohl 1988:67. The Avars took Gök Türk threats very seriously. They immediately withdrew from the Balkans, when learning that Gök Türk troops were advancing from the east. See Michael the Syrian x 21; Pohl 1988:40; Szádeczky-Kardoss 1986a:267–8.

[60] *Chronicle of Monemvasia*, p. 9; see Pohl 1988:47.

to provide a peaceful solution to the conflict. The indirect consequences were, however, more important. Most likely encouraged by the success of the Avars, the Sclavenes resumed their raids. In 578, according to Menander the Guardsman, 100,000 Sclavene warriors "devastated Thrace and many other areas."[61] The number of the invading Sclavene warriors mentioned by Menander the Guardsman is certainly exaggerated. But his account is corroborated by others. John of Biclar probably referred to this same invasion when reporting Sclavene destruction in Thrace and Avar naval attacks on the Black Sea coast. Since Avars were never at ease on sea, in sharp contrast to Sclavenes, whose sailing abilities are often mentioned by various other sources, John may have muddled Avars with Sclavenes. The scale of the raid seems to have been considerable, for according to Menander the Guardsman, the Sclavenes were still plundering in Greece ("Ελλας), when Qagan Bayan organized an expedition against their territories north of the Danube.[62]

Despite the omnipresence of the Avars, there is no reason to doubt that the raid of 578 was an independent one. The qagan himself seems to have taken very seriously the independent attitude of the Sclavene leaders. Indeed, Menander the Guardsman cites, for the first time, the name of a Sclavene chieftain, Daurentius (or Dauritas), to whom the qagan sent an embassy asking the Sclavenes to accept Avar suzerainty and to pay him tribute. The rationale behind the qagan's claims was that the land of the Sclavenes was "full of gold, since the Roman Empire had long been plundered by the Slavs, whose own land had never been raided by any other people at all." This could only mean that the arrival of the Avars to the Lower Danube, and their wars for the domination of the steppe north of the Danube Delta and the Black Sea, had no effect on the neighboring Sclavenes. The answer given by the independently minded Dauritas and his fellow chiefs to the Avar envoys may have been pure boasting designed to illustrate Menander's idea of barbarians "with haughty and stubborn spirits." It is nevertheless a plausible answer. In an episode apparently constructed as the opposite of that of Mezamer and Bayan, Menander tells us that the Sclavenes eventually slew the envoys of the qagan. Bayan now had a good reason for his long-awaited expedition. In addition, Emperor

---

[61] Menander the Guardsman, fr. 20,2. See Metcalf 1962b:135; Popović 1975:450; Whitby 1988:87. For the fall of Sirmium, see Menander the Guardsman, fr. 27,2.

[62] John of Biclar, p. 214: "Avares litora maris captiose obsident et navibus litora Thraciae navigantibus satis infesti sunt"; Menander the Guardsman, fr. 21. See also Waldmüller 1976:106; Weithmann 1978:78; Popović 1980:231; Yannopoulos 1980:332; Pohl 1988:68; Whitby 1988:87; Levinskaia and Tokhtas'ev 1991b:343; Cherniak 1991:398; Chiriac 1993:193. The exact meaning of "Ελλας is a controversial issue. Despite its vague territorial content, it is clear that Menander refers here to the southern regions of the Balkans, as an indicator for the magnitude of the Slavic raid.

Tiberius II also needed him to force the Sclavenes raiding the Balkans to return home. Tiberius ordered the *quaestor exercitus* John, who was at the same time *magister militum* (or *praefectus praetorio) per Illyricum* and apparently commanded the Danube fleet, to transport 60,000 Avar horsemen on ships along the Danube, from Pannonia to Scythia Minor. Since the Avar horsemen landed in Scythia Minor, the Sclavene villages to which Bayan set fire must have been located on the left bank, not far from the river, in eastern Walachia or southern Moldavia. Bayan laid waste the fields, which may indicate that the expedition took place in the late summer or early fall of 578. No Sclavenes "dared to face" the qagan, and many took refuge into the nearby woods.[63]

Nevertheless, Qagan Bayan's expedition against the Sclavenes did not fulfill Tiberius II's expectations. That the situation in the northern Balkans remained confused is shown by the fact that, in 579, the Avar envoy himself, together with his small Roman escort, were ambushed by Sclavene marauders on their way back from Constantinople through Illyricum.[64] According to John of Ephesus, two years later, "the accursed people of the Slavs" set out and plundered all of Greece, the regions surrounding Thessalonica (the Syrian word is *tslwnyq'*), and Thrace, taking many towns and castles, laying waste, burning, pillaging, and seizing the whole country. On the double assumption that the first Sclavene attack on Thessalonica occurred in 586 and that John died shortly after 585, Theresa Olajos proposed an emendation of the text, replacing Thessalonica with Thessaly.[65] To my knowledge, her point of view remains unchallenged. A closer examination of her assumptions, however, may lead to a different conclusion. First, John could not have died in about 585, for the last event recorded by his *Ecclesiastical History* is the acquittal of Gregory of Antioch in 588. As a consequence, he could well have had knowledge of a Sclavene raid reaching the environs of Thessalonica. Archbishop John of Thessalonica mentions an attack on the city by 5,000 Sclavene warriors attacking the city, but the currently

---

[63] Menander the Guardsman, fr. 21. Date of the Avar embassy: Litavrin 1991b:13. For Dauritas' speech, see Baldwin 1978:118. For the *quaestor exercitus* John, see Jones 1964:307; Hendy 1985:653; Szádeczky-Kardoss 1985:64; Pohl 1988:68; Levinskaia and Tokhtas'ev 1991b:346; Torbatov 1997:84–5. The use of λέγεται suggests the number of Avar horsemen may be exaggerated. For ships transporting the Avar army, see Bounegru 1983:276–7. For the probable location of the Danube fords the Avar horsemen used to cross over into Walachia, see Nestor 1965:148; Chiriac 1980:255 and 1993:198–9; Pohl 1988:68–9. For Sclavenes fleeing to the woods, see also Theophylact Simocatta VI 7.10 and *Strategikon* XI 4.38.

[64] Menander the Guardsman, fr. 25,2. For a later date, see Nystazopoulou-Pelekidou 1986:348. For Bayan and the expectations of Emperor Tiberius, see Waldmüller 1976:165; Rusu 1978:123; Ferjančić 1984:94.

[65] John of Ephesus VI 6.25; Olajos 1985:514–5. See also Grégoire 1944–5:109. Date of the invasion: Waldmüller 1976:110. John's notion of "Hellas": Weithmann 1978:88.

accepted date for this event (604) is based on Paul Lemerle's dubious interpretation of the text and his questionable chronology of the events narrated in chapters 12 through 15 of Book 1.[66] According to Lemerle, the attack of the 5,000 warriors narrated in miracle 12 must have taken place *after* the siege of Thessalonica narrated in miracles 13 to 15, which he dated to 586. He pointed to a passage of miracle 13, in which Archbishop John claimed that it was for the first time that the citizens of Thessalonica, particularly those who had not served in the army, were seeing a barbarian army so close to them that they could examine it in great detail. By contrast, as the 5,000 Sclavene warriors attacked the city by surprise, the citizens of Thessalonica could hear from a distance "certain signs of that barbarian cry to which ears were accustomed." This, Lemerle argued, was an indication that the attack of the 5,000 Sclavene warriors occurred some time after the siege of 586, for the inhabitants of the city could by now recognize the Sclavene battle cry.[67]

The evidence cited by Lemerle should be treated with great caution. First, an accurate translation of the passage referring to the Sclavene battle cry suggests a different interpretation. The ears accustomed to the barbarian cry are not necessarily those of the inhabitants of the city attacked by the 5,000 warriors. John may have referred to members of his audience, some of whom had indeed witnessed this event, as well as other, subsequent attacks. Moreover, what John says is not that the citizens of Thessalonica were able to recognize the battle cry because they had already heard it many times before, but simply that they were able to distinguish the cry from the general noise of the battle. Second, what John says about the citizens of Thessalonica seeing for the first time a barbarian army refers to the whole army of 586, including Sclavenes under the orders of the qagan, as well as other barbarians, all organized in companies of soldiers and in order of battle. What is new to the eyes of the inhabitants of the city is not the Sclavenes, but the spectacle of the Avar army.[68]

I therefore suggest that the attack of the 5,000 Sclavene warriors may as well be dated before the siege of 586. Indeed, despite claims to the

---

[66] *Miracles of St Demetrius* I 12.107–13; Lemerle 1981:40, 69, and 72.

[67] *Miracles of St Demetrius* I 12.112: καί τινα τῆς βαρβαρικῆς κραυγῆς σημεῖα διὰ τῆς ἐθάδος ἀκοῆς ἐπεγίνωσκον. For the citizens of Thessalonica and the barbarian army, see *Miracles of St Demetrius* I 13.124. On the assumption that it took place at a later date than the siege of 586, Lemerle dated the raid of the 5,000 Sclavene warriors to 604, on the sole basis of his translation of τῇ δευτέρᾳ ἡμέρᾳ τῆς ἑορτῆς ἄφνω μέσης νυκτὸς as "le lundi jour de la fête, au milieu de la nuit" (I 12.102; Lemerle 1981:72). This is plainly and simply wrong. All that Archbishop John says is that the Sclavenes attacked on the night of the second day of the festival. See Whitby 1988:119–20; Speck 1993:423; Ivanova 1995a:182.

[68] The army of 586: *Miracles of St Demetrius* I 13.117. See also Ivanova 1995a:188. For subsequent attacks on Thessalonica, see *Miracles of St Demetrius* I 12.101.

contrary, Archbishop John's narrative leaves the impression of a raid organized by "professional" warriors coming from afar, not by marauders living in the vicinity. The reaction of the inhabitants of Thessalonica is also instructive. There is no mention of any army within the city's walls. However, when an official of the prefecture gave the alarm, nobody panicked. Instead, everybody rushed home to bring his weapons and then took his assigned position on the walls. To judge from Archbishop John's evidence, the inhabitants of Thessalonica were already prepared for the attack, which they seem to have expected at any moment. I suspect this to be an indication of a serious and continuous threat on the city, of a kind which may be associated with the invasion referred to by John of Ephesus. The attack of the 5,000 Sclavene warriors occurred at a time of intense raiding, when the citizens of Thessalonica had become accustomed to barbarian onslaughts. Indeed, John of Ephesus, to whom the "accursed Slavs" were just the instrument of God for punishing the persecutors of the Monophysites, claims that they were still occupying Roman territory in 584, "as if it belonged to them." The Slavs had "become rich and possessed gold and silver, herds of horses and a lot of weapons, and learned to make war better than the Romans." I think, therefore, that Franjo Barišić was right when relating the attack of the 5,000 Sclavene warriors on Thessalonica to the events referred to by John of Ephesus.[69]

However, questions still remain. Both Archbishop John and John of Ephesus seem to describe an independent raid of the Sclavenes reaching Thessalonica and also, according to John of Ephesus, Greece. In distant Spain, John of Biclar knew that in 581, Greece had been occupied by Avars. It is known, on the other hand, that at that time the major Avar forces were concentrated at Sirmium, which actually fell in 582. Is it possible that John muddled Avars with Slavs? Taking into consideration the considerable distance at which he wrote, it is not altogether impossible. But there is additional evidence to prove the contrary. Writing at the end

---

[69] *Miracles of St Demetrius* I 12.108: διὰ τὸ παντὸς τοῦ τῶν Σκλαβίνων ἔθνους τὸ ἀπίλεκτον ἄνθος; see Lemerle 1981:71. Citizens on the walls: *Miracles of St Demetrius* I 12.107. Date of the siege: Barišić 1953:49–55; Ivanova 1995a:182. The only chronological indication is the association of this episode with that of the destroyed *ciborium* of St Demetrius' church, which John attributes to the time of Bishop Eusebius (I 6.55). Eusebius is known from letters written by Pope Gregory the Great between 597 and 603 (Lemerle 1981:27–8). The date of his appointment is not known. It must have been a long episcopate, for he is mentioned as bishop in 586, as the army of the qagan besieged Thessalonica (I 14.131). For the "accursed Slavs," see John of Ephesus VI 6.25. John of Ephesus' evidence is viewed by many as indicating the beginning of Slavic settlement in the Balkans. See Nestor 1963:50–1; Ferjančić 1984:95; Pohl 1988:82; Soustal 1991:72; *contra*: Popović 1975:450. All that John says, however, is that after four years of raiding the Sclavenes were still on Roman territory. It is not clear whether they had established themselves temporarily or on a longer term.

of the sixth century, Evagrius recorded some information on Balkan events of the 580s, which he may have obtained in Constantinople, during his visit of 588. He reports that Avars conquered and plundered cities and strongholds in Greece. The date of this raid is not given, but there is no reason to accuse Evagrius of muddling Avars and Slavs.[70]

In addition, Michael the Syrian, in a passage most likely taken from John of Ephesus, records an attack of the Sclavenes (*sqwlyn*) on Corinth, but refers to their leader as qagan. He then attributes the attack on Anchialos not to Avars, but to Sclavenes. The reference to Anchialos could be used for dating the attack on Corinth in or shortly before 584.[71] But it is very difficult to disentangle Michael's narrative and decide who exactly was raiding Greece in about 584. Michael the Syrian is a later source. He might have used John not directly, but through an interme-diary (possibly the eighth-century chronicle attributed to Dionysius of Tell Mahre). As a consequence, he might have muddled Avars and Slavs. But neither the evidence of John of Biclar, nor that of Evagrius, can be dismissed so easily on such grounds. There is good reason to suspect, therefore, that in the early 580s, Greece was raided by both Avars *and* Slavs. It is possible that some of the Slavs were under the orders of the Avars, while others, such as the 5,000 warriors storming Thessalonica, may have operated on their own.

That some Sclavene groups were under the command of the Avar qagan is also suggested by Theophylact Simocatta's report of another raid across Thrace, which reached the Long Walls. In 584, "the Avars let loose the nation of the Sclavenes." The threat seems to have been so great that Emperor Maurice was forced to use circus factions in order to garrison the Long Walls. The imperial bodyguards were led out from the city, under the command of Comentiolus, and they soon intercepted a group of Sclavenes.[72] One year later (585), Comentiolus encountered a larger group under the command of a certain Ardagastus, roaming in the vicin-ity of Adrianople. After crushing Ardagastus' warriors, Comentiolus

---

[70] John of Biclar, p. 216; Evagrius VI 10. Avars in Greece: Weithmann 1978:88; Yannopoulos 1980:333; Avramea 1997:68–9. The date of the attack is indicated by John of Biclar's mention of both Tiberius II's third regnal year and King Leuvigild's eleventh year. According to Walter Pohl (1988:76 with n. 40), John of Biclar may have indeed referred to Avar forces when mentioning Pannonia along with Greece. The raid mentioned by Evagrius may be that of 584, when Singidunum fell and the hinterland of Anchialos was ravaged; see Theophylact Simocatta I 4.1–4; Pohl 1988:77–8 and 107; Whitby 1988:110. Unlike John of Biclar, Evagrius also reports that cities and strongholds had been conquered by Avars "fighting on the parapets" (ἐξεπολιόρκησαν).

[71] Michael the Syrian x 21. See Yannopoulos 1980:366. The association between Anchialos and Greece also appears in Evagrius VI 10. There is no serious reason for accepting Zakythinos' emen-dation of Corinth into Perinthus. See Zakythinos 1945:37; Karayannopoulos 1990.

[72] Theophylact Simocatta I 7.3–6; see Mango 1997:376. The threat is also indicated by the hasty appointment of Comentiolus as *magister militum praesentalis* (Theophylact Simocatta I 7.4).

began clearing the entire region of Astike. Could Ardagastus have been under the orders of the qagan? In 584 and 585, the Avars were busy capturing cities and forts along the Danube frontier. Moreover, a few years later, as Priscus' troops chased him across his territory north of the Danube river, Ardagastus appeared as an independent leader. On the other hand, there is no reason to believe that the group of Sclavenes intercepted by Comentiolus in 584 is the same as the one of 585, which was under Ardagastus' command. The raid of 584, which was directed to Thrace, might have been part of, if not the same as, the invasion of 581 to 584, which is reported by John of Ephesus as having reached Greece, the region of Thessalonica, *and* Thrace.[73]

The situation in the years following Bayan's expedition against Dauritas seems to have been as follows, to judge from the existing evidence. The campaign itself did not have immediate results, for only one year later the Avar envoy to Constantinople was attacked by Sclavene marauders somewhere in Illyricum. But as soon as the Avars began the siege of Sirmium in 579, they may have encouraged, if not ordered, massive Slavic raids to prevent the rapid access of Roman troops to the besieged city on the northern frontier. If we are to believe John of Ephesus, this diversion kept Roman troops in check for four years, even after Sirmium was conquered by the Avars. The evidence of John of Biclar, Evagrius, and Michael the Syrian suggests, on the other hand, that, at the same time, the Avars too raided some of those regions. The peace between Tiberius II and Bayan following the fall of Sirmium in 582, by which the emperor agreed to pay an annual stipend of 80,000 solidi to the Avars, did not prevent Sclavene raids. John of Ephesus claimed that the Sclavenes were still on Roman territory in 584. The 5,000 warriors storming Thessalonica at an unknown date before 586 were certainly not obeying Avar orders. On the other hand, the Avar polity seems to have experienced social and political turmoil during this period, as a new qagan was elected in 583. Bayan's son followed his father's aggressive policy and in 584, as Emperor Maurice denied his request of increased subsidies, he attacked and conquered Singidunum, Viminacium, Augusta, and plundered the region of Anchialos, on the Black Sea coast. At the same time, according to Theophylact Simocatta, the new qagan of the Avars ordered the Sclavenes to plunder Thrace, as far as the Long Walls. The next year (585), Maurice agreed to pay increased subsidies to the Avars, which now amounted to 100,000 solidi. The affair of the Avar shaman Bookolabra troubled again Roman–Avar relations, and the qagan's troops plundered all major cities and forts along

---

[73] Date: Waldmüller 1976:128; Whitby and Whitby 1986:29 with n. 37. Avars in 584/5: Pohl 1988:77–8 and 85. Priscus' attack against Ardagastus: Theophylact Simocatta VI 7.1–5.

the Danube frontier, from Aquis to Marcianopolis. At the same time, Comentiolus was kept busy fighting Ardagastus' Sclavenes near Adrianople.[74]

That in the eyes of the Roman emperor, the Sclavenes and the Avars were two different problems, also results from the different policies Maurice chose to tackle them. The Avars were paid considerable amounts of money, when Roman troops were lacking or were unable to resist. There is nothing comparable in the case of the Slavs. Instead, Maurice preferred to use Justinian's old policies of inciting barbarian groups against each other. According to Michael the Syrian, the Romans paid the Antes for attacking and plundering the "land of the Sclavenes," which the Antes did with great success.[75] Maurice's policy might indeed have produced visible results in the case of the Sclavenes operating on their own.

But the war with the Avars continued in Thrace in 586, with indecisive victories on both sides. At the same time, an army of 100,000 Sclavenes and other barbarians obeying the orders of the qagan appeared under the walls of Thessalonica. The number of soldiers in the army besieging Thessalonica is evidently exaggerated. The attack, however, may well have been associated with the war in Thrace. Its precise date could be established on the basis of Archbishop John's reference to a Sunday, September 22, when the alarm was first given in Thessalonica. We are also told that the attack occurred at the time of the emperor Maurice. September 22 in the reign of Maurice could have fallen on a Sunday in either 586 or 597. A strong argument in favor of the latter date is the fact that Eusebius, the bishop of Thessalonica at the time of the attack, is mentioned by Pope Gregory the Great in three letters, the earliest of which is from 597. This is no indication, however, that Eusebius was appointed bishop in the 590s. He could have been bishop of Thessalonica since the 580s. Speros Vryonis has also argued that 597 should be preferred, because the poliorcetic technology and the siege machines employed during the one-week attack on Thessalonica could not have been acquired before 587. In that year, the qagan's army besieged and conquered Appiaria in Moesia Inferior, after being instructed by a certain Roman soldier named Busas as to how to build a siege engine. Theophylact Simocatta's story, however, is no more than a cliche, designed to emphasize that barbarians could have had access to high-tech siegecraft only through traitors. More important, the story clearly refers

---

[74] Avar envoy attacked by Slavs: Menander the Guardsman, fr. 25,2. Annual stipends for the Avars: Pohl 1988:75 and 82. New qagan: Pohl 1988:77–8 and 177. For the Bookolabra affair, see Theophylact Simocatta I 8.2–11.

[75] Michael the Syrian x 21. For the probable location of the "land of the Sclavenes," see Nestor 1963:53–4; Pigulevskaia 1970:214; Waldmüller 1976:123; Szydłowski 1980:234; Serikov 1991:279–80 and 289.

only to Avars, while Archbishop John describes an attack by an army of Sclavenes and other barbarians, which, though obeying the orders of the qagan, was not led by the qagan himself and apparently did not include any Avar troops.[76]

Barišić and Lemerle supported a date of 586, on the basis of a better fit of this event into the general picture of Avar–Byzantine relations in the 580s. In 586, as well as in 597, the bulk of the Avar forces led by the qagan were far from Thessalonica. But in the 590s, most, if not all, of the operations of the Avar–Byzantine war took place in the northern part of the Balkans. The 580s are the only period in which the Avars are known to have reached the southern regions of the Balkans. In addition, Archbishop John explains that the attack was ordered by the qagan, because he wanted to take revenge on Emperor Maurice, after his embassy's requests had been denied. We do not know of any such dealings preceding the campaign of 597. We do know, however, that shortly after the Avar shaman Bookolabra defected to the Romans, an Avar envoy to Constantinople, who was coming for the 100,000 solidi paid as annual subsidies to the qagan, was arrested and sent to jail by the order of the enraged emperor Maurice. This event took place just before the Avar campaign along the Danube, in 585. It would make sense to identify this incident with the failed negotiations referred to by Archbishop John as causing the attack on Thessalonica.[77]

Two years later (588), a group of Sclavene warriors, whom Theophylact Simocatta calls Getae, raided Thrace.[78] That Theophylact refers to these Sclavenes as "Getae," without any mention of Avars, may indicate an independent raid. But Theophylact also mentions Slavs, who were subordinated to the qagan. In 592, in order to conquer Singidunum, the qagan ordered the Sclavenes to build boats for his troops to cross the Danube river. The Sclavenes engaged in "timber operations" at Sirmium

---

[76] *Miracles of St Demetrius* I 13.117. See Nestor 1963:56; Avenarius 1973:13–14; Pohl 1988:105. Avar war in Thrace: Pohl 1988:85–9. For the size of the army besieging Thessalonica, see *Miracles of St Demetrius* I 13.126; see also Charanis 1976:10; Skedros 1996:17. For the association between the siege of Thessalonica and the war in Thrace, see Popović 1975:473; Whitby 1988:147. For Eusebius, the bishop of Thessalonica, see *Miracles of St Demetrius* I 14.131; Lemerle 1953:353–4 and 1981:50; Nystazopoulou-Pelekidou 1970:173; Pohl 1988:104. Appiaria episode: Theophylact Simocatta II 16.1–11; Vryonis 1981:387–90; *contra*: Pohl 1988:88. Evagrius (VI 10) clearly attests to the fact that when raiding Greece, the Avars were capable of conquering cities and strongholds by "fighting on the parapets."

[77] Barišić 1953:57–67; Lemerle 1981:49–69; see also Waldmüller 1976:123; Weithmann 1978:87; Popović 1975:450–1, 1978:622, and 1980:132; Yannopoulos 1980:339; Whitby 1988:117–18; Ivanova 1995a:186–7. Arrest of the Avar envoy: Theophylact Simocatta I 8.7–10.

[78] Theophylact Simocatta III 4.7: τὸ δὲ Γετικόν, ταὐτὸν δ'εἰπεῖν αἱ τῶν Σκλαυηνῶν. There are two other instances of "Getae" instead of Slavs (VI 6.14 and VII 2.5), but it is difficult to explain this usage. Given Theophylact's bombastic style, it may just be literary antiquarianism. For the date of this raid, see Waldmüller 1976:137; Whitby and Whitby 1986:77 with n. 14.

in that same year had their own officers, apparently appointed by the qagan. The Avar army itself consisted of a considerable number of Sclavene warriors, as suggested by the great number of prisoners captured by Priscus in 599.[79] In 603, the qagan sent Sclavene warriors to help the Lombard king Agilulf to conquer Cremona. Small Sclavene tribal units were also developing on the western frontier of the qaganate. They seem to have been clients of the qagan, for they were involved in petty warfare with the western neighbors of the Avars, the Bavarians. According to Paul the Deacon, in 592, Duke Tassilo of Bavaria raided *provincia Sclaborum* and returned home *cum maxima praeda*.[80]

WAR AGAINST THE SCLAVENES: MAURICE'S CAMPAIGNS OF THE 590S

To Roman eyes the real danger was not the Slavs under Avar authority, but the independent ones in the immediate vicinity of the frontier. All attempts to deal with them, from Justinian's building program to the practice of setting barbarian groups against each other, had borne no fruits. Maurice's reign, therefore, brought a drastic change. For the first time since Chilbudius' campaigns, the Roman army launched operations across the Danube frontier. That no effort seems to have been made to drive out the Slavs from Roman territory shows that the perceived danger was still north, not south, of the Danube frontier. The real problem was not to remove the Slavs presumably infiltrated and settled on imperial lands in the Balkans or in Greece, but to deal with those remaining beyond imperial frontiers. From Theophylact's evidence, however, it is clear that the main attraction was not booty or the extraction of tribute, but the propaganda value of relatively easy military victories which could be celebrated in Constantinople. Roman attacks were almost exclusively targeted against a relatively limited territory in

[79] Sclavenes building boats: Theophylact Simocatta VI 3.9–4.1; timber operations: VI 4.4–5. See also Whitby and Whitby 1986:162; Waldmüller 1976:140; Pohl 1988:134. Sclavene warriors in the Avar army: Theophylact Simocatta VIII 3.14–15; Mango 1997:407. According to Theophylact, Priscus took 8,000 Sclavene prisoners, besides 3,000 Avars and 6,200 other barbarians.

[80] Paul the Deacon, *Historia Langobardorum* IV 28 and IV 7. See Popović 1975:465; Waldmüller 1976:183; Fritze 1980:536–7; Bertels 1987:92–5; Pohl 1988:150. Location of *provincia Sclaborum*: Bertels 1987:93. Avar protection of Slavs against Bavarians: Paul the Deacon, *Historia Langobardorum* IV 10. The Sclavenes struck back in 610, as they defeated Duke Garibald, son of Tassilo III. Encouraged by Avars, they plundered Bavarian territories in the upper Drava valley (Paul the Deacon, *Historia Langobardorum* IV 39). The political influence of the qagan reached even farther to the north, as suggested by Theophylact Simocatta's account of the three Sclavenes captured by imperial bodyguards near Heraclea (VI 2.10–16; see Mango 1997:391). The Sclavenes belonged to a tribe living "at the boundary of the western ocean," to which the qagan had dispatched envoys, in order to levy a military force.

present-day eastern Walachia and Moldavia. They did not aim to conquer, but strictly to protect what was still viewed as the frontier of the Empire. On the other hand, operations against the Avars in Pannonia were only launched after the campaign against the Sclavenes north of the Danube, an indication of Maurice's priorities.[81]

The chronology of these events is most controversial. According to Theophylact Simocatta, our main source for this period, Maurice launched his campaign after concluding a peace with Persia, which is known to have taken place in 592.[82] At the same time, Theophylact mentions a Frankish embassy arriving in Constantinople. The embassy had been sent, according to Theophylact, by a ruler named Theodoric, but there was no ruler by that name in 592. Theodoric II became king of Burgundy only in 596. Some have argued therefore that the beginning of the campaign should be placed in 596. Since Theophylact's source for this part of his *History* is the *Feldzugsjournal*, his chronology is based on annual campaigns. The campaign against the Sclavenes could therefore be fairly well dated to 593, by counting back the years from the final campaign of Maurice's reign in 602. Moreover, Theophylact tells us that at the beginning of the campaign, Maurice appointed Priscus as *magister equitum* and Gentzon as *magister peditum*. In July 593, Priscus received a letter from Pope Gregory the Great, congratulating him for having regained the emperor's favor. It is likely, therefore, that the campaign was launched in the spring of 593.[83]

A month after leaving Heraclea (present-day Yeşilköy), Priscus crossed the Danube river, already knowing that Ardagastus was gathering Sclavene warriors for a new raid across the Danube. Taken by surprise in the middle of the night, Ardagastus barely escaped being captured. Priscus had crossed the Danube at Durostorum (present-day Silistra) and his troops encountered Ardagastus just one night after the crossing. It is possible, therefore, that Ardagastus' headquarters were located some-

[81] Goubert 1963:115; Pohl 1988:135–6. For the first time since the days of Theodosius I, the emperor led in person the first part of the campaign. Following Priscus' successful attacks, Maurice kept vigil at the church of St Sophia and "made prayers of supplication" to God to grant "more glorious trophies" (Theophylact Simocatta VI 8.3–8). Direction of Roman attacks: Janković 1981:202. The Sclavenes against whom Maurice launched his campaign were not subjects of the Avars. This results from the answer Priscus gave to the Avar envoys: the agreement and the truce with the Avars had not concluded the "Getic war" as well (Theophylact Simocatta VI 6.13). See Waldmüller 1976:142–3; Rusu 1981:23.

[82] According to the seventh-century Armenian chronicle attributed to Sebeos, after the peace was signed between Maurice and Khusro, the emperor "ordered all troops in the Eastern area to be taken across the sea and assembled against the enemy in the Thracian area" (Sebeos, p. 51).

[83] Frankish embassy: Theophylact Simocatta VI 3.6–7; Olajos 1988:167 with n. 705. Pope's letter to Priscus: Gregory the Great, ep. III 51; Nystazopoulou-Pelekidou 1970:164; Olajos 1988:171; Whitby 1988:158. For a late date of Priscus campaign, see Labuda 1950:170; Duket 1980:55. For an early date, see Ştefan 1967:255; Waldmüller 1976:142; Whitby and Whitby 1986:167; Pohl 1988:128–9.

where between the swampy Mostiştea valley, to the northeast from Durostorum, and the river Argeş, across which Ardagastus swam to escape his followers.[84]

The booty captured by Priscus was considerable enough to excite protests from the troops, when he attempted to send it all to Constantinople. Just as Dauritas and his fellow tribesmen, the Sclavenes of the 590s seem to have been prosperous. The author of the *Strategikon*, who most likely was a participant in this campaign or in those of 594 and 602, would later recommend officers of the Roman army operating north of the Danube to transport provisions found in Sclavene settlements "to our own country."[85]

Priscus himself seems to have acted as if advised by the *Strategikon*. He ordered some men to move ahead on reconnaissance, and commanded the brigadier Alexander to march into the region beyond the adjacent river Helibacia, most likely the present-day Ialomiţa river. He encountered a group of Sclavenes, who quickly made their escape in the nearby marshes and woods. All attempts to capture them failed, but Alexander found a Gepid, "who had once long before been of the Christian religion," who divulged to the Romans the place where the Sclavenes were hidden. He also told Alexander that the Sclavenes were subjects of Musocius, "who was called *rex* in the barbarian tongue" and lived thirty parasangs (93 to 111 miles) away. If the Roman army headed northeast and not west, Musocius' territory must have been located somewhere in southern Moldavia.[86]

---

[84] Theophylact Simocatta VI 7.4–5. See also Wiita 1977:334; Zasterová 1971:65. For night attacks, see the *Strategikon* IX 2.7. The normal marching speed during summer was four Roman miles (about 6 km) per hour. See Vegetius, *Epitome Rei Militaris* I 9, ed. Leo F. Stelten (New York and Bern, 1990), p. 25; Watson 1969:55 with n. 170. The distance between Silistra and the Mostiştea valley is 40 km, but the pursuit of Ardagastus seems to have been the work of horsemen, not of infantry troops.   [85] *Strategikon* XI 4.32; see Pohl 1988:140–1.

[86] Theophylact Simocatta VI 9.1: ὑπὸ Μουσωκιον τὸν λεγόμενον ῥῆγα, τῇ τῶν βαρβάρων φωνῇ For the emendation of βάρβαρον into βορβορώδη, meaning "swampy," see Whitby and Whitby 1986:169. Retreat into woods and swamps: *Strategikon* XI 4.12 and 38. Reconaissance: *Strategikon* XI 4.41. Helibacia as Ialomiţa: Cihodaru 1972:5; Comşa 1974:309; Schramm 1981:257; Whitby and Whitby 1986:171. Helibacia was large enough to pose crossing problems (see Theophylact Simocatta VII 5.7–10). Ialomiţa is the only tributary of the Danube that could pose such problems in this region. Alexander attempted to set fire to the woods to which the Sclavenes fled as soon as they saw him coming. He failed, Theophylact explains, because of the damp conditions. This detail may point to a swampy region at the confluence of Sărata and Ialomiţa, near the modern city of Urziceni. If so, Alexander might have crossed the river somewhere between present-day Snagov, near Bucharest, and Slobozia. In any case, after crossing the Danube, Priscus' army must have headed east, not west. This results from the fact that in 594, moving from west to east, Peter's army did not encounter Paspirius before reaching Helibacia (see Theophylact Simocatta VII 5.6). In ancient sources, a parasang was the distance covered in a fifth of a marching day, i.e., 3.1 to 3.7 miles. Musocius was thus at a considerable distance (about three days of marching) from Helibacia, which probably formed the border between his territory and that of Ardagastus. For Musocius' name, see Braichevskii 1953:23; Cihodaru 1972:5; Comşa 1974:310; Ditten 1978:80 with n. 2.

Alexander did not pursue his mission into Musocius' territory, for it was too far for his small-sized contingent. He re-crossed Helibacia and returned to Priscus, bringing with him the barbarian prisoners and the Gepid defector. Priscus ordered the execution of the Sclavene prisoners. The deserter agreed to beguile the Sclavene "king" in exchange for gifts. He returned to Musocius, asking to be given canoes for ferrying across the refugees from Ardagastus' territory. With 150 canoes and 30 oarsmen, the Gepid re-crossed the river Paspirius. Since the river seems to have been navigable, at least for canoes, Paspirius may refer to the lower course of the Siret river.[87]

In the middle of the night, the Gepid came to Priscus, who sent him back together with 200 soldiers under the command of the brigadier Alexander. Drunk and asleep, the Sclavenes were no match for Alexander's men. An additional Roman force of 3,000 men crossed the river on canoes captured from the Sclavenes. Just as with Ardagastus, the Roman army took the Sclavenes by surprise. But unlike Ardagastus, "king" Musocius was taken prisoner, while most of his subjects were killed. Apparently, this was not a decisive victory, for the next day, Priscus' soldiers barely escaped being destroyed by Sclavenes. Theophylact claims that Roman troops were saved only by the swift intervention of *magister peditum* Gentzon, an indication that both generals participated in the expedition north of the Danube. After this last combat, Priscus moved south of the Danube. There may have been at least one more raid by Roman troops into Sclavene territory, until Tatimer's return from Constantinople in the fall of 593.[88]

Tatimer had been sent to Maurice with the prisoners captured after Priscus had stormed Ardagastus' territory. Somewhere on his way to Constantinople, he was ambushed by Sclavenes roaming freely on Roman territory, despite Priscus' campaign north of the Danube fron-

---

[87] Priscus closely followed the counsels of the *Strategikon*: to kill the prisoners (XI 4.45) and to promise gifts to those deserters who can provide valuable informations (IX 3.8). Though Theophylact does not mention the first crossing, it is clear that in order to attack Musocius, one first needed to cross the river Paspirius (VI 9.10 and 12). The small number of oarsmen may indicate that the Gepid expected to find available oarsmen among the refugees. That Musocius agreed to help those coming from Ardagastus' territory seems to confirm the suspicions of the *Strategikon*. Its author recommends Roman officers to win over some of the Sclavene chiefs by persuasion or by gifts, then to attack the others, so that "their common hostility will not make them united or bring them together under one rule" (*Strategikon* XI 4.30). See Cankova-Petkova 1962:267. According to the *Strategikon*, all northern tributaries of the Danube were navigable (XI 4.32). Paspirius has often been identified with the Buzău river, mainly on the basis of the dubious derivation of Musocius' name from the river's ancient name, Musaios. See Iorga 1937:307; Nestor 1970:104; Comşa 1974:310; Pohl 1988:141.

[88] Theophylact Simocatta VI 9.14. Alexander's soldiers must have reached Paspirius by horse. The signal of attack was given by the Gepid "by means of Avar songs," which were apparently familiar to both Romans and Slavs (Theophylact Simocatta VI 9.10).

tier. Some Roman infantry troops were, however, stationed in the environs, for only their intervention allowed Tatimer to reach his destination. In Constantinople, Emperor Maurice decided to send him back to Priscus, with orders for his army to pass the winter season "where they were." This most likely refers to the left bank of the Danube. Priscus may have indeed crossed the Danube for a second raid against the Sclavenes. It is not known whether Maurice's decision was dictated by tactics described in the *Strategikon* or by his need to avoid military expenditures during the winter season. But as soon as "the royal utterances became known, the army was kindled by commotion." As if rehearsing for Phocas' revolt of 602, the soldiers claimed that the "hordes of barbarians [were] irresistible." The conflict was just settled and Roman troops had just returned south of the Danube, when Priscus learned that the Avars were preparing a new incursion and that the qagan had ordered Sclavenes to cross the Danube against Roman troops. It is hard to believe that these were the same Sclavenes Priscus had just defeated north of the Danube frontier. They might have been subjects to the qagan and therefore may have come from the region under his control. However, during negotiations for peace with Priscus, the qagan demanded a substantial part of the booty taken by Roman troops during the campaign of 593. He claimed that in doing so, Priscus had attacked his land and had wrought injury to his subjects. It is difficult to separate reality from mere boasting, but beyond declarations and threats, it appears that the Sclavenes had now become a bone of contention between the Empire and the qaganate.[89]

The campaign of the following year (594) was led not by Priscus, but by Maurice's brother, Peter. At Marcianopolis, Peter's advanced guard, under the command of brigadier Alexander, encountered 600 Sclavenes, returning from a raid across Moesia Inferior. The Sclavenes were carrying the booty in wagons, which they placed round as a barricade as soon as they perceived the danger. The Romans dismounted and approached the barricade. Though the Sclavenes fought fiercely, Alexander's men finally broke the barricade and slew them all. Just as the episode of Tatimer, this incident seems to indicate that Priscus' campaign against the Sclavenes north of the Danube had no effects on Slavic raiding activity. Moreover, learning that the Sclavenes were directing their attacks towards Constantinople, Maurice asked Peter to postpone his expedition across the Danube and to remain in Thrace.[90]

---

[89] Theophylact Simocatta VI 8.4–8, VI 9.1, VI 10.1–3, VI 11.5, VI 11.17; see also VIII 6.2; *Strategikon* XI 4.19. On Maurice's decision, see Pohl 1988:139.

[90] Theophylact Simocatta VII 2.1–10, VII 2.15. The forts sacked by Sclavenes (Zaldapa, Aquis, and Scopi) were all in Moesia Inferior. See Waldmüller 1976:148–9; Whitby 1988:160 with n. 30; Pohl 1988:141–2.

Peter had meanwhile reached the Danube frontier. The movements of the Roman army on the right bank, from one fort to another, are difficult to follow, for Peter often changed direction for no apparent reason. Theophylact, who seems to have been completely ignorant of Balkan geography, misunderstood his source (arguably, the *Feldzugsjournal*), and the resulting narrative is very confusing. Peter's intention may have been to patrol along the Danube, between Zaldapa and Asemus, in order to prevent Slavs from crossing the river. His troops, most likely, were already on the left bank when a reconnaissance mission was captured by Sclavene horsemen. The last city on the right bank visited by Peter was Asemus, where he attempted to remove the local garrison and to include it among his own troops. The city was located at the mouth of the river Asemus (present-day Osăm), which may suggest that Peter's confrontation with the Sclavenes occurred somewhere near the mouth of the Olt river, on the left bank. In this case, Peter may have headed east, for some time after the confrontation his troops reached the Helibacia river, which can be safely located in the vicinity of Durostorum.[91]

At the crossing of an unknown river north of the Danube (perhaps the Olt river?), Peter's army was ambushed by the Sclavenes under the command of their leader Peiragastus, whom Theophylact calls a "brigadier." The Roman troops, however, were able to land on the opposite bank and to encircle the "barbarian hordes." Peiragastus was killed and his warriors turned to flight. Without horses, the Romans were initially not able to press the pursuit, but the next day Peter dispatched a large detachment to follow the Sclavenes. Theophylact claims that the army's guides "made a great error, with the result that a water shortage beset the camp." Despite Theophylact's bombastic style, the meaning of the passage seems to be that the Roman troops found themselves in the middle of some sort of desert, for in the absence of water, soldiers "assuaged their thirst with wine." Fortunately, a Sclavene captive showed them the way to the nearby Helibacia. If Peter's troops were heading east and Helibacia is Ialomiţa, the arid country may have been the Burnaz plain between the

---

[91] Theophylact Simocatta vii 3.1.10, vii 4.8–13. Location of Helibacia: vi 8.9. Route of the Roman army: Schreiner 1985:64; Whitby and Whitby 1986:182 with n. 10. As the Roman troops approached the Danube, they encountered 1,000 Bulgar horsemen. They been sent by the qagan to protect the frontier (vii 4.1–2). According to Theophylact, Peter "reached the habitations of the Sclavenes" even before marching along the Danube (vii 2.14). Michael Whitby believes this to be an indication that Peter already crossed the Danube against the Sclavenes, although Theophylact, because of his bias against the general, did not credit him with such energetic action (Whitby and Whitby 1986:181 n. 9). If this is true, however, it is difficult to understand why Peter recrossed the river, only to monitor the barbarians from the right bank. In reality, at this point, Theophylact's text is very obscure and no conclusion can be drawn as to the relative chronology of the Roman army's movements. In addition, the river referred to in the text (vii 4.8) is not the Danube, for ποταμός only occurs singly when preceded by Ἴστρος. See Ivanov 1995b:59.

Vedea and the Argeş rivers. This would nicely dovetail with the four-day distance between Helibacia and the point where the Romans had encountered Peiragastus. Attacked by Sclavenes from the opposite bank of the Helibacia river, the Roman troops attempted to cross the river against them, but were overwhelmed and turned to flight.[92]

Since Theophylact does not tell us anything else about the expeditionary force, and only reports that Peter was soon replaced by Priscus as "general in Europe," we may presume that Peter's campaign of 594 ended in failure. This, however, did not prevent Maurice from continuing to wage war against Sclavenes on their own territory. In 598, he concluded the peace treaty with the Avars. The Danube was agreed upon not as a frontier, but "as an intermedium (μεσίτης) between Romans and Avars," for "there was provision for crossing the river against Sclavenes." That these were not mere intentions is shown by the fact that the war against the Sclavenes resumed in 602, as Peter's second-in-command, Godwin, crossed the river and "destroyed the hordes of the enemies in the jaws of the sword." In response, the qagan attacked the traditional allies of the Romans, the Antes. The Avar general Apsich was sent "to destroy the nation of the Antes." Theophylact claims that "in the course of these very events, large numbers defected from the Avars and hastened to desert to the emperor." At first glance, the text seems to suggest that because of the defection, the intentions of the qagan had not been accomplished. But Theophylact is the last source referring to Antes and the last time the title *Anticus* appears in the imperial intitulature is in 612. It is likely, therefore, that, notwithstanding numerous defections to the Romans, Apsich's campaign resulted in the destruction of the Antian polity. After 602, the Antes disappear from all historical sources.[93]

Godwin seems to have remained for a long time north of the Danube, waging war against the Sclavenes. Maurice's new orders to his troops to pass the winter in Sclavene territory were, however, received with dismay.

---

[92] Theophylact Simocatta VII 5.4 and 6–9. The Roman troops may have reached the Ialomiţa river at some point north of Bucharest.

[93] Theophylact Simocatta VII 15.12–14, VIII 6.1. For Apsich's campaign, see Litavrin 1995a:309. For the epithet *Anticus*, see Ivanov 1991a:261. Both Priscus and Peter seem to have combined the *quaestura exercitus* with the office of *magister militum per Illyricum*. Indeed, judging from Theophylact's evidence, there always was only one commander on the Balkan front. Following Zlatarski, Bulgarian scholars insist that the Antes were imperial federates in Dobrudja. See Bonev 1986:56–61. As a consequence, Gennadii Litavrin (1999) suggested that Apsich's army moved along the right bank of the Danube, without ever reaching the Antes. According to Litavrin, the fact that, as late as 612, *Anticus* was still an imperial epithet is an indication that the Antes were still the emperor's allies and federates. Though destroyed by internal strife or attacks by Bulgars, the Antes resurfaced at the end of the seventh century under a new name, the Severeis mentioned by Theophanes. Leaving aside the dubious interpretation of the archaeological evidence, Litavrin seems to ignore the fact that the epithet *Anticus*, first attested under Justinian, referred to imperial victories over the Antes, not to them being imperial allies.

Just as in 593, they caused mutiny. According to Theophylact, the soldiers were "troubled by the emperor's purpose, both because of the booty itself, and because of the exhaustion of the horses, and in addition because hordes of barbarians were surging around the land on the opposite bank of the Ister." It is true that the author of the *Strategikon* recommends attacking the Sclavenes during winter, "when they cannot easily hide among bare trees, when the tracks of fugitives can be discerned in the snow, when their household is miserable from exposure, and when it is easy to cross over the rivers on the ice."[94] The audience of the *Strategikon* consisted of generals and officers, not of the common soldiers, like those who in 602 wanted to go home. On the other hand, there is no indication that the revolt itself was caused by the allegedly increasing barbarian pressure. Godwin had just returned from a successful campaign and there is no reason to believe that the situation was in any way different from that of 593. It is still a widely spread belief, however, that Phocas' revolt caused the collapse of the Roman frontier. As a consequence, ever since Robert Roesler argued that the Slavic settlement of the Balkan peninsula south of the Danube and the Save rivers could not have taken place before the reign of Phocas, historians speak of a Slavic stream now pouring in an irresistible flood and submerging the entire peninsula. This view, however, is contradicted by all existing evidence. First, Phocas' purge of the Danubian army (Peter, Comentiolus, Praesentinus, and other officers) did not affect its discipline and morale. The seventh-century Armenian chronicle attributed to Sebeos provides clear evidence that, after overthrowing Maurice, the army returned to the Danubian front and continued "to oppose the enemy." It must have remained there until Phocas concluded a treaty with the qagan in 605, in order to transfer the army to the Persian front.[95]

Second, as Franjo Barišić has demonstrated, there is no evidence for raiding activity, by either Avars or Slavs, during Phocas' reign. By contrast, Heraclius' early regnal years witnessed some devastating incursions. Relying on information borrowed from the *historiola* of Secundus of Trento, Paul the Deacon tells us that in 610 or 611, following the conquest of Forum Iulii by the Avars, the Sclavenes devastated Istria, which

---

[94] Theophylact Simocatta VIII 6.2; *Strategikon* XI 4.19. See Theophylact Simocatta VIII 5.12.
[95] Sebeos, p. 80. See Olster 1993:69. Phocas' revolt and collapse of the Roman frontier: Roesler 1873; Ostrogorski 1959:4; Haldon 1997:37; Madgearu 1997:51. The definite withdrawal of all troops from Europe came only in 620, as Heraclius was preparing his campaign against Persia (Mango 1997:434). These troops were expected to return to Thrace after the campaign, but the conquest of Syria by the Muslims and the defeat of the Byzantine army prevented the return of the European troops. After Yarmuk, all troops were brought to Asia Minor, including those of Thrace. Thrace proper remained without any Byzantine troops until about 680, when a *hypostrategos* of Thrace, who was also count of Opsikion, is known to have attended the sixth ecumenical council. See Lilie 1977:27; Soustal 1991:76.

had been until then under Byzantine control. George of Pisidia, in a poem dedicated to Heraclius, describes the perils the new emperor was facing at the beginning of his reign. Among them, he lists the Sclavenes, gathering in hordes like wolves, and moving swiftly by land and by sea. In distant Spain, Isidore of Seville knew that at the beginning of Heraclius' reign, the Persians had conquered Syria and Egypt, and the Slavs had taken Greece from the Romans. It has been argued that Isidore's notion of *Graecia* was very vague and might have referred to what used to be known as Illyricum, rather than to Greece proper. This might indeed be the case for Isidore, but certainly does not apply to the author of Book II of the *Miracles of St Demetrius*. He knew that before attacking Thessalonica, the Sclavenes had devastated Thessaly and its islands, the islands of Greece, the Cyclades, Achaia, Epirus, and the most part of Illyricum, as well as parts of Asia. The reference to both Illyricum and Greece makes it clear that there is no confusion.[96]

THE SEVENTH CENTURY

Unfortunately, the attack on Thessalonica by Slavs previously raiding Greece is impossible to date with any precision. We are only told that it occurred under the episcopate of John, the author of Book I. The description of the territories ravaged by Sclavenes before they turned against Thessalonica is viewed by many as fitting into the picture of Heraclius' early regnal years, snapshots of which are given by George the Pisidian or Isidore of Seville. In particular, the fact that the author of Book II specifically refers to maritime raids on canoes reminds one of what George of Pisidia has to say about the Sclavene wolves. Historians agree, therefore, in dating this attack to the first decade of Heraclius' reign.[97]

For the first time, we are told that the Sclavenes brought with them their families, for "they had promised to establish them in the city after its conquest." This suggests that they were coming from the surrounding countryside, for the author of Book II used 'Sclavenes' as an umbrella-term for a multitude of tribes, some of which he knew by name: Drugubites,

---

[96] Paul the Deacon, *Historia Langobardorum* IV 40; George of Pisidia, *Heraclias* II 75–8; Isidore of Seville, p. 479; *Miracles of St Demetrius* II 1.179. Secundus and Paul: Gardiner 1983:147; Pohl 1988:9. For the raid mentioned by Isidore, see Charanis 1971:22–5; Szádeczky-Kardoss 1986b:53–4; Ivanova 1995b:356–7. The *Continuatio Hispana* places this raid in Heraclius' fourth regnal year (Szádeczky-Kardoss 1986b:54). For the *Miracles of St Demetrius*, see Koder 1986:530–1. Sclavene raids in the Aegean are also mentioned in the *Chronicon Miscellaneum* (also known as *Liber Chalifarum*), a compilation of various sources with different authors, which was preserved in an eighth-century Syrian manuscript. According to this source, a Slavic raid reached Crete and other islands in the year 934 of the Seleucid era (AD 623). See Krivov 1995.

[97] *Miracles of St Demetrius* II 1.179; see also II 4.253 and 254. Barišić (1953:86–95) dated the siege to 616, Lemerle (1981:91–4) to 615. See also Ivanova 1995a:191.

Sagudates, Belegezites, Baiunetes, and Berzetes. There are several cross references to most of these tribes in Book II. In all cases, we are left with the impression that they were a familiar presence. The Sclavenes were not just invaders, they were "our Slavic neighbors." It is hard to believe, therefore, that those tribes were responsible for the devastation of the islands of Thessaly, the Cyclades, of most of Illyricum, and of parts of Asia. Book II of the *Miracles of St Demetrius* contains two other cases of "lists of provinces," one of which betrays an administrative source.[98]

I suggest therefore that in describing a local event – the attack of the Drugubites, Sagudates, Belegezites, Baiunetes, and Berzetes on Thessalonica – of relatively minor significance, the author of Book II framed it against a broader historical and administrative background, in order to make it appear as of greater importance. When all the other provinces and cities were falling, Thessalonica alone, under the protection of St Demetrius, was capable of resistance. As in 586, the siege itself did not last more than a week. Unlike the siege of 586, however, the Sclavenes did not give up their idea of establishing themselves in Thessalonica after its conquest. More important, they now called upon the qagan for assistance. They offered rich presents and promised him much more provided that he would help them capture the city. These Sclavenes were certainly not subjects of the qagan. They were negotiating an alliance with the Avars as equals. That other Sclavenes, however, were still obeying the orders of the qagan is shown by the composition of the army the qagan eventually sent to Thessalonica.[99]

The siege of Thessalonica was definitely not an event of major importance. Even the author of Book II was aware that nobody, not even the emperor, knew about it. We are not told who that emperor was, but he must have been Heraclius, for the siege occurred not long after the one described in the first homily of Book II. Indeed, two years after being offered the alliance of the Sclavene tribes who had failed in capturing Thessalonica, the qagan marched against the city. The siege must have taken place in 617 or 618, at the latest.[100]

Eight years later, the army of the qagan was bent on capturing yet

---

[98] *Miracles of St Demetrius* II 1.180. Multitude of tribes: II 1. 179 (πλῆθος ἄπειρον). Sclavene as "our neighbors": II 3.219 and 222, II 4.231. See also Speck 1993:354. Location of the various tribes: Lemerle 1981:89–90. Lists of provinces: II 2.197 and II 5.284. At II 5.284, the author lists provinces believed to be parts of the Illyrian prefecture. There are *two* Pannoniae and *two* Daciae. According to Book II, Illyricum included Rhodope, which in fact belonged to the Thracian prefecture. The author of Book II knows that Sirmium *used* to be the capital city of Pannonia (πάλαι μητρόπολις). He had only an approximate knowledge of the sixth-century administrative geography of the Balkans (Beshevliev 1970a:287–8). This, however, may simply indicate that in the late 600s, when Book II was written, that administrative configuration was already history.

[99] *Miracles of St Demetrius* II 2.197–8. The Sclavenes attacked on the fourth day (II 1.185) and the decisive confrontation took place that same day.

[100] *Miracles of St Demetrius* II 2.210, II 2.198. See Lemerle 1981:99–100; Pohl 1988:242–3.

another city. A combined attack of Persian and Avar forces was directed against Constantinople. The Sclavenes appear as allies of the qagan. They formed the majority of troops besieging the city in the summer months of 626. Byzantine ships intercepted their fleet of canoes on August 4. However, Avar troops under the direct command of the qagan also included large numbers of Sclavenes, who were most likely his subjects. They too had canoes, which they used to attack Blachernae. The Sclavene troops included women. Their bodies were found in the Golden Horn waters after the battle. The Sclavenes attacking Blachernae must have been subjects of the qagan, for those escaping the massacre swam back across the straits to the bank where the qagan was positioned, only to be slain at his injunction. As the Sclavene squads abandoned the battlefield one after another, the defeat turned into a general retreat. Conflicts between Avars and Sclavenes seem to have followed the siege, as suggested by George of Pisidia.[101]

Avar power suffered considerably from this humiliating setback. According to Fredegar, Samo, the Frankish merchant elected king of "those Slavs who were known as Wends," proved his *utiletas* in battle against the Avars, bringing victory after victory to his subjects. Fredegar claims that Samo went to the Slavs "in the fortieth year of Chlothar's reign" (623/4) and that he ruled them for thirty-five years. Some took this at face value and concluded that the rebellion of the Wends against the Avars must have taken place before the siege of Constantinople. Others raised doubts about Fredegar's chronology and claimed that the episode of Samo postdated the humiliating defeat of the qagan under the walls of Constantinople. Even if Samo came to power in 623/4, he must have taken advantage of this defeat for consolidating his power. In 631 or 632, Samo crushed an army led by the Frankish king Dagobert. His victory encouraged a certain Dervanus, *dux gente Sorbiorum que ex genere Sclavinorum*, to declare his independence from the Franks. Ten years later, in 641, Samo was still powerful enough for Radulf, the duke of Thuringia, to seek his alliance.[102]

---

[101] George of Pisidia, *Bellum Avaricum* 197–201. Sclavene allies of the Avars: Nicephorus, *Breviarium*, p. 58 (εἰς συμμαχίαν) and *Chronicon Paschale*, p. 173. See also Litavrin 1995d:236; Ivanov 1995c:80. First day of the siege: *Chronicon Paschale*, pp. 173–4; Barišić 1954:380; Waldmüller 1976:281. See also Howard-Johnston 1995. Fleet of canoes: *Chronicon Paschale*, p. 183. For canoes brought from the Danube, see *Chronicon Paschale*, p. 174; Theodore Syncellus, *De Obsidione Avarica Constantinopolis* VI 22; Nicephorus, *Breviarium*, p. 58; George the Pisidian, *Bellum Avaricum* 409–12. For Sclavene women, see Nicephorus, *Breviarium*, p. 60. Retreat and post-siege conflicts between Avars and Sclavenes: *Chronicon Paschale*, pp. 178–9; George of Pisidia, *Restitutio Crucis* 78–81.

[102] Fredegar IV 48, 68, and 87. For Fredegar's chronology, see Szádeczky-Kardoss 1991:181; Gardiner 1978; Kusternig 1982; Pohl 1988:257. According to Fredegar, a "violent quarrel in the Pannonian kingdom of the Avars or Huns" broke during Dagobert's ninth regnal year (631/2: IV 72; see Pohl 1988:269). By that time, a duke named Walluc ruled over a "Wendish March" (IV 72; Fritze 1994:279).

Almost nothing is known about contemporary developments in the Balkans. According to the thirteenth-century *History of Split* by Thomas the Archdeacon, a certain Abbot Martin came in 641 to Dalmatia on a papal mission to redeem Christians taken captive by the Slavs. Thomas's account is based on earlier sources, none of which survives. As a consequence, it is difficult to assess the value of this information. Thomas also claims that in the mid-600s, fearing the Slavic raids, the citizens of Salona decided to move the relics of St Anastasius to Split. This may be interpreted as a decision to abandon Salona, but without any contemporary evidence, Thomas' account should be treated with great caution.[103]

Dalmatian Slavs may have been responsible for the raid of *c.* 642 into the duchy of Benevento, for Paul the Deacon describes them as having sailed across the sea. According to Paul, when Raduald, the duke of Benevento, attempted to revenge the death of Aio at the hands of the invading Slavs, he "talked familiarly with these Slavs in their own language, and when in this way he had lulled them into greater indolence for war, he fell upon them and killed almost all of them." Raduald was the son of Gisulf and had previously been duke of Forum Iulii, an area in which Slavs were a familiar presence at that time. In the 610s or the early 620s, two other sons of Gisulf, Taso and Cacco, who succeeded their father as dukes of Friuli, were ruling over *Sclavorum regionem quae Zellia appellatur.* At some point after 663, some 5,000 raided the duchy of Friuli. At about the same time, Arnefrit, the son of the Friulan duke Lupus, fled *ad Sclavorum gentem in Carnuntum, quod corrupte vocitant Carantanum.* This has rightly been viewed as the first reference to the *Carantani,* later to emerge as a strong polity under the dynasty of *dux* Boruth.[104]

Similar polities seem to have developed in the eastern Balkans. Theophanes mentions Emperor Constans II's campaign of 656/7 against *Sklavinia* (Σκλαυινία), most likely located in the hinterland of Constantinople. Such polities seem to have represented a serious threat, judging from the fact that this successful campaign, the first since 602, was accompanied by the transfer of large numbers of Sclavene prisoners to Asia Minor. The Georgian continuation of John Moschus'

---

[103] Thomas the Archdeacon, *Historia Salonitana,* pp. 29 and 34. See Katić 1950–1:101–2; Fine 1983:250. A late date for the abandonment of Salona has been recently corroborated by numismatic evidence. See Marović 1984.

[104] Paul the Deacon, *Historia Langobardorum* IV 44, 39, and 38, V 23 and 22. For the raid of 642, see also *Chronica S. Benedicti Casinensis,* ed. G. Pertz, *MGH SS* 3:200; Waldmüller 1976:347; Weithmann 1978:96. Dalmatian origin of the raid: Guillou 1973:13; Borodin 1983:57. Taso and Cacco: Hauptmann 1915:252–3; Fritze 1994:90 and 110. *Sclavorum regio Zellia:* Mal 1939:22; Bertels 1987:99–103. *Carantani* and *dux* Boruth: *Conversio Bagoariorum et Carantanorum* c. 4–5; Bertels 1987:109; Wolfram 1987:342.

Leimonarion, preserved in a ninth-century manuscript, mentions a number of Slavic villages on the western coast. Furthermore, when in 663/4 the Muslim general ʿAbd al-Rahman b. Khalid b. al Walid led a particularly successful raid against Byzantium, 5,000 Sclavene soldiers deserted from the Byzantine army and later settled in the region of Apameia, in Syria.[105]

Theophanes, our major source for this period, may have used at this point a translation of an eastern, Syrian chronicle. This may explain his emphasis on eastern developments, including those involving Slavs. There is comparatively little information on the interior of the Balkans. Both Nicephorus and Theophanes apparently employed the same source when reporting the victory of Asparuch's Bulgars over the imperial troops in 681 (678/9 by Theophanes). The Bulgars crossed the Danube and subdued the Slavic tribes in the area of "Varna, as it is called, near Odyssos and the inland territory that is there." The names of these tribes are to be found only in Theophanes. According to him, the Bulgars resettled the Severeis along their new frontier with the Empire, near the mountain pass Veregava (most likely, the Rish pass). They also moved "the so-called Seven Tribes" (αἱ λεγόμεναι ἑπτὰ γενεαί) on their southern and western frontier, against the Avars.[106]

The best-documented case of Slavic tribes established in the Balkans, however, is that of Book II of the *Miracles of St Demetrius*. The fourth miracle is an extremely valuable source for the seventh-century Balkan Slavs and without this text there would be very little to say. To the unknown author of Book II the Slavs were a familiar presence, "our Slavic neighbors." He described what might have been, in Theophanes' words, a powerful *Sklavinia*, that of the Rynchines led by "king"

[105] Theophanes, p. 347; Mango 1997:484. See Graebner 1978:44. For *Sklaviniai*, see Litavrin 1984. At the battle of Sebastopolis (692), 20,000 Slavs deserted to the Arabs (Theophanes, p. 366; Mango 1997:511). They formed the majority of Muhammad b. Marwan's troops raiding deep into Byzantine territory in 693/4 (Theophanes, p. 367; Mango 1997:513). By that time, the Sclavenes must have been a presence familiar enough for the Muslim poet al-Ahtal (*c.* 640–710) to use the golden-haired Slavs as a metaphor for danger. See Kalinina 1995. Georgian continuation of the *Leimonarion*: Ivanov 1995e. For the Slavs of 663/4, see Theophanes, p. 348; Mango 1997:487; Graebner 1975:41.

[106] Theophanes, p. 359 (Mango 1997:499); Nicephorus, p. 91. See Whitby 1982a:15; Mango 1990:15; Litavrin 1995a:25. For the location of the Veregava pass, see Soustal 1991:75 and *sub voce*. The Severeis are again mentioned by Theophanes in relation to their chief, Sklavunos, captured by Constantine V's troops on the eve of his 763/4 campaign against Bulgaria (Mango 1997:603). Cyril Mango's infelicitous translation, "(they settled) the Severeis . . . and the remaining *six* tribes, which were tributary to them" (Mango 1997:499) stands for τοὺς μὲν Σέβερεις κατῴκισαν . . . , τὰς ὑπολοίπους ἑπτὰ γενεὰς ὑπὸ πάκτον ὄντας. Mango failed to understand that the Severeis and the Seven Tribes were two separate entities and that the Seven Tribes were not tributary to the Severeis, but, most likely, to the Byzantine emperor. For the Seven Tribes, see also Tăpkova-Zaimova and Voinov 1965:38; Beshevliev 1967a:54; Cankova-Petkova 1968:157 and 1970:221–2; Koder 1978:316; Pohl 1988:277; Soustal 1991:75.

Perbundos. Other groups of Sclavenes existed in the vicinity of Thessalonica. There were Sclavenes living in the Strymon valley, while the Sagudates concluded an alliance with the Rynchines against the Empire in general, and Thessalonica in particular, as soon as they learned that the king of the Rynchines had been arrested and executed. Later on, a third tribe, the Drugubites, joined the alliance. The ensuing siege of the city is to be dated to July 25, 677, because of a clear reference to "July 25 of the fifth indiction." The Sclavenes appear as better organized than in any of the preceding sieges, with an army of special units of archers and warriors armed with slings, spears, shields, and swords. In a long story most likely derived from an oral account, the author of Book II mentions a Sclavene craftsman building a siege machine. He also mentions Sclavene tribes living at a considerable distance and not taking part in the Sclavene alliance against Thessalonica. The Belegezites, who lived near Thebes and Demetrias, even supplied the besieged city with grain.[107] The author of Book II also refers to Slavic pirates raiding as close to Constantinople as the island of Proconnesus. The emperor (whose name is not given) eventually decided to send an army to Thrace and to the "land on the opposite side," against the Strymonian Slavs. Since the siege can be dated to 677, and we are specifically told that prior to the siege the emperor was preparing for war against the Arabs, this expedition against the *Sklaviniai* of southern Macedonia must have been ordered by Constantine IV. The successful campaign took place in 678, shortly after the failure of the Arab blockade of Constantinople. Ten years later, another expedition led by Justinian II against the *Sklaviniai* reached Thessalonica, where the presence of the emperor was commemorated in inscriptions. According to Theophanes, Justinian had directed his campaign against both Bulgaria and the *Sklaviniai*. This may indicate that the *Sklaviniai* of 688/9 were clients of the Bulgar qagan. The same may be true for the Severeis and the Seven Tribes, the Slavic groups resettled by Bulgars in 681. Theophanes suggests that the Seven Tribes had until then been clients of the Byzantine emperor. In the late 600s, judging from the existing evidence, the creation of a Bulgar qaganate south of the Danube drastically altered the balance of power in the northern Balkans, while driving *Sklaviniai* into the orbit of the new state.[108]

---

[107] *Miracles of St Demetrius* II 3.219, 3.222, 4.231, 4.242, 4.255, 4.255, 4.262, 4.271–6. Supplies of grain from the Belegezites: II 4.254 and 268. The Drugubites supplied food to Kuver and his people (II 5. 289).

[108] *Miracles of St Demetrius* II 4.277, 4.278, 4.232. Date of Constantine IV's campaign: Lemerle 1981:131–3. Justinian II's campaign: Theophanes, p. 364; Mango 1997:508. Thessalonican inscription: Hattersley-Smith 1988:310. Justinian II's route: Grigoriou-Ioannidou 1982; Karayannopoulos 1989:14–15. Severeis as clients of the Byzantine emperor: Theophanes, p. 359 (ὑπὸ πάκτον ὄντας); Voinov 1956; Avenarius 1976:301–2; Waldmüller 1976:403–4; Bonev 1985:67. *Contra*: Beshevliev 1967a:57.

CONCLUSION

I began this chapter with the statement that the nature of the Slavic settlement remains obscure to many modern historians. Several conclusions follow from the preceding discussion, but the most important is that, whether or not followed by actual settlement, there is no "infiltration" and no *obscure progression*. The evidence of written sources is quite explicit about this.

Could then "migration" be an appropriate term? Modern studies have shown that migration is a structured aspect of human behavior, involving a more or less permanent change of residence. Historians, however, generally treat migration as chaotic and inherently not explicable through general principles. Recent formulations of migration as a structured behavior have established that migrations are performed by defined subgroups (often kin-recruited) with specific goals, targeted on known destinations and likely to use familiar routes. Most migratory streams develop a counterstream moving back to the migrants' place of origin.[109] The problem with applying this concept of migration to the sixth- and seventh-century Slavs is that there is no pattern of an unique, continuous, and sudden invasion. Moreover, until the siege of Thessalonica during Heraclius' early regnal years, there is no evidence at all for outward migration, in the sense of a permanent change of residence. Almost all raids reported by Procopius in the mid-sixth century were followed by a return to the regions north of the Danube frontier. At times, the Sclavene warriors may have spent the winter on Roman territory, as in 550/1. However, Menander the Guardsman makes it clear that the wealth acquired during Sclavene raids was usually carried back home, across the Danube.

John of Ephesus, on the other hand, claims that in 584, after four years of raiding, the Sclavenes were still on Roman territory. They had become "rich and possessed gold and silver, herds of horses and a lot of weapons, and learned to make war better than the Romans." This, however, could hardly be interpreted as an indication of Slavic settlement. What John had in mind were warriors, not migrant farmers. Michael the Syrian, in a passage most likely taken from John, describes a Sclavene leader who took *with him* the *ciborium* of a church in Corinth, not a chief establishing himself in the conquered city. The only evidence for such a decision is that of the Sclavene tribes besieging Thessalonica in the early years of Heraclius' reign. They had brought their families with them, for they intended to establish themselves in the city following its conquest. This also indicates that they were not coming from afar, for the prisoners they

---

[109] Lee 1966; Anthony 1990; Gmelch 1980.

had taken after the siege could return to Thessalonica carrying the booty taken by the Sclavenes from the inhabitants of the city. Moreover, some of the tribes mentioned in the second homily of Book II are described in the fourth homily as living in the immediate vicinity of the city. When did they settle there? Paul Lemerle argued that in the 610s a Slavic settlement around Thessalonica must have been a relatively recent phenomenon. How recent, however, is impossible to tell. The evidence regarding the mid-600s and the second half of that century suggests that the Sclavenes were by then already established at a short distance from the eastern frontier of the Lombard kingdom and from Constantinople. In 681, as the Bulgars moved south of the Danube, there were already Slavic groups in the eastern Balkans and around Thessalonica. Judging from the existing evidence, therefore, a true migration could have taken place only during a relatively short period of time, namely not long after Heraclius' accession to power.[110] To Theophylact Simocatta, writing about Maurice's reign on the basis of a late sixth- or early seventh-century source (the *Feldzugsjournal*), *Sklavinia* was still located north of the Danube frontier. In the mid-600s, the *Sklaviniai* moved to the outskirts of Constantinople and Thessalonica.

The survey of Slavic raiding activity during the sixth and the early seventh century points to another important conclusion. There seems to be a certain raiding pattern (Table 4). Independent Sclavene raids began in the 540s, with a long interruption after 551/2. They resumed in the late 570s and seem to have come to an end only after Maurice's campaigns north of the Danube. A new phase opened with massive raids, both on land and on sea, during the early years of Heraclius' reign. One can hardly fail to notice that this pattern coincides with major engagements of Roman armies on other fronts: in Italy, in the 540s and 550s, as well as in Persia and on the eastern front in the 570s, the 580s, and the 610s. It has indeed been shown that the pattern of information-movement across the Danube frontier proves that northern peoples often seem to have known when sectors of the Empire's defence were weakened as a result of Roman problems elsewhere. The Sclavenes of 550, who were bent on capturing Thessalonica, quickly changed their plans as soon as they learned that Germanus was in Serdica. The figures advanced by Menander the Guardsman and Archbishop John of Thessalonica for the

---

[110] John of Ephesus VI 25; *Miracles of St Demetrius* II 2.196. See Lemerle 1981:90. No evidence exists, however, that the Sclavenes established either on the frontier of the Lombard kingdom or near Constantinople came from regions located north of the Danube. Sklavinia north of the Danube: Theophylact Simocatta VIII 5.10. Whitby's unfortunate translation ("Peter prepared to move camp against the Sclavene horde") stands for Πέτρος κατὰ τῆς Σκλαυηνίας πληθὺς στρατο-πεδεύεσθαι παρεσκεύαζεν. See also Litavrin 1984:196.

Sclavene raids of the 580s were no doubt exaggerations. They suggest the efforts of these authors to explain why barbarians achieved success against the Empire in spite of being numerically and organizationally inferior to the Romans. In the 580s and the late 590s, the Sclavenes seem to have known remarkably well where to strike, in order to avoid major confrontations with Roman armies, and when to attack, in order to take advantage of the absence of troops.[111]

I would stress, however, another important conclusion following from the preceding discussion. None of the Sclavene raids in the 540s or early 550s was organized under the leadership of a chief. Procopius could distinguish "armies" from "throngs," but ignored any names of Sclavene chiefs or leaders. He claimed that the Sclavenes and the Antes "were not ruled by one man, but they [had] lived from old under a democracy, and consequently everything which involved their welfare, whether for good or for ill, was referred to the people." As the story of "phoney Chilbudius" suggests, the Antes did not even have a name for the Roman official, who was supposed to guide them into some sophisticated organization. They just called him "Chilbudius."[112]

However, writing as he did in *c.* 560, Pseudo-Caesarius knew that, though living without the rule of anyone, the Sclavenes often killed their leaders "sometimes at feasts, sometimes on travels." At the turn of the century, the picture radically changed, as the author of the *Strategikon* now recommended that Roman officers win over some of the Sclavene chiefs by persuasion or gifts, while attacking others, "so that their common hostility will not make them united or bring them together under one ruler." As soon as the Sclavene raids resumed in the late 570s, we learn of many Sclavene leaders, apparently different in status from each other. Names such as Dauritas, Ardagastus, Musocius, and Peiragastus are in sharp contrast to the lack of any chief-names in Procopius' work. Other names, such as Chatzon, Samo, Dervanus, Walluc, or Perbundos, appear in seventh-century sources. Is the absence of names in Procopius' work just an illustration of his idea of "Slavic democracy" or does this reflect some aspect of Slavic society? This question is most difficult to answer. It is hard to understand, however, why Procopius should invent the "Slavic democracy" if nothing justified the use of this concept for contemporary Slavic society. It is interesting to

---

[111] Menander the Guardsman, fr. 20,2; *Miracles of St Demetrius* I 13.117. For the pattern of information-movement, see Lee 1993:141–2.

[112] Procopius, *Wars* VII 14.22. See Benedicty 1963:46 and 1965:53; Evans 1989:63. There are many names of barbarian leaders in Procopius' *Wars*: Datios, Aordos, and Suartua, kings of the Herules (V 15.29 and 33); Torisind, king of the Gepids (VII 18.3); Auduin, king of the Lombards (VI 34.5); and Chinialon, the Cutrigur chief (VII 18.15).

Table 4 *Raiding activity in the Balkans*

Date	Group	Target	Source
493	Bulgars	Thrace	Paul the Deacon
499	Bulgars	Europe	Marcellinus Comes, Jordanes
502	Bulgars	Thrace, Illyricum	Marcellinus Comes, Theophanes
504/5	Ostrogoths	Moesia Superior	Jordanes, Procopius, Ennodius, Cassiodorus
505	Gepids (Mundo)	Dacia Mediterranea	Jordanes, Ennodius, Marcellinus Comes
518	**Antes**	Balkans	Procopius
519	Bulgars	Illyricum	Zonaras
526/7	Ostrogoths	Dacia Mediterranea	Procopius, Cassiodorus
529/30	Bulgars (Huns)	Thrace	Marcellinus Comes, John Malalas
533–45	**Antes**	Thrace	Procopius
535	Bulgars	Moesia Inferior	Marcellinus Comes
	Gepids	Moesia Superior	Procopius, John Lydus, Theophanes
	Bulgars	Scythia Minor, Moesia Inferior, Thrace	John Malalas, Theophanes
539	Huns	Illyricum, Europe, Asia Minor, Thessaly, Achaia	Procopius
540	Huns	Illyricum	Procopius
544/5	Huns	Balkans	Procopius
545	**Sclavenes**	Epirus Nova	Procopius
548	**Sclavenes**	Thrace, Illyricum	Procopius
549	**Sclavenes**	Illyricum	Procopius, Jordanes
550	Herules, Gepids, Bulgars	Dacia Mediterranea, Dalmatia	Procopius
	Sclavenes	Illyricum, Thrace	Procopius
551	Cutrigurs	Haemimons, Europe	Procopius
	Sclavenes	Illyricum	Procopius
	Sclavenes		
558	Cutrigurs, **Sclavenes?**	Scythia Minor, Moesia Inferior, Achaia, Rhodope, Europe	Agathias, John Malalas, Theophanes

Year	People	Region	Source
574	Avars	Balkans	Evagrius, Theophanes
578	**Sclavenes**	Thrace, Greece	Menander the Guardsman, John of Biclar
579	**Sclavenes**	Illyricum	Menander the Guardsman
579–82	Avars	Moesia Superior	Menander the Guardsman
581	Avars	Thrace, Greece	John of Biclar
581–4	**Sclavenes**	Greece, Macedonia, Thrace	John of Ephesus, *Miracles of St Demetrius*
584	Avars	Moesia Superior, Dacia Ripensis, Haemimons	Theophylact Simocatta
585	**Sclavenes**	Thrace, Europe	Theophylact Simocatta
585	**Sclavenes**	Haemimons	Theophylact Simocatta
586	Avars	Dacia Ripensis, Moesia Inferior, Scythia Minor	Theophylact Simocatta
586	Avars	Scythia Minor, Moesia Inferior, Haemimons, Europe, Thrace, Macedonia, Achaia	Theophylact Simocatta
588	**Sclavenes**	Macedonia	*Miracles of St Demetrius*
592	**Sclavenes**	Thrace	Theophylact Simocatta
592	Avars	Europe	Theophylact Simocatta
593	**Sclavenes**	Moesia Inferior	Theophylact Simocatta
594	**Sclavenes**	Moesia Inferior	Theophylact Simocatta
595	Avars	Moesia Superior, Dalmatia	Theophylact Simocatta
597	Avars	Dacia Ripensis, Moesia Inferior, Scythia Minor	Theophylact Simocatta
598	Avars	Moesia Inferior, Europe	Theophylact Simocatta
601/2	Avars	Istria	Paul the Deacon
609/10	Avars	Illyricum	John of Nikiu
610/11	**Sclavenes**, Avars	Istria	Paul the Deacon
610–20	**Sclavenes**	Thessaly, Greece, Cyclades, Achaia, Epirus, Illyricum, Asia	*Miracles of St Demetrius*
615	Avars	Dacia Mediterranea	*Miracles of St Demetrius*
617/18	Avars	Macedonia	*Miracles of St Demetrius*
618	Avars	Thrace	Theophanes
623	Avars	Europe	*Chronicon Paschale*
626	Avars, **Sclavenes**, Bulgars	Europe	*Chronicon Paschale*, George of Pisidia, Theodore Syncellus, Nicephorus

note that, with the exception of the quasi-legendary King Boz of the Antes, Procopius' contemporary, Jordanes, also ignores any Slavic leaders. I am inclined, therefore, to take Procopius' evidence as a strong *argumentum ex silentio*. Something had radically changed in Slavic society as the Slavic raiding activity resumed in the late 570s. A detailed discussion of this change is to be found in Chapter 7. For the moment, it is important to note that in terms of their social organization, the Sclavenes of the 580s were different from those of the 540s.[113]

Finally, there are important changes concerning the very name of the Slavs. Until the first decade of Heraclius' reign, as Sclavene groups settled on Roman territory, all sources – Greek, Latin, or Syriac – spoke exclusively of Sclavenes and/or Antes. The author of Book II of the *Miracles of St Demetrius* was the first to introduce tribal names, such as the Drugubites, the Sagudates, the Belegezites, the Berzites, and the Rynchines. Fredegar spoke of Wends and Theophanes of Severeis. The evidence is too strong to be interpreted as mere accident. The author of the *Strategikon*, a direct participant in Maurice's campaigns of the 590s, knew only of Sclavenes and Antes. The campaign diary later used by Theophylact Simocatta, but most likely written at about the same time as the *Strategikon*, also used only 'Sclavenes' and 'Antes.' In this particular case, 'Sclavenes' was an umbrella-term for various groups living beyond the frontier, in *Sklavinia*. As soon as *Sklaviniai* moved south of the Danube, the precise affiliation to any particular "tribe" became a key issue. Indeed, some "tribes" are described as hostile and bent on conquering Thessalonica, while others appear as friendly, willingly supplying food to the besieged city. The same may be true for Fredegar's Wends. As they successfully fought the Avars and elected a king for themselves, the Sclavenes, in Fredegar's eyes, became "different" and required a new name, 'Wends.' A similar conclusion follows from Theophanes' account. According to him, after crossing the Danube in 681, the Bulgars did not encounter an undifferentiated mass of 'Slavs,' but (at least) two groups, the Severeis and the Seven Tribes. The newcomers approached and treated them as two separate entities.

What all this suggests, in my opinion, is that the name 'Sclavene' was a purely Byzantine construct, designed to make sense of a complicated configuration of *ethnies* on the other side of the northern frontier of the

---

[113] For the independent (ἀναγεμόνευτοι) Sclavenes killing their leaders, see Riedinger 1969:302. Sclavene chiefs united under one ruler: *Strategikon* XI 4.30 (μοναρχία). For Boz, see Jordanes, *Getica* 247. Paul the Deacon also avoids mentioning any Sclavene leaders, though at the time he wrote the *History of the Lombards*, the Carantani were already organized as a polity under the "dynasty" of *dux* Boruth. The *Life of St Hrodbert*, bishop of Salzburg, indicates that the Carantani had a *rex* not long after Arnefrit, the son of the Friulan duke Lupus, fled *ad Sclavorum gentem in Carnuntum, quod corrupte vocitant Carantanum* (*Historia Langobardorum* V 22; *Vita Hrodberti*, p. 159).

Empire. Byzantine criteria for classifying ethnic groups were substantially different from ours. In spite of their common language, "an utterly barbarous tongue," the Sclavenes and the Antes were often at war with each other. On the other hand, the author of the *Strategikon* knew that there was more than one Sclavene king, and that Sclavene "kingdoms" were always at odds with one another. Despite obvious differences in status, the name 'Slavs' applies to both those attacking Constantinople in 626 as allies of the Avars and those who were the subjects of the qagan. It might be that 'Sclavene' was initially the self-designation of a particular ethnic group. In its most strictly defined sense, however, the "Sclavene ethnicity" is a Byzantine invention.[114]

[114] Procopius, *Wars* VII 14.26; *Strategikon* XI 4.30. For the name 'Sclavene,' see Pekkanen 1971; Schelesniker 1973:11; Schramm 1995:165.

Chapter 4

THE BALKANS AND THE DANUBE *LIMES* DURING THE SIXTH AND SEVENTH CENTURIES

No discussion of the early Slavs can avoid the very controversial issue of their role in the transformation of the Roman world that led to the "fall of the old order" and the rise of the new Empire, which historians call Byzantium.[1] The withdrawal of the Roman administration and armies from the Balkans in the early seventh century is viewed by many as a result of the Slavic *Landnahme*. More often than not, accounts of the early Slavic history focus on the destruction brought by the invading hordes to the flourishing cities of the Balkans. The classical urban culture was unable to survive the strain of the barbarian invasions. As with the Germans in the West, the Slavic "obscure progression" led to the slow dissolution of the Roman frontier and the Empire finally succumbed to the growth of forces beyond its control.

The existing evidence, written or archaeological, does not confirm this over-simplified picture. Long before the first Slavic raid attested by historical sources, the urban landscape in the Balkans began to change. It is clear, however, that some change was also taking place in the Balkans at the time of Slavic and Avar raids. The remaining question is whether or not the Slavs can be made responsible. Emphasizing almost exclusively the Roman side of the story, historians also neglected the equally impor- tant question of the Roman influence on the "invading" barbarians. The archaeological evidence of late fourth- and early fifth-century barbarian graves between the Rhine and the Loire suggests that a process of small- scale cultural and demographic change took place on both sides of the Roman frontier.[2] Can we envisage Roman–Slavic relations in a similar way? This chapter will focus on issues of urban change, with the purpose of showing that the Roman world, as Slavic warriors saw it in the 500s, was very different from the classical civilization many historians have in mind when describing their inroads. Using primarily archaeological evi-

---

[1] Whittow 1996:69–95.   [2] See Young 1992.

dence, I will focus on internal mechanisms of change. I will argue that Justinian's building program drastically altered both the network of settlements in the Balkans and the relations with barbarians, specifically with the Slavs. The idea that the implementation of the fortified frontier in the mid-500s had a profound effect on the making of the Slavs will be further developed in the last chapter.

URBAN CHANGE IN THE BALKANS

More often than not, modern studies of Late Antique cities narrowly focus upon textual evidence of public institutional change within civic urban communities, ignoring the archaeological evidence. On the other hand, archaeologists inspired by the culture-historical approach strive to link archaeological phenomena with historical narratives, with particular barbarian raids or earthquakes, and ignore the historical implication of their research.[3] Proponents of both approaches attempt to answer the controversial issue of what happened to the ancient city, the polis, during the fourth to sixth centuries.

Procopius seems to have been aware of a hierarchy of settlements in the Balkans.[4] In his *Buildings*, he carefully distinguished between three major categories: large cities, called πόλεις (such as Diocletianopolis in Thessaly and Euroia in Epirus), and new foundations such as Justiniana Prima; cities ranked lower, presumably because of their size, and called πολίχνια, such as Photike and Phoinike in Epirus Vetus; and fortified sites in the countryside, such as the forts along the Danube, or the *refugia*-type settlements in Thessaly, all known as φρούρια. A comparison between Procopius and the archaeological evidence yields no clear parallels. The city described by Procopius as Justiniana Prima has been tentatively located at Caričin Grad. The identification is most likely correct, but the entire area of the site at Caričin Grad is no larger than 4.55 ha, slightly smaller than the size of Nicopolis (5.74 ha), which Procopius calls a φρούριον (Table 5). Diana, a πολίχνιον, is even smaller (1.87 ha), while Novae, a φρούριον, covers about 32.5 ha. The only observable pattern is that settlements which Procopius lists as φρούρια tend to be rather small, between one and three hectares.

Another relevant body of evidence is that of the contemporary legislation. The urban administration during the sixth century was gradually shifting from decurions, a social group on the verge of disappearing, to a clique of local notables headed by the local bishop. Emperor Anastasius granted to the committee of local landowners, chaired by the bishop, the

---

[3] Dunn 1994:72–3.   [4] See Dagron 1984:7–8.

Table 5 *Sixth- to seventh-century sources and Balkan settlements*

Name	Procopius	Menander	Theophylact Simocatta	Area	Churches	Other
Tropaeum Traiani		—	πόλις (I 8.10)	c. 12.5 ha	4	HP
Troesmis	φρούριον (*Buildings* IV 11.20)	—	—	c. 2 ha	3	—
Noviodunum	φρούριον (*Buildings* IV 11.20)	—	—	—	1	—
Ulmetum	ὀχύρωμα (*Buildings* IV 7.17)	—	—	c. 2.1 ha	1?	—
Novae	φρούριον (*Buildings* IV 11.20)	—	πόλισμα (VII 2.19)	c. 32.5 ha	2	HP? ER
Iatrus	φρούριον (*Buildings* IV 7.6)	—	πόλις (VII 2.16; VII 13.9)	c. 2.8 ha	1	W
Nicopolis	φρούριον (*Buildings* IV 11.20)	—	(VII 13.8)	5.74 ha	2	W?
Abritus	φρούριον (*Buildings* IV 11.20)	—	—	c. 14.9 ha	2	W?
Diocletianopolis	—	—	πόλις (II 17.1)	c. 30 ha	1	HP
Philippopolis	(*Wars* VIII.21.21; *Buildings* IV.11.19)	—	πόλισμα (II 17.2)	c. 81.6 ha	1	—
Iustiniana Prima	πόλις (*Buildings* IV 1.20)	—	—	4.55 ha	8	HP ER W,T

			Size	No.	
Serdica	πόλις (Wars.VII.40.1; Buildings IV 4.3)	—	—	3	—
Sucidava	φρούριον (Buildings IV 11.20)	—	c. 2.1 ha	1	—
Ratiaria	πόλις (Buildings IV 6.24)	πόλις (1 8.10)	—	—	—
Castra Martis	χωρίον (Buildings IV 6.34)	—	1.25 ha	—	—
Diana	πολίχνιον (Buildings IV 6.6)	—	1.87 ha	—	—
Novae	ὀχύρωμα (Buildings IV 6.1)	—	1.8 ha	1	—
Smorna	φρούριον (Buildings IV 6.5)	—	0.2 ha	1	—
Campsa	φρούριον (Buildings IV 6.5)	—	0.1 ha	—	—
Taliata	φρούριον (Buildings IV 6.5)	—	1.8 ha	1	—
Sirmium	πόλις (Wars VII 33.8); πόλις (fr.12, 5.24; 12, 6.24; 12, 7.3; 25, 1.11, etc.)	πόλισμα, ἄστυ	—	—	W?

Notes: HP – house with peristyled courtyard; W – workshop; ER – episcopal residence; T – *thermae* (bath)

task of procuring grain for the city. The process continued under Emperor Justinian. Novel 8, of 535, prevented provincial governors from appointing their representatives in cities, while novel 65 of 538 concerning cities in Moesia allowed local committees of notables headed by bishops to replace the *curiales* in the urban administration. Novel 128 of 545 gave the final blow to the city councils by granting bishops, together with committees of notables, the right to assume the fiscal responsibilities of the decurions. The most important consequence of this series of decrees issued in a relatively short period of time is that they gave bishops considerable powers and enabled them not only to organize the civilian life of the cities, but also to take even larger responsibilities in the organization of the defense of both the city and the surrounding countryside. It is therefore no surprise that provinces as administrative units tend to be replaced by important ecclesiastical centers with their surrounding forts and πολίχνια. There is no Dacia Mediterranea and no Dacia Ripensis in Procopius' *Buildings*. Both provinces have been replaced by regions centered on important cities, such as Serdica, Pautalia, Naissus, Remesiana, and Aquis.[5]

CITIES: THE ARCHAEOLOGICAL EVIDENCE (FIGURE I)

Sixth-century cities on the Black Sea coast display signs of prosperity and economic activity. The presence of merchants from the East is attested by inscriptions found at Tomis and Callatis. This economic activity seems to have caused the growth of a middle class of craftsmen and merchants, who undertook most of the traditional tasks of the decurions. An inscription found in the wall at Tomis attests that *munera* on behalf of the city were carried out in the 500s by *collegia*: the *pedatura* of the city wall was erected by the city's butchers. Scythia Minor, on the other hand, was a highly militarized province. The social group most frequently referred to in fourth- to sixth-century inscriptions is the military, while great landowners seem to have been completely absent. The active economic life in coastal cities provided the means for remarkably wealthy individuals. At Histria, excavations carried since 1949 revealed a building boom and a prosperous city. Near the city's western wall a bazaar (*tabernae*) was erected in the middle of what Romanian archaeologists called the "Commercial Sector." This area has three building phases, the second of which is dated to the second third of the sixth century. Besides two large

---

[5] Maksimović 1984:156–7; Dagron 1984:10. Anastasius' legislation: *Codex Iustinianus* I 4.17 (505); Velkov 1977:79. Justinian's novel 11 of 535 specifically deals with the power of the bishop of Aquis not only over the city, but also over its territory, forts (*castella*), and parishes (*ecclesiae*) (*Corpus Iuris Civilis* III: 94). It has been argued that the change from poleis to centers for ecclesiastical and military administration cannot be dated as late as the reign of Justinian. See Poulter 1992:131. While it is true that the origins of this process may be traced back to the third century, its effects became fully visible in the Balkans during the sixth century, particularly during Justinian's reign.

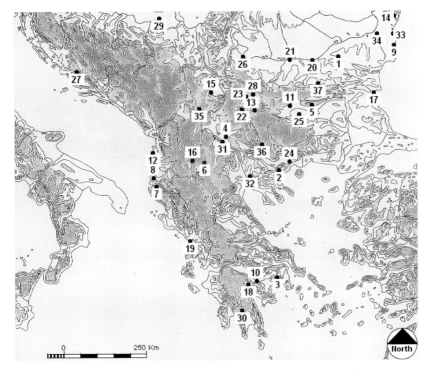

Figure 1 Location map of the principal cities mentioned in the text

1 – Razgrad (Abritus); 2 – Amphipolis; 3 – Athens; 4 – Bargala; 5 – Beroe; 6 – Bitola (Heraclea Lyncestis); 7 – Butrint; 8 – Bylis; 9 – Mangalia (Callatis); 10 – Corinth; 11 – Hissar (Diocletianopolis); 12 – Durrës (Dyrrachium); 13 – Germania; 14 – Histria; 15 – Caričin Grad (Justiniana Prima); 16 – Ohrid (Lychnidos); 17 – Mesembria; 18 – Nemea; 19 – Nicopolis; 20 – Svishtov (Novae); 21 – Gigen (Oescus); 22 – Kyustendil (Pautalia); 23 – Pernik; 24 – Philippi; 25 – Plovdiv (Philippopolis); 26 – Ratiaria; 27 – Salona; 28 – Sofia (Serdica); 29 – Sirmium; 30 – Sparta; 31 – Stobi; 32 – Thessalonica; 33 – Constanţa (Tomis); 34 – Adamclisi (Tropaeum Traiani); 35 – Ulpiana; 36 – Sandanski (Zapara?); 37 – Carevec (Zikideva?).

basilicas, it included a large number of small houses with walls of stone and clay, each room with three to seven *dolia*. Many were interpreted as storage facilities, but two of them served as smithy and bakery, respectively. Small dwellings with walls of stone and clay were also found close to the western curtain, outside the city wall.[6]

---

[6] Inscriptions attesting merchants: Popescu 1976:23, 44, and 92–3. In Odessos, the preparation of hides, presumably for export, was an important local industry. Wine seems to have been a major import: a trader from Alexandria supplied large quantities on the local market at Tomis. See Beshevliev 1964:99–100, 102–4, and 126; Popescu 1976:28. See also Velkov 1983:183; Poulter 1992:127. Walls of Tomis: Popescu 1967:170. Presence of the military in Scythia Minor: Barnea 1990:402. Histria: Condurachi 1957:243, 251, and 255, and 1967:167–8; Barnea and Vulpe 1968:473.

A wealthy residential area was unearthed in the northeastern sector of the city. "Domus I," with two building phases, was a two-floored *villa urbana* with eight rooms. Its latest phase is dated by a coin struck for Tiberius II. "Domus II," across the street from "Domus I," had a large, central courtyard and an apsed *triclinium*. A third building, "Domus V," had a bath with *caldarium* and *suspensurae* found *in situ*. In this case, the central courtyard seems to have been used for the needs of the household: an oven was built in its south eastern corner. All three houses produced the only evidence of sixth-century glass windows at Histria.[7]

"Aristocratic" houses were also found on other sites. At Adamclisi (Tropaeum Traiani), excavations carried out after 1968 near the city's eastern gate revealed three buildings, one of which, built on top of older ruins of a fourth-century house, had a central courtyard and a portico. Judging from the evidence found in this house (a stone mold and a small anvil), at least one of its rooms may have served as a workshop.[8]

The urban landscape was drastically modified by new buildings, first of all by churches. No other public buildings were found in any city of Dobrudja. At Slava Rusă (Ibida), the only monumental building erected was the three-aisled basilica with mosaic pavement. Three churches existed at Histria during the sixth century. Three new basilicas were also built at Adamclisi during the period between Anastasius' and Justinian's reigns. At Constanța (Tomis), two basilicas were erected in the late 400s and the 500s in the western part of the city. At Igliţa (Troesmis), older excavations carried out in 1865 by Ambroise Baudry and Gustave Boissière in the eastern settlement revealed the existence of three basilicas, though it remains unclear whether or not they could all be dated to the sixth century. Salvage excavations at Isaccea (Noviodunum) revealed a basilica built next to the city's northern wall. At Mangalia (Callatis), a fifth-century basilica of Syrian plan, built against the city's northern rampart, was twice renewed during the sixth century, when it probably became an episcopal church. After 600, walls of stone bonded with clay were erected in the interior, the basilica being already abandoned.[9]

---

[7] Barnea and Vulpe 1968:427; Condurachi 1957:259 and 254 fig. 3; Pippidi, Bordenache, and Eftimie 1961:238; Condurachi et al. 1970:187–8; Condurachi 1975:174–9, 176 fig. 3, and 179 fig. 4. The apsed *triclinium* was usually interpreted as a private chapel, which led to the wrong conclusion that the house belonged to the local bishop. See, more recently, Sâmpetru 1994:62. For apsed *triclinia*, see Sodini 1993:148–9.

[8] Barnea et al. 1979:106; Bogdan-Cătăniciu 1979:185; Sâmpetru 1994:33–53.

[9] Slava Rusă: Ştefan 1977:457–8. Histria: Barnea 1958:287–9 and 291–2 and 1960a:205. Adamclisi: Barnea and Vulpe 1968:470–1; Barnea et al. 1979:229. Constanța: Barnea and Vulpe 1968:466. Two lead seals were found in Constanța (Tomis), one belonging to a bishop, the other to a deacon. They must have been members of the local clergy, for ecclesiastical seals rarely moved beyond the area of their production. See Barnea 1984:97 and 99; Morrisson and Cheynet 1990:110. Igliţa and Isaccea: Barnea and Vulpe 1968:425 and 477. Mangalia: Theodorescu 1963; Pillinger 1992:97–8.

A similar picture emerges from Moesia Inferior. The late sixth-century source (the *Feldzugsjournal*) used by Theophylact Simocatta for his account of Maurice's campaigns against the Slavs and the Avars in the 590s lists thirty towns in Dacia and Moesia with a cluster of cities between Novae and Iatrus. Theophylact called them πόλεις. At Svishtov (Novae), the excavations carried out since 1960 by a joint Bulgarian–Polish team showed that in its last phase of existence, tentatively dated to the fifth or sixth century, the fourth-century building with peristyled courtyard located in the northwestern corner of the city was subdivided into smaller rooms by walls of stone bonded with clay, while its northern portico was blocked. Between 470 and 480, Novae was ruled by Theoderic the Great and it may be during this period that the episcopal basilica was built on top of the city's abandoned *thermae* (bath). With its long and wide nave, the three-aisled basilica is the largest of all early Christian churches currently known in Bulgaria. Three other basilicas were built in the eastern part of the city, north of the forum, and outside the city's walls, to the west. Around 500 the first intramural burials appeared near the episcopal basilica, probably of some wealthy sponsors. During Justinian's reign, both the basilica and the episcopal residence located on its northern side underwent substantial restoration. To the northeast, some small houses and workshops were built in stone and clay.[10]

An important city existed not far from the abandoned site at Nicopolis, on top of the Carevec hill near modern Veliko Tărnovo. It has been tentatively identified with Zikideva mentioned by Procopius. The city was built entirely during the period between Anastasius and Justinian. As a sixth-century foundation, the city plan is characterized by the absence of the forum and of any orthogonal street grid. The main orientation of the street leading to the gates does not coincide with the longitudinal axis. In addition, there is no *intervallum* (i.e., a ringroad all along the city ramparts). The city was dominated by a three-aisled basilica, which was superposed by the late medieval church of the patriarch of Tărnovo. A sixth-century burial, presumably of some high-rank clergyman or of a wealthy donor, was found outside the church, next to the apse. A single-naved church existed north of the three-aisled basilica, which was later connected with a group of houses built in stone and adobe. A reconstruction phase of the mid-sixth century transformed the small church into another three-aisled basilica, while a large, two-storied building was added to the southeast. The building included a cistern and its ground

---

[10] Theophylact's account and cities in Moesia Inferior: Schreiner 1985:62–4. For Svishtov, see Press et al. 1973:103–24; Chichikova 1983:15–6; Parnicki-Pudelko 1983:242 and 268–9 and 1984:271 and 301–2; Press and Sarnowski 1990:242–3; Kalinowski 1999.

rooms were vaulted. The church and the two-storied building were interpreted as a "monastery compound," but the existing evidence suggests that the building functioned as a hostel, rather than as cells for monks. Finally, a single-naved church to the north was attached to a cruciform building with a common portico, arguably a sixth-century martyrium. A two-storied, "aristocratic" house with peristyled courtyard and vaulted ground rooms was found nearby. Rooms built in stone and adobe were later added to the north and to the south. Other similar rooms, some equipped with cisterns, were excavated in the northern and southeastern parts of the city. The remains of a second "aristocratic" house with an apsed *triclinium* were found in the northern region. During the second habitation phase, dated to the mid-sixth century, this building was divided into three rooms, and a new *triclinium* added on its eastern side. A three-aisled church was built in front of the main city gate. The current interpretation of this odd location is that the basilica secured divine protection of that key point in the city defense. The last coin found on site was minted for Constantine IV and Tiberius (659–81), but the site seems to have been already abandoned by the beginning of Heraclius' reign.[11]

At Razgrad (Abritus), the excavations led by Teofil Ivanov focused more on the city's defenses and very little is known about its internal organization. We only know that walls of stone and brick were erected within the defenses during the fifth and sixth century. A three-aisled basilica existed east of the west gate, but its dating to the sixth century is not certain. Building VII with peristyled courtyard (also known as the "town house") produced a large number of iron implements (plowshares, sickles, pruning knife, woodcarving tools, etc.). However, their dating to the sixth century is doubtful. A wall of stone bonded with clay was erected during this period inside the abandoned *horreum*, and other similar structures appeared north and south of the *horreum*. Other buildings of similar fabric were built along the walls during the fifth and sixth century. At Gigen (Oescus), where no basilica was found so far, the portico and the courtyard's vestibule of the temple dedicated to Fortuna were subdivided during the fifth and sixth centuries and rooms were built with walls of stone bonded with clay.[12]

Some cities in Thrace, such as Philippopolis, continued to erect statues of emperors and army commanders as late as the end of the fifth century, which suggests that municipal life may have survived longer than in any other place. But even in Philippopolis, the ancient urban street grid seems

---

[11] Angelov 1962:23–5 and 1986:50–55; Hoddinott 1975:251; Tuleshkov 1988:21–2; Pisarev 1990; Dinchev 1997b.
[12] Razgrad: Ivanov 1980:77; Ivanov and Stoianov 1985:27, 31, and 33. Early Byzantine tools and implements: Popović 1994–5. Gigen: Ivanov 1974:64; Ivanov 1993:42.

to have been drastically altered. Salvage excavations in the downtown area of modern Plovdiv unearthed a considerable portion of the ancient city's forum. During the first half of the fifth century, a large three-aisled basilica was built on top of two *insulae*, thus blocking the *decumanus* and the *cardo* between them. By the end of the following century, the basilica itself was abandoned and turned into a cemetery. But the baths of the city remained in use until the late 500s. At Hissar (Diocletianopolis), an "aristocratic" house was accidentally discovered by bulldozers, which destroyed half the remains of the building. The plan was reconstructed from what was left of the foundations plus a partial excavation of the western half. The western part of this multi-roomed building was occupied by a spacious peristyled courtyard, the vestibule of which was paved with brick. It led to a large room, no doubt the *triclinium*. There is significant evidence of glass windows. Most likely, the building had two phases, the first of which could be dated to the early 400s. Beroe/Augusta Traiana also underwent major transformations during the sixth century. A house by the south gate, excavated in 1962, overlaid an older building. Two rooms produced *dolia* and probably served for storage. Another fourth-century house built at the corner of the *cardo* and the *decumanus* retained its original floor and exterior walls, but the interior was radically altered. A series of rooms were located on the southern side, with a small court with a pool faced with marble slabs, a big stone mortar, and five or six *dolia*.[13]

Little is known about cities in Haemimons and Europe, except Mesembria, the only city in the entire diocese of Thrace with five basilicas, only one of which, the church near the city's northern tower, was explored. Nothing is known about cities in the immediate vicinity of the capital, in the region of the modern frontier between Turkey and Bulgaria, except Annie Pralong's description of the early Byzantine walls at Çorlu (Tzurullum) and Kiyiköy.[14]

Before Justinian's reign, Serdica was an urban center of the foremost importance in northern Illyricum, i.e., the diocese of Dacia. The city was an important bishopric, whose last bishop, Felix, was mentioned in 594. It was a local bishop, Leontius, who, according to an inscription found in 1953, and dated to 580, sponsored the restoration of the city's aqueduct. The main cemetery of early Byzantine Serdica was located along the road to Philippopolis. The St Sophia church probably functioned as

---

[13] Plovdiv: Hoddinott 1975:291; Velkov 1977:153; Kessiakova 1989. Hissar: Hoddinott 1975:310–13 and 314 fig. 19; Gorbanov 1987; Madzharov 1989.

[14] Nesebăr: Hoddinott 1975:323; Velkov 1992:19–20. It is not without interest that Mesembria, together with Serdica, was the only city in the Balkans with a church dedicated to St Sophia. Çorlu and Kiyiköy: Pralong 1988:185–6 and 192. For other sixth-century finds in Thrace, see Bakirtzis 1989b:46.

basilica coemeterialis. Nothing is known about the city's internal organization. At Kyustendil (Pautalia), the site in the plain coexisted with a fort built some 150 meters above it, on the Hissarlyk hill. In the plain, a three-aisled, single-apsed basilica was found, with fine mosaic floor, dated to the fifth century. At Germania, Belisarius' hometown, the defenses were restored under Justinian, but nothing is known about the internal organization of the city. The same is true about Ulpiana, in Dardania. Vladislav Popović suggested that after 545 Justiniana Prima replaced Ulpiana, now rebaptized Justiniana Secunda, as metropolis of Dardania. This, he argued, was meant to eliminate any possible competition between the bishoprics of Serdica and Justiniana Prima.[15]

A similar picture emerges from the Bulgarian excavations on the Krakra hill near Pernik. Despite claims to the contrary, there is enough evidence to suspect that walls built later were erected on top of earlier, presumably sixth-century ramparts. Within the settled area, archaeologists found houses with walls of stone, mortar, and adobe, sometimes equipped with brick ovens. The settlement had two basilicas, one of which was destroyed during the second half of the sixth century. A few *exagia* indicate that at Pernik gold coins were common enough to require control. The presence of gold coins may bear witness to the presence of the military.[16]

The most important city in the region was, however, Justiniana Prima, identified with the site at Caričin Grad. The city had been built shortly before 535, as Justinian's novel 11 established an archbishopric there. The novel announced the imminent transfer of the Illyrian prefecture to Justiniana Prima, but it is unlikely that it was ever moved from Thessalonica. This may further explain the specific design of this imperial foundation in the Balkans. Excavations at Caričin Grad, which started in 1912, revealed that at first the acropolis, no larger than 1 ha, was occupied by a large episcopal church with a baptistery and a residential area to the north, perhaps an episcopal residence. The upper city is divided into four unequal parts by two main colonnaded streets meeting in a large, circular plaza surrounded by porticoes. The lower city, measuring 2.25 ha in area, was built only later, after *c.* 550. The north–south colonnaded street, which was curved to protect a large basilica with transept, continued to the south gate as a simple street without porticoes.[17]

---

[15] Sofia: Stancheva 1978:217; Velkov 1991:94. Bishop Leontius: Beshevliev 1964:2. Theuprepius, whose epitaph was found in Sofia, may have also been bishop of Serdica (see Beshevliev 1964:10). For the St Sofia church, see Sotiroff 1972; Hoddinott 1975:269; Kousoupov 1984; Chaneva-Dechevska 1984:619; Krautheimer 1986:256. Kyustendil: Hoddinott 1975:285. Germania: Bavant 1984:247. Ulpiana: Popović 1989–1990:279–80.

[16] Changova 1963; Liubenova 1981:112 and 195. *Exagia* and gold coins: Vladimirova 1985.

[17] Justiniana Prima and novel 11: Maksimović 1984:145 and 149; Döpmann 1987. For Caričin Grad, see Duval and Popović 1984:549; Bavant 1984:273; Duval 1984:407–14; Krautheimer 1986:274. Episcopal residence: Müller-Wiener 1989; *contra:* Duval 1984:417.

The upper city provided evidence for significant economic activities. Workshops and a bakery, as well as store-rooms with *dolia*, were found north of the west–east colonnaded street. An "aristocratic" house (*villa urbana*) with central courtyard and apsed *triclinium* was located just south of the three-aisled basilica in the eastern part of the upper city. Just as in Histria, the vestibule of the house had a baking oven, arguably used for the needs of the entire household. Later, some workshops, including a jeweller's shop, were built in the area between the *villa urbana* and the city's southern wall. At that time, the basilica with transept was already abandoned and a few houses with simple hearths and a baking oven were built in its ruins. Other houses with walls built in stone bonded with earth were found north of the basilica. In addition, two structures, one outside the walls, close to the south gate of the upper city, the other close to the east gate of the lower city, were interpreted as *thermae*. Soon after being built, they were abandoned and the latter's ruins were reused by houses with walls of stone bonded with clay.[18]

At Caričin Grad, as many as eight churches have come to light, all different in plan from each other, but going back to prototypes of an earlier date, drawn from Constantinople or Thessalonica and merged with local elements. The nave and the atrium of the cathedral had mosaic floors. The eastern portico of the atrium of the basilica B with cruciform plan produced three burials, a clear indication that shortly after the city's foundation, burials had already appeared in intramural contexts. Except for a capital of Proconnesian marble from the tribelon of the basilica with transept (basilica D), which bears Justinian's monogram, there are no dedicatory inscriptions of donors. All extant mosaic floors (the cathedral's baptistery, the basilica with transept, basilica E, basilica B, the cathedral, and the atrium of the upper city *thermae*) display a remarkable unity of style, which may indicate the same "workshop" of local, provincial taste. The building program at Caričin Grad seems to have been extremely ambitious and very expensive, but the actual building was left to local craftsmen working with local techniques.[19]

Like Carevec, Caričin Grad was a sixth-century foundation, with no significant building traditions. It is not without interest that when describing Justiniana Prima, though referring to administrative buildings, Procopius mentioned no civic administration, and no structures of that sort have been found. Bernard Bavant argued that the building of the city

---

[18] Mano-Zisi 1969:210 and 212; Bavant 1984:276 and 279–81.

[19] Krautheimer 1986:273; Duval 1984:410, 421–2, 432, and 480. For Proconnesian marble capitals as indications of imperial munificence, see Barsanti 1989:211. There is no indication of any Constantinopolitan work at Caričin Grad, though carvers from the Capital may have worked elsewhere in Illyricum, as well as in Crimea or on the eastern Black Sea coast. See Sodini 1984b:256; Bortoli-Kazanski 1981:63; Khrushkova 1979:134. Intramural burials at Caričin Grad: Jeremić 1994–5:183–6.

started shortly before 535 on the acropolis and in the upper city area. This building phase included the basilica with transept, the lower city *thermae*, and the basilica with triconch, located some 350 meters away from the lower city's rampart. The rampart itself was built only later, during the second half of Justinian's reign, together with the upper city *thermae*, the two-aisled basilica, and the lower city cistern. Bavant suggested that this second building phase also included some drastic alteration of the initial building program. Its main purpose seems to have been to include as many churches and public buildings as possible within the city's walls. Soon, however, many public buildings and churches (such as the basilica with transept) were abandoned and an encroachment phase seems to have taken place. This third building phase, dated after *c.* 565 until about 615, is characterized by houses with walls built in stone bonded with clay and a significant quantity of agricultural implements, which indicate that the status of the new inhabitants was now defined by agricultural occupations, rather than crafts. This phase has been traditionally attributed to a Slavic settlement following the invasions of the late sixth and early seventh centuries, but Bavant rightly pointed out that the stone-cum-clay building technique has nothing to do with sunken buildings found on contemporary sites north of the Danube river (see Chapter 6).[20]

That this building phase predates the abandonment of the city and the settlement of the Slavs in the Balkans is clearly indicated by a house found in the western portico of the once colonnaded street running from the circular plaza to the upper city's south gate. The house was built with walls of stone and clay and had a small hearth. Three *dolia* were found inside the house, all filled with grain. Two other, smaller, vessels contained dried pears and nuts. Domestic animal bones were scattered around the hearth, together with three arrow heads, an earring with basket-shaped pendant, two fibulae, and two belt-buckles. One of the two buckles has good parallels in the destruction debris of the abandoned houses of the palaestra in Anemurium, on the Cilician coast. The other buckle belongs to a type with shield-shaped end, derived from the so-called Salona-Histria class with belt-strap. Such buckles, also found at Anemurium, are especially frequent on several early Byzantine sites in the Balkans and in Crimea. Clear chronological indications are also provided by one of the two brooches, a cast fibula with bent stem. Such fibulae were produced in and associated with military sites on the Danube frontier, as evidenced by the workshop found at Turnu Severin (Drobeta). A date from Justin II's reign is secured by two hoards found at Bracigovo and Koprivec, respectively, both including such fibulae and concluding

---

[20] Procopius, *Buildings* IV 1. See Bavant 1984:282–5.

with coins struck for that emperor. A date from the late sixth century for the house in the western portico is also suggested by the bow fibula, a variant of Werner's class II C, as well as by the earring with basket-shaped pendant. Such earrings, derived from Late Roman specimens with à-jour pendant welded to the ring, were found in late sixth- or seventh-century cemeteries north of the Alps and in Pannonia, but no such finds are known from contemporary sites north of the Danube river.[21]

The evidence cited shows that the house cannot be interpreted as "Slavic infiltration into the Byzantine urban design," primarily because it predates the earliest evidence of Slavic settlements in the Balkans, known from historical sources. Instead, it seems to indicate the presence of the military (arrow heads, cast fibula with bent stem) and the shift from a purely urban to a ruralized environment. The excavations at Caričin Grad certainly bear out Procopius' description of the city's amenities, according to which it boasted churches, fountains, an aqueduct, baths, paved streets, private buildings, and colonnades. But they also show that less than fifty years after the city's foundation, Caričin Grad witnessed the same process of subdivision and encroachment visible on other, less representative, sites.[22]

At Sirmium, this process had started long before the sixth century. In the late 300s or early 400s, the city's walls had been leveled and a three-aisled basilica erected on top of them. A group of houses built with *spolia* bonded with earth surrounded the church. By the second half of the fifth century and during the sixth century, the basilica was abandoned and, on top of its ruins, new houses were built with brick fragments bonded with clay. The remains of the *villa urbana* located to the north of the hippodrome and the "aristocratic" house near the city's southern gate (probably a fourth-century imperial residence) were drastically altered to accommodate a few structures built in the stone-cum-clay technique. In both cases, this new occupation also included isolated burials, some cutting through the mosaic floor of the *villa urbana*. As the city was occupied by the Ostrogoths and then by the Gepids, most of the public buildings were abandoned, while the city itself disintegrated into small hamlets emerging in urban areas not used before.[23]

Except Sirmium, no other city on the northern frontier was systematically excavated and studied. A joint Bulgarian–Italian team began

---

[21] Mano-Zisi 1958:312–13. Buckles: Russell 1982:142–3 fig. 6/7–8 and 7/21; Uenze 1966:166; Varsik 1992:80. Cast fibula with bent stem: Bejan 1976; Uenze 1974 and 1992:156; Janković 1980:173; Curta 1992:84. See also Kharalambieva and Ivanov 1986:16; Kharalambieva and Atanasov 1991:57. Bow fibulae: Werner 1950; see also Chapter 6. Earrings with basket-shaped pendants: Kastelić 1956:127; Slabe 1986:201; Bierbrauer 1987:147; Riemer 1992:126.

[22] Mano-Zisi 1958:312. Procopius' description of Justiniana Prima: *Buildings* IV 1; Poulter 1992:125.

[23] Popović 1982:550–4.

working at Archar (Ratiaria) in 1978, but no relevant sixth-century material is known from the site. We only know that under Justinian those parts of the city were restored which had been severely damaged by the Hunnic raids of the mid-400s. An inscription ("Anastasiana Ratiaria semper floreat"), found in 1983 in the wall of the city's main gate, was initially interpreted as evidence of an earlier phase of reconstruction under Anastasius. This interpretation, however, was recently challenged by Vladislav Popović on philological grounds.[24]

Evidence of an early phase of subdivision and encroachment also comes from several Macedonian cities. At Stobi, large palatial residences with elaborate courtyards with decorated fountains, floors with pavements of mosaic or *opus sectile*, and walls covered with frescoes and, occasionally, mosaics, were still in use in the early 500s. At that time, however, the theater was only a quarry for building material. Small houses with walls of stone and clay were built in its ruins. Similar houses were found on the eastern slope of the acropolis, to the west from the theater. Stobi had five basilicas. After the early sixth-century earthquake, the episcopal church was modified to accommodate galleries built above the aisles and a large terrace was built between the church and the baptistery. Sidewalks were added beneath arcades along the eastern side of the Via Sacra and in front of the basilica's main entrance. The walls of the church were covered with marble revetment, colored stucco, and fresco. The narthex and the south aisle were repaved with fine mosaics. The care and expense needed to restore the episcopal basilica so lavishly are in sharp contrast to the refurbishment of other buildings in the city. In the aftermath of the Hunnic invasion of the mid-400s, the House of the Fuller (the name is derived from the quantity of murex-shells found to the north of the apsidal hall), built in the early 300s, was divided by rough walls of brick bonded with clay into a storehouse and a workshop. Both produced a considerable quantity of spindle whorls and loom weights. Sometime after 570, the city was abandoned before the Avars and the Slavs began raiding the area. The uniform presence of powdery grey silt, several feet deep all over the site, suggests that during the sixth century Stobi experienced extremes of cold and dry weather followed by wind-blown dust storms which aggravated the existing problem of soil erosion.[25]

At Bitola (Heraclea Lyncestis), the theater was also abandoned in the fifth century. Just as in Stobi, it became a quarry for building material and at some point after 562, a group of houses with walls of stone bonded

---

[24] Susini 1982:239; Giorgetti 1980 and 1983:19 and 33. Inscription: Velkov 1985:886; Popović 1989–90:283.

[25] Mikulčic 1974:200 and 1982:536–7; Neppi Mòdona 1974:112; Popović 1982:561–2; Wiseman 1984:310; Hattersley-Smith 1988:85, 106–9, and 123.

with clay was built in its ruins. One of them produced no less than six querns. Around the middle of the sixth century, the colonnade in front of the small basilica's baptistery was dismantled and the whole area enlarged to include a second mosaic floor, which is strikingly similar in composition to the narthex mosaic in the basilica with transept at Caričin Grad, dating from the second or third quarter of the century. When the narthex of the small basilica was later in need of repair, the large worn areas between the entrance doors on the west side of the narthex and the central door into the nave were simply patched up with bricks and mortar. Both basilicas at Heraclea Lyncestis seem to have been built with money donated by private individuals, as suggested by the nave mosaic of the large basilica and the Corinthian capital with monogram found in the small basilica. One of these donors may have owned the *villa urbana* built in the late third century in the eastern part of the city and rebuilt in the fifth and sixth century. By contrast, at Sandanski (tentatively identified with Zapara, mentioned as bishopric in 553), the inscription of the floor mosaic in the three-aisled basilica partially excavated in 1960 indicates Bishop John as the main donor. The city had three other basilicas, two of which had mosaic floors.[26]

At Ohrid (Lychnidos), although seven churches were found inside the ancient city's defenses, very little is known about its internal organization. Sometime during the fifth or sixth century, the acropolis was fortified with strong walls, but nothing is known about the lower city's street grid. The same is true for Bargala, where a large episcopal basilica was remodeled in the late 400s or early 500s. Its orientation is entirely different from all other, earlier, buildings, which suggests that the old street grid was abandoned after *c.* 500. After the destruction of the episcopal basilica, a smaller, single-naved church was built on top of its ruins, reusing many of the architectural fragments of the former building. Coins struck for Emperor Phocas indicate that this church was still in use in the early seventh century.[27]

An entirely different picture results from the examination of three Macedonian towns located on the coast: Philippi, Amphipolis (near modern Iraklitsa), and Thessalonica. At Philippi, despite numerous alterations to the structures within the *insulae* and the partial covering up of two streets, the initial grid system dominates the urban plan until the early

---

[26] Bitola: Neppi Mòdona 1974:112; Popović 1982:560 fig. 16; Hattersley-Smith 1988:184, 186, and 190; Mikulčić 1986a:237. The date 562 is that of an inscription mentioning Emperor Justinian as the sponsor for the restoration of the city's aqueduct. See Dzhidrova 1999:282. For the extramural *basilica coemeterialis* with mosaic floor, see Maneva 1981–2. Sandanski: Ivanov, Serafimova, and Nikolov 1969; Pliakov 1973:177–80. Bishop John: Pillinger 1985:298.

[27] Ohrid: Mikulčić 1974:194 and 1986a:238. Bargala: Aleksova 1969:110, 1975–78:77–9, and 1986:24.

600s. New alterations were brought to the Octagon in the first quarter of the sixth century and though small buildings obstructed the southwest street sometime after *c.* 600, the Commercial Road remained open to traffic until the ninth century. Basilica C, restored in the second quarter of the sixth century, yielded a considerable quantity of colored fragments of glass, many of which were carefully cut into different shapes and have been found in association with strips of lead. This seems to be the earliest known example of stained-glass. Pieces of colored glass were also found in the second phase of the extramural basilica, reconstructed and remodeled under Justinian. That Philippi had its own glass-making industry is suggested by a glass and metal workshop built on top of a Roman building in the southern range of the city. Basilica B (Direkler) had a cross-domed unit in addition to the vaults over the aisles, galleries, nave, and transept wings. The combination of a transept and a cross dome reminds one of the Justinianic buildings of Constantinople, in particular of St Sophia and SS. Sergius and Bacchus. Not long after the building's erection in *c.* 540, the dome collapsed and the main part of the basilica was never rebuilt, but structures on the northern and southern sides of the transept continued to be used as baptistery and small chapel, respectively. Nothing is known about further changes during the seventh century, the next piece of evidence being coin-dated to the 800s.[28]

Amphipolis had several basilicas, four of which (including a hexagonal church) were built at different times during the sixth century. By the end of that century, the acropolis was surrounded by a new wall, the west side of which was built across the narthex of basilica A of the first half of the sixth century. A fifth basilica (C) was thus left outside the encircled area. Its lavish decoration seems to have been paid for by a group of donors, as evidenced by the mosaic inscription. A small, single-naved chapel was erected in the late 500s or slightly later on the basilica's eastern side.[29]

Still more interesting is the evidence from Thessalonica. In his *Secret History*, Procopius refers to the grandfather and father of Antonina, Belisarius' wife, who had demonstrated their skills as charioteers in Thessalonica, an indication that the city's hippodrome was still in operation during the early sixth century. Archbishop John, the author of the first book of the *Miracles of St Demetrius*, mentions both the city's stadium and the theater. During the plague, shortly before the siege of 586, the sick who had taken refuge in the church of St Demetrius were making their way every morning to the baths. We are also told that Marianos, the praetorian prefect, descended from the church of St Demetrius to the

---

[28] Hattersley-Smith 1988:133, 149, 155, and 158–9.   [29] Hattersley-Smith 1988:202 and 207–8.

praetorium, which was probably located in the lower, southern, part of the city. Marianos was also depicted as donor on one of the basilica's exterior walls. Two other wealthy citizens, Menas and John, donated money for the reconstruction of the wooden roof and the *ciborium* of the basilica of St Demetrius.[30]

In addition to the episcopal basilica, several other churches were built in Thessalonica between 400 and 600: St Demetrius, Acheiropoietos, and the octagonal church near the Vardar Gate. The Rotunda was also converted into a church, now known as St George's. In the Acheiropoietos, two inscriptions surviving on the soffits in the south arcade and the central arch of the tribelon refer to private donors. St Demetrius, on the other hand, was the beneficiary of imperial patronage, as evidenced by a mutilated inscription found on the ground, near the basilica's north wall. The inscription may have been an edict issued by Justinian I. More than a century later, Justinian II granted all profits from the city's salt-pans to the same church, as evidenced by another inscription, now lost. While becoming the main focus of local patronage and occasional imperial donations, Thessalonica's new churches coexisted for a time with elements of the ancient city, such as the agora, which retained its commercial significance, as suggested by the association of the Megalophoros' western side with the copper trade from Late Antiquity through the present day. Unfortunately, none of the three Macedonian cities discussed above produced any evidence of urban habitat, since research has typically focused on either city walls or Christian monuments. The only *villa urbana* known from southern Macedonia is that explored at Tocatlis, on the island of Thasos, and dated to the fifth or sixth century. It was a two-storied building, with a large *atrium* and a fountain.[31]

The evidence of the *Miracles of St Demetrius* may help explain how Thessalonica survived as a major urban center in the Balkans. On at least two occasions, the Slavs launched attacks against the city while its citizens were busy harvesting their crops on their estates and small holdings outside the city walls. But at the same time, Thessalonica relied heavily on its rations of public grain (*annona*), as evidenced by the eighth homily of Book I. Preventing corn supplies from reaching the city must have been one of the main reasons behind the attempt of the Slavs to block

---

[30] Procopius, *Secret History* I. 11; *Miracles of St Demetrius* I 14.132 (theater), I 1.23 (*praetorium*), I 1.24 (stadium, Marianos as donor), I 3.39 (baths), I 6.60–1 (Menas and John as donors). For the stadium, see also Vickers 1971. See also Spieser 1984a:319; Hattersley-Smith 1988:63, 66, and 236. Another praetorian prefect, Hormisdas, may have been responsible for the city's impregnable walls. See Vickers 1974:251 and 254.

[31] Churches and inscriptions in Thessalonica: Popović 1982:561; Hattersley-Smith 1988:269, 304, 310, and 319; Spieser 1984a:319. Tocatlis: Sodini 1984a:357.

the port with their fleet of canoes and to attack Thessalonica by sea. This further suggests that a crucial factor in the city's survival was its role as a harbor which remained open to outside shipping. As long as Egypt was under Byzantine control, Thessalonica continued to receive regular supplies of corn to supplement the foods its population cultivated locally. With the Persian conquest of Egypt in 619, the Empire's main source of grain was lost, and the city could no longer expect shipments of public corn. Thessalonica was thus forced to depend on the products of its own hinterland and on those brought from the neighboring regions. In 677, an embassy was sent to the Belegezites of Thessaly to purchase food. One could further speculate that the survival of urban centers and regular supplies of public corn were intimately connected and that this relation may explain the collapse of Byzantine authority in the Balkans during the seventh century.[32]

Evidence for a later survival of coastal cities also comes from the western Balkans. The early Byzantine walls at Nicopolis in Epirus Vetus enclosed an area of 30 ha in the northeastern sector of the early Roman city. The towers at the west gate were similar in size to those of the large wall at Constantinople and to the larger towers at Resafa. This suggests that the building was entrusted to an imperial architect, being sponsored by the urban community and by the provincial authorities, with some imperial assistance. Nothing is known, however, about the city's internal organization, except three churches, dating to the sixth century: the "Alkison basilica" (also known as basilica B), built at some point before 518; the basilica D, perhaps contemporary; and the "Dumetior basilica" (basilica A), dated to the second quarter of the century. All show the layout of tripartite basilicas with transepts. At Butrint, the early Roman walls were still in use during the sixth century. A three-aisled basilica with mosaic floor was erected during this period on top of an earlier, large, cistern on the acropolis. A second church existed in the lower city, beside the so-called "tower gate." A considerable quantity of *spolia*, including Roman columns with Corinthian capitals, was used for this building. During Justinian's reign a circular baptistery was built inside a quadrangular structure, which is reminiscent of the great baptisteries of Italy. A splendid mosaic, one of the largest known so far from Late Antiquity, decorated the floor of the baptistery. Several details, such as red flowers on waving black stalks, suggest the work of local craftsmen, since very similar patterns were found in the small chapel attached to the narthex of the "Dumetior basilica" at Nicopolis. But the most impressive building is the triconch palace, located next to the lower city southern rampart.

---

[32] *Miracles of St Demetrius* I 13.127 and II 2.199, II 1.180, II 4.254. See also Durliat 1990:389–99.

The tri-apsidal *triclinium* opening into a large peristyle is dated to the early sixth century, but the palace seems never to have been completed. Despite the presence of small niches for statuary in the interior of the northern and eastern apses, no traces of decoration were found, while the primary occupation appears to be industrial or agricultural. Soon after the abandonment of the building project, some rooms were subdivided by walls of earth-bonded construction. By the late sixth century, the first burials appeared within the triconch or cut through the former peristyle. A midden deposit in the northern part of the building produced fragments of sixth- and early seventh-century amphoras and glassware, showing that the last phase of habitation within the ruins of formerly finer buildings was still associated with long-distance trade across the Mediterranean. Moreover, it has been suggested that the acropolis continued to be occupied after *c.* 600, although on a considerably reduced scale.[33]

At Durrës (Dyrrachium), Emperor Anastasius' hometown, the city walls were rebuilt at his order, as evidenced by brick stamps. They were still in use during the early medieval period. The same seems to be true for some of the city's public buildings and churches, as recently shown by excavations at the extramural triconch church at Arapaj. Bylis also witnessed a period of economic prosperity during the sixth century, as Viktorinos, Justinian's architect, rebuilt the city walls. Two churches, both with mosaic floors, were built during this period. The city, however, was abandoned after 600 and a rural settlement grew around a sixth-century extramural basilica at Ballshi, at a short distance from the town. A sixth-century building phase was also identified at Sarda, but the dating to this period of six houses built in stone bonded with clay remains controversial.[34]

Unfortunately, little is known about the sixth-century habitat at Salona, despite extensive excavations since the late nineteenth century. We know that in *c.* 530, the sanctuaries dedicated to Nemesis in the city's amphitheater were turned into churches, while *Porta postica* was blocked. Judging from the existing evidence, out of eight churches so far identified in Salona, only one, the Gradina, was built after 500. After partial destruction, probably in the early seventh century, the transept and the apse of the basilica at Manastirine, not far from the city, were turned into a smaller church, which Rudolf Egger called a *Notkirche*. He suggested

---

[33] Nicopolis: Gregory 1987a:260; Hellenkemper 1987:250; Krautheimer 1986:131. Butrint: Karaiskaj 1984:161; Koch 1988:124; Hodges and Saraçi 1994–5:217–23, 226–7, and 231–2.

[34] Durrës: Zheku 1972:42; Miraj 1980; Koch 1988:124 and 136; Anamali 1989:2618. Arapaj: Anamali 1993a:462–4. Bylis: Feissel 1988; Anamali 1989:2632; Muçaj 1993; Korkuti and Petruso 1993:738. Ballshi: Anamali 1988. Sarda: Spahiu 1976:154–5; Karaiskaj 1989:2647.

that this new church became the focus of religious life after the presumed destruction of Salona by the invading Slavs. But similar evidence was later found at Kapljuč and comparable alterations were identified at the basilica at Marusinac. They all confirm that the city was still inhabited by Christians during the first half of the seventh century.[35]

The *Synekdemos* of Hierocles lists about eighty cities (all called πόλεις) in the province of Achaia, apparently making Greece one of the most highly urbanized regions of the eastern Mediterranean. At Athens, the post-Herulian wall included the Acropolis, but excluded the Agora, for by that time the city's government offices and commercial center had already shifted eastward from the Agora to the less-damaged Library of Hadrian and the Roman Market. Statues of high-ranking officials were still erected in the fifth century, as evidenced by one found in the northeastern corner of the so-called Gymnasium of the Giants (in the middle of the ancient Agora). In the early 500s, a bath was built on top of an older fountain, on the southern side of a Late Roman house on the Areopagus. A collection of antique marble sculptures was found in a courtyard north of the bath. Given their specific location, which suggests they were hidden, the sculptures have been interpreted as evidence for Justinian's anti-pagan legislation of 529. Similar evidence has been recently found at Antioch and Carthage. A mosaic floor in the room south of the baths was replaced with *opus sectile* in a cruciform pattern. Another *villa urbana* was found in the southern corner of the Acropolis and has been attributed to Proclus. A large *triclinium*, a relief representing the goddess Cybele, and an altar, are viewed as sufficient evidence for this attribution. A third *villa* comes from the eastern area of the Library of Pantainos. The earlier stoa was converted into an elegant suite of small rooms belonging to a two-storied building. On the first floor, there was a large peristyled courtyard and an apsed *triclinium*. Room B on the first floor had a barrel vault and the walls of rooms A, B, and C had niches for statues. The house was included in the Late Roman fortification and was used, with alterations, until the eighth century. On the northern slope of the Acropolis, houses with inner courtyards, built in the fifth century BC, were rebuilt at some point during the fifth century AD and were still in use during the sixth century. After 600, the old colonnade of the Stoa lost its original architectural integrity and was subdivided into small rooms. In room 6, hundreds of teracotta roof tiles recovered from

---

[35] Neppi Mòdona 1974:115–16; Nikolajević 1975:92 and 94; Marin 1989:1127. See also Duval 1990:438–9. A sixth-century papyrus, now lost, attests that churches and *castella* in the hinterland of Salona were supplied with revenue from medium-sized estates on the island of Mljet, on the Adriatic coast. See Nikolajević 1971:286.

the fallen debris of the house destroyed sometime in the 630s were piled in neat rows for possible reuse. These later alterations are dated by coins of Constans II.[36]

During the sixth century, two industrial establishments were set up on either side of the Panathenaic Way, near the southeast corner of the Agora: a flour mill driven by a water wheel, which was active between *c.* 450 and *c.* 580 (the water coming from the newly restored Hadrianic Aqueduct), and a small olive mill. In contrast, the Christian reuse of buildings inside the city walls is dated comparatively later. At some point during the late 400s or the early 500s, a three-aisled basilica was erected on the foundations of the Asklepieion. The Gymnasium of the Giants was abandoned and the Olympeion and the Temple of Kronos and Rhea were converted into churches. After *c.* 580, both the Parthenon and the Erechtheion followed suit, and a three-aisled basilica was built over the ruins of the quatrefoil building of Hadrian's Library. Shortly after 500, burials were introduced within the urban area, on the south side of the Acropolis, as well as between the Odeion of Pericles and the Theater of Dionysos.[37]

The situation at Corinth was slightly different. With the questionable exception of a statue allegedly erected in honor of Constans II, no honorific inscriptions dated after *c.* 400 have been found in the forum area. Any use of the forum as a public square or for private housing ceased by 500. The corridors along the eastern and northern sides of the peristyled courtyard known as the Peribolos of Apollon were transformed in the early 500s into small rooms. A house was built in the northern half of the Great Bath on the Lechaion Road. It has been dated to the first half of the sixth century. The walls were partially built with reused material. A coin struck for Justin II gives a *terminus post quem* for the hearth in the southeast corner of the house.[38]

Corinth was twice hit by earthquakes (522 and 551) and was devastated by the plague (542). One of the buildings severely damaged by the earthquake of 551 was the H. Leonidas basilica at Lechaion, built in the mid-fifth century. Shortly after the mid-sixth century, a group of houses was built in the basilica's *atrium* and the immediate vicinity. All had water

---

[36] Shear 1973:393–4 and 397; Gregory 1984a:273; Hattersley-Smith 1988:367 and 374. Urban villas in Athens: Sodini 1984a:348–52 and 359.

[37] Hattersley-Smith 1988:377, 381, 383, and 386; Gregory 1984a:273.

[38] Biers 1985:12; Hattersley-Smith 1988:403; Ivison 1996:104. Statue: Kent 1950. The inscription is a dedication to "Flavius Constan," which could stand for Constantine, Constantius, or Constans. Kent's attribution to Constans II was disputed by Peter Charanis (1952) and defended by Kenneth Setton (1952). The attribution has been decisively rejected by Feissel and Philippidis-Braat 1985:271.

wells or cisterns in the middle of small, inner, courtyards. Some were also provided with reduced versions of *triclinia* with earthen semicircular benches. Baking ovens, querns, and *dolia* bespeak the agricultural character of this settlement. The effects of the plague are illustrated by a mass burial of over 100 adults and children, which was found in Reservoir IV at Lerna. Toward the end of the century, there is evidence of a sudden abandonment and subsequent pillaging and dismantling of buildings. A late sixth-century or early seventh-century church was erected on the hill north of the Agora. Its narthex was richly decorated in *opus sectile* pavement and colored marble revetment. A modest chapel was built on the spring house near the Asklepieion sometime after *c. 665/6*. By the mid-sixth century, burial activity was well established in the forum area, with tombs in the ruins of the fourth-century shops and baths to the rear of the South Stoa. Two sixth-century burial vaults were found in the court of the Sacred Spring of Pierene. Whether or not these burials were intramural remains an object of dispute, for it is not yet clear what exactly constituted the city of Corinth during the 500s.[39]

The evidence from other cities in Greece remains scarce. At Nemea, a sixth-century building extended over the Bath and post-fourth-century cist burials with tiles were found in the area south of the Temple of Zeus. The ruins of two churches have been identified within the Late Roman walls at Sparta. One of them, St Nikon, was probably built in the sixth century. If true, this would make Sparta the only early Byzantine city in Greece with ecclesiastical representation within its walls. Elsewhere, the archaeological evidence points to the existence of *villae urbanae*. At Mantinea, a second-century double-room building was restored during the 500s, as a bath and a large *triclinium* were added. On the other hand, smaller dwellings, often interpreted as squatter-houses, were installed in the ruins of earlier residences, as in Aixone, Argos, or Castelli Kisamos, in Crete.[40]

CHANGING CITIES, RURAL SETTLEMENTS, AND MONASTERIES

How far is it possible to generalize from this rich archaeological evidence? Despite some variation a pattern of change is easily recognizable. In most

---

[39] Lechaion: Krautheimer 1986:132–3; Sodini 1984a:372. Churches and burials: Gregory 1982a:53 and 1984a:273; Snively 1984:121; Hattersley-Smith 1988:407, 411, and 413; Ivison 1996:104 and 112. Earthquakes: Avramea 1997:45–6.

[40] Nemea: Miller 1977:3 and fig. 5; Birge, Kraynak, and Miller 1992:239. Sparta: Gregory 1982a:55; Avramea 1997:114 and 185. Mantinea, Aixone, Argos, and Castelli Kisamos: Sodini 1984a:364 and 370.

cases, ancient cities contracted and regrouped around a defensible acropolis, usually dominated by the church. The process of disintegration of the urban nucleus into small settlement areas was accompanied by subdivision into smaller rooms of formerly finer buildings, by reuse of various architectural elements, and by new buildings with mud and brick walls. Large *civitates* were replaced by comparatively smaller forts, or coexisted with them, as in the case of Pautalia. The urban population of the Balkans concentrated primarily in coastal cities, such as Dyrrachium, Mesembria, Thessalonica, or Salona, and in Constantinople.

Subdivision and encroachment on the sites of former grand buildings were not restricted to the sixth-century Balkans. Similar phenomena have been observed at Carthage ("Michigan sector"), Anemorium, and Sbeitla.[41] The same is true for the presence of burials within urban areas. At Constantinople, Justinian's legislation had already allowed intramural interments between the old and the new precincts, as well as in Blachernae and Sykae.[42] The difference, if any, between the Balkans and the rest of the Roman world is one of degree rather than quality. In any case, the process of encroachment and change of use, though different in rhythm in various parts of the Empire, seems to indicate an urban change which cannot be attributed to particular local causes, such as plague or invasion, but must have been connected to economic and administrative factors, above all to the relation of these new urban centers to the central administration. It is important to note, for example, that cities in the interior of the Balkans lack the signs of long-distance trade so evident in those of the Black Sea coast or in Greece. Phocaean Red Slip Wares (also known as Late Roman C), produced at Phocaea in western Anatolia, began to appear in significant quantities on the western Black Sea coast after 470 and remained relatively frequent until about 580. They are also abundant at Argos during the first half of the sixth century. Around 600, such wares were still in use on the site of Diocletian's palace in Split. Extensive excavations on sites in the interior, such as Ratiaria, Iatrus, Sacidava, Bregovina, and Karanovo, yielded only small quantities. All sites

[41] Cameron 1993:161. Like Thessalonica, sixth-century Chersonesus seems to have preserved the Hellenistic street grid, though some secondary streets were blocked by new religious buildings, such as the basilica "1935." The city expanded westward to the expense of an earlier cemetery. The theater in the southern part of the city was abandoned before 500. A cruciform church was erected in its ruins, either during or after Justinian's reign. Two-storied buildings were still erected during this period, such as the "Wine-dresser's House." See Bortoli-Kazanski and Kazanski 1987:448–50. Between 500 and 600, the city had at least ten churches. See Beliaev 1989:173. For the Uvarov basilica, see Kosciushko-Valiuzhinich 1902. Other churches were built during Justinian's reign at Mangup, Eski-Kermen, and Partenitae. See Zubar' and Pavlenko 1988:70.

[42] Dagron 1991:167.

in the interior, however, produced a large quantity of amphora sherds, which suggests that the relative absence of Phocaean Red Slip Ware is not an accident.[43]

This picture is confirmed by finds of lead seals. Among eighty-two sixth- to seventh-century specimens known from the northern Balkans, forty-six (56 percent) have only the name of the owner, without office or title.[44] They were most likely commercial seals.[45] The largest number were found at Constanţa (Tomis). The westernmost specimen found is that from Călăraşi, on the left bank of the Danube, just across from the important city of Silistra (Durostorum). In addition, two lead seals of clear Aegean provenance (one from Pergamon, the other from Ephesus) were found in Dobrudja. No such seal was found in the rest of the Balkans, an indication that commodities traded by seal owners did not reach the interior. The commercial circuit signalized by lead seals included but a small area easily accessible by sea. Disruption of commercial links between coastal trade centers and settlements in the interior illustrates the degree of autonomy of the northern Balkan cities, which Procopius listed by regions, rather than by provinces.

That this phenomenon was also associated with significant social changes is shown by the quality of buildings now erected within the urban area. To be sure, many buildings seem to have been abandoned, but the existence of a derelict and useless temple or gymnasium in the heart of an ancient city is no guide to the prosperity or otherwise of that city as a whole. Nor can mud and brick walls be described *ipso facto* as "barbarian." The inhabitants of early Byzantine cities displayed their wealth and status by building churches and paying for their lavish decoration with mosaic floors. Except in Thessalonica, there is no evidence for any other public buildings erected at that time. Caričin Grad (Justiniana Prima) was dominated by the acropolis on which the episcopal church was located. This further suggests that the power granted to local bishops

---

[43] Phocaean Red Slip Wares: Minchev 1983:197; Mackensen 1987:235; Poulter 1992:130; Opaiţ 1996:137. Argos: Abadie-Reynal 1989b:155. Split: Dvoržak Schrunk 1989:94. Phocaean Red Slip Wares also appear at Shkodër, in Albania; see Hoxha 1993:565. For sites in the interior, see Kuzmanov 1987:112; Böttger 1979:62; Scorpan 1978:160–1; Borisov 1988a:106; Jeremić and Milinković 1995:223. At Sadovec, there are no Phocaean Red Slip Wares. See Mackensen 1992:235.

[44] Barnea 1960b:323–4, 1966:279–81, and 1969; Nubar 1964; Culică 1975:246; Barnea 1975:159–61; Schultz 1978:100; Gaj-Popović 1980; Barnea 1981, 1982:202, 1984, 1985b:239–42, 1987a:203–4, 1987b:77–9, and 1990:316; Gerasimova-Tomova 1992:70. There is a wide variety of names, sometimes represented by more than one seal (e.g., Damianos, George Theodoulos, Leontius, and Peter). There are also cases of namesakes (four different individuals named John, three named Peter, and three named Theodore).

[45] Some may have been belonged to local merchants, as indicated by Thracian names, such as Boutzios, Bassos, or Moldozos. See Barnea 1987a.

by Justinian's legislation drastically altered the urban landscape. Newly built churches, such as that of Plovdiv (Philippopolis), often obstructed or even obliterated the old street grid. With few exceptions (e.g., Thessalonica), the forum ceased to represent the focus of building activity and was abandoned. Ancient baths were converted into churches, though *thermae* were still built anew during the 500s, as in Justiniana Prima. In some cases (Histria, Tropaeum Traiani, Diocletianopolis, Justiniana Prima, Butrint, Tocatlis, Athens, and Mantinea), archaeological excavations revealed the existence of houses with peristyled courtyards and apsed *triclinia*, used as main representative rooms. They were most likely residences of the rich, though attempts to identify their inhabitants with the new urban elite (e.g., bishops) should be treated with extreme caution. They are in sharp contrast with houses built in stone bonded with clay, which archaeologists often associate with the last building phase. That such buildings cannot be attributed to the invading Slavs, allegedly establishing themselves in the conquered and destroyed cities, is suggested by the house at Caričin Grad. Since, in some cases, such buildings encroached into earlier *villae urbanae*, they might indicate that the place of the rich was taken by the less well-off. The last decades of the Balkan cities may thus have witnessed a rise in the number of poorer citizens. Querns, spindle whorls, baking ovens, and smithies may illustrate a process of ruralization, which immediately preceded and was encouraged by the Slavic invasions. But the existing archaeological evidence suggests a much more complex picture. It is certainly difficult, if not impossible, to assess in each case the relative importance of the stone-cum-clay buildings. The absence of any agricultural tools which could be safely dated to the sixth or early seventh century is in itself significant. There is no reason to believe that these new houses or rooms built in stone bonded with clay were a hasty, if provisory, solution to the problem of countless refugees from the countryside, now savagely raided by the Slavs. Moreover, the goods found in the house at Caričin Grad suggest a military occupation which is otherwise comparable to that of contemporary forts.[46]

This trend is also recognizable in the disappearance, after *c.* 450, of medium-sized villa estates in the urban hinterland, which had provided the majority of decurions. To be sure, archaeologists identified significant numbers of *villae rusticae* and rural settlements dated to the first four centuries AD. After the middle of the fifth century, however, medium-sized estates seem to have completely disappeared. By 450, the last *villae*

---

[46] Hattersley-Smith 1988:169 and 299; Whittow 1990:18–19. Refugees from the countryside: Barnea et al. 1979:107.

rusticae, which had survived until then in the sheltered areas of Dalmatia and northeast Bosnia, were completely abandoned. The only evidence of rural *villae* comes from Akra Sophia, near Corinth, where a systematic archaeological exploration yielded a sumptuous villa with mosaic floor in room VII, probably a *triclinium*. A single fragment of hypocaust brick suggests the presence of a small bath which is otherwise unattested in the surviving architectural remains. The walls were built of rubble set in lime mortar mixed with large pebbles. A fragment of a late sixth- or early seventh-century amphora (Late Roman 2) was found embedded in the mortar of the foundations of the north wall of room VII. The owner of the villa may have been an imperial military official in charge with the defense of the near-by Hexamilion. Another *villa* was found in 1949 at Polače, on the island of Mljet in the Adriatic. It has been dated to the fifth or sixth century.[47]

On the other hand, some evidence exists that there were still large estates in the Balkans during the 500s. An inscription found near Sliven, in Bulgaria, refers to an ἐπίσπεψις, a state or church estate. By the time Procopius wrote his *Wars* there were still large herds of horses near Apri, in Thrace, probably belonging to a *domus divina*. A law of 535 shows that the St Sophia cathedral in Constantinople owned large estates and had a *scribinium* with cartularies located somewhere in Thrace. But the evidence of peasant settlements is very scarce. According to Procopius, Justinian "made the defenses so continuous in the estates (χωρία), that each farm (ἀγρός) either had been converted into a stronghold (φρούριον) or lies adjacent to one which is fortified." This has been interpreted as an indication of an important rural population in the sixth-century Balkans. Indeed, Procopius even provided an example of a village entirely transformed into a stronghold, due to Justinian's munificence. But he also described peasants becoming "makeshift soldiers for the occasion," thus suggesting that agricultural occupations were now abandoned. The only evidence for the survival of a significant peasant population comes from the immediate vicinity of the Capital. Theophylact Simocatta refers to a χωρίον some fifteen miles away from Heracleia, in Europe. The village had a large population and was a food supplier for the imperial armies. Two inscriptions found at Selymbria and Şarköy, in Thrace, refer to the estates of a certain Zemocarthos.

---

[47] Kurz 1969:99; Poulter 1983:86; Henning 1987:22–35 and figs. 7–11 (with a complete list of sites). Akra Sophia: Gregory 1985. Two other early Byzantine *villae* may have existed near Corinth and Sparta, but their date is uncertain. See Avramea 1997:127, 159, and 185. Polače: Nikolajević 1971:281; Duval 1971:109–18. A building complex found in 1930 at Breza, near Sarajevo, was interpreted as *aula* of an Ostrogothic high official, perhaps a *comes* (Basler 1993:28–9). The building is more likely a basilica.

Elsewhere the existence of open settlements with exclusively agricultural functions remains doubtful.[48]

Despite the evident bias of early Byzantine archaeology in the Balkans toward urban centers, the evidence for rural settlements is remarkably scanty. Recent excavations at Kurt Baiâr, near Slava Cercheză, in Dobrudja, not far from the presumed monastic site at Slava Rusă, unearthed a rectangular, single-roomed house built in stones bonded with clay and mud bricks. The building has two phases, dated to the fifth and sixth centuries, respectively. Salvage excavations near Novgrad, not far from the ancient site of Iatrus, have also revealed two similar structures, one of which is dated by a coin issued by Justin II. Altogether, this is all the evidence we have so far from the Balkans. There is nothing comparable to the village at Qasrin, in the Golan highlands, nothing similar to the two-storied peasant houses found in the hinterland of the city of Kyaneai, in Lycia, or to those found in the Silifke region of Cilicia. The rarity of rural settlements could be explained in reference to contemporary legislation. In 505, Emperor Anastasius was compelled to acknowledge the impossibility of collecting the *annona* in Thrace and to introduce the *coemptio*. Thirty years later, Justinian issued the novel 32, which attempted to stop an ever-accelerating decline of the peasant population in Haemimons and Moesia Inferior. Because of high-interest loan rates, peasants were compelled to forfeit their lands; some fled and some died of starvation, the general situation being described as worse than after a barbarian invasion. In that same year, Justinian's novel 33 extended the stipulation of novel 32 to Illyricum, because creditors there were taking the lands (*terrulae*) of the peasants. No improvement occurred and, ten years later, Justinian's novel 128 introduced the *epibole* to the fiscal law, in order to cope with the demographic instability of the countryside upsetting the process of tax collection. Every farmer was now burdened with liability for taxes from the abandoned land of his next-door neighbor. Justinian's successor, Justin II, twice granted tax exemptions for peasants in Moesia and Scythia Minor (novels 148 and 162). In both cases, at stake were food supplies for troops stationed in these two provinces. Whether or not barbarian invasions contributed to the rapid deterioration of the economic situation in the Balkans, the evidence cited suggests that in this region the rural class was on the verge

---

[48] *Codex Iustinianus* 1.2.24; Procopius, *Buildings* IV 1– 2, 4, and 10. Inscriptions: Velkov 1962: 60 (with n. 164) and 62. According to Agathias (v 11), the Cutrigur chieftain Zabergan, who led the invasion of 558/9, quickly reached Thrace after crossing many *deserted* villages in Moesia and Scythia Minor. For the rural population of the northern Balkans, see also Patoura 1985:206. There is no evidence to support Michel Kaplan's idea that burials found at Porto Cheli (lower town at Halieis) were those of slaves working on *villa* estates. See Rudolph 1979:297–8; Kaplan 1992:159.

of disappearing. This is substantiated by recruitment shortages, which were already visible during Justinian's reign.[49]

The rarity of rural settlements may explain the rarity of monasteries. The association between the two is strongly advocated by cases of monasteries established in densely populated regions with numerous rural communities. But the evidence for monasteries in the Balkans is very scarce. To be sure, literary sources indicate the existence of monks. During Justinian's reign, the "Scythian monks" were zealous supporters of a formula attempting to reconcile adherents of the council of Chalcedon with the Monophysites. A few decades later, at the time of Tiberius and Maurice, John Moschus wrote about hermitages around Thessalonica in his biographies of Abbot Palladius and David the Ascetic. In 592, Emperor Maurice, on the eve of his campaigns against the Sclavenes and the Avars, forbade soldiers or civil servants from becoming clerics or monks until their period of service has been completed. His edict brought a reprimand by Pope Gregory the Great, who argued that the emperor had no right to interfere with religious vocations. In response, Maurice agreed to limit the law to soldiers who had not yet served for three years. It has been argued that Maurice's edict referred to the male population of Thrace, an indirect indication of monasteries there. Though the edict was issued in connection with the Slav and Avar invasions into the Balkans, there is no evidence to support the idea that Maurice's edict referred to recruitment in Thrace. Soldiers and civil servants could have joined monasteries located anywhere else in the Empire.[50]

The archaeological evidence for monasteries is also very meager. From written sources we know that by 536 there were sixty-seven male monasteries in Constantinople and its vicinity, but archaeological investigations in the Balkans have yielded no comparable result. There is some evidence of monasteries on the Adriatic coast. A fifth-century monastic site was found on the island of Majsan, near Korčula. It was organized around two porticoed courtyards and included a small church with *memoria* containing St Maximus' relics. The site was still occupied during the second half of the sixth century, for it has also produced a Byzantine coin hoard closed under Justin II. At Isperikhovo, near Plovdiv, an early

---

[49] Kurt Baiâr: Opaiţ and Bănică 1992:105–6. Novgrad: Stefanov 1974:291–2. For other settlements, see Hood 1970; Gregory 1984b. Peasant houses in the Golan highlands, Lycia, and Cilicia: Sodini 1993:152. *Coemptio*: *Codex Iustinianus* 10.27.2; Kaplan 1992:378; Gorecki 1989:225. Recruitment shortages: Fotiou 1988.

[50] Monasteries and rural communities: Trombley 1985. "Scythian monks": Zeiller 1918:383–4; Barnea and Vulpe 1968:458–9; Moorhead 1994:125–8. Hermitages around Thessalonica: Rose 1887:15–6; Moutsopoulos 1987:129. Maurice's edict 110 of 592: Dölger 1924:13–14. See also Frazee 1982:276. Pope Gregory's reaction: *epp.* III 61, III 64, and VIII 10.

Byzantine monastery incorporated a small single-naved church with a baptistery on the southern side and another annex containing a font later added on the northwestern side. The rest of the complex consisted of a series of rooms, some roughly mortared with mud. They included a cattle shed and a baking oven. Tools for woodwork and agriculture and household pots show that soon after the church was built a group of monks settled here and cultivated the land. The complex was surrounded by a wall sometime during the sixth century. At Anevo, in the same area of Thrace, Bulgarian archaeologists recently explored another monastic complex, dated to Justinian's reign. East of the basilica at Palikura, near Stobi, in Macedonia, there was a courtyard and beyond this an octagonal baptistery and numerous other annexes. On the basis of this evidence, some believe Palikura was a monastic site. A cave monastery may have existed not far from the modern monastery Aladzha, near Varna. Its early dating to the fourth century is secured by fragments of glassware, but coins of Justinian indicate that the complex may have still been in use during the 500s. Finally, at Slava Rusă, in Dobrudja, recent excavations have unearthed a monastic complex with two single-naved churches and three building phases dated to the late fifth, early sixth, and late sixth centuries, respectively. Sometime in the last decades of the sixth century a wall was built around the complex.[51]

With this rarity of monasteries and rural settlements, the problem of urban change in the Balkans can be rephrased in new terms. It is now clear that during the sixth century, the region witnessed a serious contraction, but the complex readjustments taking place almost everywhere do not seem to have involved any rural sites. What was the role, if any, of the rural environment in the survival and, in some cases, the prosperity of sixth-century Balkan cities? There seems to be no simple answer to this question, but from the existing evidence it appears that urban life in the Balkans was not based on a thriving rural economy. All textual evidence indicates a sharp decline of the rural areas and archaeologists have not been able to identify any significant number of villages in the hinterland of the great cities. Moreover, the Church itself seems to have been rather resistant to the idea of implementing monastic communities in a region devoid of substantial rural population. If so, who fed the remaining urban population? There is no indication of agricultural work inside any of the sixth-century Balkan cities. The *Miracles of St Demetrius* suggest

---

[51] Monasteries in and around Constantinople: Gerostergios 1974:435; Frazee 1982:271. Majsan: Fisković 1981:146; Mirnik 1982; Cambi 1989:2420. Isperikhovo: Dzhambov 1956; Hoddinott 1975:297. Anevo: Dzhambov 1989:2519. Palikura: Hoddinott 1963:185; Mikulčić 1986a:233 and 246. Aladzha: Atanasov 1991:34–5. Slava Rusă: Opaiţ, Opaiţ, and Bănică 1992:113–17. For the problematic identification of churches associated with monastic sites, see Migotti 1995:125–6.

that a large city, such as Thessalonica, relied heavily on supplies of public corn, but it is dangerous to extrapolate this evidence to other Balkan cases. The explanation may lie at a more structural level, in the military and building programs implemented in the Balkans, in particular on the Danube frontier under Emperor Justinian.

THE *LIMES* AND THE SIXTH-CENTURY BALKANS

The idea of making the Lower Danube the frontier of the Roman state was an old one. It dates back to Julius Caesar. The natural and the military borders complemented each other and formed an intricate matrix of Roman imperial self-definition. In the mid-500s, Procopius of Caesarea still viewed the Danube as the barrier against barbarians, πρόβολον ἰσχυρότατον. Procopius was also a witness to the increasing differentiation between political and administrative frontiers, on one hand, and cultural boundaries, on the other. Long before the sixth century, the *limes* had ceased to be a purely military zone and had become an area of contact and exchange with populations living on the left bank of the Danube. Some argued that its main purpose was now that of a buffer zone, specifically designed to divert and to slow down, if not to stop, the invasions of the Slavs. Others believe that the Roman frontier was never intended to be a preclusive perimeter defense, but a deep zone that included the *limes* itself, the supporting provinces, and, in some cases, even the territories across the frontier. Denys Pringle's research on the African *limes* revealed a hierarchy of forts with various functions, operating on different levels in a sophisticated system of in-depth defense. The situation in the Balkans is equally instructive. According to Procopius, Justinian built or renewed more than 600 forts in the Balkans, eight times more than in the entire Asian part of the Empire. Moreover, recent excavations reveal that a number of then modern and sophisticated building techniques, such as the use of hexagonal bastions, so dear to the author of the *De Re Strategica*, were widely prevalent in the building of defenses on the Danube *limes* or in the interior.[52]

There is still a tendency among scholars to downplay the significance of this major building program or to treat Procopius' evidence with extreme suspicion. More recently, an inscription found at Ballshi (near Bylis), in Albania, clearly attests that the forts in Moesia, Scythia Minor,

---

[52] Procopius, *Buildings* IV 1.33; *De Re Strategica* 12, ed. G. T. Dennis (Washington, 1985), p. 35. For Africa, see Pringle 1981. See also Zanini 1988; Shuvalov 1991:40; Miller 1996:162. Justinian's reign coincided with the introduction of *proteichismata*; some walls were thickened and elevated and triangular or pentangular bastions were retained. Bastions were also blocked and converted into bastides. See Ovcharov 1973:14–16 and 18–19, and 1977:469; Biernacka-Lubańska 1982:219–20.

Illyricum, and Thrace were built for Justinian by his architect, Viktorinos. The evidence of this inscription suggests that Procopius should be given some credit for veracity.[53]

It has been long shown that Procopius' *Buildings* has three main themes: church building, fortifications, and water supply. Part of an imperial propaganda effort, all that Procopius describes under these topics is attributed to Justinian alone, as though the emperor personally initiated and carried it through. It is not without interest that Procopius sees a certain continuity between Justinian and his predecessors, particularly Constantine the Great. But Justinian does not follow Constantine's program in all details. "As if seeking to excuse his imperial predecessor's want of propriety," he builds an aqueduct and a public bath, churches, and a palace and stoas in Helenopolis (the native city of Constantine's mother). Not even Trajan is spared for Procopius' fault-finding approach. Unlike Justinian, the *Optimus Princeps* was "of an impetuous and active temperament and filled with resentment that his realm was not unlimited, but was bounded by the Ister River." Procopius' attitude toward Justinian's closer predecessors is also critical. The Long Walls illustrate an ill-applied strategic concept and Anastasius is blamed for the consequences of hastily erecting a fortress at Dara. He did not raise the walls of Theodosiopolis to an adequate height, in spite of rebaptizing the city after his imperial name. He relinquished Martyropolis to the Persians, "understanding that it was not possible to defend [the city] from hostile assault, since it had no defences," and died before the completion of the work at Melitene. In all those cases, Justinian is presented as having remedied the errors of his predecessors and, at least in the case of Martyropolis, as a more aggressive leader.[54]

But the tendency to exaggerate Justinian's achievements, particularly in comparison to those of his predecessors, was a feature built into the genre. The overall impression is that a sudden and overwhelming effect was brought about by Justinian's building policies. Procopius' narration is set in a timeless atmosphere, which may have been intended to suggest the permanence of the emperor's achievements. That the *Buildings* may be viewed as a panegyric is also shown by a comparison of Procopius'

---

[53] Feissel 1988; Avramea 1997:65–6. Skepticism toward Procopius' *Buildings* goes back to Edward Gibbon, who maintained that the forts mentioned by Procopius were simple towers surrounded by moats. See Evans 1996:222–3.

[54] Procopius, *Buildings* III 2.9–14, III 4.19, III 5.4– 12, IV 5–7 and 9, V 2.1–5. See also Evans 1970:223; Cameron 1985:86–7.

portrait of Justinian with other contemporary propaganda media. In the
Buildings, Justinian is "the founder of the civilized world," a builder *par
excellence*. This reminds one of an inscription from Callatis and of brick
stamps from Mesembria, both of which call Justinian φιλοκτίστης.[55]

On the other hand, with his *Buildings*, Procopius may be reflecting a
contemporary taste for the cataloguing of buildings, which is also recognizable in sixth-century chronicles and in special works about the physical history of cities. Book IV, which deals with the Balkans, looks,
however, like an annotated itinerary of the network of roads. The
Thracian list begins with the forts along the Via Egnatia. In his description of Scythia Minor, Procopius follows the old imperial road from
Tropaeum Traiani to the north.[56]

Is the *Buildings* then a purely rhetorical exercise? Some have argued
that Procopius' work is not a factual record, despite its appearance of documentary authenticity. Others believe that the *Buildings* has been under-
valued as a work of strategic insight and point to many links between
Book IV and the renaissance of military treatises in the sixth century, from
the Anonymus Byzantinus to the author of the *Strategikon*. In order to
assess Procopius' reliability, however, it is first necessary to identify his
sources. Noticing that Procopius' information is accurate and detailed,
some have argued that he found it all in the imperial archives. Others,
observing that the description in Book IV follows the network of roads,
concluded that Procopius used an official map. This may also explain why
most fort names are rendered in ablative or accusative plural (*-is*), as on
Roman *itineraria picta*. Lists of forts in Book IV are given by provinces,
which also suggests that Procopius' source may have been some sort of
administrative document. It is not without interest that when Procopius
introduced his own narrative, he had a completely different set of terms,
indicating not administrative boundaries, but the traditional ethnic geography of the Balkans, which is also identifiable in Viktorinos' inscription
from Ballshi.[57]

---

[55] Procopius, *Buildings* IV 1.17 (ὁ τῆς οἰκουμένης οἰκιστής). Inscription: Popescu 1967:170. Brick
stamps: Ognenova-Marinova 1969:109 and 111. *Buildings* as panegyric: Cameron 1985:90 and
109; Whitby 1985a:141. *Contra*: Rousseau 1998.

[56] Cameron 1985:90; Adshead 1990:108; Aricescu 1977:170.

[57] Procopius acknowledges the existence of a strategy underpinning Justinian's buildings in the
Balkans: "he made the defenses so continuous in the estates that each farm either has been con-
verted into a stronghold or lies adjacent to one which is fortified" (Procopius, *Buildings* IV 1.35).
See Cameron 1985:110; Adshead 1990:107 and 113; Evans 1972:77 and 81. For fort names in the
Buildings, see Beshevliev 1967b:278. Viktorinos' inscription: Feissel 1988:143. In his description,
Procopius starts in Illyricum with Justiniana Prima (Dardania), then moves to Dacia Mediterranea
(without naming it), then to Epirus Vetus, Hellas, Thessaly, Euboea, and Macedonia. In the lists
at IV 4, the order is different: Epirus Nova, Epirus Vetus, Macedonia, Thessaly, Dardania, Dacia
Mediterranea, and Dacia Ripensis (the latter two not being mentioned by name). Thrace is

The description of the road from Strongylum to Rhegium, which was probably the first segment of the Via Egnatia, seems to be based on personal experience. Procopius may indeed have seen that road and its exceptionally coarse paving stones, giving the appearance "not simply of being laid together at the joints," but of having actually grown together. But the description of Justiniana Prima, despite the significance of the city for the purpose of the *Buildings*, is vague and lacking in detail. In contrast to other Books, Book IV lists no churches, and the lack of coherence in the direction of the account may reflect lack of personal experience in the area. There is also some contradictory information. In his *Secret History*, Procopius claims that no buildings were restored and nothing else was done in the whole of Greece, including Athens. In the *Buildings*, we are told that all cities south of Thermopylae were made safe and their walls renewed, and Procopius cites Corinth, Athens, and Plataea. There is extensive repetition of fort names in Book IV, usually of two forts in two neighboring provinces. This suggests that Procopius' source listed a particular fort only under a particular province. Unfamiliar with Balkan geography, in particular with provincial boundaries, Procopius may have ascribed a fort to more than one province.[58]

Despite all this, however, he seems to have been well aware of what he was trying to do in Book IV. To Procopius, the Danube, when getting "close to Dacia, for the first time clearly forms the boundary between the barbarians, who hold its left bank, and the territory of the Romans, which is on the right." His emphasis on the Danube is meant to help explain that the entire strategy underlying the building program in the Balkans was centered upon the Danube. The forts built by Justinian, according to Procopius, were designed as a response to a particular kind of warfare, namely sudden attacks coming from the north. Justinian "reflected that if it should ever be possible for the enemy to break through somehow, they would fall upon fields which would be entirely unguarded, would enslave the whole population, from the youths upwards, and would plunder all their property." The defense system was therefore designed to protect the estates (χωρία) and to turn each farm

---

described in the following order: Moesia Inferior, Scythia (Minor), Europe, Rhodope. Between Scythia (Minor) and Europe, there is a section in which we are told that "all the building that was done by the emperor Justinian in Dardania, Epirus, Macedonia, and the other parts of Illyricum, also in Greece and along the river Ister has already been described by me" (*Buildings* IV 8). Procopius then resumes the description of Thrace in the following order: Europe, Rhodope, Thrace, Moesia, and ἐν τῇ μεσογείᾳ. Since Moesia includes cities that were actually located in Scythia (Minor), it is possible that ἐν τῇ μεσογείᾳ refers to the newly created *quaestura exercitus*.

[58] *Buildings* IV 2 and 8; *Secret History* 23.33. See Cameron 1985:94; Adshead 1990:108. To Procopius, "the spurs of the Caucasus range extend in one direction to the north and west and continue into Illyricum and Thrace" (*Wars* VIII 3.3).

(ἀγρὸς ἕκαστος) into a stronghold (φρούριον). Procopius thus suggests that barbarian raids were targeted not on large cities, but on "fields" in the countryside. In any case, he implies that Justinian's building program was a direct response to the impact and direction of these attacks. Some went as far as to claim that the *Buildings* may be interpreted as a "codified" map of the barbarian invasions into the Balkans, of their direction and impact.[59]

Justinian's strategy, according to Procopius, was based on three successive lines, one along the Danube, the other along the Balkans, and a third one along the Istranca Dağlar range. But a closer examination of only one sector of the defense system (the region between the Iskăr and the Ogost rivers in northern Bulgaria) reveals that during Justinian's reign, another line of defense was added between the one along the Danube and the one along the Balkans. A simple reckoning of the forts listed in Book IV (Table 6) shows that northern Illyricum received the largest number of forts in the Balkans. The highest density was that of northern Dacia Ripensis, especially in the area of the Timok valley. Many forts were in fact restored, not built anew. This may relate to the fact that Illyrian armies were often involved in wars in Italy or Pannonia and Illyricum lacked large cities on which the defense network could be centered. The solution in Illyricum seems to have been decentralization, as suggested by the absence from Procopius' account of both Dacia Ripensis and Dacia Mediterranea. Both were replaced as administrative units by regions centered on major urban centers. By contrast, Thrace had large cities in the plains, such as Diocletianopolis, Philippopolis or Beroe. Moreover, Procopius' description of Thrace lacks the division into "new" and "restored" forts. Topeiros is referred to in the lists as "new," but elsewhere we are told that Justinian only "added a great deal to the height of the wall." In Thrace, Justinian's approach was based more on administrative measures. Novel 26 gave civilian and military power to the praetorian prefect, while novel 34 extended the power of the governor of Haemimons to Moesia Inferior. Finally, the creation of the *quaestura exercitus* in 536 radically altered the old administrative structure of the

---

[59] *Buildings* IV 1 and 5. Procopius used the plural Δακίας, which referred to both Dacia Ripensis and Dacia Mediterranea, none of which was mentioned in the text. For the Danube and the strategy of the building program, see *Buildings* IV 1: "For these works have been executed with due regard for the nearness of the Ister river and for the consequent necessity imposed by the barbarians who threaten the land." For Justinian's forts and attacks from the north, see ibid.: "Indeed it was the custom of these peoples [barbarians] to rise and make war upon their enemies for no particular cause, and open hostilities without sending an embassy, and they did not bring their struggle to an end through any treaty, or cease operations for any specified period, but they made their attacks without provocation and reached a decision by the sword alone." For the *Buildings* as a "codified map" of barbarian invasions, see Ivanov 1984.

region. That Justinian's strategy described in Book IV *was* realized in practice is confirmed by the inscription of Ballshi, dedicated to Viktorinos, the imperial architect. Procopius' description may thus be viewed, in its essence, as sound. The archaeological evidence substantiates this conclusion.[60]

THE LIMES AND THE BALKANS: AN ARCHAEOLOGICAL SURVEY (FIGURE 2)

The archaeological evidence from Scythia Minor and the neighboring regions on the Black Sea coast reveals a variety of forts. At Ovidiu, ten kilometers to the north of the modern city of Constanţa, Romanian archaeologists explored a *quadriburgium* destroyed in the mid-sixth century. At Cape Kaliakra (Acrae), there were three successive defense lines across the promontory, at 1.2 km distance from the sea. New buildings with walls of stone bound with mortar were erected at Capidava as late as the last quarter of the sixth century. At Garvăn (Dinogetia), recent excavations by Alexandru Barnea confirmed that after a destruction coin-dated to 559, occupation of the fort ceased, though traces of a non-military habitation were found, which were dated sometime after 559. The three-aisled basilica built at some point during the fourth or the fifth century near the city's southern tower was restored first under Anastasius, then under Justinian. Small houses with walls of stone and adobe bonded with clay are in sharp contrast to the "aristocratic" houses of Histria. Similar buildings were also found at Musait (Sacidava), and have been dated to the late sixth and early seventh centuries. The large fort at Pantelimonu de Sus (Ulmetum) excavated before World War I by Vasile Pârvan was rebuilt by the *lanciarii iuniorii* of the imperial palace in Constantinople, as evidenced by the inscription found in one of the towers. The most interesting site, however, is Topraichioi, in central

---

[60] *Buildings* IV 11. According to Procopius, all forts along the Danube received garrisons of troops (IV 1). By contrast, the defense of Greece before Justinian's building program relied only on "some peasants from the neighborhood, [who,] when the enemy came down, would suddenly change their mode of life, and becoming makeshift soldiers for the occasion, would keep guard there in turn" (IV 2). It is not without interest that when describing the rebuilding of forts, Procopius refers to small settlements. When speaking of big cities, he describes only repairing of walls or minor works of fortification. Note that Book IV contains a rare reference to an imperial architect, Theodore, who built the fortress Episkopeia (IV 8). For the defense system between the Iskăr and the Ogost rivers in northern Bulgaria, see Poutiers 1975:61–3. Density of forts in northern Dacia Ripensis: Ivanov 1983:42–3 and 1984:49. Procopius lists names of forts under the name of the city, preceded by ὑπό, an indication that forts were under the direct administration of that city. In Dacia Mediterranea, forts are listed by regions (χώραι) belonging to various cities. Serdica had two such χώραι, one in Cabetzus, the other around an unknown city. The average distance between cities along the Danube is 50 km, that between forts, 12 km (Poutiers 1975:61). Administrative measures in Thrace: Ivanov 1984:50.

Table 6 *The fortification of the Balkans according to Procopius' Buildings* IV

	New	Restored	Total
ILLYRICUM:	92	207	394
Epirus Nova	32	26	58
Epirus Vetus	12	24	36
Macedonia			46
Thessaly		7	7
Dardania	8	61	69
(Dacia Mediterranea):		140	
near Serdica			9
Cabetzus region	1	16	17
near city?	5	23	28
near Germenne	1	6	7
near Pauta(lia)			5
Kasseta region			5
near Naissus	32	7	39
near Remesiana			30
(Dacia Ripensis):		38	
near Aquae	1	37	38
THRACE:			179
Europe			2
Rhodope			12
Thrace			35
Haemimons			53
Moesia Inferior			51
μεσογεία			26
LIMES:			85
(Moesia Superior)			28
(Dacia Ripensis)			29
(Moesia Inferior)			20
(Scythia Minor)			8

Dobrudja, where two Romanian archaeologists, Mihai Zahariade and Andrei Opaiţ, excavated a *burgus*. The nature of activity within this small fortification seems to have drastically changed in the mid-fifth century, when a considerable reduction in the quantity of weaponry is recorded. The fortification gradually lost its military nature and became a store-house for the local military *annona* with the aim of ensuring the supplies of troops passing by.[61]

[61] Ovidiu: Bucovală and Papuc 1981 and 1986. Cape Kaliakra: Dimitrov 1985:123. Capidava: Florescu and Covacef 1988–9:203. Garvăn: Barnea 1986:448 and 1984:344. For a similar situation identified at Tropaeum Traiani, see Papuc 1977:358. That the basilica at Garvăn was restored under Anastasius is indicated by bricks from the nave's pavement with stamps bearing the emperor's name. See Barnea 1958:295–6 and 1980:251. Musait: Scorpan 1974:114. Pantelimonu de Sus: Barnea and Vulpe 1968:423. Topraichioi: Zahariade and Opaiţ 1986:565, 567, and 569–71.

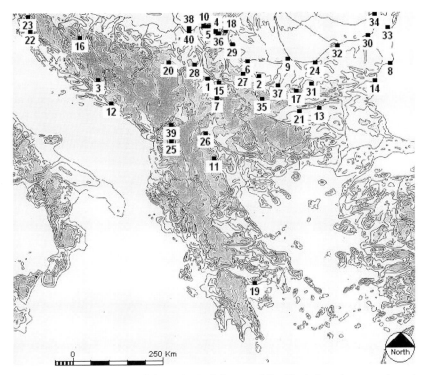

Figure 2 Location map of the principal forts and fortified churches mentioned in the text

1 – Balajnac; 2 – Berkovica; 3 – Biograci; 4 – Boljetin; 5 – Bosman; 6 – Botevo; 7 – Bregovina; 8 – Cape Kaliakra; 9 – Celei; 10 – Čezava; 11 – Debrešte; 12 – Dubrovnik; 13 – Dyadovo; 14 – Dzhanavar Tepe; 15 – Gamzigrad; 16 – Gornji Vrbljani; 17 – Gradăt; 18 – Hajdučka Vodenica; 19 – Isthmia; 20 – Jelica; 21 – Karasura; 22 – Kaštelina; 23 – Korintija; 24 – Krivina (Iatrus); 25 – Kruja; 26 – Markovi Kuli; 27 – Mikhailovgrad (Montana); 28 – Momčilov Grad; 29 – Mora Vagei; 30 – Musait (Sacidava); 31 – Nikiup (Nicopolis ad Istrum); 32 – Nova Cherna; 33 – Ovidiu; 34 – Pantelimonu de Sus (Ulmetum); 35 – Pirdop; 36 – Ravna; 37 – Sadovec (Sadovsko kale and Golemanovo kale); 38 – Sapaja; 39 – Shurdhah; 40 – Svetinja.

North of the Stara Planina range, the most striking feature is the ubiquity of fortified hilltop sites, concentrated along river valleys and the northern slopes of the mountains, occupying strongly defensive positions perched above cliffs or on top of steep-sided hills. Few have been explored by systematic excavations, but those that have (Nova Cherna, Krivina/Iatrus, Sivri Tepe near Kochovo, Zmei kale near Koprivec, Gradăt near Batoshevo, Krumovo kale near Tărgovishte, Dolno Kabda, Sadovsko kale near Sadovec, Biala, and Shumen) seem to have been substantially restored at some point during the sixth century, most likely during Justinian's reign. That, in some cases, restoration may have started earlier than that is indicated by an inscription mentioning Emperor

Anastasius, which was found at Vavovo kale near Gradec. These forts were built with walls of ashlar filled up with white mortar and rubble (*opus implectum*). Walls are massive, with towers along the circuit and double enclosures (*proteichismata*) sometimes added to earlier fortifications, as in Shumen. These forts are called πόλεις by Theophylact Simocatta. For example, he refers twice to Iatrus as a πόλις. After being destroyed by the Huns in the mid-400s, Iatrus had been abandoned for at least fifty years. When building restarted in phase D (late fifth to early sixth century), the πόλις had turned into a simple fort. The only building in stone and the largest on site is the basilica. A building with a portico (Building XXXIII), but with no apparent use as dwelling, may have had some representative role, perhaps in connection with the military commander of the garrison. In the ruins of the fourth-century *horreum*, a complex of eleven houses was built, with walls of stones and mud bricks. A two-storied house was located in the southeastern corner of the *horreum*. On top of the former *principia*, now abandoned, a workshop was erected, which had a brick-made kiln. All houses were buildings of adobe or stones bonded with clay. But the use of glass vessels (*Stengelgläser*) seems to have continued, though it remains unclear whether they were of local production or imports. During phase E, covering most of the seventh century, houses built in stone bonded with clay produced handmade pottery and a bow brooch. More important, the faunal material from this period typically contains a large number of species, particularly dog and wild animals, which suggests an increasing reliance on hunting for meat procurement.[62]

A similar picture can be drawn on the basis of excavations at Nikiup (Nicopolis ad Istrum). The Roman city had been abandoned before the early 400s. The early Byzantine fort built in the former city's southeastern corner encloses an area of 5.74 ha, little more than one fourth of the size of the Roman city (21.55 ha). Early Byzantine Nicopolis had no regular street grid and no agora surrounded by public buildings. A large basilica, built at the highest point on the eastern side of the enclosure, was the dominant feature within the defenses. A second, single-naved

[62] Theophylact Simocatta VII 2.16 and VII 13.9. Iatrus: see Mitova-Dzhonova 1968:13 and 15 fig. 4; Wachtel 1974:140; Gomolka 1976:40; Herrmann 1979a:18, 1979b:114–15, 1986a:10, and 1987a; Bierbrauer 1986:457; Döhle 1989:41; Bülow 1990:369, 372, and 383; Dinchev 1997a:50. For faunal remains, see Bartosiewicz and Choyke 1991:191. Sivri Tepe: Antonova 1970:304. Krumovo kale and Dolno Kabda: Ovcharov 1971. Biala: Dimitrov 1985:125. Vavovo kale: Velkov and Lisikov 1994:263. Shumen: Antonova 1987:55–6. For *opus implectum* and other building techniques, see Biernacka-Lubańska 1982; Poulter 1983:98–9. At Sadovsko kale, Ivan Velkov's excavations focused exclusively on the western half of the plateau and left most of the fort unearthed. As a consequence, the plan of the fort, as published in 1934, is wrongly viewed as a "classical" example of early Byzantine defense architecture in the Balkans. See Werner 1992:409.

church was still in use in the last quarter of the sixth century, as evidenced by a coin struck for Emperor Tiberius II, which was found above the nave floor. Despite clear evidence that the large basilica was destroyed by fire, the absence of metal fittings and roof-tiles from the destruction levels suggests that the church had been systematically stripped of reusable material, before being abandoned. A series of buildings running from east to west seems to have served as barracks or storehouses. In the center of the fort there was a two-roomed structure, perhaps a workshop, crudely built with limestone blocks and reused architectural fragments bonded with earth and supporting mud walls. Large "open spaces" existed along the northern side of the site, on the western side and around the basilica. There is no sign of large-scale grain cultivation and there seems to have been a shift from winter-sown cereal crops to garden cultivation of millet and legumes, which could have been grown close to the city or, conceivably, in the open land which existed inside the defenses.[63]

It has been argued that since most of the forts in Moesia Inferior were built in isolated and almost inaccessible sites, they might not have been occupied permanently. However, most of them had at least one church, sometimes with a baptistery, as in Gradăt. Moreover, houses built in the stone-cum-clay technique have been found on many sites, as has evidence of agricultural (sickles, at Gradăt) and industrial activities (a smithy in the pentagonal tower at Sadovsko kale). At Sadovsko kale, one of the rooms built against the fort's wall produced twenty-nine gold coins, while two skeletons were found in the neighboring room, in a non-burial context, together with five gold coins and silver jewels, including two bow brooches, all scattered on the room's floor. The rooms immediately next to the pentagonal tower have been interpreted as belonging to elite members of the fort's garrison, clearly caught by surprise and killed during an attack.[64]

How did the occupation on these sites end? At Nova Cherna, numerous traces of fire catastrophe were found within the *quadriburgium*, but this event is dated to the first half of the sixth century. Clear evidence of destruction by fire was found in several parts of the fort at Gradăt, the last coins found there being issued under Justinian. At Sadovsko kale, the archaeological evidence from rooms 2 and 3 clearly indicates an attack,

---

[63] Poulter 1995:40–2, 44, 46, 166, and 181. At Iatrus, the soldiers' diet seems to have included oats and peas, arguably cultivated on site. See Hajnalová 1982:232. At Voivoda, near Shumen, a house built parallel to the fort's wall has been interpreted as a grinding area. The associated agricultural tools, however, are of a much later date. See Damianov 1976:17 and 24.

[64] Gradăt: Milchev and Koicheva 1978a:60. Sadovsko Kale: Werner 1992:411. Other churches within forts: Milchev and Koicheva 1978b:25, 27, and 31; Soustal 1991:344 and 349. All were three-aisled basilicas. Houses: Milchev and Koicheva 1978a:60; Milchev and Draganov 1992:39; Uenze 1992:125; Antonova 1987:61.

which, however, does not seem to have been followed by either fire destruction or systematic plundering. The last coins found on the site are those of Maurice.[65]

The situation is slightly different on the territory of the former provinces Dacia Ripensis and Moesia Superior. Some forts were restored during Anastasius' or Justin I's reign, during Justinian's reign, or as late as Justin II's reign. Sixth-century forts were at about six kilometers from each other, in a sight distance, with *refugia* on hilltops, no farther than 150 to 200 m away from the Danube line. Many were square or rectangular in plan. The preference for angular architecture so typical of Justinian's reign is also visible. More often than not, these forts incorporate into a larger fortification an older, fourth-century *burgus*. Some forts were completely destroyed by fire at some point during the last quarter of the sixth century. Others were simply abandoned.[66]

At Gamzigrad, the imperial palace was abandoned as early as the fourth century. During Theodosius I's reign, a basilica was built on top of the southern wing of the palace, and a glass workshop was installed in the former bath. After being destroyed sometime during the sixth century, the basilica was restored and a baptistery added on its southern side. A small settlement with houses built in stone bonded with earth appeared around the church. During most of the sixth century, Gamzigrad may have functioned as a fortified village. The presence of a considerable number of querns and agricultural implements bespeaks its rural character. Bulgarian excavations at Mikhailovgrad (Montana) have revealed a house built near the northwestern tower. The house produced a significant quantity of amphora sherds and agricultural implements, as well as a scale. Fragments of bronze vessels may indicate a workshop. The settlement had only one single-naved church. Evidence of long-term occupation also comes from Golemanovo kale. The fort had between thirty-five and forty houses, in addition to about forty to fifty storage rooms. The most impressive feature of this site is the presence of two-storied houses with no heating facilities, such as I δ or the so-called "Nestor house" (named after the Romanian archaeologist Ion Nestor, who excavated it in 1937). The latter produced a hoard of seven gold coins, in addition to silver jewels (including a pectoral cross), illustrating the wealth of its

---

[65] Nova Cherna: Milchev and Angelova 1970:36; Ivanov 1974:68–9; Milchev 1977:351–7. For Gradăt, see Milchev and Koicheva 1978a:60–1. For Sadovsko kale, see Uenze 1992:127.

[66] Distance between forts: Janković 1981:208 and 211. Restoration under Anastasius or Justin I: Gabričević 1986:72. Restoration under Justinian: Uenze 1992:97; Jovanović 1982–3:328 and 330. Restoration under Justin II: Milošević and Jeremić 1986:250. For examples of angular architecture, see Kondić 1982–3a:141; Kondić 1984a:142. Incorporation of older *burgi*: Kondić 1984a:144–7. Destruction by fire: Tudor 1965:124; Uenze 1992:107 (*c.* 580). Abandoned forts: Jovanović 1982–3:330; Čermanović-Kuzmanović and Stanković 1986:455; Atanasova 1987:125; Atanassova-Georgieva 1974:167.

inhabitants. All houses were built in stone bonded with clay. The abundance of agricultural implements and spindle whorls has been too hastily interpreted as indication of a rural settlement, with no military function. Similar houses with glass windows and heating facilities were found on the acropolis of the site at Mokranjska stena, in the Iron Gates segment of the frontier. They are in sharp contrast with poorer dwellings in the lower part of the settlement.[67] Closer to the Danube line, smaller forts produced evidence of more modest dwellings. At Celei (Sucidava), on the left bank, rooms with brick ovens were built against the curtain. A two-roomed building was found in the middle of the fort, not far from a *hypocaustum* probably belonging to a larger building, now completely destroyed. A "secret fountain" outside the fort had an underground access beneath the southern wall. Small rooms built against the curtain were also found at Hajdučka Vodenica, and wattle-walled houses appeared at Bosman. At Mora Vagei, there were no buildings at all, which may suggest that soldiers lived in tents. Some forts had single-naved churches, as in Celei, with burials both inside and outside the basilica. The fort at Golemanovo kale produced an unique case of a two-storied church, included in a bastion (*peribolos*) on the northern rampart. An older church built outside the fort continued to be used during the 500s, but its baptismal function was transferred to the intramural basilica. In other cases, the church stood between the main walls and the *proteichisma*. At Berkovica, the three-aisled basilica built outside the fort, immediately next to its wall, was later incorporated into a large bastion-like structure protruding from the fort's precinct. A second church was incorporated with its apse into the fort's northeast rampart. At Botevo, a small military outpost near Ratiaria, Bulgarian archaeologists discovered in 1947 a church of cruciform plan.[68]

In addition, the northern Balkans provide two examples of fortified

---

[67] See Janković 1981:212. Gamzigrad: Srejović, Lalović, and Janković 1980:77; Popović 1982:556 and 557 fig. 13; Srejović 1986:90. Mikhailovgrad: Aleksandrov 1987:64 and 79. Because of the presence of agricultural implements, Joachim Henning (1986:107) believed the Mikhailovgrad site had no military function. For Golemanovo kale, see Uenze 1992:116–19; Werner 1992:415. Werner (1992:403) believed that the site at Golemanovo kale was not a military one because no structure was found on site that could be interpreted as *horreum*. In fact, very few, if any, *horrea* were erected on sixth-century military sites in the Balkans.

[68] "Secret fountain" at Celei: Tudor 1965:109 and 116–17. Another well was found at Bosman (Kondić 1982–3a:141 and 143). Rooms built against the walls: Jovanović 1982–3:321. Mora Vagei: Čermanović-Kuzmanović and Stanković 1986:454–5. The occupation of the site is evidenced by six *dolia* and faunal remains, the majority of which are of pig. The fort had a small port, an indication that supplies for the garrison may have come via the Danube river. Another anchorage is said to have existed at the neighboring fort at Čezava (Kondić 1984a:155), but does not appear on any of the published plans. For the church and the cemetery at Celei, see Tudor 1965:111; Tudor, Toropu, Tătulea, and Nica 1980. For the two-storied church at Golemanovo kale, see Uenze 1992:52. Berkovica: Mitova-Dzhonova 1974:342–3 and 1984:340–1. Botevo: Hoddinott 1975:242.

churches built in the middle of nowhere, apparently without any related settlements or cemeteries. At Dzhanavar Tepe, 4 km south of Varna, in Bulgaria, a single-naved basilica was built with projecting north and south rooms inscribing both apse and narthex, all in the form of powerful towers. The one on the northwestern side was a baptistery. Some have suggested Syrian influences, but there is no doubt as to the defensive character of the complex. A still more compelling example is the Stag's basilica at Pirdop, in western Bulgaria, with a massive rectangular wall with four angle towers enclosing the church. The precinct seems to have been built at the same time as the extant church. Despite claims to the contrary, the defensive character of the complex is betrayed not only by its walls and towers, but also by barrel vaults and domes replacing the timber roof during the last building phase. It is not clear why these two churches were fortified in this way. Taking into consideration their isolated location, however, it may be possible to associate them with churches built within city or fort ramparts or close to the strongest parts of the precincts.[69]

The situation in Moesia Superior is remarkably similar. Under Justinian, no less than nine new forts were built in the Iron Gates segment of the Danube *limes*, three of which incorporated older *burgi*. The only period of restoration or building indicated by coin-dated archaeological contexts is indeed that of Justinian's reign, as clearly shown by excavations at Sapaja, Saldum, Čezava, and Svetinja. Wattle-walled houses have been found at Ravna and Svetinja, near Viminacium. In the latter case, they were all similar in size and form, with surfaces ranging from twenty to twenty-seven square meters. Loom weights found in houses 1 and 3 suggest that weaving was an important activity. With the exception of house 3, which produced only seeds of millet, most samples of grain seeds from Svetinja were mixtures of wheat, rye, barley, and millet, a clear indication of three-field rotation. Supplies of corn undoubtedly came from outside the small military settlement, probably from the neighboring city of Viminacium. During the third building phase, which is coin-dated to the end of the sixth century, a smithy was established on the other side

---

[69] Dzhanavar Tepe: Pillinger 1985:285–7. The church has been dated on no solid grounds to the fifth century (Hoddinott 1975:327). Other examples of cross-shaped churches in the Balkans: Carevec (Hoddinott 1975:251), Cărkvishte (Hoddinott 1975:279), the basilica D in Caričin Grad (Duval 1984:419), and the H. David basilica in Thessalonica (Krautheimer 1986:239–40). As suggested by the Carevec basilica, such churches might have served as martyria. For Pirdop, see Hoddinott 1975:327; Mitova-Dzhonova 1974:56; Chaneva-Dechevska 1984:619; Pillinger 1985:284–5; Krautheimer 1986:251–2. Though the last building phase may be Justinianic, a final remodeling of the church seem to have occurred sometime during the last third of the sixth century. To my knowledge, there are no other examples of isolated churches in the Balkans, despite claims to the contrary (Mikulčić 1986a:244). The only other case is located outside the area under discussion, in Istria. See Šonje 1976 and 1976–8.

of the rampart. The house produced a considerable quantity of soot with iron dust and slag. Elsewhere, there is evidence of storage facilities, possibly designed for supplies of corn from other areas. At Sapaja and Čezava, despite an abundance of ceramic material testifying to the intensity of human activity, there were no buildings at all. Soldiers may have resided in tents. But the forts at Čezava, Veliki Gradac, and Boljetin were dominated by single-naved churches, the latter two with later additions of baptisteries. Fire destruction was only attested at Ravna (on the profile A-A' at the southwest wall) and dated by archaeologists to 596 on purely historical grounds. At Svetinja, the second building phase ended with heavy destruction as evidenced by a thick layer of rubble mixed with fallen parts of the upper rampart construction. This destruction has been coin-dated between 575 and 587. After restoration, the settlement in phase III was abandoned at some point after 590/1, the date of the last coin found on the site. At Saldum and Čezava, the abandonment may have taken place shortly after 592/3 and 593/4, respectively.[70]

In the interior, the evidence of forts has only recently come to light. In connection with special measures taken for the protection of the mining district in the Morava valley, several forts seem to have been built at key points. At Bregovina, near Caričin Grad, the only fully excavated building is the three-aisled basilica, which incorporated one of the fort's towers. A sixth-century coin was found in the middle of the nave. Six other, only partially excavated, structures within the fort produced evidence of the stone-cum-clay technique. The fort at Balajnac, near Niš, had a large, remarkably well-preserved, cistern, which produced a coin minted for Emperor Justinian. Very little is known about other buildings in the interior of the fort or about the date of its abandonment. Several other forts have been only partially explored in the iron ore district of

---

[70] Fire destruction at Ravna: Kondić 1982–3b:249. Abandoned sites: Popović 1987:12–13; Petrović 1982–3:133; Vašić 1990:907. Justinianic forts in northern Serbia: Vašić and Kondić 1986:555; Popović 1991:14; Vašić 1994–5. Sapaja: Dimitrijević 1982–3:47–9. Saldum: Kondić 1974:46; Petrović 1982–3:133. Transdrobeta: Vašić 1999:35. Čezava: Kondić 1974:41; Vašić 1982–3:102 and 1990:907. Miloje Vašić's subdivision of the sixth-century phase at Čezava into two sub-phases is not supported by the published archaeological profiles. For Svetinja, see Popović 1987:10; Milošević 1987:57. The construction of the bulwark across the narrow strip of land between the Dunavac and the Mlava bed is coin-dated to 542/3. New houses were built under Justin II and Maurice on both sides of the rampart. Svetinja has recently been interpreted as port, and the bulwark as wharf. See Mirković 1999:24–5. The soldiers who manned the bulwark (believed to be Gepid mercenaries, because of the stamped pottery found on the site) most probably came from Viminacium. For wattle-walled houses, see Kondić 1982–3b:249; Popović 1987:12–13; Milošević 1987:49. For samples of grain seeds, see Borojević 1987:67 and 70. For the smithy, see Popović 1987:28–31; Milošević 1987: 47. Among artifacts found in the house, there were two folles struck for Maurice in 587/8 and 590/1, respectively, in addition to parts of two armors made of small rectangular iron plates and a fragment of a comb case sheath. For storage facilities, see Vašić and Kondić 1986:558. For fort churches, see Bošković 1978:437; Kondić 1984a:155; Vašić 1990:907.

Tutin, in southern Serbia. The most impressive site in this region, however, is Jelica-Gradina, near Čačak. Within the area enclosed by walls, a building was found, with walls of stone bonded with clay. The building produced fragments of quern stones and ceramic and glass remains. The site had at least three churches, one of which was an extramural, cemeterial basilica. Basilica C had a cruciform baptistery with walls decorated with frescoes. Fragments of window glass also point to a decoration unusually lavish for a fort basilica. The church produced a pentanummion struck for Justinian between 526 and 537 and the excavator believes that the fort was built under Justinian, in the 530s. However, twelve burials within and outside basilica C had no associated finds. The Jelica-Gradina fort also had a martyrium, which produced a silver reliquary, now lost. Another group of burials – women, men, and children – was found inside basilica A. The associated grave-goods (a bronze buckle and a *Vogelfibel*) indicate a date in the 500s. A third cemetery of thirty-one burials, including a burial chamber, was found within and around the third church, most probably a *basilica coemeterialis*. A gold coin struck for Emperor Justin II was found near the burial chamber. It gives a *terminus a quo* for this cemetery. The presence of burnt layers in various parts of the site has been interpreted as an indication that habitation within the fort ended in violence, but no chronological evidence exists for this event, while the occupation of the site during the seventh century remains doubtful. Field surveys and trial excavations in the same region identified four other forts, all of which produced evidence of a sixth-century, perhaps Justinianic, occupation. The same is true for the fort at Momčilov Grad near Potočac, which produced a great number of coins issued under Justinian's reign. By contrast, the fort near Pautalia was built in the early 400s. When Procopius spoke of Justinian restoring Pautalia, he may have referred to this fort, not to the city itself.[71]

The date established on the basis of coin finds for the small fort at Dyadovo, in Thrace, excavated by a Dutch-Bulgarian team, is confirmed by an inscription found near Nova Zagora indicating substantial building activity during Justinian's reign. Radiocarbon dating of grain seeds from houses destroyed by fire at the end of the building phase C indicate that the neighboring fort at Karasura was rebuilt at some point after the early sixth century, thus confirming Procopius' textual evidence. Among all

---

[71] Forts in the Morava basin: Werner 1986:561–4. Bregovina: Popović 1989–90; Jeremić and Milinković 1995; Milinković 1999. Balajnac: Jeremić 1995. Forts in the Tutin area: Milinković 1982a, 1982b, and 1985. For Gradina and other forts in the area, see Milinković 1995 and http://arheo.f.bg.ac.yu/projekti/jelica/index.html (visit of May 29, 2000). Momčilov Grad: Brmbolić 1986. Pautalia: Goceva 1971:431. For forts in the Timok valley in eastern Serbia, see Petrović 1994–5.

churches on site, only the extramural *basilica coemeterialis* has been fully explored. More interesting is the evidence of intramural habitation. Two storage rooms containing no less than 167 amphoras and 4 *dolia* were built against the northwest wall shortly after the early sixth century. House N 10/W 10 had two stories, and the presence of a quern suggests that its first floor may have served as a mill. The great number of weapons found in N 10/W 10 does not necessarily indicate fighting, despite clear evidence that the house ended in fire, for the house's second floor may have been used as armory. Three houses with walls of stone and adobe bonded with clay were built on top of the ruins of the storage rooms erected during the building phase D. Subdivision of the area formerly designed for storage indicates that the new buildings served as dwellings. The pottery found in these houses has no analogy in the Balkans. It has been therefore interpreted as an indication of Armenian settlers brought to Thrace during the seventh century. Moreover, house S 5/W 34, dated to the same building phase as the three houses already mentioned, produced wheel-made pottery (called "Byzantine" by the German archaeologists), arrow heads, a shield, bronze and iron brooches (including fibulae with bent stem), and a stirrup, all artifacts strikingly reminding those from the house excavated at Caričin Grad in the western portico of the colonnaded street running from the circular plaza to the upper city's south gate. Just as in Caričin Grad, there is no evidence to substantiate the idea of a Slavic settlement. On the other hand, there is clear evidence that the fort at Karasura was destroyed by fire at some point after Justinian's reign. After restoration, buildings belonging to phase E were also destroyed by fire at some point during the seventh century, as evidenced by burnt layers on many house floors.[72]

Thanks to an excellent survey of the archaeological evidence in Thrace and the neighboring areas, it is possible to visualize the distribution of forts in the region south of the Stara Planina range (Figure 3). One of the most striking features of this distribution is the cluster of forts around the main mountain passes. Particular attention seems to have been paid to passes of lower altitude. Many forts were large (over 2 ha), sometimes with an extra-fortified acropolis. With only one exception, forts in the Stara Planina mountains have no churches, but many were equipped with

[72] Karasura: Procopius, *Buildings* IV 11; Wendel 1987:201 and 1992:201 and 290; Herrmann 1992:174–5; Döhle 1992:196; Böttger 1992:245 and 249; Dinchev 1997a:53. Extramural church: Schöneburg 1991. For other fort churches in Thrace, see Borisov 1988b; Soustal 1991:238, 300, and 488. Dyadovo: Boer 1988–9:9. It is not at all certain that any Armenian settlers came to Thrace during this period. According to Sebeos (pp. 70–1 and 81), Emperor Maurice had the intention to conscript the Armenian nobility to serve in the Balkans and twice attempted to settle Armenian families in Thrace, the last time just before Phocas' revolt. There is no indication, however, that the settlers ever arrived in Thrace.

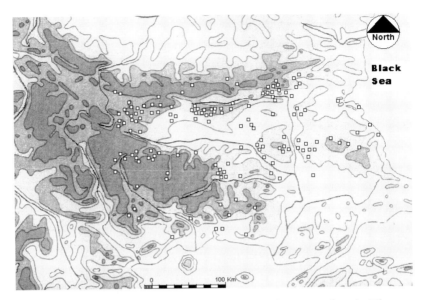

Figure 3 The distribution of known fifth- to sixth-century forts in Thrace
Lowest contour 200 m, thereafter 500 m and over 1,000 m (data after Soustal 1991).

cisterns or wells. Despite the lack of systematic excavations and relevant finds, their dating to Justinian's reign is secured by the presence of *protei-chismata*, as well as of triangular, pentagonal, and horseshoe-shaped towers.[73]

Equally interesting is the evidence from Macedonia. It is often assumed that forts in this region can easily be separated from fortified villages or *refugia* because of being apparently built by military experts. In many cases, interior amenities (cisterns, *horrea*, *armamentaria*) were identified. Typical for the Justinianic phase are the disappearance of *praetoria* and the building of interior structures against the ramparts. A date to Justinian's reign is also suggested by the presence of triangular and pentagonal

[73] *Proteichismata*: Ovcharov 1973; Biernacka-Lubańska 1982:148, 159, and 162; Gregory 1982a:260. For *proteichismata* and Justinianic fortifications in Crimea, see Veimarn 1958:10. For a case of pentangular tower in the Caucasus region, see Voronov and Bgazhba 1987:118. For the archaeological survey of Thrace, see Soustal 1991. On the Black Sea coast, two forts were identified at Sv. Nikola and Maslen nos, both on the bay of Burgas, but no excavations were carried in any of them (ibid., pp. 62–3). The main passes of lower altitude in the Stara Planina are Kotel (685 m), between the upper Ticha valley and the Luda Kamchiia, and Traianova vrata (Succi, 843 m) between the Eledzhik and the Dolna Vassilica mountains. The latter was the most important pass on the main highway across the Balkans, from Constantinople to Singidunum. Each one of these two passes was defended by ten forts, unlike passes at higher altitude (such as Troian, Zlatishki prohod, and Shipka), which had fewer.

towers, and confirmed by coin finds. All Macedonian forts have churches, either three-aisled or single-naved basilicas. Despite clear evidence of heavy destruction by fire, the fort at Markovi Kuli was twice restored. In the end, it seems to have been abandoned sometime after 601/2, the date of the last coin found in the fort's aqueduct. The same is true for the fort at Debrešte, though an exact date for its abandonment cannot be conjectured. In both cases, there is no indication that the abandonment was the result of any external threat.[74]

Elsewhere in the Balkans, the evidence is too meager to permit any conclusions. In Albania, only three forts have been identified so far from the sixth and seventh centuries: Drisht-Shkodër, Shurdhah, and Kruja. Their date was established on the basis of the presence of triangular and horseshoe-shaped towers, a feature most typical for Justinianic military architecture. Though excavations were carried at Shurdhah, the original date initially advanced for houses found in the interior has been disputed. Nor is it clear what was the relation between the famous cemetery at Kruja and the neighboring fortress. With the exception of the large fort at Isthmia, which may have accommodated soldiers and their families, the evidence from Greece is minimal.[75]

Farther to the north, forts produced evidence of occupation at the time of the Byzantine take-over in Dalmatia, during the Gothic war in Italy. Recent archaeological excavations at Dubrovnik reveal that shortly after Byzantine troops occupied the eastern Adriatic coast, a fort was built on the former island of Lave. It was immediately followed by a large

---

[74] For the use of leveling courses of brick (*opus latericum*) or alternating courses of brick and stone (*opus mixtum*), with bricks set in a bed of red mortar, as typical for the late fifth- and sixth-century military architecture, see Ovcharov 1977:470–1 and 1982:68; Gregory 1982a:258. Cisterns: Mikulčić and Bilbija 1981–2:213; Mikulčić 1986b:266. A smithy was identified at Ljubanci: Chausidis 1985–6:191. For other buildings in the interior, see Mikulčić and Nikuljska 1978:139. Houses built against the ramparts: Mikulčić 1986b:261 and 266. Triangular and pentagonal towers: Georgiev 1985–6:203–4. At Markovi Kuli, the triangular tower is coin-dated to Justinian's reign. New work was added during Justin II's reign (two coins issued between 575 and 578 date phase II). After heavy destruction, a new restoration amplified the triangular tower into a massive, polygonal bastion. This latter phase is coin-dated to the last regnal years of Justin II or to Tiberius II's reign. See Mikulčić and Nikuljska 1978:139 and 141; Mikulčić and Nikuljska 1979:72. Fort churches: Mikulčić and Bilbija 1981– 1982:214; Rauhutowa 1981:45–8; Spasovska-Dimitrioska 1981–2:170–1; Mikulčić 1986a:266. The three-aisled basilica at Venec had a baptistery, that of Debrešte was built next to an episcopal residence.
[75] Forts in Albania: Komata 1976:182; Anamali 1993a:455–7; Hoxha 1993:555–6. Shkodër produced brick stamps with Justinian's monogram. Triangular towers also appear at Qafa. The three-aisled basilica from Zaradishtë produced a relatively large number of coins minted for Justin I and Justinian, but its chronology is not clear. For Shurdhah, see also Spahiu 1976:154–5 and 158; Karaiskaj 1989:2647. For the cemetery at Kruja, see Anamali and Spahiu 1963. That families of soldiers may have resided within forts is suggested by the presence of intramural female and child burials. See Kardulias 1988:208 and 1992:284; Milinković 1995. Military sites in Greece: Ober 1987:226.

extramural, three-aisled basilica, built on the site of the modern city cathedral. This fort appears to be the largest on the Adriatic coast and in mainland Montenegro, comparable in size to such cities as Dyrrachium, Onhezmos, and Butrint. At some point after 536, but before 597, the bishop of neighboring Epidauros was transferred to the new basilica erected under the eastern ramparts of the fort. Dubrovnik thus became a bishopric and, perhaps, a lesser center of Justinian's administration of the coastal region.[76]

In Slovenia, no settlements existed during the fifth and sixth centuries, other than hillforts. The abandonment of settlements in the lowlands was accompanied by drastic changes in the economic profile of those communities, with a greater emphasis on pastoralism. At Ajdovski gradec, faunal remains mainly consisted of bones of sheep and goat, followed at a distance by pig and cattle. A date established for the forts in the northwestern Balkans during Justinian's reign seems to be confirmed by finds of coins and fibulae. In most cases, the fort's interior contained relatively large, open spaces, probably under cultivation. At Tinje, houses were cut in rock, with wattle or wooden superstructure. One of them, no. 4, produced a hoard of agricultural implements, with socketed shares, a mattock, and a scythe. At Rifnik, houses were built in stone bonded with clay. One of them, built very close to the church, produced evidence of glass windows. Another house may have served as a smithy. Houses built in stone bonded with clay were also found at Ajdovski gradec. House A had four rooms and produced exceptional artifacts: a bronze bowl, stamped pottery, *spatheia*, a marble mortar, and a silver pin. It has been interpreted as an episcopal residence. House D had a single room with a heating system with channels under the floor of lime mortar. House E produced a considerable number of tools (awl, knife, whetstones, saws), which suggests that the building may have been a workshop. Handmade pottery was found in house G, built immediately close to the precinct. A multi-roomed building was also found at Gornji Vrbljani, in western Bosnia. It had an inner courtyard, an oven, and a kitchen. No other buildings were apparently built on the site. By contrast, at Korinjski hrib, in Slovenia, some of the towers of the precinct may have served as dwellings, as suggested by the existence of hearths. Another tower contained a cistern. At Rifnik and Korintija, on the island of Krk, the cisterns were cut in rock. At Ajdovski gradec, Biograci, and Kaštelina, on the island of Rab, the cisterns were part of the precinct. Almost all forts have at least

---

[76] Stevović 1991:142, 147, and 150; see also Cambi 1989:2400 and 2402. Even before the Gothic war, a defense line was built on the left bank of the Neretva river, with forts at Debelo brdo, Bobovac, Usora-Bosna, and Zecovi near Prijedor. At the same time mining activites resumed at Bosanski Novi. See Basler 1993:17–18.

one single-naved church located on the highest point of the settlement. But Christian congregations on the northern shore of the Adriatic, in the Alpine region farther north and in Bosnia, clung to architectural types established in the early fourth century. Box churches without apses, the altar pushed forward into the nave and a semicircular clergy bench behind the altar, have been found at Rifnik and Ajdovski gradec. It is often assumed that the occupation of the forts in the northwestern Balkans ceased sometime before or shortly after 600, as a consequence of Avar or Slavic attacks. At a closer examination of the published material there is no indication of destruction by fire, except at Gornji Vrbljani, for which, however, there is no indication of date.[77]

In many cases, the exact dates for the building, restoration, destruction, or abandonment of the Balkan forts were established on the basis of isolated coins or hoards. Hoards are particularly important in this context, since they are often associated with impending disaster caused by barbarian raids. It might be worthwhile, therefore, to take a fresh look at the numismatic evidence before drawing the final conclusion of this chapter.

INFLATION IN THE BALKANS AND THE END OF THE *LIMES*: THE EVIDENCE OF COIN HOARDS

Hoards are generally believed to have been deposited close to the date of the latest coin. An unusual clustering of coin hoards within a short span of time is often interpreted as indicating some severe threat to the region. Plotted on maps, hoards were often used for tracing movements of armies or peoples and areas of social and military unrest. They were thus viewed as mute testimonies to misfortunes, calamities, or tragedies. It comes as no surprise, therefore, that archaeologists made extensive use of coin hoards for tracing barbarian invasions into the Balkans, especially when coin hoards were found in or near destroyed forts.[78] Despite the extensive use of numismatic evidence for documenting Slavic invasions, very few scholars attempted to map hoards in order to show in detail how far away they lay from the conjectural routeways and focal areas of settlement.

[77] Ciglenečki 1987a:107 and 1987b:272 and 285. See also Bierbrauer 1984:53–4. For pastoralism, see Petru 1978:226. For faunal remains at Ajdovski gradec, see Knific 1994:215. Intramural open spaces: Ciglenečki 1979:463 and 1987b:114–15. Coins and fibulae: Bolta 1978:515; Čremošnik 1987–8:94. Tinje: Ciglenečki 1987b:44. Rifnik: Bolta 1978:511. Ajdovski gradec: Knific 1994:212 and 216. Gornji Vrbljani: Ciglenečki 1987a:107; Basler 1993:33. Korinjski hrib: Ciglenečki 1987a:274 and 1987b:101–3. Korintija: Tomičić 1986–7:151. Kaštelina: Tomičić 1988–9:33. Fort churches: Tomičić 1986–7:151 and 1988–9:30–2; Faber 1986–7:123. Church architecture in Dalmatia, Bosnia, and Istria: Krautheimer 1986:179; Bolta 1978:515; Knific 1994:212; Bratož 1989:2381; Basler 1993:48.

[78] Kent 1974:202; Banning 1987:7; Metcalf 1991:141. See also Curta 1996:65–78. What follows is primarily based on this study.

Even fewer examined large numbers of hoards in order to assess from their size and age-structure how soon after the *terminus post quem* their conceal-ment is likely to have been. Some observed that not every incursion pro-voked hoarding. Moreover, the evidence of sixth-century hoards suggests that coin hoarding continued in relatively quiescent periods.[79] The dep-osition of low denomination copper coins has been attributed to eco-nomic factors. Inflation had a particularly marked effect on the radiate, making it practically worthless. Large hoards of radiates may thus have been originally buried for safe-keeping, but not retrieved because infla-tion had rendered them valueless or they were already worthless and were buried as a means of disposal.[80]

The early Byzantine Empire operated a closed economy, in which the monetary value of coins was officially sanctioned. It is often assumed that copper coins which passed beyond the sphere of control of the issuing authority lost their value, because coinage in that metal was almost uni-formly of a fiduciary nature. Exporting copper beyond the imperial fron-tiers would have immediately dropped its value to that of its bullion content.[81] If this is true, however, it is very difficult to explain the pres-ence of coin hoards, primarily of copper, in the regions beyond the Danube frontier of the Empire, where historical sources locate the Sclavenes. These sources suggest that beginning with the 570s the raids of the Slavs considerably increased and changed in both direction and effects. Some argued that until 602 the most destructive invasions were in the southern region of the Balkans and that Roman sites in the north survived until Heraclius' early regnal years. Did, then, invasions of the Cutrigurs, Avars, and Slavs result in such clear-cut changes in the pattern of coin-hoarding in various provinces that we can identify particular moments when these provinces were overrun? The distribution of hoards in the Balkans would at best indicate that large tracts in the western and central parts were not touched by invasions at all (Figure 4).[82]

As shown in Chapter 3, the diocese of Thrace was systematically raided

[79] For the use of hoards for documenting Slavic invasions, see Metcalf 1962a and 1962b; Iurukova 1969b; Popović 1975 and 1980; Nystazopoulou-Pelekidou 1986; Madgearu 1997. Out of more than 200 hoards known so far from the Balkans, not a single one produced a *terminus a quo* to be associated with the serious Cutrigur raid of 558/9. Conversely, coin hoarding in the Balkans increased particularly after 565 and before 580, at a time when, according to historical sources, there was no major Slavic invasion or any other barbarian attack across the Lower Danube. See Curta 1996:80 and 103–4.

[80] Aitchison 1988:273–4; Berghaus 1987:16. For an interesting study of coin hoarding and burying in relation to economic recession, see Mikołajczyk 1982. See also Sarvas 1981. Samuel Pepys's diary (1667) is the cautionary tale most frequently cited against hastily associating hoards with invasions. See Higbed 1967; Casey 1986:53–5.

[81] Hendy 1985:257; Aitchison 1988:270. *Contra:* Pottier 1983:225; Morrisson 1989:251. For coin cir-culation in the Balkans, see Duncan 1993.

[82] Popović 1980:257; Metcalf 1991:140; Curta 1996:76 and 178 fig. 1. For the Sclavene raid of 548, which reached Durrës (Epidamnus, Dyrrachium), see Procopius, *Wars* VII 29.1–3.

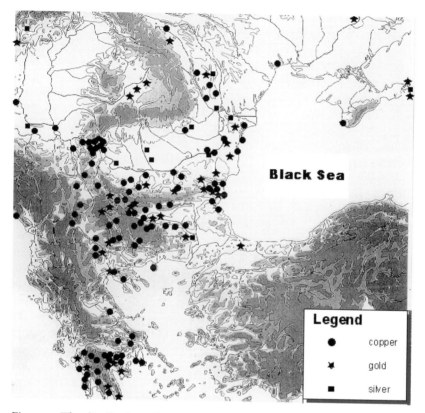

Figure 4 The distribution of sixth- to seventh-century Byzantine coin hoards in Southeastern Europe.

by Cutrigurs and Sclavenes in the late 400s and the early 500s, as well as by Sclavenes and Avars in the late 500s. One would expect to find a large number of hoards in an area under such a serious threat. The distribution of sixth-century hoards in the Balkans reveals, however, a striking difference between central regions, such as Serbia and Macedonia, and the eastern provinces included in the diocese of Thrace (Figure 5). With just one exception, there is no hoard in the eastern Balkans with a *terminus post quem* before 600. The latest coins found in Thracian hoards were either struck for Justin I or, more often, pre-550 issues of Justinian. The number of hoards drastically dropped in the following decades and hoards completely disappeared between 580 and 680.[83] One can easily find similar examples in Thessaly and the western provinces of the Balkans,

[83] Curta 1996:94–5 and 180 fig. 3. The exception is the ill-published Mezek hoard with a last coin probably struck during the second half of Justinian's reign (Iurukova 1969b:262).

for which clear evidence exists that they were also raided by Avars and Sclavenes. However, no hoard was found on the territory of Epirus Vetus, Prevalitana, and Epirus Nova, while Thessaly is ranked close to the eastern provinces. By contrast, the largest number of hoards is that from Greece, which was seriously threatened only after *c.* 580.

A considerable number of sixth- and early seventh-century hoards were found in urban contexts, in Caričin Grad (Justiniana Prima), Pustogradsko (Stobi), Adamclisi (Tropaeum Traiani), Athens, Corinth, or Salona. Others were found in Roman camps, particularly in the Iron Gates area of the Danube frontier.[84] In cases where coins were associated with other artifacts, we can discern a certain pattern. While two hoards with the last coin issued under Justin II include cast fibulae with bent stems,[85] hoards of silver of the late 600s contain silver earrings with star-shaped pendants of a type usually found in the late 500s.[86] Archaeological observations thus suggest the existence of certain regularities in hoarding activity. A closer examination of the numismatic data may verify this hypothesis. Many hoards of copper have a *terminus post quem* between the reign of Anastasius and the early years of Justinian's reign, with a peak shortly before and after 530 (Figure 6). The number of hoards decreased dramatically after 535 and a new increase took place only after 570. By contrast, the seventh century witnessed a significant increase, particularly after 670, in the number of hoards of silver, silver and copper, or silver and gold.

On the basis of a detailed statistical analysis of the age-structure of Balkan hoards it is possible to explain this hoarding pattern by drawing comparisons between various regions in the Balkans.[87] Hoards from both Greece and Dobrudja with latest coins minted before 570 include fairly large numbers of minimi (i.e., lowest copper denominations) and so-called "barbarian imitations." These hoards were often interpreted as indicating continuous raids by Cutrigurs, Antes, or Sclavenes, but the examination of hoards with last coins struck *after* 570 suggests a different solution.[88] This latter group of hoards typically includes a much smaller number of coins, usually lesser fractions of the follis, issued in the late

---

[84] Cities: Popović 1984b:61–9 and 77–9; Barnea et al. 1979:22 and fig. 2; Popović 1978:620 with n. 79; Metcalf 1962b:138–44 and 145–6; Avramea 1983:52 and 54–6; Mirnik 1981:89; Marović 1984. Forts: Jovanović 1984; Popović 1984b:23–6, 71–2, and 75–7; Minić 1984; Kondić 1984b.

[85] Bracigovo: Uenze 1974:485–6; Koprivec: Milchev and Draganov 1992:39. For a recent discussion of this group of fibulae, see Curta 1992:83–5 and Uenze 1992:154–8.

[86] Zemianský Vrbovok: Svoboda 1953; Radomerský 1953. Silistra: Angelova and Penchev 1989. Priseaca: Butoi 1968. For earrings with star-shaped pendants, see Comşa 1971; Aibabin 1973; Čilinská 1975.   [87] Curta 1996:84–97.

[88] "Barbarian imitations": Iurukova 1969a; Gaj-Popović 1973; Zhekov 1987. For the interpretation of pre-570 hoards as signalizing barbarian raids, see Preda and Nubar 1973:81; Popović 1978:610; Poenaru-Bordea and Ocheşanu 1980:387.

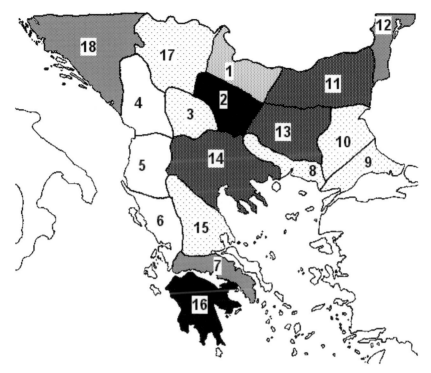

Figure 5 The distribution of sixth- and seventh-century Byzantine coin
hoards in the Balkans, plotted by provinces

Blackened areas – over twenty hoards; white areas – no hoards. The descending scale of grays
indicates the frequency of hoard finds. Provinces: 1 – Dacia Ripensis; 2 – Dacia Mediterranea; 3 –
Dardania; 4 – Praevalitana; 5 – Epirus Nova; 6 – Epirus Vetus; 7 – Achaia (without Peloponnesus);
8 – Rhodope; 9 – Europe; 10 – Haemimons; 11 – Moesia Inferior; 12 – Scythia Minor; 13 –
Thrace; 14 – Macedonia; 15 – Thessaly; 16 – Achaia (Peloponnesus); 17 – Moesia Superior; 18 –
Dalmatia.

400s and early 500s. Since accumulation had often begun in the early 500s
and continued until the reigns of Justin II or Tiberius II, the owners of
these hoards seem to have deliberately avoided lower denominations, no
doubt because of the growing inflation. Indeed, by the time hoards concluded in the 570s and 580s, 1/4, 1/8, and 1/40 fractions of the follis were
already valueless and probably out of circulation.[89] If so, then hoards

---

[89] The last nummia were struck under Emperor Maurice, but both the nummion and the pentanummion had become rare during Justinian's reign. See Morrisson 1989:250. The regional stress
in the copper coinage supply may have caused small-scale production of leaden imitations of low
denominations. See Culică 1976–80; Morrisson 1981; Weiser 1985.

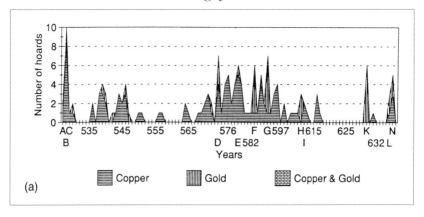

(a)

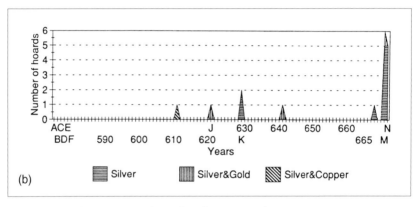

(b)

Figure 6 The mean number of sixth- to seventh-century Byzantine coin
hoards found in Eastern Europe

including very low denominations, with latest coins struck shortly before
570, as well as a large number of saving hoards with minimi from Greece
dated after 570, may have never been retrieved by their owners not necessarily because of external threats, but because they had become valueless.[90] After 540, there is a general decline in the number of coins and no
coins minted between 545 and 565 made their way to the regions beyond
the Danube frontier. In Greece, on the other hand, hoards with latest
coins minted before 570 display a significant decrease in both the number
and the value of coins. In 554, coin circulation seems to have completely

[90] Inflation during Justinian's reign was encouraged by the financial ability of John the Cappadocian,
who levied a supplement to the land tax, called the "air tax" which added 3,000 lb of gold to the
annual revenue, in order to balance the budget grievously threatened by the Persian wars. See
Jones 1964:284.

ceased. By contrast, hoards dated after 570 indicate a continuous circulation between 540 and 560. Despite minor variations at the regional level, the trend is visible throughout the entire Balkan peninsula. By 540, a dearth of copper seems to have become most serious in the northern Balkans, but the evidence of hoards shows that Greece and Scythia Minor also felt the impact of the crisis.

What caused this sudden change from inflation to lack of copper currency? The crisis coincides with the unpopular reform of 542, when Peter Barzymes, Justinian's *comes sacrarum largitionum*, decreased the number of folles to 180 per solidus. In addition, in 545, Peter Barzymes was compelled by the failure of the Egyptian harvest to make extensive compulsory purchases of wheat in Thrace, Bithynia, and Phrygia. Dismissed in 546, he came back in 554/5 and held office until 562. Although the financial situation was very difficult, he was able to supply Narses with sufficient funds for paying off the arrears which had accumulated in Italy and for raising the considerable army with which Justinian eventually defeated the Ostrogoths. In addition, between 545 and 562 Peter raised 7,500 pounds of gold which were instrumental in buying the final peace with Persia.[91] The general decrease in coin circulation in the Balkans and the proportional increase of low or very low denominations may have something to do with these strains. The drastic decrease in the number of coins after 542/3 may have also been associated with the plague and the subsequent famine in Constantinople.[92] The lack of any coin finds dated to 554/5 may also be connected with the project of another reform, that of 553, which aimed at decreasing the weight of the half-follis. The project had to be abandoned after street riots broke out in Constantinople.[93] The evidence of hoards, however, suggests an alternative interpretation.

In the central Balkans, in Dobrudja, and north of the Danube frontier, the number of hoards with latest coins struck under Emperor Justinian is very small. The first half of Justinian's reign, however, witnessed the largest number of Thracian hoards, all found in or near small-sized forts along the roads from Philippopolis to Diocletianopolis and Beroe. This has traditionally been interpreted as indicating Slavic raids, which reached a peak around 550. Indeed, Procopius' evidence suggests that the raids of both Cutrigurs (in 551) and Sclavenes (in 549, 551, and, possibly, 545) focused on the diocese of Thrace (see Chapter 3). However, his account highlighted only those Sclavenes who approached the walls of

---

[91] Procopius, *Secret History* 25.12. Monetary reform of 542: Whitting 1973:106; Grierson 1982:46–47. For Peter Barzymes' career, see Jones 1964:295–6; Delmaire 1989:269.
[92] For the plague, see Durliat 1989. For its effect on mint output, see Pottier 1983:241.
[93] See Pottier 1983:241; Morrisson 1986:115.

Constantinople and completely ignored concurrent developments in Illyricum. On the other hand, there are no hoards from the last fifteen years of Justinian's reign (550–65), a period in which the eastern Balkans were ravaged by the invading Cutrigurs, although Slavic raids seem to have completely ceased.[94]

The dwindling of the hoarding activity between 545 and 565 coincides in time with the implementation of Justinian's defense system in the Balkans. On the basis of Procopius' evidence, the completion of this building program can be dated shortly before 558. A connection between Justinian's building program and contemporary hoards is substantiated by their archaeological association with small-size forts. Justinian's gigantic project in the Balkans and its execution must have strained the local coin circulation. The increasing number of payments and other monetary transactions brought by this economic conjuncture had serious consequences especially on small savings, such as found in hoards of radiate. This may also explain the sharp decline in accumulation, as fewer coins were now withdrawn from circulation. Throughout the Balkans, hoarding developments match the picture given by stray finds. In both cases, the number of coins in the late 540s and in the 550s drastically dropped, although to different ratios in Greece, Macedonia, Serbia, and Dobrudja. North of the Danube frontier, circulation of coins practically ceased between 545 and 560, a clear indication that relations between the two banks of the river were interrupted as a consequence of Justinian's building program (Figures 7–8).[95] This conclusion is supported by finds of gold coins north of the Danube. Thirteen specimens are known so far from the first half of Justinian's reign. By contrast, there are only seven gold coins from the rest of Justinian's reign, as well as from Justin II's and Tiberius II's reigns (Figures 9–12).[96]

Despite the occasional presence of gold coins, no hoards of gold were found in the regions adjacent to the Danube frontier. Hoards of early sixth-century solidi were found, however, at a considerable distance from the Danube frontier, in the steppes north of the Black Sea and on the Baltic Sea shore. Many include large numbers of light-weight solidi, which may have been specifically minted for paying mercenaries

[94] Curta 1996:90–1 and 93–7. For the association between Thracian and Macedonian hoards and incursions of Sclavenes and Cutrigurs, see Iurukova 1969b:257 and 259; Popović 1978:262; Poenaru-Bordea 1976.
[95] Stray finds of coins of Anastasius and Justin I in present-day Romania are relatively numerous, but the largest number of coins are those of Justinian. See Butnariu 1983–1985. Out of 96 coins of Justinian known from *barbaricum* (Eastern Europe), 54 are Romanian finds. Forty specimens were published with exact dates. Only eight of them were minted after 550.
[96] Gold coins in *barbaricum*: Butnariu 1983–5; Huszár 1955; Kropotkin 1962 and 1965; Gassowska 1979; Kos 1986; Fiala 1989; Stoliarik 1992.

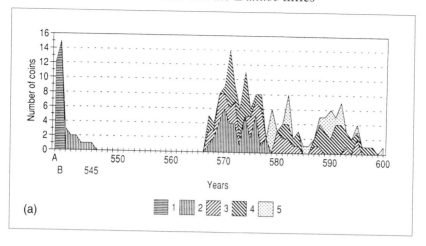

(a)

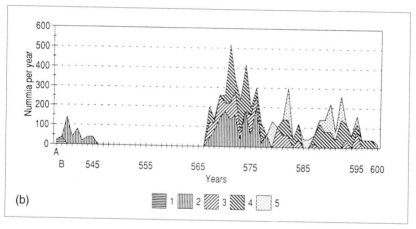

(b)

Figure 7 The mean number of coins (a) and nummia per year (b) in hoards
found in Romania
1–Cudalbi; 2–Gropeni; 3–Unirea; 4–Horgeşti; 5–Movileni.

recruited in *barbaricum*.[97] Late sixth-century hoards of gold found south
of the Danube frontier, in the Balkans, have a different composition.
They typically include between five and nine solidi each, with all coins
struck in Constantinople within a short span of time. It has been suggested that such hoards represent payments to the army known as *donativa*. Under Tiberius II, the accessional *donativum* was indeed 9 solidi and

---

[97] Kropotkin 1962:231–2 and 253; Frolova and Nikolaeva 1978; Laser 1982:106–10. See also Fagerlie
1967; Gaul 1984. For the interpretation of light-weight solidi, see Hahn 1989:165–7; Smedley
1988:129. See also Hahn 1981:97.

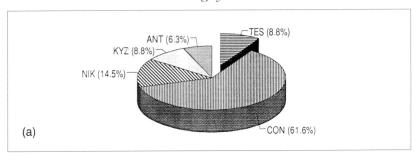

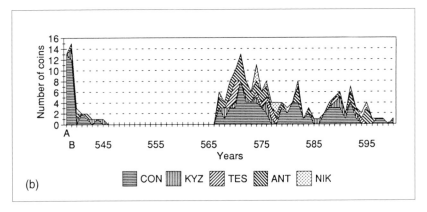

Figure 8 The frequency (a) and the mean number of coins per year (b) issued
in mints represented in hoards found in Romania

the quinquennial one 5 solidi. *Donativa* were still paid in 578 and the
practice of ceremonial payments to the army may have survived as late
as 641.[98] In addition, the distribution of late sixth-century hoards of
solidi within the Balkans coincides with the shift of military operations
from the eastern to the western Balkans, which took place in the late
570s and early 580s in connection with the siege of Sirmium by the Avars
and the Sclavene raids into Greece. Hoards of five to nine solidi may
therefore be seen as an example of the correlation between mint output
and hoarding, on one hand, and military preparations, on the other. Such
hoards indicate the presence of the Roman army, not Avar or Slavic
attacks. Their concealment is not necessarily the result of barbarian raids,
because their owners may have kept their savings in cash in a hiding place

[98] Curta 1996:86 and 103; Hendy 1985:188 and 646–7. According to Wolfgang Hahn (1981:96–7),
   the 23-carat solidi introduced by Maurice were specifically struck for his quinquennial *donativum*
   of 587.

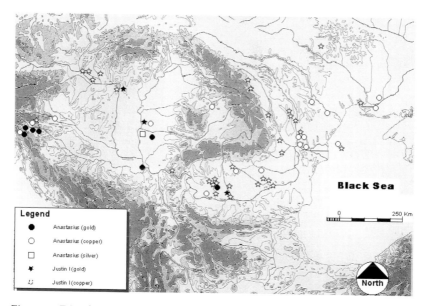

Figure 9 Distribution of stray finds of coins of Anastasius and Justin I north of the Danube frontier

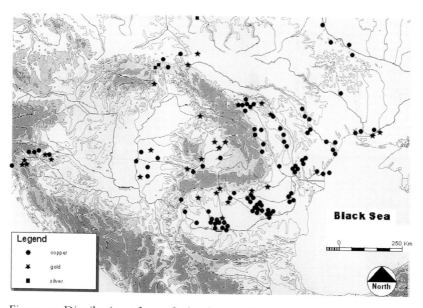

Figure 10 Distribution of stray finds of coins of Justinian north of the Danube frontier

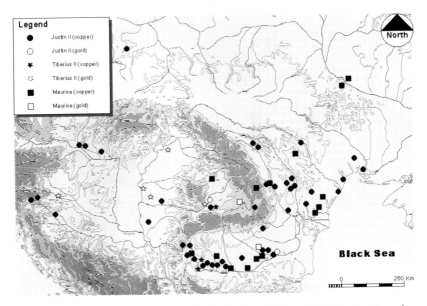

Figure 11 Distribution of stray finds of coins of Justin II, Tiberius II, and Maurice north of the Danube frontier

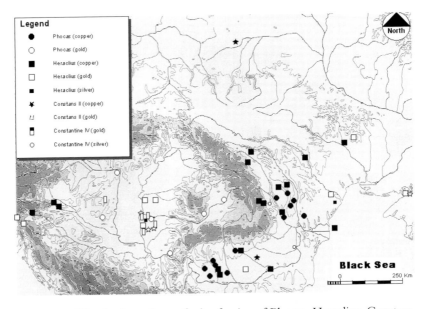

Figure 12 Distribution of stray finds of coins of Phocas, Heraclius, Constans II, and Constantine IV north of the Danube frontier

custodiae causa, not *ob metum barbarorum*.[99] In contrast with the abundance of low value coinage, finds of late sixth-century gold coins are extremely rare in the regions beyond the Danube frontier. This may indicate that few such savings fell into the hands of Sclavene or Avar marauders. The chronology of gold hoards, on the other hand, is different from that of hoards of radiate. While the number of hoards of copper considerably diminished after *c.* 600, small quantities of gold, possibly *donativa*, were still hoarded in the early seventh century.[100]

During the early 600s, both copper and gold continued to reach the regions north of the Danube. By 620, however, the distribution of the new silver coinage, the hexagram, provides a true measure of disruption. Only two hexagrams are known so far from the Balkans. By contrast, a large number of silver coins were found north of the Danube (Figures 4 and 12). The majority were struck for Constans II and Constantine IV. Many hoard specimens are freshly minted and die-linked, which may indicate that they did not change hands much after leaving the mint. Hoards of hexagrams have been interpreted as bribes or gifts sent directly from Constantinople to some barbarian, most likely Bulgar, chieftains. Viewed against the background of general decline, if not total cessation, of coin circulation in the Balkans, these shipments of silver to the regions north of the Danube are in sharp contrast to the small accumulations of copper in sixth-century hoards on both sides of the Danube frontier of the Empire.[101] They delineate a different distribution network for the Byzantine coinage, itself the result of changing military and political circumstances.[102]

CONCLUSION

Justinian, or, more probably, one of his Vaubans named Viktorinos, designed the defense system of the Balkans as a network of three inter-related fortification lines. This plan is spelled out by Procopius, and

---

[99] For the association between mint output and military operations, see Metcalf 1976:92. For hoards of gold and the presence of the military, see also Poenaru-Bordea and Ocheşanu 1983–5:180; Iurukova 1992b:287. See also Okamura 1990:51.

[100] Gerasimov 1959:263; Iurukova 1980; Avramea 1983:58 and 65; Marović 1984:302. For an unusually rich hoard, see also Iurukova 1992a; Fiedler 1994a: 31 with n. 2.

[101] Curta 1996:109–16. The two hexagrams found south of the Danube are those from the Valea Teilor hoard. See Oberländer-Târnoveanu 1980:163–4. For the hexagram, see Yannopoulos 1978; see also Hahn 1978–9. For hexagrams found north of the Danube, see Radomerský 1953; Fiala 1986; Mitrea 1975; Bonev 1985; Somogyi 1997.

[102] This is further substantiated by the two ceremonial issues from a late seventh-century hoard and by Emperor Constantine IV's seal, all found in Silistra (Bulgaria). See Angelova and Penchev 1989:40; Barnea 1981. For the Silistra "coins" as ceremonial tokens for the anniversary of either Rome (April 21) or Constantinople (May 11), see Hahn 1975:156.

archaeological investigations proved the existence of three successive lines of fortifications along the Danube, the Stara Planina range, and the high ridges of Istranca Dağlar. The system may have been implemented shortly after the devastating Cutrigur invasion of 539/40. The major part of this grandiose building program was already finished in 554, when Procopius ended Book IV of his *Buildings*. This program was later extended to the northwestern Balkans, following the defeat of the Ostrogoths and the conquest of Dalmatia. In the central Balkans, Justinian laid a stronger emphasis on the second line of defense, for the largest number of forts were found around the main mountain passes across the Stara Planina. Many forts in the northern and central Balkans were quite small. Among seventy forts found in Bulgaria until 1977, more than half were less than 1 ha, and among those, the majority had no more than 0.5 ha.[103] A tabulation of some of the most important forts mentioned in the archaeological survey, for which exact data on the occupied area is available, confirms this conclusion (Table 7). Moreover, a closer examination of the tabulated forts shows that most of those built along the Danube frontier, in either Moesia Superior or Dacia Ripensis, were remarkably small. By contrast, forts built in Macedonia, in Scythia Minor, or Achaia tend to be large, over 1 ha. How could this situation be explained?

One way to answer this question is to tackle the problem of the troops used to man these forts. On the basis of archaeological research at Isthmia, Nick Kardulias has recently argued that estimates of the military population of sixth-century forts should be based on a coefficient of 1.8 to 2.7 square meters per man, which corresponds to calculations based on the archaeological evidence from the Late Roman forts at Lejjun, on the Arabian frontier, and at Thamughadi, in North Africa, as well as to the sleeping space in modern, standard US-army 25-man barracks for enlisted men. Figures obtained by using this coefficient show that most small forts did not hold more than a *numerus* (or *tagma*), the basic tactical unit of the early Byzantine army, with numbers varying from 100 to 500 men. Garrisons at large forts, such as Krivina (Iatrus), Jelica, Isthmia, or Nikiup (Nicopolis), may have held maximum forces ranging between 2,000 and 4,000. By contrast, adding up the lowest estimated numbers of soldiers for all garrisons of forts with known area, which were found in the Iron Gates segment of the Danube frontier, we obtain a total force of slightly more than one legion with an operational strength of 5,000 men (Figure 13).[104]

---

[103] Ovcharov 1982:22. For Justinian's plan, see Procopius *Buildings* IV 1.

[104] Kardulias 1988:207, 1992:282–3, and 1993. A sixth-century military treatise (*De Re Strategica*, p. 9) recommends that "the men in the garrison should not have their wives and children with them." However, "if a fort is extremely strong, so that there is no danger of its being besieged, and we can keep it provisioned without any problems, then there is no reason why the men cannot have their families reside with them." Indeed, the only evidence for the presence of women and children in sixth-century forts comes from large ones, such as Isthmia and Jelica.

The Balkans and the Danube limes

Table 7 *Sixth-century Balkan forts: area and estimated number of soldiers*

Fort	Province	Area (in hectares)	Estimated number of soldiers
Nikiup	Moesia Inferior	5.74	3,589 to 3,651
Venec	Macedonia	3.00	1,876 to 1,908
Pčinja	Macedonia	3.00	1,876 to 1,908
Krivina	Moesia Inferior	2.80	1,751 to 1,781
Debrešte	Macedonia	2.80	1,751 to 1,781
Isthmia	Achaia	2.71	1,694 to 1,724
Balchik	Scythia Minor	2.60	1,626 to 1,654
Dolojman	Scythia Minor	2.50	1,563 to 1,590
Pantelimon	Scythia Minor	2.20	1,375 to 1,399
Enisala	Scythia Minor	2.00	1,250 to 1,272
Karataš	Dacia Ripensis	1.87	1,169 to 1,189
Vavovo	Moesia Inferior	1.80	1,125 to 1,145
Korinjski	Dalmatia	1.80	1,125 to 1,145
Kaliakra	Scythia Minor	1.70	1,063 to 1,081
Korintija	Dalmatia	1.70	1,063 to 1,081
Momčilov g.	Dacia Mediterranea	1.50	938 to 954
Saldum	Moesia Superior	1.36	850 to 865
Kaštelina	Dalmatia	1.30	813 to 827
Kula	Dacia Ripensis	1.25	781 to 795
Dvorište	Macedonia	1.00	625 to 636
Sapaja	Moesia Superior	0.86	538 to 547
Nova Cherna	Moesia Inferior	0.81	506 to 515
Vrbljani	Dalmatia	0.66	413 to 420
Sadovec	Dacia Ripensis	0.65	406 to 413
Sivri Tepe	Moesia Inferior	0.50	312 to 318
Zelenikovo	Macedonia	0.50	312 to 318
Cetacea	Dacia Ripensis	0.47	294 to 299
Ovidiu	Scythia Minor	0.37	231 to 235
Ljubičevac	Dacia Ripensis	0.36	225 to 229
Dyadovo	Thrace	0.36	225 to 229
D. Butorke	Dacia Ripensis	0.33	206 to 209
Ljubanci	Macedonia	0.30	188 to 191
Glamija	Dacia Ripensis	0.28	169 to 172
Milutinovac	Dacia Ripensis	0.27	168 to 171
Ravna	Moesia Superior	0.24	150 to 153
Bosman	Moesia Superior	0.20	125 to 127
Mora Vagei	Dacia Ripensis	0.03	19

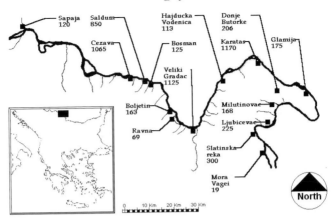

Figure 13 Sixth-century forts in the Iron Gates segment of the Danube *limes*, with estimated numbers of soldiers

It has been argued that Justinian depended on local farmers, serving as a kind of peasant militia, to defend his walls and forts in the Balkan peninsula.[105] Both the absence of rural settlements and the great number of forts, especially in the northern Balkans, show this conclusion to be wrong. It would not have made much sense for the state to undertake such expensive building projects, only to leave defense of these fortifications in the hands of local militias. Whether or not the troops which manned the forts remained there for a longer term cannot be decided on the basis of the archaeological evidence alone. But the general picture obtained from this evidence is one of rather permanent garrisons, at least in medium to large forts, with houses, amenities, and churches.

The evident association of smaller forts with the regions in the northern Balkans does not indicate that the defenders were fewer. Justinian's building program was designed to increase the potential of the existing troops by dividing and subdividing them into smaller units capable of manning the newly built or restored forts. Frontier areas, such as the mining district at the border between Dacia Ripensis and Moesia Superior, received special treatment with barrier walls and towers built across the outlets of the tributaries into the Danube.[106] An important role was that of the Danube fleet. Theophylact Simocatta shows that in the

---

[105] Rosser 1985:253.

[106] Werner 1986:562. Elsewhere in the Balkans, barrier walls seem to have been either earlier constructions (the Hexamilion) or designed to protect water supplies (the Long Walls). See Gregory 1982b:21; Harrison 1974:247; Crow 1995:117. For the Long Walls as predating Anastasius' reign, see Croke 1982 and Whitby 1985b.

late sixth century, Securisca was still an important center for producing boats and rafts for the army. Archaeological excavations indicate that the location of forts on the right bank of the Danube was influenced by the location of major ports of the Danube fleet. The Danube fleet was under the command of the *quaestor exercitus*, the office created by Justinian in 536 by combining two Balkan provinces, Scythia Minor and Moesia Inferior, and two provinces overseas, Caria and Cyprus, into a single administrative unit in which the fleet played an obviously crucial role. Moreover, since the *quaestor exercitus* was not only the most important military commander of the Thracian diocese, but also the most important administrative office in that region, some historians suggested that the *quaestura Iustiniana exercitus* was an antecedent of the first theme, the Karabisianoi.[107]

In contrast to other regions, where Justinian's program simply consisted of restoring older constructions, the building activity in the northern Balkans seems to have been taken more seriously. Local quarries, such as those of oolitic limestone in the Svishtov-Ruse area, supplying all sites in the Iantra valley, provided most of the building materials. Who took the responsibility for all these forts? Frank Wozniak suggested that local aristocrats and their personal armies took the provincial defense into their own hands. If true, this hypothesis would still have to account for the problem of how forts were supplied with ammunition, weapons, and food. Themistius' evidence from the fourth century suggests an important role of the central government and the imperial administration. There are some indications that the system was still in use during the sixth century.[108]

Ever since A. H. M. Jones interpreted the *quaestura exercitus* as an administrative reform designed to ensure a continuous food supply for troops stationed on the Thracian border, scholars insisted that the attributions of the *quaestor* were primarily financial. He was directly responsible for the *annona* of the army in Moesia Inferior and Scythia Minor. In addition, lead seals found in the region point to communication of some regularity between the two Balkan provinces included in the *quaestura exercitus* and the central government. Thirteen imperial seals, nine of

---

[107] Theophylact Simocatta VIII 6.7. The major ports of the Danube fleet were Ratiaria, (Se)curisca, and Transmarisca. See Mitova-Dzhonova 1986:506. For the Karabisianoi, see Szádeczky-Kardoss 1985:61 and 63.

[108] Themistius, *Oratio* 10.136, trans. P. Heather and J. Matthews (Liverpool, 1991), 44; Velkov 1987:147. For an earlier example of central distribution, see Whittaker 1994:103 and 105. For a detailed discussion of *annona* in the early Byzantine period, see Durliat 1990:37–282. For local aristocrats and sixth-century forts, see Wozniak 1982:204 and 1987:265. For marble quarries in Macedonia, see Keramidchiev 1981–2:123. For stone-cutting workshops in Thrace, see Vaklinova 1984:647–8.

which are from Justinian, demonstrate that officials in Scythia Minor received letters and written orders from the emperor.[109]

Even more interesting is the evidence of amphoras. Egyptian papyri show that the daily food ratio for a soldier consisted of three pounds of bread, two pounds of meat, two *sextarii* of wine and 1/8 *sextarii* of olive oil. At least three elements of this ratio were commodities usually transported in amphoras. The capacity of these vessels varied minimally, as suggested by a few measurements taken, and never exceeded forty to fifty liters, the majority ranging between fifteen and twenty-five liters. There are two basic types according to the shape: squat or globular, and oblong or elongated. The first type, subdivided into Late Roman 2 (LR 2), Kuzmanov XIX = Scorpan XIII, and Kuzmanov III = Scorpan VI, is well represented in sixth-century Balkan forts. LR 2 amphoras were produced in the Aegean and were used for transporting either wine (as indicated by grape seeds found in some cargo amphoras on the Yassi Ada shipwreck) or olive oil. Such amphoras were quite common on sixth-century sites in Greece (e.g., Argos), as well as in northern and central Balkan forts. The same is true for Kuzmanov III = Scorpan VI, a type well represented at Ratiaria and Cape Kaliakra. As for the Kuzmanov XIX = Scorpan XIII amphoras, presumably used for transporting wine, they were found in great quantities at Krivina (Iatrus) and Voivoda. No globular amphoras were found in the Balkans in seventh-century contexts.[110]

Elongated amphoras of a type known as Late Roman 1 (LR 1) were also a familiar presence. Produced in Cilicia, near Antioch, in Cyprus, as

---

[109] Imperial seals: Barnea 1984:95; Schultz 1978:100; Culică 1975:246; Barnea 1982:202; Gerasimova-Tomova 1992:70; Barnea 1969:29–30. A seal of Justinian of unknown provenance, now in the National Museum at Sofia, may have been found in Bulgaria. See Mushmov 1934. By contrast, only one imperial seal is known from the interior (Gaj-Popović 1980:165). Similarly, only one seal of Justinian was found in Crimea. See Sokolova 1991:204. The sigillographic evidence from the Balkans includes an abundance of official seals: prefects, eparchs, consuls, *chartularii*, *magistri*, and *a secretis*. They must have belonged to the local administration. Three seals belong to *stratelates*, one of whom may have been the last king of the Gepids, Cunimund. By contrast, the sigillographic evidence from Crimea produced no seals of prefects, eparchs, consuls, or military officials. Attributions of the *quaestor exercitus*: Jones 1964:280; Torbatov 1997:78 and 80.

[110] Daily food ratios: Böttger 1990:926; Torbatov 1997:82 with n. 4. For early Byzantine amphoras, see Hautumm 1981:38; Böttger 1988:73–4; Bakirtzis 1989a:73; Van Doorninck 1989:248 and 252; Conrad 1999. LR 2 amphoras reached Ireland and England and made their way into Avar burials and local settlements north of the Danube frontier. See Hautumm 1981:43–4; Iakobson 1979:14; Cantea 1959:22; Mitrea, Eminovici, and Momanu 1986–7:224. This distribution suggests that LR 2 amphoras carried some precious substance, arguably a liquid, not just plain grain supplies. Balkan finds of LR 2: Abadie-Reynal 1989b:53; Kuzmanov 1974:313, 1978:21, and 1987:115; Jeremić and Milinković 1995:224 fig. 31; Uenze 1992:302; Mackensen 1992:252; Popović 1987:13. For Kuzmanov XIX=Scorpan XIII amphoras, see Böttger 1990:926; Kuzmanov 1985:25.

well as in Rhodes, they were used for transporting wine, oil, or grain. They were the commonest of all amphoras at Argos, in Greece, Constantinople, and on many military sites in the Balkans. They were also found in great quantities in Crimea and on the eastern Black Sea coast. The Yassi Ada shipwreck produced a large number of LR 1 amphoras, though in relatively fewer quantities than the LR 2 type. Unlike this latter type, LR 1 amphoras are also known from early seventh-century contexts. A closely similar type, Kuzmanov XV = Scorpan XII is one of the three types found at Krivina (Iatrus), but it is also known from early Byzantine forts on the eastern Black Sea coast and in Crimea. A second variant of the elongated type is known under the rather improper name of *spatheion*. *Spatheia* were most probably produced in the east Mediterranean area and may have been used for carrying olive oil, though other commodities, such as *garum* or honey, may not be excluded. Such amphoras were relatively rare at Argos and in Constantinople. The Yassi Ada shipwreck produced only two specimens. But they were very common in the northern Balkans, and the only type of early Byzantine amphoras found on hilltop sites in Slovenia.[111]

By contrast, types produced in Palestine (Late Roman 4 to 6), which were common in the western Mediterranean area and in Gaul, where they certainly transported wine, are comparatively much rarer. Only a few fragments were found in Constantinople, at Histria, Novae, and at Cape Kaliakra. Large quantities come from Argos and from some other sites in Greece, where LR 1 and LR 2 do not occur too frequently. Catherine Abadie-Reynal first attempted to explain this difference in distribution patterns by pointing to different distribution networks. She argued that Palestinian amphoras, particularly the so-called "Gaza amphora" (LR 4), seem to indicate "free-market commerce," for they crossed the Mediterranean and reached Gaul in significant quantities. Their relatively lower frequency in the Aegean area and total absence in the Balkans (except a few trade centers on the coast) suggest that the Balkans were an area of state-run distribution. The frequency curves for LR 1, LR 2, and *spatheion*-type amphoras seem therefore to support the hypothesis of *annona*-type distributions to the army. This is also suggested

---

[111] LR 1 amphoras: Mackensen 1992:252; Hautumm 1981:64; Hayes 1992:64; Jovanović 1982–3:325; Popović 1987:13; Opaiţ 1984:320; Kuzmanov 1974:312 and 1978:22; Iakobson 1979:14; Van Doorninck 1989:247; Alfen 1996. For Kuzmanov XV=Scorpan XII amphoras, see Böttger 1990:926; Iakobson 1979:12. Böttger (1988:74) suggested that the Kuzmanov XV amphora was produced in the Balkans, but no evidence exists to support this idea. For *spatheia*, see Mackensen 1992:252; Böttger 1990:926; Borisov 1985:42; Jovanović 1982–3:325; Mackensen 1987:258; Knific 1994:220. By contrast, in Gaul, particularly at Marseille, *spatheia* appear in great quantities in fifth-century deposits, but are very rare in the 500s and early 600s. See Bonifay and Piéri 1995:97.

by the constant association of these amphoras with military sites, as well as by their relatively homogeneous typology.[112]

That the sixth-century *limes* still relied on the central distribution of grain is shown by legislative measures taken by emperors from Anastasius to Justin II. All attempted to provide a solution to the irremediable problem of making a much impoverished and depopulated region of the Empire capable of producing enough food for the troops coming to its defense. Approaches to this problem ranged from compulsory collection of the *annona* to tax exemptions, but in all cases at stake were food supplies for troops stationed in Thrace or Moesia Inferior. Some have even and rightly assumed that the very creation of the *quaestura exercitus* in 536 was a solution to the problem of helping Scythia Minor and Moesia Inferior feed their troops with supplies from the rich overseas provinces. That none of these measures proved to be successful is indirectly shown by the *Strategikon*. Its author, an experienced military officer, not only knew that the Sclavenes buried "their most valuable possessions" in secret places, but also recommended that "provisions found in the surrounding countryside should not simply be wasted," but shipped on pack animals and boats to "our own country." The evidence of the *Strategikon* is archaeologically confirmed by the changing consumption patterns. In addition to shipments of *annona*, the soldiers of the fort at Iatrus relied heavily on hunting for meat procurement. Garden cultivation of millet and legumes at Iatrus and Nicopolis, as well as the occasional presence of agricultural implements elsewhere, suggest that the *annona* was not sufficient for the subsistence of the frontier troops. On the other hand, that Roman soldiers may have relied on food captured from the enemy is also a good indication of the ongoing crisis.[113]

A project of gigantic proportions and overall excellent execution, Justinian's system failed to provide the expected solutions because its maintenance would have required efforts far beyond the potential of the Roman state, particularly of the Balkan provinces. Clearly what seems to

---

[112] See Abadie-Reynal 1989b:159. For finds in Gaul, see Bonifay, Villedieu, Leguilloux, and Raynaud 1989:31. For Novae, see Klenina 1999:87. For finds in Histria, see Pippidi, Bordenache, and Eftimie 1961:241. The cargo on the Yassi Ada shipwreck has been associated with food supplies for the army, perhaps in connection with the *quaestura exercitus*. It is possible that the ship sunken off the southwest coast of Turkey shortly after 625 transported *annona* distributions to the Byzantine army in the East. See Alfen 1996:213.

[113] *Strategikon* XI 4.8 and 32. See Velkov 1962:58–9; Torbatov 1997:80. Roman armies and populace were twice supplied with food by the Avars, first after the fall of Sirmium, as the conquering Avars supplied the desperately starving besieged with "bread and wine" (John of Ephesus v.32); and then during a five-day truce for the celebration of Easter, in 598, "when famine was pressing hard on the Romans" and the qagan "supplied the starving Romans with wagons of provisions" (Theophylact Simocatta VII 13.3–4). By contrast, the Avars, unlike Germanic federates, never received supplies of grain from the Romans. See Pohl 1991b:599.

have happened after Justinian's death, if not earlier, is that the emperor's building program, whose implementation coincides with the last phase of a sharp decline of the rural population, proved to be an unbearable burden for the provincial administration. When the central distribution of *annona* completely ceased, maintaining the troops on the frontier became impossible. During Maurice's reign, the Roman army on the Danube frontier twice mutinied, and the second rebellion brought about the emperor's rapid fall. In both cases, at stake was the deterioration of the living standards and the social status of the field army as a consequence of Maurice's intended reforms.

But when did the system eventually collapse? The *communis opinio* is that as soon as Phocas' rebellion broke out, the *limes* crumbled and the Slavic tide invaded the Balkans. This idea, however, does not stand against the archaeological evidence. The year 602 has no archaeological significance for the early Byzantine settlements in the northern Balkans. Most cities and forts along the Danube frontier had already suffered heavy destruction by fire at some point between Justinian's and Maurice's reigns, at least twenty years before Phocas' rebellion. In many cases, destruction was followed by rebuilding. We have seen that the number of forts apparently abandoned without any signs of violence by far exceeds that of forts presumably sacked and destroyed by barbarians. Moreover, recent research shows that Phocas' purge of the Danubian army did not prevent it from returning to the Danubian front after overthrowing Maurice, in order to continue operations against the Avars and the Slavs. It remained there until Phocas concluded a treaty with the qagan in 605, in order to transfer the army to the Persian front. In 620, Heraclius definitely moved all troops from Europe to the eastern front. The general withdrawal of troops from the Balkan front thus coincides in time with the definite cessation of grain supplies (*annona*) from Egypt, now occupied by the Persians. The effects of the latter on grain supplies for Thessalonica are well, if indirectly, documented by the *Miracles of St Demetrius*. The Arab conquest of Syria and the subsequent developments prevented the return of the army to Thrace. The Thracian troops would be relocated in western Anatolia and Thrace remained without any troops until 680 or 690, when the Thracian theme first emerged. By that time, Justinian I's system of defense was already history.[114]

---

[114] Sebeos, p. 80. See Olster 1993:69. For the archaeological significance of AD 602, see Shuvalov 1989. For the creation of the Thracian theme, see Lilie 1977:27.

Chapter 5

BARBARIANS ON THE SIXTH-CENTURY
DANUBE FRONTIER: AN ARCHAEOLOGICAL
SURVEY

Following the collapse of the Hunnic polity in the mid-fifth century, and the military and political recovery of the Empire in the late fifth and early sixth centuries, the northern frontier along the Danube became a key element of early Byzantine foreign affairs. The fifth, sixth, and seventh centuries were also a period of dramatic changes among the Empire's northern neighbors. For the making of the Slavic *ethnie*, these changes were particularly crucial. Justinian's defensive program on the Danube frontier triggered the social and political effects that led to the process of ethnic formation described in the last chapter. Equally important was the Empire's relationship with the neighbors of the Slavs, the Gepids, the Lombards, the Cutrigurs, and the Avars. The boom which has taken place in medieval archaeology over the last few decades has made this relationship far more visible than was possible on the basis of written sources alone. The purpose of this chapter is to examine the results of archaeological investigations and the problems raised by their interpretation. Emphasis will be laid upon the use of material culture for building group identity or creating symbols of power. I will first examine the evidence from the sixth-century Carpathian basin and neighboring regions, followed by a brief survey of Avar archaeology. The last section of this chapter is devoted to the archaeology of the steppe north of the Black Sea and to problems of chronology and interpretation of hoards of silver and bronze, which are relevant for the archaeological assemblages discussed in the next chapter.

THE CARPATHIAN BASIN

Attila's death and the rapid demise of the Huns opened the way for the rise of new political forces in the Middle Danube region. The Gepids were among the first to take advantage of the power vacuum. Their king, Ardaric, who ruled between 451 and 455, became the new ally of

Emperor Marcian, and the Gepids were now paid 100 lb of gold solidi annually. In 471, they occupied Pannonia Secunda (present-day Srem and Slavonia), but were attacked in 504 by an Ostrogothic army led by Count Pitzas. The Gepids attempted to regain Sirmium, but Vitigis ousted them in 528. As the Gothic war started in Italy, however, they eventually occupied Sirmium and Bassiana. They allied themselves with the Franks and began raiding into the Balkans. In response, Emperor Justinian decided to give the Lombards the annual subsidies until then paid to the Gepids. The Gepids were defeated in 547 by an allied Lombard–Byzantine–Herul force, and again, in 551 or 552, by Lombards alone. They were led by petty kings ruling over the eastern part of the Carpathian basin. In the late 480s, Thrapstila was "king" of Sirmium, followed at his death by his son, Thrasaric. Cunimund, who ruled between 560 and 567, also resided in Sirmium, together with the Arian bishop of the Gepids. In Sirmium, Cunimund minted silver imitations of Byzantine and Ostrogothic coins.[1]

Following their victory over the Herules in *c.* 507, the Lombards moved south of the Danube's middle course into Pannonia. At some point after 526, they seem to have established themselves permanently in that region. They were most likely federates, since they appear as defending the Danube frontier, much like Suebians before them. In addition, Justinian allowed them to expand between the Sava and the Drava rivers, which brought them very close to Sirmium and to other Gepid settlements. Wacho, the king of the Lombards, had close ties to the Merovingian rulers in Reims. His eldest daughter, Wisigarda, married Theudebert in *c.* 530, while his younger daughter, Walderada, became the wife of Theudebert's son, Theudebald (547–55). In addition, the collapse of the Thuringian "kingdom," following Theudebert's victory of 534 or 535, brought large numbers of Thuringians within the area controlled by Lombards. Auduin, who ruled from 547/8 to 560/5, married Rodelinda, the daughter of Herminafred, the last Thuringian king.[2]

The first to speak of "Gepid culture" in relation to sixth-century artifacts found in the Hungarian plain (east of the Tisza river) was József Hampel, the founder of medieval archaeology in Hungary. The first cemetery was excavated in the early 1900s by Gábor Csallány at

---

[1] Procopius, *Wars* VII 33.8–11; *Secret History* 18.16–19. See also Bóna 1956:235 and 1976:16 and 71; Pohl 1980:289; Christou 1991:56. For the succession of Gepid kings, see Kiss 1989–90. During their raid of 539, the Gepids of Thrasaric killed *magister militum* Calluc (Jordanes, *Romana* 387). To Jordanes, the Lombards were the allies of the emperor against the Gepids (*Romana* 386). The chronology of the Lombard–Gepid wars has been disputed. Most scholars, however, adopted 547 for the first confrontation, 549 for the second, and 551 for the third war. See Christou 1991:84, 91, and 95; Pohl 1997:90.

[2] Christou 1991:59 and 62; Bóna 1990b:14–15. For Frankish–Lombard relations, see also Werner 1962:136.

The making of the Slavs

Berekhát, near Szentes. By 1925, Károlyi Eperjesy had unearthed the cemetery at Csanád-Bökény, the first to be coin-dated to the late fifth century. Shortly after World War II, Kurt Horedt began working at Moreşti, in Transylvania, the first fully excavated, sixth-century, settlement in the Carpathian basin. The "Gepid culture," however, came to be more often associated with burial assemblages. In his still unrivaled monograph of 1961, Dezsö Csallány listed 275 cemeteries with more than 1,900 burials and an immense quantity of artifacts. Kurt Horedt first emphasized the association of the "Gepid culture" with contemporary assemblages in Germany and France and called it the easternmost *Reihengräber* group.[3]

By contrast, the evidence of sixth-century burials in Transdanubia (i.e., the region west of the Middle Danube and presumably inhabited by Lombards) is comparatively meager. Only seventeen cemeteries are known so far in western Hungary with about 400 burials dated to the period of the Lombard presence in Pannonia. Ever since Joachim Werner subdivided the archaeological material attributed to the Lombards into three chronological phases, artifact-categories from Pannonia are viewed as different from those of Italy and the region north of the Danube river. Recent studies, however, have produced a far more complex picture. Instead of a uniform, unidirectional, migration movement, archaeologists now emphasize ties maintained between regions north and south of the Middle Danube. After *c.* 450, a new burial pattern made its appearance in Bohemia, Moravia, and Slovakia. Warriors were buried with large numbers of weapons (swords, spears, arrow heads, shield bosses, and axes). Close contacts were maintained with Merovingian Gaul, as indicated by the glass beaker found at Zohor, and with the Scandinavian world, as exemplified by the cross-brooch found at Orasice. A significant change in fashion is also visible in female burials. Besides a pair of brooches at shoulders, women wore one or two additional fibulae attached to leather straps hanging from the belt and adorned with amber or glass beads. That occupation of the area north of the Danube continued even after the Lombards established themselves in Pannonia is shown by finds of stamped pottery in Moravia. On the other hand, strong ties were maintained with the regions further to the north. This results, for example, from the unusual association at Kajdacs of thirty-eight inhumations with ten contemporary cremation burials. Further confirmation comes from finds of handmade pottery similar to that produced in central

[3] Hampel 1905:776; Bóna 1979a:10; Csallány 1961:17; Horedt 1979a. See also Horedt 1977. The term *Reihengräberkreis* was coined in 1858 by Ludwig Lindenschmidt and was used to describe funerary assemblages of the Merovingian period. The German archaeologist Joachim Werner first attempted to build a chronology for this archaeological horizon. See Werner 1935.

Bohemia. Some archaeologists laid a particular emphasis upon a variety of small, handmade pots, which were found only in children's burials. Such pots were hastily classified as Slavic, Prague-type pottery, in an attempt to provide an archaeological illustration to Procopius' story of Hildigis and his retinue of Sclavene warriors (see Chapter 3). Similar pots, however, appear in contemporary children burials east of the Tisza river, in "Gepidia." This further indicates that deposition of handmade pots should be interpreted in terms of age status, not ethnicity. István Bóna rightly rejected the interpretation of handmade pots in connection with the episode of Hildigis, by pointing to substantial chronological differences.[4]

Cemeteries in "Lombardia" appear along the right bank of the Danube, between Vienna and Budapest, often near already abandoned Roman forts, but no associated settlements have been found. Contacts with the western Frankish world increased during this period, as indicated by the growing number of Frankish–Alamannic brooches, which are otherwise absent from both Bohemian–Moravian and later Italian assemblages. The same is true for finds of swords with damascened blades (such as that from Tamási), which point to production centers in the Rhine valley.[5] Unlike the Frankish *Reihengräberkreis*, cemeteries in western Hungary produced a relatively large quantity of *millefiori* beads. Such beads were produced in Italy or in some other place in the eastern Mediterranean. By contrast, amber beads almost disappear from funerary assemblages, though connections with Scandinavia certainly continued, as evidenced by the introduction of the so-called "animal Style I" for the decoration of local types of brooches or by finds of bracteates (e.g., burial 21 at Várpalota). Scandinavian connections, perhaps mediated via "Lombardia," are also visible in funerary assemblages within the Empire's frontiers. A pair of Scandinavian brooches was found in association with a freshly minted

---

[4] See Bóna 1979b:393–4 and 1979a:24; Menghin 1982:59–60; Christie 1995:37. Phasing of the archaeological evidence: Werner 1962; Tejral 1990:231. North Danubian phase: Tejral 1975. Contacts with Merovingian Gaul and Scandinavia: Pieta 1987:394–5; Zeman 1987:521. Female dress: Bóna 1976:41; Zeman 1987:521. The stamped pottery was produced only in Pannonia and only after *c.* 530 (Werner 1962:54). Kajdacs: Bóna 1979b:395; Menghin 1982:60. Handmade pottery: Werner 1962:60; Bóna 1979b:399–400.

[5] Lombard occupation of abandoned Roman sites: Bóna 1976:33. Sixth-century settlements in Bohemia and Moravia: Vojtěchovská and Pleinerová 1997; Čižmář 1997. Replicas of two brooches from Várpalota and Hegykö were found at Haulchin (Belgium) and Wiesbaden (Germany). See Werner 1962:62; Kühn 1974:1076–86 and 1094–106. Conversely, tongs-shaped fibulae, which are typical for funerary assemblages in Bohemia and Moravia, occasionally appear in the West (Kühn 1974:827–40). For damascened sword blades, see Bóna 1978:112. The most powerful example of Lombard–Frankish contacts is that from Mosonszentjános (northwestern Hungary). One of two burials found there produced a Frankish bell-beaker of Rhenish origin and a wooden bucket with plate escutcheon mounts with anthropomorphic heads, which are also allied to an extensive group in the Rhenish area. See Bóna 1976:72–4; Menghin 1982:66–7.

solidus of Justinian (dated after 538), in a female burial in Gračanica (Kosovo, Yugoslavia). Their closest analogy is the fibula from Skodborgus (Denmark), which was found together with B- and D-bracteates, dated to the early sixth century.[6] Archaeologists traditionally divide "Gepidia" into three areas: the Tisza plain, north Serbia, and Transylvania. Large sixth-century settlements excavated in Transylvania include sunken buildings (*Grubenhäuser*) with a superstructure supported by five, six, or, sometimes, even more posts, but without any heating facility. Such buildings were common in contemporary settlements of Central and Western Europe. The earliest, but also richest, burials, dated to the second half of the fifth century also come from Transylvania. High-status burials, with many types of often costly grave-goods, may indicate the presence of a power center, perhaps the most important in the area during the half-century following the demise of Attila's Hunnic Empire.[7]

By 500, however, the distribution of wealth changed dramatically. Rich and isolated graves were replaced by relatively large cemeteries, and costly objects of gold by other, comparatively simpler, status markers. Unlike fifth-century funerary assemblages, such markers often appear in women's graves. Among the most important were silver eagle-headed buckles, lavishly decorated with niello and cabochons and equally luxurious silver or gilded silver brooches of the Aquileia class. Both artifact-types also occur in contemporary funerary assemblages in Crimea, which

[6] *Millefiori* beads: Tomka 1980:22; Koch 1974; Fiedler 1992:81. Amber beads: Bóna 1956:213; Werner 1962:82. Bracteates: Haseloff 1981:702; Werner 1962:80; Bóna 1976:pl. 80. Gračanica: Popović and Čerškov 1956:319–20; Vinski 1968:106 and pls. II–III; Haseloff 1981:238–41 and pl. 32/1. Werner assigned the pair of fibulae to a Kentish variant of square-headed brooches, but no such specimen is known from Anglo-Saxon England. See Werner 1970:77; Hines 1997. That contacts with Scandinavia may have been mediated via "Lombardia" is shown by the large, single, fibula from Gračanica, with its footplate inspired by brooches of the Cividale, Ravenna, and Castel Trosino classes (Kühn 1974:1187–91, 1217–24, and 1239–48). In addition, the Gračanica burial produced a buckle and two belt straps for which the closest analogies are those from the second burial at Mosonszentjános. I wish to thank Dr Mihailo Milinković (University of Belgrade) for his kind assistance in reconstructing the exact position of the grave-goods found at Gračanica and for sharing with me his excellent knowledge of sixth-century archaeological assemblages in Yugoslavia.

[7] Bóna 1976:29–30; Cseh 1986:205. Settlements in Transylvania: Horedt 1979a; n. a. 1955a; Vlassa et al. 1966; Gaiu 1994; Bârzu 1994–5; Zaharia 1994–5. There are no fully excavated, sixth-century settlements in the Tisza region, only isolated buildings. See Cseh 1997. *Grubenhäuser* similar to those from Transylvania were found in Germany (Bärhorst, Gladbach, Weimar, and Irl), England (West Stow), and Belgium (Brebières). See Kiss 1992:59. For late fifth-century, high-status burials, see Harhoiu 1982:587. The Hunnic gold, or at least a good part of it, most likely fell into the hands of the anti-Hunnic coalition of 454. Knowing that the Gepid king Ardaric was the leader of this coalition, it is tempting to associate the "princely graves" at Apahida I and II (with objects weighing more than 1 kg and 2.4 kg gold, respectively) with the late fifth-century Gepid royal seat. See Kiss 1987b:58 and 61.

points to long-distance contacts with "Gepidia." A small number of sixth-century Byzantine coins suggests that, in material culture terms, relations with the Empire had comparatively less importance.[8]

By contrast, contacts with Scandinavia were much stronger. Nils Åberg suggested that a true commercial network existed between sixth-century Gotland and Italy, in which "Gepidia," particularly after the conquest of Sirmium, played a major role. Two eagle-headed buckles were found at Tylkowo, a sixth-century cemetery in Mazuria, while Joachim Werner rightly pointed to "imports" from "Gepidia" found in the warrior burial at Taurapilis (Lithuania). An equal-armed brooch found in grave no. 84 at Szentes-Nagyhegy, in Hungary, is a typical specimen of the animal Style I (phase B) in east Sweden, which dates from the early sixth century. To the same direction points the buckle accidentally found at Gyula, near the present-day Hungarian–Romanian border, which was certainly produced in Scandinavia in a style strikingly similar to local fibulae decorated in animal Style I. Finally, the square-headed brooch with foot-plate bar, which was found in burial no. 124 at Szolnok-Szandaszöllös, is a unique continental specimen of a purely Scandinavian series of the early 500s. Such contacts were probably the result of a variety of factors, ranging from gift-exchange and exogamy to traveling craftsmen. It is much more difficult to identify trade connections. In any case, once they reached "Gepidia," few Scandinavian and Baltic goods were further redistributed into neighboring regions.[9]

This is most evident from the examination of sixth-century amber finds within the Carpathian basin. Unlike contemporary funerary assemblages in western Pannonia, burials in eastern Hungary and

---

[8] According to István Bóna (1976:72), the main cause for the radical changes taking place around AD 500 was that "the majority of Gepids had lost their clan rights as many were hit by poverty, wealth and power being concentrated in the hands of a small group of nobles relying on their small armed retinues." With no serious, quantitative, study of "Gepid" funerary assemblages, although plausible, Bóna's interpretation is no more than pure speculation. It is true, however, that in Transylvania changing burial patterns were accompanied by the rise of hillforts, a phenomenon probably linked to dramatic social changes. See Horedt 1957, 1964, and 1969; Harhoiu 1982:590. No such forts were found in the Tisza region, which produced, however, the richest and largest sixth-century cemeteries. Eagle-headed buckles: Rusu 1959; Bóna 1976:13–15. Brooches of the Aquileia class: Kühn 1965:95–101; Harhoiu 1982:589 and 1990:187. Contacts with Crimea: Ambroz 1968:14 and 17; Aibabin 1990:32–5. Sixth-century Byzantine coins in "Gepidia": Bóna et al. 1993:77.

[9] Trade network: Åberg 1953:90 and 100–1; Hines 1984:277. Tylkowo: Rusu 1959:12. Taurapilis: Werner 1977. Szentes-Nagyhegy: Csallány 1961:59–62 and pls. xxxix/5 and xli/1; Åberg 1953:102; Haseloff 1981:187–8. The animal Style I decoration of this fibula is very similar to that of "Lombard" fibulae in western Hungary (e.g., burial no. 8 from Bezenye). Gyula: Csallány 1961:113 and pl. cxcii/2; Haseloff 1981:702. Szolnok-Szandaszöllös: Csallány 1961:211 and pl. ccxlvi/1; Haseloff 1981:701; Hines 1984:271–2 and 1997:28 and pl. 102a.

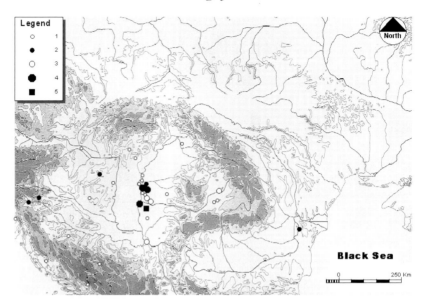

Figure 14 Distribution of amber beads in late fifth- or sixth-century burial
assemblages within the Carpathian basin and neighboring areas
1 – 1 specimen; 2 – between 2 and 10 specimens; 3 – between 10 and 20 specimens; 4 – between
30 and 40 specimens; 5 – over 100 specimens

Transylvania produced a large number of amber beads, often in more
than one specimen and in combination with glass or chalk beads. The
largest quantity in a single cemetery (138 in total) is from Kiszombor,
but neighboring cemeteries (Szentes-Nagyhegy, Berekhát, Szentes-
Kökényzug, Szöreg) also produced large numbers of amber beads. A
distribution map of all known finds (Figure 14) shows a concentration
in "Gepidia," especially in the region on the left bank of the Tisza,
between the Körös/Criş and the Maros/Mureş rivers. Despite the lack
of any characterization studies, it is possible that these beads were made
of succin amber, which is found on the shores of the Baltic Sea. That
amber traveled along the Vistula trade route is demonstrated by amber
deposits, such as that found at Basonia, but none could be dated later
than *c.* 450. The distribution map shows that if amber beads were
imported into "Gepidia" from the Baltic coast, comparatively few were
allowed to pass further, which may indicate that they were used,
between *c.* 500 and *c.* 565, as markers of group identity in "Gepidia."
This is also suggested by the distribution of amber beads dated to the

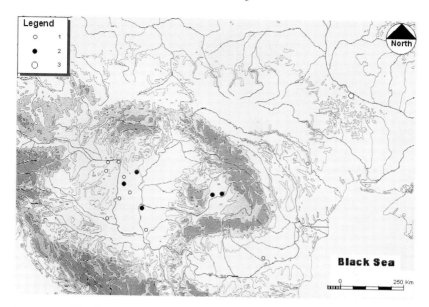

Figure 15 Distribution of amber beads in seventh-century assemblages within
the Carpathian basin and neighboring areas
For symbols, see Figure 14

Early Avar period (*c.* 570 to *c.* 670), which sharply contrasts with the
previous, more localized distribution (Figure 15).[10]

As shown in Chapter 1, emblemic style often marks and maintains
boundaries and transmits a clear message to a defined target population.
It becomes highly visible particularly in times of sociopolitical stress and
between-group competition and hostility. Archaeological finds in
Hungary and the neighboring regions, which could be dated to the late
fifth century or to the first two-thirds of the sixth century, concentrate
either on the right bank of the Danube or on the left bank of the Tisza
river (Figure 16).[11] There are few known finds in the land between the
two rivers and no sites of a fortified nature. This area was interpreted as

---

[10] Amber beads in Pannonia: Csallány 1961:272. Provenance analysis: Pétrequin et al. 1987:280–2.
For contacts between Merovingian Gaul and the Baltic coast, see also Kazanski 1991b. Almost 50
percent of the beads found in cemeteries in the northern Caucasus region and in Crimea were
made of amber from the Kurzem coast. See Krumphanzlová 1992:361; Deopik 1961:204 table 1.
Deposits of amber: Wielowiejski 1987:77–9 and 83. Early Avar amber beads: Tóth and Horváth
1992:205–6. Amber beads found in Early Avar assemblages were interpreted as markers of the
identity of Gepid communities under Avar rule. See Kiss 1996:197.
[11] Data after Menghin 1982 and Bóna et al. 1993.

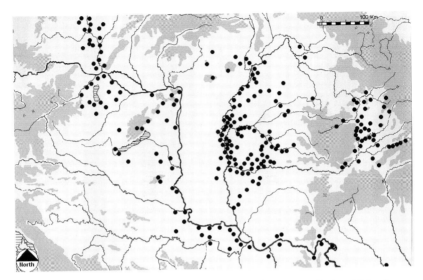

Figure 16 Distribution of late fifth- and sixth-century finds within the
Carpathian basin

a "no man's land" separating the Lombards from the Gepids. There was
undoubtedly significant interaction across this buffer zone. The construction of male identity in both "Lombardia" and "Gepidia" operated with
the same artifact-categories, which is most visible from the dress of the
deceased at burial or from the provision of military gear. With few exceptions (such as the damascened blades from Tamási), there is no difference
between swords found in warrior graves in western Pannonia and
"Gepidia," despite Jordanes' claim that the *ensis* was a typically Gepid
weapon. In both cases, these were double-edged weapons, ranging from
80 to 100 centimeters in length. In both areas, as elsewhere in Europe,
shield deposition signalized male adulthood. Both west of the Danube
and east of the Tisza river the prevalent type of shield boss was indeed
not different from contemporary Anglo-Saxon or west Merovingian
specimens with convex cone, straight wall, and five flange rivets.[12]

Helmets of the Baldenheim class, which were also used by Roman

---

[12] For the "no man's land" between Lombards and Gepids, see Werner 1962:116; Christie 1995:55.
Wacho, the Lombard king, married Austrigusa, the daughter of the Gepid king (Paul the Deacon,
Historia Langobardorum I 21). The episode of Hildigis also points to interaction between Lombards
and Gepids. For the *ensis* as a Gepid weapon *par excellence*, see Jordanes, *Getica* 50; Csallány 1961:96
fig. 1; Cseh 1990a:30; Kiss 1992:52. For the distribution of graves with swords in pre-Avar
"Gepidia," see Kiss 1992:96 fig. 1. Shields and shield deposition: Hübener 1989:94; Dickinson
and Härke 1992:13–17 and 69. It is true, however, that well-datable burial contexts in western
Pannonia show that by the mid-sixth century there was a change in shape of shield bosses from

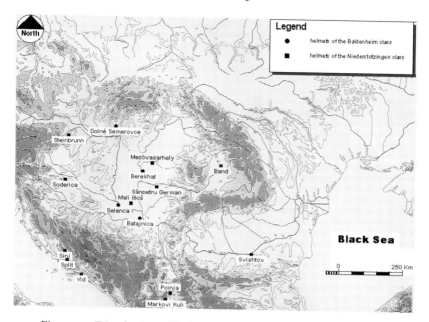

Figure 17 Distribution of helmets within the Carpathian basin and
neighboring areas

army officers, were found in both "Lombardia" (Dolné Semerovce and
Steinbrunn) and "Gepidia" (Batajnica and Berekhát) (Figure 17). Such
rare and expensive artifacts, which clearly signalize high social status, are
easy to distinguish from slightly later helmets of the Niederstotzingen
class, for which parallels could be found as far as Bokchondong in South
Korea.[13]

Interaction between "Lombardia" and "Gepidia" is even more visible,
when we examine finds of stamped pottery. There are about forty

sugar-loaf to convex-coned, presumably under the influence of Gepid and Byzantine weapons
(Werner 1962:80). Both forms of shield bosses were still in use during the Early Avar period; see
Kiss 1992:52.

[13] Baldenheim helmets: Vinski 1957:pls. I–VII/7 and 1982:pls. I/I, VII/2–3, X/2, and IX/I; Csallány
1961:pls. LI/8, LXXXV/3, and LIX/5; Kiss 1983; Maneva 1987; Pieta 1987:394; Mikulčić and
Nikuljska 1979:69 fig. 4; Georgiev 1985–6:210 fig. 6/3; Press et al. 1973:137 figs. 1–2; Bóna
1976:50 fig. 11. See also Böhner 1993:206. The Ostrogothic kings Totila and Theodahad were
represented on their own, respective, coinage as wearing Baldenheim-type helmets. Similar
helmets appear in very rich burials in Western Europe. For the rich decoration of the Bitola
helmet, which imitates coin-studded jewelry, see Marinescu 1996:294. Niederstotzingen helmets:
Kovács 1913:281 fig. 13; Maneva 1987:102; Cseh 1990a:30; Dörner 1960:fig. 3/1; Vinski 1982:pl.
XV. Such helmets originated in the Far East. See Werner 1988. Their appearance in eastern and
central Europe, as well as in Italy, is attributed to the Avars. See Vinski 1982:14; Maneva 1987:102;
Swietosławski 1993:284; Kryganov 1990:76.

stamped vessels found in "Gepidia" and some thirty pots from
"Lombardia." Pots with stamped decoration were certainly produced
locally, as evidenced by the kiln and the associated potsherds found at
Törökszentmiklós, in eastern Hungary. Such pottery was only rarely
found in settlements, which may indicate its exclusively funerary use. All
known finds of stamped pottery come from male burials. No die-study
exists of stamped vessels from cemeteries in western Pannonia and
"Gepidia", to be compared with C. J. Arnold's analysis of stamped urns
from Anglo-Saxon cemeteries. The methodology used by Attila Kiss for
identifying sixth-century stamps that were also used during the Early
Avar period is based on the macroscopic comparison of the stamps presented in the form of a presence/absence diagram. According to Kiss,
there are five stamps which appear on both "Gepid" and "Lombard"
vessels and four stamps which appear on "Gepid," but not on "Lombard,"
pottery. In reality, though most likely cut in different dies and with different frequency, almost all stamps were used in both areas. In the absence
of die-studies, however, it is difficult to decide whether or not and to
what extent dies moved from one site to the other, following family or
kin connections. In any case, judging from the evidence available from
published photographs and/or drawings, it seems there was no specific
clustering. Stamp patterns, if not dies, were used on both sides of the "no
man's land" between the Danube and the Tisza.[14]

Clear material culture distinctions were maintained, however, in a
wide range of artifact-categories found in women's graves. As in many
other cases in sixth-century Europe, female apparel may have been used
as internal and external badge as well as a reminder of ethnic identity.
While cemeteries in western Pannonia produced no specimens of any
kind, various types of earrings, especially those with polyhedral cube,
were particularly frequent in "Gepidia."[15] Unlike graves in "Lombardia,"

[14] The presence of an antler die within the early Byzantine fort at Momčilov Grad (Brmbolić
1986:fig. 37) indicates that decorated pottery was also produced within the Empire's frontiers. For
the production of stamped pottery in "Gepidia," see Cseh 1990b. The kiln at Törökszentmiklós
produced decorated pots which are die-linked to stamped vessels of unknown provenance, now
in the National Museum in Budapest (Cseh 1990b:236). Settlement finds of stamped pottery:
Horedt 1979b:pl. 37/1; Popović 1987:22 fig. 17/7, 9–12; Bârzu 1994–5:288 fig. 14/8, 12, and 19.
Burial finds: Simoni 1977–8:231; Knific 1994; Kiss 1984:135; Bóna 1990b. See also Kiss 1992:55
and 77–9. Die-link studies: Arnold 1983 and 1988. The lattice circle, which is viewed as a typically Lombard stamp, occurs frequently on handmade, sixth-century pottery in southeast and
southwest Germany (Werner 1962:60). Two stamps, the lattice lozenge and the simple lattice rectangle, are particularly frequent on pottery found in Italy. Stamped pottery also appears in early
Avar ceramic assemblages, but there are no die-linked specimens. See Vida 1990–1:133, 1995:104,
and 1999:37 with n. 16.
[15] Female apparel as marker of ethnic identity: Sasse 1990:48; Strauß 1992:70; Dickinson 1993:39;
Hines 1994:52. See also Pancake 1991:46. For the absence of earrings in Transdanubia, see Sági
1964:396. Earrings with polyhedral cube: Horedt 1979b; Slabe 1986:201; Bierbrauer 1987:150;
Cseh 1990a:29–30; Uenze 1992:163. For other types of earrings, see Kiss 1992:52–3 and 1996:309.

where single-layered combs were preferred, women and children in "Gepidia" were buried with double-layered ones in their hair.[16] Unlike Lombard women's graves, Gepid ones had no straps with fastened jewels, though they occasionally produced reliquaries attached to the belt. In "Lombardia," after *c.* 530, there were no burials, either of children or of women, with artificially deformed skulls. By contrast, artificial cranial deformation, a practice introduced by the Huns in the early 400s, was maintained in "Gepidia" during most of the sixth century.[17]

No other artifact-category, however, is more relevant in relation to the construction of ethnic boundaries than brooches. The distribution of all types of bow fibulae which were in use during the first two-thirds of the sixth century (Figure 18) shows a sharp contrast between the area west of the Danube and the region east of the Tisza river.[18] A particularly popular class of brooches in "Gepidia" was the Gurzuf type, which also occurs in Crimea and Mazuria, an indication of long-distance contacts established with "Gepidia."[19] However, the most popular fibulae were those of the Hahnheim class, many of which have parallels in Germany or France. There are two variants of this class, apparently of local production and use.[20] A related, also very popular, type of brooch was that of the Krainburg class.[21] Brooches of this class appear in Crimea, Mazuria, Germany, and France. Specimens with a slightly different decoration

---

[16] See Bóna 1956:213 and 1976:43. Such combs were produced locally. See Dumitraşcu 1982.

[17] Reliquaries: Csallány 1961:pl. xxxix/4. Lack of skull deformation in "Lombardia": Zeman 1987:524. Skull deformation in "Gepidia": Cseh 1990a:60. On skull deformation and ideals of female beauty, see the interesting remarks in Mikić 1992–3:197–8. Artificial cranial deformation is also attested in contemporary cemeteries in the western Balkan area. See Pilarić 1975; Slabe 1978; Vuga 1980. For "Hunnic" artificial cranial deformation, see Werner 1956. For artificial cranial deformation in Merovingian Gaul, see Crubézy 1990. The practice is also attested in Crimea, where it is associated with both female and male burials. See Kropotkin 1959:190. For a cross-cultural perspective on artificial cranial deformation and its relation to social status, see Garrett 1988.

[18] Data compiled from Csallány 1961; Kühn 1974; Werner 1962; and Bóna 1990b. In what follows, I left aside cast fibulae with bent stems and crossbow brooches, which were particularly frequent in "Gepidia." The same is true for fifth-century brooch types, such as Alkofen or Krefeld (Kühn 1974:571–5 and 587–95).

[19] Kühn 1974:728–42. Assigned brooches: Csánád-Bökény, Kiszombor (grave 88), Moreşti, Novi Banovci, Pecica, Szentes-Rákoczi utca, Szentes-Kökényzug (graves 49 and 66), Berekhát (graves 2 and 43), Szentes-Nagyhegy (grave 22), and Sânnicolau Mare. Specimens produced in Crimea may have imitated "imports" from "Gepidia" (Aibabin 1990:20–1).

[20] Kühn 1974:799–811. Assigned brooches: Hódmezővásárhely-Gorzsa (grave 94), Magyartés, Szentes-Kökényzug (grave 56), Berekhát (grave 274), Tarnaméra, and Jankovo (grave 13). Despite Kühn's claims to the contrary, it is possible that this class of fibulae originated in the West, sometime before or after 500, and was later "imported" to "Gepidia." For local variants, see Horedt 1979a:183. Some authors compared one of these variants with the so-called "Slavic" brooches of Werner's class II, a comparison rejected by Werner himself. See n.a. 1954:210; Horedt 1977:258; Werner 1950:167.

[21] Kühn 1974:758–66. Assigned brooches: Beregovo, Csongrád-Kettöshalmi, Dunaföldvár, Kistelek, Oradea, Szentes-Nagyhegy (grave 77), Szentes-Kökényzug (graves 29 and 50), Tiszaroff (grave 1), and Tiszaladány.

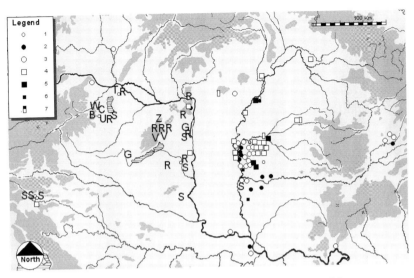

Figure 18 Distribution of sixth-century fibulae within
the Carpathian basin

1 – disc-brooches; 2 – Gurzuf class; 3 – Hahnheim class and variants; 4 – Krainburg class; 5 –
Reggio Emilia class; 6 – Szentes-Berekhát class; 7 – Wittislingen class; B – Burghagel class; C –
Cividale class; G – Goethe class; R – Ravenna class; S – S-shaped brooches; T – Castel Trosino
class; V – Trivières class; U – Ulm class; W – Wiesbaden class; Z – *Zangenfibeln*

were also found in Italy, where they were interpreted as "imports" from
"Gepidia."[22] Conversely, fibulae of the Reggio Emilia class may have
been Ostrogothic "imports" into "Gepidia."[23] Two specimens of the
Suuk Su group, that of Kiszombor (grave 146) and that of Magyartés,
have analogies in Spain. Two other classes, Pfullingen and Wittislingen,
originated in the West.[24] By contrast, S-shaped fibulae and disc-brooches
are very rare in the area east of the Tisza river.[25]

The range of brooch classes in "Lombardia" is also very wide. A

22 Kühn 1974:758–66. For Italian specimens, see Bierbrauer 1975:284 and pl. XXIII/2 and
   1978:221–2 and pl. XCIII/7.3.
23 Kühn 1974:718–26. Assigned brooches: Szentes-Nagyhegy (grave 8), Berekhát (grave 105 and
   stray find), and Tiszafüred.
24 Kühn 1974:510–46 (Suuk Su), 639–48 (Pfullingen), and 891–4 (Wittislingen). Only one specimen of the Pfullingen class is known, that of grave 247 at Kiszombor. Wittislingen brooches:
   Gyöngyös, Oradea, Szarvas, Ószöny. The only known analogy for the fibulae from Berekhát
   (grave 202), Tiszafüred (grave 1), and Bočar (grave 4) is the specimen found at Mainz (Kühn
   1974:288 no. 190). They all form Kühn's class Szentes-Berekhát (Kühn 1974:1275–8). Three other
   brooches (Morești, Novi Banovci, and Szentes-Kökényzug, grave 29), which belong to Kühn's
   class Taman (Kühn 1974:766–79), have no analogies outside "Gepidia."
25 S-shaped fibula: Szöreg (grave XI). Disc-brooches: Tiszafüred (grave 1) and Hódmezővásárhely
   (grave 77).

brooch of Kühn's Burghagel class was found at Hegykö (grave 21). Its closest analogy is a fibula from Besançon.[26] Frankish analogies may also be cited for two specimens of the Trivières class, found at Várpalota (grave 5) and Jutas. This is also true for the fibula of Kühn's Ulm class found at Fertöszentmiklós, for the *Zangenfibel* found at Várpalota (grave 13), and for the fibula of Kühn's Wiesbaden class found at Hegykö (grave 4). The only specimen of the Gurzuf class, which was so popular in contemporary "Gepidia," was found at Szentendre. From the same cemetery (grave 33) comes the only specimen of the Hahnheim class found west of the Danube river. By contrast, the number of S-shaped and disc-brooches is comparatively larger. The distribution of fibulae west of the Danube river is also characterized by a relatively large number of brooches without any analogies outside "Lombardia," except Italy. Kühn's Goethe, Cividale, Ravenna, and Castel Trosino classes are cases in point.[27]

The distribution of all these types speaks for itself. Completely different, but coexisting, types of brooches were in use and fashion on each side of the "no man's land" between the Danube and the Tisza river. We can clearly speak of two different "styles" of brooch-use and assume that they convey information about relative identity of the brooch owners. The patterns and contrasts created did not produce, however, ethnically specific artifact-categories. Very few, if any, brooch classes were creations *ex nihilo* and many were either "imports" or produced as replicas of "imported" specimens. In other words, no particular class could be *a priori* diagnosed as either "Gepid" or "Lombard." The ethnic boundary emerged from the manipulation of specific types, without assigning an "ethnic value" to any of them. More important, this coincides in time with increasing rivalry between the two groups, following the Lombard settlement of the land between the Sava and the Drava rivers, not far from Sirmium, now in Gepid hands. The Lombard–Gepid wars of the mid-sixth century may have contributed to the consolidation of emblemic styles on the Lombard–Gepid frontier. According to Theophylact Simocatta, the final confrontation between Alboin and Cunimund was

---

[26] Brooches in "Lombardia": Tejral 1990. Burghagel class: Kühn 1974:965–70.

[27] Kühn 1974:689–94 (Ulm class), 827–40 (*Zangenfibeln*), 996–1006 (Goethe class), 1076–86 (Wiesbaden class), and 1094–106 (Trivières class), 1187–91 (Cividale class), 1217–24 (Ravenna class), and 1239–48 (Castel Trosino class). Two specimens of the Hahnheim class were found in Mistřín and Vienna (see Werner 1962:68). S-shaped fibulae: Kajdacs (grave 2), Rácálmás (graves 16 and 20), Fertöszentmiklós (grave 9), Mohács (grave 5), Kranj (several specimens). Disc-brooches: Hegykö (graves 18 and 21), Bezenye (grave 3), Kajdacs (grave 2), Kranj (graves 193/1907, 43, 58, and 66). Goethe fibulae: Keszthely (grave B) and Rácálmás (grave 2). Cividale class: Hegykö (grave 18). Ravenna brooches: Bezenye (grave 20), Várpalota (graves 1, 17, and 19), Kápolnásnyék, Szentendre (graves 29 and 56), Kajdacs (grave 2), Tamási (grave 6), Rácálmás (grave 16), and Fertöszentmiklós (grave 9). Castel Trosino class: Bezenye (grave 8).

The making of the Slavs

caused by Rosimunda, the daughter of the Gepid king, who was kidnapped by Alboin. This may suggest that aristocratic women played a major role in the display of emblemic styles.[28]

THE AVARS

Few events in the medieval history of East Central Europe were given more importance by historians than the annihilation of the Gepid and, later, Lombard "kingdoms" and the conquest of the Carpathian basin by the Avars. To many, the year 568 is the beginning of the Middle Ages, an East European equivalent of 476. Archaeologists working within a culture-historical framework maintain that AD 568 represents an important chronological marker and cultural watershed.[29]

József Hampel was the first to acknowledge the existence of two chronological horizons in the archaeological material attributed to the Avars. András Alföldi first pointed to the importance of Byzantine coins found in burials for the phasing of the "Avar culture." Despite recent caveats, some fifty Byzantine coins found as either funerary offerings or ornamental objects in rich male burials still underpin the entire chronological system of Avar archaeology.[30] There are more than 50,000 burials dated to the period between c. 570 (the foundation of the Avar qaganate) and c. 800 (the collapse of the Avar qaganate following Charlemagne's victories). On the basis of her analysis of the Alattyán cemetery, Ilona Kovrig first divided this period into three phases, namely Early (568–650/60), Middle (650/60–700), and Late Avar (700–92). Only the first phase can be coin-dated, but Kovrig believed that some Early Avar assemblages, especially those associated with coins minted for Justinian, Justin II, or Tiberius II, were earlier than the first half of the seventh century. This claim, however, proved to be groundless, given the underlying problems of the chronological association of coins and artifacts and of their respective use-life.[31]

---

[28] Theophylact Simocatta VI 10.8.

[29] Pohl 1988:52–7. In István Bóna's words (1976:105), the year 568 was the end of "almost 600 years' rule by successive Germanic tribes in the Carpathian basin."

[30] See Hampel 1905; Alföldi 1934. For the use of Byzantine coins for the chronology of Avar assemblages, see Bóna 1990a:113. Separating the Early Avar material from the Middle Avar one, however, is a very difficult, if not impossible, task. Coins are not always good guides to chronological studies. For example, a bracelet with trumpet-shaped ends was found at Szentendre in association with a coin minted for Emperor Phocas (607–10). Its closest parallel is that from the Zemiansky Vrbovok hoard, which also produced miliaresia struck for Emperor Constantine IV (668–9). See Bálint 1993:201. For the Szentendre burial, see also Garam 1992:138–9.

[31] Kovrig 1963. See also Bóna 1971:291; Sós 1973:86. The existence of an Early Avar phase had already been postulated by Dezsö Csallány, who was also the first to assign artifact-categories to

The number of Byzantine coins produced so far by Early Avar assemblages, on the other hand, is remarkably small. As a consequence of various treaties with the Empire, Byzantine payments to the Avars between 568 and 626 totalled at least 6 million solidi. It is very likely that a good part of this incredible wealth was later redistributed within the Avar qaganate as gifts. It is possible that the majority of these coins were melted to provide raw material for gold jewelry, for the exact weight of the largest earrings with pyramid-shaped pendants, which are so typical for Early Avar assemblages, is equivalent to either eight or ten light solidi. Since the use of gold, instead of the usual silver, is restricted to a few exceptionally rich burials, it is possible that supplies of Byzantine gold became the monopoly of a small elite headed by the qagan. If this is true, it may be more productive to treat Early Avar assemblages as indicative of social stratification, than to continue to draw lists of chronologically sensitive artifact-categories.[32]

Some authors ascribe archaeological assemblages to the Early Avar period on the basis of their alleged analogies from Central Asia or the Middle East, but rarely can contemporary parallels for Early Avar artifact-categories be found outside the Carpathian basin.[33] Equally unique are burials with both human and horse skeletons. Swords with P- or 3-shaped sheath attachments are typical for the earliest assemblages attributed to Avar warriors, but all of them predate their frequently cited East

this archaeological phase. See Csallány 1946–8. Middle Avar assemblages produced Avar imitations of non-identifiable Byzantine coins. See Bóna 1980:34. For Early Avar assemblages with coins of Justinian, Justin II, and Tiberius II, see Garam 1990:138–9. For a critique of Kovrig's chronology based on coins, see Bálint 1989:149 and 1993:246. The Kunágota burial, which produced a light-weight solidus of Justinian, is now dated to the first third of the seventh century. See Garam 1995:127.

[32] Pohl 1991b:598. For a list of treaties and payments of gold to the Avars, see Pohl 1988:502. Unlike Goths, Lombards, or Gepids, the Avars never received payments in food. Like coins, finds of Byzantine jewels are equally rare in Avar assemblages. For the weight equivalence between Avar earrings and solidi, see Bóna 1990a:117. For gold as a monopoly of the Avar elite, see Garam 1990:258. For Avar assemblages as indicative of social stratification, see Szentpéteri 1993a and 1993b.

[33] Bálint 1989:149 and 1993:214; Garam 1990:253. A clear Central Asian origin may be claimed only for bone artifacts, such as needle cases, buckles, awls, or belt pendants. See Sekeres 1957; Bóna 1980:52 and 54. Of "Asian" origin may also be finds of single earrings with male skeletons, the deposition of the belt (without buckle), sword, and quiver on the right side of the skeleton, with the bow on top of the coffin. See Bálint 1993:217–18 and 237; Tomka 1995:83. The only parallels for the deposition of armor slats are those from the Altai region and the Tuva basin (Bóna 1980:45). By contrast, there is no "Asian" element in the decoration of belt-buckles and plates. Silver rosette-mounts, which appear frequently in Early Avar assemblages, have no analogies outside the Carpathian basin, except two rich burials in Ukraine (Malo Pereshchepino and Glodosy). See Bálint 1993:234; Sós and Salamon 1995:33. In addition, the use of earrings by adult males most likely imitated Sassanian practices (Bóna 1980:39). Attempts to identify Central Asian Avars by means of physical anthropology bore no fruits. See Tóth 1967.

The making of the Slavs

European or Central Asian analogies.[34] It is also difficult to demonstrate a Central Asian origin for the wheel-made grey ware, which was produced only during the Early Avar period in southwest Hungary.[35]

Both bow-shaped stirrups and stirrups with elongated attachment loops, which are viewed as typical for Early Avar assemblages and the earliest European stirrups, were found in the Kudyrge cemetery in Tuva (west of Lake Baikal, near the Chinese–Russian–Mongolian frontier). Turkic archaeology, however, is notoriously lacking any firmly established chronological system. As a consequence, there is no possibility of deciding whether or not such stirrups were brought by the Avar horsemen from Central Asia or "invented" by them in the Carpathian basin. The majority of Early Avar burials were found either in isolation or in small groups of graves. In the absence of large cemeteries, which would permit an analysis of frequency, distribution, and toposeriation of artifact-categories, the relative chronology of the Early Avar period remains problematic.[36]

Another major difficulty is the dating of Middle Avar assemblages. On the exclusive basis of burial evidence and without sufficient settlement finds for comparison, it is almost impossible to discriminate between (late) Early and Middle Avar artifact-categories, although it is clear that the second half of the seventh century witnessed some dramatic cultural change. The Middle Avar phase was first identified within the Kisköre-Halastó cemetery, but its best-known monuments are the rich burials of the so-called Tótipuszta–Dunapentele–Igar group. Dated by means of coins minted for Emperors Constans II and Constantine IV, these burials have close analogies in extremely rich funerary assemblages from

[34] For burials with human and horse skeletons, see Bóna 1979c:18–19. For swords with P- or 3-shaped sheath attachments, see Bálint 1993:219; Ambroz 1986. The date of the Avar specimens is given by the warrior burial found at Szegvár-Sápoldal, in which a double-edged sword with P-shaped sheath attachments was associated with an imitation of a solidus struck for Emperor Maurice. Another, similar specimen was found in burial 2 at Kiszombor O, in association with a solidus struck for Emperor Phocas. The latest P-shaped sheath attachments known so far are those from the horseman burial at Iváncsa, dated to the late seventh century, but such artifacts were already rare by AD 630 (Garam 1992:157). Swords with 3-shaped sheath attachments, such as found in Early Avar assemblages, have no parallel outside the Carpathian basin, except the rich burial at Malo Pereshchepino.

[35] Vida 1990–91:133 and 1999:42–63. István Bóna claimed a Central Asian origin for this ceramic category, but other authors pointed to possible parallels in sixth-century ceramic assemblages in Romania, of the so-called Ipoteşti-Cândeşti culture. See Vékony 1973. For ceramic categories with clear Central Asian analogies, see Vida 1992.

[36] Truly Avar stirrups first occurred in Merovingian burials in southern and western Germany during the second third of the seventh century. Replicas of Avar stirrups with elongated attachment loops were produced there as early as the second half of the seventh century. See Bott 1976:227. For Turkic archaeology, see Bálint 1989:242–3 and 249. Large Avar cemeteries only appear after c. 650 (Bóna 1971:292). For large cemeteries with Early Avar material, see Salamon and Erdelyi 1971; Sós and Salamon 1995; Kiss 1996; Bárdos 1995. Toposeriation: Djindjian 1985.

Ukraine, which will be discussed in the following section of this chapter (Voznesenka, Malo Pereshchepino, Glodosy, and Zachepilovki).[37] These astonishing parallels at such a great distance were interpreted as evidence for the migration into the Avar qaganate, by the late seventh century, of a Bulgar group fleeing the civil war inside the western Turkic qaganate. But there are also signs of remarkable continuity between the Early and the Middle Avar assemblages, particularly in western Hungary. Beginning with the last decades of the Early Avar period, belt buckles and plates were decorated with an original variant of the animal Style II, characterized by the frequent occurrence of the dentil pattern. Single-edged sabres, of a type commonly dated to the Middle Avar period, were found in at least three Early Avar contexts, that of the Sânpetru German burial (dated by means of a perforated coin struck for Heraclius and Heraclius Constantine), that of burial 259 from Kölked-Feketekapu, and that of grave x from Tarnaméra-Urak düllö. Combat axes, though typical for the Middle, but especially for the Late, Avar period, are also known from Early Avar contexts and from seventh-century assemblages in Italy and Albania.[38]

The understanding of Avar history and archaeology is crucial for the problem of Slavic ethnicity, particularly because, as shown in Chapter 3, in the aftermath of the Avar conquest, numerous groups of Sclavenes became subjects of the qagan. The subject of Avar–Slavic relations is extremely controversial. The debate has often been embittered by nationalistic claims, but there is also little understanding of how the Early Avar society and qaganate operated. As far as written sources allow us to tell, the territorial division following the conquest of the Carpathian basin resembles a Turkic scheme (of Chinese inspiration) based on *ēl* ("the peace zone"), including all territories under the qagan's direct rule, and *yāgī*, the territory of the enemy, who refuses to obey the qagan's orders.

---

[37] The first to postulate the existence of the chronological phase now known as Middle Avar was the Hungarian archaeologist Gyula Lászlo (1955). For the culture change of the mid-seventh century, see Bálint 1993:201. The most important marker of this change is the shift from swords to sabres and combat axes, an indication of changing warfare practices. In addition, the Middle Avar period coincides with the introduction of a new decoration style primarily based on the interlaced pattern. See Bálint 1989:156–60; Garam 1992:158–9. For Middle Avar sabres and their Sassanian parallels, see also Bálint 1978:184. For the Tótipuszta–Dunapentele–Igar group, see Garam 1976:129 and 140; Fülöp 1988 and 1990; Müller 1989. Avar settlements: Bóna 1968. The first (Late) Avar sunken building was excavated in 1962 by Otto Trogmayer at Bokros (Bóna 1971:313). The monograph of the site at Dunaújváros remains the only comprehensive study of (Early and Middle) Avar settlements. See Bóna 1973.

[38] Sânpetru German: Dörner 1960; Kölked-Feketekapu: Kiss 1996:230 and 232; Tarnaméra-Urak düllö: Szábo 1965:42 and 69 pl. VIII/1–3. See also Bálint 1992:339. For the theory of the Bulgar migration, see Bálint 1989:169. For the transition from double-edged swords to sabres, see Simon 1991 and 1991–2. Combat axes: Kiss 1996:238 and 318. Avar variant of animal Style II: Nagy 1988 and 1995.

The Avars viewed the Danube river as the frontier between *yāgī* and *ēl*. Qagan Bayan considered the Sclavenes in Walachia to be part of the *ēl*. Ethnic cleavage within the *ēl* may not be easily identifiable, particularly because the Avars themselves were subdivided into clans and tribes. The archaeological evidence substantiates this complex picture. Recent studies show that within the Carpathian basin, various artifact-categories, particularly dress accessories, have a restricted, localized, distribution, and, in fact, there are few items which could be considered "Avar" on the basis of their wide distribution.[39]

THE STEPPE NORTH OF THE BLACK SEA

There was no heir to the Hunnic "Empire" north of the Black Sea. Beginning with the late 500s, Cutrigurs, Utigurs, Saragurs, and Onogurs appear to have shared both the control over the steppe and the interest of historical sources. The first to mention the Cutrigurs were Procopius and Agathias. Both referred to them as "Huns." A German historian of the Romantic era, however, claimed that the Cutrigurs and the Utigurs were Bulgars. To many, his claim is still indisputable truth, despite the fact that no source referring to Bulgars mentions the Cutrigurs and vice versa. The Bulgars appear in written sources as early as the mid-fourth century, but only in the region north of the Caucasus mountain range.[40]

By contrast, the "Hunnic" Cutrigurs were constantly located in the area close to Crimea and to the northern shore of the Black Sea. They probably controlled the entire steppe corridor up to the Danube river. Since Menander the Guardsman is the last source to mention the Cutrigurs, they most likely did not survive politically in the aftermath of the Avar invasion. During the last years of Justinian's reign, the control of

---

[39] Bracelets with trumpet-shaped ends of the so-called Szentendre type are a case in point. The majority of specimens known so far come from Transdanubia (Sós and Salamon 1995:41). The same is true about buckles of Ibler's classes Pécs and Nagyharsány. See Ibler 1992:138 and 143. For Avar–Slavic relations, see Avenarius 1973 and 1987; Fritze 1980; Tyszkiewicz 1989. *Yāgī* and *ēl*: Göckenjan 1993. Avar clans and tribes, see *Strategikon* XI 2.34–5. Non-Avar groups within the Avar qaganate: Pohl 1988:225–36. On the basis of their archaeological distribution, scholars postulated the existence of a buffer zone between Middle Avar cemeteries in south and southeast Slovakia and presumably Slavic settlements with Prague-type pottery to the north. These cemeteries were interpreted as Avar outposts in Transdanubia against Samo and his "kingdom." See Zábojník 1988:401–2.

[40] Zeuss 1837:713–14; Romashov 1992–4:218. John of Antioch refers to Bulgars in relation to events taking place in 480 in the Lower Danube region, while other sources mention the first Bulgar raid across the Danube in 499. They subsequently appear as the allies of the Gepids. Dezsö Simonyi argued, therefore, that these were not Cutrigurs, but a separate group of Bulgars who came to Pannonia with the Huns and remained there until the arrival of the Avars. See Simonyi 1964. This theory was very popular in the 1960s and 1970s and had a considerable influence upon interpretations of the Early Avar archaeological evidence. See Csallány 1963; Fettich 1972; Beshevliev 1981:85–6. Following István Bóna's devastating critique, this interpretation is now abandoned. See Bóna 1981.

the steppe was disputed between Utigurs and Cutrigurs, but the rise of the Gök Türk Empire brought the Utigurs, the Onogurs, and other groups under the domination of the western qaganate. At the same time, the Cutrigurs became subjects of Bayan, the qagan of the Avars. The two "Empires" most likely collided on the Don river. As the civil war broke within the western Gök Türk qaganate after the death, in 630, of the yabghu qagan T'ung, two confederations were competing for power and control over the steppe north of the Caucasus range: the Bulgars, under the leadership of a heir of the Dulo, the leading clan of the left division of the western qaganate, and the Khazars, led by a member of the charismatic clan Ashina of the Turkish qaganate, associated with the right division. The Bulgar qaganate established shortly after 630 by Koubratos, who concluded a treaty with Emperor Heraclius, probably reached the Dnieper river to the west, which is viewed as an indication that, in the first half of the seventh century, the steppes between the Dnieper and the Danube rivers were still controlled by the Avars.[41]

As in many other cases, the archaeological evidence does not fit the picture drawn by historians on the basis of written sources. The steppe north of the Black Sea has not produced so far any materials from the late fifth century. Finds of the following period (sixth to seventh century) fall into one of Ambroz's groups IV, V, and VI. Group IV, which Ambroz viewed as representing the "lower class," the "commoners" of the steppe society, consists of burials with no weapons, but with perforated buckles, mounts, and strapends, all datable to the late sixth and early seventh centuries (Veliki Tokmak, Akkerman, Bilozerka). By contrast, group V includes only extraordinarily rich burials, such as Malo Pereshchepino, Kelegeia, and Glodosy. In group VI, Ambroz included burials such as Sivashs'ke, Kostogryzovo, Kovalevka, and Iablonia, in which a human skeleton (often a male) was commonly associated with that of a horse or with parts of a horse skeleton (skull and legs).[42]

---

[41] Szádeczky-Kardoss 1986a:153–62. Koubratos' Bulgaria: Pletneva 1980:27–9; Bozhilov and Dimitrov 1995. Cutrigurs north of the Black Sea: Golden 1980:261; Bálint 1989:14. Last mention of the Cutrigurs: Menander the Guardsman, fr. 12.6. As the Tang dynasty came to power with Turkic assistance, almost all sources for the history of the Gök Türk qaganate are Chinese. They have been collected by Edouard Chavannes (1969, first published in 1903). The death of the yabghu qagan T'ung coincides with the collapse of the eastern qaganate. For the ensuing civil war, see also Golden 1980:37–42 and 1982:40–1 and 50–4; Bálint 1989:239–40; Whittow 1996:222.

[42] Ambroz 1981; Orlov 1985; Baran and Kozlovskii 1991:235. The continuity of the steppe "Hunnic culture" of the early fifth century well into the sixth century has recently been advocated by A. V. Bogachev (1996). The evidence cited, however, is far from conclusive. Most sixth- to eighth-century funerary assemblages in the steppe north of the Black Sea were found in the area between the Danube and Dnieper rivers. There are comparatively fewer finds in Left Bank Ukraine and virtually no finds between the Don and the Volga rivers. See Dimitrov 1987:63; Bálint 1989:102. For a rare instance of perforated belt mounts in Left Bank Ukraine, see Lipking 1974:145–7. For the steppe east of the Don river, see Bezuglov 1985.

Ambroz's tripartite scheme, which was designed to provide an easy model for understanding the society of the steppe nomads, does not seem, however, to stand against the existing evidence. First, many burials of Ambroz's fourth group are female graves (Khristoforovka, Malaia Ternovka, Akkerman, Veliki Tokmak), which can easily explain the absence of weapons. Second, burials of groups VI and V do not coincide in time. Besides an extensive array of gold and silver grave-goods, extremely rich burials, such as Kelegeia, Malo Pereshchepino, and Zachepilovki, also produced Byzantine gold coins, often in relatively great numbers. In all three cases, the last coins were minted for Emperor Constans II (641–68).[43]

The dating of group VI is more difficult, for there are no coin finds, with the exception of Iosipivka, which produced a perforated coin of Heraclius and Heraclius Constantine (613–41). All other graves can be dated only on the basis of perforated belt mounts and straps. Such dress accessories signalize the use of a belt with multiple, secondary, straps, which was first used in Sassanian Persia, as indicated by the Taq-i Bustan reliefs dated to Khusro II's reign (590–628). The belt with multiple straps did not originate in the steppe milieu, for the earliest assemblages with belt mounts from the early sixth century were found in Transcaucasia. The number of graves with belt mounts and strapends increased suddenly in the mid-500s in both Transcaucasia and Crimea.[44] Perforated specimens, commonly known as "Martynovka mounts" became popular in the steppes north and northeast of the Black Sea only in the second half of the sixth century and the early seventh century.[45]

---

[43] Malo Pereshchepino: Werner 1984a. Kelegeia: Bálint 1989:95. Glodosy: Smilenko 1965. Zachepilovki: Smilenko 1968. Voznesenka: Grinchenko 1950; Bálint 1989:92–4. The interpretation of the Malo Pereshchepino assemblage as burial has been disputed, for no human bones were found on site. See Kazanski and Sodini 1987:72; Schulze-Dörrlamm 1987b. Joachim Werner argued in favor of a funerary assemblage, pointing to fragments of gold sheet bearing traces of wood, which he interpreted as casket mounts. Knowing that the assemblage was accidentally found in 1912 and no systematic excavations were ever carried out on the site, there is no way to decide whether or not Malo Pereshchepino was a specific, ritual, site of a kind illustrated by the Voznesenka assemblage. By contrast, the site at Glodosy produced cremated fragments of a male skeleton (twenty to forty years old). See Smilenko 1965:7–10. Joachim Werner (1984a:17) also argued that all sixty-eight coins found at Malo Pereshchepino belonged to a "ceremonial or marriage belt," for they were each perforated and decorated with a cabochon applied on the obverse. See also Bálint 1985:139–40. For the coins found at Kelegeia, see Kropotkin 1962:37.

[44] Werner 1974:132; Somogyi 1987:138; Bálint 1992:327 and 1993:220; Fiedler 1994a:35 and 46. Judging from the iconography of the Taq-i Bustan reliefs, the number of secondary straps indicated social rank, for the use of as many as ten or twelve straps was restricted to the king, while lesser nobles wore only three to six straps. Belts as symbols of social status appear in contemporary Byzantium. See Martini and Steckner 1993:134–6. For examples of buckles used in association with belts with multiple straps, see Schulze-Dörrlamm 1987a:802 and 803 fig. 63; Bálint 1992:324 and 438 pl. 2/1.

[45] Nándor Fettich was the first to link the Martynovka hoard to assemblages with perforated belt mounts. He also coined the phrase "Martynovka mounts." At Mokraia balka, in Transcaucasia, perforated belt mounts appear in the second interment phase of the cemetery, dated with coins

Nevertheless, the use of a buckled belt became so strongly associated with the horsemen of the steppe that an early seventh-century Egyptian papyrus referred to such dress accessories as "Bulgar belts." The distribution of perforated belt mounts and strapends confirms this association (Figure 19). Belts with "Martynovka mounts" were in use in the Balkan provinces of the Empire during the sixth century, as demonstrated by their presence in both forts and burial assemblages excavated south of the Danube river. They were in use in "Gepidia" even before the arrival of the Avars, as shown by burial no. 29 at Szentes-Nagyhegy, in which a "Martynovka mount" was found in association with a Sucidava belt-buckle, a dress accessory most typical for early Byzantine forts of the Justinianic age. In Avar assemblages dated shortly after *c.* 600, "Martynovka mounts" are a familiar presence.[46]

Assemblages with perforated belt mounts and strapends are therefore earlier than rich burials such as Malo Pereshchepino, Zachepilovki, or Glodosy, which include only mounts and strapends with granulated ornament. The best analogies for these burials are both late Early Avar assemblages, such as Bócsa and Kunbábony (dated to the second third of the seventh century), or Middle Avar assemblages of the so-called Tótipuszta–Dunapentele–Igar group, some of which produced coins minted for the emperors Constans II and Constantine IV. They are also paralleled by the earliest archaeological evidence attributed to the Bulgars in Bulgaria, namely that from burial no. 5 from Madara. Gold belt mounts and strapends with granulated ornament found in this burial are considered as the latest of their kind.[47]

The different date and interpretation of these two groups of burials in the steppes north of the Black Sea becomes even more evident when we introduce another class of evidence, that of hoards of silver and bronze

---

of the Sassanian king Kavad I (488–531). See Afanas'ev 1979:47. Perforated mounts were also found in neighboring forts built under Emperor Justinian. See Afanas'ev 1975:53 and 60. In Crimea, perforated belt mounts were in use in the mid-sixth century, as suggested by their association with coins of Justinian. See Repnikov 1906:15–16; Afanas'ev 1979:47. The analysis of the Suuk Su cemetery indicates that access to belts with perforated mounts was restricted to adults, both female and male. See Uenze 1992:170. For perforated mounts at Skalistoe, see Veimarn and Aibabin 1993:12–3.

[46] For "Bulgar belts" in the papyrus Erzherzog Rainer 9010, see Wessely 1889:242; Setton 1950:524; Bálint 1992:415. Buckled belts have often been associated with trousers or tights, a garment believed to have been introduced by barbarian soldiers of the Roman army. See Russell 1982:146. However, as the Taq-i Bustan reliefs suggest belts with multiple straps were worn with tunics. See Martini and Steckner 1993:133. In other cases, perforated belt mounts (such as Somogyi's class A 9) may have been used to attach shoe straps. See Bálint 1992:357. Perforated belt mounts in forts: Opaiţ 1990:46 fig. 18/53–7; Uenze 1992: pl. 11/1–5, 8–10, 14–17. "Martynovka mounts" in burial assemblages: Petre 1987:pl. 130 fig. 207 d–e; Alexandrescu and Vîlceanu 1962:402 fig. 5/1; Vaklinova 1989:136 fig. 2. Szentes-Nagyhegy: Csallány 1961:50–1 and pl. xxv/14.

[47] Bócsa and Kunbábony: Tóth and Horváth 1992. Tótipuszta–Dunapentele–Igar group: Garam 1976:140 and 1995:129. Madara: Fiedler 1992:143–4 and 1994a:47; Garam 1988:162 and 167. For analogies in Transcaucasia, see Atavin and Paromov 1991.

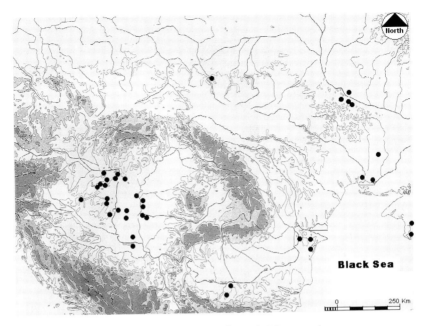

Figure 19 Distribution of perforated, Martynovka-type
belt straps

(Figures 20–3). A. A. Spicyn called them "Antian antiquities," because he
believed their distribution matched Procopius and Jordanes' description
of the Antes. His idea had a remarkable influence on the development of
Soviet archaeology, particularly after World War II. Many embraced G.
F. Korzukhina's very influential suggestion that both the distribution and
the composition of hoards of silver and bronze from the forest-steppe belt
were different from those of rich burials of the steppe area. No hoards
were found in the steppe area and none included either weapons or horse
gear. By contrast, no burial produced such artifacts as bow fibulae or earrings with star-shaped pendant. This contrast has been interpreted as an
indication of two different ethnic groups: the nomads (burials) and the
Slavic Antes (the hoards). The distribution in the area north of the Black
Sea of sixth- and seventh-century burials and hoards of silver and bronze,
respectively, are indeed in sharp contrast (Figure 24).[48]

A cluster analysis of eighteen hoards of silver and bronze and five
burials by means of chi-square distance, which accounts for differences in

---

[48] Spicyn 1928; Korzukhina 1955:69 and 71–2. Spicyn attributed to the Antes not only hoards, but
also burials with bow fibulae. For an example of burial with bow fibulae in Left Bank Ukraine,
see Aksenov and Babenko 1998:113. By contrast, M. I. Artamonov (1969) attributed both hoards
and burials to the (Cutrigur) nomads. For a critique of Artamonov's theories, see Tret'iakov 1971.

total quantity of types in the assemblage, gives, however, a picture radically different from that suggested by Korzukhina (Figure 25).[49] Rich burials belong to the same cluster as hoards of silver and bronze, such as Kharyvki and Zemiansky Vrbovok. With a correspondence analysis, a technique recently introduced to archaeology, the relationships between hoards, between artifact-categories, and between artifact-categories and hoards may be all analyzed together and represented in the same scattergram or series of scattergrams produced by the plotting of pairs of orthogonal axes. What catches the eye at first on the scattergram showing the relationships between assemblages is the clear segregation between hoards and burials (Figure 26). An examination of the second scattergram, which represents relationships between artifact-categories found in both hoards and burials, indicates this split to be a chronological one (Figure 27). Burials are characterized by the presence of swords with typical cross-bars, similar to those depicted on seventh- and eighth-century Soghdian silverware or in fresco scenes at Afrasiab and Pendzhikent. Earrings with bead-pendants, such as found at Malo Pereshchepino, Glodosy, and Zachepilovki, are typically associated with Middle Avar assemblages. A specimen of this category was found at Ozora-Tótipuszta in association with a solidus minted for Emperor Constantine IV.[50]

By contrast, hoards are characterized by the presence of repoussé bronze pendants, an artifact-category frequently encountered in Early Avar assemblages, but not later. Such pendants were only found with female burials. They might have belonged to corolla-type head-dresses

---

[49] Iakhniki: Braichevskii 1952a:45–6. Khacki: Bobrinskii 1901:147–8 and pl. xiv. Kharyvki: Berezovec 1952. Koloskovo: Liapushkin 1961:186–7 and 185 fig. 87. Kozievka: Rybakov 1953:66–7. Krylos: Kropotkin 1970 and 1971. Malii Rzhavec: Rybakov 1953:74–6 and 75 fig. 16. Martynovka: Prikhodniuk et al. 1991; Pekarskaja and Kidd 1994. Nova Odessa: Rybakov 1953:67 and 69 fig. 13. Pastyrs'ke: Braichevskii 1952b. Poltava: Braichevskii 1952a:46–7. Sudzha: Rybakov 1949. Veliki Kuchurov (Kuczurmare): Noll 1974; Gschwantler 1993. Velikie Budki: Romanova 1983:311; Goriunova 1987:85–7. Vyl'khovchik: Prikhodniuk 1980:129 and 99 fig. 61. Zalesie: Ugrin 1987. Zemiansky Vrbovok: Svoboda 1953. I left aside two hoards, which included only one or two artifact-categories: Grigoryvka, with only five earrings with star-shaped pendant; and Halič, with a necklace and two earrings with star-shaped pendant. See Prikhodniuk 1980:131; Garam 1980:172 and fig. 7. Not considered was the hoard from Tépe, for which I have been unable to find complete information. See, however, Thomas 1988:143. My analysis also excludes hoards of Sassanian silver, such as Khoniakovo, Pavlovka, and Sloboda Limarovka, for which see Bieńkowski 1929 and Bálint 1989:106 and 108–9. Despite lack of irrefutable evidence, I assumed that the finds from Martynovka and Kharyvki were hoards, not burials. See Kidd and Pekarskaya 1995.

[50] Swords with cross-bars: Ambroz 1986:63; L'vova and Semenov 1985:83. For earrings with bead-pendant, see Garam 1992:150. The correspondence analysis belongs to a group of data reduction methods, which became popular in the archaeological literature in the late 1980s. The method was first developed in the 1960s in France by J. P. Benzécri and his team of the laboratory for the Mathematical Statistics at the University of Paris VI. The first to adopt the correspondence analysis were Scandinavian archaeologists. See Bølviken et al. 1982. Its adoption by American and British archaeologists came comparatively later. For the algebra, see Shennan 1990:283–6; Ringrose 1992. For various statistical methods and their use in archaeology, see also Djindjian 1990.

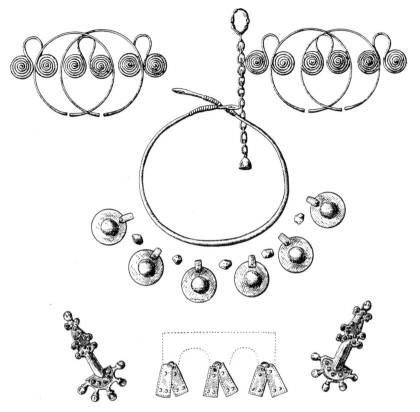

Figure 20 An early seventh-century hoard of silver and
bronze from Sudzha
Source: Rybakov 1953: 64 fig. 11.

or head-bands or might have trimmed veils or lappets hanging from the head-dress. Hoards produced other artifact-categories typically associated with Early Avar assemblages, such as "Martynovka mounts" and "Slavic" bow fibulae. The latter will be discussed in detail in the following chapter. Brooches with bent stems, such as those found at Koloskovo, Nova Odessa, Gaponovo, or Kozievka, have good parallels in seventh-century funerary assemblages in Albania.[51]

---

[51] Repoussé bronze pendants: Szatmári 1980:100–1; Comşa 1984:70; Kiss 1996:201; Fiedler 1996:206–8. The closest parallel for the silver bow brooch with peacocks from Martynovka is that found in an Early Avar female burial at Kölked (Kiss 1996:201). For fibulae in seventh-century assemblages in Albania (the so-called "Koman culture"), see Goriunov and Kazanskii 1978:26; Vinski 1971:388; Uenze 1992:153–4.

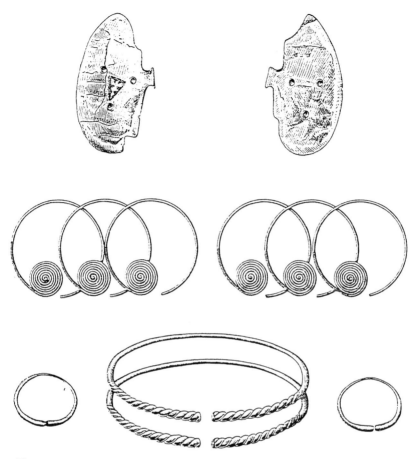

Figure 21 An early seventh-century hoard of silver and bronze from Malii
Rzhavec
Source: Rybakov 1953: 75 fig. 16.

Burials such as Glodosy, Voznesenka, Kelegeia, and Malo
Pereshchepino also produced Sassanian silverware. Hoards often display
sets of Byzantine stamped silverware manufactured as *largitio* objects for
imperial distribution. Four control stamps on the base of the Martynovka
cup are from the reign of Justin II, possibly from 577, when Theodore
Petrus was the *comes sacrarum largitionum.* The closest analogy for the large
goblet is the chalice found at Kaper Koraon, stamped in 605–10. Five
stamps on the base of the large silver bucket (*situla*) from Veliki Kuchurov
are from 613–29/30. Like most other groups of silver plate in "barbarian"

Figure 22 An early seventh-century hoard of silver and bronze from Khacki
Source: Bobrinskii 1901: p. XIX

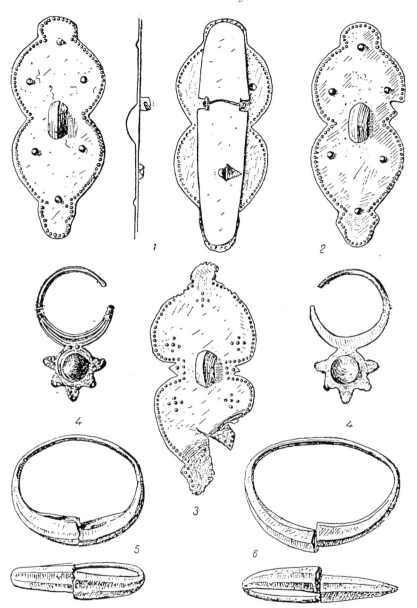

Figure 23 A seventh-century hoard of silver from Pastyrs'ke

Source: Braichevs'kii 1952b: pl. 1.

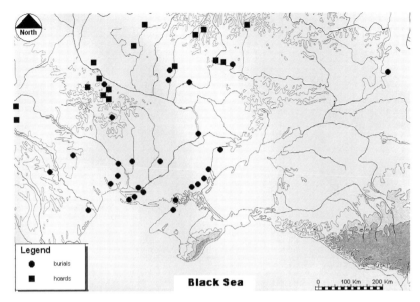

Figure 24 Distribution of sixth- to seventh-century burials and hoards in the area north of the Black Sea

Europe, such as Sutton Hoo or finds from the Kama region, hoards display almost complete functional sets, with large plates, drinking vessels (goblets, cups, or bowls), and washing vessels (buckets, ewers, or basin). Since stamps not only guaranteed silver purity, but also authorized release of state silver, hoards with stamped Byzantine silverware are good indicators of the distribution of people important enough to own them. As diplomatic gifts or some other form of imperial largesse, Byzantine silver indicates that hoards with "Martynovka mounts" were not equivalent to "burials of commoners," but truly symbolized the highest social status.[52]

However, not all hoards of silver and bronze were contemporary. A seriation of seventeen hoards reveals two groups, with the Martynovka hoard at an intermediary position (Figure 28). Applying a correspondence analysis to the same data, it becomes clear that we are actually dealing with three different groups (Figure 29). The second scattergram representing relationships between artifact-categories indicates three

[52] Painter 1988:104; Mango 1992:214–15 and 1995:80–1. A goblet similar to that from Martynovka was found in a sixth-century fort near Haskovo (Bulgaria). See Gerasimova-Tomova 1987. For the Veliki Kuchurov *situla*, see Gschwantler 1993:177 and 178 fig. 6. There is no known analogy for the control stamp on the Krylos silver bowl (Kropotkin 1971:68). For the silver spoon from Martynovka, see Hauser 1992:56. Such artifacts signalize social status, not Christian beliefs, since they were certainly not baptismal spoons. See Simoni 1988:82; Hauser 1992:81. *Contra*: Petrikovits 1966:181; Dănilă 1986:91.

218

Similarity Coefficient: Jaccard
Number of Neighbours considered: 8

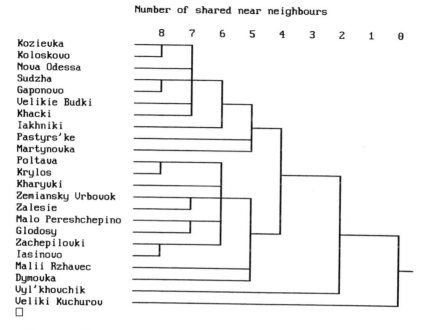

Figure 25 Cluster analysis of eighteen hoards of silver and bronze and five burials found in the area north of the Black Sea, in relation to the artifact-categories found in them

different chronological phases (Figure 30). Velikie Budki, Kozievka, Koloskovo, Nova Odessa, Gaponovo, Sudzha, Khacki, Iakhniki, and Malii Rzhavec are all earlier than Martynovka, Pastyrs'ke, Poltava, and Kharyvki, which, in turn, are earlier than Krylos, Zalesie, Veliki Kuchurov, and Zemiansky Vrbovok. Earlier hoards are characterized by repoussé bronze pendants, "Slavic" bow fibulae, "Martynovka mounts," lead mounts, and brooches with bent stems, while later hoards include earrings with bead or star-shaped pendants. The association of earrings with star-shaped pendants with miliaresia of Constans II in the Zemianský Vrbovok hoard and with hexagrams of Constantine IV in the almost contemporary coin hoard of Priseaca, shows that the third phase represented on the first scattergram coincides in time with rich burials, such as Malo Pereschepino or Zachepilovki.[53]

---

[53] Earrings associated with coins of Constans II and Constantine IV: Svoboda 1953:33–108; Mitrea 1975. Earrings with star-shaped pendants also appear in late seventh-century funerary assemblages in Albania. See Anamali 1993b:443.

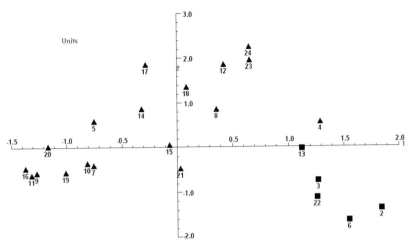

Figure 26 Correspondence analysis of eighteen hoards of silver and bronze and five burials found in the area north of the Black Sea
2 – Dymovka; 3 – Glodosy; 4 – Veliki Kuchurov; 5 – Iakhniki; 6 – Iasinovo; 7 – Khacki; 8 – Kharyvki; 9 – Koloskovo; 10 – Gaponovo; 11 – Kozievka; 12 – Krylos; 13 – Malo Pereshchepino; 14 – Malii Rzhavec; 15 – Martynovka; 16 – Nova Odessa; 17 – Pastyrs'ke; 18 – Poltava; 19 – Sudzha; 20 – Velikie Budki; 21 – Vyl'khovchik; 22 – Zachepilovki; 23 – Zalesie; 24 – Zemianský Vrbovok. Triangles represent hoards, rectangles represent burials

That Martynovka should be placed somewhere between the earliest and the latest hoards is suggested by the chronology of the nine anthropomorphic and zoomorphic mounts, traditionally said to have been used for the decoration of the saddle. Such mounts were found in late sixth- and early seventh-century burials at Pregradnaia and Kugul (North Caucasus), in association with "Martynovka mounts." Similar specimens come from three early seventh-century burials in the Castel Trosino cemetery in Italy. Moreover, zoomorphic mounts were also found in the Malo Pereshchepino assemblage, dated to the second half of the seventh century, and in a collection of mounts from Thessaly, also from the seventh century.[54]

The interpretation of this pattern is most difficult, because of the lack of contextual information. It is clear, however, that the meaning behind hoards of silver and/or bronze did not remain constant. That the same

[54] Saddle mounts: Lászlo 1955:276–84; Ambroz 1989:78–80; Swietosławski 1993:284; Kidd and Pekarskaya 1995:352. See also Vallet 1995:335; Werner 1953 and 1984a:29; Kidd 1992. For a saddle mount from Sardis wrongly interpreted as *Tierfibel*, see Waldbaum 1983:117 and pl. 43/688. For finds from the Crkvine cemetery near Salona, see Vinski 1967:17 and 1970:701–2 and 703 fig. 1. A bronze model for the production of saddle mounts was found in the Biskupija hoard (Croatia). See Korošec 1958b.

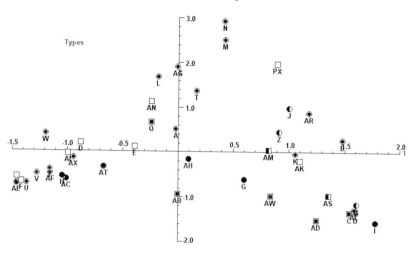

Figure 27 Correspondence analysis of artifact-categories from eighteen hoards of silver and bronze and five burials found in the area north of the Black Sea A – armlet with enlarged ends; AB – spear; AC – "Martynovka mounts"; AD – bridle bit; AE – brooch with bent stem; AF – "Slavic" bow brooch; AG – shield-shaped bow brooch; AH – pseudo-buckle; AI – chain; AK – cup; AL – finger-ring; AM – horse-harness mounts; AN – silver ingot; AO – neckring with embossed decoration; AP – collar; AR – necklace; AS – stirrup; AT – silver sheet strapend; AV – cast strapend with scrollwork decoration; AW – sword; AX – earring with spiral-end; AZ – seashells; B – hinge bracelet; C – arrow-head; D – amber beads; E – glass beads; F – jingle bells; G – cast belt mounts; H – buckle (Sucidava class); I – rectangular buckle; J – chalice; K – silver or gold coin; L – silver wire earring; M – earring with star-shaped pendant; N – earring with globe-pendant; O – earring with bead pendant; P – silver goblet; Q – helmet cheek-piece; R – jug; S – lead mounts; T – neckring with widened ends; U – hat-shaped pendant; V – repoussé bronze pendant; W – circular bronze pendant; Y – spectacle-shaped pendant; Z – silver plate

type of hoard may be found in areas hundreds of kilometers apart raises important questions about demographic mobility, spread of fashions, and, ultimately, the significance of hoards. It is also interesting to note that later hoards were found north of the Carpathian basin, while earlier ones cluster in the Middle Dnieper area. Spicyn's interpretation cannot be accepted, for the simple reason that no hoard can be dated earlier than *c*. 600. At that time, according to the literary sources analyzed in Chapter 3, the Antes had already ceased to exist politically. If not ethnicity, then what? There is nothing in these hoards that is obviously utilitarian, and in most cases we can use the evidence of contemporary funerary assemblages to infer that some, if not all, artifact-categories were female dress-accessories. Later hoards present some connections with contemporary, very rich, burials, which seem to have been male graves, for they produced weapons and horse gear. The lack of representation of high-status

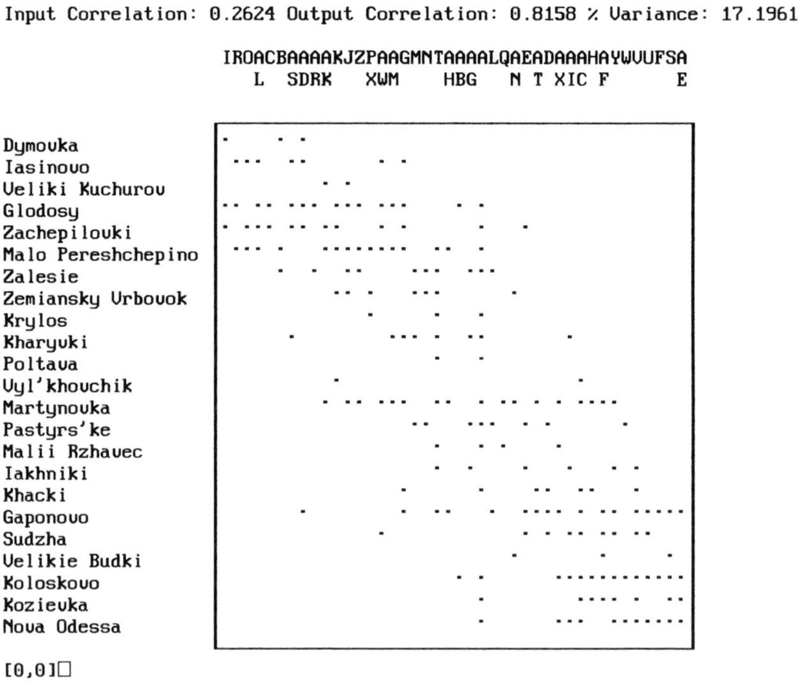

Input Correlation: 0.2624 Output Correlation: 0.8158 % Variance: 17.1961

```
IROACBAAAAKJZPAAGMNTAAAALQAEADAAAHAYWUUFSA
   L  SDRK   XWM    HBG   N T XIC F      E
```

```
Dymouka
Iasinovo
Veliki Kuchurou
Glodosy
Zachepilouki
Malo Pereshchepino
Zalesie
Zemiansky Urbovok
Krylos
Kharyuki
Poltava
Uyl'khouchik
Martynouka
Pastyrs'ke
Malii Rzhavec
Iakhniki
Khacki
Gaponovo
Sudzha
Velikie Budki
Koloskovo
Kozievka
Nova Odessa
```

[0,0]□

Figure 28 Seriation of seventeen hoards found in the area north of the Black
Sea

For abbreviations, see Figure 27

women in burials at this time suggests that, unlike the situation in the
Carpathian basin, women were not vehicles for displaying the status of
their husbands. What, then, is the significance of hoards, at least of
earlier ones, in which female dress accessories played such an important
role?

Hoards of silver were certainly not collections of raw silver or "hack-
silver." There are no broken objects and no metalworking residues. The
deliberate choice of items, usually found in pairs or more than two specimens, and the value attached to Byzantine silver seem to indicate conspicuous consumption of a type known to anthropologists as potlatch. In
times of social and political stress, such consumption may have served a
number of functions, such as celebrating rites of passage or succession to
office. It certainly was the privilege of an aristocratic group and probably
involved the provision of food and of certain other valuables that did not

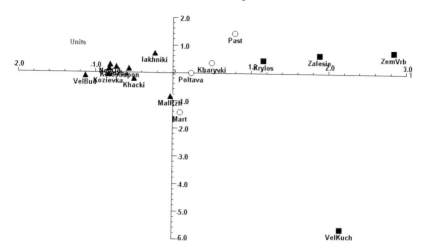

Figure 29 Correspondence analysis of seventeen hoards found in the area
north of the Black Sea
Legend: phase I − triangle; phase II − oval; phase III − rectangle

survive in the archaeological record.[55] Lavish offerings such as hoards of
silver, involving the deposition in locations from which items could not
be recovered, might have provided a way of fixing status and of claiming
the prestige associated with it. Initially, female dress accessories were as
common currency for this type of social behavior as women were for displaying the status of their husbands. Contemporary male burials (with or
without horse skeletons) are comparatively much poorer than hoards of
silver. In the late 600s, however, men assumed this role for themselves and
extremely rich burials with a vast array of gold (rather than silver) grave-
goods dwarfed displays of wealth through hoarded silver.

CONCLUSION

There are at least three important conclusions to be drawn from this
sweeping survey of the archaeology of the Carpathian basin and the

---

[55] Artifacts in the Khacki hoard were wrapped in silk (Bobrinskii 1901:147). It is tempting to associate the burial of earlier hoards, for which a date may be tentatively assigned to *c.* 630, with the
beginning of the civil war within the western division of the Gök Türk Empire and the subsequent rise of the Bulgar qaganate. However, both were located in Left Bank Ukraine and the
steppe north of the Caucasus mountains, at a considerable distance from the main concentration
of hoards in the Middle Dnieper area. Moreover, the hoarding phenomenon clearly continued
through the second half of the seventh century, as hoards were buried in Volhynia and Slovakia.

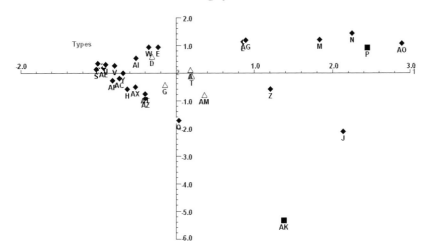

Figure 30 Correspondence analysis of seventeen hoards found in the area
north of the Black Sea and their respective artifact-categories
For abbreviations, see Figure 27

steppe north of the Black Sea. First, in all cases discussed in this chapter, material culture may be and was indeed used for the construction of social identities. Despite interaction across the buffer zone between the Danube and the Tisza rivers, clear material culture distinctions were maintained in a wide range of artifacts. The nature and function of these distinctions is very similar to those identified by Ian Hodder in the Baringo district of Kenya. As in East Africa, material culture contrasts were maintained in order to justify between-group competition and negative reciprocity. Displays of emblemic styles were particularly important at the time of the Lombard–Gepid wars in the mid-500s. More often than not, such styles were associated with the status of aristocratic women, wives, daughters, or mothers of "kings." This may be a result of the special emphasis laid on public representation of group identity, but may also be an indication of the intricate relationship between ethnic and gender identity.

The examination of hoards of silver and bronze also shows that women were symbolic vehicles for the construction of social identities. In this case, however, it is more difficult to decide precisely what kind of identity was constructed through displays of female dress accessories. Unlike the Carpathian basin, the specific way in which identity was expressed was not funerary assemblage but lavish offering of silver and bronze artifacts, which may have represented a particular form of potlatch.

However, just as with displays of wealth in rich female graves, deposition of hoards may have served as "tournaments of value."[56] Like funerals, hoards were used for social display mainly during periods of instability when the status of the individual needed underlining. An important route to social advancement was most likely access to foreign goods, such as Byzantine silver plate. Within the Empire, the social status which silver plate conferred or reflected was often seen in terms of wealth and power. The donation of family silver to be recycled into liturgical silver or given to the poor became a literary *topos*. In "barbarian" contexts, transactions in which silver plate was symbolically displayed were certainly different. To claim that acquisition, imitation, and use of Roman silver plate reflects the degree to which barbarians were Romanized[57] is simply to ignore that the symbolic system changed with the changing contexts in which imported objects were employed. There can be no doubt, however, that Byzantine silver plate *was* viewed as "exotic" and "precious" for an image of power, for stamped objects were only produced for imperial distribution. The ability to acquire fine *largitio* objects carried a considerable premium. The same is true for objects of possibly Sassanian origin, such as the Zemiansky Vrbovok bowl. On the other hand, that hoards of silver conveyed an image of power much stronger than grave-goods may be deduced from the fact that some contain several sets of ornaments, which suggests that such collections were the property of more than one person. In other words, hoards of silver and bronze may have permitted a more "extravagant" display of metalwork than the provision of grave-goods.

Finally, the survey of the archaeological evidence from the Carpathian basin and the steppe north of the Black Sea strongly suggests that in order for material culture to participate in the construction of social identities, artifacts need to be given meaning in social context. Swords with P-shaped sheath attachments or stirrups with elongated attachment loops were not "Avar" because of being of Central Asian origin, but because of being used in a specific way in specific transactions (such as display of grave-goods) in the new social milieu in which Avar warriors found themselves after *c.* 570. Similarly, there are no specific "Lombard" or "Gepid" brooches, for many fibulae found in female burials on both sides of the "no man's land" either were "imported" from distant locations or imitated such exotic imports. There is, therefore, no "phenotypic" expression of a preformed ethnic identity, though identity *is* constructed by manipulating *certain* artifact-categories. The value of each of these artifact-categories depended less on questions of supply and origin than on the social strategies employed by those who used them. On the other

---

[56] The phrase is that of Bradley 1990:139.   [57] Mango 1995:81.

hand, objects that are the prerogative of an elite may be imitated by lower-ranking groups. "Citations" from the material culture discourse which can be identified in rich burials or hoards may be found in completely different contexts, such as settlements. As I will argue in the last chapter, just as in the case of "Lombard" and "Gepid" identities, Slavic ethnicity may have been communicated through displays of objects whose use was restricted to local elites. In such cases, artifacts similar to those found in Ukrainian hoards are not mere analogies. They have become metaphors.

Chapter 6

ELITES AND GROUP IDENTITY NORTH OF THE DANUBE FRONTIER: THE ARCHAEOLOGICAL EVIDENCE

If the social label of various ethnic identities in *barbaricum*, both East and West, can be pinned down to material culture, matters are more difficult when it comes to the symbols by which Slavic ethnicity may have been expressed. Archaeologists, from Ivan Borkovský to Volodymyr Baran, have focused on specific artifacts, particularly pottery, in an effort to reconstruct a "Slavic culture" by which Slavic ethnicity may be then identified at any place and time. In the first chapter, I discussed the problems and difficulties involved in this approach. I will attempt now to show that, just as with contemporary Gepids, Lombards, or Bulgars, no particular item was ethnically specific to the Slavs. Material culture, nevertheless, played a crucial role in building ethnic boundaries. The social mechanisms by which artifacts were manipulated and used for statements of group identity may well have been at work in "Sclavinia," just as in "Lombardia" or "Gepidia."

A survey of Slavic archaeology is beyond the scope of this work. By default, a discussion of Slavic ethnicity will entail only certain aspects of the Slavic culture, if such a thing ever existed. Instead of a standard description of material culture items, which is the current practice with monographs on the Slavic culture,[1] I will focus on only three issues, which I believe are relevant for the formation of a Slavic *ethnie*.

First, I will examine problems of chronology, which are fundamental for the understanding of changes in material culture and their historical background. Much too often, archaeologists have imposed the rigid framework of written sources on the archaeological record, without acknowledging chronological discrepancies. Second, I will focus on a specific group of bow fibulae, which the German archaeologist Joachim Werner first called "Slavic" brooches.[2] More than any other artifact-category (with the exception, perhaps, of pottery), this group of fibulae

---

[1] E.g., Parczewski 1993.   [2] Werner 1950.

has been used to "illustrate" Slavic ethnicity and the migration of the Slavs has been reconstructed on the basis of their map distribution. Since fibulae, as well as other dress accessories, particularly those of the female dress, became badges of group identity during the confrontation between Gepids and Lombards in the Middle Danube area, it is theoretically possible that Slavs too used brooches as symbols of ethnic identity. Unlike the contemporary situation in the Carpathian basin, however, the distribution of various subgroups of "Slavic" brooches and their chronology suggest a much more complex mechanism of appropriation of the symbolism attached to these dress accessories.

Finally, I will take into consideration changes in material culture, which might be considered as emblemic style. I will focus on buildings and pottery, with an emphasis on pottery decoration and clay pans, a ceramic category associated with the consumption of special foods, particularly flat loaves of bread. My intention is to show that, just as with "Slavic" brooches, the introduction of a "standard" form of sunken building equipped with a single heating facility (either stone or clay oven), the generalization of certain styles of pottery decoration, as well as the intrasite distribution of clay pans, might all have been connected with the rise of elites. This argument will have a key role in asserting the association between chiefs and ethnicity, which is the major point of the concluding chapter of this book.

DATING THE CHANGE: WHERE WERE THE EARLIEST SLAVS?

Ever since Ivan Borkovský identified the Slavic pottery (the Prague type), archaeologists have used ceramic assemblages for dating the early Slavic culture. Iurii V. Kukharenko and Irina P. Rusanova rebaptized Borkovský's type "Korchak-Zhitomir" on the basis of extensive excavations in the 1950s and 1960s in the Zhitomir Polesie, south of the Pripet marshes. Ukrainian sites replaced those of central Bohemia as the earliest phase of the Slavic culture, and Soviet archaeologists made all possible efforts to demonstrate that the pottery found at Korchak and other sites in the Teterev valley, east of Zhitomir, was based on local traditions going back to the early Iron Age. The pottery type identified by Irina Rusanova by means of statistical analysis became the main and only indicator of Slavic ethnicity in material culture terms.[3] At any place and time, finds of Korchak-Zhitomir-type pottery would indicate the existence of an early, sixth-century, phase of Slavic habitation. Archaeologists from other countries, such as Romania or Bulgaria, quickly embraced Rusanova's

---

[3] Rusanova 1976.

theories, and used the Korchak-Zhitomir pottery as a diagnostic type for their own research. More often than not, this involved visual, intuitive, comparison of vessel shape or rims with those found at Korchak and used by Rusanova in her work on the early Slavic culture.

Rusanova's ideas were further developed by Polish and Slovak archaeologists, who focused on rim sherds, since whole vessels rarely came out of excavated settlements.[4] Rim attributes were now a favourite trait for the analysis of Slavic ceramics, and newly discovered sites were dated on the basis of the presence or absence of certain lip forms in the ceramic assemblage.[5] Sherds, however, represent only random and arbitrary subdivisions of the vessel shapes. They are not discrete units of cultural behavior and should not be used as *ad hoc* boundaries for defining design elements. Variability in primary forms, such as shapes, usually in gross functional terms, is more likely than secondary variables (lip, base, or appendages) to inform about change in function, activities, and production. Ethnoarchaeological studies of modern communities of potters show that significant differences in rim form and size may appear even within a single-size class of vessels produced by specialist potters.[6]

There are, however, other major problems with Rusanova's approach. As is often the case in archaeology, it remains unclear whether the meaning of types, as imposed by archaeologists on to a group of artifacts, is only in the mind of the classifier, or, as Rusanova believed, nominal categories discovered by archaeologists by means of statistical identification of combinations of attributes may have also been recognized by manufacturers and users in the past. If the mental template used by the "original" Slavic potters in the Zhitomir Polesie was the Korchak-Zhitomir type, it remains unclear why and how it remained unchanged, almost frozen in tradition, long after the Slavs reached the limits of their alleged expansion.[7]

[4] See Parczewski 1993; Fusek 1994.
[5] See, for instance, Podgórska-Czopek 1991; Postică 1994; Fusek 1995:28. Despite her efforts to establish a pottery classification based on the statistical ordering of whole vessels, Rusanova (1976:11) claimed that rim and lip variations ultimately provided the most valuable chronological information. Without the information provided by the base, however, the primary breakdown of vessel types is impossible. See Froese 1985:239.
[6] Rice 1987:279 and 1989:113. See also Richards 1982:40. Other studies show that, in all shape classes, effective capacity (i.e., maximum volume of material that is normally placed in a vessel) and use are strongly correlated with orifice diameter. Liquid separation, for instance, is made possible by outflaring rims, but not by vertical or insloping rims, which suggests that rim variation is primarily functional, not stylistical. See Shapiro 1984:696; Hally 1986:279–80. For sherds as *ad hoc* boundaries for defining design elements, see Skibo, Schiffer, and Kowalski 1989:401.
[7] Cowgill 1990:67–74; Neverett 1991:32. The idea that types were entirely constructed by archaeologists was first advanced by J. A. Ford (1954). By contrast, A. Krieger (1944) and A. Spaulding (1953 and 1982) believed that types were mental templates of prehistoric manufacturers and users. For the "emic" nature of types, see also Tschauner 1985 and Rice 1987:283.

For the purpose of this chapter, however, chronological problems are of comparatively greater importance. Rusanova and her followers emphasized ceramic attributes, because settlements excavated in the Teterev valley produced very few, if any, metal artifacts to be used for building relative chronologies and dating the sites. Rusanova assigned a date to the handmade urns found in cremation burials in eastern Volhynia (Miropol', Chernyakhov, Korchak) by visually comparing them with pots found in Bohemia and believed by Borkovský to be "very old." For dating the ceramic assemblages from settlements excavated at Korchak, she relied upon information provided by the stratigraphical excavations at the nearby hillfort of Khotomel'.

Kukharenko and Rusanova's work at Khotomel' was based on a heavily stratified site, which was divided into standard sized units and dug in arbitrary, horizontal levels. Even if they destroyed much stratigraphic data that could have been used to reconstruct the site's own history, their technique was appropriate in relation to Rusanova's frequency-based method of analysis. Like many before her, Rusanova considered archaeological layers as containing objects peculiar to each stratum ("index-fossils") which could be used to identify deposits of the same date in other localities. The percentage of cultural remains which were comparable with more recent forms of objects was expected to decrease as the lower and earlier deposits were examined. Rusanova employed a rudimentary form of seriation, very similar to the "battleship curves" used by contemporary American archaeologists, in order to convert percentage frequencies of pottery categories into a relative order. She then developed an evolutionary scheme for the handmade pottery, assuming that simple vessel shapes were earlier than complex ones. Vessel categories established in this way were then dated by means of metal objects, in association with which they were found in each arbitrarily excavated level. The earliest level at Khotomel' is from the late seventh and early eighth centuries. But despite clear evidence that the medieval history of the site had begun long after the "migration of the Slavs," Rusanova decided that the earliest pottery found at Khotomel' *must* have been of the sixth century, because it displayed ceramic profiles similar to those of pots found on fourth-century sites of the Chernyakhov culture.[8]

With serious methodological flaws and without acknowledging the impossibility of using vessel shapes or rims as chronological markers, Rusanova's conclusions should be regarded with extreme suspicion. One major problem with the exclusive use of ceramic types in chronological studies is the implicit assumption of strong covariation of all attributes

---

[8] Rusanova 1958:44–5, 1968:581, and 1973b:21. Arbitrary horizontal stratigraphy: Praetzellis 1993. For metal artifacts from the earliest layers at Khotomel', see Sedov 1982:198 pl. xxiv/4–8, 10–29.

through the life of a type. There is, however, no indication of the actual degree of covariation.[9] In addition, in the absence of metal objects or alternative methods of dating (such as dendrochronology), no exact date could be assigned to any one of the settlements excavated at Korchak. The pottery found there, which was classified as Korchak-Zhitomir, has no chronological value in itself. In other words, there is no indication that this pottery represents the earliest phase in the development of the Prague-Korchak-Zhitomir type. It cannot be considered as the earliest evidence of Slavic settlements. Moreover, Rusanova was not capable of recognizing much earlier materials excavated at Korchak, which were taken to be of the sixth century. In fact, her monograph on sixth- to ninth-century "Slavic antiquities" in eastern Volhynia lists ceramic assemblages that are likely to be of a much earlier date. For example, the decoration with notches on a clay band applied to the vessel's shoulder, such as found in features 4 and 8 at Korchak I, and in features 7, 8, and 13 at Korchak VIII, is typical for ceramic assemblages of the Wielbark culture, dated to the first three centuries AD. No such decoration was found on any site attributed to the Slavs and clearly dated to the sixth or seventh century. A slightly later date may be ascribed to vessels decorated with clay knobs on the shoulder, which are typical for Dytynych-Trishin assemblages of western Ukraine.[10]

Mis-dating archaeological sites is, by no means, a problem restricted to Soviet archaeology. In Romania, the site at Ipoteşti gave its name to the Ipoteşti-Cândeşti culture, the archaeological culture "invented" by Romanian archaeologists in order to illustrate the life of the civilized Romanians before the arrival of the savage Slavs. The site produced a relatively large quantity of wheel-made pottery and comparatively fewer sherds of handmade pottery, which could arguably be attributed to the Slavs. Eager to use this argument in demonstrating an earlier date for the ceramic assemblage at Ipoteşti – much earlier than the date of the Slavic migration – Romanian archaeologists failed to notice that one of the two sunken buildings excavated there produced a coin issued for the Roman

---

[9] See Plog and Hantman 1986:89.
[10] Ceramic decoration with notches on a clay band: Rusanova 1963:46–9 and 47 fig. 8, and 1973b:pls. 5/11, 7/7, and 6/3. Wielbark parallels: Jaskanis 1996:108 and pl. IV/22.1; Wołągiewicz 1993:149–57. Further indication of Rusanova's wrong dating of the site at Korchak I is an iron knife of Minasian's class I. Such knives were particularly frequent on fourth- and fifth-century sites in the area between the Upper Dnieper and the Volga. See Rusanova 1973b:pl. 32/5; Minasian 1980:69. For vessels with clay knobs on shoulders, see Baran 1984–7:81. Such vessels were found at Zelenyi Gai (Ukraine), a site that also produced stamped pottery of the Early Avar period. This is most likely an indication of two occupation phases. A vessel with perforated handles found in a sunken hut at Horodok (a settlement wrongly believed to be from the sixth and seventh centuries), suggests a much earlier date, perhaps in the first centuries AD. See Prikhodniuk 1975:124 pl. XIV/11; Vinokur and Prikhodniuk 1974. For Dytynych-Trishin assemblages, see Baran 1973:27–9 and 28 fig. 1.

emperor Nerva (96–8), but no artifacts clearly dated to the sixth century. At Botoşana, one of the most important sixth- and seventh-century sites in Romania, one of the thirty-one sunken buildings excavated there by Dan Gh. Teodor produced a fourth-century fibula with bent-stem which is typical for assemblages of the Chernyakhov culture. The same is true for the iron fibula with bent stem found in a sunken building at Kavetchina, near Kamianec Podil's'kyi (Khmiel'nyc'kyi region, Ukraine), which was recently used by O. M. Prikhodniuk and L. V. Vakulenko as an argument in favor of the idea that the early Slavic culture originated in late fourth- and early fifth-century Chernyakhov assemblages in Podolia.[11]

A strong commitment to the culture-historical paradigm, with its emphasis on using written sources for dating the archaeological record, may have been responsible for the mis-dating of several Balkan sites. The ever-changing date of the early Slavic culture in Bulgaria is particularly evident in Zhivka Văzharova's work. Under the influence of Rusanova, according to whom the earliest Slavic settlements in Bulgaria could not antedate the presumably sixth-century sites in the Zhitomir Polesie, Văzharova initially gave up the idea of associating the ceramic assemblages found at Dzhedzhovi Lozia with the Prague and Korchak-Zhitomir cultures. However, the work of Atanas Milchev and Stefka Angelova on the early Byzantine site at Nova Cherna prompted her to change attribution. She now argued that at Garvan, near Silistra, the earliest phase should be dated to the late sixth and early seventh centuries. The site, however, produced clear evidence of a much later date, such as ninth- and tenth-century ceramic kettles and pottery with lustred decoration. Văzharova attributed twenty-four features (twenty sunken buildings and four ovens) to the sixth and seventh centuries, but no artifact was found in any of them which could be dated with some degree of certainty. The presence of clay pans and potsherds decorated with either notches or finger impressions on the lip may suggest that at least some assemblages at Garvan coincided in time with late sixth- and early seventh-century archaeological assemblages in Romania, Moldova, and Ukraine. In reality, the earliest phase at Garvan may well be of the late seventh or early eighth century. In the absence of datable artifacts, Văzharova's conclusions

---

[11] Vakulenko and Prikhodniuk 1984:82 and 57 fig. 32/9, and 1985. Botoşana: Teodor 1984a:22–4 and 108 fig. 29/4. The Kavetchina fibula belongs to the so-called "Gothic" class of brooches with bent stem, most typical for fourth-century mortuary assemblages of the Chernyakhov milieu. See Curta 1992:85–6. Unlike Botoşana, the site at Kavetchina produced no sixth-century artifacts. Chernyakhov sites in Podolia: Baran 1973. Ipoteşti: Roman and Ferche 1978. No indication exists of an earlier occupation, and salvage excavations unearthed only two settlement features. The extent of the original settlement is unknown. Doubts about the archaeological and historical value of the materials excavated at Ipoteşti were recently cast by Petre Diaconu (1993:299).

should be regarded with extreme caution, particularly because the ceramic chronology of the Garvan site was established on the basis of visual comparison with rim sherds of handmade pottery found at Nova Cherna.[12]

To many archaeologists, Greece appears as the ideal territory for testing hypotheses on the migration of the Slavs, because of the expected association of "Slavic" artifacts with well-datable contexts of the early Byzantine sites. Unfortunately, the appealing culture-historical paradigm has prevented a serious archaeological analysis of the existing evidence. This is most obvious in the case of the French excavations at Argos. The ceramic assemblage from the ruins of Bath A was dated with surprising precision to AD 585. The only basis for this dating was the association of this assemblage with debris, which were hastily interpreted in connection with Slavic raids into Greece, known from written sources. Since, following this invasion, a settlement of the Slavs would have been inconceivable for various reasons, the French archaeologist Pierre Aupert claimed that the "Slavic ware" testified to a temporary camp established by the Slavic marauders in the ruins of the city, just before returning to their homes north of the Danube river. The relatively large quantity of "Slavic ware" found at Argos and on various other sites in Greece sharply contradicts Aupert's views. In addition, his interpretation, which was rapidly embraced by other scholars, is based on a blatant error of dating. To be sure, the ceramic assemblage of Bath A at Argos is extremely difficult to date in the absence of closed finds and metal objects. In this particular case, however, the best guide for, at least, an approximate dating is the pottery decoration. A pot found during excavations at Koutroumbis, as well as other fragments of pottery made on a tournette (a turntable device turned with the hands) display a particular type of incised decoration with combed, vertical lines, sometimes cutting through the adjacent horizontal lines. No such decoration was found on any category of pottery (either wheel- or handmade) on any sixth- or early seventh-century site north of the Danube river. A recent analysis of the pottery from early medieval cemeteries in the Lower Danube region

[12] Văzharova 1968 and 1986:70 with n. 1, 80 and 83 fig. 2 (ceramic kettles and pottery with lustred decoration), 137 and fig. 140/1–4 (clay pans), 156 and fig. 165/1–5 (sherds with notches and finger impressions on the lip). See also Rusanova 1978:142; Angelova 1980. Văzharova attributed four settlement features to the late seventh- or early eighth-century habitation phase at Garvan. Since she also dated twenty-four features to the sixth and seventh centuries, one is led to the conclusion that the site had three phases of occupation. In fact, neither the stratigraphy of the site, nor the material resulting from excavations, substantiate this implication. Nova Cherna: Milchev and Angelova 1970. To be sure, in the last few decades, an increasing number of early Byzantine sites in the Balkans produced small quantities of handmade pottery: Böttger 1979:34–5; Ştefan, Barnea, and Mitrea 1962:676; Scorpan 1978:160–1; Barnea et al. 1979:192 and 226; Diaconu 1959; Andrei Opaiţ 1991:157 and 1996:105; Vilceanu and Barnea 1975. See also Hayes 1992:53; Rautman 1998.

shows, however, that this decoration is particularly frequent on pots found in eighth- and ninth-century burials and settlements in southeast Romania and northeast Bulgaria.[13]

Such a late date should also be assigned to the "Slavic" pottery from the cremation cemetery found at Olympia, which many regard as the only "hard" piece of archaeological evidence for the presence of the Slavs in Greece. Despite previous caveats by Ion Nestor and Jean-Pierre Sodini, Speros Vryonis recently dated the site to the late sixth and early seventh centuries, on the basis of Văzharova's classification of the early Slavic pottery from Bulgaria. Like Rusanova's, Văzharova's classification is based on vessel shape. By contrast, Nestor and Sodini rightly pointed to vessel decoration. Six pots published by Vryonis, five of which were certainly used as urns, have the same pattern of combed decoration as the pottery from Argos. That at least some burials at Olympia should be dated to the eighth rather than the sixth or seventh century, is further suggested by three spindle-shaped glass beads found in grave 9. They belong to a category known to archaeologists as *Melonenkernperle*, which is typical for Late Avar assemblages (*c.* 700–800), but often appears in later contexts dated to the early ninth century. In any case, there is no indication of a date earlier than *c.* 700.[14]

Elsewhere in Greece, the archaeological context points to a date in the 600s, most probably in the second half of the century. This is the case of the mortuary assemblages found in Corinth, Philippi, Edessa, Athens, and Porto Cheli. Nothing, however, was found in any of these assemblages, which may be associated with the "Slavic culture" north of the Danube river. By contrast, many artifact-categories have good analogies in Avar assemblages. There is, therefore, no serious basis for the bizarre claim that such burials belong to seventh-century Slavic *foederati*, to whom the Byzantine emperor had made grants of land.[15]

Where, then, were the earliest Slavs (Figure 31)? Drawing on an earlier

---

[13] Aupert 1980:380–1 nos. 23–34 and figs. 15–20, 22–4, and 30; Fiedler 1992:153. See also Baratte 1984:170–1 and 178; Vryonis 1992:26–7 and 33. For "Slavic ware" in Greece, see Aupert and Bottini 1979:626 and fig. 14; Kilian 1980:283 and 284 fig. 2; Etzeoglu 1989.

[14] Vryonis 1992:36; Kovrig 1963:164–5; Čilinská 1975:87; Fiedler 1992:188 and 190. For combed decoration, see the urns of graves I, III, IX, 9, and 29, and one pot with no grave attribution (Vryonis 1992:figs. 38, 8, 2, 9, 37, and 29). Potsherds with a similar decoration (vertical and oblique combing) were found in Mušići (Bosnia), a site long viewed as the earliest Slavic settlement in former Yugoslavia. Several Late Avar settlements in Slovakia produced pottery with similar ornamental patterns. See Čremošnik 1975:109 fig. 7/a; Bialeková 1960:815 fig. 290/4; Budinský-Krička 1990:95, 98 and pls. XI/11 and XVI/10, 11; Fusek 1991:pl. VI/17; Meřínský 1993:12 fig. 5/1. Olympia and the earliest Slavic settlement in Greece: Bouzek 1971; Vryonis 1992:33. See also Nestor 1969:144; Baratte 1984:170 with n. 33.

[15] Ivison 1996. For seventh-century assemblages in Greece, see Davidson 1937:230, 232, and 235; Davidson 1974; Gounaris 1984:47, 52, and 54; Petsas 1969:307; Travlos and Frantz 1965; Rudolph 1979:297–8. In addition, a seventh-century settlement was recently identified at Isthmia. See Gregory 1993. The debate over the seventh-century burials at Corinth goes back to the contro-

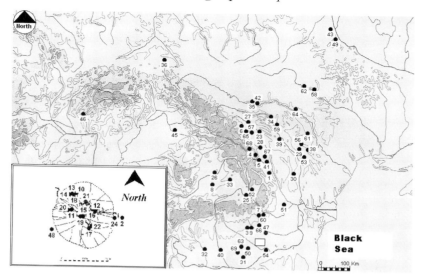

Figure 31 Location map of principal sites mentioned in the text (insert: sites found in Bucharest)

1 – Bacău; 2 – Bălăceanca; 3 – Băleni-Români; 4 – Borniş; 5 – Borşeni; 6 – Botoşana; 7 – Bozieni; 8 – Bratei; 9 – Brăteştii de Sus; 10 – Bucharest-Băneasa; 11 – Bucharest-Ciurel; 12 – Bucharest- Colentina; 13 – Bucharest-Străuleşti; 14 – Bucharest- Dămăroaia; 15 – Bucharest-Foişorul Mavrocordaţilor; 16 – Bucharest-Soldat Ghivan Street; 17 – Bucharest-Lunca; 18 – Bucharest-Măicăneşti; 19 – Bucharest-Mihai Vodă; 20 – Bucharest-Militari; 21 – Bucharest-Tei; 22 – Bucharest-Văcăreşti; 23 – Budeni; 24 – Căţelu Nou; 25 – Cernat; 26 – Cipău; 27 – Cucorăni; 28 – Davideni; 29 – Dănceni; 30 – Dodeşti; 31 – Dulceanca; 32 – Făcăi; 33 – Filiaş; 34 – Gordineşti; 35 – Rashkov; 36 – Grodzisko Dolne; 37 – Gutinaş; 38 – Hansca; 39 – Iaşi; 40 – Ipoteşti; 41 – Izvoare-Bahna; 42 – Kavetchina; 43 – Kiev; 44 – Kodyn; 45 – Lazuri; 46 – Ludanice; 47 – Malu Roşu; 48 – Mihăileşti; 49 – Obukhyv; 50 – Olteni; 51 – Oreavu; 52 – Poian; 53 – Proscuriani; 54 – Radovanu; 55 – Gorecha; 56 – Recea; 57 – Rus-Mănăstioara (Udeşti); 58 – Samchincy; 59 – Şapte-Bani (Hucea); 60 – Sărata Monteoru; 61 – Selişte; 62 – Semenki; 63 – Sfinţeşti; 64 – Skibincy; 65 – Suceava; 66 – Târgşor; 67 – Valea Neagră; 68 – Vânători-Neamţ; 69 – Vedea

suggestion by Każimierz Godłowski, the Ukrainian archaeologist Volodymyr Baran has recently argued that the earliest assemblages, which could be attributed to the Slavs, are those of the Upper Prut and Upper Dniester area. He cited Irina Rusanova and Boris Timoshchuk's work at Kodyn, near Chernivtsi, in Ukraine, where handmade pottery allegedly

versy between Kenneth Setton (1950, 1952) and Peter Charanis (1950, 1952). Both were driven by a strong desire to read culture-history in the archaeological record and, at least in Charanis' case, to prove the authenticity of the Chronicle of Monemvasia by archaeological means. The chronology of the Corinth burials is based on buckles of the Nagyharsány, Corinth, Boly-Želovce, and Bologna classes. See Werner 1955; Hessen 1974; Ibler 1992:143–4; Varsik 1992:83 and 86–9. Of particular interest is also the knuckle-guard of the sword from the burial of the "Wandering Soldier." Similar specimens were found in Middle Avar burials and in the rich funerary assemblages from Malo Pereshchepino, Glodosy, Voznesenka, and Kelegeia. See Ambroz 1986:63; Kazanski and Sodini 1987:78; Kiss 1987a; Simon 1995:117.

235

of the Prague type was found in association with an iron crossbow brooch. A second crossbow brooch with twisted bow was found not far from the sunken building 21, which also produced handmade pottery. Both fibulae belong to the Prague class. Crossbow brooches of this kind were particularly frequent in two regions of East Central Europe: the Carpathian basin and the Baltic area of Mazuria and Lithuania. Specimens similar to that of Kodyn 10 come from Transylvania. Another was found in a grave of the Berekhát cemetery on the left bank of the Tisza river. A good analogy for the second brooch was found in a sunken building at Battonya, together with fine, grey wheelmade pottery with lustred decoration which was common in "Gepidia" around AD 500. A late fifth- and early sixth-century settlement excavated at Bratei (Transylvania) produced two more analogies. At Taurapilis, in Lithuania, a Prague-type crossbow brooch was found in association with a buckle with scrollwork decoration and a sword of Menghin's class A, both dated to the second half of the fifth century. Crossbow fibulae of the Prague class were also found in early Byzantine hillforts in the Balkans and in some of their associated cemeteries. On the basis of the two fibulae from Kodyn, Baran argued that the early Slavic culture originated in Podolia, not in Polesie, as claimed by Rusanova. He maintained that no other region of the Slavic *oikumene* produced assemblages as early as those of the Upper Prut and Upper Dniester area. In conclusion, this must have been the Slavic *Urheimat*.[16]

Leaving aside the fact that Baran's argument is built on the evidence of only two brooches, there are several other chronological markers of the late fifth and early sixth centuries in the neighboring regions. Notwithstanding the absence of closed finds to be assigned to phase D3 (third quarter of the fifth century) and phase E (last quarter of the fifth century), the two crossbow brooches from Kodyn are not the only late fifth-century artifacts in the region east and south of the Carpathians. A fibula with semicircular head-plate, similar to late fourth- and early fifth-

---

[16] Baran 1994:6; Godłowski 1979:424. Kodyn brooches: Rusanova and Timoshchuk 1984:22, 48, and 21 fig. 19/2. That Kodyn 10 should be dated to the late fifth or early sixth century is also suggested by the presence of fine, grey wheelmade ware. This ceramic ware was found in great quantities on contemporary sites in "Gepidia" and archaeologists were able to identify at least one production center. See Cseh 1990b. As a consequence, Rusanova's and Baran's claims that this ware is indicative of Chernyakhov traditions in the early Slavic culture have no archaeological substance. For crossbow brooches, see Schulze-Dörrlamm 1986:600–3; Corman 1998:37. For finds in Transylvania, see Horedt 1979a:pl. 41/5, 7; Bârzu 1994–5:290 fig. 16/11, 13, and 17. Berekhát: Csallány 1961:82 and pl. LXXXI/2. Battonya: Szábo and Vörös 1979:225 fig. 9/1. Taurapilis: Werner 1977. Balkan specimens: Gomolka-Fuchs 1982:pl. 55/243, 244, 249, 255, and 257–8; Liubenova 1981:169 fig. 108/1, 2; Kharalambieva 1991:34 fig. 11. Two crossbow brooches of the Prague type were found in the Middle Dnieper area. See Tret'iakov 1974:97 fig. 16/1; Kazanski 1992:fig. 1/21, 22.

Elites and group identity

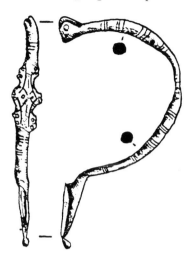

Figure 32 Crossbow brooch from Moleşti-Râpa Adâncă (Moldova)
Drawing, courtesy of Ioan Tentiuc, Museum of Archaeology, Chişinău.

century silver- or bronze-sheet brooches, was found in a grave at Sărata Monteoru. Another grave of the same cemetery produced a small brooch similar to late fifth-century fibulae of the Vyškov class. The Sărata Monteoru cemetery also produced a bronze buckle with embossed decoration, of a type that was popular in the Mediterranean area during the late fifth century. A crossbow brooch of the Viminacium type was recently found in a small settlement excavated at Moleşti, near Cimişlia (Moldova)(Figure 32). Brooches of the Viminacium class could be dated to the late fifth or early sixth century. The best analogies for a brooch with bent stem found at Moldoveni, in Romanian Moldavia, are the so-called Emmanuel fibula from Salona and a similar specimen found in a late fifth-century burial in Jerusalem. A similar dating was advanced for another brooch with bent stem found at Târgşor, near Ploieşti, in south Romania. An almost identical fibula found at Dragosloveni, in a sunken building, is probably of the same date.[17]

[17] Comşa 1972:fig. 4/2. Sărata Monteoru: Fiedler 1992:82; 84; 83 fig. 11/5, 7; and 85 fig. 12/3. Vyškov class: Bierbrauer 1989:151 and 155. Buckles with embossed decoration: Kazanski 1994:161. Moleşti: Ioan Tentiuc, 'Otchet o rabotakh iuzhnoslavianskoi arkheologicheskoi ekspedicii OE i IAN MSSR na poselenii Moleshty-Rypa adynka', an archaeological report in the archives of the Institute of Ancient History and Archaeology, Chişinău, 1990. I am grateful to Dr Tentiuc from the Archaeological Museum in Chişinău for allowing me to see the still unpublished material found at Moleşti-Râpa Adâncă and to reproduce his brooch drawing. Viminacium class: Schulze-Dörrlamm 1986:606–8; Kharalambieva and Atanasov 1991:44–5. The closest analogy of

237

What all this brief survey shows is that we only now begin to conceptualize in archaeological terms the period between the demise of the Hunnic "Empire" and the first Slavic raids known from historical sources. Due to the absence of closed finds, archaeologists have been unable to pin down those assemblages which may be dated to the late fifth or early sixth century, but the situation might well change in the near future.[18] The Kodyn brooches are not unique, but because they were found in closed finds, they are invaluable elements for building a relative chronology of contemporary archaeological assemblages.

A seriation by correspondence analysis of 327 settlement features (sunken buildings, kilns, ovens, and pits) in relation to forty-two chronologically sensitive artifact-categories (including various types of pottery decoration), clearly shows that Kodyn 10 and Kodyn 21, which produced crossbow brooches, should be separated from assemblages of both the same site and other regions (Figure 33). After being abandoned as a house, Kodyn 10 served as a rubbish pit. Materials found in the filling are therefore later than those found on the house's floor. Despite the presence of a crossbow brooch, a sherd of handmade pottery with finger impressions on the lip, which was found in the filling of Kodyn 10, caused the inclusion of this sunken building in the second phase of the seriation, though still far from the main cluster at the tip of the parabola (Figure 34).

A much smaller group of units belong to the third phase. An examination of the scattergram showing the relationships between artifact-categories (Figure 35) indicates that this phase should be dated much later than the other two, primarily because of the exclusive presence of flint steels. The flint steel found in feature 4 at Bucharest-Militari was associated with a scraping tool (Henning's class P2). The earliest specimens of this tool, dated to the fourth and fifth centuries, come from southern Siberia, but similar implements frequently occur in sixth- and seventh-century warrior burials from the present-day Tuva autonomous region.

Footnote 17 (*cont.*)

the Moleşti fibula is the specimen from the Lug II settlement near Pen'kyvka (Ukraine). See Berezovec 1963:fig. 18/4. The Moleşti fibula is not the only fifth-century artifact found in Moldova. The neighboring site at Hansca, near Chişinău, produced a bronze mirror of the Chmi-Brigetio type, which may be dated to the mid-400s (Figure 38/7). See Rafalovich 1972c:33 fig. 3/8; Corman 1998:50; see also Werner 1956:18. Moldoveni: Mitrea 1973:664 fig. 1/1; Uenze 1992:151. Târgşor: Teodorescu 1971:126 fig. 2/2; Harhoiu 1990:204. A fibula of this kind was found in the early Byzantine fort at Gabrovo in a fifth-century context. See Koicheva and Kharalambieva 1993:pl. 1/5. Another brooch from Târgşor is a fifth-century equal-armed fibula (Teodorescu 1971:126 fig. 2/1).

[18] Beginning with issues of Anastasius, Byzantine coins reappeared north of the Danube river after a long interruption. A relatively large number of coins struck for the emperors Anastasius and Justin I were found in Romania, Moldova, and Ukraine. However, since old issues remained in circulation long after leaving the mint, they do not prove anything, for it is impossible to decide whether or not these coins reached the regions where they were found during the reigns of the emperors for whom they were minted.

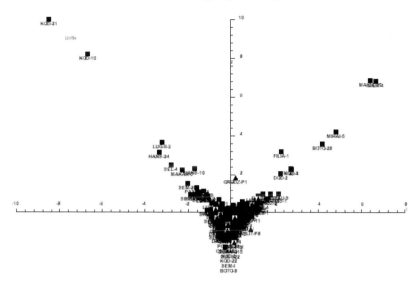

Figure 33 Seriation by correspondence analysis of 327 settlement features in
relation to categories of artifacts with which they were associated
For site name abbreviations, see Appendix A

In Europe, scraping tools occur in eighth-century burials in the Lower
Don area. Along with certain axe-types, they have recently been interpreted as social status markers for second-rank Khazar warriors, the so-
called *afsad*. In the Middle Danube region, such tools were also found
with warrior graves dated to the Middle Avar period. A date in the late
seventh or early eighth century should be assigned to the mortuary
assemblage from grave 7 at Aradka, which produced a flint steel very
similar to those from settlement features of the third group. The same is
true for two flint steels from Kalaja Dalmaces and Kruja, in Albania. Of
a slightly earlier date is the flint steel from grave 5 at Unirea
(Transylvania). In conclusion, phase III may be dated to the second half
of the seventh century, possibly to the late 600s.[19]

The majority of the seriated settlement features cluster in the second
phase. A zoomed detail of the scattergram showing relationships between

[19] Flint steels: Zirra and Cazimir 1963:69 fig. 17/1–2; Teodor 1984a:97 fig. 18/2 and 1984b:30 fig.
6/8; Rusanova and Timoshchuk 1984:73 pl. 13/6; Nagy 1959:pl. II/3; Ippen 1907:17 fig. 25;
Anamali and Spahiu 1963:6 fig. 1; Roska 1934:124 fig. 2 C/7. Grave 5 from Unirea produced an
iron clasp used for attaching the quiver to the belt, a good analogy of which was found in the rich
warrior grave at Kunbábony, dated to the second or last third of the seventh century. See Tóth
and Horváth 1992:160; Kaminskii 1986:28–9. Scraping tools: Henning 1981:69 and 1989:91;
Kovács 1981:92–3 and 100; Mogil'nikov 1981:26 and 124 fig. 20/39; Makhitov 1981:25 and 116
fig. 13/58; Afanas'ev 1993:141–2.

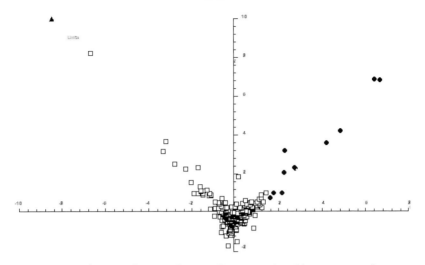

Figure 34 Phasing of 327 settlement features seriated by correspondence
analysis in relation to categories of artifacts with which they were associated
Legend: phase I – triangle; phase II – rectangle; phase III – oval

artifact-categories (Figure 36) indicates those which are closely associated
with this phase. At least six artifact-categories (specially marked in order
to be easily identified) can assist us in estimating the date of the second
phase. In addition, two settlement features from Botoşana (nos. 13 and
20) produced coins struck for Emperor Justinian. Both are folles minted
in Constantinople before the monetary reform (i.e., between 527 and
538). Coins dated to the first half of Justinian's reign were found on
several other sites, though none in a closed find comparable to the
Botoşana settlement features. These coins can only provide a *terminus a
quo*, for it is impossible to know how long they circulated before enter-
ing the archaeological deposit through loss or discarding. As shown in
Chapter 4, hoards closed before *c.* 570 include a fairly large number of
pieces issued between the reign of Anastasius and the first part of
Justinian's reign. Folles minted during this period were occasionally collected even after *c.* 570, unlike lower denominations, which seem to have
become valueless and probably went out of circulation. This warns us
against pushing the numismatic evidence too far. All that Justinian's folles
from Botoşana can tell us is that the archaeological context in which they
were found cannot be dated earlier than AD 527.[20]

---

[20] See Butnariu 1983–5:217–18. It is true that no Romanian hoard closed after *c.* 570 contains coins
antedating Justinian's monetary reform of 538. Some hoards buried next to the Danube frontier
display, however, a different pattern. Veliki Gradac, with the last coin minted in 594/5, has two

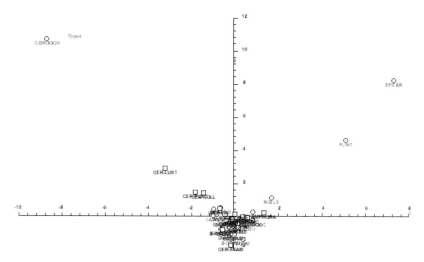

Figure 35 Seriation by correspondence analysis of forty-two artifact-categories
found in sixth- and seventh-century settlement features

CAKES – clay lumps; 2-COMB – double-layered bone comb; AMPHORA – sherds of LR 1 or
LR 2 amphoras; ARROW – arrow head; B-AMU – bone amulet; B-FIBULA – bow-fibula; B-
NEEDLE – bone needle; B-SCRAP – bone scrapper; B/A-AWL – bone or antler awl; BEADS-I
– small-sized glass beads; BEADS-II – glass beads with eye-shaped inlays; BS-BROOCH – brooch
with bent stem; C-BROOCH – crossbow brooch; CER-COLL – handmade or wheelmade pots
with collar; CER-COMB – wheelmade pottery with combed decoration; CER-GROO –
wheelmade pottery with grooves; CER-LUST – wheelmade pottery with lustred decoration;
CER-PUNC – handmade pottery with punctuation depressions; CER-STAM – handmade or
wheelmade pottery with stamped decoration; CER-STRI – handmade pottery decorated with
striations; COIN-I – sixth-century coin; CRUC – crucible; FLINT – flint steel; I-AWL – iron
awl; I-KNIFE – iron knife; IBS- BROO – iron brooch with bent stem; IMP-FIN – handmade
pottery with finger impressions on rims; KNOBS – handmade pots with knobs on shoulders;
LADLE – clay ladle; LOOM – loom weights; MOLD – stone or bone mold; NP-OBUCK – oval
buckle without plate; NP-RBUCK – rectangular buckle without plate; PANS – clay pans;
QUERN – rotary quern; ROLLS – clay rolls (found in the oven); SICK – sickle; SLA-DEC –
handmade or wheelmade pottery with notches on rims; SPEAR – spear-head; SPINDLE –
spindle whorl; VERT-INC – handmade pottery with vertical incisions; WHET – whetstone

That phase II must be dated later than that is suggested by artifact-
categories marked as special. Beads with eye-shaped inlays first occur in
Early Avar burial assemblages in Hungary and remained popular through
the Middle Avar period. The earliest known beads of this kind are those
of grave 2 at Szentendre, in which they were found together with a tremissis minted for Emperor Justin II, and those of grave 116 at Jutas, which
were associated with a copper coin struck for Emperor Phocas.

coins issued for Anastasius, three for Justin I, and one pre-reform coin of Justinian. In the
Murighiol hoard, twelve out of thirty-eight identifiable coins are pre-reform issues. See Minić
1984; Cristina Opaiţ 1991:478–9.

Handmade pottery with stamped decoration, such as that from Poian and Cernat, was also found on Early Avar sites in Bohemia, Moravia, and Slovakia.[21] Single- or double-layered combs are rare on early medieval sites in Eastern Europe, but relatively frequent in Central Europe, particularly on sixth-century sites. They remained popular during the Early Avar period, as well as later. A late sixth-century settlement at Ludanice (Slovakia) produced clear evidence of comb production. A comb-case similar to that found at Davideni, which is decorated on either side with an incised and punched geometrical pattern, comes from grave 33 of the Early Avar cemetery at Pécs-Köztemetö.[22]

Amphora sherds were found on several sites south and east of the Carpathian mountains.[23] Many belong to LR 1 and LR 2 amphoras (Figure 37).[24] Both types may be dated to the sixth and seventh centuries. With LR 2 amphoras, a narrower dating is possible on the basis of

[21] For beads with eye-shaped inlays, see Garam 1992:151; Kiss 1996:197. Such beads are relatively common in contemporary assemblages in Romania. At Sărata Monteoru, 14 percent of all beads are with eye-shaped inlays (Fiedler 1992:80). Handmade pottery with stamped decoration: Székely 1992:267 fig. 16/1–2 and 285 fig. 26/B 4; Klanica 1993:87; Hromada 1991. The cremation cemetery at Bratislava-Dubravka produced a bronze bracelet, which is typical for early seventh-century assemblages in northern Italy. See Werner 1991.

[22] Mitrea 1974–6:fig. 18/1–2; Kiss 1977:96 and pl. xxxvi/33; see also Popović 1984a. For finds in Eastern Europe, see Vakulenko and Prikhodniuk 1984:96; Rejholcová 1990:380. For a list of Early Avar finds, see Kiss 1996:190. For Ludanice, see Fusek, Staššiková-Štukovská, and Bátora 1993:33.

[23] Amphora finds on various sites in Bucharest: Constantiniu 1965a:90–1; Turcu and Marinescu 1968:125 fig. 6/8; Cantea 1959:33–4; Dolinescu-Ferche and Constantiniu 1981:319 fig. 16/3, 6; Constantiniu 1963:83–4; Vasilica Sandu, 'Bălăceanca, archeological report', paper presented at the 28th National Archaeological Conference (Satu Mare, May 12–15, 1994). Dulceanca: Dolinescu-Ferche 1974:figs. 85/6–8 and 99–100, 1986:137 fig. 10/9, 10, and 1992:136 fig. 5/5, 6, 139 fig. 8/9, 11–14, 18–19, 143 fig. 12/8, 144 fig. 13/4, 5, 20, 146 fig. 15/2–5, 148 fig. 17/2, 4–5. Other finds: Bârzu 1994–5:285 fig. 11/11; Mitrea, Eminovici, and Momanu 1986–7:224; Rafalovich 1972c:38 fig. 8/8; Toropu 1976:212; Vakulenko and Prikhodniuk 1984:61 fig. 34/10, 64 fig. 37/10, 15; Rusanova and Timoshchuk 1984:18 fig. 12/3; Dolinescu-Ferche 1973; Rafalovich 1972b:127. Early Avar burials produced only LR 1 amphoras, while local replicas of such amphoras were found in Middle Avar assemblages. See Tettamanti 1980:158; Vida 1990–1:134, 1993:279–80, and 1999:90–3.

[24] Amphoras of the Scorpan IX=Kuzmanov XVI=Antonova V=Opaiţ B-Id class, though common in late sixth-century deposits in Dobrudja, do not appear north of the Danube. They were only found in the Middle Dnieper area. Two specimens were found in Kiev, one at Kyselivka, the other on the Podyl; a third specimen on the opposite bank, at Svetil'ne. See Shovkoplias 1957:101 and 1963:140. A fourth amphora was found in a Kievan suburb, at Vishgorod (Prikhodniuk 1980:130). Other classes are also represented. A specimen of the LR 1 class comes from A. V. Bodianskii's excavations at Iaicevoi-Zaporizhzhia, on the Lower Dnieper, and a fragment of LR 2 was associated with pottery with lustred decoration in a sunken building found at Budishche, near Cherkassy (Prikhodniuk 1980:130 and 127). Just as with contemporary specimens found in Cornwall and Ireland, amphoras found in regions so far away from their production centers in the eastern Mediterranean area point to trade relations. That Byzantine ships were sailing on the Lower Dnieper in the early seventh century is suggested by the anchor found at Khorticia, near Zaporizhzhia. See Shapovalov 1990. Its closest analogy is the anchor of the Yassi Ada shipwreck.

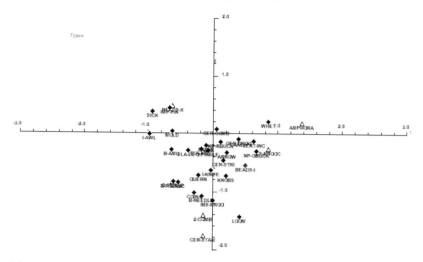

Figure 36 Zoomed detail of the seriation by correspondence analysis of forty-two artifact-categories found in sixth- and seventh- century settlement features

Triangles indicate special artifact-categories discussed in the text. For abbreviations, see Figure 35

the presence or absence of a pointed tip, a feature that disappeared after *c.* 550. Specimens with combed decoration in the form of wavy lines should be dated to the second half of the sixth century and the early seventh century. Unfortunately, finds of amphora tips are rare, the most frequently encountered sherds being those of shoulders or bodies. However, excavations at Bucharest-Mihai Vodă produced a LR 2 amphora tip, which suggests that the ceramic assemblage found there should be dated to the first half of the sixth century. Most other fragments have wavy combed decoration, a detail pointing to a date in the late sixth or early seventh century.[25]

The fibula with bent stem found in an oven at Bucharest-Militari belongs to a group which includes almost identical specimens from sites along the Lower Danube (Prahovo/Aquis, Korbovo, Krivina/Iatrus, Izvoarele-Pârjoaia, and Adamclisi). This may indicate a center of local production, probably at Prahovo. Since all specimens with known archeological context (except the Bucharest brooch) come from early Byzantine forts, such fibulae may be associated with the implementation

---

[25] Cantea 1959:33–4; Mackensen 1992:241 and 244. See also Scorpan 1977:274; Opaiţ 1984:316; Van Doorninck 1989:248. At Iatrus, the ratio between sherds of amphora body, rim, base (or tip), and handle is 16.4:1:0.2:0.5. See Wendel 1986:114.

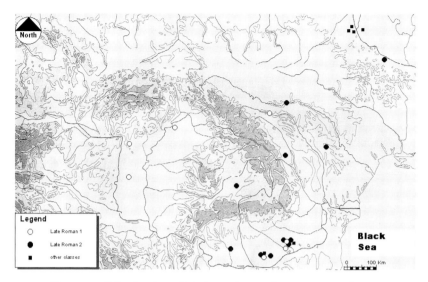

Figure 37 Distribution of sixth- and seventh-century amphoras

of Justinian's building program in the northern Balkans and should therefore be dated to the mid-500s.[26]

Another fibula with bent stem from Bucharest-Militari was found in a
sunken building, together with handmade pottery with finger impressions and notches on the lip. All known parallels come from military sites
along the Danube frontier of the Empire. They are all of the same size
and have identical decoration, which strongly suggests they were produced in the same workshop, probably at Prahovo.[27]

Analogies for the fibula with bent stem found in a sunken building at
Poian, together with a clay pan and a single-layered comb, are only
known from two burial assemblages in "Gepidia" dated to the first half
of the sixth century (grave 102 at Berekhát and grave 146 at Kiszombor).
Unlike these two specimens, however, the Poian brooch displays a characteristic hook at the end of the bow, which is viewed by some scholars
as an indication of a slightly later date, probably in the mid- or late sixth
century.[28]

---

[26] Uenze 1992:147–8 and 151; Curta 1992:87. Bucharest-Militari: Sgîbea-Turcu 1963:379 pl. II.
Production center: Janković 1980:177; Gencheva 1989:34. Balkan finds: Kharalambieva and
Atanasov 1991:56 pl. VIII/4; Kharalambieva 1989:pls. II/6, 7 and III/6, 9; Gomolka-Fuchs 1982:pl.
55/269; Kharalambieva and Ivanov 1986:pl. III/18; Koicheva and Kharalambieva 1993:pl. VII/2–4.
[27] Sgîbea-Turcu 1963:379 pl. II/1. Balkan finds: Janković 1981:126 fig. 70 and pls. XVI/3 and XVI/1;
Uenze 1992:pl. 3/5; Kharalambieva 1989:pl. III/4–5.
[28] Székely 1992:269 fig. 17/6; Csallány 1961:pls. LXXV/1 and CXXXV/2; Uenze 1992:149–51.

Three fibulae with bent stem found at Davideni also indicate a date in the late 500s. One of them has a characteristically trapezoidal foot, which is reminiscent of the gold fibula found at Markovi Kuli in a small hoard, together with a buckle of the Sucidava class, which may not be earlier than *c.* 550 or later than *c.* 600. A second fibula from Davideni was found in association with a pectoral cross. The fibula is made of iron, instead of bronze. Such fibulae appear in late sixth-century contexts in Balkan hill-forts. At Markovi Kuli, one such fibula was found in association with two coins issued for Emperor Justin II (dated 575/6 and 577/8, respectively). Finally, the third specimen found at Davideni is also made of iron and has no exact analogy. The closest parallels are a fibula from Heraclea (Yeşilköy) and another from an unknown location in Romania. All three have a wide bow and a comparatively narrower foot, a feature which reminds one of iron and bronze brooches found in seventh-century mor-tuary assemblages in Albania and the neighboring region (the so-called "Koman culture").[29]

Cast fibulae with bent stem are even stronger indications of a late date. Despite slight ornamental variations, this group of fibulae is remarkably homogeneous. Its dating to the reign of Justin II (565–78) is secured by specimens associated with hoards of copper concluding with coins issued for that emperor (Bracigovo and Koprivec). Fibulae of this kind were found in great numbers in forts, particularly in the northern Balkans. It has been suggested that they were part of the military uniform. However, specimens found in mortuary assemblages, always with female skeletons, indicate that cast fibulae with bent stem were worn by women, arguably by wives of soldiers. Such fibulae were produced locally in workshops like the one found at Turnu-Severin (Drobeta), on the left bank of the Danube. Since the specimens found at Bârlăleşti and Hansca (Figure 38/6) are unique, it is also possible that replicas of such fibulae were pro-duced in Barbaricum.[30]

---

[29] Davideni: Mitrea 1974–6:fig. 15/1, 3, and 4. Analogies for the first fibula: Mikulčić and Bilbija 1981–2:213 fig. 7; Janković 1981:pl. XVI/5; Kharalambieva 1989:pl. II/7; Kharalambieva 1992:134 pl. III/12. Analogies for the second fibula: Mikulčić and Nikuljska 1979:148 fig. 17; Dimitrov et al. 1974:55 fig. 23; Uenze 1992:pl. 2/8; Kharalambieva and Ivanov 1986:pl. II/15–16; Poulter 1988:83 fig. 10/11; Kharalambieva and Atanasov 1991:pls. IV/8, 9 and VI/8; Koicheva and Kharalambieva 1993:pls. I/9, II/5, and III/10, 12. For a production center for this group of fibulae, see Uenze 1992:150; Koicheva and Kharalambieva 1993:61. Analogies for the third fibula: Popescu 1941–44:503 fig. 10/115; Vinski 1971:388; Goriunov and Kazanskii 1978:26; Uenze 1992:149; Văzharova 1971:46 and 1973:265.

[30] Bârlăleşti: Coman 1969:309 fig. 16/4. Hansca: Rafalovich 1972c:33 fig. 3/6. Turnu-Severin: Bejan 1976. Coin-hoards with cast fibulae with bent stem: Milchev and Draganov 1992:39 and fig. 5; Uenze 1974:485–6. See also Curta 1992:84–5. In addition, the "Nestor house" at Sadovec produced a cast fibula with bent stem and coins struck for Justin II (Uenze 1992:156). For the specimen found in a sunken building at Bacău and its Balkan analogies, see Mitrea and Artimon

All this archaeological evidence suggests that the major part of the seriated settlement features, which were ordered into the second phase, should be dated to the second half or the last third of the sixth century and to the early seventh century. It is important to emphasize that some assemblages may be of an earlier date, possibly of the first half of the sixth century. A LR 2 amphora tip was found at Bucharest-Mihai Vodă. Salvage excavations at Sfinţeşti produced fragments of grey gritty ware (Kuzmanov I 4), which appeared around or just before the middle of the fifth century, but became popular shortly after 500. Both sites seem to have been occupied during the first half of the sixth century. Without sufficient artifacts from the first half of the sixth century, archaeologists are not yet capable of differentiating the earlier material from later assemblages. It is not unlikely, however, that a significant number of ceramic assemblages with no associated metal artifacts are earlier than c. 550.[31]

One important conclusion resulting from this analysis is that during the second half of the sixth century and the first decades of the seventh, a relatively large number of sites appeared east and south of the Carpathians, which displayed a similar set of artifact-categories. On many, occupation must have begun much earlier, as suggested by finds in Kodyn and Bucharest-Mihai Vodă. Others continued to be occupied during the seventh century, as in Bucharest-Militari. On the evidence of the selected sites, it seems that the dramatic increase in number of sites took place during the second half of the sixth century, shortly after the implementation of Justinian's building program in the Balkans. As shown in Chapter 4, this is also the period in which the number of coins from both hoards and stray finds suddenly began to increase. More important, Slavic raids resumed during this period on a very large scale, often under the leadership of Slavic "kings" (Chapter 3). Social and political change seems to have coincided with material culture change, a coincidence which will be discussed in detail in the following chapter. That this coincidence is no accident is shown by the analysis of another artifact-category associated with settlement features of the second phase: "Slavic" bow fibulae.

Footnote 30 (*cont.*)
  1971:242 fig. 13/1; Barnea et al. 1979:218 fig. 169/10.2; Kharalambieva 1989:pls. IV/1, 3, 8, and VI/1–3 and 7–8; Kharalambieva 1992:pl. III/6–7; Kharalambieva and Ivanov 1986:pl. I/2, 4, and 5; Kharalambieva and Atanasov 1991:55 pl. VII/1; Brmbolić 1986:fig. 31; Janković 1981:pls. XIV/2–6, 8–13 and XV/1–10, 12; Gabričević 1986:86 fig. 19/8; Uenze 1992:pl. 3/8, 14, pl. 4/2, and pl. 122/15, 16. For the specimen from Suceava-Şipot and its analogies, see Comşa 1972:14 fig. 4/3; Janković 1981:pl. XIV/7; Kharalambieva 1989:pl. V/9. For finds south of the Stara Planina, see Gencheva 1989:35. A cast fibula with bent stem was found in Constantinople. See Gill 1986:266 and fig. V.
31 Dolinescu-Ferche 1967:130 fig. 3/1, 3. Grey gritty ware: Kuzmanov 1985:47 and 1992:213; Borisov 1988a:100; Hayes 1992:54. See also Vékony 1973:213.

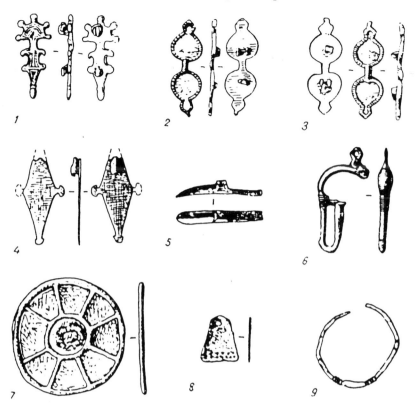

Figure 38 Metal artifacts from fifth- to seventh-century sites in Moldova
Source: Rafalovich 1972c: 33 fig. 3.

"SLAVIC" BOW FIBULAE IN EASTERN EUROPE

A German archaeologist, Herbert Kühn, first called the bow fibula an early medieval artifact *par excellence.*[32] Textbooks and art history studies use it to illustrate sections dedicated to the Dark Ages. There are probably thousands and hundreds of thousands of bow fibulae in European museum collections. A still greater number of specimens come out of archaeological excavations and their incredible diversity defies any attempts to establish unequivocal typologies.

The first classification of bow fibulae found in Eastern Europe was produced by Joachim Werner, who also attached the label "Slavic" to the

[32] Kühn 1965.

name of this class of artifacts. Werner divided his corpus into two classes (I and II), further subdivided into groups (A, B, C, etc.), on the basis of presumably different terminal lobes, shaped in the form of either human face ("mask") or animal head. A quick glimpse at those brooches ascribed by Werner to his respective classes, however, yields no positive result. There is no significant correlation between variables used by Werner and the brooches he discussed. More important, Werner's approach is rooted in Gustav Kossina's concept of *Siedlungsarchäologie* (see Chapter 1). He used artifacts to identify "cultures." The distribution of artifacts was then interpreted as reflecting "cultural provinces," which he further viewed as coinciding with settlement areas of tribal or ethnic groups. The distribution of bow fibulae in Eastern Europe convinced Werner that the migration of the Slavs may have been responsible for the spread of this dress-accessory in areas so afar from each other as Ukraine and Greece.[33]

An important element of his theory was the idea that unlike the "Germanic" ethnic dress, "Slavic" bow fibulae were usually worn not in pairs, but singly, and that they were more likely to be found in association with cremation (the presumably standard burial rite of the early Slavs) than with skeleton graves.[34] A large number of his "Slavic" bow fibulae have been found prior to World War II in a limited area in Mazuria, in archaeological assemblages which were foreign to anything both Werner and Soviet archaeologists viewed as typically "Slavic." Aware that his theory of the Slavic migration would not work with Mazurian brooches, Werner proposed that in this case bow fibulae be interpreted as a result of long-distance trade between Mazuria and the Lower Danube region, along the "amber trail." In accordance with the widely spread belief that mortuary practices were an indication of status hierarchy, he believed that bow fibulae found in Mazurian graves marked the status of the rich "amber lords" of the North.[35]

Werner's ideas were taken at their face value by many archaeologists

---

[33] Werner 1950:166 and 172, 1960, and 1984b. Werner's class I includes also brooches with animal-head terminal lobe (e.g., Werner 1950:pls. 29 and 31). Before Werner, the Soviet archaeologist Boris Rybakov had already ascribed these brooches to the early Slavs, but because of linguistic and ideological barriers, his work was far less influential in Europe than Joachim Werner's. See Rybakov 1948.

[34] Though Herbert Kühn (1956) provided a considerable number of examples from East Prussia, in which pairs of identical brooches were found in association with cremation, Werner (1960:115) persisted in his idea that "Slavic" bow fibulae were typically worn singly, not in pairs.

[35] Werner 1950:167 and 1984b:74–7. This idea goes back to the work of the Latvian archaeologist Eduard Šturms (1950:22), who first claimed that during the early Middle Ages the present-day Olsztyn district of Poland possessed Europe's richest amber resources. As shown in Chapter 5, connections between the Baltic region and the Carpathian basin are well illustrated by finds of amber beads, which were particularly frequent in "Gepidia." For mortuary practices as indicating status hierarchy, see Binford 1971:15. Olsztyn group: Okulicz 1989; Mączyńska 1998:88–9.

and never seriously questioned. Despite heavy criticism, his interpretation of the "Slavic" bow fibulae is the scholarly standard in many countries of Eastern Europe, where a strong undercurrent of German archaeological tradition is still apparent. To be sure, despite occasional errors of attribution, Werner's classification is still valid and will be used in the following analysis. The principal question that remains to be tackled is whether the introduction of "Slavic" bow fibulae can be explained in terms of migration. Werner's dating of the entire corpus to the seventh century, an important element of his theory, is a starting point for discussing this group of artifacts.[36]

Werner's group I B (Veţel-Coşoveni), which I examined in detail elsewhere, can be subdivided into two series. One of them includes brooches similar to a gilded specimen with lavish scrollwork decoration, which is said to have been found at Constantinople and is now in a private collection in Switzerland. Fibulae with similar, but more modest, decoration were found in Bulgaria, Romania, and East Prussia. Formal parallels for fibulae of this group may also be found among specimens of Kühn's Aquileia class, particularly those of the Lower Danube area and Crimea, all of which are from the second half of the fifth century. These fibulae display two kinds of ornamentation, one resulting in coloristic effects (garnet inlay and mercury gilding), the other in textural effects consisting of chip-carving, scrollwork decoration on both head- and foot-plate. The scrollwork is reminiscent of the so-called Gáva-Domolospuszta-style metalwork of the late fifth century. A *Prunkfibel* with typically Early Avar decoration in animal Style II, which was found at Coşoveni together with two silver earrings with star-shaped pendants and a silver collar, was used by Werner to date the entire corpus of "Slavic" bow fibulae to the seventh century. However, the Coşoveni brooch should be treated as an exceptional specimen of the I B group, in terms of both decoration and archaeological context.[37]

A date to the early seventh century may be assigned only to the second

---

[36] When it comes to chronology, Werner's thesis is self-contradicting. He dated all "Slavic" bow fibulae to the seventh century, including those of Mazuria, which he explained by means of trade relations. However, he also claimed that regular trade relations between the Danube region and the North were interrupted shortly before 600 by the arrival of Avars and Slavs. See Werner 1984b; Okulicz 1973:565; Dąbrowski 1975:196; Kulakov 1990:45; Teodor 1992:128. For alternative views, see Menke 1990; Fiedler 1992; Curta 1994b; and Vagalinski 1994. Contacts between Mazuria and the Danube region continued even after the conquest of the Carpathian basin by the Avars, as shown, for example, by ornament links between metalwork found on Early Avar and Mazurian sites. See Urbańczyk 1977.

[37] Werner 1950:150–2 and 157. Swiss fibula and its analogies: Werner 1960:119 and pl. 2; Curta 1994b:245–7 and 260; Mikhailov 1977:317–18 and pl. 7; Simonova 1970:75 and 76 fig. 1; Kühn 1981:317 no. 502 and pl. 75/502. Gáva-Domolospuszta style: Bierbrauer 1975:140; Menke 1986; Harhoiu 1990:187. Coloristic and textural ornamentation effects: Leigh 1991:107.

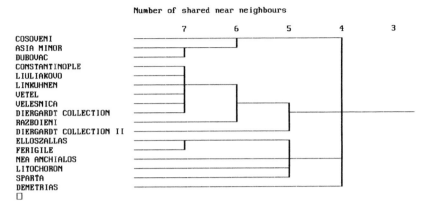

Figure 39 Cluster analysis of seventeen brooches of Werner's group I B, in
relation to their ornamental patterns

series of the I B group, which is represented by four brooches found in
Greece (Litochoron/ Dion, Sparta, Demetrias, and Nea Anchialos). This
is suggested by the crisp style decoration of the Nea Anchialos fibula and
by the closest analogy for all four fibulae, which was found in an Early Avar
grave of the Ellöszállás cemetery. A cluster analysis by the Jaccard coefficient of similarity shows indeed that fibulae of Werner's group I B fall into
two variants, each defined by different ornamental patterns (Figure 39).
When plotting on a map the nearest-neighbor relationships resulting from
this analysis, it becomes clear that the two variants, though related to each
other, have different distributions (Figure 40). In terms of ornamental patterns, fibulae found in Romania seem to represent the intermediary link
between the two variants, since fibulae found in Greece or in Hungary are
not direct analogies of the Constantinopolitan brooch.[38]

Werner's group I C (Figure 41/3, 6; Figure 42) is characterized by a
foot-plate in the form of a lyre with one or two pairs of bird-heads. The
only known parallel to this specific feature are buckles of the seventh-
century Boly-Želovce class. However, there is evidence that at least some
specimens of group I C must be of an earlier date. The I C brooches
found in graves 8 and 30 of the Mazurian cemetery at Kielary were

[38] The crisp style decoration of the Nea Anchialos fibula is reminiscent of a horse shaped figurine
from the Biskupije hoard, dated to the seventh century, and of a copper-alloy "votive hand"
recently auctioned in New York. See Werner 1953:5 and pl. 4/4; Korošec 1958b; Kidd 1992:511
and 514 fig. 5e. Ellöszállás: Sós 1963:315 and 314 fig. 5b.

250

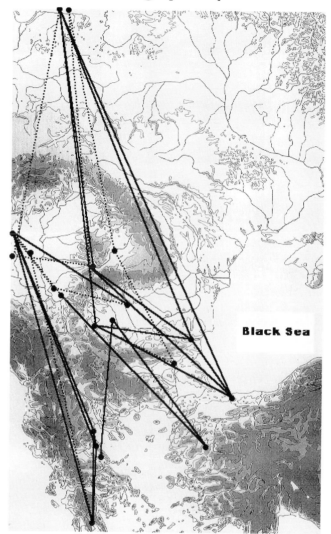

Figure 40 Plotting of the nearest-neighbor similarity of seventeen brooches of
Werner's group I B

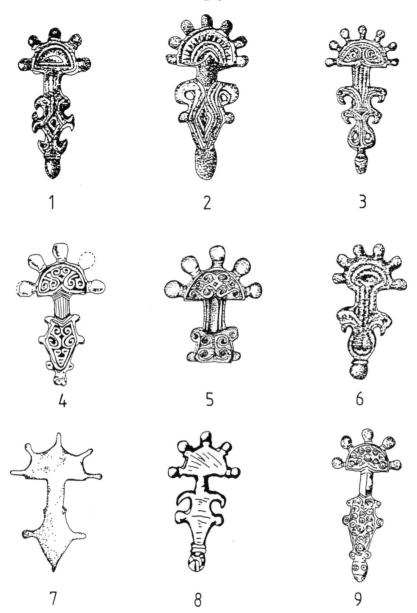

Figure 41 Examples of "Slavic" bow fibulae
Bratei (1, 2), Gâmbaş (3), Vârtoape (4), Pietroasele (5), Poian (6), Butimanu (7), Selişte (8), and Dănceni (9).
Drawings by author

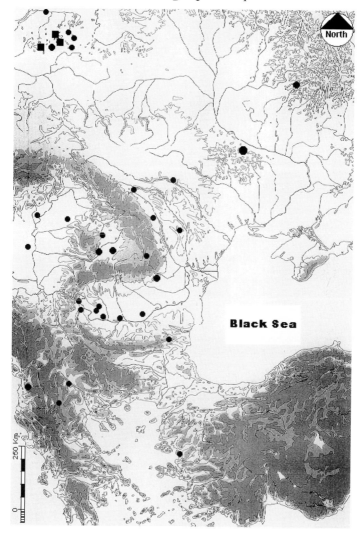

Figure 42 Distribution of "Slavic" bow fibulae of Werner's group I C
For legend, see Figure 50

associated with crossbow fibulae, which are typical for sixth-century assemblages in the Baltic region and in Finland. By 550, fibulae of Werner's I C group were also in fashion in Transylvania, as indicated by a specimen found in grave 113 at Bratei together with a buckle of the Sucidava class. Specimens with two pairs of bird-heads (Corneşti, Gâmbaş, Kruja) are, no doubt, the latest of the entire group. In a female burial at Kruja (Albania), two such fibulae were associated with a buckle of the Corinth class, which cannot be dated earlier than *c.* 600. At Gâmbaş, two other specimens were found in association with earrings with star-shaped pendants, similar to those found in the Priseaca hoard, which also produced hexagrams of Constantine IV.[39]

What catches the eye on the plotting of the cluster analysis of forty-one brooches of Werner's group I C in relation to their shape and ornamental pattern (Figures 43–4) is that there are very few specimens without analogies from Mazurian cemeteries. These cemeteries also produced the earliest specimens of Werner's group I C. Among brooches with two pairs of bird-heads, which are significantly later than the others, the one with the most elaborated decoration (niello triangles on all edges, paw-shaped head-plate knobs, etc.) is a fragmentary specimen from Tumiany. Brooches found on Mazurian sites (Tumiany, Tylkowo, Kielary) are almost identical, sometimes to such minute details as the terminal lobe. One can hardly avoid the conclusion that they were all worked by the same jeweller or by jewellers working after the same model. Brooches found in the Middle Dnieper region, in Romania, or in the western Balkan area are all dated later and display a much simplified version of the Mazurian decoration. We should note, however, that similar, if not identical, fibulae are now found at greater distance, without any Romanian intermediary. Furthermore, four brooches of a small series (Lăuni, Paşcani, Chernyvka, and Sărata Monteoru) are all alike, but have comparatively fewer links with the rest of the group. This may indicate a locally produced series. In any case, everything points to the precedence taken by Mazurian specimens.[40]

---

[39] Corneşti: Pálko 1972:677–8 and pl. 1/5. Gâmbaş: Horedt 1958:97–8 and 79 fig. 15/8, 9. Kruja: Anamali and Spahiu 1979–80:61–2 and pl. 7/11, 12. Boly-Želovce buckles: Ibler 1992:143–4. Kielary: Kühn 1981:177 and 179, pls. 38/237 and 39/243. Crossbow brooches: Bitner-Wróblewska 1991:236. Another I C fibula was found in grave 1185 at Sărata Monteoru in association with a brooch, which is reminiscent of the early fifth-century Bratei class. See Nestor and Zaharia 1960:513 and 511 fig. 1/7; Bierbrauer 1989:141–7. A I C fibula found in a cremation burial at Tumiany was associated with an envelope-shaped belt mount, most typical for late sixth-and early seventh-century weapon graves on the island of Bornholm. See Kulakov 1989:192 and 255 fig. 39/3; Jørgensen 1999:149 and 153 fig. 9/4.

[40] Tumiany: Kühn 1981:111 and pl. 21/135. Lăuni: Spiru 1970:531 and fig. 2. Paşcani: Biţă 1985. Chernyvka: Timoshchuk, Rusanova, and Mikhailina 1981:91 and fig. 7. Sărata Monteoru: Nestor and Zaharia 1959:517 fig. 3. For other Mazurian specimens, see Kühn 1981:57, 59 (Mragowo), 107, 109–11 (Tumiany), 177, 179–81, 184–5 (Kielary), 221 (Mietkie), and 310 (Tylkowo).

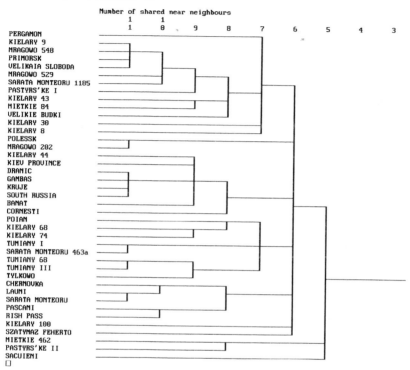

Figure 43   Cluster analysis of forty-one brooches of Werner's group I C, in
relation to their shape and ornamental patterns

Fibulae of Werner's group I D (Figures 41/2 and 45) are modeled after
late fifth- and early sixth-century brooches of the Aquileia and
Hahnheim classes. An early date seems to be confirmed by a pair of
brooches found in grave 126 at Basel-Kleinhüningen, dated to the late
400s and the early 500s, which are very similar to Werner's group I D.
When we examine the plotting of the cluster analysis of thirty-four
brooches of this group in relation to their decoration (Figures 46–7), it
becomes clear that most specimens have analogies in Mazuria. At a closer
look, almost all parallels to late fifth-century brooch ornamentation are
also from Mazuria. Besides a I D fibula, grave 46 of the Tumiany cemetery produced a brooch imitating the early fifth-century Vinarice class.
The fibula found in grave 85 at Kielary was associated with silver strapends from the first half of the sixth century. Outside Mazuria, specimens

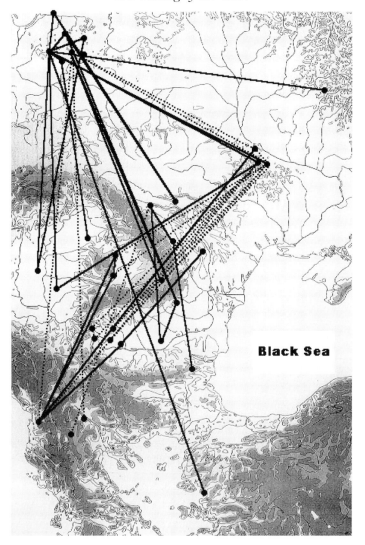

Figure 44 Plotting of the nearest-neighbor similarity of forty-one brooches of
Werner's group I C

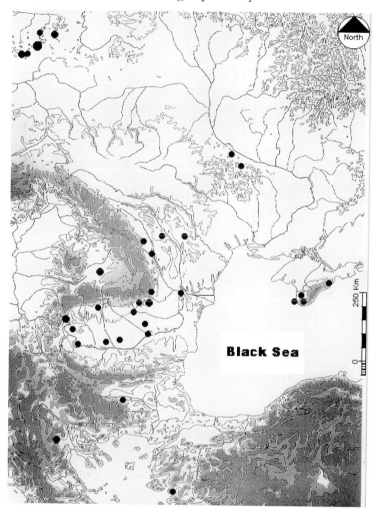

Figure 45 Distribution of "Slavic" bow fibulae of Werner's group I D
For legend, see Figure 50

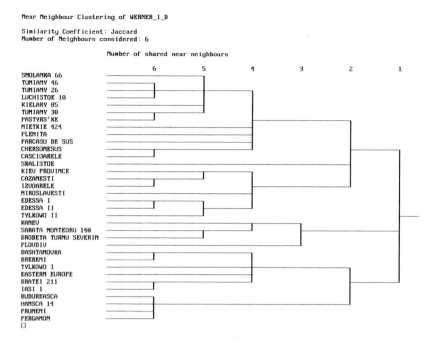

Figure 46 Cluster analysis of thirty-four brooches of Werner's group I D, in relation to their ornamental patterns

of Werner's class I D are of a much later date, most likely of the late sixth century. This is the case of the fibula from the burial chamber 10 at Luchistoe (Crimea), which was found together with silver sheet brooches with trapezoidal head-plate (Ambroz's class II b) and a buckle with eagle-headed plate (Ambroz's class IV). Both have been dated to the late 500s and early 600s. An even later date may be assigned to the pair of I D brooches found at Edessa, in Greece, together with a buckle of the Syracuse class, which cannot be earlier than c. 600.[41]

Although I D fibulae were also found in the Middle Dnieper area, there are no analogies between them and Crimean brooches. In both areas, however, there are strong links to Mazurian specimens. By contrast, Romanian brooches have closer links to each other than to outside specimens. This may suggest the existence of a local production.

[41] Basel-Kleinhüningen: Roth and Theune 1988:34. Tumiany: Jaskanis and Kachinski 1981:47 no. 47 and pl. 47/3; Kühn 1974:565–71. Kielary: Kühn 1981:183 no. 259 and pl. 41/259; Åberg 1919:98. Luchistoe: Aibabin 1990:22 and 199 fig. 20/6. Edessa: Petsas 1969:307 and fig. 320/ε, η.

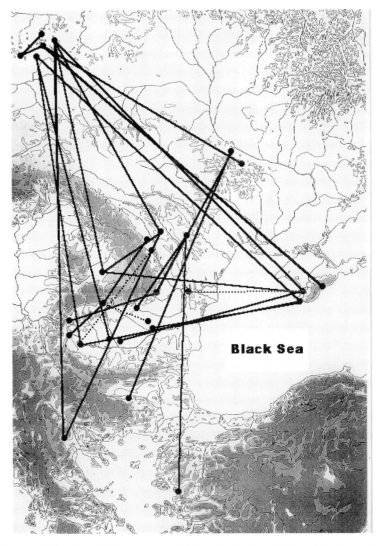

Figure 47 Plotting of the nearest-neighbor similarity of thirty-four brooches
of Werner's group I D

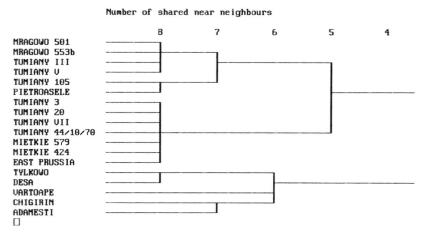

```
Near Neighbour Clustering of pietroasele

Similarity Coefficient: Jaccard
Number of Neighbours considered: 8

                  Number of shared near neighbours

                   8        7        6        5        4
MRAGOWO 501     ──────────┐
MRAGOWO 553b    ────────┐ │
TUMIANY III     ──────┐ │ │              ┌────────────
TUMIANY V       ──────┤ │ ├──────────────┤
TUMIANY 105     ──────┤ │ │              │
PIETROASELE     ──────┘ │ │              │
TUMIANY 3       ──────┐ │ │              │            ┌──
TUMIANY 20      ──────┤ │ │              │            │
TUMIANY VII     ──────┤ │ │              │            │
TUMIANY 44/10/70────────┘ │              │            │
MIETKIE 579     ──────┐   │              │            │
MIETKIE 424     ──────┤   │              │            │
EAST PRUSSIA    ──────┘   │              │            │
TYLKOWO                                  │            │
DESA            ──────────┐              │            │
VARTOAPE        ────────┐ ├──────────────┤            │
CHIGIRIN        ──────┐ │ │              │            │
ADAMESTI        ──────┤ │ │              │            │
               []   ──┘ └─┘
```

Figure 48 Cluster analysis of eighteen brooches of Werner's group I F, in relation to their ornamental patterns

Moreover, there is at least one variant (represented by specimens found at Hansca, Budureasca, and Pruneni), which has no parallels in either Mazuria or Crimea. Production of this series may have involved the use of hard models, such as the silver-alloy model found at Bucharest-Tei, which is remarkably similar to the Hansca brooch.[42]

In sharp contrast to other series, Werner's group I F (Pietroasele) may have originated in Romania (Figures 41/4–5, 48, and 49). Fibulae of this group were modeled after specimens of the Aquileia class and decorated with scrollwork inspired by Gáva-Domolospuszta metalwork, both from the late fifth century. Brooches cast in silver, with careful chip-carving in standard Gáva-Domolospuszta style, were found at Pietroasele and Bucharest-Băneasa. By contrast, Mazurian brooches present a grossly simplified version of this ornament. Only two brooches found at Mrągowo (graves 501 and 553b) have analogies outside Mazuria. No Romanian specimen was found in a datable archaeological context, but the unique association of a I F brooch with another of Werner's group I D in grave 424 at Mietkie suggests that the two groups coexisted. If, as

---

[42] Bucharest-Tei: Rosetti 1934:207 fig. 1/4. Hansca: Rafalovich 1972c:32–3, 196–7, 32 fig. 2, and 33 fig. 3/1. Budureasca: Teodor 1992:138 no. 3 and 147 fig. 6/3. Pruneni: Comşa 1972:15. For fibulae from Crimea and the Middle Dnieper area, see Ambroz 1970:74. Models in early medieval metalworking: Capelle and Vierck 1971:51 and 86–7; Hines 1984:183 and 1997:211–13; Roth 1986:46 and 48; Mortimer 1994.

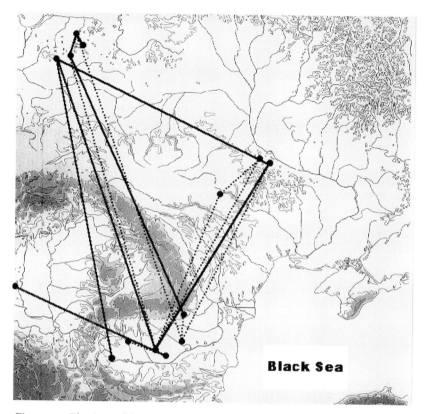

Figure 49 Plotting of the nearest-neighbor similarity of eighteen brooches of
Werner's group I F

suggested by their archaeological context, some Mazurian I D brooches
may be dated to the sixth century, then the burial assemblage at Mietkie
could also be dated to that century as well. That the Werner I F group is
of an earlier date than the others, perhaps from the first half of the sixth
century, is also suggested by the fact that no such fibulae were found in
Early Avar burial assemblages in Hungary.[43]

The main characteristic of Werner's group I G (Figures 41/1, 50, 51,
and 52) is the tongs-shaped foot-plate, most probably inspired by early
and mid-sixth-century *Zangenfibeln*. A large number of specimens, all
found in Mazuria, display an elaborate ornamentation, which suggests
links with Werner's group I C (paw-shaped head-plate knobs, ribs on
bow, etc.). No specimen of this series was found outside Mazuria, though

[43] Pietroasele: Curta and Dupoi 1994–5. Bucharest-Băneasa: Constantiniu 1965a:77–8 and 92 fig.
18. Mrągowo: Kühn 1956:95 and pl. 24/7, 12. Mietkie: Kulakov 1989:181 and 230 fig. 14/1.
According to Manfred Menke (1990:151), the brooch found at Keszthely predates the migration
of the Avars.

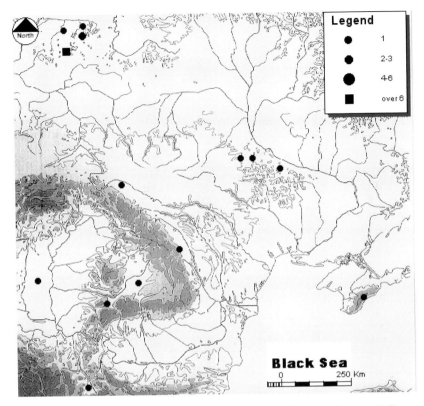

Figure 50 Distribution of "Slavic" bow fibulae of Werner's group I G

the Dem'ianyv fibula displays a vaguely similar decoration on the foot-plate. This brooch is closely linked to four other specimens (Bratei, Davideni, Kiskörös, Caričin Grad), but not to those from the Middle Dnieper region or Crimea. This is a picture completely different from that given by the distribution of I F fibulae. Werner's group I G should therefore be dated much later than I F, but not later than, at least, some brooches of group I D. This results from the association of a brooch of Werner's group I D with a I G fibula in Luchistoe, burial chamber 10.[44]

---

[44] Dem'ianyv: Baran 1972:52 fig. 18/9. Bratei: Teodor 1992:138 no. 1. Davideni: Mitrea 1995:126 fig. 2/2. Kiskörös: Csallány 1961:230 and pl. 272/8. Caričin Grad: Mano-Zisi 1954–5:178 fig. 38. Luchistoe: Aibabin 1990:22 and 199 fig. 20/2. For fibulae of Werner's group I G and *Zangenfibeln*, see Popović 1984a:174. For *Zangenfibeln*, see also Kühn 1965:pl. 82/19.1–27 and 1974:840. Such fibulae were still in use during the Early Avar period, as evidenced by the specimen found in a female grave at Várpalota (Werner 1962:65). For other possible parallels, see Petre 1966:265; Ibler 1992:144.

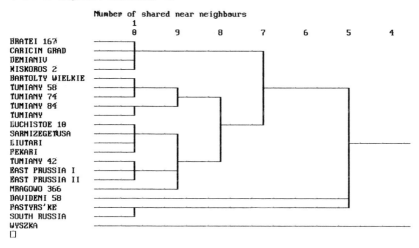

Near Neighbour Clustering of sarmizegetusa-kiskoros

Similarity Coefficient: Jaccard
Number of Neighbours considered: 10

Number of shared near neighbours

Figure 51 Cluster analysis of twenty-one brooches of Werner's group I G, in relation to their ornamental patterns

The same is true for Werner's group I H (Figure 41/7, 8; Figure 53). This group is characterized by extreme simplification and, with few exceptions, by the absence of any textural ornamentation. Group I H is not very common in Mazurian cemeteries. A sixth-century date for this group is suggested by the association of a fibula found at Iatrus (Krivina) with a sixth-century bronze coin. At Pruneni, a I H fibula was found together with a brooch of Werner's group I D. Finally, the Selişte brooch was associated with a repoussé bronze pendant, a dress accessory which appears in late sixth- and early seventh-century Ukrainian hoards of silver and bronze and in Early Avar assemblages in Hungary.[45]

A date in the late sixth or early seventh century may be assigned to Werner's group I J (Figure 54). This is supported by the association of the Óföldeák brooch with glass beads with eye-shaped inlays in an Early Avar burial assemblage. Fibulae of Werner's group I J may have been produced with copper-alloy models, such as that found in a jeweller's grave at Felnac, together with a complete set of models for belt plates. Some of these models may be linked to identical belt plates found in Early Avar

---

[45] Iatrus: Herrmann 1979a:114–15 and 114 fig. 46/a. Pruneni: Fiedler 1992:100 no. 24. Selişte: Rafalovich and Lapushnian 1973:131 fig. 9/6.

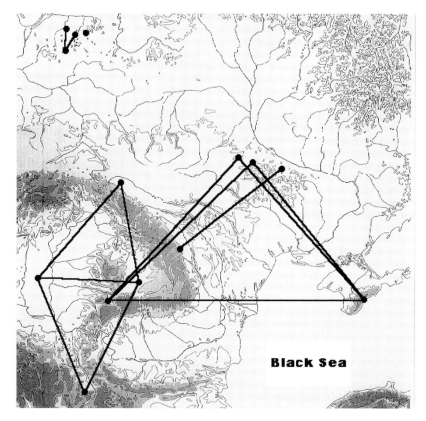

Figure 52 Plotting of the nearest-neighbor similarity of twenty-one brooches
of Werner's group I G

mortuary assemblages together with solidi of Heraclius. The Felnac
assemblage may therefore be dated to the 630s.[46]

A typical feature for Werner's group II C (Figure 41/9; Figure 55) is
the circle-and-spot decoration, which Werner himself viewed as a "cheap
imitation" of the scrollwork ornament. Brooches of this group may be
dated to the second half of the sixth century on the basis of the association of a specimen found at Carevec with a cast fibula with bent stem
dated to Justin II's reign. The same is true for the fibula found in a house

---

[46] Óföldeák: Csallány 1961:138 and pl. 191/16 and 259/1. Felnac: Dömötör 1901:63 pl. I/5, 7;
Hampel 1900:pl. II/5. For dated belt-plates from Hajdudorog and Sânpetru German, see Garam
1992:155 and 160.

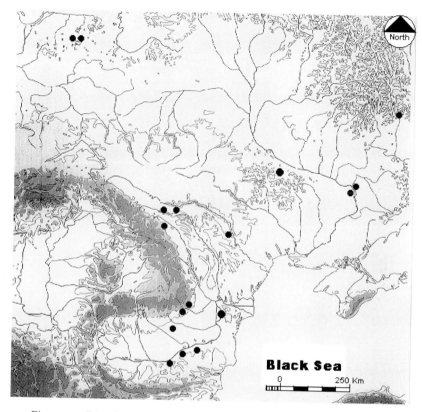

Figure 53 Distribution of "Slavic" bow fibulae of Werner's group I H
For legend, see Figure 50

at Caričin Grad, which, besides a cast fibula with bent stem, also produced an earring with basket-shaped pendant of the Allach class, dated
to *c.* 600. At Szigetszentmiklós-Háros, a II C fibula was found together
with two gold earrings with globe pendants. Such earrings were found
at Szentendre in association with a tremissis struck for Justin II. The fibula
from grave 86 at Suuk Su, in Crimea, was found in association with a
bronze coin issued for Emperor Maurice and dated to 597–602. To the
same date point the hat-shaped and repoussé bronze pendants found at
Luchistoe (burial chambers 38 and 54) and Mokhnach. Such artifacts are
common with late sixth- and early seventh-century hoards of silver and
bronze, such as Sudzha and Nova Odessa (Chapter 5). Crimean brooches
coincide in time, for many were found in association with the same

Figure 54 Distribution of "Slavic" bow fibulae of Werner's group I J
For legend, see Figure 50

artifact-categories (silver sheet brooches, repoussé bronze pendants, buckles with eagle-headed plates).[47]

When examining the plotting of the cluster analysis of thirty-five brooches of Werner's group II C (Figures 56–7), it becomes readily obvious that, with few exceptions, all specimens are linked to Crimean brooches. All fibulae found in hoards in Left Bank Ukraine or in Early Avar burials in Hungary have analogies in one of the four Crimean cemeteries (Eski Kermen, Luchistoe, Suuk Su, and Artek) which produced such brooches. Moreover, there is a striking resemblance between the

---

[47] Carevec: Kharalambieva 1993:25 and 26 fig. 1/1. Caričin Grad: Mano-Zisi 1958:312–13 and 327 fig. 39. Szigetszentmiklós-Háros: Sós 1961:51 and 40 fig. 11/1. Suuk Su: Repnikov 1906:23 and pl. VIII/4. Luchistoe: Aibabin 1990: 22 and 196 fig. 17/5, 6. Mokhnach: Aksenov and Babenko 1998:113–14 and 114 fig. 3/1–2. For circle-and-spot decoration as imitation of scrollwork, see Werner 1950:163. Allach earrings: Bierbrauer 1987:147; Riemer 1992:126.

Figure 55 Distribution of "Slavic" bow fibulae of Werner's group II C
For legend, see Figure 50

fibula from the Martynovka hoard and the specimens found at Cherkassy and Luchistoe 36, including the characteristic rectangular lattice pattern on the foot-plate. The only difference is that instead of circle-and-spot, the Martynovka fibula is covered with scrollwork ornamentation. That this correspondence also points to a coincidence in time is demonstrated by the association of the Martynovka fibula with a silver cup bearing four stamps dated to Justin II's reign. Crimean burials with bow fibulae include "citations" from contemporary hoards of silver and bronze, such as female dress accessories. By contrast, there are no fibulae of this group in Mazuria.[48]

---

[48] Cherkassy: Werner 1950:160 and pl. 37/12. Luchistoe: Aibabin 1990:pp. 22 and 196 fig. 17/3. The northernmost specimen of this series was recently found in a hillfort near Mogilev (Belarus). See Sedin 1995:163 and 162 fig. 3.

Near Neighbour Clustering of WERNER II C (DANCENI-SUUK SU)

Similarity Coefficient: Jaccard
Number of Neighbours considered: 20

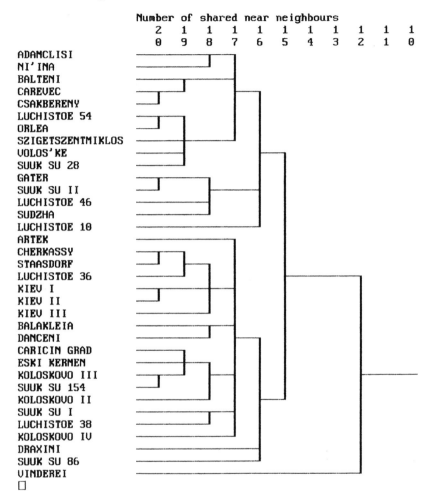

Figure 56 Cluster analysis of thirty-five brooches of Werner's group II C, in relation to their ornamental patterns

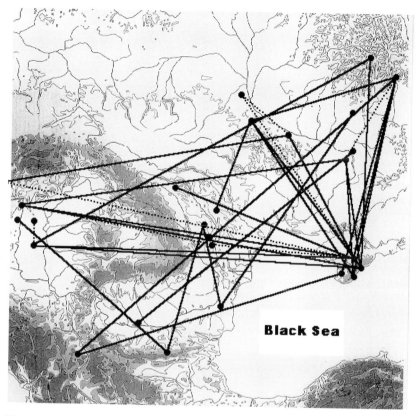

Figure 57 Plotting of the nearest–neighbor similarity of thirty-five brooches of
Werner's group II C

What immediately follows from this analysis is that all bow fibulae considered here were "in fashion" around year 600, though they certainly
enjoyed different popularity rates (Table 8). This is even true in spite of
their different distribution patterns. Though no fibulae of Werner's
groups I C and I J were worn in Crimea, and, accordingly, no Mazurian
site yielded any II C brooches, all groups occurred at different moments
in time in the Lower Danube region. As plottings of various cluster
analyses show, fibulae found in this region have multiple links to brooches
from distant areas, such as Mazuria or Crimea. The dissemination of the
ornamental patterns described by these plottings may indicate the extent
of social connections between manufacturers, clients, or wearers. Linked
pieces of ornamental metalwork are likely to emphasize the extent of the
movement of people and, therefore, of contact.

Table 8 *Chronology of "Slavic" bow fibulae*

Werner's class	500	525	550	575	600	625	650	675	700	725
I C	———————— · · · · · · · · ————————————————— · · ·
I D	———————————— · · · · · · · ————————————— · · · ·
I H	· · · · · · · · · · · · · · · ——————————————— · · · · ·
I F	· ·
II C	· · · · · · · · · · · · · · ————————————— · · ·
I J	· · · · · · ———————————— · · · ·
I G	· · · · · · · · ———————— · · · ·
I B	· ————————

Notes:
dots: date range possible but uncertain
bold line: firm date range

During the first half of the sixth century, brooches of group I F, such as found in the southern area of present-day Romania (Pietroasele, Bucharest-Băneasa), were imitated by brooches found in Mazuria and in the Middle Dnieper area. At about the same time, brooches of group I D, the earliest specimens of which are those of Mazuria, may have served as models for those found in Romania and the Middle Dnieper region. In Mazuria, at least, these two groups coexisted, as shown by the assemblage of grave 424 at Mietkie. During the 500s, smaller and more simple replicas of the I D series were produced in Romania and the neighboring regions (Hansca, Budureasca, Pruneni, Bucharest-Tei).

Brooches of group I C, which probably originated in Mazuria, made their way into Romanian assemblages dated to the second half of the sixth century. At that time, I D brooches were still in fashion, as indicated by the association of the two groups in the assemblage of grave 211 at Bratei. It is possible that in the meantime, I B brooches, which most likely originated in the Balkans, had already reached Mazuria.[49]

Probably during the reigns of Justin II and Maurice, the first brooches of group II C appeared in Crimean mortuary assemblages, as circle-and-spot replicas of contemporary brooches with scrollwork decoration, such as that found at Martynovka. Brooches of Werner's group II C rapidly spread to the Balkans, to Hungary and to Left Bank Ukraine, but not to Mazuria. By the end of the sixth century, I G brooches appeared in Crimea and some other places, which were similar with, but not identi-

---

[49] Mietkie: Kühn 1956:90 and 95, pl. xxii/ii.7 and xxiv/8. Bratei: Teodor 1992:137; and Eugenia Zaharia (personal communication, 1992). For linked pieces of ornamental metalwork as indicating movement of people, see Arnold 1997:140–1.

cal to, a specifically Mazurian series. Shortly before or after *c.* 600, a distinct series of the group I B was produced, which substituted the scroll-work decoration with a purely geometric pattern. This is also the period in which the exceptional *Prunkfibel* from Coşoveni was manufactured. After 600, I D brooches similar to those in fashion in Mazuria during the sixth century appeared in Greece (Edessa) and Crimea (Luchistoe). This coincided in time with the introduction of I C brooches with two pairs of bird-heads, such as those from Gâmbaş and Kruja, and of I H brooches with three or five knobs.

It appears that early sixth-century distributions were more localized than late sixth- or early seventh-century ones, when we see a greater degree of interconnectedness. The apparent patterning among groups of brooches and types of ornament raises some important questions. Theoretically, the dissemination of a brooch-form or of ornamental details may take place at any time through the movement from one area to the other of either brooches (as gifts or trade), with or without their owners, of models for brooches, or, finally, of craftsmen carrying manufactured brooches or models.[50] Werner believed that "Slavic" bow fibulae reached Mazuria in exchange for amber. In reality, many Mazurian specimens antedate their analogies found outside Mazuria. In addition, there are no finds of Baltic amber on any sixth- and seventh-century site in eastern and southern Romania. By contrast, the majority of amber beads in the Danube region are those from contemporary assemblages in "Gepidia."

Another interpretation favors the idea of moving craftsmen. Prevailing views about the organization of production in the early Middle Ages are still based on the idea of itinerant specialists. Finds of models, such as those from Bucharest-Tei and Felnac, were believed to be sufficient proof for itinerant craftsmen carrying durable bronze or leaden models, which presumably allowed the creation of the brooch design in two-piece clay molds. There are indeed some examples of bow fibulae which accord with the idea of models being used, but there are more examples which do so only partially, if at all. There is little evidence for the physical copying of an existing brooch, though some parts of brooches may have been reproduced very closely, probably by some mechanical means, such as templates. Furthermore, the metallographic analysis of one brooch from the Ukrainian site Pastyrs'ke yielded different alloy compositions for the head- and foot-plate, respectively. That each brooch may have been made from its individual model makes the idea of an itinerant craftsman carrying bronze or leaden models for each brooch pair a nonsense.

[50] Leigh 1991: 117; Hines 1997:213; Arnold 1997:145.

In addition, there is clear evidence of local production. A soapstone mold for bow fibulae was found, along with other smelting implements, in a sunken building at Bernashivka, near Mohyliv Podils'kyi (Ukraine). Although, to my knowledge, there is no matching brooch for the mold from Bernashivka except the pair of brooches found in burial chamber 10 at Luchistoe, the mold itself suggests that production was based on a different technology than that implied by the existence of bronze or lead-alloy models. Models presuppose two model- and mold-making pieces. A stone mold excludes the use of models, because the technique employed in this case is the lost-wax process. Regional variation is certainly possible and we should probably envisage multiple technologies being used at the same time for the production of the same class of artifacts.[51]

The absence of exact replication with many groups of bow fibulae is a strong indication that each brooch or pair of brooches was produced as required, probably for only one occasion at a time. This shifts the emphasis from manufacturer to user or wearer. In Mazurian graves, bow fibulae were never associated with spurs. Eduard Šturms first interpreted this dichotomy as indication of gender division: bow fibulae were usually found in female graves, while spurs may have been male attributes. Within the Merovingian world, bow fibulae found with women, usually late adolescents or adults (twenty to forty years old), suggest a "threshold of acquisition" exactly comparable with access to shields and/or swords (*spatha* or *sax*) among weapon-bearing men. This arguably took place at marriage. Furthermore, the absence of brooches or other dress-fasteners from other female graves might lead to the conclusion that access to brooches was also dependent upon social status.[52]

The existing archaeological evidence shows that brooches worn with the female dress were easily visible, probably the most visible accessories, a particular sort of badge. They may have played an important communicative role particularly in public, "beyond-the-households" contexts of social action.[53] This is substantiated by a comparison of distributions for

---

[51] Lost-wax procedure: Franke 1987. Itinerant specialists: Werner 1970; Capelle and Vierck 1971; Teodorescu 1972. Metallographic analysis: Prikhodniuk 1994:63. Local production of fibulae: Dąbrowski 1980; Vinokur 1994. For the pair of brooches from Luchistoe that match the Bernashivka mold, see Aibabin 1984:239 and fig. 1.

[52] Sasse 1990:48 and 56. Brooches and female burials: Šturms 1950:21; Jaskanis and Kachinski 1981:31; Strauß 1992:70; Dickinson 1993:39. Studies based on microwear analysis suggest that there is a direct correlation between the degree of use and the age of the wearer, which may indicate that the same brooches acquired at betrothal or marriage were then worn during the rest of the lifetime. See Martin 1987:278 and 280; Nieke 1993:129; *contra:* Clauss 1987:530 and 564. The early ninth-century *Lex Thuringorum* clearly states that brooches (*nuscae*) were inherited by daughters from their mothers (ed. Claudius von Schwerin (Hannover: Hahnsche Buchhandlung, 1918), c. 28, tit. 6.6).   [53] The phrase "beyond-the-households" context is that of Conkey 1991.

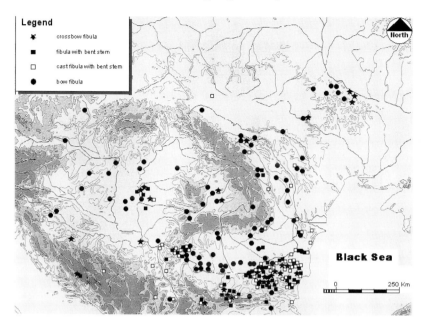

Figure 58 Distribution of principal classes of fibulae in the Lower Danube
region

various classes of sixth- and seventh-century brooches on both sides of
the Danube frontier. Uwe Fiedler noted a sharp contrast between the distribution of Aquileia brooches and that of "Slavic" bow fibulae.[54] The
contrast is even more evident when we take into consideration other
classes, such as simple and cast fibulae with bent stem (Figure 58). Despite
continuous interaction, there is a tendency for bow fibulae to cluster
north of the Danube river. By contrast, finds of fibulae with bent stem
and cast fibulae concentrate in early Byzantine forts south of the river.
This suggests that bow fibulae communicated a locative imagery, which
went beyond the simple delimiting of a space of origin. Like bow fibulae
in the Carpathian basin (Chapter 5), they may have been used for building ethnic boundaries. On the other hand, the manner in which decorative patterns displayed by bow fibulae were interchanged and new ones
occasionally added indicated a sort of heraldry, perhaps denoting individual descent groups. If this is true, linked patterns of brooch ornamentation may point to long-distance relations between such groups, perhaps
exogamy.

[54] Fiedler 1992:91–105.

273

Bow fibulae may thus indicate movement of people. This movement, however, was not a migration in the true sense of the word. Networks of linked fibulae may testify to a different form of mobility, that of gifts or of women married to distant groups in forging alliances. There are two reasons for favoring this approach. First, the movement of ornamental patterns is not that of a unidirectional movement of people, but a two-way transfer: some brooch-forms traveled north, others moved south, often at about the same time. Second, there is no fibula which may be ascribed to any one region alone, despite the precedence taken at times by Mazuria or Crimea in the dissemination of new forms. As soon as a new group emerged, linked specimens spread rapidly over wide distances, a phenomenon which could hardly be explained by means of itinerant specialists or transmission of models. Moreover, there is no chain of communication between the main areas of dissemination and, at times, no links exist between fibulae found in adjacent territories.

Everything points to the conclusion that "Slavic" bow fibulae were not simply symbols of social status or gender, but badges of power. This was the power of those able to establish long-distance relations and thus to yield influence. Like amber beads or Scandinavian brooches in "Gepidia," "Slavic" bow fibulae may have started by being exotic enough to produce prestige. They did not become "Slavic," therefore, until some time after contact with a distant dissemination center, especially Mazuria, was established. Soon thereafter, a transferred "model" was copied in less sophisticated forms apparently in response to an exclusively local demand. It is no accident that all groups coexisted shortly before and after *c.* 600. This is the period in which symbols of personal identity seem to have been in higher demand. Brooch-forms borrowed from other cultural settings were now culturally authenticated and an "emblemic style" emerged, which existed only in the repetitions and contrasts created by the replication of ornamental patterns or forms.

The social meaning attached to these dress accessories may have also been fixed in time, as the rise of Slavic "kings," many of whom were able to mobilize large numbers of warriors in successful raids across the Danube, necessitated markers of sharper social differentiation. What distinguishes the area south and east of the Carpathian mountains on a distribution map is the fact that a large number of bow fibulae were found in settlements, not in mortuary assemblages (Figure 59). Despite systematic excavations and, in some cases, a considerable number of settlement features unearthed, no settlement produced more than one brooch. In most cases, the building in which this brooch was found was also the one with the richest furnishings, which may indicate that access to brooches as symbols of identity was restricted to elites. More important, the intra-

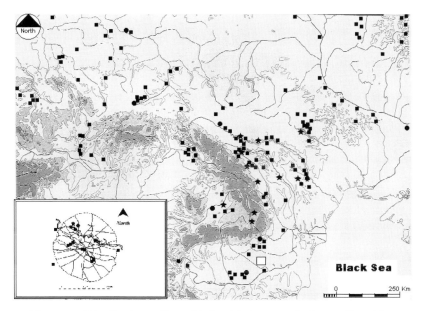

Figure 59 Distribution of bow fibulae (circle: stray find; star: found in a
sunken building) in relation to sixth- and seventh-century settlements
(rectangle)
Insert: the territory of modern Bucharest

site distribution of artifacts, as I will show in the next section, points to
the use of material culture, including brooches, for the construction of a
new social hierarchy.

Not all "Slavic" bow fibulae should be dated to the seventh century, as
Werner once believed. Some, like group I F, were in fashion in the early
500s. For many groups, the earliest specimens are those from Mazuria,
which suggests that they were neither Slavic inventions, nor products of
early Byzantine workshops.[55] The dissemination of bow fibulae to the
Lower Danube region, as well as to other areas, is likely to indicate long-
distance contacts between communities and to signalize the rise of individuals having the ability both to entertain such contacts and to employ
craftspersons experienced enough to replicate ornamental patterns and
brooch-forms. Instead of treating "Slavic" bow fibulae as "index-fossils"
for the migration of the Slavs, we should therefore regard them as indicators of contacts established by such individuals and as symbols of social
identity.

[55] Slavic inventions: Werner 1950. Byzantine artifacts: Petre 1966; Pallas 1981.

275

GRUBENHÄUSER, POTS, AND CLAY PANS: MATERIAL CULTURE
IN ACTION

Some 100 sixth- and seventh-century settlements have been excavated so far in Romania, Ukraine, Moldova, Poland, and Slovakia. Only a few were systematically explored. There are even fewer cases in which research was designed on a micro-regional scale from the beginning. It is not easy to generalize from this patchy evidence, but a settlement pattern is already visible. In Slovakia, as well as in Walachia (southern Romania), settlements are located on the lowest river terraces, below the 200– or 300-meter contour, at the interface between everglades and higher ground. In Walachia, this specific settlement pattern did not go unnoticed by contemporary sources. The largest number of settlements are sited on rich soils, stagnogleys or chernozems. Those which have been systematically excavated proved to be no larger than 0.5 to 2 hectares, with a small number of features per habitation phase, ranging from ten to fifteen.[56]

Though still limited, micro-regional research offers some glimpse into the phenomenon of settlement mobility. Suzana Dolinescu-Ferche's work at Dulceanca, near the modern city of Alexandria (Romania), admirably demonstrates how sixth- and seventh-century settlements were relocated. The first identifiable occupation at Dulceanca was a fifteen-feature settlement, which was abandoned at some point during the 500s. A new settlement grew at 1 km distance from the old one, on the bank of the Burdea creek (Dulceanca II). During the second half of the sixth century, this settlement moved to the south (Dulceanca III). It was smaller (nine features), of briefer duration, and more dispersed. Another seventh-century settlement was installed here some time after the previous one was abandoned. It is apparent from all this that Dulceanca was not a village but a series of shifting hamlets. It is very likely that these transfers were brought about by the condition of arable land losing its fertility after repeated cultivation without manuring, and regaining it only after several years.[57]

[56] *Strategikon* XI 4.38: "The settlements (τὰ χωρία) of the Slavs and Antes lie in a row along the rivers, very close to one another. In fact, there is practically no space between them, and they are bordered by forests, swamps, beds of reeds." Suzana Dolinescu-Ferche's work in the Vedea valley of southern Romania is a unique and excellent example of micro-regional research. See Dolinescu-Ferche 1967, 1973, 1974, 1984, 1986, 1992, and 1995. For settlement location, see Šalkovský 1988:387; Dolinescu-Ferche 1984:122–3. For the number of residential units per habitation phase, see Pleinerová 1980:51; Timoshchuk 1985:12. Settlements in Walachia tend to have larger numbers (twenty to thirty) of sunken buildings per occupation phase (Dolinescu-Ferche 1984:124).

[57] Pleinerová 1980:53–4; Beranová 1976:437 and 1984:12. For a description of "itinerant agriculture," see Stahl 1980:61. Dulceanca I: Dolinescu-Ferche 1974. Dulceanca II: Dolinescu-Ferche

Elites and group identity

Two types of buildings were found on settlements of this period. Ground-level buildings were only found at Dulceanca I, but this may only be the result of exceptionally careful methods of excavation of that site. The largest proportion of settlement features were, however, sunken buildings of the kind known in Germany as *Grubenhäuser* and in Russia as *poluzemlianki* (Figures 60, 61, and 62). The Russian word refers to a structure partially dug into the ground, often less than 1 m deep. The structure had a gable roof, as suggested by postholes found on either two or all sides of the pit. Table 9 shows that this was, by no means, a general rule. Relatively large settlements, such as Dulceanca II or Filiaş, produced no buildings with posts, while others had considerably fewer buildings without posts. Despite comparatively smaller number of cases with posts in Walachia (Bucharest-Băneasa, Bucharest-Militari, Bucharest-Străuleşti, and Dulceanca), there seems to be no regional pattern. Moreover, a few seventh-century, or even later, sites produced evidence of tent-like, circular buildings, with one central and a multitude of surrounding posts, which were interpreted as yurts.[58]

The actual *Grubenhaus* was erected over a rectangular pit, ranging in size from four to over twenty-five square meters of floor area. Table 10 shows the degree of variation within each listed settlement. A pattern is easily discernable. On sixth- and seventh-century sites east and south of the Carpathians, the majority of sunken buildings were under fifteen square meters of floor area. The same is true for contemporary settlements in "Gepidia," such as Bratei or Moreşti. By contrast, all wattle-

---

1986. Dulceanca III and IV: Dolinescu-Ferche 1992. Despite claims to the contrary, there is no evidence, neither at Dulceanca, nor on any other site in Walachia, of slash-and-burn agriculture, which is archaeologically visible through evidence of woodland, growing cereals, and high proportions of hunted animals. Judging from the existing evidence, the dominant pattern seems to have been some flexible form of natural fallow sequence in which arable lands were periodically left to lie fallow for a varying number of years, sometimes for a period sufficient for old fields to turn back to waste land. No parts of plows were found on any sixth-century site, and the number of agricultural tools is very limited. The plowshares cited by Igor Corman (1998:30–1) and Magdalena Beranová (1976:433–4) are not of the sixth and seventh centuries. That cultivation of cereals was the basic economic activity is, however, confirmed not only by contemporary sources (cf. *Strategikon* XI 4.5), but also by the relatively large number of querns found on sixth- and seventh-century sites, all of which belong to Minasian's class I. See Minasian 1978:104 and 110. Very few, if any, such implements appear on contemporary sites in the Middle and Upper Dnieper area, where querns were found only on seventh- and eighth-century sites. See Sedov 1982:40.

[58] The largest number of buildings with posts, often in six-, seven-, eight-, and nine-post array, were found at Moreşti, Kodyn, and Botoşana. The first two sites also produced evidence of an earlier occupation phase, dated to the late fifth or early sixth century, which suggests that such buildings are older than those without posts. On the other hand, the absence of postholes does not necessarily indicate buildings without posts, for the ethnographic evidence demonstrates that buildings often had posts, which left no trace in the archaeological record. See Rappoport 1975:114; Timoshchuk 1978:188. Yurts: Văzharova 1971:18; Bóna 1973:68; Čremošnik 1980:137 and 140. Dulceanca I: Dolinescu-Ferche 1974:63–80. Regional patterns: Rappoport 1972:229; Pleinerová 1979:631.

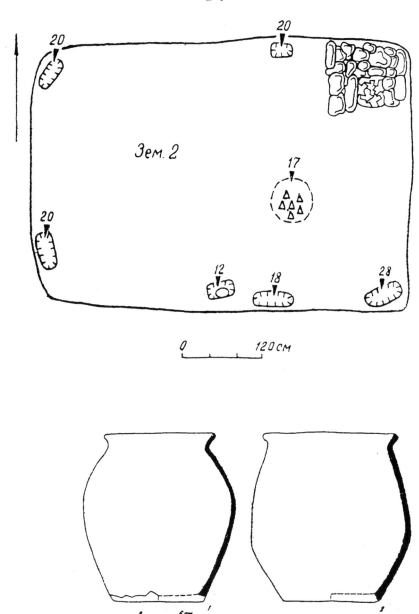

Figure 60 Selişte, six-post array in sunken building 2 with stone oven; plan and associated artifacts

Source: Rafalovich 1972b: 132 figs. 7–8 (re-combined).

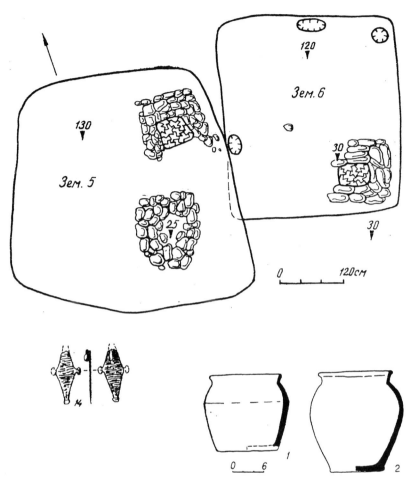

Figure 61 Selişte, sunken buildings 5 and 6 with stone ovens; plans and
artifacts found in sunken building 5

Source: Rafalovich 1972b: 136 fig. 11.

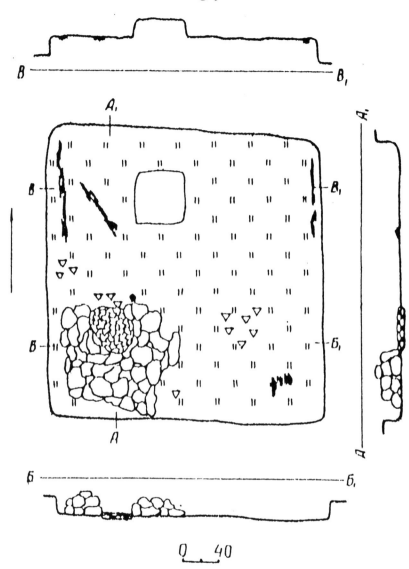

Figure 62 Recea, sunken building with stone oven; plan and profiles
Source: Rafalovich 1972c: 64 fig. 10.

Table 9 *Sunken buildings in sixth- and seventh-century settlements*

Settlement	Buildings with posts										Total	Buildings without posts
	1	2	3	4	5	6	7	8	9	>=10		
Bacău	1	1	2			1					5	3
Biharea	1						1				2	0
Botoşana		3	1	1	2	4	2	6	2	1	22	1
Bratei	7	8	2	2	1						20	50
Bucharest-Băneasa											0	9
Bucharest-Ciurel	1		2								3	6
Bucharest-Ghivan			2		1						3	11
Bucharest-Măicăneşti											0	8
Bucharest-Militari											0	8
Bucharest-Străuleşti											0	7
Căţelu Nou	2	1									3	5
Cernat											0	4
Cucorăni							2				2	4
Dănceni				1							1	0
Davideni	1			1	1						3	27
Dipşa		1									1	8
Dodeşti		1	1								2	4
Dulceanca I	2										2	18
Dulceanca II											0	13
Dulceanca III											0	8
Dulceanca IV											0	13
Filiaş											0	33
Gorecha						1	1	1			3	0
Gutinaş		1									1	6
Hansca	1										1	11
Iaşi-Nicolina											0	3
Izvoare-Bahna											0	7
Kavetchina	1			1	1						3	20
Kiev		1									1	2
Kodyn	9	5	3	3	4	5	4	6	2	1	42	9
Lazuri											0	2
Malu Roşu											0	2
Mălăeşti				1							1	0
Moreşti		7	2		6	5	1		1	1	23	13
Obukhyv		1									1	2
Oreavu											0	1
Poian	1										1	15
Recea	1										1	1
Şapte-Bani (Hucea)							1			1	6	
Selişte			2				1				3	3
Semenki											0	8
Skibincy			1					1			2	0

Table 10 *Size of sunken buildings from sixth- and seventh-century settlements by floor area*

Settlement	4–10	10–15	15–20	20–5	over 25	Total number of buildings
Cernat	4					6
Cucorăni	1	2	2			7
Gutinaş	1	5	1			7
Selişte	2	3	1			14
Izvoare-Bahna	3	3	1			7
Bucharest-Ciurel	3	3	1	1		10
Bacău	3	2	1	1		8
Filiaş	5	15	11			40
Botoşana	4	17	3			31
Poian	5	7	3	1		32
Davideni	8	9	2			46
Moreşti	11	16	4	2	1	37
Kavetchina	15	4	2	1		37
Kodyn	16	12	2	1	1	32
Bratei	34	18	5			74
Budeni		3				3
Dodeşti		5				6
Dipşa		6	2			17
Kiev		2	1			3
Semenki		3	1	2	2	14
Svetinja			1	2	3	7

Note: There is a difference between numbers of buildings within size categories and the total number of buildings because there is not enough information for all houses within each individual settlement to allow ordering within any one of the size categories given in the table.

walled houses found on the early Byzantine site at Svetinja, near Viminacium (see chapter 4) are over twenty square meters of floor area. To explain this pattern is not easy, but an experiment stemming from excavations of the early medieval settlement at Březno, near Prague, might offer some hints. The building experiment consisted of two houses, which were exact replicas of two sunken buildings excavated on the site, one of the late sixth or early seventh century, the other of the ninth. The sixth- to seventh-century feature was relatively large (4.20 x 4.60 m) and deep (80 cm under the original ground). The excavation of the rectangular pit represented some fifteen cubic meters of earth. The excavation, as well as other, more complex, operations, such as binding horizontal sticks on the truss or felling and transport of trees, required a minimum of two persons. The building of the house took 860 hours, which included the felling of trees for rafters and the overall preparation of the wood. Building the actual house required 2.5 cubic meters of wood (ash, oak, and beech). In itself, the superstructure swallowed two cubic meters of wood. Three to four cubic meters of clay were necessary for daubing the walls and reeds harvested from some 1,000 square meters, for the covering of the superstructure. Assuming sixty to seventy working hours per week and a lot more experience and skills for the early medieval builders, the house may have been built in three to four weeks.[59]

The experiment clearly demonstrated that a house like that could accommodate a family of no more than five (the experimental family included two adults and two children), provided that the available room was divided and certain activities were assigned fixed places. This suggests that, despite claims to the contrary, the basic social unit represented in sixth- and seventh-century settlements was the minimal family. The average settlement may have consisted therefore of some fifty to seventy individuals. This further suggests that the lowest level at which the archaeological evidence from settlements should be interpreted is most likely that of descent groups. Occasional finds of intrasite graves of infants, which were buried next to sunken buildings, points to the same direction.[60]

The most important characteristic of sixth- and seventh-century sunken buildings in Eastern Europe is the presence of a stone oven placed in one of the corners and built directly on the floor. At a micro-regional level, there seems to be some consistency in terms of the position of the oven within the house, though it is not clear whether this should be interpreted as a practical response to local conditions (such as wind direction) or as emblemic style. Volodymyr Baran claimed that the stone oven was a Slavic ethnic badge, for the earliest examples of *Grubenhäuser* equipped

---

[59] Pleinerová 1986:113–14 and 139. Various prohibitions (e.g., selection of the building site, propitious time for starting the building, etc.), as well as a number of ritual practices pertaining to the symbolism attached to the house, some of which are known from the ethnographic evidence, may have considerably delayed the building process. See Vareka 1994.

[60] Intrasite children burials: Dolinescu-Ferche 1992:133; Bóna 1973:72. Four other intrasite burials were found at Korchak IX and Teterevka (Rusanova 1973b:4). In the absence of datable artifacts, their chronology is uncertain. For residential units and minimal families, see Rappoport 1975:154; Prikhodniuk 1988:189; Timoshchuk 1990b:184; Parczewski 1993:113. See also Čilinská 1980:80–1; Litavrin 1987:36. Many scholars believe that the extended family group is archaeologically visible through long-houses (*Wohnstallhäuser*), a feature typical for early medieval sites in Central Europe. See Baran, Maksimov, and Magomedov 1990:122–3; Heather 1991b:58. According to B. A. Timoshchuk, however, the extended family group may also be associated with sunken buildings surrounding a central area, as on the Ukrainian sites Kodyn II and Semenki. See Timoshchuk 1990a:132. For estimated numbers of inhabitants, see Timoshchuk 1985:12; for slightly larger estimates, see Baran 1986:168.

with such ovens were found in association with fourth-century sites in that area of the Chernyakhov culture, in which Baran believed the early Slavic culture originated. Others emphasized the contrast between "Slavic" *Grubenhäuser* with stone ovens and sunken buildings found on early medieval sites in Central and Western Europe, which had no heating facility. That a strong relationship existed between sunken buildings and stone ovens is confirmed by the Březno building experiment mentioned above, which also included measurements of heating during winter time (January through early February). In temperatures below zero centigrade, a replica of a late sixth- and early seventh-century sunken building with stone oven offered protection of some six to seven degrees centigrade. Intensive heating during more than two weeks, which required 1.35 cubic meters of wood, increased the average temperature inside the house from seven to fourteen degrees centigrade. Between twelve and eighteen cubic meters of wood may have been necessary to maintain this temperature through the cold season. The experiment demonstrated that thermal isolation was considerably enhanced by sinking the floor below the ground level. This concern with maintaining a comfortable temperature for indoor activities may also be recognized in cases where ovens were built in clay, not in stone, as in all four settlements at Dulceanca. Such ovens were often associated with clay rolls found in great numbers on the hearth, which may have served for retaining heat within the oven area. There are also examples of sunken buildings equipped with two ovens, only one of which produced clay rolls (as in Dulceanca II). The other must have been used for cooking.[61]

If regional variation in oven building can easily be detected, it is much more difficult to explain it, for no one-to-one relationship seems to exist between the kind of oven preferred and resources available. Clay ovens often occur in regions which were otherwise rich in stone, sometimes in association with stone ovens, either within the same settlement or even within the same building. A distribution map of sixth- and seventh-century heating facilities (Figure 63) suggests that the contrast is not simply one between buildings with stone or clay ovens and buildings without ovens, as Peter Donat once suggested. Many sixth-century forts in the Balkans produced evidence of brick ovens, but not of stone or clay ones. The remarkable cluster of clay ovens in Walachia, close to the

[61] Dolinescu-Ferche 1995:173–6. Clay rolls: Tel'nov 1991:159; Dolinescu-Ferche 1995:163; Corman 1998:27. Clay ovens: Dolinescu-Ferche 1995:162; Gavritukhin 1993:110. Březno experiment: Pleinerová 1986:145, 148, and 152–3. In a constantly inhabited building, the temperature may have been even higher, for additional heating may have been given by taking in domestic animals, such as sheep or goat. In addition to heating, some eighteen cubic meters of firewood per year may have been necessary for cooking. Stone ovens and Slavs: Tel'nov 1991:161–2; Baran 1986:170; Vakulenko 1983:176; Donat 1980:57.

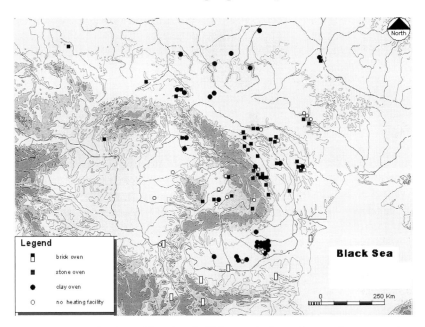

Figure 63 Distribution of heating facilities on sixth- and seventh-century sites

Danube frontier, may therefore represent not just a local adaptation of the standard sunken building with stone oven, but a stylistic variation.[62]

This may also be true when we examine another class of evidence, that of pottery. As shown in the first chapter, it was often believed that Slavic ethnicity was "represented" by the Prague type, reified as ethnic badge. The Romanian archaeologist Ion Nestor asserted that potsherds exhibiting rilling or, in the case of bases, concentric striations caused by removing the vessel while the wheel was still turning, were either "imports" or later developments of the early Slavic culture.[63] Soviet and Bulgarian archaeologists emphasized handmade pottery as a hallmark of Slavic ethnicity. Some even insisted that the Slavic pottery is characterized by the use of specific tempers, such as crushed sherds. Suzana Dolinescu-Ferche's excavations at Dulceanca I proved, however, that local potters fired both handmade and wheelmade pottery in the same kiln. There are few studies based on textural or petrological analysis and even fewer in which the focus is the basic technique used for constructing the pot. The potter may have divided the pot conceptually into

[62] Donat 1980; Šalkovský 1993:73.
[63] Nestor 1969:141–7. For a recent version of this theory, see Corman 1998:64–5.

285

various parts and used different sequences for building the vessel, such as "opening" the lump of clay by inserting fingers and squeezing the clay (pinching technique) or constructing the vessel from upside down, using one or more slabs of clay (slab modeling). From a cognitive point of view, these are fundamental aspects which link pottery-making to other aspects of culture and permeate very large areas of the activity of any group of people. In terms of a *chaîne opératoire* approach, it is interesting to note that all handmade pots from the Ukrainian site at Rashkov were made using the coiling technique. More studies are needed, however, for making comparisons which may be relevant for the question of ethnic identity.[64]

Another possibility is to treat pots as tools, for their shapes and, to a certain extent, their decoration are constrained by their intended contexts and conditions of use. Recent studies have shown a strong correlation between volume and shape of vessels found on many early medieval sites. The Březno experiment demonstrated that three-liter pots were the most suitable for cooking soups and porridges, while one-liter pots served as containers for milk and for manipulation. All cooking operations were performed using a set of eleven pots of different shapes and three vessels of wood. This is also confirmed by ethnographic studies, which reveal that full vessel assemblages in present-day communities typically consist of between eight and twenty morphological vessel types.[65]

The experiment suggests that early medieval pottery-making may have operated on the basis of "prototypic shapes," mental models of the potter's preference for morphological set attributes, which could be recognized in vessels belonging to the same family. Other studies show that despite variation in size, functionally equivalent vessels in various ceramic

---

[64] Baran 1988a:52. *Chaîne opératoire* approach: Richards 1982:35; Rice 1987:124–7; Guthnick 1988:91–3; Cowgill 1990:73; Van Der Leeuw 1994. For a classification of medieval pottery on the basis of fabric, see McCorry and Harper 1984. Slavs and crushed-sherd tempered pottery: Rafalovich 1972c:137; Rusanova 1973b:12. Dulceanca kiln: Dolinescu-Ferche 1969. Such kilns were capable of producing and maintaining temperatures over 800 degrees centigrade. See Pleiner 1988. In most other cases, handmade pots were fired using the clamp method, i.e., a bed of fuel, then pottery, and finally more fuel on top. Temperatures attained by such bonfires range between 600 and 800 degrees centigrade. For an archaeological example of open firing, see Rafalovich 1972c:138.

[65] In archaeological contexts, however, it is impossible to use potsherds for making statements about parent population assemblages, for the number of pots from which we have a sample is unknown and one cannot tell what proportion of the population is missing. See Orton 1993:178. Pots as tools: Braun 1980 and 1983; Shapiro 1984; Smith 1988. For the relation between form and content in ceramic classification, see also Zedeño 1985. For the correlation between volume and shape, see Bialeková and Tirpaková 1983. Vessel assemblages in present-day communities: Hally 1986:273 and 275. Březno experiment: Pleinerová 1986:162; Pleinerová and Neustupny 1987:90–101 and 119 pl. III. The use of wooden vessels is archaeologically confirmed. See Fusek, Staššiková-Štukovská, and Bátora 1993:34.

assemblages display identical proportions. There are many methods for shape representation for boundary retrieval and display using pattern matching to provide automatic retrieval. However, handmade pots from early medieval ceramic assemblages in Eastern Europe are typically asymmetrical, which suggests that approaches based on vessel ratios should be preferred to those based on vessel profiles. The advantage of using ratios is that they eliminate all differences which would arise in comparing vessels of similar shape but different size. In Eastern Europe, the most popular approach to shape analysis based on vessel ratios is that pioneered by the Russian archaeologist Vladimir Gening, who inspired Irina Rusanova's analysis of early Slavic pottery. The method is still used, with slight variations, by archaeologists working with sixth- and seventh-century ceramic assemblages in Romania, Moldova, Slovakia, and Poland. Genning's approach consists of a number of basic measurements made from scale drawings of vessels (Figure 64), which are then used to derive shape variables, viewed as ratios between these measurements. Classification is obtained by applying the Robinson coefficient of agreement to the matrix of shape variables. Classes of pottery are thus derived, which are then considered as chronologically sensitive and used for dating sites.[66]

The classification of sixth- and seventh-century pots found on East European sites raises two major problems. One is that of dating, which I already discussed in a previous section of this chapter. The other is that of the mental template, a combination of technological, functional, cognitive, and cultural factors, which in the eyes of many archaeologists was specific to the early Slavs, and only to them. The idea of a mental template was behind Borkovský's Prague type and Rusanova's Zhitomir-Korchak type. Rusanova and others made extensive use of statistical methods for shape analysis, in order to approximate as closely as possible that combination of mechanical and aesthetical executions, which, in their eyes, formed a definite structural pattern in the minds of the early

---

[66] Gening 1973:120–3 and 132, and 1992. For a mathematical description of the Brainerd–Robinson method of ordering assemblages, see Shennan 1990:191–2. For Rusanova's application of Genning's approach, see Rusanova 1976:10–1. For its further application in Eastern Europe, see Teodor 1996; Postică 1994:15–16; Fusek 1994 and 1995; Parczewski 1993:31–2. See also Tirpaková and Vlkolinská 1992. For a similar approach in American archaeology, see Froese 1985. J. D. Richards (1982) applied a similar method for the classification of Anglo-Saxon urns. For vessel proportions in ceramic analysis, see Stehli and Zimmermann 1980; Whallon 1982; Madsen 1988:17. For methods of shape representation using pattern matching, see Kampffmeyer et al. 1988. For an automatic artifact classification using image analysis techniques (the Generalized Hough Transform) to extract the initial information for classification, see P. Durham, P. H. Lewis, and S. J. Shennan, "Classification of Archaeological Artifacts Using Shape," on the web site of the University of Southampton (http://www.ecs.soton.ac.uk/research/rj/1994/im/lewis/phl.html, visit of May 18, 2000).

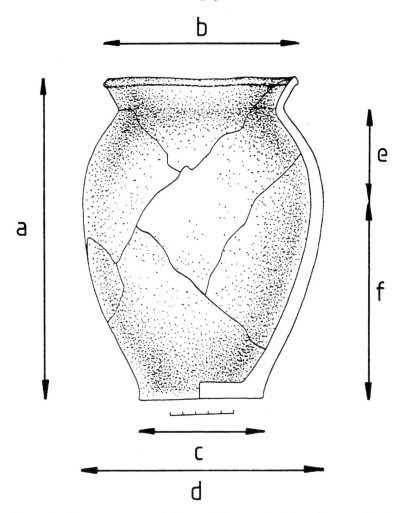

Figure 64 Measurements used for vessel shape analysis based on vessel ratios
a – maximum vessel height; b – rim diameter; c – base diameter; d – maximum vessel diameter;
e – height from neck to shoulder; f – height to maximum diameter
Drawing by author.

medieval potters. In order to test the idea of template expression, I selected 112 vessels from various sites in Romania, Ukraine, and Moldova, both handmade and wheelmade. Some of these pots were found in archaeological assemblages with no certain date (Korchak IX). Others were associated with burial assemblages in "Gepidia," which have nothing to do with the "Slavic culture" (Bistriţa). Another pot was found

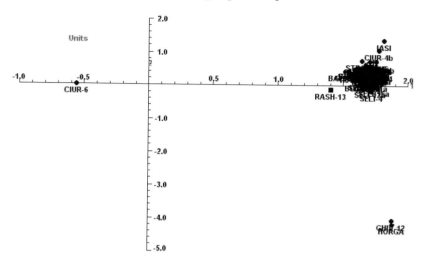

Figure 65 Correspondence analysis of 112 vessels in relation to eight ratios
proposed by Gening 1992
For site name abbreviations, see Appendix B

during excavations on the early Byzantine site at Capidava. All pots were
classified according to two sets of variables proposed by Vladimir Gening
and Michał Parczewski, respectively (Figures 65 and 66).[67]
Both plots show a strong resemblance between almost all pots considered, regardless of where they were found. Two zoomed details of these
plots indicate that very similar proportions were used for the manufacture of both handmade and wheelmade pots (Figures 67 and 68). Can this
pattern be interpreted as a template, in Borkovský and Rusanova's sense?
In my opinion, the answer must be negative for a variety of reasons. First,
Borkovský and Rusanova insisted that the Prague type is a specific class
of handmade pottery, but this series of plots clearly shows that both handmade and wheelmade pots were shaped similarly. Second, the Březno
experiment and the fact that very similar shapes appear in ceramic assemblages considerably different in date suggest that vessel shape is primarily
determined by vessel use and is not a function of "ethnic traditions."
Furthermore, the experiment demonstrated that contents of all pots had
to be mixed frequently as the cooking was mostly carried out at the
hearth by the oven, so that only half of the pot was usually exposed to
fire. This seems to point to a certain correlation between use of cooking

[67] For a detailed description of the ratios used in this analysis, see Gening 1992:50–1; Parczewski
1993:32. Korchak IX: Rusanova 1973b:pls. 8/7, 17, 18 and 9/1, 16, 20. Bistriţa: Gaiu 1992:117
fig. 2/23 and 119 fig. 4/1. Capidava: Scorpan 1968:fig. 22b.

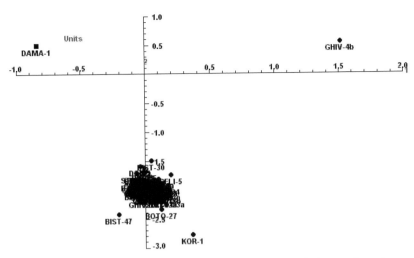

Figure 66 Correspondence analysis of 112 vessels in relation to six ratios
proposed by Parczewski 1993
For site name abbreviations, see Appendix B.

ovens and vessel shape and size. If so, the allegedly prototypic shape
should be interpreted in relation to food preparation, not to "emblemic
style." Third, archaeologists working on distinguishing artifact variability
that reflects differences in consistent practices or templates from "accidental" variability normally focus on single assemblages or, at the most,
on assemblages from the same site. As the example from Rashkov shows,
procedural modes pertaining to the manufacture of pots may have existed
at the individual site level. A limited number of distinct practices and
templates may have been in use in any given community. It is unknown
whether or not such isomorphism existed between sites, particularly
between those located at considerable distance from each other, such as
Rashkov and Dulceanca.[68]

We may be in a better position when examining not vessel shape, but
vessel decoration. Ethnographic evidence indicates that pottery decoration may be used for building ethnic boundaries. Stamped pottery was
used in both "Lombardia" and "Gepidia" and no specific clustering of
stamps or dies was found on either side of the "no man's land" between
the Danube and the Tisza rivers (Chapter 5). However, when compared

---

[68] See Baran 1986:52; Cowgill 1990:72. See also Corman 1998:62. Detailed analyses of ceramic
assemblages from sites dated by dendrochronology point to a long use-life of most pottery types.
See Donat 1986:85. Březno experiment: Pleinerová 1986:162. Most of the pots selected for my
analysis were found on the hearth, by the oven's door.

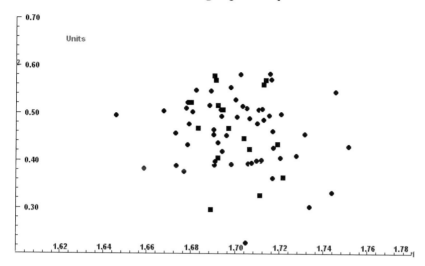

Figure 67 Zoomed detail of the correspondence analysis of handmade (circle) and wheelmade (rectangle) vessels in relation to eight ratios proposed by Gening 1992

to the distribution of pots with finger impressions or notches on the lip, which were found on contemporary sites, the distribution of stamped pots reveals an interesting contrast (Figure 69). There is a significant cluster of vessels with finger impressions or notches east of the Carpathians, while stamped decoration is especially abundant within the Carpathian basin. The earliest specimens of handmade pottery with finger impressions or notches on the lip (Figure 70) were found in association with artifacts of the second half of the sixth century.[69]

This decoration became popular, however, after *c.* 600. Potsherds with finger impressions and notches were found at Bucharest-Militari in association with a jingle bell very similar to those from contemporary hoards of silver and bronze in Ukraine (Chapter 5) and a sixth-century fibula with bent stem. At Dodeşti, potsherds with similar decoration were associated with a bronze buckle with three lobes, a dress accessory most frequently associated with early seventh-century *Reihengräberkreis* and Early Avar assemblages. At Hansca, fragments of such pottery were associated with a pair of equal-armed brooches (Figure 38/2, 3), which cannot be dated earlier than *c.* 650. This is also confirmed by finds from the Early

---

[69] Pottery decoration and ethnic boundaries: Işfănoni 1991. Only a few examples exist of finger impressions or notches on seventh- to ninth-century sites in Poland, Slovakia, east Germany, and Bohemia. See Madyda-Legutko and Tunia 1991:85; Corman 1998:66.

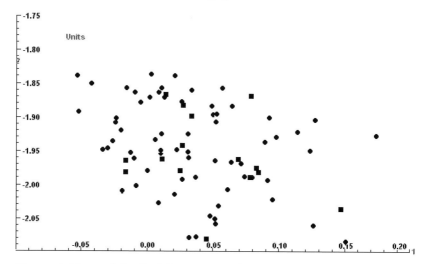

Figure 68 Zoomed detail of the correspondence analysis of handmade (circle) and wheelmade (rectangle) vessels in relation to six ratios proposed by Parczewski 1993

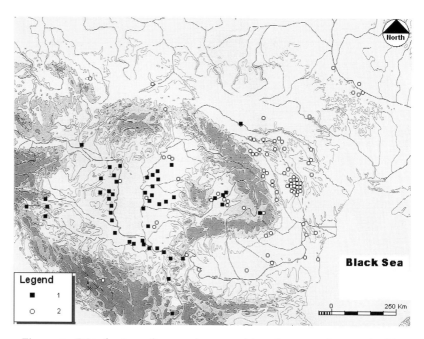

Figure 69 Distribution of stamped pottery (1) and pottery decorated with finger impressions or notches on lip (2)

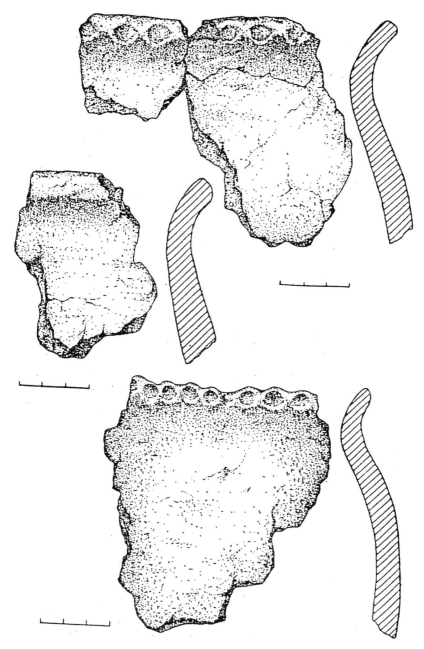

Figure 70 Examples of handmade pottery with finger impressions on lip
Source: Tel'nov 1985: 97 fig. 4.

Avar site at Dunaújváros and by mortuary assemblages in Crimea, where pots with finger impressions and notches on the lip were associated with Martynovka mounts. The distribution of finds strongly suggests that this type of decoration was used in the late 500s and early 600s to mark ethnic boundaries.[70]

An interesting case is that of signs incised on both pots and spindle whorls. More often than not, such signs consist of simple crosses, sometimes followed by a wavy line, or swastikas. There are also images of fish and even short inscriptions.[71] That such signs may have carried a Christian symbolism has already been suggested. In the light of the existing evidence, this is a plausible interpretation. Two pectoral crosses and a few molds for producing such artifacts were found north of the Danube river. Identical crosses with a distinct Christian symbolism were popular on contemporary sites in the central and western regions of the Balkans. Besides being used as pectorals, they were often attached to dress pins or earrings. Molds similar to those found north of the Danube come from early Byzantine forts. As for the pottery decoration, it is interesting to note that very similar, if not identical, signs were found on various sites located far from each other (e.g., crosses with "tails" at Bacău and Dulceanca). The handmade pottery on which such signs were incised is, however, of indisputably local production. This suggests the existence of a cross-regional set of symbols shared by potters and/or users of pottery, despite an arguably localized production. The relatively large number of cases indicates that this was a widespread phenomenon, which coincides in time with the use of finger impressions and notches.[72]

---

[70] Bucharest-Militari: Zirra and Cazimir 1963:63. Dodeşti: Teodor 1984b:46 fig. 18/1, 4, 6, 47 fig. 19/3, 31 fig. 8/1. Bronze buckles with three lobes: Swoboda 1986. Hansca: Tel'nov and Riaboi 1985:116 fig. 6 and 117 fig. 7. Equal-armed brooches: Godłowski 1980:83 and 99 fig. 15; for a much later dating, see Ambroz 1993:182. Dunaújváros: Fiedler 1994b:307–16. Crimea: Baranov and Maiko 1994:98.

[71] Simple crosses: Mitrea and Artimon 1971:246 fig. 16/7–8 and 247 fig. 17/1–2; Teodor 1991:133 fig. 15/1, 3–6; Teodor 1984a:126 fig. 47 and 121 fig. 42/3; Nestor and Zaharia 1973:195; Constantiniu 1965a:93; Dolinescu-Ferche and Constantiniu 1981:314 fig. 12/3; Constantiniu 1965b:178 fig. 85/2; Morintz and Rosetti 1959:pl. xxxi/5; Mitrea 1974–6:fig. 5/3 and Mitrea 1994:322 fig. 23/4; Teodor 1984b:47 fig. 19/7; Dolinescu-Ferche 1992:150 fig. 19/2 and 143 fig. 12/10; Mitrea, Eminovici, and Momanu 1986–7:243 fig. 10/1, 4 and 246 fig. 13/5; Coman 1971a:481 fig. 2/4, 5; Timoshchuk and Prikhodniuk 1969:77 fig. 4/3, 4; Mitrea 1980:444 fig. 11/2; Vakulenko and Prikhodniuk 1984:46 fig. 21/15; Baltag 1979:pl. xxxviii/3; Székely 1975:pl. xxxvi/1; Rafalovich and Lapushnian 1974:132 fig. 11/6; Teodor 1991:133 fig. 15/1, 4. Crosses followed by wavy lines: Dolinescu-Ferche 1974:fig. 52/2; Rosetti 1934:210 fig. 5/4; Teodor 1991:138 fig. 19/2. Swastikas: Zaharia 1994–5:349 fig. 13/7; Dolinescu-Ferche 1979:189 fig. 4/21; Dolinescu-Ferche and Constantiniu 1981:309 fig. 9/6; Teodor 1991:125 fig. 7/8, 9; Dolinescu-Ferche 1974:fig. 70/1; Berezovec 1963:fig. 19. Images of fish: Teodor 1984a:98 fig. 19/5 and 1991:130 fig. 12/5. Inscriptions: Teodorescu 1971:109; Teodor 1991:137 fig. 19/1, 8.

[72] At Bucharest-Ciurel, both kinds of decoration were associated in sunken building 2A. The same is true for Davideni 42 and Dodeşti 1. See Dolinescu-Ferche 1979:185 and 206–7; Mitrea

The study of ethnicity as a mode of action has recently caused a shift in emphasis from group boundaries to group experience, as ethnicity is now viewed as a phenomenon of the *Alltagsleben*. Foodways is an important aspect of this new line of research, for food preparation is a daily activity involving habitual dispositions, which, according to some authors, are key elements in understanding how ethnicity is created and recreated through material culture.[73] Very few things are known about diet in the 500s and 600s, but one aspect deserves particular attention. It has long been noted that a characteristic of sixth- and seventh-century ceramic assemblages in Romania, Ukraine, Moldova, and, to a lesser degree, Bulgaria, is the presence of clay pans (Figure 71). As the ethnographic evidence suggests, these handmade vessels served for baking flat loaves of wheat or millet bread. As a consequence, use of clay pans indicates cultivation of wheat or millet, which is also mentioned in contemporary sources. A long-held belief has been that clay pans are specific Slavic artifacts and that their presence signalizes that of the migrating Slavs.[74] Soviet archaeologists argued that early medieval pans derive from clay discs, often found in ceramic assemblages of the Zarubinec culture of the first centuries AD. They were also common on third- and fourth-century sites in the Desna basin and in Left Bank Ukraine. Such discs, however, served as lids for cooking pots or urns, not for baking, which makes the alleged typological link very problematic.[75]

1994:307, 309, and 311; Teodor 1984b:22–3. For incised signs as Christian symbols, see Coman 1971b; Barnea 1985a; Teodor 1991. Pectoral crosses: Baran 1988a:21 fig. 12/7; Mitrea 1974–6:fig. 14/1. For similar crosses in the Balkans, see Vinski 1968:pls. III, IV/19, and VII/30; Simoni 1989:pl. 4/4; Prendi 1979–80:pl. IX/V.22. Molds for pectoral crosses: Teodor 1984a:99 fig. 20/1; Constantiniu 1966:675 fig. 5/3; Preda 1967. For finds of molds in the Balkans, see Uenze 1992:164 fig. 9/6; Dănilă 1983:559.

[73] Bentley 1987. For *Alltagsleben*, see Greverus 1978; Räsänen 1994; Tebbetts 1984.
[74] *Strategikon* XI 4.5: the Sclavenes "possess an abundance of all sorts of . . . produce, which they store in heaps, especially common millet (κέγχρος) and Italian millet (ἔλυμος)." Clay pans and Slavs: Skružný 1964; Babić 1972:114–15; Herrmann 1986b:270; Zábojník 1988:419; Szőke 1995:54. Until very recently, clay pans were still produced by women in various regions of the Balkans, such as Bosnia, Macedonia, and Bulgaria. In all those regions, pans remained in use as long as the baking of the bread on an open hearth survived. See Filipović 1951:6 and 159; Bratiloveanu-Popilian 1968. Manual-rotation mills (quern stones) also bear out an overwhelming emphasis on growing bread cereals and on flour-based foods. On sixth- and seventh-century sites east and south of the Carpathians, they were typically associated with clay pans.
[75] Clay discs used as vessel lids first appear in Early Iron Age (Hallstatt B1–B3) assemblages in Slovakia and Volhynia. Both discs and pans are absent from ceramic assemblages of second- and third-century sites in Walachia and Moldova and from the pottery of the subsequent Chernyakhov culture. See Moscalu 1983:87 and 89; Rafalovich 1972c:132 and 151. Clay discs used as urn lids: Symonovich 1975:22 with n. 18; Rusanova 1973a:5; Lipking 1974:144, 149, and 145 fig. 4/46. Clay discs in Zarubinec assemblages: Tret'iakov 1974:66–7; Maksimov and Terpilovskii 1993:111. For clay discs in third- and fourth-century assemblages in the Desna region and Left Bank Ukraine, see Symonovich 1969:88 and 90 fig. 2; Goriunov 1974:124–5; Sukhobokov 1975:35; Terpilovskii 1984:28; Abashina 1986:79; Baran, Maksimov, and Magomedov 1990:147.

Figure 71   Examples of clay pans
Source: Rafalovich 1972c: 152 fig. 25.

By contrast, true pans first occur in sixth- and seventh-century assemblages (Figure 72). The earliest specimens were found on Romanian sites. A mid- or late sixth-century fibula with bent stem was associated with clay pans in the assemblage of the sunken building 20 at Poian. At Botoşana, a sunken building produced fragments of clay pans and a coin struck for Emperor Justinian. At Bacău, fragments of clay pans found in sunken building 6 were associated with a cast fibula with bent stem, dated to Justin II's reign. At Davideni, clay pans were associated with early seventh-century "Slavic" bow fibulae. A glass bead with eye-shaped inlays, typical for Early and Middle Avar assemblages, was found together with fragments of clay pans at Dulceanca II.[76]

To judge from the existing evidence, clay pans and the associated foods

[76] Poian: Székely 1992:263. Botoşana: Teodor 1984a:31 and 128 fig. 49/1, 3. Bacău: Mitrea and Artimon 1971:236. Dulceanca: Dolinescu-Ferche 1986:148 fig. 21/9, 11. Davideni: Mitrea 1994:305 and 321 fig. 22/7, 9; 1994–5:446. The association of clay pans with bow fibulae is also attested at Hansca and Semenki. See Rafalovich 1968:97 and 100; Khavliuk 1974:207. For clay pans as a sixth-century phenomenon, see also Rafalovich 1974:97–8; Sukhobokov and Iurenko 1978:133; Kravchenko 1979:86; Jelínková 1990:257 and 1993:79.

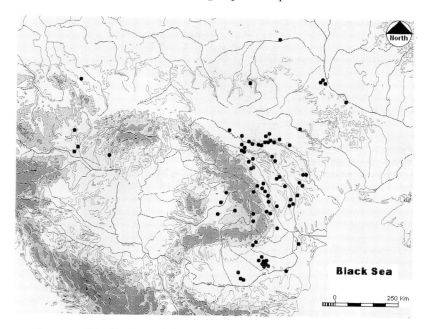

Figure 72 Distribution of clay pans on sixth- and seventh-century sites

(flat loaves of bread) were first introduced in the late 500s on sites east and south of the Carpathians, not far from the Danube river. Clay pans represent no more than 3 to 4 percent of the entire ceramic assemblage found on any given site. Moreover, the distribution of clay pans within the site is not uniform. Not all settlement features produced clay pans and their distribution is not random. An examination of the settlement pattern of a few sixth- and seventh-century sites suggests that this is no accident.

Ever since Gordon R. Willey introduced the concept, settlement pattern analysis has been viewed as the strategic point for interpreting archaeological cultures as reflecting various institutions of social interaction and control. Since the late 1930s, a similar concept has guided Soviet archaeologists. According to current views, the distribution of storage pits and work areas on a given site directly reflects social relations within that community. Storage pits grouped within or next to individual sunken buildings, such as found at Hansca, are believed to be an indication of private consumption, if not property. By contrast, storage pits found at Seliște, which were located far from any other settlement feature, have been interpreted as indicating communal property (Figure

297

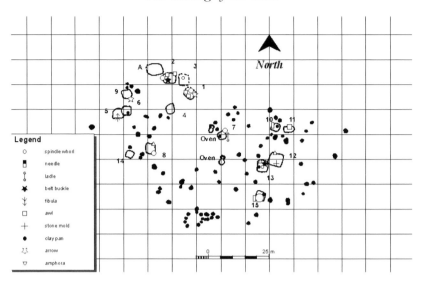

Figure 73 Selişte, intrasite distribution of artifacts
Irregular black spots indicate storage pits

73). Needless to say, in both cases, there is no clear chronological relation between storage pits (usually devoid of any refuse material) and the rest of the settlement. In addition, such an approach entirely ignores the intrasite distribution of artifacts.[77]

People's decisions on how to organize the use of space within their residences and settlements may indeed be influenced by the socioeconomic organization of the group. This influence, however, is mediated by the kind of activities performed on the site at a given date. "Activity," in this context, must be understood as a specific task resulting in the deposition of clustered diagnostic archaeological remains. The spatial correlate to activity is the activity area, defined as an archaeologically consistent, spatially clustered, association of artifacts and/or ecofacts in a minimally dated archaeological horizon.[78] At Selişte (Figure 73), two groups of sunken buildings were located on either side of a large, central place with only one building surrounded by two ovens. Five sunken buildings in the eastern part of the site (nos. 10, 11, 12, 13, and 15) produced all needles, most of the amphora sherds, and all clay pans found on site. By contrast, all arrow heads, awls, and dress accessories (beads and bow fibula) were

---

[77] Settlement pattern analysis: Willey 1953 and 1989; Trigger 1970. Soviet variant: Timoshchuk 1990a:129; Prikhodniuk 1988:189. Storage pits and social structure: Timoshchuk 1985:12; Baran 1987:64 and 1988b:16–17; Prikhodniuk 1988:191; Hayden and Gargett 1990:16.

[78] See Ferring 1984:117.

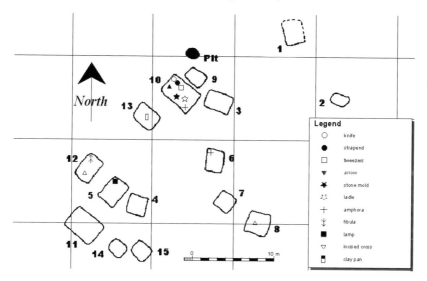

Figure 74 Bucharest-Soldat Ghivan Street, intrasite distribution of artifacts

found on the western side of the settlement. Furthermore, three of the
five buildings in the east (nos. 10, 13, and 15) had no heating facility. This
may indicate that, unlike structures in the western part of the settlement,
which were equipped with stone ovens, buildings in the east were not
permanently used. Perhaps they were not dwellings. The almost exclusive association of clay pans and amphora sherds with this settlement
sector suggests that some sort of activities were performed there, which
involved consumption of special foods.[79]

Though on a comparatively smaller scale, the site at Bucharest–Soldat
Ghivan Street (Figure 74) shows an arrangement very similar to that of
Seliște. Settlement features, all of which had clay ovens, were placed
around a large area devoid of any structures. A large building on the
northern side produced all tools and weapons found on site, while a
neighboring structure had the only fragments of clay pans. No such artifacts occurred in the south. A "Slavic" bow fibula, a potsherd with an
incised cross, which were found in building 12, and a handmade lamp
found in building 5, are in sharp contrast with the artifact distribution to
the north.[80]

At Poian (Figures 75–6), the distribution of dress accessories (combs,
a bow fibula, and a brooch with bent stem) deviates from that of tools

[79] Rafalovich 1972b; Rafalovich and Lapushnian 1974.
[80] Dolinescu-Ferche and Constantiniu 1981.

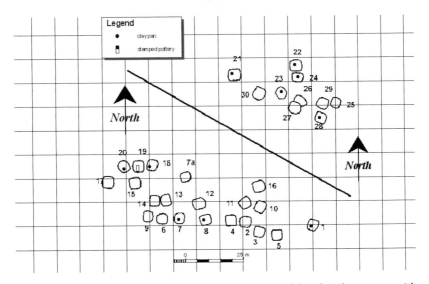

Figure 75 Poian, intrasite distribution of clay pans and handmade pottery with
stamped decoration
The bold line separates the northern from the southern sectors of the settlement, located at 700 m
from each other

(chisel, awls) and querns. A group of three buildings in the southern part
of the settlement (nos. 18, 19, and 20) produced most items of the first
category, but also the only fragments of handmade pottery with stamped
decoration. A similar arrangement may be seen at Dulceanca I (Figure
77). The site consists of three sunken buildings with clay ovens and twelve
ground-level buildings without any heating facility, all arranged in a loose
semicircle around a central place dominated by a kiln. A sunken building on the northern side produced all dress accessories and jewels (beads,
brooch, finger-ring, and bracelet) found on site, while another, on the
southern side, was associated only with tools (whetstone, mold, and
spindle whorls). At Dulceanca II (Figure 78), a site with sunken buildings arranged in a circle around two ovens, sherds of clay pans and
amphoras cluster on the southern side of the settlement, while tools
occur mostly in the northern sector.[81]

The site at Davideni consists of two groups of sunken buildings, in the
past presumably separated by a creek. The larger group to the north
includes the largest structures found on site, but also some of the smallest

[81] Poian: Székely 1992. Dulceanca I: Dolinescu-Ferche 1974:63–90. Dulceanca II: Dolinescu-
Ferche 1986.

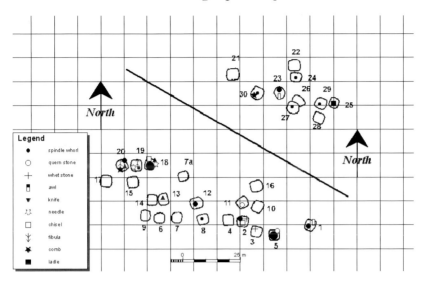

Figure 76 Poian, intrasite distribution of non-ceramic artifacts
The bold line separates the northern from the southern sectors of the settlement, located at 700 m
from each other

buildings, such as no. 38 (only 8.25 square meters of floor area), which
was located in the middle of a central, open area. Though too small to
accommodate a family, Davideni 38 had two heating facilities, a stone
oven and an open hearth (Figure 79).[82] This structure produced no tools
and no dress or personal accessories, only a few sherds of handmade
pottery and clay pans (Figures 80, 81, 82, and 83). It is interesting to note
that most other buildings surrounding the central area were equipped
with two heating facilities. Davideni 42, a large structure of over sixteen
square meters of floor area, had three ovens, two of stone and one of clay.
There is only one structure with two heating facilities in the smaller group
of buildings to the south. This group, however, was associated with three
open-air ovens. Like no. 38, many sunken buildings surrounding the
central area to the north produced large numbers of clay pans. Four of
them (nos. 33, 35, 36, and 39) also produced the majority of tools found
on site. The largest number of spindle whorls and needles were also found
in this area. Sunken building 41, which was next to Davideni 42, produced
a "Slavic" bow fibula and a fragment of a double-layered comb. Judging
from the intrasite distribution of artifacts, the central area on the northern side of the settlement may have been a locus of industrial activities,

[82] This is also true for Davideni 31 (6.19 square meters), with two clay ovens.

301

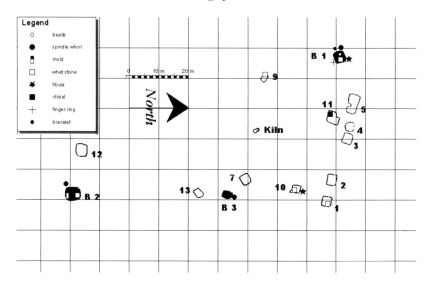

Figure 77 Dulceanca I, intrasite distribution of artifacts
Filled contours indicate sunken huts (B 1, B 2, and B 3), numbers refer to ground-level buildings

such as smelting and, possibly, production of dress accessories. It was also an area of special activities involving consumption of special foods. Clay pans were more frequently associated with features equipped with two or three ovens (nos. 27, 31, 34, 37, 38, and 42), which were located in this region. A comparison of the distribution of clay pans (Figure 83) to that of faunal remains (Figure 84) may strengthen the point. Consumption of flat loaves of bread substantially differed from that of meat. Moreover, processing of cereal-based foods is more complex than meat preparation and, consequently, more demanding in terms of space and equipment.[83] As in Seliște, clay pans may signalize the existence at Davideni of an area of communal activities involving, among other things, production and consumption of flat loaves of bread. It is reasonable to believe that structures equipped with more than one heating facility were associated with such activities, particularly if we think of Davideni 38 and other neighboring structures, which were too small to serve as dwellings.[84]

The analysis of the intrasite distribution of artifacts on these sites reveals a systematic organization and use of space, which further generates a specific site structure and a patterned arrangement of artifacts. The

---

[83] The Březno experiment indicated that for a day of an exclusively cereal menu, the experimenting family of four needed 1.7 kg of flour, which the wife processed in some two hours of grinding. See Pleinerová 1986:161–2.   [84] Mitrea 1972, 1974–6, 1992, and 1994.

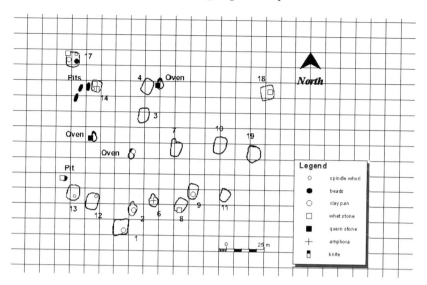

Figure 78 Dulceanca II, intrasite distribution of artifacts

most important characteristics of this arrangement are the presence of the central, open area and the polarization of the artifact distribution. All sites examined are examples of sociopetal settlements, in which the communal front region, where activities involving the entire community are performed, is placed at the center.[85] This area may have served as the stage for communal activities and ceremonies involving consumption of special foods, such as feasts or assemblies. As the center for intervillage social, religious, or economic events, the communal front region may have acquired a special public character as the symbol for the community as a whole. It is important to note that artifact-categories which may have been used to express cross-regional identities, such as clay pans, pottery decorated with incised signs, or "Slavic" bow fibulae, were especially associated with the communal front region. The intrasite distribution of artifacts at Selişte, Bucharest-Soldat Ghivan Street, and Davideni indicates, however, that bow fibulae, though found close to the communal front region, were part of artifact assemblages which suggest that, unlike most other neighboring buildings, no craft activities were undertaken there. If "Slavic" bow fibulae were symbols of power, such assemblages may represent either a dominant descent group or the head of the entire community. While the status of these individuals is reflected in the

[85] For the concept of "communal front region," see Oetelaar 1993:664. See also Pleinerová 1980:52.

303

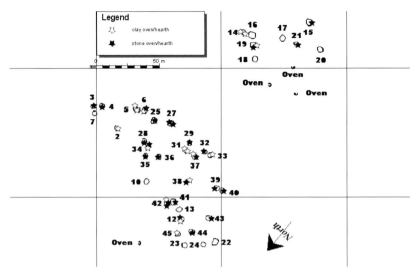

Figure 79 Davideni, intrasite distribution of heating facilities

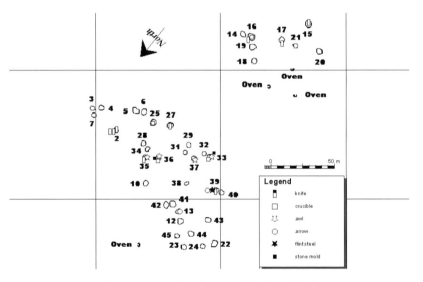

Figure 80 Davideni, intrasite distribution of tools and other non-ceramic artifacts

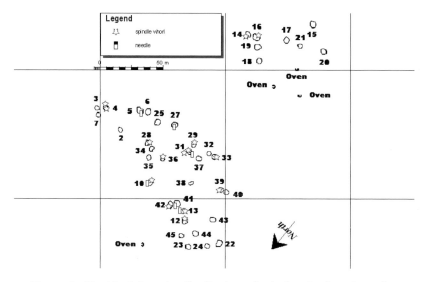

Figure 81 Davideni, intrasite distribution of spindle whorls and needles

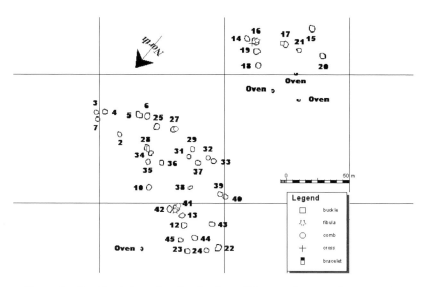

Figure 82 Davideni, intrasite distribution of dress and personal accessories

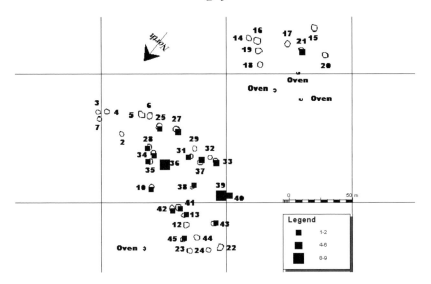

Figure 83 Davideni, intrasite distribution of clay pans

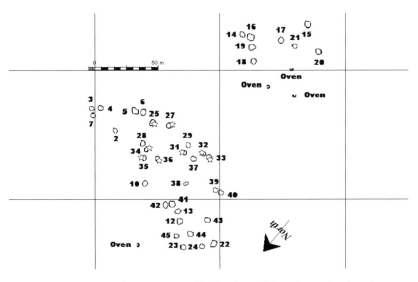

Figure 84 Davideni, intrasite distribution of faunal remains (stars)

marked contrasts revealed by the intrasite distribution of artifacts, bow fibulae, many of which have analogies in such distant location as Mazuria or Crimea, indicate their claims to an overarching, supra-regional identity. The communal front region was thus not only a locus of communal activity, but also an arena of social competition, a "beyond-the-households context" for displays of symbols of leadership.

CONCLUSION

The archaeological study of identity and status is often based on the analysis of burial assemblages, notably of the nature and symbolism of grave goods. The extensive use of cremation, rather than inhumation, as well as the possible use of funerary rites that may have left no trace in the archaeological record, prevented the use of such data for Slavic archaeology.[86] The data on which this chapter is based derive primarily from settlement excavations. Despite this bias, there are some important conclusions to be drawn for the reconstruction of social organization and ethnic identity.

First, there is already enough evidence to move away from the migrationist model which has dominated the discipline of Slavic archaeology ever since its inception (Chapter 1). A retreat from migrationism is necessary simply because the available data do not fit any of the current models for the study of (pre)historic migration. Cultural correspondences were too often explained in terms of long-distance migration, despite lack of any clear concept of migration to guide such explanations. Recent research in anthropology and other social sciences laid a strong emphasis on discriminating between such diverse phenomena as seasonal population movements, "scouting," and outward migration. It has become increasingly evident that migrations across ecological or cultural boundaries would require considerable planning on the part of the migrants, and should leave substantial and clear archaeological evidence. "'Cultures'," as one archaeologist noted, "do not migrate. It is often only a very narrowly defined, goal-oriented subgroup that migrates."[87] To speak of the Prague culture as the culture of the migrating Slavs is, therefore, a nonsense.

Furthermore, the archaeological evidence discussed in this chapter does not match any long-distance migratory pattern. Assemblages in the

---

[86] Zoll-Adamikowa 1980:948 and 1983. The long awaited publication of the large cemetery at Sărata Monteoru may bring significant changes to current views on status and identity expressed through mortuary displays. For an interesting study based exclusively on cemeteries, see Losert 1991.

[87] Anthony 1990:909. For the archaeological model of (pre)historic migrations, see Rouse 1986; Stark, Clark, and Elson 1995.

Lower Danube area, both east and south of the Carpathian mountains, antedate those of the alleged Slavic *Urheimat* in the Zhitomir Polesie, on which Irina Rusanova based her theory of the Prague-Korchak-Zhitomir type. More recent attempts to move the *Urheimat* to Podolia and northern Bukovina are ultimately based on the dating of crossbow brooches found at Kodyn and some other places. These brooches, however, are not the only late fifth- or early sixth-century artifacts in the area. Despite lack of closed finds comparable to those at Kodyn, there are good reasons to believe that at least some archaeological assemblages in south and east Romania go back as early as *c.* 500. The evidence is certainly too meager to draw any firm conclusions, but from what we have it appears that instead of a "Slavic culture" originating in a homeland and then spreading to surrounding areas, we should envisage a much broader area of common economic and cultural traditions. The implementation of an agricultural economic profile, which is so evident on later sites, is very likely to have involved some short-distance movement of people. The dominant type of economy seems to have been some form of "itinerant agriculture" which encouraged settlement mobility. Suzana Dolinescu-Ferche's research at Dulceanca brilliantly illustrates this model. Such population movements, however, cannot be defined as migration. There is simply no evidence for the idea that the inhabitants of the sixth- and early seventh-century settlements in Romania, Moldova, and Ukraine were colonists from the North.[88]

Nor does the idea of a "Slavic tide" covering the Balkans in the early 600s fit the existing archaeological data. South of the Danube river, no archaeological assemblage comparable to those found north of that river produced any clear evidence for a date earlier than *c.* 700. By contrast, there is no doubt that many early Byzantine forts in the Balkans were abandoned only during Heraclius' early regnal years (Chapter 4). The ceramic assemblages found at Argos and Olympia have nothing to do with these developments, for there are good reasons to believe they are of a much later date. It is unlikely that either the small settlement at Mušići or the cremation cemetery at Olympia existed at the time of the final withdrawal of Roman armies from the Balkans. The archaeological assemblages at Garvan may also be of a much later date than assumed by the archaeologist who led excavations there. Though both Greece and Albania produced clear evidence of seventh-century burial assemblages, they have nothing in common with the "Slavic culture" north of the Danube river.

---

[88] Slavic *Urheimat* in Podolia and Bukovina: Baran 1978, 1981, 1991, and 1994. See also Godłowski 1979. For Dulceana, see n. 57. For settlement mobility, see also Ștefan 1968.

Elites and group identity

The analysis of a considerable number of settlement features found in Romania, Moldova, and Ukraine has shown, on the other hand, that the second half of the sixth century and the early seventh century was a period of crucial change in the culture history of communities leaving north of the Danube river. While the existence of many settlements may have begun at a much earlier date, it is precisely during this period that they came to share a number of stylistic traits which may have been associated with emblemic styles. Pots ornamented with finger impressions or notches on the lip, clay pans, and *Grubenhäuser* with stone or clay oven are just a few examples of regional styles which became the norm in the late 500s and early 600s. Not all represented ethnicity, as suggested by Christian symbols incised on pots. Others may have represented cross-regional identities, as in the case of "Slavic" bow brooches with their ornamental patterns pointing to long-distance social contacts. Symbols drawn from "exotic" milieus may have been culturally authenticated and transformed into "native" symbols. The production of local series of bow fibulae, some imitating larger or more sophisticated specimens, may indicate this process. As such "imports" were "internalized," emulation of elite styles may have contributed to the dissemination of ornamental patterns.

Second, the analysis of intrasite distributions of artifacts suggests that with the agricultural economy established as a dominant subsistence pattern, processing and consumption of special, cereal-based foods, such as flat loaves of bread, became an essential ingredient of communal activities. The principal locus for these activities was now the communal front region of the settlement. Finds of tools and clay pans cluster around this region. This may have also been an arena for ceremonies orchestrated to convey complex messages of group identity.

It is against this background that the relative status of those who wore "Slavic" brooches becomes visible in both social and archaeological terms. Since fibulae were primarily female dress accessories, it is likely that, as with contemporary hoards of silver and bronze in Ukraine, women were symbolic vehicles for the construction of social identity. Just what kind of identity was symbolized is a matter of how "Slavic" bow fibulae are to be interpreted. Wearing a Mazurian or a Crimean brooch may have given the wearer a social locus associated with images of power. Wearing a local reproduction of such a fibula was, no doubt, a very different statement, though still related to status. Beyond emulation, therefore, "Slavic" bow fibulae, particularly much cruder specimens, without complicated scrollwork ornaments, may have conveyed a message pertaining to group identity. Whether living within the same region or widely scattered, adherence to a brooch style helped to integrate isolated individuals within a group whose social boundaries criss-crossed those of local communities. At the same time, brooches articulated a hierarchy of identities both within and between those communities. Production of bow fibulae involved knowledge of complicated technological processes and access to them was certainly restricted by the ability either to procure such items from distant locations or to employ a craftsman with enough experience and skill to replicate ornamental patterns and brooch-forms. Just as with "Lombard" and "Gepid" brooches, "Slavic" bow fibulae were not "phenotypic" expressions of a preformed ethnic identity. There were no Slavic fibulae *per se*. Access to and manipulation of such artifacts, however, may have been strategies for gaining admission into a group of people known to Byzantine authors as "Slavs."

Chapter 7

"KINGS" AND "DEMOCRACY": POWER IN EARLY SLAVIC SOCIETY

One of the most persistent stereotypes about the early medieval history of Eastern Europe is that, at the time of their migration, the Slavs were organized in a "polyarchic tribal society with no elevated notion of sovereignty." No Clovis or Theoderic arose among the Slavs to gather their scattered communities into a state and attempt a symbiosis with the Greco-Roman civilization of Byzantium. Incapable of organizing themselves on the state level, the Slavs could not escape being conquered by Goths, Huns, or Avars, who thus eliminated any incipient aristocracy the Slavs may have developed. The idea of the political inferiority of the Slavs in the Middle Ages, in contrast with a Germanic stratified society, is not new. It may be traced back as far as Herder's notion of a "democratic," egalitarian Slavic society. Today, the notion of the politically "primitive" Slavs of the early Middle Ages is a commonplace. This idea is primarily based on Procopius' frequently cited description of the Sclavenes and the Antes in the mid-500s: "For these nations, the Sclavenoi and Antae, are not ruled by one man, but they have lived from of old under a democracy (ἐν δημοκρατία ἐκ παλαιοῦ βιοτεύουσι), and consequently everything which involves their welfare, whether for good or for ill, is referred to the people (ἐς κοινὸν ἄγεται)". Some have argued that "democracy" is derisively applied here to what, in Procopius' eyes, might have been the opposite of Byzantine monarchy. Others blame Procopius for being an unqualified witness, who could not distinguish between acephalous societies and "primitive democracies." Some others, particularly among Soviet historians, believe Procopius to have described what is now known under the Marxist concept of "military democracy."[1]

---

[1] Procopius, *Wars* VII 14.22. Procopius' democracy as "military democracy": Braichesvkii 1953:22; Cankova-Petkova 1962:267; Benedicty 1965:61–2. See also Litavrin 1985:101; Havlík 1985:176. Procopius' democracy and Byzantine monarchy: Benedicty 1963:46–7 and 1965:53; Havlík 1985:174. Procopius and "primitive democracies": Evans 1989:63. For the political inferiority of the early Slavs, see Obolensky 1971:57; Anderson 1977:216 and 285; Pohl 1988:94; Alexander 1994:205–6. See also Grafenauer 1960:94; Richards 1986:327.

There is still much confusion about this account and no attempt has been made to take a fresh look at historical sources referring to Sclavenes and Antes in the light of modern anthropological thought. My purpose in this chapter is to examine these questions from the scarce evidence that we have. This evidence has usually been analyzed by historians as an undifferentiated body of information. It is assumed that, despite their own biases towards what constituted a "civilization" and a "barbarian" mode of life, the authors of our sixth- and seventh-century sources gave a reliable picture of the newcomers. I discussed both biases and accounts in Chapter 2. My intention here is to focus on what little textual evidence exists on descriptions of polity or society. I will first take into consideration two major theses about early medieval Slavic society, namely the "military democracy" and the "segmentary society" and I will analyze their basic tenets against the evidence of historical sources. By emphasizing the mechanism of the accumulation of power in the hands of the Slavic "kings," I will then focus on the applicability of the modern concept of chiefdom to Slavic society and compare Slavic leaders with both their Germanic counterparts and "classical" examples of big-men and great-men, on the basis of a theory of symbolic power.

"MILITARY DEMOCRACY": USEFUL CONCEPT OR PROCUSTEAN BED?

Procopius' account of the Slavic "democracy" became a favorite historiographical theme in the days of the Slavic Congress in Prague (1848). Both Palacký and Šafářik interpreted Procopius' text as referring to a distinctive quality of "Slavdom," as opposed to the aggressiveness and brutality of the Germans. To Niederle, the Slavic "democracy" was as a pristine form of ancestral, Indo-European social structure based on social equality and cooperation between large families. He imagined these families as identical to the Balkan *zadruga*, "discovered" by Western ethnographers in the late nineteenth century. Like Niederle, many still argue that the peculiar social organization of the early Slavs prevented centralization of economic and political power, despite clear evidence that the *zadruga* was a much later phenomenon.[2]

By contrast, Soviet historians of the late 1930s referred to early Slavic society only as a "military democracy." As such, the early Slavic society would by no means be different from the Germanic one. The concept was first introduced to the academic discourse by Lewis Morgan. In his

[2] See Palacký 1868:74–89; Schafarik 1844: I, 17. For the Slavic *zadruga*, see Schrader 1901:73; Niederle 1923:26 and 1926:173; Cross 1948:17; Richards 1986:326. *Zadruga* as a recent phenomenon: Baumann 1982; Todorova 1993:133–58.

Ancient Society (1877), Morgan described the "military democracy" as the transitional stage from kin-based societies to state societies. According to him, the military democracy presupposed the existence of an elected and removable chief, a council of the elders, and a popular assembly. Frederick Engels first gave the concept its economic and social meaning. To Engels, "military democracy" concerned war and organization for war, since those were now "regular functions of the life of the peoples who began to regard the acquisition of wealth as one of the main purposes in life." He considered population pressure to be the primary cause for the emergence of the military democracy. Engels insisted that the military democracy contained both elements of the kin-based society and, *in nuce*, the principles of class-based state society. Not surprisingly, Soviet historians fully endorsed Engels' definition. To them, Procopius' notion of Slavic democracy was just "military democracy" *avant la lettre*. Since Engels emphasized warfare, Soviet historians used the *Strategikon* to argue that the Slavic "military democracy" implied a particular form of slavery, which they described as "patriarchal." Warfare brought a large number of captives, who became slaves. Such slaves, however, played no determining role in production, and, in time, they were set free.[3] Drawing on Engels' suggestion, S. P. Tolstov argued that the military democracy represented the final stage of primitive society, the last step before class society. The theory of the "military democracy" gradually lost its popularity after World War II and during the 1960s was exposed to harsh criticisms from both Soviet and Western Marxists. The wide variety of political forms and structures described by anthropologists and ethnographers made the rigid scheme derived from Engels' work a totally inadequate concept. Some have argued that, if at all, the "military democracy" has some conceptual value only when applied to the military tribal organization. With much of its initial appeal long dissipated, the military democracy was now replaced by the "Germanic mode of production" as a model for the description of decentralized stratified societies. Since there is no critical evaluation of the "military democracy" thesis in relation to Slavic

---

[3] *Strategikon* XI 4.4: "They do not keep those who are in captivity among them in perpetual slavery, as do other nations. But they set a definite period of time for them and then give them the choice either, if they so desire, to return to their own homes with a small recompense or to remain there as free men and friends." "Patriarchal slavery": Kuchma 1978:7; Sverdlov 1977:47–8, 50, and 54; Litavrin 1984:193. Military democracy: Engels 1968:581; Guhr and Schlette 1982:910; Guhr 1984; Peršic 1988:150. "Military democracy" in Soviet historiography: Levchenko 1938; Mishulin 1939; Gorianov 1939a and 1939b. See also Herrmann 1982:15. A Polish historian, Gerard Labuda (1949), first applied the concept to Samo, Fredegar's "king" of the Slavs. V. D. Koroliuk (1970) described all medieval Balkan states as "military democracies." Labuda's interpretation of Samo's state is still prevalent and the concept remains popular in Eastern Europe, even after the demise of the Communist regimes. See Čilinská 1980:80; Parczewski 1993:114.

society, it is necessary to examine the arguments and to discuss the relevance of this theory.[4]

True, historical sources, particularly the *Strategikon*, describe warfare as one of the most important features of early Slavic society. This, however, is an indication of the Byzantine authors' concern with the military organization of those whom they described as the enemy of the Empire. John of Ephesus, in a furious outburst, even complained that during their invasion of 581, the Sclavenes had learned to make war better than the Romans. Both John and the author of the *Strategikon* refer to the javelin as the favorite weapon of the Sclavene warriors. Procopius and the *Strategikon* considered ambushes, sudden attacks, and the stratagem of the feigned retreat to be typically "Slavic." At the time, however, Roman troops were themselves equipped with "Slavic javelins" and knew how to combat Sclavenes, using their own stratagems. It is true that the author of the *Strategikon* had only praises for the treatment of prisoners by Sclavenes and seems to have suggested that the Sclavenes were only concerned with "a small recompense" in exchange for freeing their captives. Both Procopius and Theophylact Simocatta, however, describe scenes of mass slaughter, in which captives were intentionally and systematically decimated, apparently with no concern for their "economic" value. To some, one important characteristic of the "Germanic mode of production" is that societies organized in this way often supply tribute-based states with slaves drawn from neighboring kin-organized groups. All Slavic raids known from historical sources aimed at and resulted in the capture of a great number of prisoners. No indication exists, however, of Sclavenes raiding neighboring territories in order to supply the Empire with slaves.[5]

---

[4] Tolstov 1935:206. See Guhr and Schlette 1982:914; Khazanov 1974:134 and 144; Herrmann 1982:17; Peršic 1988:85. "Germanic mode of production": Bromley 1979:207; Gailey and Patterson 1988:81; Krüger 1988; Kristiansen 1991:19–20. The "Germanic mode of production" has been elaborated with reference to the Sahara-Sahel nomadic herders (Bonte 1977) and the Maasai of East Africa (Rigby 1985). To be sure, the "Germanic mode of production" is neither identical with nor a more fashionable substitute of the "military democracy." Marx (1965:75–80) defined the "Germanic mode of production" in opposition to the "Asiatic" one, as characterized, among others, by a significant expansion of private property, with dispersed, self-sufficient, family groups coming together only for reasons of defense.

[5] John of Ephesus VI 25; *Strategikon* XI 4.4, 9, 11, 13, 25, 29, and 39, XII 2.5; Procopius, *Wars* VI 26.18, VII 14.25, VII 38.11–23; *Buildings* IV 7.12–13; Theophylact Simocatta VII 2.3 and 9. The late sixth-century military treatise known as *De Militari Scientia* lists Sclavenes and Antes, along with Saracens, Persians, and Scythians, as examples of nations making extensive use of ambushes. See Ivanov 1988. Slaves and "Germanic mode of production": Gailey and Patterson 1988:82. For Slavic raids and prisoners, see Procopius, *Wars* VII 13.24, VII 29.1, VII 38.20, VII 40.45; John of Ephesus VI 25; Theophylact Simocatta I 7.3–6 and VII 2.1. The qagan of the Avars boasted of having freed a great number of Roman prisoners he had found north of the Danube, during his punitive expedition of 578 (Menander the Guardsman, fr. 21; cf. 25.1). By contrast, the very name of the Sclavenes

An important argument for interpreting early Slavic society as a military democracy is the existence of the chief's retinue of warriors. According to Menander the Guardsman, the attack of the Avars in 578 was directed against Daurentius and "the chiefs of his people (τοὺς ὅσοι ἐν τέλει τοῦ ἔθνους)." Some argued that this particular passage indicated the existence of a tribal aristocracy, whose authority was presumably based on wealth differentials. That Daurentius was a warrior leader is beyond any doubt. Furthermore, the existence of Sclavene chiefs as primarily military leaders is well documented by Theophylact Simocatta. There is, however, no evidence for the council of the elders, one of the institutions both Morgan and Engels viewed as a necessary condition for the existence of a military democracy. Nor can Menander the Guardsman's evidence be used to postulate the existence of a political hierarchy, in which the power of the military leader was checked by that of the "chiefs of his people." On the other hand, when Procopius refers to "the people" or to public affairs, there is no indication of chiefs. Where chiefs appear, there is no indication of their clear-cut separation from the agrarian substrate.[6]

The model of the military democracy presupposes a form of tribal military organization, characterized by the existence of a military leader. This is, however, in sharp contrast with the lack of coordination of many Sclavene raids. At several times, different groups of warriors seem to have operated on their own, without any master strategy or division of military tasks (see Chapter 3). Nor does the practice of slaying the prisoners fit this picture, and even less so the cannibalism reported by Pseudo-Caesarius.[7] It is also difficult to understand why Sclavenes are constantly referred to as using rather "primitive" military equipment, though John of Ephesus did not fail to notice their adaptability to Roman warfare and weaponry. Insofar as the existence of military democracy is presumed, it is also difficult to explain the contradictory evidence of the *Strategikon* with reference to Sclavene "kings." The author of this treatise suggests that Roman generals should win over some of these "kings" by persuasion or gifts, but considers Sclavenes, in

---

seems to have been at the origin of the word "slave" in both Greek and Latin. See Verlinden 1937:125; Schelesniker 1973:7; Köpstein 1979:72; Nystazopoulou-Pelekidou 1986:358. To my knowledge, the only instance of Sclavenes selling their prisoners of war is the episode reported in Book II of the *Miracles of St Demetrius* (II 4.249). In this case, however, prisoners were sold to other Sclavenes, not to the Byzantines.

[6] Menander the Guardsman, fr. 21; Procopius, *Wars* VII 14.21–2. See also Benedicty 1965:53. "Military democracy" and the retinue of warriors: Benedicty 1963:49–50 and 54–5, and 1965:66; Pohl 1988:127. See also Sverdlov 1977:57.

[7] Riedinger 1969:302: "The Sclavenes . . . with pleasure consume the breasts of women, full of milk, dashing infants with rocks like rats" (English translation quoted from Bačić 1983:152).

general, to have no regard for treaties, "which they agree more out of fear than by gifts."[8]

In Engels' terms, military democracy was a form of social organization typically associated with the gradual disintegration of communal ownership and with the emergence of private ownership and exploitation based on tribute and clientship. Recent theorists stress the decentralized form of subsistence production, with village communities or farms scattered across the landscape and household-based relations of production. Although there seems to be no definite stratification, as Tolstov once believed, wealth differentials may truly exist in the "Germanic mode of production." Chiefs set themselves apart from the agrarian substrate and rule through a retinue of warriors. The warrior chief or king controls and exploits the farming communities through tribute and taxation. As a hallmark of a complex pre-state society, many scholars emphasize the importance of inter-regional market-places (emporia, ports-of-trade), where trading activities were controlled by kings or chiefs.[9]

There is no indication of trading communities, let alone towns, in historical sources concerning the early Slavs. Where available, the archaeological evidence of hillforts could hardly be dated prior to the eighth or ninth centuries. The author of the *Strategikon* refers to the "abundance of all sorts of . . . produce" and livestock that Roman armies might expect to find in Sclavene villages. We are told that the Sclavenes used to bury their most valuable possessions in secret places (τὰ ἀναγκαῖα τῶν πραγμάτων αὐτῶν ἐν ἀποκρύφῳ χωννύουσιν), keeping nothing unnecessary in sight. Can this be an indication of storage facilities under the chief's control, as some have argued? Nothing in the passage indicates that this might be the case. By contrast, the passage is reminiscent of another in Book II of the *Miracles of St Demetrius*. Its author knew that every house left deserted in a Sclavene village near Thessalonica contained reserves of corn, pulses, and utensils. This dovetails with the archaeological evidence presented in Chapter 6, which suggests that late sixth- and early seventh-century communities living north of the Danube river were characterized by an economic profile strongly oriented toward agriculture and consumption of cereal-based foods. That Sclavene communities south of

[8] *Strategikon* XI 4.30 and 14. The author of the *Strategikon* knew that there were many "kings" at odds with one another, but does not seem to have overruled the possibility of seeing them brought together under one ruler (μοναρχία) (XI 4.30). For the adaptability of Sclavenes to Roman warfare and weaponry, see John of Ephesus VI 25. For Sclavene weaponry, see Procopius, *Wars* VII 14.25; *Strategikon* XI 4.11.

[9] Emergence of private ownership and exploitation: Herrmann 1982:20 and 1987b:263–4. Decentralized mode of production: Kristiansen 1991:19–20; Gailey and Patterson 1988:81. Ports-of-trade: Engels 1968:581; Guhr and Schlette 1982:915; Hodges and Whitehouse 1983:92–3. See also Smith 1976.

the Danube were able to produce food in large quantities is demonstrated, on the other hand, by the fact that, at the order of the emperor, the Drugubites were capable of feeding the entire population returning from the Avar qaganate under the leadership of Kuver. It is therefore very likely that keeping all valuable possessions in "secret places" was just a response to frequent inroads by outsiders, including Roman armies.[10]

Procopius, when briefly describing the religion of the Sclavenes, claimed that they sacrifice to "one god, the maker of the lightning . . . cattle and all other victims." If taken at its face value, this passage may be, and has indeed been, interpreted as referring to conspicuous consumption, but it could hardly be invoked as an argument for accumulation of wealth. To Emperor Leo the Wise, writing in the early 900s, the Sclavenes appeared as completely indifferent toward accumulation. Emperor Leo specifically referred to land property, which in late ninth- or early tenth-century Byzantium was a key factor for defining social status. Other sources, however, emphasize accumulation of chattels as a consequence of continuous raiding into the Roman provinces resulting in considerable amounts of booty. As shown in Chapter 4, collection of Byzantine coins is attested by a relatively large number of Romanian hoards. It would be difficult, however, to associate these hoards with accumulation of wealth. With a rampant inflation in the mid-sixth century, the amounts accumulated in hoards were worth slightly more than one or two *modii* of Egyptian wheat. Exotic wealth and the associated external ideologies may have been used as status-defining markers and as political currency in manipulating political relationships. This might have been the case of fibulae with bent stem or pectoral crosses discussed in Chapter 6. There is no indication, however, that such artifacts participated in the construction of power or of class-society, in any way comparable to the model of "military democracy."[11]

---

[10] *Strategikon* XI 4.5 and 8; *Miracles of St Demetrius* II 4.280 and II 5.289–90. See also Litavrin 1987:38–9; Ivanova 1980:86. Hillforts: Pohl 1992:15; Staňa 1985. The earliest medieval hillforts found in Eastern Europe, such as Szeligi, Hacki (Poland), and Zimno (Ukraine), were more likely loci of communal social and religious ceremonies, not "royal centers." See Kobyliński 1989:309 and 1990:152 and 155.

[11] Procopius, *Wars* VII 14.23–4; Leo the Wise, *Tactica* XVIII 106: "They much prefer even short rations, than bearing with difficulty the other burdens of farming, because they prefer to lead a rather free and careless existence rather than to acquire property or costly food through great effort" (English translation from Wiita 1977:276). See also Burmov 1963:61. Emperor Tiberius succeeded in persuading the qagan of the Avars to organize a punitive expedition against Dauritas and "the chiefs of his people," because Bayan knew the Avars would find "the land full of gold (πολυχρήματον), since the Roman Empire had long been plundered by Sclavenes, whose land, however, had never been raided by other people at all" (Menander the Guardsman, fr. 21). For sixth-century prices in Byzantium, see Morrisson 1989:239–60. A *modius* was about 15 kg. For use of livestock by pastoralists in payment or sacrifice at naming ceremonies, circumcisions, weddings, and funerals, see Ausenda 1995:27–8. Conspicuous consumption:

Because it attempts to define society in terms of the impact of war and trade on economic relations that might have offered the path for transformation into a class-based society, the theory of the "military democracy" is inappropriate for a description of early Slavic society. Marxist theorists tend to limit research on "pre-capitalist" formations to scholastic discussion about the typology of modes of production and generally employ a restricted definition of economic interest (as a historical product of capitalism), without acknowledging that the theory of strictly economic practice is simply a particular case of a general theory of practice. In reality, "economic calculations" should be extended to all the goods, material and symbolic, without distinction, that present themselves as rare and worthy of being sought after in a particular social formation.[12]

The current literature on chiefdoms depicts them as institutions depending upon the interlocking of three major components of power: control over economy, military force, and ideology. It is precisely economic control that is absent from any description of early Slavic society. There are, however, clear cases of accumulation of "symbolic capital." John of Ephesus describes the Sclavenes of the early 580s as becoming rich and possessing "gold and silver, herds of horses and a lot of weapons," in sharp contrast to the "simple people" they used to be, who never dared "to leave the woods." The same phenomenon might have been at work in the episode of a Sclavene chief narrated by Michael the Syrian. During their raid into Greece, the Sclavenes carried off on carts the holy vessels and *ciboria* from devastated churches. In Corinth, however, one of their leaders took the great *ciborium* and using it as a tent, made it his dwelling. In doing so, he might have imitated the qagan of the Avars, who sat on a throne under a canopy when receiving embassies from Constantinople. The Sclavene chief seems to have clearly grasped the symbolic potential of the otherwise useless stone *ciborium*, shaped as it was like a canopy over a throne. This further suggests that, at least in this case, simple accumulation of "material capital" cannot account for the process of power concentration.[13]

Footnote 11 (*cont.*)
 Ivanova and Litavrin 1985:47. Conspicuous, presumably ritual, consumption of liquor may also be derived from Theophylact's account of "king" Musocius. The Sclavene "king" was captured by Roman troops in the middle of a night of the year 593, as he was "drunk and debilitated by liquor, since on that day there had been a funeral celebration for his departed brother in accordance with their [Sclavene] custom" (VI 9.12). For liquor consumption at funerary celebrations, see Goehrke 1992:146. [12] Bourdieu 1994:173 and 194.
[13] John of Ephesus VI 25; Michael the Syrian X 21; Menander the Guardsman, fr. 27. See also Nikolajević 1983:803. In Byzantine literature, disrespect for holy instruments or clothes, especially those usually kept in churches, is a stereotypical complaint against barbarians. See Serikov 1991:289. In the 570s, the throne of the Byzantine emperor was usually associated with the throne

"Kings" and "democracy"

The idea of military democracy indirectly suggests the potential for secondary state formation, that is, a social formation which is pushed toward a higher form of organization by an external power which has already been raised to statehood. There are, however, no attempts to examine the connections between Slavic chiefdoms and Roman frontiers. Moreover, the "military democracy" model only accounts for what is viewed as a transitional stage to state-level society. No explanation is given for the emergence of the presumed Slavic military democracy from "primitive society." Dissatisfaction with this model may explain why, more recently, historians following the pervasively Romantic ideas of Palacký and Šafářik have focused on a specific, historically determined, "Slavic way of life," which may be used for describing long-term historical processes in Eastern Europe. In contrast with highly stratified and centralized societies of the Germanic successor states, the early Slavs have emerged in recent literature as the medieval "segmentary society" *par excellence*.[14]

SEGMENTARY SOCIETY: IDEOLOGY OR ACTUALITY?

When historians speak of the "segmentary society" of the early Slavs they usually refer to the *Strategikon*, whose author claimed that Sclavenes were unable to fight a battle standing in close order or present themselves on open and level ground. This lack of strategy, he argued, was a direct consequence of their political organization: "Owing to their lack of government (ἄναρχα) and their ill feeling toward one another (μισ-άλληλα ὄντα) they are not acquainted with an order of battle (οὐδὲ τάξιν γιγνώσκουσιν)." "Lack of government," it has been argued, refers to a segmentary lineage system. The underlying idea of such a system is that the functions of maintaining cohesion, social control, some degree of "law and order," which normally depend on specialized agencies, with sanctions at their disposal, can be performed with tolerable efficiency, simply by the "balancing" and "opposition" of constituent groups. Societies that Emile Durkheim coined "segmentary" are thus

---

of Christ, particularly after Justin II initiated the building of a new throne in the imperial palace (the so-called Chrysotriklinos). Justin II's coins emphasize this quasi-religious theme of the *enthroned emperor*, already glorified by Flavius Cresconius Corippus in his poem on the ceremonial of the emperor's rise to power. For more details on contemporary imperial imagery, see Cameron 1981:221. The phrase "symbolic capital" is that of Pierre Bourdieu. For the components of power in chiefdoms, see Earle 1989:86.

[14] Nystazopoulou-Pelekidou 1986:354: "en effet, les tribus slaves – malgré leur vie sédentaire en Grèce de plus de cinquante ans – n'avaient pas encore dépassé l'état des sociétés primitives dont parle déjà au tournant des VI-e/VII-e siècles le Stratégikon de Maurice – c'est-à-dire l'état des sociétés 'ségmentaires' qu'a si bien décrit Emile Durkheim." Instead of Durkheim, Walter Pohl (1988:126) cited Pierre Clastres (1977). See also Richards 1986:332.

characterized by a paradoxical configuration: complex social organization, but lack of hierarchy, of super-ordination and subordination. Evans-Pritchard has called this "ordered anarchy." What is usually referred to as "segmentary society," however, is one that is in some way structured in terms of descent, in terms of *lineage*. The segmentary lineage model has as its premises a genealogical ordering of political alliances based on the principle of complementary opposition. Lineages are relative social entities, arising only when aroused by competition. Marshall Sahlins has argued that a segmentary lineage system is a predatory organization confined to societies in migration, for, as a social means of intrusion and competition in an already occupied ecological niche, it develops specifically in a tribal society which is moving against other tribes. The invading nucleus is eventually joined by people of related segments and all distribute themselves according to genealogical distance, paralleling their original positions.[15]

At first glance, Slavic settlements north of the Danube river seem to fit this model perfectly. In the early 500s, Procopius described the scattered, "pitiful hovels," of the Sclavenes. At the turn of the century, everything changed: the settlements of the Sclavenes and Antes were now laying in rows along the rivers, so close to each other that "there was practically no space between them." Just as the Tiv of more recent times, the Sclavenes violently reacted against any attempts to impose on them rulers from the outside. The author of the *Strategikon* knew that the Sclavenes and the Antes were "both independent, absolutely refusing to be enslaved or governed, least of all in their own land."[16] Emperor Leo the Wise witnessed the same stubborn resistance:

> Even if they had crossed over [the Danube] and been compelled to accept servitude, they did not wish to be happily persuaded by an outsider, but through some method by their own people. They would rather be led to destruction by a leader of their own tribe than to be enslaved and submit to Roman laws

[15] *Strategikon* XI 4.12 and 16. See *Strategikon* XI 4.9 and 19; Procopius, *Wars* VII 22.3 and 5, VII 38.7, VII 40.7; *Buildings* IV 7.12–13 and 17; Theophylact Simocatta VII 4.13–VII 5.1, VII 5.8. See also Zasterová 1971:51–2; Kuchma 1978:8. For "lack of government" and the segmentary lineage system, see Pohl 1988:126. Segmentary societies: Durkheim 1893:150; Evans-Pritchard 1940:181; Fortes and Evans-Pritchard 1940:296. See also Sigrist 1967. For segmentary society as structured in terms of lineage, see Munson 1989:387. See also Evans-Pritchard 1953:26. For the segmentary lineage in political action, see Lindholm 1985:21; Ausenda 1995:19. Segmentary lineage system and migration: Sahlins 1961:323 and 337–8. See also Sigrist 1967:43 and 98; Holy 1979:12.

[16] *Strategikon* XI 4.1 and XI 4.38. Procopius, *Wars* VII 14.24 and 29. See also Benedicty 1965:75. For the Tiv, see Bohannan 1958:11; Sigrist 1967:198–200 and 217–18. The chroniclers of the Fourth Crusade described in similar terms the Milings and the Ezerites of Peloponnesus. Both were "un gent de voulenté et n'obeissent a nul seignor" (*Livre de la Conqueste de la Princée de l'Amorée*, cited by Weithmann 1978:117).

nor have they received the sacrament of the baptism of the Savior until our time, in this case giving way to some extent in the practice of their ancient freedom.[17]

Sclavenes may in fact unite to attack or repel an enemy at one time, but may also fragment into feuding factions at another, quarreling over land or personal injuries. The former case is illustrated by "king" Musocius, who agreed to provide assistance for rescuing the Sclavenes from the neighboring territory of Ardagastus, previously attacked by the Romans. The Sclavene tribes living around Thessalonica allied themselves in order to defend "king" Perbundos, arrested by Byzantine authorities. It is with this fact in mind that the author of the *Strategikon* recommended that Roman generals use any possible means to thwart Sclavenes from uniting "under one ruler." Emperor Tiberius' idea to incite Avars against the Sclavenes, "so that all of those who were laying waste Roman territory would be drawn back by the troubles at home, choosing rather to defend their own lands," was based on the same assumption. However, the "massing effect" may evaporate in the absence of a common danger: "When a difference of opinion prevails among them, either they come to no agreement at all or when some of them do come to an agreement, the others quickly go against what was decided. They are always at odds with each other (πάντων ἐναντίων ἀλλήλων φρονούντων)."[18] When the defensive objectives that had induced confederation have been accomplished, the confederation dissolves again into its several segments, and leaders that had emerged now fall back into social oblivion or retain only local influence. Ardagastus might have achieved enough fame beyond his primary group, enough indeed to be influential among neighboring, related, segments, and to organize raids across the Danube with other warriors coming from distant regions. But once his territory was devastated by Roman troops in 593, Ardagastus narrowly escaped capture and his name, which he had begun to build, rapidly vanished from Byzantine sources and, we may presume, from among Sclavenes.[19]

Can we then apply the model of the segmentary lineage system to the

---

[17] Leo the Wise, *Tactica* XVIII 99; English translation from Wiita 1977:259. See also Pseudo-Caesarius, *Eratopokriseis*, in Riedinger 1969:302; Zasterová 1971:59; Pohl 1988:126.

[18] *Strategikon* XI 4.14; see also XI 4.30. The phrase "massing effect" is that of Marshall Sahlins. For Musocius, see Theophylact Simocatta VI 9.6. For Perbundos, see *Miracles of St Demetrius* II 4.231. For Emperor Tiberius and the Avar attack against the Sclavenes, see Menander the Guardsman, fr. 21.

[19] Theophylact Simocatta VI 7.5; see Zasterová 1971: 78–9. Ardagastus had also organized the expedition crushed by Comentiolus under the walls of Adrianople, in 585 (Theophylact Simocatta I 7.5).

Sclavene case? In other words, was the early Slavic society structured in terms of descent? Inspired by Pierre Clastres' model of the "Society against the State," Walter Pohl derived a segmentary system from the presumed absence of social mechanisms contributing to the consolidation of royal authority. Unlike the highly centralized model of Germanic society, the early Slavic society was characterized by a form of leadership, which typically enhanced "tribal hierarchies," without replacing them. Soviet historians cited the *Strategikon* as evidence for their claims that the Slavic society was a "military democracy." Pohl used the same source for advocating the idea of a "segmentary society."[20]

What he obviously ignored is that lineage theory and segmentation are not at all the same thing. The former deals with sequences of events at the level of observation, in particular with the appearance of groups, whereas the second deals with formal relations that characterize the types of events possible. The segmentary lineage model has been strongly criticized by historically minded anthropologists precisely for reifying local ideology to the level of social theory. In other words, in assuming that segmentary societies ignore hierarchy and political leadership, anthropologists did not, in fact, refer to a set of empirical facts about actual behavior, but to a set of actors' ideas about their political relations or to the anthropologists' own set of ideas about the actors' representations.[21]

Can our sources prove the existence of a segmentary lineage system? They have almost nothing to offer to anthropologists dealing with lineage theory. We are completely ignorant about what social mechanisms were responsible for the descent structure of the early Slavic society. We know that "king" Musocius attended a funeral ceremony for his departed brother, in accordance with the Sclavene custom. This, however, does not tell us anything about the structure of kin groups. Menander the Guardsman, on the other hand, narrates an episode of the Avar conquest, in which the leaders of the Antes, under the pressure of Avar incursions, decided to sent an embassy to the Avars and appointed as ambassador Mezamer "the son of Idariz and brother of Kelagast." If we are to believe the Cutrigur who had joined the Avars and incited them to kill the ambassador, Mezamer was "the most powerful of all amongst the Antes (οὗτος ὁ ἀνὴρ μεγίστην ἐσότι περιβέβληται δύναμιν ἐν ΄Ανταις)." Irrespective of what exactly was Mezamer's office, it seems evident that,

---

[20] Pohl 1988:126–7, based on *Strategikon* XI 4.1.
[21] Dresch 1986:309; Lindholm 1985:21. See also David Turton's comments to Giorgio Ausenda's paper (Ausenda 1995:47): "The Langobards obviously had a descent construct but this could have had other uses apart from group recruitment. *It would be wrong to assume that, because they had a descent construct, they necessarily had groups that were recruited by means of it. The fara may have been a* local group of assorted kin and affines organized around an 'agnatic core' (emphasis added)."

according to Menander the Guardsman, his status was derived from lineage. In this case, however, the organization of the Antes was more a ranked than a segmentary society.[22]

It has been observed that a segmentary structure of society involves a segmentary structure of space, the minimal unit of which represents the "primary tribal segment," as the smallest multifamily group that collectively exploits an area of tribal resources and forms a residential entity. How large was a segment? The author of the *Strategikon* understood that for an invasion into Sclavene territory to be successful, a fairly large force should be dispatched against each settlement (χωρίον). For attacking a settlement, he recommended the use of one or two bandons, i.e. 400 to 800 men, some going about pillaging, while others kept guard over them. He even insisted that it was not wise to detach more bandons, even if the settlement happened to be a large one, thus implying that 400 to 800 men were a sufficiently large force to overcome any possible resistance. We may safely presume therefore that the population of a Sclavene χωρίον was slightly inferior in size to the attacking Roman force, assuming that the estimations of the *Strategikon* are based only on the military potential of the enemy, that is, on the number of warriors, not on the total number of inhabitants.[23] This is indirectly confirmed by the episode of the Roman soldiers slaughtered by Peiragastus' warriors in 594. Theophylact Simocatta relates that Peter, the general of the Roman army, had ordered his army to cross the Danube, not knowing that the Sclavenes had prepared an ambush. The first 1,000 men were killed, but Peter eventually managed to cross over his entire army. The Sclavenes were eventually forced to withdraw, as Peiragastus was killed in the encounter. The Sclavene army may thus have been slightly larger than the unit (a μοῖρα or brigade) of 1,000 men that first crossed the river. As a consequence, the warriors Peiragastus had under his command may have represented three to four χωρία. These warriors seem to have come from a distance. Indeed, after Peiragastus's death, Peter's troops began chasing the remnants of his army across the Sclavene territory, without encountering any settlement. When viewed against the background of the *Strategikon*, this episode suggests therefore that the force the Romans encountered in 594

---

[22] Menander the Guardsman, fr. 3. For Musocius, see Theophylact Simocatta VI 8.12.
[23] *Strategikon* XI 4.43. This estimate is much larger than that derived from the archaeological evidence discussed in Chapter 6. An average number of inhabitants per settlement, ranging between fifty and seventy, was inferred from excavations of *Grubenhäuser* with under fifteen square meters of floor area. It is possible, however, that a χωρίον was not a single settlement, but a cluster of settlements. Segmentary structure of space: Balandier 1970:53; Sahlins 1961:325; Dirks, Eley, and Ortner 1994:13. Bulgarian historians claimed the Slav settlers in the Balkans were divided into numerous separate families, bound not so much by their common descent, as by their life together. See Koledarov 1969:125 and 127–8; Cankova-Petkova 1962:266.

did not represent a single segment. In other words, Peiragastus was not one of those "kings" living close to the Roman frontier, to be won by persuasion or gifts, so that "their common hostility will not make them united."[24]

The archaeological evidence may also indicate a segmentary organization of space. Groups of households found on sixth- and seventh-century sites north of the Danube river may have been communal villages of a kind described by Henri H. Stahl for early modern Romania. The family organization of the communal village allowed sons to found their own households and settle down near their parents, clear land, and build houses together, but the households lived separately, as small individual families. Once a family group was established, by clearing or simply taking over a certain part of the territory, it grew, biologically and socially, until it formed a hamlet. The group expressed its solidarity by invoking an ancestor, whose name was sometimes invented or derived from that of the hamlet. Paul Bohannan has found the same mechanism in the spatial distribution of Tiv primary segments in western Africa and his model may be applied to the Slavs. In this case, however, the early Slavic society was by no means unique, for the principle of segmentation existed in many other early medieval societies. Emile Durkheim has already classified Germanic tribes as "polysegmental societies doubly compounded."[25]

It remains unclear how much of what we know from Byzantine sources should be viewed as a set of empirical facts about actual behavior. It is logical to believe that the author of the *Strategikon* had a better (most likely first-hand) knowledge about Sclavenes than Procopius. In spite of significant differences, however, when the author of the *Strategikon* claims that Sclavenes were always at odds with each other, this is a well-worn *topos*, used by many before him, including Procopius.

The model of the "segmentary society" ignores historical process. It is very unlikely that the Sclavene society had remained "frozen" in its "primitive," segmentary, stage during contact with the Empire. Though Byzantine sources make it clear that Sclavenes had their own "kings," advocates of this model described the Sclavene society as characterized by social mechanisms inhibiting the rise of political leadership. In fact, by ideologically defining any political action as an affair of segments in

[24] Theophylact Simocatta VII 5.1; *Strategikon* XI 4.30. It is interesting to note that Theophylact (or his source) calls Peiragastus a brigadier (ταξίαρχος), i.e. commander of a division (μέρος) with three brigades.
[25] Durkheim 1958:84: a "polysegmental society doubly compounded" results from the "juxtaposition or fusion of several simply compounded polysegmented societies." For the Lombard society as segmentary, see Ausenda 1995. For communal villages, see Stahl 1980:44; Timoshchuk 1985:15; Bohannan 1958.

balanced opposition and not an affair of particular individuals, the notion of the segmentary lineage structure allows for the emergence of men entrusted with considerable authority and wielding great political power. As long as political leadership remains personal and does not become institutionalized into an office, it can be accounted for within the given ideology and the ideological dictum of egalitarianism upheld in spite of considerable political inequality on the ground. The fact that so little attention has been paid to political leadership in societies classified as having segmentary lineage structures, such as that of the Sclavenes, and the fact that inequality of status, political authority, and power have been consistently underplayed in historical analysis is a typical consequence of mistaking the ideology for actuality.[26]

GREAT-MEN, BIG-MEN, AND CHIEFS

In a passage describing the savage Sclavenes, in contrast to the peaceful Physonites, Pseudo-Caesarius claimed that the Sclavenes "call each other with the howl of wolves (τῇ λύκων ὠρυγῇ σφᾶς προσκαλούμενοι)." A Greek linguist, Phaedon Malingoudis, has interpreted the passage as referring to lycanthropy and pertaining to a system of beliefs and rituals, the essential part of which was a ritual transformation of the young warrior into a wolf. The "howling wolves" appear in various other sources, always in connection with warfare. On the other hand, the author of the *Strategikon* knows that, while in Sclavene territory, Roman troops should expect sudden attacks from young Sclavene warriors (οἱ νεώτεροι αὐτῶν). In encounters, they shout (κράζοντες) all together and if their opponents begin to give way at the noise, they attack violently. The inhabitants of Thessalonica were all accustomed to the Sclavene battle cry, after being attacked three times by Sclavene warriors.[27]

It is difficult to decide from this evidence whether or not Malingoudis' interpretation of Pseudo-Caesarius is correct. He seems to suggest that the "howling wolves" may have gone through a kind of initiation that is often associated with secret brotherhoods of warriors, the *Männerbünde* which Georges Dumézil's studies of Indo-European mythologies have rendered famous. It is not impossible, but the evidence is too scarce to make the point convincing. If Malingoudis is right, this evidence would rather suggest that the "howling wolves" were some sort of "age sets," pan-tribal social groupings of young warriors, which cross-cut kinship and descent ties. Some authors pointed to the state-building potency of

---

[26] Lederman 1990:10; Pohl 1988:126–7. See also Holy 1979:19.
[27] Riedinger 1969:302; *Strategikon* XI 4.12 and 39; *Miracles of St Demetrius* I 14.138, I 1.185, and II 4.235–6. See Malingoudis 1990:90–1; Stange-Zhirovova 1980–1; Steindorff 1985.

these associations, since they usually break through the kinship and neighborhood organization of society.[28]

Pseudo-Caesarius' evidence, nevertheless, is important for another reason. Writing in the 560s (see Chapter 2), he was familiar with the region of the Danube frontier, which suggests he had access to first-hand information. Thus, he is the first author to refer to Sclavene chiefs, who were often killed at feasts or on travels, that is during peacetime (συνεχῶς ἀναιροῦντες συνεστιώμενοι ἢ συνοδεύοντες τὸν σφῶν ἡγεμόνα καὶ ἄρχοντα). This seems to indicate that strategies chiefs employed to expand their prominence and draw followings were checked by their kinsmen. Pseudo-Caesarius used this example to show that the Sclavenes were living by their own law and without the rule of anyone (ἀνηγεμόνευτοι), a remark which dovetails with the evidence of other sources. That the purge of would-be tyrants took place during feasts further suggests that chiefs were coordinators of communal ceremonies.[29]

Ever since Elman Service defined chiefdoms as "redistributional societies with a permanent central agency of coordination," chiefs have been viewed as the prevailing characteristics of the social organization in early medieval Europe, which had existed beyond the Roman frontiers and persisted into the migration period. According to current anthropological views, chiefdoms are regionally organized societies with a centralized decision-making hierarchy coordinating activities among several village communities.[30]

Were all Sclavene "kings" of the sixth and seventh century truly chiefs? The terminology employed by Greek sources is very complex and difficult to interpret. Though already used with reference to Sclavenes by Pseudo-Caesarius, the author of the *Strategikon*, and the author of Book II of the *Miracles of St Demetrius*, and with reference to Antes by Menander the Guardsman, the term ἄρχων appears with some consistency only in ninth- and tenth-century sources, such as Theophanes Confessor and Constantine Porphyrogenitus. An archon was a ruler with full, regionally organized authority.[31] To the unknown author of Book II of the

---

[28] Schürtz 1902:324; Lowie 1961; Krader 1968:99; Ausenda 1995:25. For *Männerbünde*, see Dumézil 1969 and Przyluski 1940. Beliefs in lycanthropy were widely spread and by no means restricted to Indo-Europeans. See Eliade 1973; Comba 1991.

[29] Riedinger 1969:302; Procopius, *Wars* VII 14.22; *Strategikon* XI 4.30. See also Benedicty 1963:50. For examples of strategies responsible for the creation and maintenance of regional polities, see Earle 1989:84–5; Webster 1975:466.

[30] Service 1971:134; Hodges 1982:187; Haldon 1993:213. See also Earle 1987:288; Townsend 1985:144; Earle 1989:84.

[31] Riedinger 1969:302; *Miracles of St Demetrius* II 4.271–3; Menander the Guardsman, fr. 5.2; *Strategikon* XI 4.21. See also Kuchma 1991:388. For ἄρχων, see Ferluga 1982. It is not without interest that the translation of ἄρχων in the tenth-century Old Church Slavonic version of *Eratopokriseis* is *knyaz* (prince). See Benedicty 1963:54; Duichev 1957.

Miracles of St Demetrius, Chatzon, the leader of the Sclavenes who besieged Thessalonica, was an "exarch" (ἔξαρχος). The word would later be used in the *Life of St Gregory Decapolites* with reference to Sclavene leaders who were subordinates of the Byzantine emperor. Menander the Guardsman calls Dauritas' "fellow chiefs" ὅσοι ἐν τέλει τοῦ ἔθνους and ἡγεμόνες. Ἡγεμών is a term Menander employs frequently to refer to barbarian leaders. Ambrus and Alamundar, the chiefs of the Saracens subject to the Romans, Sandilkh, the chief of the Utigurs, and Sarosius, the king of the Alans, were also ἡγεμόνες. The same is true, however, for leaders with an obviously different status, such as Sigisbert, the king of the Franks, Sizilbul and Turxanthos, both qagans of the Turks, and Bayan, the qagan of the Avars. By contrast, Alboin, the king of the Lombards, is a μόναρχος, just like Arsilas, the eldest ruler of the Turks. This suggests that those to whom Menander refers as ὅσοι ἐν τέλει τοῦ ἔθνους were not subordinates, or in any way inferior in rank, to Dauritas. All seem to have enjoyed a similar status and joined into what might be best described as a tribal confederation.[32]

Theophylact Simocatta, who wrote in the late 620s on the basis of a source written in the late 500s, has the widest variety of terms. The rulers of the Sclavenes living "at the boundary of the western Ocean" are ἐθνάρχαι, a term Theophylact only employed for rulers of distant, almost legendary, tribes. Both Peiragastus, the tribal leader of 594, and the "appointed officers" of the Sclavenes under Avar rule are ταξιάρχοι. This is a word Theophylact commonly applies to subordinate commanders of the Roman army. Peiragastus, however, is also a φυλάρχος, like Ogyrus and Zogomus, the "tribal chiefs" of the Ghassanid Arabs.[33] Finally, Musocius is a 'ρῆξ. The only other instance in which Theophylact Simocatta employs this word is in reference to the king of the Lombards. The author of the *Strategikon* employed the same word for the Sclavene "kings," in general. Less than a century later, the unknown author of Book II of the *Miracles of St Demetrius* applied the same title to both Perbundos and the "kings" of the Drugubites. The word was often used in late Roman sources in reference to independent barbarian leaders.

---

[32] Menander the Guardsman, fr. 21; see Levinskaia and Tokhtas'ev 1991b:348. For other ἡγεμόνες, see Menander the Guardsman, fr. 2.1, 4.2, 5.1, 6.1, 9.3, 11, 12.4, and 19.1. The same term is used for Alamundar by Theophylact Simocatta (III 17.7). For μόναρχος, see Menander the Guardsman, fr. 12.1 and 19.1. For ἔξαρχος, see the *Miracles of St Demetrius* II 1.193; Weiss and Katsanakis 1988:136. See also Antoljak 1982:386; Ivanova 1987:61.

[33] Φυλάρχος: Theophylact Simocatta VII 4.13 and II 2.5. Ἐθνάρχης was also the ruler of the "nation of Kolch," who was defeated and killed in battle by the qagan of the Turks (VII 8.6). For Sclavene ταξιάρχοι, see VI 2.12, VII 5.4, VI 4.5. For other ταξιάρχοι, see II 12. 7 (Ansimuth, a Roman brigadier in Thrace), VI 8.9 (Alexander, a brigadier in Priscus' army), and II 3.1 (Vitalius, a Roman commander on the eastern front).

Such leaders had significant power over their fellow tribesmen, a feature easily recognizable in Musocius' case: "But the Gepid described everything and revealed things in detail, saying that the prisoners *were subjects of Musocius*, who was called *rex* in the barbarian tongue (ὑπὸ Μουσώκιον τὸν λεγόμενον ῥῆγα, τῇ τῶν βαρβάρων φωνῇ) [emphasis added]." It is interesting to note that Menander the Guardsman, and the author of Book II of the *Miracles of St Demetrius* referred to ἡγεμόνες and ἄρχοντες only in plural, whereas ῥῆξ was bestowed on individuals, often known by name (Musocius, Perbundos). This suggests that there were many Sclavene leaders at any one time, but not all had the same kind of power. While Pseudo-Caesarius' leaders were killed at feasts or on travels, arguably by their fellow tribesmen, "king" Musocius is explicitly said to have had "subjects."[34]

In anthropological terms, this variety of leadership forms may be best described as the coexistence of three different sorts of power. Anthropologists distinguish chiefs, whose powers are largely ascribed and coincide with privileged control of wealth, from big-men, whose powers are largely achieved and derived from the manipulation of wealth, and great-men, whose powers may be largely ascribed or achieved, but are not based upon the control of wealth. The distinction between chiefs and big-men goes back to Marshall Sahlins, who depicted the typical Melanesian leader as a "big-man," because he achieved his position in a context of egalitarian ideology and competition, and his Polynesian counterpart as a chief, because he succeeded to a hereditary position in a context of social hierarchy. "Big-man" arose as a conceptual model primarily because of the need to differentiate between self-made leaders and ascribed chiefs. Big-men are leaders who organize feasts and festivals, daring warriors and commanders in warfare, aggressors in interpersonal and intergroup conflict, orators, directors of communal work and enterprise, men of authority who arbitrate disputes within the community, ritual practitioners, magicians, and sorcerers. Some dominate by their physical strength, particularly in contexts where leading warriors are politically important, some by force of character. The concept of big-man leadership was applied outside Melanesia when achievement rather than ascribed leader status was under discussion. Big-men are more likely to arise in exchange activities involving the entire community. When they compete as peers, the stakes are prestige, wealth, or even physical

---

[34] Theophylact Simocatta VI 9.1 and VI 10.13; *Strategikon* XI 4.30; *Miracles of St Demetrius* II 4.231 and II 4.235–6. For Musocius, the Sclavene "king," see also Benedicty 1963:51 and 1965:66; Havlík 1974:184–5; Ivanova 1987:58. Given that the term ῥῆξ appears in several independant sources, L. M. Whitby's argument (1982b:428) that Theophylact apparently misused a Latin term is untenable. See also Baldwin 1977; Ivanova 1980:88 and 101.

well-being of their respective social groups, not just the leader's own status.[35]

More recently, Maurice Godelier took as a starting point that the big-men system is derived from the great-men system. To Godelier, a big-man belongs within a peculiar institutional system, in which the principle of competitive exchange takes precedence over the principle of war. By contrast, the great-man advances alone toward the enemy lines, followed by a handful of assistants, and engages in single combat with any warrior prepared to match his skill and strength. He gains prestige, a name for himself, and admiration, but not wealth. In times of war, his authority is unquestioned; in peacetime his function disappears, but his prestige remains.[36]

As described by Theophylact Simocatta, Ardagastus fits well the model of the great-man. No particular title is attached to his name, though he appears twice in Theophylact's narrative. Ardagastus had a remarkable physical size and strength, which helped him avoid being captured by Romans in 593. He had a "territory" of his own, which Priscus' troops devastated in that same year. It is interesting to note that the inhabitants of this χώρα are never referred to as his subjects, only as "Sclavene hordes" or his "followers." Ardagastus may have been a warrior leader, "specializing" in the organization of raids across the Danube. Warriors from afar may have come to his "territory" and joined him in his plundering expeditions. No mention is made of a village and, if we are to believe Theophylact Simocatta, Ardagastus was on the point of launching a new raid against the Roman provinces, when Priscus' attack took him by surprise. Ardagastus also led the raid of 585, which was intercepted by Comentiolus not far from Adrianople. Ardagastus was perceived as a real threat, which results from the fact that his χώρα was the first target of Priscus' operations across the Danube. Ardagastus' power was most likely achieved, with his remarkable physical strength at the basis of this political prominence. He had already begun to build a name for himself, when Priscus' expedition put an end to his career. Though he may have survived the Roman aggression, Ardagastus fell back into social oblivion, for nothing is reported about him in the otherwise well-documented events of the following decade.[37]

Can we bestow the title of great-men upon other Sclavene leaders?

[35] Sahlins 1963. See also Allen 1984:20; Khazanov 1985:86; Brown 1990:97 and 100; Lederman 1990:6; Whitehouse 1992:118; Wason 1994:45. [36] Godelier 1986:105 and 109–10.
[37] Theophylact Simocatta I 7.3–6, VI 7.1, 3, and 5, VI 9.1 and 6. See also Zasterová 1971:78–9; Avenarius 1991:29. The correct translation of τὰ τῶν Σκλαυηνῶν πλήθη ἀπόδημα is "the Sclavene hordes from abroad," not "(Ardagastus was sending) the Sclavene hordes abroad," as Michael and Mary Whitby have it. In this case, ἀπόδημα is an adjective modifying πλήθη, not an adverb.

Peiragastus is briefly mentioned by Theophylact in relation to Peter's campaign north of the Danube. He was therefore a contemporary of Ardagastus. To the author of the *Feldzugsjournal*, which served as the main source for Theophylact's narrative in Book VII (see Chapter 2), Peiragastus was a "brigadier." The word, which often appears in relation to subordinate commanders of the Roman army, indicates that the author of this campaign diary was himself a military or was writing for one. That Peiragastus is called by the same name as commanders of the Roman army also suggests he was just a military leader. It is true that he is then called "the tribal leader (φύλαρχος) of that barbarian horde." Knowing that the same term is applied to two Saracen leaders, who appear in Book II, it is possible that it was Theophylact (who wrote much later), not the author of the *Feldzugsjournal*, who applied the word to Peiragastus. Moreover, what we know about him from Theophylact refers exclusively to the military confrontation with Peter's troops. Mention is made of forces under his command, but significantly enough, unlike Ardagastus, Peiragastus had no "territory." Immediately after his death in battle, the Sclavenes "turned to flight" and the Roman troops were concerned with pursuing them, not with ravaging neighboring villages that might have existed in the area. We may conclude that Peiragastus and his "horde" had come from afar in what might have been an expedition against Peter's army. It is likely, therefore, that Peiragastus was nothing more than a warrior leader.[38]

The association between Pseudo-Caesarius' leaders and feasting suggests they were big-men. Generation of debt and the prospect of future gain for all supporters are the critical aspects for understanding the emergence of accumulators through competitive feasting. This seems to be supported by the archaeological evidence, particularly by the intrasite distribution of artifacts discussed in Chapter 6. We have seen that big-men are prominent in those contexts in which personification or embodiment of collective interest and responsibility is not only possible, but becomes a recurrent practice. They play a key role in "making" groups. Their oratorical interventions during meetings, together with private persuasions, transform actions that would otherwise be construed as merely personal into collective ones as well. This applies to Menander the Guardsman's Dauritas and to Fredegar's Samo. Both appear as speaking in the name of their respective groups, boldly proclaiming their independence and thus "creating" their new identity. Unlike Dauritas, Samo's *utilitas* won him not only the admiration of the Wends, but also his election as their "king." The Wendish *rex* proved his skills as commander in warfare, his

---

[38] Theophylact Simocatta VII 4.13 and 5.4.

prudence and courage always bringing victory to the Wends. A self-made leader, Samo forged alliances with several Wendish families, marrying no less than twelve Wendish women, "who bore him twenty-two sons and fifteen daughters." He was involved in long-distance trade and his economic and political influence produced not only wealth and high status, but also strong alliances, particularly after the debacle of the Frankish army at *castrum Wogastisburc*.[39]

More than twenty years earlier, another *rex*, Musocius, had "subjects," that he could send to reconnoitre or to give assistance to refugees from neighboring territories. Strong ties of loyalty linked this "king" to his subjects, as suggested by the episode of the Sclavene prisoners, who, though interrogated under torture, did not betray their chief. Unlike Samo, however, Musocius' chiefdom was territorially more limited. In order to destroy this chiefdom, all Priscus needed to do was to capture Musocius and to devastate his village. By contrast, the power of Perbundos, "king" of the Rynchines (τοῦ Ῥυγχίνων ῥηγός, τοὔνομα Περβούνδου), was built upon a special relationship with the Byzantine imperial authority. Chief Perbundos wore the dress of the Byzantine aristocracy and fluently spoke Greek. Arrested and brought to Constantinople, he found well-connected friends to help him out of trouble. Like Musocius, Perbundos was also very popular. When he was finally captured and executed, all "Sclavene nations" (τὰ Σκλαβίνων ἔθνη) around Thessalonica rose in rebellion and attacked the city.[40]

The examples of Musocius, Perbundos, and especially Samo show the importance for chiefdoms of direct or indirect contact with a previously existing state. The most important means by which a decentralized system could enter the orbit of the Roman "Commonwealth" was the *foedus*, a pact between Romans and barbarians whereby the latter could settle on Roman territory in return for serving as a military buffer against other barbarians. An interesting example is Procopius' episode of the "phoney Chilbudius." When his story "was carried about and reached the entire nation of the Antes (Ἄνται σχεδὸν ἅπαντες, κοινὴν δὲ εἶναι τὴν πρᾶξιν ἠξίουν)," Chilbudius was forced to take on a false identity, claiming that he was a Roman general. Under this cloak, he was immediately sent to Constantinople to negotiate a treaty with Justinian, by

---

[39] Menander the Guardsman, fr. 21; Fredegar IV 48 and 68. Dervan, *dux gente Surbiorum*, "placed himself and his people under the rule of Samo." See also Havlík 1974:183; Avenarius 1987:73; Fritze 1994:281 with n. 1736. Though Samo's rank, wealth, and status hinged on achievement, his rank was not inherited. No mention is made of any of his twenty-two sons becoming a "king" after Samo's death, despite clear evidence that the Frankish chronicler outlived the Wendish leader. Accumulators and competitive feasting: Hayden and Gargett 1990:14 and 16. Big-men and group making: Lederman 1990:10; Rousseau 1985:41

[40] Theophylact Simocatta VI 8.14 and VI 9.1; *Miracles of St Demetrius* II 4.231, 233–7, and 242.

which the Antes received an old Roman city, Turris, as well as stipends, in exchange for becoming the emperor's allies (ἔνσπονδοι) and protecting the Danube frontier against Hunnic inroads.[41]

Whatever the source for this story and the degree to which Procopius reworked the account (see Chapter 2), it is clear that in his eyes the Antes, who "are not ruled by one man, but . . . lived from old under a democracy," needed a chief in order to negotiate the *foedus* with Justinian. "Chilbudius" was not a person, but an office, by which their acephalous, de-centralized system (Ἄνται . . . ἅπαντες) could turn into a loyal ally of the emperor. Some time later, when the Antes were attacked by Avars (see Chapter 3), they already had ἄρχοντες and an ambassador of "noble" origin. The episode of the powerful Mezamer, "son of Idariz and brother of Kelagast," points to the existence of conical clans, one of the most important social characteristics of chiefdoms. Several segments were now ranked relative to each other, and their leaders, true chiefs, hold offices in an extensive polity, capable of military mobilization against the Avars.[42]

CONCLUSION

There is no indication of Slavic chiefs before *c.* 560. Notwithstanding his detailed description of Slavic society, Procopius knew nothing about them. He carefully recorded, however, the names of several other barbarian leaders in the area, especially kings of the Gepids, Herules, and Lombards, or Cutrigur chieftains. That this is no accident is shown by Procopius' claim that both Sclavene and Antes "are not ruled by one man, but they lived from old under a democracy."[43] No Slavic raid recorded in the *Wars* seems to have been organized by military leaders and the story of the "phoney Chilbudius," with its emphasis on the false identity of the would-be chief of the Antes resonates with Procopius' notion of Slavic "democracy". The Slavic ethnographic *excursus*, which is probably based on his interviews with Sclavene and Antian mercenaries in Italy, is the longest in all of Procopius' work. As a consequence, the absence of Slavic leaders cannot be explained by either Procopius' lack of interest or his hostility towards those whom he viewed as nomads (see Chapter 2). His image of the Slavs is much more favorable than that of their neighbors in Procopius' *oikumene*. But he seems to have denied political leadership

---

[41] Procopius, *Wars* VII 13.24–6 and 14.1–6. For chiefdoms and neighboring states, see Kipp and Schortman 1989. For the role of the Roman frontier in state formation in *barbaricum*, see Willems 1989:43–4.
[42] Procopius, *Wars* VII 14.22; Menander the Guardsman, fr. 3. For conical clans and chiefdoms, see Yoffee 1993:62.   [43] Procopius, *Wars* VII 14.22.

only to the Slavs. There is no reason to believe, however, that Procopius deliberately omitted the names of Slavic military leaders, when he was so attentive in distinguishing Sclavene "throngs" from Sclavene "armies" (see Chapter 3).

The first political leaders appear in Pseudo-Caesarius' *Eratopokriseis*, which was written in the 560s. The largest number and the widest variety of leadership forms, however, occur in sources regarding the last quarter of the sixth century. Names of individual chiefs suddenly appear in Menander the Guardsman, *Strategikon*, and Theophylact Simocatta. In sharp contrast to the picture given by Procopius, the author of the *Strategikon* even suggests that Sclavene chiefs may at times unite and accept, albeit temporarily, being "ruled by one man." This is also the period in which chiefs emerged, who spoke in the name of their respective groups, boldly proclaiming their independence. It is also during this period that chiefs, often mentioned by name, were leading more or less successful raids across the Danube. These were the raids which most strikingly coincided with major engagements of the Roman armies in the east. The chiefs knew where and when to strike, in order to avoid major concentrations of Roman troops. This strongly suggests that among all three categories of leaders discussed in this chapter, which may have possibly existed at that time, warrior leaders (great-men) were the most common.

The end of the sixth century is also the period in which we can see increasing competition between chiefs. The author of the *Strategikon* knew that there were many Sclavene "kings, always at odds with each other," a useful political detail for any Roman general who happened to wage war against any one of them. What were the stakes of this competition, we can only guess. As shown in Chapter 6, the second half of the sixth century was a period of dramatic change in the material culture of communities living north of the Danube river. Shortly before and after AD 600, symbols of personal identity were in higher demand. The greatest number of links between ornamental patterns displayed by bow fibulae found in Romania, Crimea, and Mazuria is that of specimens dated to this period. Long-distance connections, as well as the display of *different* patterns on various groups of "Slavic" bow fibulae point to social competition. If the intrasite distribution of artifacts in the common front region of the sites analyzed in Chapter 6 can, in any way, be associated with competitive feasting, which is a typical feature for big-man leadership, we may be able to visualize some aspects of this competition. War, however, was the overwhelming concern of those who, though unable to fight in ordered battle, were nevertheless extremely skillful in ambushing Roman troops. That Slavic society was geared up for warfare is evident from the significant quantity of weapons, especially arrow and spear-heads, that were found on sixth- and seventh-century sites.[44] It is therefore possible that at least some of the evidence for destruction by fire, which sixth- to seventh-century sites in Romania, Moldova, and Ukraine occasionally produced, is the result of inter-group conflicts. After all, as the author of the *Strategikon* observed, in the Slavic "democracy", "nobody is willing to yield to another."[45]

---

[44] *Strategikon* XI 4.30. It was often noted that "Slavic" settlements produced no weapons (e.g., Dolinescu-Ferche 1984:145). The archaeological evidence, however, gives a different picture. Arrows: Dolinescu-Ferche 1979:205 fig. 22/15; Rosetti 1934:212 fig. 7/4; Dolinescu-Ferche and Constantiniu 1981:322 fig. 18/9; Turcu and Ciuceanu 1992:200; Teodor 1980:fig. 31/8; Mitrea 1974–6:figs. 16/1 and 15/5 and 1994:328 fig. 27/5; Teodor 1984b:29 fig. 6/7; Dolinescu-Ferche 1986:fig. 22/21, 22; Székely 1974–6:pl. x/24 and 25; Toropu 1976:211; Rafalovich and Lapushnian 1974:133 fig. 10/15; Rafalovich 1968:96 fig. 29/8. Spears: Zirra and Cazimir 1963:60; Constantiniu 1965b:182; Székely 1992:pl. X/8; Vakulenko and Prikhodniuk 1984:68 fig. 38/1. For a battle-axe, see Vakulenko and Prikhodniuk 1984:68 fig. 39/9.

[45] *Strategikon* XI 4.14. Heavy destruction by fire of numerous buildings is evident at Bucharest-Măicăneşti and Kavetchina. By contrast, only two buildings of the large settlement at Davideni were destroyed by fire. The same is true for Selişte and Dulceanca III.

CONCLUSION: THE MAKING OF THE SLAVS

As its title suggests, the subject matter of this book is not the Slavs, but the process leading to what is now known as "the Slavs." This process was a function of both ethnic formation and ethnic identification. In both cases, the "Slavs" were the object, not the subject. The preceding chapters have presented a series of perspectives on the history and archaeology of the Lower Danube area during the sixth and seventh centuries. Each approached a different aspect of the process of constructing a Slavic *ethnie* and each highlighted specific themes and arguments. This chapter will review those themes, but will also attempt to string them all together into a tripartite conclusion. In doing so, it will focus on the major issues presented in the introduction: the migration and the making of the Slavs. Though in agreement with those who maintain that the history of the Slavs began in the sixth century, I argue that the Slavs were an invention of the sixth century. Inventing, however, presupposed both imagining or labeling by outsiders and self-identification.[1]

MIGRATION

A brief examination of the historiography of the "Slavic problem" yields an important conclusion: the dominant discourse in Slavic studies, that of "expert" linguists and archaeologists, profoundly influenced the study of the early Slavs. Though the evidence, both historical and archaeological, presented itself in a historical light, historians were expected merely to comb the written sources for evidence to match what was already known from the linguistic-archaeological model. Because this model was based on widely spread ideas about such critical concepts as culture, migration, and language, the basic assumptions on which the model was based were rarely, if ever, questioned. One such assumption was that

---

[1] Ivanov 1991c and 1993.

ethnies, like languages, originate in an *Urheimat* and then expand over large areas through migration. Migration was defined in the terms of the *Kulturkreis* school, as the relatively rapid spread of racial and cultural elements. This led many scholars to abandon a serious consideration of the historical evidence and to postulate instead a Slavic *Urheimat* located in the marshes of the Pripet river. Chased from their homeland in the North by the rigors of the harsh climate, the Slavs then inundated Eastern Europe. A Slavic homeland implied, however, that the history of the Slavs was older than the first Slavic raids known from historical sources. The cornerstone of all theories attempting to project the Slavs into prehistory was Jordanes' *Getica*. Jordanes equated the Sclavenes and Antes with the Venethi also known from much earlier sources, such as Pliny the Elder, Tacitus, and Ptolemy. This made it possible to claim the Venedi of Tacitus, Pliny, and Ptolemy for the Slavic history. It also provided a meaning to archaeological research of "Slavic antiquity." A Polish linguist, Tadeusz Lehr-Spławiński, first suggested that the archaeological culture of the Vistula basin during the first century BC to the first century AD, which was known as the Przeworsk culture, was that of Tacitus' Venedi. Soviet archaeologists argued that the Slavic Venethi were the majority of the population in the area covered by the Chernyakhov culture of the fourth century AD. They claimed that by AD 300, the Antes separated themselves from the linguistic and archaeological block of the Venedi, and were soon followed by the Sclavenes. More often than not, therefore, the task of the archaeologist was to illustrate conclusions already drawn from Jordanes' account of the Slavic Venethi.

Without any doubt, Jordanes had in mind contemporary concerns when describing barbarians living beyond imperial frontiers. He also used written, ancient sources regarding the regions under his scrutiny. When applying such sources, however, what was his concept of geography? What was he thinking about the ethnographic material provided by his sources in the light of what was known to him about recent developments in those same regions? Why did he use three different names for what was apparently one group of people? In Chapter 2, as well as elsewhere, I attempted to answer these questions while addressing issues of authorship and chronology of sources. My argument is that instead of being an eyewitness account, Jordanes' description of Sclavenes and Antes was based on two or more maps with different geographical projections, the imaginary space of which he filled with both sixth-century and much earlier ethnic names he found in various sources. This seriously diminishes the value of the most important piece of evidence invoked by advocates of both a considerable antiquity of the Slavs and their migration from the North. Moreover, no source dated before Justinian's reign

(527–65) refers to Slavs or Slavic Venethi. Despite some overlap in time-spans covered by Procopius' *Wars* and the chronicle of Marcellinus Comes (including the continuation to 548 added by another author), there is no mention of Slavs in the chronicle. Procopius, on the other hand, made it very clear that a "Slavic problem" arose, along with others, only during Justinian's reign.[2]

The Slavs did not migrate from the Pripet marshes because of hostile environmental conditions. Nor did they develop forms of social organ-ization enabling them to cope with such conditions and presumably based on cooperation and social equality (*zadruga*). Niederle's thesis does not stand against the existing evidence and has at its basis an outdated concept of migration. That the migrationist model should be abandoned is also suggested by the archaeological evidence examined in Chapter 6. No class of evidence matches current models for the archaeological study of (pre)historic migration. More important, assemblages of the Lower Danube area, where, according to the migrationist model, the Slavs migrated from the Pripet marshes, long antedate the earliest evidence available from assemblages in the alleged *Urheimat*. Short-distance pop-ulation movements, but not migration, must have accompanied the implementation of a form of "itinerant agriculture," which, though not based on the slash-and-burn method, may have encouraged settlement mobility.

That the Slavs were present on the northern bank of the Danube before the implementation of Justinian's building program in the mid-500s is demonstrated by their raids known from Procopius. It will prob-ably remain unknown whether or not any of the groups arguably living in contemporary settlements excavated by Romanian archaeologists called themselves Sclavenes or Antes. This, however, was the region from which Romans recruited mercenaries for the war in Italy. This is also the region that produced the largest number of coins struck under Emperors Anastasius and Justin I, as well as during Justinian's early regnal years. A small number of hoards with last coins minted during this period was also found in this area. It is hard to judge from the existing evidence, but from what we have it appears that the Slavic raids mentioned by Procopius originated in this same region. This may also explain why Chilbudius' campaigns of the early 530s targeted against Sclavenes, Antes, and Cutrigurs were directed to a region not far from the Danube river.

We are fortunate to have first-hand sources of information for the late 500s and the early 600s, such as the *Strategikon*, and the campaign diary used by Theophylact Simocatta's Books VI–VIII. In both cases, our

---

[2] Procopius, *Secret History* 18.20–1.

knowledge, however restricted, of what was going on north of the Danube river is based, almost certainly, on eyewitness accounts. Neither Theophylact nor the author of the *Strategikon* knew any other area of Slavic settlements except that located north of the Danube frontier. Furthermore, no clear evidence exists of an outright migration of the Slavs (Sclavenes) to the regions south of the Danube until the early years of Heraclius' reign. Phocas' revolt of 602 was not followed by an irresistible flood of Sclavenes submerging the Balkans. In fact, there are no raids recorded during Phocas' reign, either by Sclavenes or by Avars. By contrast, large-scale raiding activities resumed during Heraclius' early regnal years. This is also confirmed by the archaeological evidence discussed in Chapter 4. Some forts along the Danube or in the interior were destroyed by fire at some point between Justinian's and Maurice's reigns. In many cases, however, restoration followed destruction and forts were abandoned at various dates without signs of violence. After Maurice's assassination, Phocas' army returned to the Danube and remained there at least until 605, if not 620. This is clearly attested by Sebeos and does not contradict in any way what we know from the archaeological and numismatic evidence. The earliest archaeological evidence of settlement assemblages postdating the general withdrawal of Roman armies from the Balkans is that of the 700s. This suggests that there was no "Slavic tide" in the Balkans following the presumed collapse of the Danube frontier. In addition, the archaeological evidence confirms the picture drawn from the analysis of written sources, namely that the "Slavs" were isolated pockets of population in various areas of the Balkans, which seem to have experienced serious demographic decline in the seventh century.

The discussion in Chapter 4 has been based on the concept that the disintegration of the military system in the Balkans, which Justinian implemented in the mid-500s, was the result not so much of the destruction inflicted by barbarian invasions, as of serious economic and financial problems caused both by the emperor's policies elsewhere and by the impossibility of providing sufficient economic support to his gigantic building program of defense. This conclusion is substantiated by the analysis of sixth-century Byzantine coin hoards, which suggest that inflation, not barbarian raids, was responsible for high rates of non-retrieval.

ETHNICITY AND *ETHNIE*: THE VIEW FROM THE INSIDE

After Chilbudius' death in 533, there was a drastic change in Justinian's agenda in the Balkans. From this moment until Maurice's campaigns of the 590s, no offensive strategy underpinned imperial policies in the area. Instead, Justinian began an impressive plan of fortification, of a size and quality the Balkans had never witnessed before. The project, or at least the most important part of it, was probably completed in some twenty years. It was completed in its basic lines when Procopius finished Book IV of his *Buildings*. In addition, Justinian remodeled the administrative structure of the Balkans and created the *quaestura exercitus* in order to support both financially and militarily those border provinces which were most affected by his building program. He also shifted military responsibilities from army generals to local authorities, especially bishops (novel 11).

These measures were not taken in response to any major threat, for Roman troops were still in control of the left bank of the Danube, possibly through bridge-heads such as those of Turnu Severin (Drobeta) and Celei (Sucidava). This is shown by the edict 13, issued in 538, which clearly stated that troops were still sent (if only as a form of punishment) north of the Danube river, "in order to watch at the frontier of that place."

In addition to military and administrative measures, Justinian offered his alliance to the Antes (*foedus* of 545) and began to recruit mercenaries from among both Sclavenes and Antes for his war in Italy. All this suggests that Chilbudius' campaigns of the early 530s opened a series of very aggressive measures on the Danube frontier, which were meant to consolidate the Roman military infrastructure in the Balkans. It is during this period of aggressive intrusion into affairs north of the Danube frontier that Sclavenes and Antes entered the orbit of Roman interests. Justinian's measures were meant to stabilize the situation in *barbaricum*, which is why the *foedus* with the Antes was only signed after the end of the war between Antes and Sclavenes. Whether or not he intended to create a buffer zone between the Danube frontier and the steppe corridor to the northeast, Justinian's goal was only partially fulfilled. Two devastating invasions of the Cutrigurs, in 539/40 and 558/9, respectively, broke through both Justinian's system of alliances and his fortified frontier. None of the subsequent Sclavene raids can be compared in either size or consequences to the Cutrigur invasions. However, knowing that the first recorded raid of the Sclavenes is in 545, it is possible that Sclavene raiding was a response to Justinian's aggressive policies, with both the fortified frontier and his barbarian allies. The Sclavenes may have felt encouraged by the Cutrigur breakthrough of 540, but it is no accident that their first raid coincided with Justinian's alliance with the Antes.

The interruption of Sclavene raids coincides with the completion of the building program. With the exception of Zabergan's invasion of 558/9, there were no raids across the Danube for twenty-five years. This is an indication of the efficiency of the defensive system, consisting of

339

three interrelated fortification lines, the strongest of which was not along the Danube, but along the Stara Planina. Later, this grandiose program was extended to the northwestern Balkans, following the defeat of the Ostrogoths and the conquest of Dalmatia. Along the Danube and in the immediate hinterland, forts were relatively small (less than 1 hectare of enclosed area). Each one may have been garrisoned by a *numerus* (*tagma*), the minimal unit of the early Byzantine army, with up to 500 men. This may explain why small armies of Sclavenes (such as those responsible for the raids in the late 540s and early 550s) had no problems taking a relatively large number of forts. It also explains why Sclavene or Avar armies, no matter how large, moved with remarkable speed after crossing the Danube, without encountering any major resistance. The excavation of forts and the estimation of the number of soldiers who may have manned these forts in the Iron Gates area indicate that the entire sector may have relied for its defense on forces amounting to some 5,000 men, the equivalent of a Roman legion.[3] If, as argued in Chapter 7, the population of a Sclavene χωρίον was somewhat inferior in size to one or two bandons (400 to 800 men), we may be able to visualize the effort of mobilizing warriors for a successful raid across the Danube, which a great-man like Ardagastus may have faced. It is hard to believe that any chief was able to raise an army of 100,000, as maintained by Menander the Guardsman.[4] The 5,000 warriors who attacked Thessalonica at some point before 586, nevertheless, is a likely figure. In any case, there is no reason to doubt the ability of Archbishop John, who may have been an eyewitness, to give a gross estimate of the enemy's force. If so, then this indicates that raids strong enough to reach distant targets, such as Thessalonica, usually aimed at mobilizing a military force roughly equivalent to a Roman legion. Furthermore, there is no evidence, until the early regnal years of Heraclius, of an outright migration of the Slavs (Sclavenes) to the region south of the Danube river.[5] No evidence exists that Romans ever tried to prevent the crossing, despite the existence of a Danube military fleet. Moreover, all major confrontations with Sclavene armies or "throngs" took place south of the Stara Planina mountains.

Nevertheless, the efficiency of the fortified frontier, at least in its initial phase, cannot be doubted. During the last fifteen years of Justinian's reign, no Slavic raid crossed the Danube. The implementation of the for-

[3] This figure may have been even smaller if, as suggested in Chapter 4, some forts were inhabited by soldiers with their families. [4] Menander the Guardsman, fr. 20,2.
[5] Forts, at least those of medium and large size, were permanently occupied, but the number of soldiers actually manning these forts may have considerably varied in time. Judging from the general picture of military operations in the 500s, it is likely, however, that this number was often too small. By contrast, during the fourth century no less than 15,000 *milites ripenses* were in charge with the Danube frontier in Dobrudja. See Aricescu 1977:189.

tified frontier seems to have been accompanied by its economic "closure." This is shown by the absence of both copper and gold coins dated between 545 and 565 in both stray finds and hoards found in Romania. The economic "closure" was not deliberate, for it is likely that the strain on coin circulation, which is also visible in hoards found south of the Danube frontier, was caused by the very execution of Justinian's gigantic plan. Fewer coins were now withdrawn from circulation, and even fewer found their way into hoards. It is possible, however, that the implementation of the fortified frontier strained not only the coin circulation within and outside the Empire, but also economic relations between communities living north and south of the Danube frontier, respectively.

The evidence of hoards shows that most were equivalent to the cost of one or two *modii* of Egyptian wheat. We can speculate that hoards found north of the Danube were payments for small quantities of grain sold to soldiers in sixth-century forts south of the Danube. In any case, these hoards, which primarily consist of copper, testify to trading activity. Stray finds of coins struck for Justinian and his followers, some of which were found in settlement contexts, confirm the hypothesis that Byzantine coins were used for commercial and non-commercial transactions in communities living north of the Danube. Whether or not these coins were used as "primitive money," their very existence presupposes that copper coinage was of some value even outside the system which guaranteed its presumably fiduciary value. If so, the inflation delineated by the analysis of hoards found in the Balkans (south of the Danube river), which became visible especially after 550, as the purchasing power of the follis decreased drastically, as well as the economic strains on the general circulation of goods, may have affected also the owners of the Romanian hoards. It is interesting to note, therefore, that between 545 and 565 the coin circulation was interrupted both north and south of the Danube river. This interruption was most probably accompanied by a strong crisis in trading activities across the Danube and a subsequent scarcity of goods of Roman provenance, which may have been obtained by such means and played, as shown in Chapter 6, an important role as prestige goods.[6] This may have increased the level of social competition and encouraged the rise of leaders whose basis of power was now warfare. It is most probably during this period that we can see the first signs of emblemic styles in the material culture changes described in Chapter 6. Great-men, like

---

[6] It is important to note that trading activities signalized by stray finds and hoards found north of the Danube frontier did not cease after 602. Copper coins of Phocas and Heraclius continued to appear south and east of the Carpathians, which suggests that at that time the forts from which these coins were coming had not yet been abandoned.

Ardagastus, and big-men, like the leaders mentioned by Pseudo-Caesarius, represented different responses to these historical conditions. These two forms of power may not only have coexisted, but also have been used by the same individuals. One way or another, both forms implied access to prestige goods, the quantity of which, if we are to believe Menander the Guardsman, was considerable. It is because he knew that he would find the land of the Sclavenes "full of gold" that Bayan, the qagan of the Avars, decided to launch his punitive expedition against Dauritas and his fellow chiefs. It is because of prestige goods, such as gold, silver, horses, and weapons, that the Sclavene warriors of 581, according to John of Ephesus, were still ravaging the Balkan provinces in 584. Finally, the evidence of amphoras found on sites north of the Danube frontier, many of which are from the second half of the sixth century, points to the same direction. Olive oil, wine, or *garum* were as good for showing off as horses and weapons. However, Byzantium was not the only source of prestige goods. The study of "Slavic" bow fibulae in Chapter 6 highlighted multiple and very complicated networks for the procurement of such goods. Finally, the analysis of hoards of silver in Chapter 4 and that of silver and bronze in Chapter 5 suggests that around AD 600, this was by no means a unique phenomenon.

The majority of sites found next to the Danube frontier and in the neighboring regions of Romania, Moldova, and Ukraine produced a relatively large number of artifacts that indicate a date in the second half of the sixth century or in the early seventh century. Though many such sites may have come into existence at an earlier date, artifacts displaying emblemic styles, such as "Slavic" bow fibulae became popular only after *c.* 550. Such dress accessories point to long-distance relations with communities in Mazuria and Crimea, which may indicate gifts or matrimonial alliances. Specimens brought from such distant locations into the Lower Danube area were quickly imitated in less sophisticated ornamentation, apparently in an effort to respond to an increasing local demand of symbols of group identity. Since "Slavic" bow fibulae from Romania were primarily found in settlements and since there is always only one fibula per settlement, it is possible that these dress accessories were symbols of social identity, which served as markers of social status for the newly emerging elites. The analysis of the intrasite distribution of artifacts presented in Chapter 6 reveals the existence, on many sociopetal sites, of a communal front region, which was both a locus of communal activities involving consumption of special foods (flat loaves of bread) and an arena of social competition, a "beyond-the-household" context for displays of leadership symbols. It is tempting to relate the results of this analysis, particularly the connection between bow fibulae and the communal front region, to the evidence of Pseudo-Caesarius, who associated chiefs with feasting. The mechanisms by which some of the big-man-like leaders known from written sources may have reached power had probably to do with the orchestration of communal ceremonies, of feasts and assemblies, in which those leaders played a crucial role.

The earliest changes in material culture which can be associated with emblemic styles and arguably represent some form of group identity postdate by a few decades the first mention of Sclavenes and Antes in historical sources. Can we call (Slavic) ethnicity this identity constructed by material culture means? The analysis presented in Chapter 5 shows that material culture may have been and indeed was used for the construction of ethnicity. Despite intensive interaction across the "no man's land" between the Tisza and the Danube, clear material culture distinctions were maintained in a wide range of artifacts. Material culture contrasts were created and maintained in order to justify between-group competition. As a consequence, emblemic styles were particularly visible during the Lombard-Gepid wars of the mid-500s. Because group identity, and especially ethnicity, necessitated public displays of such styles, artifacts used for the construction of ethnicity were, more often than not, associated with the female apparel, in particular with that of aristocratic women. The same is true for hoards of silver and bronze in the Middle Dnieper area. In addition, hoards emphasize that an important route to social advancement was access to foreign goods, such as Byzantine silver plate. Finally, ethnicity, as defined in the first chapter, presupposes an orientation to the past, determined by charismatic entrepreneurs, who gather adherents by using familiar amalgamative metaphors. The inspiration for many ornamental patterns on "Slavic" brooches were fifth-century decorative patterns, such as the Gáva-Domolospuszta scrollwork, brooch forms of the Aquileia class, or pairs of bird heads. At least bird heads can be viewed as "citations" from the "heroic" past, for this decoration was typically associated with artifacts dated to the times of Attila's Hunnic Empire.[7]

To judge from the existing evidence, the rise of the local elites was coincidental with the dissemination of emblemic styles which may have represented some form of group identity. It is very likely that this is more than simple coincidence. Big-men and chiefs became prominent especially in contexts in which they embodied collective interest and responsibility. Chiefs like Dauritas and Samo "created" groups by speaking and taking action in the name of their respective communities. Political and military mobilization was the response to the historical conditions

---

[7] See Werner 1956:72–3; Bierbrauer 1994:147; Kazanski 1993.

created by the implementation of the fortified frontier on the Danube. In this sense, the group identity represented by emblemic styles was a goal-oriented identity, formed by internal organization and stimulated by external pressure. The politicization of cultural differences is, no doubt, one of the most important features of ethnicity. Repeated production and consumption of distinctive styles of material culture may have represented ethnic identity. The construction of ethnicity was, however, linked to the signification of social differentiation. Changing social relations impelled displays of group identity. The adoption of the dress with bow fibulae was a means by which individuals could both claim their membership of the new group and proclaim the achievement and consolidation of elite status.[8]

Can we put the name "Slavic" to this (or these) ethnic identity(-ies)? As suggested in Chapter 3, the Sclavene ethnicity is likely to have been an invention of Byzantine authors, despite the possibility, which is often stressed by linguistically minded historians, that the name itself was derived from the self-designation of an ethnic group. It is interesting to note that this ethnic name (*slovene*) appeared much later and only on the periphery of the Slavic linguistic area, at the interface with linguistically different groups. Was language, then, as Soviet ethnographers had it, the "precondition for the rise of ethnic communities"?[9] In the case of the Slavic *ethnie*, the answer must be negative, for a variety of reasons. First, contemporary sources attest the use of more than one language by individuals whom their authors viewed as Antes or Sclavenes. The "phoney Chilbudius" was able to claim successfully a false identity, that of a Roman general, because he spoke Latin fluently, and Perbundos, the "king" of the Rynchines, had a thorough command of Greek. In fact, language shifts were inextricably tied to shifts in the political economy in which speech situations were located.[10] Just how complicated this political economy may have been is shown by the episode of the Gepid taken prisoner by Priscus' army, during the 593 campaign. He was close to the Sclavene "king" Musocius and communicated with him in the "king's language." Formerly a Christian, he betrayed his leader and cooperated with Priscus, presumably using Latin as the language of communication. Finally, both the Gepid traitor and Musocius' Sclavene subjects, who were lured into the ambush set by Roman troops, were accustomed to Avar songs, which were presumably in a language different from both Slavic and Latin.

---

[8] For a slightly different interpretation of the "Slavic culture," see Corman 1998:109.
[9] Kozlov 1974:79. Among the ethnic groups using *slovene* as a name were the Slovenes of Novgorod, the Slovincy (or Kashubians) of the Baltic area, the Slovaks, and the Slovenes of Slovenia. See Ivanov and Toporov 1980:14; Schramm 1995:199.   [10] See Urciuoli 1995.

Second, Common Slavic itself may have been used as a *lingua franca* within and outside the Avar qaganate. This may explain, in the eyes of some linguists, the spread of this language throughout most of Eastern Europe, obliterating old dialects and languages. It may also explain why this language remained fairly stable and remarkably uniform through the ninth century, with only a small number of isoglosses that began to form before Old Church Slavonic was written down.[11] This is also confirmed by the fact that Old Church Slavonic, a language created on the basis of a dialect spoken in Macedonia, was later understood in both Moravia and Kievan Rus'. The same conclusion can be drawn from the episode of Raduald, duke of Benevento, reported by Paul the Deacon and discussed in Chapter 3. Raduald, who had previously been duke of Friuli, was able to talk to the Slavs who had invaded Benevento, coming from Dalmatia across the sea. Since the duchy of Friuli had been constantly confronted with Slavic raids from the neighboring region, we may presume that duke Raduald learned how to speak Slavic in Friuli. His Slavic neighbors in the north apparently spoke the same language as the Dalmatian Slavs.[12]

Slavic was also used as a *lingua franca* in Bulgaria, particularly after the conversion to Christianity in 865. It is only the association with this political development that brought Slavic into closer contact with other languages. This explains why, despite the presumed presence of Slavic-speaking communities in the Balkans at a relatively early date, the influence of Common Slavic on the non-Slavic languages of the area – Romanian,[13]

---

[11] See Lunt 1985:203; Birnbaum 1992:7 and 1993:359. Lunt (1997:36) believes that the migration of the Slavs forced "bands from different areas" of a relatively small homeland to adapt their language to further communication, each one giving up peculiarities and substituting equivalent characteristics of their neighbors or comrades. The closing of a more or less uniform development of Slavic is set at the approximate time of the "fall of the weak jers" (i.e., the disappearance of the reduced vowels ь and ъ in certain well-defined positions) and the subsequent "vocalization of the strong jers" (i.e., the development of these reduced vowels to regular full vowels in other positions). See Birnbaum 1975:4. This sound shift cannot be dated earlier than *c.* 600 and some linguists argue that it should be dated to the tenth, if not twelfth, century. Another *terminus ad quem* for the late Common Slavic is the palatalization of velars, a phenomenon which, according to some scholars, did not take place before *c.* 600. Finally, the metathesis of the liquids began only after *c.* 750 and was complete before *c.* 900 (Birnbaum 1975:228 and 232). One of the most frequently cited arguments for a late date of Common Slavic is Charlemagne's name (Carolus), which presents in all modern Slavic languages (in which the name designates the "emperor") a similar and archaic phonetical treatment. See Ivanov 1976:44; Pătruţ 1976:187.

[12] Paul the Deacon, *Historia Langobardorum* IV 39 and 44.

[13] The greater part of Slavic loans in Romanian seem to be of literary origin (Church literature, charters, and popular literature). See Nandriş 1939. Only fifteen words can be attributed to a Common Slavic influence on the basis of their phonetical treatment. For a complete list and discussion, see Mihăilă 1973:16; Duridanov 1991:15. All fifteen words appear in all Romanian dialects, both north and south of the Danube river. See Mihăilă 1971:355. One of the earliest loans is *şchiau* (pl. *şchei*), a word derived from the Slavic ethnic name (Latin *Sclavus*), which is commonly applied to Bulgarians. See Hurdubeţiu 1969; Petrovics 1987. No other word of a very long

Albanian,[14] and Greek[15] – is minimal and far less significant than that of Bulgarian, Serbo-Croatian, and Macedonian. The absence of a significant influence of Common Slavic in the Balkans is also evident from the small number of Balkan place names of Slavic origin, which could be dated on phonetical grounds, with any degree of certainty, before *c.* 800.[16]

As with material culture emblemic styles, the Slavic language may have been used to mark ethnic boundaries. The emblematic use of Slavic, however, was a much later phenomenon and cannot be associated with the Slavic *ethnie* of the sixth and seventh centuries.[17] Slavs did not become Slavs because they spoke Slavic, but because they were called so by others.

THE SLAVIC *ETHNIE*: THE VIEW FROM THE OUTSIDE

All written sources of the sixth century and some of the seventh use exclusively Sclavenes and/or Antes to refer to groups living north of the Lower Danube. Though the author of the *Strategikon* specifically mentioned that there were many "kings," which suggests more than one political and, presumably, ethnic, identity, there are no other names besides Sclavenes and Antes.[18] Moreover, despite the fact that the Antes were since 545 the allies of the Empire, the author of the *Strategikon* listed them among potential enemies. By contrast, the first tribal names (Drugubites, Sagudates, Belegezites, etc.) appear almost concomitantly in Book II of the *Miracles of St Demetrius* and in Fredegar. In both cases, the difference between *ethnies* was important, because of differing political

Footnote 13 (*cont.*)

 list of Slavic loans in Romanian can be dated earlier than the ninth century. See Bărbulescu 1929; Pătruţ 1968, 1971, and 1974:104–5, 121, and 241; Mańczak 1988. For a statistics of Slavic loans in Romanian, see Rosetti 1954:12; Pătruţ 1971:301 with n. 10. Some phonological and morphological features, such as pre-ioticization or the vocative case, may indeed be the result of Slavic language contact, but there is no way of establishing a chronological framework for these phenomena. See Petrucci 1999:53, 56–7, 105–8, 118, and 130. Moreover, phonological features long considered to have been borrowed from Common Slavic proved to be segments that developed internally. See Petrucci 1995.

[14] As in Romanian, the transformation of /n/ into /r/ (a linguistic phenomenon known as rotacization) ended before the largest number of Slavic loans entered Albanian. See Brâncuş 1989. Only three words have been identified as certainly Common Slavic loans. See Hamp 1970; Ylli 1997. As in Romanian, the word *Shqâ* in the Geg dialect of northern Albania refers to any Slavic-speaking group of the Orthodox faith, particularly to Bulgarians. See Mihăilă 1973:16; Schramm 1995:192.

[15] Among all non-Slavic languages in the Balkans, Greek has the smallest number of Slavic loans. Gustav Meyer (1894) identified only 273 words of Slavic origin. See also Popović 1959:718; Bornträger 1989. The majority of Slavic loans seems to have entered Greek between the eighth and the eleventh century. The number of Common Slavic features, however, is comparatively higher in place names. See Malingoudis 1985 and 1987.   [16] Schramm 1981:160.

[17] See Eastman and Reese 1981.

[18] The same is true for the contemporary source used by Theophylact Simocatta for his account of Priscus' and Peter's campaigns north of the Danube river in the 590s.

interests linked with various ethnicities. Some of the tribes described in Book II of the *Miracles of St Demetrius* were among those besieging Thessalonica. They were viewed as savage, brutish, and heathen. Others, like the Belegezites, were friendly and, at times, potential and important allies, who were able to supply the besieged city with food. To Fredegar, the Wends were different from the rest of the Slavs because of their successful revolt against the Avars, and, more important, because of their role in the demise of Dagobert's power. The same is true for Theophanes' account of the Bulgar migration. The two Slavic groups mentioned in connection with the conquest by Asparuch's warriors of northeastern Bulgaria have specific tribal names, because they were treated differently by both Byzantium and the conquering Bulgars. The Severeis were resettled on the frontier between the Bulgar qaganate and Byzantium, while the ἑπτὰ γενεαί,[19] who until then had probably been clients of the Byzantine emperor, were moved on the western frontier against the Avars.

In all those cases, ethnicity was a function of power in a very concrete and simple way. *Ethnies* were not classified in terms of language or culture, but in terms of their military and political potential. Names were important, therefore, because they gave meaning to categories of political classification. If this is true, however, then "Antes" were also a similar example, since from 545 to 602, they played a completely different role for imperial policies on the Danube frontier than the Sclavenes. The Antes were constantly allies of the Romans, while Sclavenes always appeared on the side of their enemies. A different Antian ethnicity may thus have existed irrespective of the common, "utterly barbarous," language, which, according to Procopius, both *ethnies* used.[20] Emperor Maurice's campaigns of the late 500s against all potential and true enemies (Avars and Sclavenes) may have blurred this difference or at least made it negligible. In the eyes of the author of the *Strategikon*, the Sclavenes and the Antes not only had the same customs, weapons, and tactics, but both were treated as potential enemies.

In the light of these remarks, the very nature of a Sclavene ethnicity needs serious reconsideration. Procopius and later authors may have used this ethnic name as an umbrella-term for various groups living north of the Danube frontier, which were neither "Antes," nor "Huns" or "Avars". Jordanes did the same, though unlike others, he chose an ancient name, the Venethi, probably because he believed that the contemporary configuration of *gentes* beyond the limits of the Empire was a conse-

---

[19] Whether or not this was the real name of this group or simply a phrase employed by Theophanes for some sort of tribal confederation, he made it clear that they were a category separate from the Severeis. [20] Procopius, *Wars* VII 14.26.

quence, if not a reincarnation, of that described by ancient authors such as Tacitus or Ptolemy. To him, in other words, the barbarians of the sixth century, unless touched by the course of Gothic history, were frozen in time and space, basically the same and in the same places as viewed by the ancient authors. That no Slavic ethnicity existed in the eyes of any sixth- or seventh-century Byzantine author, which could be compared to the modern concept of ethnicity, is shown by Pseudo-Caesarius' usage of the term "Sclavenes". To him, the opposite of "Sclavenes" is 'Ριπιανοί, which was not an *ethnie*, but a name for the inhabitants of the Roman province of Dacia Ripensis.[21] The contrast is that between a group living north and another living south of the Danube frontier, to which Pseudo-Caesarius referred by the biblical name Physon. His focus was on the specific location, within one and the same climate, of groups supposedly different in customs and religious life. The same is true for the author of the *Strategikon*. If Sclavenes were discussed in a different chapter than Avars, it is because, in his eyes, they had radically different social and political systems and, as a consequence, different forms of warfare. Roman generals, therefore, ought to learn how to fight them differently. Nevertheless, when it comes to real raids, the evidence discussed in Chapter 3 reveals that many authors were not at ease pinning down who exactly was ravaging Thrace in the 580s and who, at the same time, was in Greece.

This, I must emphasize, is in sharp contrast to other authors' concepts of Slavic ethnicity.[22] That to our sixth- and seventh-century authors, ethnicity was an instrument to differentiate between enemies and allies is also shown by Theophylact Simocatta's episode of the Gepid captured by Priscus' army in 593. To the author of the *Feldzugsjournal* used by Theophylact as a source for Priscus' campaign, this "Gepid" was different from "Sclavenes," even if he had chosen to live among them and was a friend, if not a subject, of "king" Musocius. His "Gepid" ethnicity became apparent and important only when it became necessary to make a difference between him, a former Christian, and the other, "Sclavene" prisoners, who refused to reveal the location of their chief's village. Unlike them, the "Gepid" deserter would become a key factor for the successful conclusion of Priscus' campaign. Viewed from this perspective,

---

[21] For a different, but unconvincing, interpretation of 'Ριπιανοί, see Dragojlović 1972–1973.

[22] See Pohl 1988:107–8. In relation to the Slavic raids of the 580s, and especially to the evidence of the *Chronicle of Monemvasia*, Walter Pohl believed that the reason for which many authors muddled Avars and Slavs was the fluidity of the early medieval concept of ethnicity. Those who viewed themselves politically closer to the Avars, chose to leave at the end of the raid, together with the qagan. Those who presumably remained and settled in Greece, became Slavs. The analysis presented in Chapter 3 shows, however, that this interpretation does not stand against the existing evidence.

ethnicities were just labels attached to various actors in historically determined situations. Like all labels, they were sometimes misleading. The author of the *Strategikon* warns against those still claiming to be "Romans" ('Ρωμαῖοι), but who "have given in to the times," forgot "their own people," and preferred "to gain the good will of the enemy," by luring Roman armies into ambushes set by the Sclavenes. To the experienced soldier who wrote the *Strategikon*, any ethnicity, including a Roman one, should be treated with extreme suspicion, if not backed by a politically correct affiliation.[23]

Byzantine authors seem to have used "Sclavenes" and "Antes" to make sense of the process of group identification which was taking place under their own eyes just north of the Danube frontier. They were, of course, interested more in the military and political consequences of this process than in the analysis of Slavic ethnicity. Chiefs and chief names were more important than customs or culture. When customs and culture came to the fore, as in the case of the *Strategikon*, it was because its author believed that they were linked to the kind of warfare preferred by Sclavenes and Antes. A similar concept may have guided Procopius in writing his Slavic *excursus*. It is because of their military skills that the Sclavenes and the Antes caught the attention of the Roman authors. As early as 537, Sclavene mercenaries were fighting in Italy on the Roman side. The first Sclavene raid recorded by Procopius predates by only five or six years the publication of the first seven books of the *Wars*. In his work, Procopius viewed the Sclavenes and the Antes as "new" and their presence in the Lower Danube region as recent. Although he constantly referred to Sclavenes in relation to Huns or other nomads, there is no indication that he believed them to have recently *come* from some other place. That he considered them to be "new" can only mean that they had not, until then, represented a political force worth being treated like the Lombards, the Gepids, the Cutrigurs, and other "allies" surrounding the Empire. It is because he thought the Sclavenes and the Antes were not politically important (or, at least, not as important as Lombards, Gepids, or Cutrigurs) that Procopius failed to record any chief names. To be one of Justinian's ἔνσπονδοι, one needed first to have a "king." The irony behind the episode of the "phoney Chilbudius," with its plot setting imitating that of a neo-Attic comedy, is that the Antes, who eventually became Justinian's ἔνσπονδοι, did not have a true leader, for they had "lived from old under a democracy."

The making of the Slavs was less a matter of ethnogenesis and more one of invention, imagining and labeling by Byzantine authors. Some

---

[23] *Strategikon* XI 4.31.

form of group identity, however, which we may arguably call ethnicity, was growing out of the historical circumstances following the fortification of the Danube *limes*. This was therefore an identity formed in the shadow of Justinian's forts, not in the Pripet marshes. There are good reasons to believe that this identity was much more complex than the doublet "Sclavenes-Antes" imposed by the Byzantine historiography. Book II of the *Miracles of St Demetrius* and Fredegar's chronicle give us a measure of this complexity. That no "Slavs" called themselves by this name not only indicates that no group took on the label imposed by outsiders, but also suggests that this label was more a pedantic construction than the result of systematic interaction across ethnic boundaries. The first clear statement that "we are Slavs" comes from the twelfth-century *Russian Primary Chronicle*.[24] With this chronicle, however, the making of the Slavs ends and another story begins: that of their "national" use for claims to ancestry.

---

[24] Cross and Sherbowitz-Wetzor 1953:63.

Appendix A

LIST OF SETTLEMENT FEATURES USED IN THE SERIATION BY CORRESPONDENCE ANALYSIS

Abbreviations used in the following list are those of fig. 33.

Bacău-6: Bacău-Royal Court, sunken building 6; Mitrea and Artimon 1971:236; 242 fig. 13/1; 249 fig. 19/5/6.

Bacău-7: Bacău-Royal Court, sunken building 7; Mitrea and Artimon 1971:236, 239; 229 fig. 4; 242 fig. 13/3–4; 245 fig. 15/6; 246 fig. 16/7–8; 250 fig. 20/3, 4, 6.

Bacău-9: Bacău-Royal Court, sunken building 9; Mitrea and Artimon 1971:239; 230 fig. 5; 242 fig. 13/5–6; 243 fig. 14/1, 4, 6; 246 fig. 16/1–3, 9; 247 fig. 17/1–2; 248 fig. 18/2, 5; 249 fig. 19/3–4; 250 fig. 20/7–8.

Bahna-7: Izvoare-Bahna, sunken building 7; Mitrea 1978:207; 231 fig. 1/2; 236 fig. 6/4–12; 237 fig. 7/1–3, 5–6, 10; 238 fig. 8/4, 10, 14–16.

Bahna-8: Izvoare-Bahna, sunken building 8; Mitrea 1978:207–8; 231 fig. 1/3; 236 fig. 6/1–2.

Bahna-20: Izvoare-Bahna, sunken building 20; Mitrea 1983:429, 433; 430 fig. 1/1; 431 fig. 2/1–3; 432 fig. 3/1–5.

Bako-22: Bakota, sunken building 22; Vinokur 1980:870 and fig. 3.

Bako-35: Bakota, sunken building 35; Vinokur 1980:870; 872 fig. 5A.

Bane-1: Bucharest-Băneasa, sunken building 1; Constantiniu 1965a:89, 89–90, 92.

Bane-2: Bucharest-Băneasa, sunken building 2; Constantiniu 1965a:90.

Bane-3: Bucharest-Băneasa, sunken building 3; Constantiniu 1965a:79, 90–1; 83 fig. 8; 87 fig. 12/2.

Bane-4: Bucharest-Băneasa, sunken building 4; Constantiniu 1965a:89, 91–3; 80 fig. 3; 81 fig. 4; 93 fig. 19/1–6.

Bane-5: Bucharest-Băneasa, sunken building 5; Constantiniu 1965a:79, 92.

Bane-8: Bucharest-Băneasa, sunken building 8; Constantiniu 1965a:79, 93–4.

Bane-12: Bucharest-Băneasa, sunken building 12; Constantiniu 1965a:79, 94.

Bane-15: Bucharest-Băneasa, sunken building 15: Constantiniu 1965a:79, 85; 83 fig. 7.

Bane-20: Bucharest-Băneasa, sunken building 20: Constantiniu 1965a:79, 95.

Appendix A

Bors-1: Borşeni, sunken building 1; paper presented by Ioan Mitrea and Gh. Dumitroaia at the 29th National Conference of Romanian Archaeology, Cluj-Napoca, May 11–14, 1995.

Bors-2: Borşeni, sunken building 2; paper presented by Ioan Mitrea and Gh. Dumitroaia at the 29th National Conference of Romanian Archaeology, Cluj-Napoca, May 11–14, 1995.

Bors-4: Borşeni, sunken building 4; paper presented by Ioan Mitrea and Gh. Dumitroaia at the 29th National Conference of Romanian Archaeology, Cluj-Napoca, May 11–14, 1995.

Boto-1: Botoşana, sunken building 1; Teodor 1984a:22–4, 52–4; 83 fig. 3 a; 84 fig. 5/1; 96 fig. 17/3; 103 fig. 24/8; 104 fig. 25/7; 107 fig. 28/1; 108 fig. 29/1, 4; 109 fig. 30/4, 10; 110 fig. 31/1, 5, 7; 111 fig. 32/3; 113 fig. 34/5; 114 fig. 35/1, 4, 5, 7; 117 fig. 38/1; 122 fig. 43/1; 128 fig. 49/8.

Boto-2: Botoşana, sunken building 2; Teodor 1984a:24–5; 82 fig. 3/6; 96 fig. 17/4.

Boto-4: Botoşana, sunken building 4; Teodor 1984a:25–6; 82 fig. 3 d; 98 fig. 19/3; 101 fig. 22/3; 109 fig. 30/6; 117 fig. 38/3; 123 fig. 44/4; 124 fig. 45/7.

Boto-5: Botoşana, sunken building 5; Teodor 1984a:26; 83 fig. 4 a; 84 fig. 5/3; 96 fig. 17/2; 104 fig. 25/2; 117 fig. 38/4; 124 fig. 45/2.

Boto-6: Botoşana, sunken building 6; Teodor 1984a:26–7; 83 fig. 4 b; 103 fig. 24/9; 117 fig. 38/6.

Boto-7: Botoşana, sunken building 7; Teodor 1984a:27; 83 fig. 4 c; 84 fig. 5/4; 104 fig. 25/1; 105 fig. 26/3; 124 fig. 45/5.

Boto-8: Botoşana, sunken building 8; Teodor 1984a:28; 85 fig. 6; 103 fig. 24/3; 109 fig. 30/5; 123 fig. 44/7.

Boto-9: Botoşana, sunken building 9; Teodor 1984a:28–9; 85 fig. 6; 95 fig. 16/1; 96 fig. 17/1; 101 fig. 22/3; 108 fig. 29/2; 111 fig. 32/15; 112 fig. 33/2, 8; 113 fig. 34/1, 7; 114 fig. 35/2; 115 fig. 36/4, 7; 117 fig. 38/2, 5, 7; 122 fig. 43/7; 124 fig. 45/1; 125 fig. 46; 126 fig. 47.

Boto-10: Botoşana, sunken building 10; Teodor 1984a:29– 30; 83 fig. 4 d; 84 fig. 5/6; 104 fig. 25/3; 107 fig. 28/6; 127 fig. 48/4.

Boto-12: Botoşana, sunken building 12; Teodor 1984a:30–1; 86 fig. 7 b; 87 fig. 8/2; 98 fig. 19/1; 101 fig. 22/6; 102 fig. 23/6; 105 fig. 26/5; 111 fig. 32/4; 118 fig. 39/1; 127 fig. 48/2.

Boto-13: Botoşana, sunken building 13; Teodor 1984a:31; 86 fig. 7 c; 98 fig. 19/2; 101 fig. 22/1; 103 fig. 24/5; 109 fig. 30/1, 3; 110 fig. 31/6; 119 fig. 40/1–3; 127 fig. 48/3; 128 fig. 49/1, 3.

Boto-14: Botoşana, sunken building 14; Teodor 1984a:31–2; 86 fig. 7 d; 96 fig. 17/10; 97 fig. 18/3; 98 fig. 19/9; 101 fig. 22/2; 103 fig. 24/6; 108 fig. 29/3; 110 fig. 31/2; 114 fig. 35/6; 115 fig. 36/2–3; 119 fig. 40/4–6; 123 fig. 44/2; 128 fig. 49/7.

Boto-15: Botoşana, sunken building 15; Teodor 1984a:32–3; 88 fig. 8/3; 95 fig. 16/3; 104 fig. 25/8; 107 fig. 28/3; 122 fig. 43/5.

Boto-16: Botoşana, sunken building 16; Teodor 1984a:33–4; 87 fig. 8/4; 88 fig 9 a; 96 fig. 17/7; 98 fig. 19/7; 95 fig. 16/2; 102 fig. 23/3; 120 fig. 41/2; 122 fig. 43/8; 123 fig. 44/3.

Appendix A

Boto-17: Botoşana, sunken building 17; Teodor 1984a:34; 84 fig. 25/6; 87 fig. 8/5; 88 fig. 9 c; 96 fig. 17/5; 97 fig. 18/8; 98 fig. 19/3; 101 fig. 22/4; 103 fig. 24/2; 116 fig. 37/3, 6; 127 fig. 48/6.

Boto-18: Botoşana, sunken building 18; Teodor 1984a:35; 87 fig. 8/6; 88 fig. 9 d; 96 fig. 17/6; 98 fig. 19/10; 99 fig. 20/6; 105 fig. 26/2; 123 fig. 44/1; 122 fig. 43/4.

Boto-19: Botoşana, sunken building 19; Teodor 1984a:35–6; 89 fig. 10 d; 91 fig. 12/1; 97 fig. 18/5; 103 fig. 24/4; 104 fig. 25/4; 112 fig. 33/7; 115 fig. 36/1; 120 fig. 41/1.

Boto-20: Botoşana, sunken building 20; Teodor 1984a:36–7; 89 fig. 10 a; 91 fig. 12/2; 98 fig. 19/14; 99 fig. 20/2, 4–5; 100 fig. 21/2; 112 fig. 33/5; 116 fig. 37/5; 120 fig. 41/3–4; 127 fig. 48/1; 105 fig. 26/1; 109 fig. 30/2.

Boto-22: Botoşana, sunken building 22; Teodor 1984a:37–8; 89 fig. 10 b; 91 fig. 12/4; 98 fig. 19/5; 102 fig. 23/1; 106 fig. 27/1; 107 fig. 28/5; 123 fig. 44/5.

Boto-23: Botoşana, sunken building 23; Teodor 1984a:38–9; 90 fig. 11 a; 91 fig. 12/5; 97 fig. 18/4; 98 fig. 19/2; 106 fig. 27/4–5; 108 fig. 29/5; 109 fig. 30/9,11; 110 fig. 31/3; 111 fig. 32/1–2; 121 fig. 42/3; 122 fig. 43/6.

Boto-25: Botoşana, sunken building 25; Teodor 1984a:39–40; 90 fig. 11 b; 98 fig. 19/6; 99 fig. 20/3; 103 fig. 24/7; 112 fig. 33/1,3; 115 fig. 36/6; 121 fig. 42/1; 122 fig. 43/3; 127 fig. 48/5.

Boto-26: Botoşana, sunken building 26; Teodor 1984a:40; 92 fig. 13 a; 94 fig. 15/1; 107 fig. 28/4.

Boto-27: Botoşana, sunken building 27; Teodor 1984a:40–1; 92 fig. 13 b; 94 fig. 15/2; 97 fig. 18/7; 99 fig. 20/1; 100 fig 21/1 a–c; 102 fig. 23/5; 109 fig. 30/7; 121 fig 42/4.

Boto-28: Botoşana, sunken building 28; Teodor 1984a:41–2; 92 fig. 13 c; 94 fig. 15/3; 97 fig. 18/2; 98 fig. 19/8; 106 fig. 27/6; 108 fig. 29/6; 110 fig. 31/4; 121 fig. 42/2; 123 fig. 44/6.

Boto-30: Botoşana, sunken building 30; Teodor 1984a:42–3; 93 fig. 14 b; 94 fig. 15/5; 96 fig. 17/9; 98 fig. 19/11; 102 fig. 23/4; 105 fig. 26/4; 106 fig. 27/2–3; 113 fig. 34/2–3,8; 115 fig. 36/5; 116 fig. 37/4; 128 fig. 49/2,6.

Boto-31: Botoşana, sunken building 31; Teodor 1984a:43–4; 93 fig. 14 c; 94 fig. 15/6; 95 fig. 16/6; 96 fig. 17/8; 97 fig. 18/1, 6; 102 fig. 23/2; 113 fig. 34/4, 6; 116 fig. 37/1–2; 121 fig. 42/5.

Brat-O2: Bratei, oven 2; Bârzu 1994–5:268; 278 fig. 4/4.

Brat-P1: Bratei, pit 1; Bârzu 1994–5:268.

Brat-P16: Bratei, pit 16; Bârzu 1994–5:268; 292 fig. 18/1; 294 fig. 20/1; 295 fig. 21/1.

Brates: Brăteştii de Sus; Tudor and Chicideanu 1977:136–7; 146; 138 fig. 8; 148 fig. 15; 149 fig. 16/8–15.

Budeni: Budeni, pit 1; Teodor 1978:147; 159 fig. 11.

Cernat-1: Cernat, sunken building 1; Székely 1992:281; 282 fig. 23/B1.

Cernat-2: Cernat, sunken building 2; Székely 1992:281; 282 fig. 23/B2.

Cernat-3: Cernat, sunken building 3; Székely 1992:281; 283 fig. 24.

Cernat-4: Cernat, sunken building 4; Székely 1992:281; 285 fig. 26/B 4.

Appendix A

Chepa-2: Chepa, sunken building 2; Kotigoroshko 1977:87–8; 83 fig. 3/6; 91 fig. 9/34; 92 fig. 10/8, 9.

Chern-5: Chernovka, sunken building 5; Timoshchuk, Rusanova, and Mikhailina 1981:91 and figs. 7–8.

Ciur-1A: Bucharest-Ciurel, sunken building 1A; Dolinescu-Ferche 1979:185; 201–5; 186 fig. 1; 187 fig. 2; 188 fig. 3.

Ciur-1B: Bucharest-Ciurel, sunken building 1B; Dolinescu-Ferche 1979:185–8, 207, 209; 208 fig. 25/H 1B; 193 fig. 8; 194 fig. 9.

Ciur-2A: Bucharest-Ciurel, sunken building 2A; Morintz 1961:659–60, 661; 660 fig. 2–3; Dolinescu-Ferche 1979:185 and 206–7; 189 fig. 4; 190 fig. 5; 191 fig. 6; 192 fig. 7.

Ciur-3: Bucharest-Ciurel, sunken building 3; Dolinescu-Ferche 1979:191–4, 210, 216; 208 fig. 25/H 3; 195 fig. 11; 196 fig. 12.

Ciur-4: Bucharest-Ciurel, sunken building 4; Morintz and Roman 1962:766; 759 fig. 4/2, 3, 5, 10–11; Dolinescu-Ferche 1979:194–6, 210–11; 208 fig. 25/H 4; 197 fig. 13; 198 fig. 14; 199 fig. 15/1.

Ciur-5: Bucharest-Ciurel, sunken building 5; Dolinescu-Ferche 1979:196, 211–12; 208 fig. 25/H 5; 200 fig. 16; 201 fig. 17.

Ciur-6: Bucharest-Ciurel, sunken building 6; Morintz 1961:662; 661 fig. 4; Morintz and Roman 1962:759 fig. 4/9; Dolinescu-Ferche 1979:196, 212; 208 fig. 25/H 6; 199 fig. 15/2–13.

Ciur-7: Bucharest-Ciurel, sunken building 7; Dolinescu-Ferche 1979:196–8, 212–13, 216; 202 fig. 18; 203 fig. 19.

Ciur-8: Bucharest-Ciurel, sunken building 8; Morintz and Roman 1962:766; Dolinescu-Ferche 1979:198–200, 213–15, 216; 203 fig. 20; 204 fig. 21; 205 fig. 22.

Corpa: Corpaci, sunken building; Tel'nov 1985:104–5.

Dama: Bucharest-Dămăroaia, kiln; Rosetti 1934:211–12; 207 fig. 1/6–9; 210 fig. 5/1–4; 211 fig. 6; Morintz and Rosetti 1959:33–4; pl. xxxi/6.

Cuco-2: Cucorăni, sunken building 2; Teodor 1975:151, 154; 152 fig. 18/a; 198 fig. 59/1, 3; 199 fig. 60/12, 16; 200 fig. 61/4–7; 201 fig. 62/6.

Cuco-4: Cucorăni, sunken building 4; Teodor 1975:151; 152 fig. 18b; 198 fig. 59/4, 6; 200 fig. 61/3, 16.

Cuco-17: Cucorăni, sunken building 17; Teodor 1975:151; 153 fig. 19/a; 198 fig. 59/8; 199 fig. 60/5–6, 13; 200 fig. 61/10, 12; 201 fig. 62/7.

Cuco-19: Cucorăni, sunken building 19; Teodor 1975:151–2; 153 fig. 19/b; 198 fig. 59/5; 199 fig. 60/3–4, 7–9, 11, 16; 200 fig. 61/1, 8, 9, 14, 15; 201 fig. 62/3–5.

Cuco-20: Cucorăni, sunken building 20; Teodor 1975:152; 154 fig. 20; 198 fig. 59/2, 7; 199 fig. 60/1–2, 10, 15, 17; 200 fig. 61/11, 13; 201 fig. 62/1–2.

Danc-1: Dănceni, sunken building 1; Rafalovich and Golceva 1981:128–31; 128 fig. 3; 129 fig. 4; 130 fig. 5/1, 2; 131 fig. 6.

Danc-78: Dănceni, sunken building 78; Dergachev, Larina, and Postică 1983:130; 129 fig. viii/9.

Appendix A

David-3: Davideni, sunken building 3; Mitrea 1974–6:66, 76–7; figs. 5/3, 7–8; 10/1.

David-5: Davideni, sunken building 5; Mitrea 1974–6:67, 69, 73, 79; figs. 6/1, 4, 11; 7/2; 10/4; 17/1; 19/1.

David-8: Davideni, sunken building 8; Mitrea 1974–6:67, 70; figs. 5/5–6; 7/4, 6; 12/6; 16/8, 9; 19/5, 11.

David-9: Davideni, sunken building 9; Mitrea 1974–6:67, 73–5, 77; figs. 6/2, 8; 7/5; 8/4; 9/2; 11/11.

David-10: Davideni, sunken building 10; Mitrea 1974–6:67, 73, 76, 78; figs. 6/9, 12; 8/3, 5, 8; 10/7, 8; 13/6; 14/7; 17/2, 3, 7; 19/2, 3.

David-13: Davideni, sunken building 13; Mitrea 1974–6:67, 70, 73–4, 77–9, 83; figs. 4/9; 5/4, 5; 11/11–13; 12/7; 15/5; 17/4, 12.

David-14: Davideni, sunken building 14; Mitrea 1974–6:66, 69–70, 77–8; figs. 11/4–6; 13/4, 7; 14/18; 17/11.

David-16: Davideni, sunken building 16; Mitrea 1974–6:66, 69, 74, 88; figs. 9/2; 11/3; 13/3; 14/1, 14; 15/3; 17/8; 19/6, 10.

David-17: Davideni, sunken building 17; Mitrea 1974–6:69, 82; figs. 15/5–6; 16/2–4; 19/7, 13.

David-21: Davideni, sunken building 21; Mitrea 1974–6:66, 69, 73–4; figs. 8/7–8; 9/8, 10, 11/16.

David-25: Davideni, sunken building 25; Mitrea 1992:204–5; figs. 2; 3/1; 6/1–2, 4; 7/1–3; 8/1–6; 11/1–4, 7.

David-27: Davideni, sunken building 27; Mitrea 1992:209–11; figs. 3/2; 4; 9/1–3, 5–7; 10/1–6; 12/2–4, 7, 9, 11, 12; 13/2, 5, 8, 11–13; 14/1–4.

David-28: Davideni, sunken building 28; Mitrea 1992:211–12; figs. 5/1; 9/1; 12/1, 5, 8, 10; 13/1, 3, 4, 6, 10; 14/6, 7.

David-30: Davideni, sunken building 30; Mitrea 1994:281, 283; 282 fig. 2; 300 fig. 11/1; 304 fig. 13/1; 306 fig. 14/21, 33, 36; 310 fig. 16/13; 312 fig. 17/2.

David-31: Davideni, sunken building 31; Mitrea 1994:283, 285; 284 fig. 3/1; 300 fig. 11/2; 304 fig. 13/15; 329 fig. 28/2, 5, 7.

David-33: Davideni, sunken building 33; Mitrea 1994:285, 287, 289; 284 fig. 3/3; 304 fig. 13/9, 14, 27; 306 fig. 14/26; 308 fig. 15/1, 2, 7, 13; 310 fig. 16/1, 2; 312 fig. 17/11; 314 fig. 18/4; 318 fig. 20/2; 329 fig. 28/3, 4, 6; 330 fig. 29/3, 7.

David-35: Davideni, sunken building 35; Mitrea 1994:291, 293; 284 fig. 3/4; 306 fig. 14/2–4, 6, 13, 19–20, 29, 37; 308 fig. 15/14; 310 fig. 16/3, 8, 10–12, 14; 312 fig. 17/5, 8; 318 fig. 20/4; 329 fig. 28/1; 330 fig. 29/5, 8–10.

David-36: Davideni, sunken building 36; Mitrea 1994:293, 295; 286 fig. 4/1; 304 fig. 13/2, 3, 6, 10, 12, 16, 20, 24, 28; 306 fig. 14/7, 8, 11, 14, 39; 308 fig. 15/6, 8; 310 fig. 16/6, 7, 9; 312 fig. 17/1, 3, 4, 6, 7, 9; 314 fig. 18/1, 2, 5, 6; 318 fig. 20/3, 8; 329 fig. 28/8, 9; 330 fig. 29/1, 4.

David-37: Davideni, sunken building 37; Mitrea 1994:295, 297; 286 fig. 4/2; 304 fig. 13/4–5, 7, 18, 19, 25; 306 fig. 14/1, 5, 24, 25, 31, 32, 35, 41, 42; 312 fig. 17/12; 314 fig. 18/7; 318 fig. 20/1, 5, 6; 330 fig. 29/6.

David-38: Davideni, sunken building 38; Mitrea 1994:299, 301, 303; 288 fig. 5; 294

fig. 8; 304 fig. 13/3; 316 fig. 19/1, 4; 320 fig. 21/7; 321 fig. 22/5; 325 fig. 25/1, 5; 328 fig. 27/1, 3, 5, 7.

David-41: Davideni, sunken building 41; Mitrea 1994:305, 307; 290 fig. 6; 294 fig. 8; 304 fig. 13/22; 320 fig. 21/1, 3; 321 fig. 22/1, 4, 7–9; 322 fig. 23/5, 8; 324 fig. 24/3; 325 fig. 25/3, 4; 326 fig. 26/1, 3, 4.

David-42: Davideni, sunken building 42; Mitrea 1994:307, 309, 311; 290 fig. 6; 296 fig. 9/1; 304 fig. 13/23; 322 fig. 23/1, 2, 4, 6, 7; 324 fig. 24/1, 5, 8; 326 fig. 26/5, 6.

David-46: Davideni, sunken building 46; Mitrea 1994:315, 317; 292 fig. 7/3.

David-58: Davideni, sunken building 58; Mitrea 1994–5:446 and fig. 1/2.

Dod-1: Dodeşti, sunken building 1; Teodor 1984b:22–3; 27 fig. 5/a; 31 fig. 8/1, 2, 5; 33 fig. 9/2; 34 fig. 10/1; 37 fig. 11; 42 fig. 15/3, 6; 46 fig. 18/1–2, 4, 6; 47 fig. 19/1–4, 7.

Dod-2: Dodeşti, sunken building 2; Teodor 1984b:23; 27 fig. 5/b; 33 fig. 9/5; 34 fig. 10/3; 42 fig. 15/2, 4–5; 46 fig. 18/3, 5.

Dod-3: Dodeşti, sunken building 3; Teodor 1984b:23–4; 27 fig. 5/c; 29 fig. 6/7, 9; 33 fig. 9/1; 34 fig. 10/4; 39 fig. 13/1–5; 42 fig. 15/1; 43 fig. 16/1–2, 6.

Dod-4: Dodeşti, sunken building 4; Teodor 1984b:24–5; 27 fig. 5/d; 29 fig. 6/1–3, 10–11; 30 fig. 7; 31 fig. 8/3, 6, 7; 33 fig. 9/3, 4; 40 fig. 14/3–4; 43 fig. 16/3, 5.

Dul-III1: Dulceanca III, sunken building 1; Dolinescu-Ferche 1992:128; 129 fig. 2/1; 136 fig. 5; 137 fig. 6; 138 fig. 7.

Dul-II2: Dulceanca II, sunken building 2; Dolinescu-Ferche 1986:124, 130–2, 150; 125 fig. 2/2; 135 fig. 8.

Dul-II3: Dulceanca II, sunken building 3; Dolinescu-Ferche 1986:124; 130–2, 150; 125 fig. 2/3; 136 fig. 9/1–2, 4–10; fig. 24/1.

Dul-III4: Dulceanca III, sunken building 4; Dolinescu-Ferche 1992:128; 129 fig. 2/2; 139 fig. 8.

Dul-III5: Dulceanca III, sunken building 5; Dolinescu-Ferche 1992:128, 130; 130 fig. 3/1; 141 fig. 10; 142 fig. 11; 143 fig. 12/1–2.

Dul-II6: Dulceanca II, sunken building 6; Dolinescu-Ferche 1986:124, 130–2; 126 fig. 3/4; 137 fig. 10; 138 fig. 11.

Dul-II7: Dulceanca II, sunken building 7; Dolinescu-Ferche 1986:124, 130–2, 150; 126 fig. 3/3; 139 fig. 12.

Dul-II8: Dulceanca II, sunken building 8; Dolinescu-Ferche 1986:124, 130–2, 150; 126 fig. 3/2; 140 fig. 13; 141 fig. 14/1–14, 17; fig. 24/10.

Dul-II9: Dulceanca II, sunken building 9; Dolinescu-Ferche 1986:124, 130–2, 150; 127 fig. 4/1; 142 fig. 15.

Dul-II10: Dulceanca II, sunken building 10; Dolinescu-Ferche 1986:124, 130–2; 150; 127 fig. 4/3; 143 fig. 16.

Dul-III11: Dulceanca III, sunken building 11; Dolinescu-Ferche 1992:131; 132 fig. 4/6; 144 fig. 13/16–24.

Dul-II12: Dulceanca II, sunken building 12; Dolinescu-Ferche 1986:124, 130–2, 150; 127 fig. 4/2; 144 fig. 17.

Appendix A

Dul-II13: Dulceanca II, sunken building 13; Dolinescu-Ferche 1986:128, 130–2, 150; 127 fig. 4/5; 145 fig. 18.

Dul-II14: Dulceanca II, sunken building 14; Dolinescu-Ferche 1986:128, 130–2; 129 fig. 5/1; 146 fig. 19/1–15; fig. 24/8.

Dul-II17: Dulceanca III, sunken building 17; Dolinescu-Ferche 1992:131, 133; 132 fig. 4/1; 146 fig. 15; 147 fig. 16.

Dul-II18: Dulceanca II, sunken building 18; Dolinescu-Ferche 1986:128–9; 129 fig. 5/3; 138 fig. 11/15.

Dul-II19: Dulceanca II, sunken building 19; Dolinescu-Ferche 1986:128; 129 fig. 5/4; 149 fig. 22; 150 fig. 23/1–5.

Dul-II20: Dulceanca III, sunken building 20; Dolinescu-Ferche 1992:133; 132 fig. 4/5; 148 fig. 17.

Dul-II22: Dulceanca III, sunken building 22; Dolinescu-Ferche 1992:133; 129 fig. 2/4; 149 fig. 18.

Dulc-I-1: Dulceanca I, sunken building 1; Dolinescu-Ferche 1974:81, 83; figs. 83–8; 91/1–4; 92; fig. 115/7.

Dulc-I-2: Dulceanca I, sunken building 2; Dolinescu-Ferche 1974:83, 85–7; figs. 93 and 115/5; figs. 94–106.

Dulc-K: Dulceanca I, kiln; Dolinescu-Ferche 1974:73–6; figs. 68–73; 115/4.

Dulc-O6: Dulceanca III, oven 6; Dolinescu-Ferche 1992:130–1; 130 fig. 3/2; 143 fig. 12/3–19.

Dulc-P2: Dulceanca III, pit 2; Dolinescu-Ferche 1992:128; 132 fig. 4/4; 140 fig. 9.

Dulc-P15: Dulceanca II, pit 15; Dolinescu-Ferche 1986:128; 141 fig. 14/16.

Duna-O15: Dunaújváros, sunken building 15; Bóna 1973:22–3; 23 fig. 1/3–6; pl. 32/9.

Duna-O18: Dunaújváros, sunken building 18; Bóna 1973:25–6; pls. 1/16–22; 19/6; 21/1; 29/5; 32/7, 13; 35/3.

Duna-O25: Dunaújváros, sunken building 25; Bóna 1973:30; pl. 2/5–8.

Duna-O30: Dunaújváros, sunken building 30; Bóna 1973:33; pls. 3/6; 28/1, 4, 5, 8; 32/3.

Duna-O32: Dunaújváros, sunken building 32; Bóna 1973:34; pl. 3/7–11.

Duna-O38: Dunaújváros, sunken building 38; Bóna 1973:37; pls. 4/6–11; 14/5; 32/18.

Duna-O39: Dunaújváros, sunken building 39; Bóna 1973:38; pls. 4/12–18; 26/2; 29/4, 6; 32/6; 35/5, 6.

Duna-O42: Dunaújváros, sunken building 42; Bóna 1973:39–40; pls. 5/3, 5–11; 23/1–4; 30/4; 32/2; 33/5.

Duna-O46: Dunaújváros, oven 46; Bóna 1973:42.

Duna-O56: Dunaújváros, sunken building 56; Bóna 1973:48–9; pls. 7/15–16; 25/5; 35/10.

Duna-O57: Dunaújváros, sunken building 57; Bóna 1973:49–50; pls. 8/1–10; 25/6–8; 28/7; 29/1, 3; 30/3; 32/4–5.

Appendix A

Duna-O61: Dunaújváros, sunken building 61; Bóna 1973:58; pl. 11/1–3.

Duna-O62: Dunaújváros, oven 62; Bóna 1973:59; pl. 11/4–18.

Duna-O66: Dunaújváros, sunken building 66; Bóna 1973:60; pl. 12/17–23.

Filia-1: Filiaş, sunken building 1; Székely 1974–6:43; pls. I/1–5; II/4, 7–9.

Filia-7: Filiaş, sunken building 7; Székely 1974–6:37– 8; pls. IV/1, 1a, 4–11; V/12; VI/10, 14, 15, 17; VII/11, 12, 14, 16–18.

Filia-15: Filiaş, sunken building 15; Székely 1974–6:38; pls. II/1; V/1, 4–6, 8, 13–15; VII/4, 7, 9; IX/1, 7, 8, 11, 12; X/6.

Filia-21: Filiaş, sunken building 21; Székely 1974–6:39; pl. V/2, 3.

Filia-22: Filiaş, sunken building 22; Székely 1974–6:39; pls. VIII/1–23; X/2–3, 17, 24.

Filia-23: Filiaş, sunken building 23; Székely 1974–6:39–40; pl. X/10.

Filia-25: Filiaş, sunken building 25; Székely 1974–6:40.

Filia-30: Filiaş, sunken building 30; Székely 1974–6:40; pls. III/7, 9; X/5, 11, 19, 20.

Filia-31: Filiaş, sunken building 31; Székely 1974–6:40.

Filia-32: Filiaş, sunken building 32; Székely 1974–6:41.

Filia-33: Filiaş, sunken building 33; Székely 1974–6:41; pl. I/12.

Filia-34: Filiaş, sunken building 34; Székely 1974–6:41.

Filia-36: Filiaş, sunken building 36; Székely 1974–6:41; pls. II/3–5; III/10; VI/1–2, 6–8.

Filia-37: Filiaş, sunken building 37; Székely 1974–6:41–2; pls. III/3; IV/1, 3; X/15–16.

Filia-38: Filiaş, sunken building 38; Székely 1974–6:42; pl. III/5, 11.

Filia-41: Filiaş, sunken building 41; Székely 1974–6:42; pl. III/6.

Ghiv-3: Bucharest-Soldat Ghivan Street, sunken building 3; Dolinescu-Ferche and Constantiniu 1981:299, 302; 301 fig. 6; 302 fig. 7.

Ghiv-5: Bucharest-Soldat Ghivan Street, sunken building 5; Dolinescu-Ferche and Constantiniu 1981:297, 303–5, 319–20; 306 fig. 8; 319 fig. 16/7 a–b.

Ghiv-8: Bucharest-Soldat Ghivan Street, sunken building 8; Dolinescu-Ferche and Constantiniu 1981:305, 307; 309 fig. 9.

Ghiv-10: Bucharest-Soldat Ghivan Street, sunken building 10; Dolinescu-Ferche and Constantiniu 1981:293–4, 297, 307, 309, 311, 318–23; 310 fig. 10; 312 fig. 11; 319 fig. 16/1–3, 5; 321 fig. 17/16; 322 fig. 18/7, 9, 12–13; 323 fig. 19/1.

Ghiv-11: Bucharest-Soldat Ghivan Street, sunken building 11; Dolinescu-Ferche and Constantiniu 1981:293–4, 297, 311, 319; 298 fig. 4/4; 300 fig. 5/1–3; 319 fig. 16/6.

Ghiv-12: Bucharest-Soldat Ghivan Street, sunken building 12; Dolinescu-Ferche and Constantiniu 1981:293–4, 297, 311, 313, 324; 296 fig. 3/5; 298 fig. 4/7; 314 fig. 12; 323 fig. 20.

Ghiv-13: Bucharest-Soldat Ghivan Street, sunken building 13; Dolinescu-Ferche and Constantiniu 1981:293, 297, 313, 317; 296 fig. 3/3; 300 fig. 5/8; 315 fig. 13; 316 fig. 14; 318 fig. 15.

Gord-1: Gordineşti, sunken building 1; Tel'nov 1985:91–2.

Appendix A

Gord-2: Gordineşti, sunken building 2; Tel'nov 1985:92–3; 94 fig. 1; 95 fig. 2.

Gord-4: Gordineşti, sunken building 4; Tel'nov 1985:94–5; 96 fig. 3; 97 fig. 4.

Gord-6: Gordineşti, sunken building 6; Tel'nov 1985:99– 100; 101 fig. 6; 102 fig. 7.

Gore-21: Gorecha, sunken building 21; Rusanova and Timoshchuk 1984:85 pl. 36/9–17.

Grodz-1: Grodzisko Dolne, sunken building 1; Podgórska-Czopek 1991:17–18; 17 fig. 6; pls. XIX–XXII.

Grodz-2: Grodzisko Dolne, sunken building 2; Podgórska-Czopek 1991:18–19; 19 fig. 7; pls. XXII–XXVI.

Grodz-P1: Grodzisko Dolne, pit 1; Podgórska-Czopek 1991:15–17; 15 fig. 5; pls. V–XVII.

Gut-2: Gutinaş, sunken building 2; Mitrea, Eminovici, and Momanu 1986–7:221–2; 235 fig. 2/2; 236 fig. 3/2; 243 fig. 12/1, 2, 4; 244 fig. 11/1, 2, 4; 245 fig. 12/1, 2, 4; 248 fig. 15/1, 2, 4.

Gut-3: Gutinaş, sunken building 3; Mitrea, Eminovici, and Momanu 1986–7:222–3; 238 fig. 5/1; 245 fig. 12/5, 8; 247 fig. 14/2, 3, 6; 247 fig. 14/2, 3, 6; 250 fig. 17/5.

Gut-5: Gutinaş, sunken building 5; Mitrea, Eminovici, and Momanu 1986–7:224–5; 237 fig. 4/1; 239 fig. 6; 245 fig. 12/3, 7; 246 fig. 13/4, 6; 247 fig. 14/1, 5; 249 fig. 16/4; 250 fig. 17/2, 6.

Gut-6: Gutinaş, sunken building 6; Mitrea, Eminovici, and Momanu 1986–7:225–7; 240 fig. 7/1; 241 fig. 8; 243 fig. 10/3; 244 fig. 11/3; 246 fig. 13/8–9; 248 fig. 15/3, 6; 250 fig. 17/3, 12–14.

Gut-7: Gutinaş, sunken building 7; Mitrea, Eminovici, and Momanu 1986–7:227–8; 240 fig. 7/2; 242 fig. 9; 246 fig. 13/1–3, 5, 7, 10; 248 fig. 15/5; 249 fig. 16/2, 6; 250 fig. 17/4, 7–11.

Hans-1: Hansca, sunken building 1; Rafalovich 1973:145–6; 145 fig. 6.

Hans-10: Hansca, sunken building 10; Tel'nov and Riaboi 1985:109; 110 fig. 2.

Hans-11: Hansca, sunken building 11; Tel'nov and Riaboi 1985:114, 117; 116 fig. 6; 117 fig. 7.

Hans-24: Hansca, sunken building 24; Rafalovich 1973:151.

Hans-26: Hansca, sunken building 26; Rafalovich 1973:153; 154 fig. 11/7–12; I. A. Rafalovich, "Otchet o polevykh rabotakh Reutskoi rannesrednevekovoi arkheolog-icheskoi ekspedicii v 1970 g.," archaeological report in the archives of the Institute of Ancient History and Archaeology, Chişinău, 1972, fig. 17/9, 11.

Hlin-1: Hlincea, sunken building 1; n.a. 1953a:326–7; 324 fig. 11.

Horo-P2: Horodok, pit 2; Timoshchuk and Prikhodniuk 1969:75; 74 fig. 3/6.

Iasi-1: Iaşi-Crucea lui Ferenţ, sunken building 1; Teodor 1971:120; 127 fig. 3/2; 128 fig. 4/1–3, 5–6, 11–12, 15.

Ivan-1: Ivancea, sunken building 1; Vlasenko 1985:146–7; 142 fig. 1/7, 8–10, 14, 15, 17; 144 fig. 3/1.

Ivan-P1: Ivancea, pit 1; Vlasenko 1985:145; 142 fig. 1/2; 144 fig. 3/4.

Appendix A

Kav-2: Kavetchina, sunken building 2; Vakulenko and Prikhodniuk 1984:62, 75; 46 fig. 21; 64 fig. 37/10, 15; 66 fig. 38/4, 8, 31, 34, 40.

Kav-7: Kavetchina, sunken building 7; Vakulenko and Prikhodniuk 1984:76–7; 49 fig. 24; 64 fig. 37/9, 11.

Kav-9: Kavetchina, sunken building 9; Vakulenko and Prikhodniuk 1984:77–8; 64 fig. 37/6; 66 fig. 38/5, 16– 17, 20, 26.

Kav-11: Kavetchina, sunken building 11; Vakulenko and Prikhodniuk 1984:78; 66 fig. 38/33.

Kav-12: Kavetchina, sunken building 12; Vakulenko and Prikhodniuk 1984:78; 51 fig. 26; 66 fig. 38/6.

Kav-13: Kavetchina, sunken building 13; Vakulenko and Prikhodniuk 1984:78–9; 52 fig. 27; 66 fig. 38/3, 14, 15, 28, 41.

Kav-18: Kavetchina, sunken building 18; Vakulenko and Prikhodniuk 1984:80; 61 fig. 34; 66 fig. 38/7, 23.

Kav-25: Kavetchina, sunken building 25; Vakulenko and Prikhodniuk 1984:81; 56 fig. 31; 64 fig. 37/14; 66 fig. 38/10, 12, 13, 21, 22, 25.

Kav-27: Kavetchina, sunken building 27; Vakulenko and Prikhodniuk 1984:82; 57 fig. 32; 66 fig. 38/38; 68 fig. 39/4, 5, 8, 9.

Kav-29: Kavetchina, sunken building 29; Vakulenko and Prikhodniuk 1984:82; 58 fig. 33; fig. 37/4; 66 fig. 38/39; 68 fig. 39/1–3, 7.

Kav-P20: Kavetchina, pit 20; Vakulenko and Prikhodniuk 1984:85; 62 fig. 35/16; 66 fig. 38/2.

Kiev-8: Kiev-Obolon', sunken building 8; Shovkoplias and Gavritukhin 1993:54; 55 fig. 2/1–5.

Kiev-26: Kiev-Obolon', sunken building 26; Shovkoplias and Gavritukhin 1993:54; 55 fig. 2/6–12; 56 fig. 3.

Kod-1: Kodyn II, sunken building 1; Rusanova and Timoshchuk 1984:53; 78 pl. 22/1–2.

Kod-2: Kodyn II, sunken building 2; Rusanova and Timoshchuk 1984:54; 78 pl. 22/3–7.

Kod-3: Kodyn I, sunken building 3; Rusanova and Timoshchuk 1984:46 and 22; 73 pl. 13/1–7.

Kod-4: Kodyn I, sunken building 4; Rusanova and Timoshchuk 1984:22 and 54; 73 pl. 13/6; 78 pl. 23/1–6.

Kod-5: Kodyn I, sunken building 5; Rusanova and Timoshchuk 1984:54; 18 fig. 13/3; 78 pl. 23/7–10.

Kod-7: Kodyn I, sunken building 7; Rusanova and Timoshchuk 1984:55; 18 fig. 12/2; 20 fig. 16/8; 78 pl. 23/12–21.

Kod-10: Kodyn I, sunken building 10; Rusanova and Timoshchuk 1984:22, 48; 21 fig. 19/2; 74 fig. 14/5–18.

Kod-11: Kodyn I, sunken building 11; Rusanova and Timoshchuk 1984:29, 48–9; 20 fig. 16/5; 74 fig. 15/1–12.

Appendix A

Kod-12: Kodyn II, sunken building 12; Rusanova and Timoshchuk 1984:36, 56; 18 fig. 12/3; 32 fig. 23/2; 69 pl. 6/3–5; 80 pl. 26/1–4.

Kod-13: Kodyn I, sunken building 13; Rusanova and Timoshchuk 1984:49; 12 fig. 7/4; 15 fig. 11/1; 75 pl. 16.

Kod-14: Kodyn I, sunken building 14; Rusanova and Timoshchuk 1984:49–50; 20 fig. 17/6; 74 pl. 15/12–16.

Kod-19: Kodyn II, sunken building 19; Rusanova and Timoshchuk 1984:40, 58; 20 fig. 16/2; 39 fig. 28/2; 71 pl. 9/3; 81 pl. 28/8–18.

Kod-20: Kodyn I, sunken building 20; Rusanova and Timoshchuk 1984:34, 51; 20 fig. 17/3; 21 fig. 18/1, 5; 76 pl. 18/2–9.

Kod-21: Kodyn I, sunken building 21; Rusanova and Timoshchuk 1984:30, 51, 22; 18 fig. 12/4; 21 fig. 19/2; 76 pl. 18/10–14.

Kod-23: Kodyn I, sunken building 23; Rusanova and Timoshchuk 1984:51–2; 39 fig. 28/1; 71 pl. 9/1; 76 pl. 19/5–11.

Kod-27: Kodyn II, sunken building 27; Rusanova and Timoshchuk 1984:59; 82 pl. 30/8–11.

Kod-28: Kodyn II, sunken building 28; Rusanova and Timoshchuk 1984:59–60; 21 fig. 18/4; 82 pl. 30/12.

Kod-29: Kodyn I, sunken building 29; Rusanova and Timoshchuk 1984:17, 53; 21 fig. 18/2, 6.

Kod-31: Kodyn II, sunken building 31; Rusanova and Timoshchuk 1984:60; 20 fig. 17/1; 29 fig. 21; 69 pl. 6/3–4; 82 pl. 31/1–3.

Kod-36: Kodyn II, sunken building 36; Rusanova and Timoshchuk 1984:61; 18 fig. 15/3–4; 83 pl. 33/5–7.

Kod-45: Kodyn II, sunken building 45; Rusanova and Timoshchuk 1984:30 and 62; 84 pl. 35/4–11.

Lug-I-1: Pen'kyvka-Lug I, sunken building 1; Berezovec 1963:157–8; Prikhodniuk 1980:50 fig. 28/1–2.

Lug-I-2: Pen'kyvka-Lug I, sunken building 2; Berezovec 1963:158.

Lug-I-5: Pen'kyvka-Lug I, sunken building 5; Berezovec 1963:160; figs. 8/3; 9/4; 27/1; Prikhodniuk 1980:50 fig. 28/6,7.

Lug-I-6: Pen'kyvka-Lug I, sunken building 6; Berezovec 1963:160–1; fig. 27/2; Prikhodniuk 1980:52 fig. 29.

Lug-I-7: Pen'kyvka-Lug I, sunken building 7; Berezovec 1963: 161, 163; figs. 10/11; 27/3; Prikhodniuk 1980:53 fig. 30.

Lug-I-10: Pen'kyvka-Lug I, sunken building 10; Berezovec 1963:164; fig. 27/6.

Lug-I-12: Pen'kyvka-Lug I, sunken building 12; Berezovec 1963:164–5; fig. 27/8; Prikhodniuk 1980:33 figs. 11–12.

Lug-I-13: Pen'kyvka-Lug I, sunken building 13; Berezovec 1963:165; fig. 27/9; Prikhodniuk 1980:34 fig. 13.

Lug-I-16: Pen'kyvka-Lug I, sunken building 16; Berezovec 1963:165–6; figs. 10/4, 5, 12; 28/1, 4; Prikhodniuk 1980:62 fig. 39/3–10.

Appendix A

Lug-I-17: Pen'kyvka-Lug I, sunken building 17; Berezovec 1963:166; figs. 2/2; 28/2; Prikhodniuk 1980:63 fig. 40.

Lug-I-18: Pen'kyvka-Lug I, sunken building 18; Berezovec 1963:166–7; figs. 12/8; 13/4; 28/3; Prikhodniuk 1980:35 fig. 14.

Lug-I-19: Pen'kyvka-Lug I, sunken building 19; Berezovec 1963:167; fig. 9/10; Prikhodniuk 1980:36 fig. 15.

Lug-I-20: Pen'kyvka-Lug I, sunken building 20; Berezovec 1963:167–9; fig. 28/6; Prikhodniuk 1980:64 fig. 41.

Lug-I-21: Pen'kyvka-Lug I, sunken building 21; Berezovec 1963:169; fig. 28/5; Prikhodniuk 1980:55 fig. 32.

Lug-I-25: Pen'kyvka-Lug I, sunken building 25; Berezovec 1963:171; figs. 14/1, 7; 29/4; Prikhodniuk 1980:65 fig. 42/1–5, 7, 8, 10.

Lug-I-26: Pen'kyvka-Lug I, sunken building 26; Berezovec 1963:171–2; figs. 14/6; 29/5; Prikhodniuk 1980:65 fig. 42/6, 9, 11, 12.

Lug-I-27: Pen'kyvka-Lug I, sunken building 27; Berezovec 1963:172; fig. 29/6; Prikhodniuk 1980:65 fig. 43/1–3.

Lug-I-29: Pen'kyvka-Lug I, sunken building 29; Berezovec 1963:172–3; figs. 2/3; 15/2; 29/3; Prikhodniuk 1980:65 fig. 43/4–8.

Lug-I-30: Pen'kyvka-Lug I, sunken building 28; Berezovec 1963:173; figs. 10/18; 29/2; Prikhodniuk 1980:65 fig. 43/9–10.

Lug-II-1: Pen'kyvka-Lug II, sunken building 1; Berezovec 1963:178; figs. 2/4; 16/1.

Lug-II-2: Pen'kyvka-Lug II, sunken building 2; Berezovec 1963:178; fig. 17/10, 11.

Lug-II-3: Pen'kyvka-Lug II, sunken building 3; Berezovec 1963:178; figs. 16/4; 17/12; 18/3, 4.

Lug-II-4: Pen'kyvka-Lug II, sunken building 4; Berezovec 1963:178–9; figs. 17/1; 31/1.

Lug-II-7: Pen'kyvka-Lug II, sunken building 7; Berezovec 1963:180; figs. 16/2, 5; 17/4; Prikhodniuk 1980:56 fig. 33.

Lug-II-9: Pen'kyvka-Lug II, sunken building 9; Berezovec 1963:181; figs. 31/5; 16/3; 17/14.

Lunca: Bucharest-Lunca-Văcăreşti, oven 3; Sandu 1992:190–1; 184 pl. xiv/5–8, 10.

Makar-5: Pen'kyvka-Makaryv Ostryv, sunken building 5; Linka and Shovkoplias:240; fig. 5/3.

Makar-6: Pen'kyvka-Makaryv Ostryv, sunken building 6; Linka and Shovkoplias:240; fig. 2/1–9.

Mihai-5: Mihăileşti, sunken building 5; Turcu 1992b:234 and 236; 232 pl. II/2; 235 pl. IV; 237 pl. VI/6–8.

Milit-3: Bucharest-Militari, sunken building 3; Zirra and Cazimir 1963:56, 60; 66 fig. 14/2.

Milit-4: Bucharest-Militari, sunken building 4; Zirra and Cazimir 1963:56, 60, 63; 69 fig. 17/1–2, 6–7.

Appendix A

Milit-5: Bucharest-Militari, sunken building 5; Zirra and Cazimir 1963:56, 60, 62–3; 69 fig. 17/1–2, 4–5, 8; Turcu 1992a:fig. XIV.

Milit-6: Bucharest-Militari, sunken building 6; Zirra and Cazimir 1963:56, 60, 63; 64 fig. 12/1, 2; 69 fig. 17/3; Sgîbea-Turcu 1963:373, 378–80; 379 pl. II/1.

Milit-P8: Bucharest-Militari, pit 8; Turcu 1992a:50.

Obu-6: Obukhyv, sunken building 6; Abashina 1986:80 and 82; 79 fig. 6/1; 81 fig. 7/6, 17, 25; 82 fig. 82/3, 4.

Olt-2: Olteni, sunken building 2; Dolinescu-Ferche 1973:205 and 206 fig. 3; 207 fig. 4/1–3, 9; 208 fig. 5.

Pastyr-1: Pastyrs'ke, sunken building; Braichevskii 1955:69–70; 72 fig. 5/1, 2.

Pastyr-2: Pastyrs'ke, sunken building; Braichevskii 1955:70–1; 72 figs. 5/3, 4; 6.

Poian-5: Poian, sunken building 5; Székely 1992:251; 252 fig. 5/B5; 253 fig. 6; 254 fig. 7/B5.

Poian-8: Poian, sunken building 8; Székely 1992:259.

Poian-13: Poian, sunken building 13; Székely 1992:261.

Poian-17: Poian, sunken building 17; Székely 1992:263; 264 fig. 13/B17.

Poian-18: Poian, sunken building 18; Székely 1992:263; 265 fig. 14.

Poian-19: Poian, sunken building 19; Székely 1992:263, 266, 268; 266 fig. 15; 267 fig. 16.

Poian-20: Poian, sunken building 20; Székely 1992:263; 269 fig. 17.

Poian-21: Poian, sunken building 21; Székely 1992:268; 262 fig. 12/B21.

Poian-23: Poian, sunken building 23; Székely 1992:268, 271; 270 fig. 18/B23.

Poian-24: Poian, sunken building 24; Székely 1992:271; 272 fig. 19/B24.

Poian-29: Poian, sunken building 29; Székely 1992:274.

Poian-30: Poian, sunken building 30; Székely 1992:274.

Sam-II: Samchincy, house II; Khavliuk 1963:346; figs. 4/10, 11; 13/3; 14/7, 8.

Sam-13: Samchincy, sunken building 13; Khavliuk 1961:197–8; 198 fig. 9; 199 fig. 10/8; Khavliuk 1963:345; fig. 14/10.

Sel-1: Selişte, sunken building 1; Rafalovich 1972b:130–1; 124 fig. 2/2; 130 fig. 6/1, 3, 4.

Sel-2: Selişte, sunken building 2; Rafalovich 1972b:131, 133, 134; 132 figs. 7–8; 133 fig. 9; 133 fig. 10/8, 13.

Sel-4: Selişte, sunken building 4; Rafalovich 1972b:134–5.

Sel-5: Selişte, sunken building 5; Rafalovich 1972b:135, 137; 133 fig. 10/14; 136 fig. 11; 137 fig. 12/2.

Sel-6: Selişte, sunken building 6; Rafalovich 1972b:137–9; 130 fig. 6/6; 136 fig. 11; 137 fig. 12/1; 138 fig. 13/1.

Sel-7: Selişte, sunken building 7; Rafalovich 1972b:139–40; 138 fig. 13/1, 4; 139 fig. 14; 140 fig. 15/1, 2.

Sel-8: Selişte, sunken building 8; Rafalovich and Lapushnian 1971:362; Rafalovich 1973:138–9.

Sel-9: Selişte, sunken building 9; Rafalovich and Lapushnian 1971:362; Rafalovich 1973:139–140; 40 fig. 3/3.

Sel-10: Selişte, sunken building 10; Rafalovich and Lapushnian 1973:129–30; 130 fig. 8/1; 131 fig. 9/3, 9.

Sel-13: Selişte, sunken building 13; Rafalovich and Lapushnian 1973:133–4; 130 fig. 8/3; 133 fig. 10/5.

Sel-15 Selişte, sunken building 15; Rafalovich and Lapushnian 1974:130–1 and 133; 131 fig. 10; 132 fig. 11.

Sem-I: Semenki, sunken building I; Khavliuk 1961:188; 190 fig. 3/1–4.

Sem-VI: Semenki, sunken building VI; Khavliuk 1963:335–6; figs. 6/8; 13/8; 14/3, 4.

Sem-VII: Semenki, sunken building VII; Khavliuk 1963:336, 338; 195 fig. 6/9; 332 fig. 12/1; 338 fig. 17/4.

Sem-VIII: Semenki, sunken building VIII; Khavliuk 1974:207; 202 fig. 11/1, 2.

Sem-15: Semenki, sunken building 15; Khavliuk 1974:199; 198 fig. 9/15; 199 fig. 10/5, 10.

Sem-20: Semenki, sunken building 20; Khavliuk 1974:204; 198 fig. 9/20; 202 fig. 11/22.

Sem-21: Semenki, sunken building 21; Khavliuk 1974:204; 203 fig. 12/7.

Sem-22: Semenki, sunken building 22; Khavliuk 1974:204; 198 fig. 9/22; 202 fig. 11/3, 20.

Sem-29: Semenki, sunken building 29; Khavliuk 1974: 207; 202 fig. 11/11, 13.

Sfint: Sfinţeşti, sunken building 1; Dolinescu-Ferche 1967:127–31; 128 fig. 1; 129 fig. 2; 130 fig. 3; 131 fig. 4; 131 fig. 5.

Skib-1: Skibincy, sunken building 1; Khavliuk 1974:188–9; 189 fig. 5/12.

Skib-2: Skibincy, sunken building 2; Khavliuk 1974:189–90; 189 fig. 5/1, 3, 5, 6.

Skib-3: Skibincy, sunken building 3; Khavliuk 1974:190; 189 fig. 5/2, 4, 7, 8, 9, 11–13; 191 fig. 6/1.

Skib-4: Skibincy, sunken building 4; Khavliuk 1974:190; 191 fig. 6/2.

Spin: Spinoasa, sunken building 5; Niţu, Zaharia, and Teodoru 1960:532–3; 533 fig. 2; 534 fig. 3/2; 534 fig. 4/1, 10–13.

Stec-3: Stecyvka, sunken building 3; Petrov 1963b:214; 215 fig. 2/2.

Stec-5: Stecyvka, sunken building 5; Petrov 1963b:214; 215 fig. 2/4.

Stec-8: Stecyvka, sunken building 8; Petrov 1963b:216; 217 fig. 3/3.

Stec-9: Stecyvka, sunken building 9; Petrov 1963b:216, 218; 221 fig. 4/1; 223 fig. 5/1, 2, 4; 224 fig. 6/2.

Stec-10: Stecyvka, sunken building 10; Petrov 1963b:218; 221 fig. 4/2.

Stec-11: Stecyvka, sunken building 11; Petrov 1963b:218; 221 fig. 4/3; 222 fig. 6/6; 223 fig. 8; Prikhodniuk 1980:57 fig. 34.

Strau-8: Bucharest-Străuleşti, sunken building 8; Constantiniu 1965b:174, 176, 184, 187; 178 fig. 85/2–3.

Strau-9: Bucharest-Străuleşti, sunken building 9; Constantiniu 1963:83–4; 83 fig. 6.

Strau-17: Bucharest-Străuleşti, sunken building 17; Constantiniu 1963:84, 96; 85 fig. 7b.

Strau-21: Bucharest-Străuleşti, sunken building 21; Constantiniu 1965b:174, 176, 182, 186; 180 fig. 87/4.

Suce-2: Suceava-Şipot, sunken building 2; Matei 1962:151–8; 152 fig. 2; 156 figs. 4–5; 157 fig. 6.

Suce-4: Suceava-Şipot, sunken building 4; Teodor 1970:381–2; 380 fig. 5.

Targ-5: Târgşor, sunken building 5; Constantinescu 1960:168–72; 169 pl. 1; 170 fig. 2; 171 fig. 3; 173 fig. 4.

Tere-21: Teremcy, sunken building 21; Baran 1988a:72; 73 fig. 33.

Ude-P2: Udeşti, pit 2; Matei and Rădulescu 1973:274–5, 277; 274 fig. 7/1,3,4; 275 fig. 8/2.

Vana-2: Vânători-Neamţ, sunken building 2; Corman 1994:302, 307; 303 fig. 2/L 2; 304 fig. 3/1–4, 6; 305 fig. 4/1–4, 6–7; 306 fig. 5.

Vaca: Bucharest-Văcăreşti, sunken building 3; Turcu and Ciuceanu 1992:199–200; 198 pl. 1/10, 11 a–b.

Appendix B

HANDMADE AND WHEELMADE POTS USED FOR SHAPE ANALYSIS

Abbreviations used in the following list are those of figs. 65 and 66.

Bacău-1: Bacău (Romania), sunken building 1; Mitrea and Artimon 1971:241 fig. 12/1.

Bacău-2a: Bacău (Romania), sunken building 2; Mitrea and Artimon 1971:241 fig. 12/2.

Bacău-2b: Bacău (Romania), sunken building 2; Mitrea and Artimon 1971:241 fig. 12/4.

Bacău-4: Bacău (Romania), sunken building 4; Mitrea and Artimon 1971:241 fig. 12/3.

Bane: Bucharest-Băneasa (Romania), settlement find; Constantiniu 1965a:90 fig. 15.

Bist-30: Bistriţa (Romania) grave 30; Gaiu 1992:117 fig. 2/23.

Bist-47: Bistriţa (Romania), grave 47; Gaiu 1992:119 fig. 4/1.

Boto-1: Botoşana, Suceava district (Romania), sunken building 1; Teodor 1984a:117 fig. 38/1.

Boto-5: Botoşana, Suceava district (Romania), sunken building 5; Teodor 1984a:117 fig. 38/4.

Boto-9a: Botoşana, Suceava district (Romania), sunken building 9; Teodor 1984a:117 fig. 38/2.

Boto-9b: Botoşana, Suceava district (Romania), sunken building 9; Teodor 1984a:117 fig. 38/5.

Boto-9c: Botoşana, Suceava district (Romania), sunken building 9; Teodor 1984a:117 fig. 38/7.

Boto-9d: Botoşana, Suceava district (Romania), sunken building 9; Teodor 1984a:125 fig. 46.

Boto-12: Botoşana, Suceava district (Romania), sunken building 12; Teodor 1984a:111 fig. 32/4.

Boto-16: Botoşana, Suceava district (Romania), sunken building 16; Teodor 1984a:120 fig. 41/2.

Boto-19: Botoşana, Suceava district (Romania), sunken building 19; Teodor 1984a:120 fig. 41/1.

Appendix B

Boto-20a: Botoşana, Suceava district (Romania), sunken building 20; Teodor 1984a:127 fig. 48/1.

Boto-20b: Botoşana, Suceava district (Romania), sunken building 20; Teodor 1984a:99 fig. 20/4.

Boto-23a: Botoşana, Suceava district (Romania), sunken building 23; Teodor 1984a:111 fig. 32/1.

Boto-23b: Botoşana, Suceava district (Romania), sunken building 23; Teodor 1984a:121 fig. 42/2.

Boto-25: Botoşana, Suceava district (Romania), sunken building 25; Teodor 1984a:121 fig. 42/1.

Boto-27: Botoşana, Suceava district (Romania), sunken building 27; Teodor 1984a:121 fig. 42/4.

Boto-31: Botoşana, Suceava district (Romania), sunken building 31; Teodor 1984a:121 fig. 42/5.

Bozieni: Bozieni, Buzău district (Romania), settlement find; Teodorescu 1971:128 fig. 4/4.

Capi: Capidava, Constanţa district (Romania) stray find; Scorpan 1968:fig. 22b.

Ciur-1Aa: Bucharest-Ciurel (Romania), sunken building 1A; Dolinescu-Ferche 1979:186 fig. 1/5.

Ciur-1Ab: Bucharest-Ciurel (Romania), sunken building 1A; Dolinescu-Ferche 1979:187 fig. 2/3.

Ciur-1B: Bucharest-Ciurel (Romania), sunken building 1B; Dolinescu-Ferche 1979:193 fig. 8/3.

Ciur-2Aa: Bucharest-Ciurel (Romania), sunken building 2A; Morintz 1961:660 fig. 2/1.

Ciur-2Ab: Bucharest-Ciurel (Romania), sunken building 2A; Morintz 1961:660 fig. 2/2.

Ciur-2Ac: Bucharest-Ciurel (Romania), sunken building 2A; Morintz 1961:660 fig. 2/3.

Ciur-2Ad: Bucharest-Ciurel (Romania), sunken building 2A; Dolinescu-Ferche 1979:191 fig. 6/1.

Ciur-2B: Bucharest-Ciurel (Romania), sunken building 2B; Dolinescu-Ferche 1979:194 fig. 10.

Ciur-3a: Bucharest-Ciurel (Romania), sunken building 3; Dolinescu-Ferche 1979:196 fig. 12/1.

Ciur-3b: Bucharest-Ciurel (Romania), sunken building 3; Dolinescu-Ferche 1979:195 fig. 11/1.

Ciur-3c: Bucharest-Ciurel (Romania), sunken building 3; Dolinescu-Ferche 1979:195 fig. 11/6.

Ciur-3d: Bucharest-Ciurel (Romania), sunken building 3; Dolinescu-Ferche 1979:195 fig. 11/11.

Ciur-4a: Bucharest-Ciurel (Romania), sunken building 4; Dolinescu-Ferche 1979:198 fig. 14/1.

Appendix B

Ciur-4b: Bucharest-Ciurel (Romania), sunken building 4; Dolinescu-Ferche 1979:199 fig. 15/1.

Ciur-4c: Bucharest-Ciurel (Romania), sunken building 4; Dolinescu-Ferche 1979:197 fig. 13/13.

Ciur-5a: Bucharest-Ciurel (Romania), sunken building 5; Dolinescu-Ferche 1979:201 fig. 17/1.

Ciur-5b: Bucharest-Ciurel (Romania), sunken building 5; Dolinescu-Ferche 1979:200 fig. 17/1.

Ciur-6: Bucharest-Ciurel (Romania), sunken building 6; Morintz and Roman 1962:759 fig. 4/6.

Ciur-8a: Bucharest-Ciurel (Romania), sunken building 8; Dolinescu-Ferche 1979:205 fig. 22/1.

Ciur-8b: Bucharest-Ciurel (Romania), sunken building 8; Dolinescu-Ferche 1979:203 fig. 20/1.

Ciurel 1: Bucharest-Ciurel (Romania), settlement find; Comşa 1972:10 fig. 1/10.

Ciurel 2: Bucharest-Ciurel (Romania), settlement find; Comşa 1972:11 fig. 2/2.

Ciurel 3: Bucharest-Ciurel (Romania), settlement find; Teodor 1972:32 fig. 3/7.

Ciurel 4: Bucharest-Ciurel (Romania), settlement find; Morintz and Roman 1962:765 fig. 4/1.

Craiova: Craiova (Romania), stray find; Toropu 1976:209.

Cuco-4a: Cucorăni, Botoşani district (Romania), sunken building 4; Teodor 1975:198 fig. 59/6.

Dămă-1: Bucharest-Dămăroaia (Romania), settlement find; Rosetti 1934:210 fig. 5/1.

Dămă-2: Bucharest-Dămăroaia (Romania), settlement find; Rosetti 1934:210 fig. 5/4.

Davi-12: Davideni, Neamţ district (Romania), sunken building 12; Mitrea 1974–6:fig. 11/1.

Davi-26: Davideni, Neamţ district (Romania), sunken building 26; Mitrea 1992:fig. 7/4.

Davi-39a: Davideni, Neamţ district (Romania), sunken building 39; Mitrea 1994:316 fig. 19/1.

Davi-39b: Davideni, Neamţ district (Romania), sunken building 39; Mitrea 1994:316 fig. 19/4.

Davi-40: Davideni, Neamţ district (Romania), sunken building 40; Mitrea 1994:316 fig. 19/3.

Dod-1: Dodeşti, Vaslui district (Romania), sunken building 1; Teodor 1984b:42 fig. 15/6.

Dod-3: Dodeşti, Vaslui district (Romania), sunken building 3; Teodor 1984b:42 fig. 15/1.

Gheor: Sfântu Gheorghe-Iernut, Mureş district (Romania), settlement find; Vlassa et al. 1966:405 fig. 6/9.

Appendix B

Ghiv-4a: Bucharest-Soldat Ghivan Street (Romania), sunken building 4; Constantiniu and Dolinescu-Ferche 1981:103 fig. 2/7.

Ghiv-4b: Bucharest-Soldat Ghivan Street (Romania), sunken building 4; Dolinescu-Ferche and Constantiniu 1981:103 fig. 2/9.

Ghiv-7a: Bucharest-Soldat Ghivan Street (Romania), sunken building 7; Dolinescu-Ferche and Constantiniu 1981:298 fig. 4/6.

Ghiv-7b: Bucharest-Soldat Ghivan Street (Romania), sunken building 7; Dolinescu-Ferche and Constantiniu 1981:298 fig. 4/9.

Ghiv-7c: Bucharest-Soldat Ghivan Street (Romania), sunken building 7; Dolinescu-Ferche and Constantiniu 1981:298 fig. 4/2.

Ghiv-11a: Bucharest-Soldat Ghivan Street (Romania), sunken building 11; Dolinescu-Ferche and Constantiniu 1981:298 fig. 4/4.

Ghiv-11b: Bucharest-Soldat Ghivan Street (Romania), sunken building 11; Dolinescu-Ferche and Constantiniu 1981:300 fig. 5/3.

Ghiv-12: Bucharest-Soldat Ghivan Street (Romania), sunken building 12; Dolinescu-Ferche and Constantiniu 1981:298 fig. 4/7.

Ghiv-14: Bucharest-Soldat Ghivan Street (Romania), sunken building 14; Dolinescu-Ferche and Constantiniu 1981:298 fig. 4/8.

Ghiv-16a: Bucharest-Soldat Ghivan Street (Romania), sunken building 16; Dolinescu-Ferche and Constantiniu 1981:300 fig. 5/5.

Ghiv-16b: Bucharest-Soldat Ghivan Street (Romania), sunken building 16; Dolinescu-Ferche and Constantiniu 1981:300 fig. 5/4.

Ghiv-16c: Bucharest-Soldat Ghivan Street (Romania), sunken building 16; Dolinescu-Ferche and Constantiniu 1981:298 fig. 4/1.

Ghiv-16d: Bucharest-Soldat Ghivan Street (Romania), sunken building 16; Dolinescu-Ferche and Constantiniu 1981:300 fig. 5/6.

Ghiv-16e: Bucharest-Soldat Ghivan Street (Romania), sunken building 16; Dolinescu-Ferche and Constantiniu 1981:298 fig. 4/10.

Horga: Horga, Vaslui district (Romania), sunken building; Coman 1971b:fig. 2/2.

Iaşi: Iaşi-Crucea lui Ferenţ (Romania), sunken building 1; Teodor 1971:128 fig. 4/11.

Kor-1: Korchak IX, Zhytomyr region (Ukraine), sunken building 1; Rusanova 1973b:pl. 8/7.

Kor-4a: Korchak IX, Zhytomyr region (Ukraine), sunken building 4; Rusanova 1973b:pl. 8/17.

Kor-4b: Korchak IX, Zhytomyr region (Ukraine), sunken building 4; Rusanova 1973b:pl. 8/18.

Kor-5: Korchak IX, Zhytomyr region (Ukraine), sunken building 5; Rusanova 1973b:pl. 9/1.

Kor-7: Korchak IX, Zhytomyr region (Ukraine), sunken building 7; Rusanova 1973b:pl. 9/16.

Kor-M: Korchak IX, Zhytomyr region (Ukraine), grave; Rusanova 1973b:pl. 9/20.

Appendix B

Malu-1: Malu Roşu-Fierbinţi, Ialomiţa district (Romania), sunken building; Filipescu 1984:130 pl. 1/1.

Malu-2: Malu Roşu-Fierbinţi, Ialomiţa district (Romania), sunken building; Filipescu 1984:130 pl. 1/2.

Mili-1: Bucharest-Militari, settlement find; Teodor 1972:36 fig. 5/10.

Mili-2: Bucharest-Militari (Romania), settlement find; Teodor 1972:30 fig. 1/3.

Mili-3: Bucharest-Militari (Romania), settlement find; Zirra and Cazimir 1963:67 fig. 15/1.

Rash-13: Rashkov III, Chernivtsi region (Ukraine), sunken building 13; Baran 1988a:151 pl. xxx/9.

Rash-22: Rashkov III, Chernivtsi region (Ukraine), sunken building 22; Baran 1988a:151 pl. xxxiii/3.

Rash-25: Rashkov III, Chernivtsi region (Ukraine), sunken building 35; Baran 1988a:152 pl. xxxv/1.

Rash-30: Rashkov III, Chernivtsi region (Ukraine), sunken building 30; Baran 1988a:152 pl. xxvi/1.

Sărat-1: Sărata-Monteoru, Buzău district (Romania), cemetery find; n.a. 1955b:510 fig. 11/1.

Seli-1: Selişte, Orhei district, settlement find (Moldova); Rafalovich and Lapushnian 1973:114 fig. 2/1.

Seli-2: Selişte, Orhei district, settlement find (Moldova); Rafalovich and Lapushnian 1973:133 fig. 10/1.

Seli-3: Selişte, Orhei district, settlement find (Moldova); Rafalovich and Lapushnian 1973:133 fig. 10/2.

Seli-4: Selişte, Orhei district, settlement find (Moldova); Rafalovich and Lapushnian 1973:133 fig. 10/3.

Seli-5: Selişte, Orhei district, settlement find (Moldova); Rafalovich 1974:126 fig. 8/1.

Seli-12a: Selişte, Orhei district, sunken building 12 (Moldova); archaeological report in the archives of the Archaeological Institute in Chişinău.

Seli-12b: Selişte, Orhei district, sunken building 12 (Moldova); archaeological report in the archives of the Archaeological Institute in Chişinău.

Seli-12c: Selişte, Orhei district, sunken building 12 (Moldova); archaeological report in the archives of the Archaeological Institute in Chişinău.

Seli-16a: Selişte, Orhei district, sunken building 16 (Moldova); Rafalovich 1974:126 fig. 8/2.

Seli-16b: Selişte, Orhei district, sunken building 16 (Moldova); Rafalovich 1974:126 fig. 8/3.

Seli-P73: Selişte, Orhei district, pit 73 (Moldova); Rafalovich 1974:126 fig. 8/4.

Strău 1: Bucharest-Străuleşti (Romania), settlement find; Teodor 1972:fig. 4/1.

Strău 2: Bucharest-Străuleşti (Romania), settlement find; Teodor 1972:fig. 32/2.

Strău 3: Bucharest-Străuleşti (Romania), settlement find; Teodor 1972:fig. 32/3.

Appendix B

Strău 4: Bucharest-Străuleşti (Romania), settlement find; Teodor 1972:fig. 32/4.

Strău 5: Bucharest-Străuleşti (Romania), settlement find; Teodor 1972:fig. 32/6.

Strău 6: Bucharest-Străuleşti (Romania), settlement find; Teodor 1972:fig. 32/8.

Uzhho: Uzhhorod-Halaho, Zakarpatska region (Ukraine), sunken building; Peniak 1980:34 fig. 10/2.

Uzhho-1: Uzhhorod-Halaho, Zakarpatska region (Ukraine), grave 1; Peniak 1980:34 fig. 10/1.

REFERENCES

PRIMARY SOURCES

Agathias. *Historiae.* Ed. Rudolf Keydell. Corpus Fontium Historiae Byzantinae, Series Berolinensis 2. Berlin: De Gruyter, 1967.

Chronicle of Monemvasia. Ed. Ivan Duichev. Palermo: Istituto Siciliano di Studi Bizantini e Neoellenici, 1976.

Chronicon Paschale. Ed. L. Dindorf. Bonn: E. Weber, 1831. Trans. Michael Whitby and Mary Whitby. Liverpool: Liverpool University Press, 1989.

Constantine Porphyrogenitus. *De Administrando Imperio.* Ed. Gyula Moravcsik. Trans. R. J. H. Jenkins. Washington: Dumbarton Oaks Center for Byzantine Studies, 1967.

Conversio Bagoariorum et Carantanorum. Ed. Herwig Wolfram. Vienna: Böhlau, 1979.

Corpus Iuris Civilis. Ed. Paul Krüger, Theodor Mommsen, Rudolf Schöll, and Wilhelm Kroll. 3 vols. Berlin: Weidmann, 1954.

Evagrius. *Historia Ecclesiastica.* Ed. Joseph Bidez and Léon Parmentier. London, 1898; reprint Amsterdam: A. M. Hakkert, 1964.

Fredegar. *Chronicon.* Ed. Bruno Krusch, MGH: SRM 2:1–193; Book IV, ed. and trans. J. M. Wallace-Hadrill. London: Nelson, 1960.

George of Pisidia. *Poems.* Ed. A. Pertusi. Ettal: Buch- Kunstverlag, 1959.

Gregory the Great. *Registrum Epistolarum.* Ed. P. Ewald and L. M. Hartmann. *MGH: Epistolae* 1.2. Berlin: Weidmann, 1887/99.

Isidore of Seville. *Historia Gothorum Wandalorum Sueborum.* Ed. Theodor Mommsen. *MGH: AA* 11. Chronica Minora 2:267–303. Berlin: Weidmann, 1894.

John of Biclar. *Chronica.* Ed. Theodor Mommsen. *MGH: AA* 11. Chronica Minora 2:211–39. Berlin: Weidmann, 1894.

John of Ephesus. *Historia Ecclesiastica.* Ed. E. I. Brooks. Paris, 1935. Trans. E. I. Brooks. Paris: E. Typographeo Reipublicae, 1936.

John Lydus. *On Powers.* Ed. Anastasius C. Bardy. Philadelphia: American Philosophical Society, 1982.

John Malalas. *Chronographia.* Ed. Ludwig Dindorf. Bonn, 1831. Trans. Elizabeth Jeffreys, Michael Jeffreys, and Roger Scott. Byzantina Australensis 4. Melbourne: Australian Association for Byzantine Studies, 1986.

Jonas of Bobbio. *Vita Columbani.* In *Vitae Columbani Abbatis Discipulorumque Eius Libri II.* Ed. Bruno Krusch. In *MGH: SS* 37:1–294. Leipzig: Impensis Bibliopoli Hahniani, 1905.

References

Jordanes. *Romana et Getica*. Ed. Theodor Mommsen. *MGH: AA* 5.1. Berlin, 1882. Trans. Charles C. Mierow. New York: Speculum Historiale, 1960.

Leo the Wise. *Tactica*. PG 107:672–1120.

Martin of Braga. *Opera*. Ed. E. Barlow. New Haven: Yale University Press, 1950.

Menander the Guardsman. *Historia*. Ed. R. C. Blockley. ARCA: Classical and Medieval Texts, 17. Liverpool: F. Cairns, 1985.

Michael the Syrian. *Chronicon*. Ed. Jean B. Chabot. Paris: E. Typographeo Reipublicae, 1963.

Miracles of St Demetrius. Ed. Paul Lemerle. Paris: Centre National de la Recherche Scientifique, 1979.

Nicephorus. *Breviarium*. Ed. Cyril Mango. Washington: Dumbarton Oaks,1990.

Paul the Deacon. *Historia Langobardorum*. Ed. Georg Waitz. *MGH: SS* 48. Hannover, 1878. Trans. William D. Foulke. Philadelphia: University of Pennsylvania Press, 1974.

Procopius of Caesarea. *Wars*. Ed. J. Haury. Trans. H. B. Dewing. 5 vols. Cambridge: Harvard University Press, 1914–28.

Secret History. Ed. J. Haury. Trans. H. B. Dewing. Cambridge: Harvard University Press, 1935.

Buildings. Ed. J. Haury. Trans. H. B. Dewing. Cambridge: Harvard University Press, 1940.

Pseudo-Caesarius. *Eratopokriseis*. Ed. Rudolf Riedinger. Byzantinisches Archiv, 12. Munich: Beck, 1969.

Sebeos. *Historia*. Trans. R. Bedrosian. New York: Sources of the Armenian Tradition, 1985.

Strategikon. Ed. George T. Dennis and Ernst Gamillscheg. Vienna, 1981. Trans. George T. Dennis. Philadelphia: University of Pennsylvania Press, 1984.

Theodore Syncellus. *De Obsidione Avarica Constantinopolis*. Ed. Samuel Szádeczky-Kardoss and Thérèse Olajos. Brussels: Latomus, 1990.

Theophanes. *Chronographia*. Ed. Carl de Boor. 2 vols. Leipzig, 1883–5. Trans. Cyril Mango and Roger Scott. Oxford: Clarendon Press, 1997.

Theopylact Simocatta. *Historia*. Ed. Carl de Boor and Peter Wirth. Stuttgart, 1972. Trans. Mary and Michael Whitby. Oxford: Clarendon Press, 1986.

Thomas the Archdeacon. *Historia Salonitana*. Ed. F. Rački. Monumenta spectantia historiam Slavorum meridionalum, 26. Zagreb: Ex Officina Societatis Typographicae, 1894.

Victor of Tunnunna. *Chronica*. Ed. Theodor Mommsen. *MGH: AA* 11. Chronica Minora 2:184–206. Berlin: Weidmann, 1894.

Vita Amandi. Ed. Bruno Krusch. *MGH: SRM* 5:395–485. Hannover: Impensis Bibliopolii Hahniani, 1910.

Vita Davidi Thessaloniciensis. Ed. Valentin Rose. Berlin: A. Asher, 1887.

Vita Hrodberti Episcopi Salisburgensis. Ed. W. Levinson, *MGH: SRM* 6:140–62. Hannover: Impensis Bibliopolii Hahniani, 1913.

Vita Sancti Marini. Ed. B. Sepp. Regensburg: J. & C. Mayr, 1892.

Vita Zotici. In Aubineau 1975.

References

SECONDARY SOURCES

Abadie-Reynal, Catherine 1989a. "Les amphores protobyzantines d'Argos (IV–e–VI–e siècles)." In *Recherches*, pp. 47–56.

1989b. "Céramique et commerce dans le bassin égéen du IV-e au VII-e siècle." In *Hommes*, pp. 143–62. Vol. 1.

Abashina, N. S. 1986. "Rann'oslov'ianske poselennia Obukhiv VII na Stugni." *Arkheolohiia* 53:72–86.

Åberg, Nils 1919. *Ostpreußen in der Völkerwanderungszeit*. Uppsala: Akademiska bokhandeln.

1953. *Den historiska relationen mellan folkvandringstid och Vendeltid*. Stockholm: Wahlström & Widstrand.

Adshead, Katherine 1990. "Procopius' poliorcetica: continuities and discontinuities." In *Reading the Past in Late Antiquity*, pp. 93–119. Ed. Graeme Clark et al. Rushcutters Bay: Australian National University Press.

Afanas'ev, G. E. 1975. "Poseleniia VI–IX vv. raiona Kislovodska." *SA* 3:53–61.

1979. "Khronologiia mogil'nika Mokraia Balka." *KSIA* 158:43–51.

1993. "Sistema social'no-markiruiushchikh predmetov v muzhskikh pogrebal'nikh kompleksakh Donskikh alan." *RA* 4:131–44.

Aibabin, A. I. 1973. "K voprosu o proiskhozhdenii serezhek Pastyrskogo tipa." *SA* 3:62–72.

1984. "Raskopki rannesrednevekovykh mogil'nikov v gornom Krymu." In *Arkheologicheskie otkrytiia 1982 goda*, pp. 239–40. Ed. B. A. Rybakov. Moscow: Nauka.

1990. "Khronologiia mogil'nikov Kryma pozdnerimskogo i rannesrednevekovogo vremeni." *MAIET* 1:5–68.

Aitchison, N. B. 1988. "Roman wealth, native ritual: coin hoards within and beyond Roman Britain." *WA* 20, no. 2:270–83.

Aksenov, V. S., and L. I. Babenko 1998. "Pogrebenie VI–VII vekov n.e. u sela Mokhnach." *RA* 3:111–21.

Aksenova, E. P., and M. A. Vasil'ev 1993. "Problemy etnogonii slavianstva i ego vetvei v akademicheskikh diskussiakh rubezha 1930–1940–kh godov." *SovS* 2:86–104.

Aleksandrov, Georgi 1987. "Rezultati ot razkopkite na krepostta Montana (1971–1982)." In *Montana*, pp. 54–85. Ed. Velizar Velkov. Sofia: BAN.

Aleksova, Blaga 1969. "Pridones od istražuvanjata vo Bargala-Bregalnica za osvetluvanjeto na istorijata na južnite Sloveni." In *Simpozijum*, pp. 105–14.

1975–8. "Bargala: arkheološki istražuvanja 1966–1976." *Zbornik*:75–91.

1986. "Novi istražuvanja na baptisteriumot vo Bargala." In *Mélange*, pp. 29–38.

Alexander, Eugene M. 1994. "Early Slavic invasions and settlements in the area of the Lower Danube in the sixth through the eighth centuries." PhD Dissertation. New York University.

Alexandrescu, Petre, and D. Vîlceanu 1962. "Şantierul Histria." *MCA* 8:401–2.

Alfen, Peter G. van 1996. "New light on the 7th-c. Yassi Ada shipwreck: capacities and standard sizes of LRA1 amphoras." *JRA* 9:189–213.

Alföldi, András 1934. "Zur historischen Bestimmung der Awarenfunde." *Eurasia Septentrionalis Antiqua* 9:285–307.

References

Allen, Michael 1984. "Elders, chiefs, and Big Men: authority legitimation and political evolution in Melanesia." *AE* 11, no. 1:20–41.

Allen, P. 1979. "A new date for the last recorded events in John of Ephesus' Historia ecclesiastica." *Orientalia Lovaniensia Periodica* 10:251–4.

Alverson, Hoyt S. 1979. "The roots of time: a comment on utilitarian and primordial sentiments in ethnic identification." In *Ethnic Autonomy – Comparative Dynamics. The Americas, Europe and the Developing World*, pp. 13–17. Ed. R. L. Hall. New York, Oxford, and Toronto: Pergamon Press.

Ambroz, A. K. 1968. "Dunaiskie elementy v rannesrednevekovoi kul'ture Kryma (VI–VII vv.)." *KSIA* 113:10–23.

1970. "Iuzhnye khudozhestvennye sviazi naselenie verkhnogo Podneprov'ia v VI v." In *Sosedi*, pp. 70–4.

1981. "Vostochnoevropeiskie i sredneaziatskie stepi V-pervoi poloviny VIII v." In *Stepi*, pp. 10–23.

1986. "Kinzhaly VI–VII vv. s dvumia vystupami na nozhnakh." *SA* 4:53–73.

1989. *Khronologiia drevnostei Severnogo Kavkaza V–VII vv.* Moscow: Nauka.

1993. "K proiskhozhdeniiu Dneprovskikh antropozoomorfnykh fibul." *RA* 2:179–84.

Amory, Patrick 1993. "The meaning and purpose of ethnic terminology in the Burgundian laws." *EME* 2, no. 1:1–28.

1994. "Names, ethnic identity, and community in fifth- and sixth-century Burgundy." *Viator* 25:1–34.

1997. *People and Identity in Ostrogothic Italy, 489– 554.* Cambridge: Cambridge University Press.

Anamali, Skënder 1988. "La basilique de Ballshi (Albanie)." *BSAF*:131–5.

1989. "L'état actuel des recherches sur l'origine des villes du Moyen Age en Albanie." In *Actes XI*, pp. 2617– 35. Vol. III.

1993a. "Architettura e decorazione tardoantica in Albania." *CCARB* 40:447–74.

1993b. "Oreficerie, gioielli bizantini in Albania: Komani." *CCARB* 40:435–46.

Anamali, Skënder, and Hëna Spahiu 1963. "Varrëza e herëshme mesjëtare e Krujes." *Buletin i Universitetit Shtëror te Tiranës* 17, no. 2:3–85.

1979–80. "Varrëza arbërore e Krujes." *Iliria* 9– 10:47–103.

Anderson, Perry 1977. *Passages from Antiquity to Feudalism.* London: NLB.

Anfert'ev, A. N. 1986. "Drevneishee svidetel'stvo o rasselenii slavian (Iord. Get. 34–35)." In *The 17th International Byzantine Congress. Abstracts*, pp. 9–12. New Rochelle: Aristide D. Caratzas.

1991. "Iordan." In *Svod*, pp. 98–169. Vol. I.

Angelov, Dimităr 1981. "Die bulgarischen Slawen und die Nomaden (VI.–XII. Jh.). Nach Angaben von schriftlichen Quellen." In *Pliska*, pp. 7–15. Vol. III.

Angelov, Nikola 1962. "Spasitelni razkopki na Carevec prez 1961 g." *Arkheologiia* 4, no. 4:20–9.

1986. "Antichno i rannovizantiisko selishte." In *Istoriia na Veliko Tărnovo*, pp. 43–95. Ed. Petăr Petrov. Sofia: BAN.

Angelova, Stefka 1980. "Po văprosa za rannoslavianskata kultura na iug i na sever ot Dunav prez VI–VII v." *Arkheologiia* 12, no. 4:1–12.

Angelova, Stefka, and Vladimir Penchev 1989. "Srebărno săkrovishte ot Silistra." *Arkheologiia* 31, no. 2:38–43.

References

Anthony, David 1990. "Migration in archaeology: the baby and the bathwater." *AAnth* 92:895–914.

1995. "Nazi and eco-feminist prehistories: ideology and empiricism in Indo-European archaeology." In *Nationalism, Politics, and the Practice of Archaeology*, pp. 82–96. Ed. Philip Kohl and Clare Fawcett. Cambridge: Cambridge University Press.

Antoljak, Stjepan 1982. "Militär-administrative Organisation der makedonischen Sklavinien." *JÖB* 32, no. 2:383–90.

Anton, Hans Hubert 1994. "Origo gentis – Volksgeschichte. Zur Auseinandersetzung mit Walter Goffarts Werk 'The Narrators of Barbarian History'." In *Historiographie*, pp. 263–307.

Antonova, Vera 1970. "Vizantiiska krepost na vrăh Sivri Tepe, Shumenski okrăg." *IBAI* 32:303–5.

1987. "Shumenskata krepost prez rannovizantiiskata epokha." *GMSB* 13:53–68.

Aricescu, A. 1977. *Armata în Dobrogea romană*. Bucharest: Editura militară.

Arnold, C. J. 1983. "The Sancton-Baston potter." *Scottish Archaeological Review* 2:17–30.

1988. "Early Anglo-Saxon pottery of the 'Illington-Lackford' type." *Oxford Journal of Archaeology* 7, no. 3:343–59.

1997. *An Archaeology of the Early Anglo-Saxon Kingdoms*. London and New York: Routledge.

Artamonov, M. I. 1969. "Etnicheskata prinadlezhnost i istoricheskoto znachenie na pastirskata kultura." *Arkheologiia* 11, no. 3:1–10.

1971. "Arkheologicheskaia kul'tura i etnos." In *Problemy istorii feodal'noi Rossii. Sbornik statei k 60–letiiu prof. V. V. Mavrodina*, pp. 16–32. Ed. A. L. Shapiro. Leningrad: Izdatel'stvo Leningradskogo Universiteta.

Atanasov, Georgi 1991. "Rannovizantiiski skalni cărkvi i manastiri v Iuzhna Dobrudzha." *Arkheologiia* 23, no. 3:33–43.

Atanasova, Iordanka 1987. "Il castellum Castra Martis a Kula." *Ratiariensia* 3–4:119–26.

Atanassova-Georgieva, Iordanka 1974. "Le quadriburgium de la forteresse Castra Martis en Dacia Ripensis." In *Actes IX*, pp. 167–72.

Atavin, A. G., and Ia. M. Paromov 1991. "Bolgarskoe pogrebenie c zolotym poias-nym naborom iz Nizhnego Prikuban'ia". In *Drevnosti Severnogo Kavkaza i Prichernomor'ia*, pp. 151–5. Ed. A. P. Abramov et al. Moscow: Moskovskii ark-heologicheskii informacionnyi centr.

Aubineau, Michel 1975. "Zoticos de Constantinople, nourricier des pauvres et ser-viteur des lepreux." *Analecta Bollandiana* 93:67–108.

Aupert, Pierre 1980. "Céramique slave à Argos (585 ap. J.-C.)." In *Etudes argiennes*, pp. 373–94. Athens: Ecole Française d'Athènes.

Aupert, Pierre, and Paola B. Bottini 1979. "Philippes. L'édifice avec bain dans la zone AT.BE 55.63." *BCH* 103:619–27.

Ausenda, Giorgio 1995. "The segmentary lineage in contemporary anthropology and among the Langobards." In *After Empire. Toward an Ethnology of Europe's Barbarians*, pp. 15–50. Ed. G. Ausenda. San Marino: Boydell Press.

Avenarius, Alexander 1973. "Die Awaren und die Slawen in den Miracula Sancti Demetrii." *Vyzantina* 5:11–27.

References

1976. "Awarische Überfälle und die byzantinischen Provinzen am Balkan im 7. Jahrhundert." In *Actes XIV*, pp. 299–305. Vol. III.

1987. "'Gosudarstvo Samo': problemy arkheologii i istorii." In *Struktura*, pp. 66–74.

1991. "Avary i slaviane. 'Derzhava Samo'." In *Gosudarstva*, pp. 26–37.

Avramea, Anna 1983. "Νομισματικοὶ θεσαυροὶ καὶ μεμονωμένα νομίσματα ἀπὸ τὴν Πελοπόννησο (ΣΤ'-Ζ' αἰ.)." *Symmeikta* 5:49–89.

1997. *Le Peloponnèse du IV-e au VIII-e siècle. Changements et persistances*. Paris: Publications de la Sorbonne.

Babić, Boško 1972. "Crepulja, crepna, podnica–posebno značajan oslonac za atribuciju srednjovekovnih arheoloških nalazišta balkanskog poluostrova slovenima poreklom sa istoka." In *Materijali IX. Simpozijum srednjevekovne sekcije Arheološkog društva Jugoslavije*, pp. 101–23. Ed. Danica Dimitrijević. Belgrade: Arheološko društvo Jugoslavije/Narodni Muzej Prilep.

Bačić, Jakov 1983. "The emergence of Sklabenoi (Slavs), their arrival on the Balkan peninsula, and the role of the Avars in these events: revised concepts in a new perspective." PhD Dissertation. Columbia University, New York.

Bakalov, Georgi 1974. "Les ouvrages d'Agathias de Myrenée comme source de l'histoire des territoires balkaniques pendant la première moitié du VI-e siècle." *EB* 2–3:196–207.

Bakhmat, K. P. 1964. "Vykentyi Viacheslavovich Khvoika." *Arkheolohiia* 17:188–95.

Bakirtzis, Ch. 1989a. "Byzantine amphorae." In *Recherches*, pp. 73–7.

1989b. "Western Thrace in the early Christian and Byzantine periods: results of archaeological research and the prospects, 1973–1987." *ByzF* 14:41–58.

Balandier, Georges 1970. *Political Anthropology*. New York: Pantheon Books.

Baldwin, Barry 1977. "Theophylact's knowledge of Latin." *Byzantion* 47:357–60.

1978. "Menander Protector." *DOP* 32:101–25.

1981. "Sources for the Getica of Jordanes." *RBPH* 59:141–5.

Baldwin, Stuart J. 1987. "Roomsize patterns: a quantitative method for approaching ethnic identification in architecture." In *Conference 18*, pp. 163–74.

Bálint, Csanád 1978. "Vestiges archéologiques de l'époque tardive des Sassanides et leurs relations avec les peuples de la steppe." *ActaArchHung* 30:173–212.

1985. "Über die Datierung der osteuropäischen Steppenfunde des frühen Mittelalters. Schwierigkeiten und Möglichkeiten." *MAIUAW* 14:137–47.

1989. *Die Archäologie der Steppe. Steppenvölker zwischen Volga und Donau vom 6. bis zum 10. Jahrhundert*. Vienna and Cologne: Böhlau.

1992. "Kontakte zwischen Iran, Byzanz und der Steppe. Das Grab von Üç Tepe (Sowj. Azerbajdžan) und der beschlagverzierte Gürtel im 6. und 7. Jahrhundert." In *Awarenforschungen*, pp. 309–496.

1993. "Probleme der archäologischen Forschung zur awarischen Landnahmen." In *Probleme*, pp. 195–273. Vol. I.

Baltag, Gheorghe 1979. "Date pentru un studiu arheologic al zonei municipiului Sighişoara." *Marisia* 9:75–106.

Banks, Marcus 1996. *Ethnicity: Anthropological Constructions*. London and New York: Routledge.

Banning, E. G. 1987. "Cache and bury. The archaeology of numismatics." *Canadian Numismatic Journal* 32, no. 1:5–9.

References

Baran, Iaroslav V., and A. A. Kozlovskii 1991. "Die Nomaden der südrussischen Steppen im 1. und beginnenden 2. Jahrtausend n. Chr." In *Gold der Steppe. Archäologie der Ukraine*, pp. 233–8. Ed. Renate Rolle, Michael Müller-Wille, and Kurt Schietzel. Neumünster: Karl Wachholtz.

Baran, Vladimir D. 1968. "Nekotorye itogi izucheniia ranneslavianskikh drevnostei verkhnego Podnestrov'ia i zapadnoi Volynii." *ArchRoz* 20:583–93.

1972. *Ranni slov'iani mia Dnestrom i Pripiat'iu*. Kiev: Naukova Dumka.

1973. "Siedlungen der Černjachov-Kultur am Bug und oberen Dnestr." *ZfA* 7:24–66.

1978. "Slaviane v seredine I tysiacheletiia n.e." In *Problemy*, pp. 5–39.

1981. "K voprosu ob istochkakh slavianskoi kul'tury rannego srednevekov'ia." *AAC* 21:67–88.

1984–7. "Ranneslavianskie poseleniia Podnestrov'ia i Zapadnoi Volyni." *SlA* 30:75–86.

1985. "Prazhskaia kul'tura." In *Karta*, pp. 76–85.

1986. "Die frühslawische Siedlung von Raškov, Ukraine." *Beiträge zur Allgemeinen und Vergleichenden Archäologie* 8:73–175.

1987. "Rannesrednevekovye drevnosti slavian Iugo-Vostochnoi Evropy (problemy slozheniia, periodizacii i social'noi struktury)." In *Trudy*, pp. 52–66. Vol. 1.

1988a. *Prazhskaia kul'tura Podnestrov'ia po materialam poselenii u s. Rashkov*. Kiev: Naukova Dumka.

1988b. "Slavianskaia derevnia rannego sredn[e]veko'ia (po materialam poseleniia V–VII vv. u s. Rashkov)." In *Drevnosti slavian i Rusi*, pp. 12–18. Ed. B. A. Timoshchuk. Moscow: Nauka.

1990. "Prazhskaia kul'tura." In *Arkheologiia Prikarpat'ia, Volyni i Zakarpat'ia (ranneslavianskii i drevnerusskii periody)*, pp. 59–68. Ed. V. V. Aulikh, R. S. Bagrii, and V. D. Baran. Kiev: Naukova Dumka.

1991. "Entstehung und Ausbreitung der frühslawischen Kulturen." In *Starigard/Oldenburg. Ein slawischer Herrschersitz des frühen Mittelalters in Ostholstein*, pp. 29–51. Ed. Michael Müller-Wille. Neumünster: Karl Wachholtz.

1994. "Slov'ians'ky rann'oseredn'ovichny kultury ta ikhny pidosnovi." In *Zbirnyk*, pp. 5–13.

Baran, V. D., E. L. Gorokhovskii, and B. V. Magomedov 1990. "Cherniakhovskaia kul'tura i gotskaia problema." In *Slaviane i Rus' (v zarubezhnoi istoriografii)*, pp. 30–78. Ed. P. P. Tolochko et al. Kiev: Naukova Dumka.

Baran, V. D., E. V. Maksimov, and B. V. Magomedov 1990. *Slaviane iugo-vostochnoi Evropy v predgosudarstvennoi period*. Kiev: Naukova Dumka.

Baranov, I. A., and V. V. Maiko 1994. "Srednedneprovskie elementy v kul'ture naseleniia rannesrednevekovoi Tavriki." In *Zbirnyk*, pp. 96–103.

Baratte, François 1984. "Les témoignages archéologiques de la présence slave au sud du Danube." In *Villes*, pp. 164–80.

Bărbulescu, Ioan 1929. *Individualitatea limbii române şi elementele slave vechi*. Bucharest: Editura Casei Şcoalelor.

Bárdos, Edit 1995. "La necropoli di Zamárdi." In *Avari*, pp. 151–63.

Barišić, Franjo 1953. *Čuda Dimitrija Solunskog kao istoriski izvori*. Belgrade: Srpska Akademija Nauka.

References

1954. "Le siège de Constantinople par les Avares et les Slaves en 626." *Byzantion* 24:371–95.

1965. "'Monemvasijska hronika' o doseljavanju Avaro-Slovena na Peloponez 587." In *Godišnjak III Centar za balkanološka ispitivanja*, pp. 95–109. Vol. 1. Sarajevo: Naučno društvo Bosne i Hercegovine.

1969. "Proces slovenske kolonizacije istočnog Balkana." In *Simpozijum*, pp. 11–27.

Barlow, E. 1950. *Martini Episcopi Bracarensis Opera Omnia*. New Haven: Yale University Press.

Barnea, Alexandru 1984. "Dinogetia III. Precizări cronologice." *Peuce* 9:339–46.

1986. "La forteresse de Dinogetia à la lumière des dernières fouilles archéologiques." In *Akten 13*, pp. 447–50.

1990. "Changements sociaux et économiques dans la province de Scythie (IV–VI–e s.)." *Balcanica* 5:399–403.

Barnea, Alexandru et al. 1979. *Tropaeum Traiani I. Cetatea*. Bucharest: Editura Academiei RSR.

Barnea, Ioan 1958. "Monumente de artă creştine pe teritoriul RPR." *Studii Teologice* 10, nos. 5–6:287–310.

1960a. "Monumente de artă creştine pe teritoriul RPR." *Studii Teologice* 12, nos. 3–4:201–31.

1960b. "Sigilii bizantine inedite din Dobrogea." *SCN* 3:323–32.

1966. "Noi sigilii bizantine la Dunărea de Jos." *SCIV* 17, no. 2:277–97.

1969. "Plombs byzantins dans la collection Michel C. Soutzou." *RESEE* 7, no. 1:21–33.

1975. "Sigilii bizantine de la Noviodunum (II)." *SCN* 6:159–65.

1980. "Dinogetia – ville byzantine du Bas-Danube." *Vyzantina* 10:239–87.

1981. "Sceau de Constantin IV empereur de Byzance, trouvé à Durostorum." *RRH* 20:625–8.

1982. "Sigilii bizantine inedite de la Durostorum-Dorostolon." *Pontica* 15:201–12.

1984. "Sigilii bizantine din colecţia MIRSR." *SCN* 8:95–104.

1985a. "Le christianisme sur le territoire de la RSR au III–e–XI–e siècles." *EB* 1:92–106.

1985b. "Sigilii bizantine inedite din Dobrogea (II)." *Pontica* 18:235–48.

1987a. "Antroponime traco-dace pe sigilii bizantine." *Thraco-Dacica* 8, nos. 1–2:203–6.

1987b. "Sceaux byzantins de Dobroudja." *SBS* 1:77–88.

1990. "Sigilii bizantine inedite din Dobrogea (III)." *Pontica* 23:315–34.

Barnea, Ioan, and Radu Vulpe 1968. *Romanii la Dunărea de Jos*. Bucharest: Editura Academiei RSR.

Barnish, S. J. B. 1984. "The genesis and completion of Cassiodorus' *Gothic History*." *Latomus* 43:336–61.

Barsanti, Claudia 1989. "L'esportazione di marmi dal Proconneso nelle regioni pontiche durante il IV–VI secolo." *Rivista dell'Istituto Nazionale di Archeologia e Storia dell'Arte* 12:91–220.

Barth, Fredrik (ed.) 1969. *Ethnic Groups and Boundaries: The Social Organisation of Culture Difference*. Bergen and London: Universitets Forlaget and George Allen and Unwin.

1994. "Enduring and emerging issues in the analysis of ethnicity." In *Anthropology*, pp. 11–32.

References

Bartlett, Robert 1993. *The Making of Europe. Conquest, Colonization, and Cultural Change 950–1350*. Princeton: Princeton University Press.

Bartosiewicz, L., and A. M. Choyke 1991. "Animal remains from the 1970–1972 excavations of Iatrus (Krivina), Bulgaria." *ActaArchHung* 43:181–209.

Bârzu, Ligia 1994–5. "La station no. 1 de Bratei, dép. de Sibiu (IVe–VIIe siècles)." *Dacia* 38–9:239–95.

Basler, Duro 1993. *Spätantike und frühchristliche Architektur in Bosnien und der Herzegowina*. Vienna: Verlag der Österreichischen Akademie der Wissenschaften.

Baudot, Marcel 1928. "La question du Pseudo-Frédégaire." *Le Moyen Age* 29:129–70.

Baumann, Mariusz 1982. "From problems of the origin and collapse of Yugoslavian zadruga." *Ethnologia Polona* 8:131–41.

Bavant, Bernard 1984. "La ville dans le nord de l'Illyricum (Pannonie, Mésie I, Dacie et Dardanie)." In *Villes*, pp. 245–88.

Bejan, Adrian 1976. "Un atelier metalurgic de la Drobeta-Turnu Severin." *AMN* 13:257–68.

Beliaev, S. A. 1989. "Baziliki Khersonesa (itogi, problemy i zadachi iz izucheniia)." *VV* 50:171–81.

Benedicty, Robert 1963. "Die auf die frühslawische Gesellschaftsbezügliche byzantinische Terminologie." In *Actes XIIa*, pp. 45–55. Vol. II.

1965. "Prokopios' Berichte über die slavische Vorzeit. Beiträge zur historiographischen Methode Prokopios von Kaisareia." *Jahrbuch der Österreichischen Byzantinischen Gesellschaft* 14:51–78.

Bentley, G. Carter 1987. "Ethnicity and practice." *CSSH* 29, no. 1:25–55.

Beranová, Magdalena 1976. "Osadnictwo i gospodarska na terenie Czech w VI–VIII w." *Kwartalnik Historii Kultury Materialnej* 24, no. 3:429–39.

1984. "Types of Slavic agricultural production in the 6th–12th centuries." *Ethnologia Slavica* 16:7–48.

Berezovec, D. T. 1952. "Kharyvs'kii skarb." *Arkheolohiia* 6:109–19.

1963. "Poseleniia ulichei na r. Tiasmine." In *Obrazovaniia*, pp. 145–208.

Berghaus, P. 1987. "Coin hoards: methodology and evidence." In *Numismatics and Archaeology*, pp. 12–23. Ed. Parmeshwari Lal Gupta and Amal Kumar Jha. Maharashtra: Indian Institute of Research in Numismatics.

Bertels, Klaus 1987. "Carantania. Beobachtungen zur politisch-geographischen Terminologie und zur Geschichte des Landes und seiner Bevölkerung im frühen Mittelalter." *Carinthia* 177:87–190.

Beshevliev, Veselin 1964. *Spätgriechische und spätlateinische Inschriften aus Bulgarien*. Berlin: Akademie Verlag.

1967a. "Zu Theophanis Chronographia 359, 5–17." *ByzF* 2:50–8.

1967b. "Zur Topographie der Balkanhalbinsel in Prokops Werk De aedificiis." *Philologus* 111:267–82.

1970a. "Randbemerkungen über die 'Miracula Sancti Demetrii'." *Vyzantina* 2:287–300.

1970b. *Zur Bedeutung der Kastellnamen in Prokops Werk "De aedificiis"*. Amsterdam: Adolf M. Hakkert.

1981. *Die protobulgarische Periode der bulgarischen Geschichte*. Amsterdam: Adolf M. Hakkert.

Bezuglov, S. I. 1985. "Pogrebenie kochevnika VII v. n.e. na Nizhnem Donu." *SA* 2:248–52.

References

Bialeková, Darina 1960. "Staroslovanská osada v Siladiciach." *ArchRoz* 15:810–16, 827–8, 833.

1968. "Zur Datierung der oberen Grenze des Prager Typus in der Südwestslowakei." *ArchRoz* 20:619–25.

Bialeková, Darina, and Anna Tirpaková 1983. "Preukazateľnosť používania rímskych mier pri zhotovovaní slovanskej keramiky." *SlovArch* 31, no. 1:121–47.

Bieńkowski, Piotr 1929. "O skarbie srebrnym z Choniakowa na Wołyniu." *Swiatowit* 13:149–81.

Bierbrauer, Volker 1975. *Die ostgotischen Grab- und Schatzfunde in Italien.* Spoleto: Centro Italiano di Studi sull'Alto Medioevo.

1978. "Reperti ostrogoti provenienti da tombe o tesori della Lombardia." In *I Langobardi e la Lombardia*, pp. 214–23. Milan: Palazzo Reale.

1984. "Jugoslawien seit dem Beginn der Völkerwanderung bis zur slawischen Landnahme: die Synthese auf dem Hintergrund von Migrations- und Landnahmevorgängen." In *Jugoslawien. Integrationsprobleme in Geschichte und Gegenwart. Beiträge des Südosteuropa-Arbeitskreises der Deutschen Forschungsgemeinschaft zum V. Internationalen Südosteuropa-Kongreß der Association Internationale d'Etudes du Sud-Est-Européen Belgrad, 11.–17. September 1984*, pp. 49–97. Ed. Klaus–Detlev Grothusen. Göttingen: Vandenhoeck & Ruprecht.

1986. "Iatrus-Krivina. Ein spätantikes Kastell an der unteren Donau. Bemerkungen zu den ersten beiden Bänden der Gesamtpublikation." *Germania* 64:441–64.

1987. *Invillino-Ibligo in Friaul I. Die römische Siedlung und das spätantik-frühmittelalterliche Castrum.* Munich: C. H. Beck.

1989. "Bronzene Bügelfibeln des 5. Jahrhunderts aus Südosteuropa." *JMV* 72:141–60.

1994. "Archäologie und Geschichte der Goten vom 1.–7. Jahrhundert. Versuch einer Bilanz." *FS* 28:51–171.

Biernacka-Lubańska, Malgorzata 1982. *The Roman and Early Byzantine Fortifications of Lower Moesia and Northern Thrace.* Wrocław, Warsaw, Cracow, Gdańsk, and Łódź: Zaklad Narodowy im. Ossolińskich.

Biers, Jane C. 1985. *The Great Bath on the Lechaion Road.* Princeton: American School of Classical Studies.

Binford, Lewis R. 1971. "Mortuary practices: their study and their potential." In *Approaches to the Social Dimensions of Mortuary Practices*, pp. 6–29. Ed. James A. Brown. Memoirs of the Society for American Archaeology, Washington: Society for American Archaeology.

Birge, D. E., L. H. Kraynak, and St. G. Miller 1992. *Excavations at Nemea. Topographical and Architectural Studies.* Berkeley and Los Angeles: University of California Press.

Birnbaum, Henrik 1975. *Common Slavic. Progress and Problems in its Reconstruction.* Columbus, OH: Slavica Publishers.

1986. "Weitere Überlegungen zur Frage nach der Urheimat der Slaven." *Zeitschrift für Slavische Philologie* 46:19–45.

1992. "Vom ethnolinguistischer Einheit zur Vielfalt: die Slaven im Zuge der Landnahme der Balkanhalbinsel." *SF* 51:1–19.

1993. "On the ethnogenesis and protohome of the Slavs: the linguistic evidence." *Journal of Slavic Linguistics* 1, no. 2:352–74.

Biță, Traian 1985. "O fibulă digitată de la Pașcani-Fîntînele." *AM* 10:99–100.

References

Bitner-Wróblewska, Anna 1991. "Between Scania and Samland. From studies of sty-listic links in the Baltic Basin during the Early Migration Period." *Fornvännen* 86:226–41.

Blockley, R. C. 1985. *The History of Menander the Guardsman*. Liverpool: F. Cairns.

Bobrinskii, A. A. 1901. *Kurgany i sluchainye arkheologicheskie nakhodki bliz mestechka Smely*, vol. III. St Petersburg: Balashev.

Boer, J. G. de 1988–9. "An early Byzantine fortress on the tell of Dyadovo." *Talanta* 20–1:7–15.

Bogachev, A. V. 1996. "K voprosu o pozdnei date drevnosti 'gunnskogo kruga'." *RA* 3:186–9.

Bogdan, Ioan 1894. *Însemnatatea studiilor slave pentru români*. Bucharest: Carl Göbl.

Bogdan-Cătăniciu, Ioana 1979. "Die letzte Siedlungsphase der Civitas von Tropaeum Traiani bei Adamclisi (6.–7. Jh. u.Z.)." *SF* 38:184–90.

Bohannan, Paul 1958. "Extra-processual events in Tiv political institutions." *AAnth* 60:1–12.

Böhner, Kurt 1993. "Zur Herkunft der frühmittelalterlichen Spangenhelme." In *Actes XIIb*, pp. 199–207. Vol. IV.

Bolşacov-Ghimpu, A. A. 1969. "La localisation de la forteresse Turris." *RESEE* 7, no. 4:686–90.

Bolta, Lojze 1978. "Rifnik, provinzialrömische Siedlung und Gräberfeld." *AV* 29:510–16.

Bølviken, Erik et al., 1982. "Correspondence analysis: an alternative to principal components." *WA* 14: 41–60.

Bóna, István 1956. "Die Langobarden in Ungarn. Die Gräberfelder von Várpalota und Bezenye." *ActaArchHung* 7:183–242.

1968. "Abriss der Siedlungsgeschichte Ungarns im 5.–7. Jahrhundert und die Awarensiedlung von Dunaújváros." *ArchRoz* 20:605–18.

1971. "Ein Vierteljahrhundert Völkerwanderungszeitforschung in Ungarn." *ActaArchHung* 23:265–336.

1973. *VII. századi avar települések és Árpád-kori magyar falu Dunaújvárosban*. Budapest: Akadémiai kiadó.

1976. *The Dawn of the Dark Ages. The Gepids and the Lombards in the Carpathian Basin*. Budapest: Corvina.

1978. "Neue Langobardenfunde in Ungarn." In *Problemi*, pp. 109–15.

1979a. "Gepiden in Siebenbürgen – Gepiden an der Theiss (Probleme der Forschungsmethode und Fundinterpretation)." *ActaArchHung* 31:9–50.

1979b. "Die langobardische Besetzung Südpannoniens und die archäologischen Probleme der langobardisch-slawischen Beziehungen." *Zeitschrift für Ostforschung* 28:393–404.

1979c. "A Szegvár-sápoldali lovassír. Adatok a korai avar temetkézesi szokasókhoz." *ArchÉrt* 106:3–32.

1980. "Studien zum frühawarischen Reitergrab von Szgevár." *ActaArchHung* 32:31–95.

1981. "Das erste Auftreten der Bulgaren im Karpatenbecken. Probleme, Angaben und Möglichkeiten." *Studia Turco-Hungarica* 5:79–112.

1990a. "Byzantium and the Avars: the archaeology of the first 70 years of the Avar era." In *Baltic*, pp. 113–18.

1990b. "I Langobardi in Pannonia." In *I Langobardi*, pp. 14–73. Ed Giàn Carlo Menis. Milan: Electa.

References

Bóna, István et al. 1993. *Hunok-Gepidák-Langobardok. Történeti régészeti tézisek és címszavak.* Szeged: Magyar Östörténeti Könyvtár.

Bonev, Chavdar 1983. "Les Antes et Byzance." *EB* 3:109–20.

1985. "Nachalo dunaiskoi Bolgarii v svete nekotorykh arkheologicheskikh dannykh i monetnykh nakhodok." *EB* 21, no. 2:62–76.

1986. "Anti i slovini v Dobrudzha prez VI v." In *Rusko-bălgarski vrăzke prez vekovete*, pp. 56–61. Ed. G. G. Litavrin and D. Angelov. Sofia: BAN.

Bonifay, Michel, and Dominique Piéri 1995. "Amphores du V-e au VII-e s. à Marseille: nouvelles données sur la typologie et le contenu." *JRA* 8:94–120.

Bonifay, M., F. Villedieu, M. Leguilloux, and Cl. Raynaud et al. 1989. "Importations d'amphores orientales en Gaule (V–e–VII–e siècle)." In *Recherches*, pp. 17–46.

Bonte, P. 1977. "Non-stratified social formations among pastoral nomads." In *The Evolution of Social Systems*, pp. 173–200. Ed. J. Friedman and M. J. Rowlands. London: Duckworth.

Bopp, Franz 1833. *Vergleichende Grammatik des Sanskrit, Send, Armenischen, Griechischen, Lateinischen, Litauischen, Altslavischen, Gothischen und Deutschen.* Berlin: Ernest Dümmler.

Borisov, Boris D. 1985. "Rannovizantiiski amfori (IV–VI v.) ot Slivenski okrăg." *Arkheologiia* 27, no. 1:38–45.

1988a. "Issledovaniia rannevizantiiskoi keramiki iz Slivenskogo okruga." *Thracia* 8:90–118.

1988b. "Starokhristianskite baziliki (IV–VI v.) krai s. Karanovo, Burgaska oblast." *Arkheologiia* 30, no. 3:38– 46.

Borkovský, Ivan 1940. *Staroslovanská keramika ve střední Evrope. Studie k počátkům slovanské kultury.* Prague: Nákladem vlastním.

Bornträger, Ekkehard W. 1989. "Die slavischen Lehnwörter im Neugriechischen." *Zeitschrift für Balkanologie* 25:8– 25.

Borodin, O. R. 1983. "Slaviane v Italii i Istrii v VI–VIII vv." *VV* 44:48–59.

Borojević, Ksenija 1987. "Analiza ugljenišanog semenja sa lokaliteta Svetinja." *Starinar* 38:65–71.

Bortoli-Kazanski, Anne 1981. "La repartition du marbre de Proconnèse en Crimée à l'époque paléochretienne." In *Geographica Byzantina*, pp. 55–65. Ed. Hélène Ahrweiler. Paris: Centre de Recherches d'Histoire et Civilisation Byzantines.

Bortoli-Kazanski, Anne, and Michel Kazanski 1987. "Les sites archéologiques datés du IV-e au VII-e siècle au nord et au nord-est de la Mer Noire: état des recherches." *T&MByz* 10:437–89.

Bošković, Đurđe 1978. "Aperçu sommaire sur les recherches archéologiques du limes romain et paléobyzantin des Portes de Fer." *MEFRA* 9:425–63.

Bott, Hans 1976. "Bemerkungen zum Datierungsproblem awarenzeitlicher Funde in Pannonien vorgelegt am Beispiel des Gräberfeldes von Környe." *BJ* 176:201–80.

Böttger, Burkhard 1979. "Die Gefäßkeramik aus dem Kastell Iatrus." In *Iatrus*, pp. 33–148. Vol. 1.

1988. "Ölamphoren in Mösien und Spanien: Analogie gleich Analogie?." *WZRostock* 37:73–5.

1990. "Zur Lebensmittelversorgungen des niedermösischen Kastells Iatrus (4.–6. Jh.)." In *Akten 14*, pp. 925–30.

1992. "Zu den Ergebnissen der Untersuchungen an den spätantiken Schichten im Nordwestsektor des Kaletohügels von Karasura." *ZfA* 26:233–49.

References

Bounegru, Octavian 1983. "Tipuri de nave la Dunărea de Jos în secolele IV-VII e.n." *Pontica* 16:273–9.

Bourdieu, Pierre 1994. "Structures, habitus, power. Basis for a theory of symbolic power." In *Culture/Power/History. A Reader in Contemporary Social Theory*, pp. 155–99. Ed. Nicholas B. Dirks, Geoff Eley, and Sherry B. Ortner. Princeton: Princeton University Press.

Bouzek, Jan 1971. "Slovanske pohřebiště v Olympii." *ArchRoz* 23:99–101.

Bozhilov, Ivan 1975. "Kăm istoricheskata geografiia na severozapadnoto Chernomorie." *INMV* 11:27–36.

Bozhilov, Ivan, and Khristo Dimitrov 1995. "Protobulgarica (zametki po istorii protobolgar do serediny IX v.)." *Byzantinobulgarica* 9:7–61.

Brachmann, Hansjürgen 1979. "Archäologische Kultur und Ethnos. Zu einigen methodischen Voraussetzungen der ethnischen Interpretation archäologischer Funde." In *Von der archäologischen Quelle zur historischen Aussage*, pp. 101–21. Ed. Joachim Preuss. Berlin: Akademie Verlag.

1983. "Die Funde der Gruppe des Prager Typs in der DDR und ihre Stellung im Rahmen der frühslawischen Besiedlung dieses Gebietes." *SlA* 29:23–64.

Bradley, D. R. 1966. "The composition of the Getica." *Eranos* 64:67–79.

Bradley, Richard 1990. *The Passage of Arms. An Archaeological Analysis of Prehistoric Hoards and Votive Deposits*. Cambridge and New York: Cambridge University Press.

Braichevskii, M. Iu 1952a. "K voprosu o geneticheskikh sviazakh iuvelirnogo remesla antov i Kievskoi Rusi." *KSIA* 1:43–9.

1952b. "Pastirs'kii skarb 1949 r." *Arkheolohiia* 7:161–73.

1953. "Ob 'antakh' Psevdomavrikiia." *Sovetskaia Etnografiia* 2:21–36.

1955. "Novy rozkopki na Pastirs'komu gorodishchy." *Arkheologichni pam'iatki URSR* 5:67–76.

1983. "Slaviane v Podunav'e i na Balkanakh v VI–VII vv. (po dannym pis'mennykh istochnikov)." In *Dnestr*, pp. 220–47.

Brâncuș, Grigore 1989. "Rotacismul din limba română." *Thraco-Dacica* 10, nos. 1–2:173–80.

Bratiloveanu-Popilian, Marcela 1968. "Cirimna, o vatră portativă." *RM* 5, no. 6:554–5.

Bratož, Rajko 1989. "The development of the early Christian research in Slovenia and Istria between 1976 and 1986." In *Actes XI*, pp. 2345–88. Vol. III.

Braun, David P. 1980. "Experimental interpretation of ceramic vessel use on the basis of rim and neck formal attributes." In *The Navajo Project. Archaeological Investigations Page to Phoenix 500 KV Southern Transmission Line*, pp. 171–231. Ed. Donald C. Fiero et al. Flagstaff: Museum of Northern Arizona.

1983. "Pots as tools." In *Archaeological Hammers and Theories*, pp. 107–34. Ed. James A. Moore and Arthur S. Keene. New York and London: Academic Press.

Braun, David P., and Stephen Plog 1982. "Evolution of 'tribal' social networks: theory and prehistoric North American evidence." *AAnt* 47, no. 3:504–25.

Briusov, A. Ia. 1956. "Arkheologicheskie kul'tury i etnicheskie obshchnosti." *SA* 26:5–27.

Brmbolić, Marin 1986. "Ranovizantijsko utvrðenje na Juhoru." *ZNM* 12:199–216.

Bromley, Julian, and Viktor Kozlov 1989. "The theory of ethnos and ethnic processes in Soviet social sciences." *CSSH* 31:425–38.

References

Bromley, Yu V. 1979. "Problems of primitive society in Soviet ethnology." In *Toward a Marxist Anthropology. Problems and Perspectives*, pp. 201–14. Ed. Stanley Diamond. The Hague, Paris, and New York: Mouton.

Brown, Paula 1990. "Big man, past and present: model, person, hero, legend." *Ethnology* 29:97–115.

Bruche-Schulz, Gisela 1993. "Marr, Marx and linguistics in the Soviet Union." *Historiographia Linguistica* 20, nos. 2–3:455–72.

Buchignani, Norman 1987. "Ethnic phenomena and contemporary social theory: their implications for archaeology." In *Conference 18*, pp. 15–24.

Bucovală, Mihai, and Gheorghe Papuc 1981. "Date noi despre fortificaţia de la Ovidiu-Municipiul Constanţa (campania 1980)." *Pontica* 14:211–16.

1986. "Cercetări arheologice efectuate în fortificaţia romano-bizantină de la Ovidiu (mun. Constanţa)." *MCA* 16:169–71.

Budinský-Krička, Vojtech 1963. "Sídlisko z doby rímskey a zo začiatkov stahovania národov v Prešove." *SlovArch* 11:5–58.

1990. "Novye materialy dlia izucheniia drevneslavianskoi keramiki na poseleniiakh vostochnoi Slovakii." *SlovArch* 38:89–146.

Bülow, G. von 1990. "Die Besiedlung des Kastells Iatrus im 6. Jh. u.Z." *Balcanica* 5:367–89.

Burmov, Alexander 1963. "Zur Frage der gesellschaftlich-ökonomischen Verhältnisse bei den Südostslawen während des 6. und 7. Jahrhunderts." In *Actes XIIa*, pp. 57–62. Vol. II.

Bury, J. B. 1906. "The treatise 'De Administrando Imperio'." *ByzZ* 15:517–77.

Butnariu, Viorel M. 1983–5. "Răspîndirea monedelor bizantine din secolele VI-VII în teritoriile carpato-dunărene." *BSNR* 77–9, nos. 131–3:199–235.

Butoi, Mihai 1968. "Un tezaur de monede şi obiecte de podoabă din secolul al VII-lea descoperit în comuna Priseaca-Slatina." *Studii şi Comunicări* 1:97–104.

Byers, A. Martin 1991. "Structure, meaning, action and things: the duality of material culture mediation." *Journal for the Theory of Social Behavior* 21, no. 1:1–29.

Bølviken, Erik et al. 1982. "Correspondence analysis: an alternative to principal components." *WA* 14:41–60.

Cambi, Nenad 1989. "Nuove scoperte di archeologia cristiana in Dalmazia." In *Actes XI*, pp. 2389–440. Vol. III.

Cameron, Averil 1970. *Agathias*. Oxford: Clarendon Press.

1981. "Images of authority: elites and icons in late sixth century Byzantium." In *Byzantium and the Classical Tradition. University of Birmingham Thirteenth Spring Symposium of Byzantine Studies 1979*, pp. 205–34. Ed. Margaret Mullett and Roger Scott. Birmingham: Centre for Byzantine Studies University of Birmingham.

1985. *Procopius and the Sixth Century*. Berkeley and Los Angeles: University of California Press.

1993. *The Mediterranean World in Late Antiquity AD 395–600*. London and New York: Routledge.

Cankova-Petkova, Genoveva 1962. "Gesellschaftsordnung und Kriegskunst der slawischen Stämme der Balkanhalbinsel (6.–8. Jh.) nach den byzantinischen Quellen." *Helikon* 2:264–70.

1968. "Sur l'établissement des tribus slaves du groupe bulgare au sud du Bas-Danube." *EH* 4:143–66.

References

1970. "L'établissement des Slaves et Protobulgares en Bulgarie du nord-est actuelle et le sort de certaines villes riveraines du Danube." *EH* 5:219–39.

1987. "Zur Textgestaltung des Strategikon des Maurikios." In *Texte und Textkritik. Eine Aufsatzsammlung*, pp. 73–5. Ed. Jürgen Dummer. Berlin: Akademie Verlag.

Cantea, Gh. 1959. "Cercetările arheologice pe dealul Mihai Vodă și împrejurimi." In *București*, pp. 93–143.

Capaldo, Mario 1983. "Un insediamento slavo presso Siracusa nel primo millennio d. C." *Europa Orientalis* 2:5–17.

Capelle, Torsten, and Hayo Vierck 1971. "Modeln der Merowinger- und Wikingerzeit." *FS* 5:41–100.

Casey, P. J. 1986. *Understanding Ancient Coins. An Introduction for Archaeologists and Historians*. Norman and London: Oklahoma Press University.

Čermanović-Kuzmanović, Aleksandrina, and Svetozar Stanković 1986. "La forteresse antique Mora Vagei près de Mihajlovac. Fouilles de 1981." *DS* 3:453–66.

Cesa, M. 1982. "Etnografia e geografia nella visione storica di Procopio di Cesarea." *Studi Classici e Orientali* 32:189–215.

Chaneva-Dechevska, N. 1984. "Die frühchristliche Architektur in Bulgarien." In *Actes X*, pp. 613–23. Vol. II.

Changova, Iordanka 1963. "Prouchvaniia v krepostta Pernik." *Arkheologiia* 5, no. 3:65–73.

Chapman, Malcolm, Maryon Mcdonald, and Elizabeth Tonkin 1989. "Introduction." In *History and Ethnicity*, pp. 1–21. Ed. Elizabeth Tonkin, Maryon Mcdonald, and Malcolm Chapman. London and New York: Routledge.

Chappell, David 1993. "Ethnogenesis and frontiers." *Journal of World History* 4, no. 2:267–75.

Charanis, Peter 1950. "The chronicle of Monemvasia and the question of the Slavonic settlements in Greece." *DOP* 5:141–66.

1952. "On the capture of Corinth by the Onogurs and its recapture by the Byzantines." *Speculum* 27:343–50.

1971. "Graecia in Isidore of Seville." *ByzZ* 46:22–5.

1976. "The Slavs, Byzantium and the historical significance of the First Bulgarian kingdom." *BS* 17:5–24.

Chausidis, Nikos 1985–6. "Novootkrieni docnoantički tvrdini na Skopska Crna Gora." *MAA* 10:183–97.

Chavannes, Edouard 1969. *Documents sur les Tou-Kiue (Turcs) occidentaux*. Taipei: Ch'eng Weg.

Cherniak, A. B. 1991. "Ioann Biklarskii." In *Svod*, pp. 394–9. Vol. I.

Cheshko, S. V. 1993. "Etnicheskaia istoriia slavian s tochki zreniia problem etnologii." *SovS* 2:15–22.

Chichikova, M. 1983. "Fouilles du camp romain et de la ville paléobyzantine de Novae (Mésie inférieure)." In *Bulgaria*, pp. 11–18.

Chichurov, I. S. 1980. *Vizantiiskie istoricheskie sochineniia: "Khronographiia" Feofana, "Breviarii" Nikifora. Teksty, perevod, kommentarii*. Moscow: Nauka.

Childe, Gordon Vere 1956. *Piecing Together the Past: The Interpretation of Archaeological Data*. London: Routledge and Kegan Paul.

Chiriac, Costel 1980. "Cîteva considerații asupra tezaurului de monede bizantine de la Gropeni (jud. Brăila)." *Istros* 1:257–62.

1993. "Expediția avară din 578–579 și evidența numismatică." *AM* 16:191–203.

References

Christie, Neil 1995. *The Lombards. The Ancient Longobards*. Oxford and Cambridge: Blackwell.

Christou, Konstantin P. 1991. *Byzanz und die Langobarden. Von der Ansiedlung in Pannonien bis zur endgültigen Anerkennung (500–680)*. Athens: S. D. Basilopoulos.

Chropovský, Bohuslav, and Alexander Ruttkay 1988. "Archäologische Forschung und Genese des slowakischen Ethnikums." *Studia Historica Slovaca* 16:15–63.

Chrysanthopoulos, E. 1957. "Τὰ βιβλία Θαυμάτων τοῦ ᾽Αγίου Δεμετρίου, τὸ Χρόνικον τῆς Μονεμβασίας καὶ αἱ σλαβικαὶ ἐπιδρόμαι εἰς τὴν ᾽Ελλάδα." *Theologia* 28:115–57.

Chrysos, Evangelos 1987. "Die Nordgrenze des byzantinischen Reiches im 6. bis 8. Jahrhundert." In *Völker*, pp. 27–40.

——— 1989. "Legal concepts and patterns for the barbarians' settlement on Roman soil." In *Barbaren*, pp. 7–23.

Ciglenečki, Slavko 1979. "Kastel, utrjeno naselje ali refugij?." *AV* 30:459–72.

——— 1987a. *Höhenbefestigungen aus der Zeit vom 3. bis 6. Jh. im Ostalpenraum*. Ljubljana: Slovenska Akademija Znanosti in Umetnosti.

——— 1987b. "Das Weiterleben der Spätantike bis zum Auftauchen der Slawen in Slowenien." In *Völker*, pp. 265– 86.

Cihodaru, Constantin 1972. "Oştirea bizantină în Cîmpia munteană la sfirşitul secolului VI şi toponomastica." *Analele ştiinţifice ale Universităţii "Al. I. Cuza". Secţiunea IIIa: Istorie* 18:2–7.

Čilinská, Zlata 1975. "Frauenschmuck aus dem 7.–8. Jahrhundert im Karpatenbecken." *SlovArch* 23, no. 1:63–96.

——— 1980. "Zur Frage des Samo-Reiches." In *Rapports*, pp. 79–86. Vol. II.

Čizmář, Miloš 1997. "Langobardský sídlištní objekt z Podolí, okr. Brno-Venkov. K problematice langobardských sídlišt' na Morave." *ArchRoz* 49, no. 4:634–42.

Clastres, Pierre 1977. *Society against the State. The Leader as Servant and the Humane Use of Power among the Indians of the Americas*. New York: Urizen Books.

Clauss, Gisela 1987. "Die Tragsitte von Bügelfibeln. Eine Untersuchung zur Frauentracht im frühen Mittelalter." *JRGZ* 34:491–603.

Cohen, Abner 1969. *Custom and Politics in Urban Africa. A Study of Hausa Migrants in Yoruba Towns*. London: Routledge and Kegan Paul.

Cohen, Anthony P. 1993. "Culture as identity: an anthropologist's view." *New Literary History* 24, no. 2:195–209.

Coman, Ghenuţă 1969. "Cercetări arheologice din sudul Moldovei cu privire la sec. V–XI." *SCIV* 20, no. 2:287– 314.

——— 1971a. "Evoluţia culturii materiale din Moldova de sud în lumina cercetărilor arheologice cu privire la secolele V–XIII." *MemAnt* 3:479–97.

——— 1971b. "Mărturii arheologice privind creştinismul în Moldova secolelor VI–XII." *Danubius* 5:75–100.

Comba, Enrico 1991. "Wolf warriors and dog feasts: animal metaphors in Plains military societies." *European Review of Native American Studies* 5, no. 2:4–48.

Comşa, Maria 1960. "Slavii." In *Istoria Romîniei*, pp. 728–54. Ed. C. Daicoviciu et al. Vol. I. Bucharest: Editura Academiei RPR.

——— 1971. "Quelques données concernant les rapports des territoires nord-danubiens avec Byzance aux VI–VIII–e siècles." *RESEE* 9, no. 3:377–90.

——— 1972. "Directions et étapes de la pénétration des Slaves vers la Péninsule Balkanique aux VI–e–VII–e siècles avec un regard spécial sur le territoire de la Roumanie." *Balcanoslavica* 1:9–28.

References

1973. "Die Slawen im karpatischen-donauländischen Raum im 6.–7. Jahrhundert." *ZfA* 7:197–223.

1974. "Unele considerații privind situația de la Dunărea de Jos în secolele VI–VII." *Apulum* 12:300–18.

1984. "Bemerkungen über die Beziehungen zwischen den Awaren und den Slawen im 6.–7. Jahrhundert." In *Interaktionen*, pp. 63–74.

Condurachi, Emil 1957. "Histria à l'époque du Bas-Empire d'après les dernières fouilles archéologiques." *Dacia* 1:243–63.

1967. "Deux édifices publics d'Histria byzantine." In *Charisterion eis Anastasion K. Orlandon*, pp. 162–8. Vol. IV. Athens: Bibliotheke tes en Athenais Archaiologikes Hetaireias.

1975. "Quelques maisons byzantines des villes pontiques." In *Studies in Memory of David Talbot Rice*, pp. 171–83. Ed. G. Robertson and G. Henderson. Edinburgh: Edinburgh University Press.

Condurachi, Emil et al 1970. "Șantierul arheologic Histria." *MCA* 9:186–90.

Conkey, Margaret W. 1991. "Contexts of action, contexts for power: material culture and gender in the Magdalenian." In *Engendering Archaeology. Women and Prehistory*, pp. 57–92. Ed. Joan M. Gero and Margaret W. Conkey. Oxford and Cambridge, Mass.: Basil Blackwell.

Conrad, Sven 1999. "Zu Typologie und Funktionsbestimmung der Amphoren aus dem Kastell Iatrus." In *Limes*, pp. 174– 88.

Constantinescu, Nicolae 1960. "Noi observații în legătură cu stratul prefeudal de la Tîrgșor." *SCIV* 11, no. 1:167– 75.

Constantiniu, Margareta 1963. "Săpăturile de la Bucureștii Noi 1960." *CAB* 1:77–104.

1965a. "Șantierul arheologic Băneasa-Străulești." *CAB* 2:75–98.

1965b. "Săpăturile de la Străulești-Măicănești. Așezarea feudală II." *CAB* 2:174–89.

1966. "Elemente romano-bizantine în cultura materială a populației autohtone din partea centrală a Munteniei în secolele VI–VII." *SCIV* 17, no. 4:665–78.

Cordell, Linda S., and Vincent J. Yannie 1991. "Ethnicity, ethnogenesis, and the individual: a processual approach toward dialogue." In *Processual and Postprocessual Archaeologies. Multiple Ways of Knowing the Past*, pp. 96–107. Ed. Robert W. Preucel. Carbondale: Southern Illinois University.

Corman, Igor 1994. "Săpăturile arheologice de la Vânători-Neamț." *AM* 17:301–8.

1998. *Contribuții la istoria spațiului pruto-nistrian în epoca Evului Mediu timpuriu.* Chișinău: Cartdidact.

Ćorović-Ljubinković, Mirjana 1972. "Les Slaves du centre balkanique du VI-e au XI-e siècle." *Balcanoslavica* 1:43–54.

Cowgill, George L. 1990. "Artifact classification and archaeological purposes." In *Mathematics*, pp. 61–78.

Crabtree, Pam J. 1990. "Zooarchaeology and complex societies: some uses of faunal analysis for the study of trade, social status, and ethnicity." *AMT* 2:155–205.

Čremošnik, Irma 1970. "Istraživanja u Mušićima i Žabljaku i prvi nalaz nastarijih slavenskih naselja kod nas." *GZMBH* 25:45–117.

1975. "Die Untersuchungen in Mušići und Žabljak. Über den ersten Fund der ältesten slawischen Siedlung in Bosnien." *WMBHL* 5:91–176.

1980. "Tipovi slavenskih nastambi nadenih u sjevero-istočnoj Bosni." *AV* 31:132–58.

References

1987–8. "Rimsko utvrdenje na gradini u Biogracima kod Lištice." *GZMBH* 42–3:83–128.

Croke, Brian 1982. "The date of the Anastasian Long Wall." *Greek, Roman, and Byzantine Studies* 20:59–78.

1987. "Cassiodorus and the Getica of Jordanes." *CPh* 82:117–34.

1990. "The early development of Byzantine chronicles." In *Studies in John Malalas*, pp. 27–38. Ed. Elizabeth Jeffreys, Brian Croke, and Scott Roger. Sydney: Australian Association for Byzantine Studies.

Cross, Samuel Hazzard 1948. *Slavic Civilization through the Ages*. Cambridge, Mass.: Harvard University Press.

Cross, Samuel Hazzard, and Olgerd P. Sherbowitz-Wetzor 1953. *The Russian Primary Chronicle: Laurentian Text*. Cambridge, Mass.: Medieval Academy of America.

Crow, J. G. 1995. "The Long Walls of Thrace." In *Constantinople*, pp. 110–19.

Crubézy, Eric 1990. "Merovingian skull deformations in the southwest of France." In *Baltic*, pp. 189–208.

Csallány, Dezsö 1946–8. "Szegedi avarkori sírleletek és a hun-bolgár ivókürtök régészeti kapcsolatai." *ArchÉrt* 75–9:350–61.

1961. *Archäologische Denkmäler der Gepiden im Mitteldonaubecken*. Budapest: Akadémiai kiadó.

1963. "A kuturgur-bolgárok (-hunok) régeszeti hagyatékanak meghátarozása." *ArchÉrt* 90:21–38.

Cseh, János 1986. "Adatok kengyel környékének V–VI. századi települesi viszonyaihóz." *ArchÉrt* 113:190–206.

1990a. "Adatok az V.–VII. századi Gepida emlékanyag egységéhez." *Szolnok Megyei Múzeumok Évkönyve* 7:29–80.

1990b. "Gepida fazekaskemence Törökszentmiklóson." *ArchÉrt* 117:223–40.

1997. "Gepida település Rákóczifalva határában." *CAH*:173–94.

Culică, Vasile 1975. "Plumburi comerciale din cetatea romano-bizantină de la Izvoarele (Dobrogea). I." *Pontica* 8:215–62.

1976–80. "Imitaţii locale ale unor monede din epoca romano-bizantină descoperite în Dobrogea." *BSNR* 70–4, nos. 124–8:253–61.

Curta, Florin 1992. "Die Fibeln der Sammlung 'V. Culică'." *Dacia* 36:37–97.

1994a. "The changing image of the Early Slavs in the Rumanian historiography and archaeological literature. A critical survey." *SF* 53:225–310.

1994b. "On the dating of the 'Veţel-Coşoveni' group of curved fibulae." *Ephemeris Napocensis* 4:233–65.

1996. "Invasion or inflation? Sixth- to seventh-century Byzantine coin hoards in Eastern and Southeastern Europe." *Annali dell'Istituto Italiano di Numismatica* 43:65–224.

1997. 'Slavs in Fredegar and Paul the Deacon: medieval 'gens' or 'scourge of God'?." *EME* 6, no. 2:141–67.

1999. "Hiding behind a piece of tapestry: Jordanes and the Slavic Venethi." *JGO* 47:1–18.

Curta, Florin, and Vasile Dupoi 1994–5. "Über die Bügelfibel aus Pietroasele und ihre Verwandten." *Dacia* 38–9:217–38.

Dąbrowski, Krzysztof 1975. "Archäologische Untersuchungen in Tumiany, Kr. Olsztyn." *ZfA* 9:265–79.

References

1980. "Nouvelles données concernant l'orfèvrerie sur le territoire de la voïvodie d'Olsztyn (Pologne)." *ArchPol* 19:235–41.

Dagron, Gilbert 1984. "Les villes dans l'Illyricum protobyzantin." In *Villes*, pp. 1–20.

1991. "'Ainsi rien n'échappera à la réglementation'. Etat, Eglise, corporations, confréries: à propos des inhumations à Constantinople (IVe–Xe siècle)." In *Hommes*, pp. 155–82. Vol. II.

Damianov, Stefan 1976. "Prouchvaniia na sgrada no. 8 ot kasnoantichniia grad pri s. Voivoda, Shumensko." *GMSB* 2:17–27.

Dănilă, Nicolae 1983. "Tipare de turnat cruci din secolele IV–VI, descoperite pe teritoriul României." *Biserica Ortodoxă Română* 101, nos. 7–8:557–61.

1986. "Precizări privind linguriţele 'euharistice' din secolele IV–VI, descoperite în România." *Glasul Bisericii* 45:80–92.

David, Nicholas, Judy Sterner, and Kodzo Gavua 1988. "Why pots are decorated." *CAnth* 29, no. 3:365–89.

Davidson, G. R. 1937. "The Avar invasion of Corinth." *Hesperia* 6:227–39.

Davidson, Gladys Weinberg 1974. "A wandering soldier's grave in Corinth." *Hesperia* 43:512–21.

Delmaire, J. 1989. *Les responsables des finances imperiales au Bas-Empire romain (IV–e–VI–e s.). Etudes prosopographiques.* Brussels: Latomus.

Dennis, George T. 1981. "Flies, mice, and the Byzantine crossbow." *BMGS* 7:1–5.

Dennis, George T., and Ernst Gamillscheg 1981. *Das Strategikon des Maurikios.* Vienna: Verlag der Österreichischen Akademie der Wissenschaften.

Deopik, V. B. 1961. "Klassifikaciia bus Iugo-Vostochnoi Evropy VI–IX vv." *SA* 3:209–32.

Dergachev, V. A., O. V. Larina, and Gheorghe I. Postică 1983. "Raskopki 1980 g. na mnogosloinom poselenii Dancheny I." In *Arkheologicheskie issledovaniia v Moldavii v 1979–1980 gg.*, pp. 112–36. Ed. I. A. Borziak. Kishinew: Shtiinca.

Derzhavin, N. S. 1944. *Proiskhozhdenie russkogo naroda.* Moscow: Sovetskaia nauka.

Diaconu, Petre 1959. "Un nou tip ceramic din epoca romano-bizantină." *SCIV* 10, no. 2:487–90.

1979. "Autour de la pénétration des Slaves au sud du Danube." In *Rapports*, pp. 165–9. Vol. I.

1993. "Sur les nécropoles danubiennes (VIe–Xe siècles)." *Dacia* 37:291–300.

D'iakonov, A. 1946. "Izvestiia Ioanna Efesskogo i siriiskikh khronik o slavianakh VI–VII vekov." *VDI* 1:20– 34.

Díaz-Andreu, Margarita 1996. "Constructing identities through culture. The past in the forging of Europe." In *Identity*, pp. 48–61.

Díaz-Andreu, Margarita, and Timothy Champion 1996. "Nationalism and archaeology in Europe: an introduction." In *Nationalism and Archaeology in Europe*, pp. 1–23. Ed. Margarita Díaz-Andreu and Timothy Champion. Boulder and San Francisco: Westview Press.

Dickinson, Tania M. 1993. "Early Saxon saucer brooches: a preliminary overview." *ASSAH* 6:11–44.

Dickinson, Tania, and Heinrich Härke 1992. *Early Anglo-Saxon Shields.* London: Society of Antiquaries of London.

Dimitrijević, Danica 1982–3. "Sapaja, rimsko i sredniuvekovno utvrðenje na ostrovu kod Stare Palanke." *Starinar* 33–4:29–62.

References

Dimitrov, D. P. et al. 1974. "Arkheologicheski razkopki v iztochniia sektor na Nove prez 1967–1969 g." *IBAI* 34:138–76.

Dimitrov, Dimităr Il. 1987. "Ob osnovykh protobulgarskikh gruppakh v stepiakh Evropy v VI–VII vv." *BHR* 15, no. 1:58–70.

Dimitrov, Marin 1985. "Rannovizantiiski ukrepleniia po Zapadniia briag na Cherno more (V–VII v.)." *Dobrudzha* 2:120–8.

Dinchev, Vencislav 1997a. "Household substructure of the early Byzantine fortified settlements on the present Bulgarian territory." *ArchBulg* 1, no. 1:47–63.

——— 1997b. "Zikideva – an example of Early Byzantine urbanism in the Balkans." *ArchBulg* 1, no. 3:54–77.

Dirks, Nicholas B., Geoff Eley, and Sherry B. Ortner 1994. "Introduction." In *Culture/Power/History. A Reader in Contemporary Social Theory*, pp. 3–45. Ed. Nicholas B. Dirks, Geoff Eley, and Sherry B. Ortner. Princeton: Princeton University Press.

Ditten, Hans 1978. "Zur Bedeutung der Einwanderung der Slawen." In *Byzanz im 7. Jahrhundert. Untersuchungen zur Herausbildung des Feudalismus*, pp. 73–160. Ed. F. Winckelmann. Berlin: Akademie Verlag.

——— 1991. "Soziale Spannungen in dem von Slawen bedrohten Thessalonike des ausgehenden 6. und des 7. Jh. n. Chr. Zu den Wechselwirkungen zwischen äusserer Bedrohung und inneren Verwicklungen." In *Volk und Herrschaft im frühen Byzanz. Methodische und quellenkritische Probleme*, pp. 18–32. Ed. F. Winckelmann. Berlin: Akademie Verlag.

Djindjian, François 1985. "Seriation and toposeriation by correspondence analysis." *PACT. Revue du Groupe européen d'études pour les techniques physiques, chimiques et mathématiques appliquées à l'archéologie* 11:119–35.

——— 1990. "Ordering and structuring in archaeology." In *Mathematics*, pp. 79–92.

Döhle, Bernhard 1989. "Zur spätrömischen Militärarchitektur: das Limeskastell Iatrus (Moesia Secunda)." *Archeologia* 40:41–54.

——— 1992. "Zu den spätantik-mittelalterlichen Befestigungsanlagen auf dem Kale von Carassura." *ZfA* 26:181–97.

Dölger, Franz 1924. *Regesten der Kaiserurkunden des oströmischen Reiches von 565–1453*, vol. 1. Munich: Oldenbourg.

Dolinescu-Ferche, Suzana 1967. "Un complex din secolul al VI-lea la Sfinţeşti." *SCIV* 18, no. 1:127–34.

——— 1969. "Cuptorul de ars oale din sec. VI e.n. de la Dulceanca (jud. Teleorman)." *SCIV* 20, no. 1:117–24.

——— 1973. "Aşezarea din sec. VI e.n. de la Olteni-judeţul Teleorman, 1966." *MCA* 10:203–8.

——— 1974. *Aşezări din secolele III şi VI e.n. în sud-vestul Munteniei. Cercetările de la Dulceanca*. Bucharest: Editura Academiei RSR.

——— 1979. "Ciurel, habitat des VI–VII–e siècles d.n.è." *Dacia* 23:179–230.

——— 1984. "La culture 'Ipoteşti-Cîndeşti-Ciurel' (V–e–VII–e siècles). La situation en Valachie." *Dacia* 28:117–84.

——— 1986. "Contributions archéologiques sur la continuité daco-romaine. Dulceanca, deuxième habitat du VI-e siècle d.n.è." *Dacia* 30:121–54.

——— 1992. "Habitats du VI-e et VII-e siècles de notre ère à Dulceanca IV." *Dacia* 36:125–77.

References

1995. "Cuptoare din interiorul locuinţelor din secolul al VI-lea e.n. de la Dulceanca." *SCIV* 46, no. 2:161–92.

Dolinescu-Ferche, Suzana, and Margareta Constantiniu 1981. "Un établissement du VI-e siècle à Bucarest." *Dacia* 25:289–329.

Dolukhanov, Pavel M. 1996. *The Early Slavs. Eastern Europe from the Initial Settlement to the Kievan Rus.* London and New York: Longman.

Dömötör, Lászlo 1901. "Ujabb lemezsajtoló bronzminták fönlakról." *ArchÉrt* 21:62–6.

Donat, Peter 1980. *Haus, Hof und Dorf in Mitteleuropa vom 7. bis 12. Jahrhundert. Archäologische Beiträge zur Entwicklung der bäuerlichen Siedlungen.* Berlin: Akademie Verlag.

1986. "Probleme der Gliederung und Chronologie altslawischer Keramik." In *Mélange*, pp. 81–7.

Döpmann, Hans-Dieter 1987. "Zur Problematik von Justiniana Prima." In *Christentum*, pp. 221–32.

Dörner, Egon 1960. "Un mormînt de epocă avară la Sînpetru German." *SCIV* 11, no. 2:423.

Dostál, Antonín 1966. "Les problèmes linguistiques dans l'oeuvre de Lubor Niederle." *VPS* 6:7–31.

1967. "Lubor Niederle a jazyko vedne bádání." *ArchRoz* 18:147–53.

Dragadze, T. 1980. "The place of 'ethnos' theory in Soviet anthropology." In *Soviet and Western Anthropology*, pp. 161–70. Ed. Ernest Gellner. New York: Columbia University Press.

Dragojlović, Dragoljub 1972–3. "Psevdo-Cezarijevi fisonci ili podunavci." *RVM* 21–2:29–34.

Dresch, Paul 1986. "The significance of the course events take in segmentary systems." *AE* 13:309–24.

Duichev, Ivan 1942. "Balkanskiiat iugoiztok prez părvata polovina na VI vek." *Belomorski Pregled* 1:229–70.

1953. "Le témoignage de Pseudo-Césaire sur les Slaves." *SlA* 4:193–209.

1957. "La versione paleoslava dei Dialoghi dello Pseudo-Cesario." *Studi Bizantini e Neoellenici* 9:89–100.

1960. "Les Slaves et Byzance." In *Etudes historiques à l'occasion du XI-e Congrès international des sciences historiques Stockholm, août 1960*, pp. 31–77. Sofia: BAN.

1976. *Cronaca di Monemvasia.* Palermo: Istituto Siciliano di Studi Bizantini e Neoellenici.

1980. "Some remarks on the Chronicle of Monemvasia." In *Charanis Studies. Essays in Honor of Peter Charanis*, pp. 51–9. Ed. Angeliki E. Laiou-Thomadakis. New Brunswick: Rutgers University Press.

Duket, T. A. 1980. "A study in Byzantine historiography. An analysis of Theophanes' Chronographia and its relationship to Theophylact's History. The reign of Maurice and the seventh century to 711." PhD Dissertation. Boston College.

Dumézil, Georges 1969. *Heur et malheur du guerrier. Aspects mythiques de la fonction guerrières chez les Indo-Européens.* Paris: Presses Universitaires de France.

Dumitraşcu, Sever 1982. "O locuinţă-atelier de lucrat piepteni (sec. VI e.n.) descoperită la Biharea." *Crisia* 12:107–21.

References

Dümmler, Ernst 1856. "Über die älteste Geschichte der Slawen in Dalmatien (549–928)." *Sitzungsberichte* 20:353–430.

Duncan, G. L. 1993. *Coin Circulation in the Danubian and Balkan Provinces of the Roman Empire AD 294–578.* London: Royal Numismatic Society.

Dunn, Archibald 1994. "The transition from polis to kastron in the Balkans (III–VII cc.): general and regional perspectives." *BMGS* 18:60–80.

Duridanov, Ivan 1991. "Die ältesten slawischen Entlehnungen im Rumänischen." *BE* 34, nos. 1–2:3–19.

Durkheim, Emile 1893. *De la division du travail social.* Paris: F. Alcan.

1958. *The Rules of Sociological Method.* Chicago: Free Press.

Durliat, Jean 1989. "La peste au VI-e siècle. Pour un nouvel examen des sources byzantines." In *Hommes,* pp. 107–25. Vol. I.

1990. *De la ville antique à la ville byzantine. Le problème des subsistances.* Rome: Ecole Française de Rome.

Duval, Noël 1971. "Palais et forteresses en Yougoslavie: recherches nouvelles." *BSAF*:99–129.

1984. "L'architecture réligieuse de Tsaritchin Grad dans le cadre de l'Illyricum oriental au VIe siècle." In *Villes,* pp. 399–481.

1990. "Le culte des martyrs de Salone à la lumière des recherches récentes à Manastirine." *CRAI* 18:432–53.

Duval, Noël, and Vladislav Popović 1984. "Urbanisme et topographie chrétienne dans les provinces septentrionales de l'Illyricum." In *Actes X,* pp. 624–30. Vol. I.

Dvornik, Francis 1949. *The Making of Central and Eastern Europe.* London: Polish Research Centre.

1956. *The Slavs, their Early History and Civilization.* Boston: American Academy of Arts and Sciences.

Dvoržak Schrunk, Ivančica 1989. "Dioklecijanova palaca od 4. do 7. stoljeća u svjetlu keramičkih nalaza." *VAMZ* 22:91–105.

Dzhambov, I. 1989. "Un centre chrétien découvert récemment en Thrace. L'oppidum près de Sopot (du VI-e au XIII-e siècle) et l'identification de Kopsis." In *Actes XI,* pp. 2511–19. Vol. III.

Dzhambov, Khristo 1956. "Rannokhristiianska cărkva pri s. Isperikhovo, Peshterska okoliia." *Godishnik na Narodniia Arkheologicheskii Muzei Plovdiv* 2:175–92.

Dzhidrova, Ljubinka 1999. "Heraclea Lyncestis i problemiot na hronologijata i interpretacija." *MAA* 15:269–91.

Earle, Timothy K. 1987. "Chiefdoms in archaeological and ethnohistorical perspective." *ARA* 16:279–308.

1989. "The evolution of chiefdoms." *CAnth* 30, no. 1:84–8.

1990. "Style and iconography as legitimation in complex chiefdoms." In *Uses,* pp. 73–81.

Eastman, Carol M., and Thomas C. Reese 1981. "Associated language: how language and ethnic identity are related." *General Linguistics* 21, no. 2:109–16.

Eeckaute, Denise, Paul Garde, and Michel Kazanski 1992. "Slaves." In *Encyclopaedia Universalis,* pp. 76–100. Vol. XXI. Paris: Encyclopaedia Universalis.

Eggers, Hans Jürgen 1950. "Das Problem der ethnischen Deutung in der Frühgeschichte." In *Ur- und Frühgeschichte als historische Wissenschaft. Festschrift zum 60. Geburtstag von Ernst Wahle,* pp. 49–59. Ed. H. Kirchner. Heidelberg: Carl Winter.

References

Eisner, Jan 1948. *Lubor Niederle*. Prague: Nákladem České Akademie Ved u Umení a Praže.

Elferink, M. A. 1967. "Tyche et Dieu chez Procope de Césarée." *AClass* 10:111–34.

Eliade, Mircea 1973. "The Dacians and wolves." In *Zamolxis. The Vanishing God. Comparative Studies in the Religions and Folklore of Dacia and Eastern Europe*, pp. 1–20. Ed. Mircea Eliade. Chicago: University of Chicago Press.

Engels, Frederick 1968. *Selected Works in One Volume*. New York: International Publishers.

Ensslin, W. 1929. "s.v. Slaveneinfälle." In *Paulys Realencyclopädie der classischen Altertumwissenschaft*, pp. 696–706. Ed. August Friedrich von Pauly. Vol. II. Stuttgart: J. B. Metzler.

Eriksen, Thomas Hylland 1991. "The cultural contexts of ethnic differences." *Man* 26:127–44.

Esse, Douglas L. 1992. "The collared pithos at Megiddo: ceramic distribution and ethnicity." *Journal of Near Eastern Studies* 51, no. 2:81–103.

Etzeoglu, Rodoniki 1989. "La céramique de Karyoupolis." In *Recherches*, pp. 151–6.

Evans, Huw M. A. 1989. *The Early Medieval Archaeology of Croatia AD 600–900*. Oxford: BAR.

Evans, J. A. S. 1969. "The dates of the Anecdota and the De aedificiis of Procopius." *CPh* 44:29–30.

1970. "Justinian and the historian Procopius." *Greece and Rome* 17:218–23.

1972. *Procopius*. New York: Twayne Publishers.

1996. *The Age of Justinian. The Circumstances of Imperial Power*. London and New York: Routledge.

Evans-Pritchard, Edward 1940. *The Nuer: A Description of the Modes of Livelihood and Political Institutions of a Nilotic People*. Oxford: Oxford University Press.

1953. "The character of the Nuer." In *Primitive Heritage: An Anthropological Anthology*, pp. 326–9. Ed. Margaret Mead and Nicolas Calas. New York: Random House.

Evert-Kapessowa, Halina 1963. "Quelques remarques sur la colonisation slave." In *Actes XIIa*, pp. 78–81. Vol. II.

Faber, Aleksandra 1986–7. "Osvrt neka utvrdeja otoka Krka od vremena prethistorije do antike i srednjek veka." *Prilozi* 3–4:113–40.

Fagerlie, Joan M. 1967. *Late Roman and Byzantine Solidi Found in Sweden and Denmark*. New York: American Numismatic Society.

Falkenhausen, Vera von 1995. "Arethas in Italien?." *Byzantinoslavica* 56:359–66.

Fallmerayer, J. Ph. 1845. *Fragmente aus dem Orient*, vol. II. Stuttgart and Tübingen: J. C. Cotta.

Fedorov, G. B. 1960. *Naselenie Prutsko-Dnestrovskogo mezhdurech'ia v I tysiacheletii n.e.* Moscow: Izdatel'stvo Akademii Nauk SSSR.

Feissel, Denis 1988. "L'architecte Viktôrinos et les fortifications de Justinien dans les provinces balkaniques." *BSAF*:136–46.

Feissel, Dennis, and Anne Philippidis-Braat 1985. "Inventaires en vue d'un recueil des inscriptions historiques de Byzance, III. Inscriptions du Péloponnèse (à l'exception de Mistra)." *T&MByz* 9:367–95.

Ferjančić, Božidar 1984. "Invasions et installations des Slaves dans les Balkans." In *Villes*, pp. 85–109.

Ferluga, Jadran 1982. "Archon. Ein Beitrag zur Untersuchung der südslawischen

References

Herrschertitel im 9. u. 10. Jh. in lichte der byzantinischen Quellen." In *Tradition als historische Kraft*, pp. 254–66. Ed. N. Kamp and J. Wollasch. Berlin and New York: De Gruyter.

Ferring, C. Reid 1984. "Intrasite spatial patterning: its role in settlement-subsistence systems analysis." In *Intrasite Spatial Analysis in Archaeology*, pp. 116–26. Ed. Harold J. Hietala. Cambridge and London: Cambridge University Press.

Fettich, Nándor 1972. "Vestiges archéologiques slaves de l'époque des grandes migrations dans le bassin des Carpathes – relations koutourgoures." *MAIUAW* 1:85–97.

Fiala, Anton 1986. "K objavu miliarense Constansa II. z pokladu zo Zemianského Vrbovku." *Numismatický Sborník* 17:15–20.

1989. "Byzantské mince na Slovensku (6.–12. storocie)." *Slovenská Numizmatika* 10:57–64.

Fiedler, Uwe 1992. *Studien zu Gräberfeldern des 6. bis 9. Jahrhunderts an der unteren Donau*. Bonn: R. Habelt.

1994a. "Die Gürtelbesatzstücke von Akalan. Ihre Funktion und kulturelle Stellung." *IBAI* 37:37–47.

1994b. "Zur Datierung der Siedlungen der Awaren und der Ungarn nach der Landnahme. Ein Beitrag zur Zuordnung der Siedlung von Eperjes." *ZfA* 28: 307–52.

1996. "Die Slawen im Bulgarenreich und im Awarenkhaganat. Versuch eines Vergleichs." In *Verhältnisse*, pp. 195–214.

Filipescu, Bogdan 1984. "Cercetări în staţiunea arheologică Malu-Roşu, com. Fierbinţi-tîrg, jud. Ialomiţa." *Cercetări arheologice* 7:129–35.

Filipović, Milenko S. 1951. *Ženska keramika kod balkanskih naroda*. Belgrade: Srpska Akademija Nauka/Etnografski Institut.

Fine, John V. A. 1983. *The Early Medieval Balkans. A Critical Survey from the Sixth to the Late Twelfth Century*. Ann Arbor: University of Michigan Press.

Fisković, Cvito 1981. "Ranosrednjevjekovne ruševine na Majsanu." *SP* 11:137–62.

Flannery, K. V. 1982. "The golden Marshalltown: a parable for the archaeology of the 1980s." *AAnth* 84:265–78.

Florescu, Radu, and Zizi Covacef 1988–9. "Stratigrafia Capidavei romane tîrzii şi feudale timpurii." *Pontica* 21–2:197–247.

Ford, J. A. 1954. "On the concept of types." *AAnth* 56, no. 1:42–57.

Formozov, A. A. 1993. "Arkheologiia i ideologiia (20–30–e gody)." *Voprosy Filosofii* 2:70–82.

Förster, Richard 1877. "Kaiser Hadrian und die Taktik des Urbicius." *Hermes* 12:449–71.

Fortes, M., and E. Evans-Pritchard 1940. *African Political Systems*. London: Oxford University Press.

Fortier, Anne-Marie 1994. "Ethnicity." *Paragraph* 17, no. 3:213–23.

Fotiou, A. 1988. "Recruitment shortages in the VIth century Byzantium." *Byzantion* 58:65–77.

Franke, Helmut 1987. "Zur Herstellung der Kerbschnittfibel von Groß Köris, Kr. Königs Wusterhausen." *Veröffentlichungen des Museums für Ur- und Frühgeschichte* 21:237–41.

Franklin, Natalie R. 1989. "Research with style: a case study from Australian rock art." In *Approaches*, pp. 278–90.

References

Frazee, Charles A. 1982. "Late Roman and Byzantine legislation on the monastic life from the fourth to the eighth centuries." *Church History* 51, no. 3:263–79.

Fritze, Wolfgang H. 1980. "Zur Bedeutung der Awaren für die slawische Ausdehnungsbewegungen im frühen Mittelalter." In *Studien zur Völkerwanderungszeit im östlichen Mitteleuropa*, pp. 498–545. Ed. Gerhard Mildenberger. Marburg: J. G. Herder.

1994. *Untersuchungen zur frühslawischen und frühfränkischen Geschichte bis ins 7. Jahrhundert*. Frankfurt a.M., Berlin, and Bern: Peter Lang.

Froese, Patricia 1985. "Pottery classification and sherd assignment." In *Decoding Prehistoric Ceramics*, pp. 229–42. Ed. Ben A. Nelson. Carbondale and Edwardsville: Southern Illinois University Press.

Frolova, N. A., and E. Ia Nikolaeva 1978. "Il'ichevskii klad monet 1975 g." *VV* 39:173–9.

Fülöp, Gyula 1988. "Awarenzeitliche Fürstenfunde von Igar." *ActaArchHung* 40:151–90.

1990. "New research on finds of Avar chieftain-burial at Igar, Hungary." In *Baltic*, pp. 138–46.

Fusek, Gabriel 1991. "Včasnoslovanske sidlisko v Nitre na Mikovom dvore." *SlovArch* 39, nos. 1–2:289–328.

1994. "Analyse der Formen des handgemachten Keramikgeschirrs als Beitrag zur relativen Chronologie." In *Slawische Keramik in Mitteleuropa vom 8. bis zum 11. Jahrhundert. Internationale Tagungen in Mikulčice, 25.–27. Mai 1993*, pp. 19–27. Ed. Čenek Staňa. Vol. II. Brno: Archäologisches Institut.

1995. "Formanalyse vollständiger Gefäß oder ein weiterer Versuch, frühmittelalterliche Keramikgefäß aus der Slowakei zu klassifizieren." In *Slawische Keramik in Mitteleuropa vom 8. bis zum 11. Jahrhundert. Terminologie und Beschreibung. Internationale Tagung in Mikulčice, 24.–26. Mai 1994*, pp. 15–33. Ed. Lumil Polaček. Vol. II. Brno: Archäologisches Institut.

Fusek, Gabriel, Danica Staššiková-Štukovská, and Jozef Bátora 1993. "Neue Materialien zur Geschichte der ältesten slawischen Besiedlung der Slowakei." *Archaeoslavica* 2:25–51.

Gabričević, Martin 1986. "Rtkovo – Glamija I – une forteresse de la Basse époque. Fouilles de 1980–1982." *DS* 3:71–91.

Gailey, Christine Ward, and Thomas C. Patterson 1988. "State formation and uneven development." In *State and Society. The Emergence and Development of Social Hierarchy and Political Centralization*, pp. 74–85. Ed. John Gledhill, Barbara Bender, and Mogens Trolle Larsen. London, Boston, and Sydney: Unwin Hyman.

Gaiu, Corneliu 1992. "Le cimetière gépide de Bistriţa." *Dacia* 36:115–24.

1994. "Aşezarea din secolul al VI-lea de la Dipşa, jud. Bistriţa-Năsăud." *Revista Bistriţei* 7:91–107.

Gajdukević, V. F. 1971. *Das Bosporanische Reich*. Berlin: Akademie Verlag.

Gaj-Popović, Dobrila 1973. "The appearance of the barbarized folises (folles) in the 6th century in the Balkan Peninsula." *Balcanoslavica* 2:95–100.

1980. "Olovni pečat cara Iustinijana." *Numizmatičar* 3:165–8.

Ganzer, Burkhard 1990. "Zur Bestimmung des Begriffs der ethnischen Gruppe." *Sociologus* 40, no. 1:1–18.

References

Ganzha, A. I. 1987. "Etnicheskie rekonstrukcii v sovetskoi arkheologii 40–60 gg. kak istoriko-nauchnaia problema." In *Issledovanie social'no-istoricheskikh problem v arkheologii*. *Sbornik nauchnykh trudov*, pp. 137–58. Ed. S. V. Smirnov and V. F. Gening. Kiev: Naukova Dumka.

Garam, Eva Sz 1976. "Adatok a középavar kor és az avar fejedelmi sírok régészeti és történeti kérdéseihez." *FA* 27:129–47.

———. 1980. "VII. századi aranyékszerek a Magyar Nemzeti Múzeum gyüjteményeiben." *FA* 31:157–74.

———. 1988. "A Mautthner gyüjtemény granulációdíszes koraavar kisszívége." *FA* 39:159–72.

———. 1990. "Bemerkungen zum ältesten Fundmaterial der Awarenzeit." In *Typen der Ethnogenese unter besonderer Berücksichtigung der Bayern*, pp. 253–72. Ed. H. Friesinger and F. Daim. Vol. ii. Vienna: Verlag der Österreichischen Akademie der Wissenschaften.

———. 1992. "Die münzdatierten Gräber der Awarenzeit." In *Awarenforschungen*, pp. 135–250. Vol. i.

———. 1995. "Sepolture di principi." In *Avari*, pp. 125–31.

Gardiner, K. H. J. 1978. "Notes on the chronology of Fredegar Book IV." *Parergon* 20:40–4.

———. 1983. "Paul the Deacon and Secundus of Trento." In *History and Historians in Late Antiquity*, pp. 147–54. Ed. B. Croke and A. Emmett. Sydney: Pergamon Press.

Garrett, John 1988. "Status, the warrior class, and artificial cranial deformation." In *The King Site. Continuity and Contact in Sixteenth Century Georgia*, pp. 35–46. Ed. Robert L. Blakely. Athens and London: University of Georgia Press.

Gassowska, Eligia 1979. *Bizancjum a zemie północno-zachodnio-słowiańskie we wczesnym średniowieczu*. Wrocław, Warsaw, Cracow, and Gdańsk: Wywadnictwo Polskiej Akademii Nauk.

Gaul, Jerzy 1984. "The circulation of monetary and non-monetary currency in the West-Baltic zone in the 5th and 6th centuries AD." *ArchPol* 23:87–105.

Gavritukhin, Igor' O. 1993. "Ranneslavianskie pamiatniki v raione Zimnevskogo gorodishcha." *Archaeoslavica* 2:99–112.

Geary, Patrick J. 1983. "Ethnic identity as a situational construct in the Early Middle Ages." *Mitteilungen der Anthropologischen Gesellschaft in Wien* 113:15–26.

Gellner, Ernest 1988. *State and Society in Soviet Thought*. Oxford and New York: Basil Blackwood.

Gencheva, Evgeniia 1989. "Za tipologicheskoto razvitie na kăsnorimskite fibuli s podvito krache v Iuzhna Bălgariia." *Arkheologiia* 31, no. 4:30–6.

Gening, Vladimir F. 1973. "Programma statisticheskoi obrabotki keramiki iz arkheologicheskikh raskopok." *SA* 1:114–35.

———. 1992. *Drevniaia keramika: metody i programmy issledovaniia v arkheologii*. Kiev: Naukova Dumka.

Georgiev, Zoran 1985–6. "Gradište, s. Pčinija – docnoantički i ranovizantiski kastel." *MAA* 10:199–214.

Gerasimov, Todor 1959. "Kolektivni nakhodki ot moneti prez 1956 i 1957 g." *IBAI* 22:356–66.

Gerasimova-Tomova, Vasilka 1987. "Ein Silberkelch aus dem Dorf Nova Nadežda,

References

Bezirk Haskovo, aus der Zeit des Kaisers Justinian I. (527–565)." In *Christentum*, pp. 307– 12.

1992. "Bleiplomben aus Durostorum." In *Schwarzmeerküste*, pp. 69–72.

Gerostergios, Asterios N. 1974. "The religious policy of Justinian I and his religious beliefs." PhD Dissertation. Boston University.

Giardino, Marco 1985. "Ceramic attribute analysis and ethnic group composition: an example from Southeastern Louisiana." PhD Dissertation. Tulane University.

Gill, M. V. 1986. "The small finds." In *Excavations at Saraçhane in Istanbul*, pp. 226–77. Ed. R. M. Harrisson. Vol. I. Princeton: Princeton University Press.

Gimbutas, Marija 1971. *The Slavs*. New York and Washington: Praeger.

Gindin, L. A. 1987. "Znachenie lingvo-filologicheskikh dannykh dlia izucheniia rannikh etapov slavianizacii karpato-balkanskogo prostranstva." In *Struktura*, pp. 22–6.

1988. "Problema slavianizacii karpato-balkanskogo prostranstva v svete semanticheskogo analiza glagolov obitaniia u Prokopiia Kesariiskogo." *VDI* 3:173–82.

Ginkel, Jan Jacob van 1995. "John of Ephesos. A monophysite historian in sixth-century Byzantium." PhD Dissertation. Rijksuniversiteit Groningen.

Giorgetti, D. 1980. "Colonia Ulpia Traiana Ratiaria." *Ratiariensia* 1:13–34.

1983. "Ratiaria and its territory." In *Bulgaria*, pp. 19–39.

Giuffrida, C. 1985. "Disciplina Romanorum. Dall'Epitome di Vegezio allo Strategikon dello Pseudo-Mauricius." In *Le trasformazioni della cultura nella tarda antichità. Atti del convegno tenuto a Catania, Università degli studi, 27 sett.–2 ott. 1982*, pp. 837–61. Vol. II. Catania: Jouvence.

Gmelch, George 1980. "Return migration." *ARA* 9:135–59.

Goceva, Z. 1971. "Nouvelles données sur le système de fortification à Pautalia dans l'antiquité tardive." In *Acta Conventus XI Eirene, 21–25 oct. 1968*, pp. 429–34. Warsaw: Ossolineum.

Göckenjan, Hansgerd 1993. "Die Landnahme der Awaren aus historischer Sicht." In *Probleme*, pp. 275–302. Vol. I.

Godelier, Maurice 1986. *The Making of Great Men. Male Domination and Power Among the New Guinea Baruya*. Cambridge and Paris: Cambridge University Press and Editions de la Maison des Sciences de l'Homme.

Godłowski, Każimierz 1979. "Die Frage der slawischen Einwanderung in östliche Mitteleuropa." *Zeitschrift für Ostforschung* 28:416–47.

1980. "Zur Frage der völkerwanderungszeitlichen Besiedlung in Pommern." *Studien zur Sachsenforschung* 2:63–106.

1983. "Zur Frage der Slawensitze vor der grossen Slawenwanderung im 6. Jahrhundert." In *Slavi*, pp. 257– 302.

Goehrke, Carsten 1992. *Die Frühzeit des Ostslawentums*. Darmstadt: Wissenschaftliche Buchgesellschaft.

Goffart, Walter 1963. "The Fredegar problem reconsidered." *Speculum* 38:206–41.

1988. *The Narrators of Barbarian History (AD 550–800). Jordanes, Gregory of Tours, Bede, and Paul the Deacon*. Princeton: Princeton University Press.

1989. "The theme of 'the barbarian invasions' in late antique and modern historiography." In *Barbaren*, pp. 87–107.

Gojda, Martin 1991. *The Ancient Slavs. Settlement and Society*. Edinburgh: Edinburgh University Press.

References

Gołab, Zbigniew 1992. *The Origins of the Slavs. A Linguist's View.* Columbus, Ohio: Slavica Publishers.

Golden, Peter B. 1980. *Khazar Studies. An Historico-Philological Inquiry into the Origins of the Khazars.* Budapest: Akadémiai kiadó.

1982. "Imperial ideology and the sources of political unity among the pre-Cinggisid nomads of western Eurasia." *AEMA* 2:37–76.

Gomolka, Gudrun 1976. "Bemerkungen zur Situation der spätantiken Städte und Siedlungen in Nordbulgarien und ihrem Weiterleben am Ende des 6. Jahrhunderts." In *Studien*, pp. 35–42.

Gomolka-Fuchs, Gudrun 1982. "Die Kleinfunde vom 4. bis 6. Jh. aus Iatrus." In *Iatrus*, pp. 149–74. Vol. II.

Gorbanov, Petǎr 1987. "Die antike und frühmittelalterliche Stadt Diocletianopolis im Lichte der neuen archäologischen Forschungen." In *Christentum*, pp. 293–6.

Gorecki, Danuta 1989. "The Thrace of Ares during the sixth and seventh centuries." *ByzF* 14:221–35.

Gorianov, B. T. 1939a. "Slaviane i Vizantiia v V–VI vv. nashei ery." *IZ* 10:101–10.

1939b. "Slavianske poseleniia VI v. i ikh obshchestvennyi stroi." *VDI* 1:308–18.

Goriunov, E. A. 1974. "Nekotorye drevnosti I tys. n.e. na Chernigovshchine." In *Drevnosti*, pp. 119–25.

Goriunov, E. A., and M. M. Kazanskii 1978. "O proiskhozhdenii shirokoplatinchatykh fibul." *KSIA* 155:25–31.

Goriunova, V. M. 1987. "K voprosu ob oloviannykh ukrasheniiakh 'antskikh' kladov." In *Arkheologicheskie pamiatniki epokhi zheleza vostochnoevropeiskoi lesostepi. Mezhvuzovski sbornik nauchnykh trudov*, pp. 85–93. Ed. A. D. Priakhin. Voronezh: Izdatel'stvo Voronezhskogo Universiteta.

Goubert, Paul 1963. "Les guerres sur le Danube à la fin du VI-e siècle d'après Ménandre le Protecteur et Théophylacte Simocatta." In *Actes XIIa*, pp. 115–24. Vol. II.

Gounaris, G. 1984. "Χαλκινὸς πορπὴ ἀπὸ τὸ Ὀκταγονὸ τῶν Φιλιππῶν καὶ τὴν Κεντρικὴ Μακεδονία." *Vyzantiaka* 4:49–59.

Graebner, Michael 1975. "The Slavs in Byzantine population transfers of the seventh and eighth centuries." *EB* 11, no. 1:40–52.

1978. "The Slavs in Byzantine Europe – absorption, semi-autonomy and the limits of Byzantinization." *Byzantinobulgarica* 5:41–55.

Grafenauer, Bogo 1952. "Prilog kritici izvejštaja Konstantina Porfirogeneta o doseljenje Hrvata." *Historijski Zbornik* 5:1–56.

1960. "Zgodnjefevdalna družbena struktura Jugoslavenkih narodov in njen postanek." *ZC* 14:35–95.

Granić, B. 1925. "Die Gründung des autokephalen Erzbistums von Justiniana Prima durch Kaiser Justinian I im Jahre 535 n.Chr." *Byzantion* 2:123–40.

Graves, Paul 1995. "Flakes and ladders: what the archaeological record cannot tell us about the origins of language." *WA* 26, no. 2:158–71.

Graves-Brown, Paul 1996. "All things bright and beautiful? Species, ethnicity, and cultural dynamics." In *Identity*, pp. 81–95.

Greatrex, Geoffrey 1994. "The dates of Procopius' works." *BMGS* 18:101–14.

1995. "Procopius and Agathias on the defences of the Thracian Chersonese." In *Constantinople*, pp. 125–9.

References

Grégoire, H. 1944–5. "L'origine et le nom des Croates et des Serbes." *Byzantion* 17:88–118.

Gregory, Timothy 1982a. "Fortification and urban design in early Byzantine Greece." In *City*, pp. 43–64.

1982b. "The fortified cities of Byzantine Greece." *Archaeology* 35:14–21.

1984a. "Cities and social evolution in Roman and Byzantine southeast Europe." In *European Social Evolution*, pp. 267–76. Ed. J. Bintliff. Bradford: University of Bradford.

1984b. "Diporto: an early Byzantine maritime settlement in the Gulf of Korinth." *Deltion tes Christianikes Archaiologikes Hetaireias* 12:287–304.

1985. "An early Byzantine complex at Akra Sophia near Corinth." *Hesperia* 54:411–28.

1987a. "The early Byzantine fortifications of Nikopolis in comparative perspective." In *Nikopolis*, pp. 253–61.

1987b. "The fortress at Isthmia at the end of Antiquity." *AJA* 91:319–20.

1993. "An Early Byzantine (dark-age) settlement at Isthmia: preliminary report." In *Corinthia*, pp. 149–60.

Greverus, Ina-Maria 1978. *Kultur und Alltagswelt. Eine Einführung in Fragen der Kulturanthropologie*. Munich: C. H. Beck.

Grierson, Ph. 1982. *Byzantine Coins*. London, Berkeley, and Los Angeles: Methuen and University of California Press.

Grigoriou-Ioannidou, M. 1982. "Ἡ ἐκστρατεία τοῦ Ἰουστινιάνου Β κατὰ τῶν Βουλγάρων." *Vyzantiaka* 2:113–24.

Grinchenko, V. A. 1950. "Pam'iatka VIII st. kolo s. Voznesenki na Zaporizhzhi." *Arkheolohiia* 2:37–63.

Gschwantler, Kurt 1993. "Der Silbereimer von Kuczurmare – ein Meisterwerk frühbyzantinischer Toreutik." In *Syrien. Von den Aposteln zu den Kalifen*, pp. 175–9. Ed. E. M. Ruprechtberger. Mainz: Von Zabern.

Guhr, Günter 1984. "Das Wesen der militärische Demokratie bei Morgan sowie bei Marx und Engels", *EAZ* 25:229–56.

Guhr, Günther, and Friedrich Schlette 1982. "Die militärische Demokratie nach L. H. Morgan." *Zeitschrift für Geschichtswissenschaft* 30, nos. 10–11:909–15.

Guillou, André 1973. "Migration et présence slaves en Italie du VI-e au XI-e siècle." *ZRVI* 14–15:11–16.

Günther, Linda-Marie 1992. "Gallicus sive Anticus: zu einem Triumphaltitel Justinians I." *Tyche* 7:89–91.

Guthnick, E. 1988. "Zur Terminologie und Technologie der Töpferscheiben." *EAZ* 29:89–115.

Hahn, Wolfgang 1975. *Moneta Imperii Byzantini. Von Justinus II. bis Phocas (565–610)*. Vienna: Verlag der Österreichischen Akademie der Wissenschaften.

1978–9. "Review of P. Yannopoulos, 'L'hexagramme. Un monnayage byzantin en argent du VII-e siècle' (Louvain-la-Neuve, 1978)." *Jahrbuch für Numismatik und Geldgeschichte* 28–9:159–62.

1981. "A propos de l'introduction des solidi légers de 23 carats sous Maurice." *Bulletin de la Société Française de Numismatique* 36, no. 7:96–7.

1989. "Zur Frage der reduzierten Solidi unter Justinianus I." *Geldgeschichtliche Nachrichten* 24, no. 132:164–7.

References

Hajnalová, Eva 1982. "Archäobotanische Funde aus Krivina." In *Iatrus*, pp. 207–35. Vol. II.

Haldon, John 1993. *The State and the Tributary Mode of Production*. London and New York: Verso.

1997. *Byzantium in the Seventh Century. The Transformation of a Culture*. Cambridge: Cambridge University Press.

Halecki, Oskar 1950. *The Limits and Divisions of European History*. London and New York: Sheed & Ward.

Halkin, François 1973. "Un nouvel extrait de l'historien byzantin Ménandre?." In *Zetesis. Album amicorum aangeboden aan E. de Strycker*, pp. 664–7. Antwerpen: De nederl. Boekhandel.

Hally, David 1986. "The identification of vessel function: a case study from northwest Georgia." *AAnt* 51, no. 2:267–95.

Hamp, Eric P. 1970. "Early Slavic influence in Albanian." *BE* 14, no. 2:11–17.

Hampel, József 1900. "Emlekék és leletek. Ujabb hazai az avar uralom korából." *ArchÉrt* 20:117–25.

1905. *Alterthümer des frühen Mittelalters aus Ungarn*, vol. II. Braunschweig: F. Vieweg und Sohn.

Harhoiu, Radu 1982. "Zu den Siedlungsverhältnisse in Rumänien im 5. und 6. Jahrhundert n. Chr." In *Palast*, pp. 587–91.

1990. "Chronologische Fragen der Völkerwanderungszeit in Rumänien." *Dacia* 34:169–208.

Harrison, R. M. 1974. "To makron Teichos, The Long Wall in Thrace." In *Congress 8*, pp. 244–8.

Haseloff, Günther 1981. *Die germanische Tierornamentik der Völkerwanderungszeit. Studien zu Salin's Stil I*. Berlin and New York: Walter de Gruyter.

Hattersley-Smith, Kara 1988. "Byzantine public architecture, between the fourth and the early seventh centuries AD, with special reference to the towns of Macedonia." PhD Dissertation. University of Oxford.

Hauptmann, Ludmil 1915. "Politische Umwälzungen unter den Slowenen vom Ende des sechsten Jahrhunderts bis zur Mitte des neunten." *Mittheilungen des Instituts für Oesterreichische Geschichtsforschung* 36:229–87.

Hauser, Stefan R. 1992. *Spätantike und frühbyzantinische Silberlöffel. Bemerkungen zur Produktion von Luxusgütern im 5. bis 7. Jahrhundert*. Münster: Aschendorffsche Verlagsbuchhandlung.

Haussig, H. W. 1953. "Theophylakts Exkurs über die skythischen Völker." *Byzantion* 23:275–462.

Hautumm, Wolfgang 1981. *Studien zu Amphoren der spätrömischen und frühbyzantinischen Zeit*. Fulda: Wolfgang Hautumm.

Havlík, Lubomír E. 1974. "Slovanská 'barbarská království' 6. století na území Rumunska." *Slovanský Prehled* 3:177–88.

1985. "Die Byzantiner über die Verfassung der Slawen im 6. und 7. Jahrhundert." In *Eirene*, pp. 173–7.

Hayden, Brian, and Rob Gargett 1990. "Big man, big heart? A Mesoamerican view of the emergence of complex society." *Ancient Mesoamerica* 1:3–20.

Hayes, J. W. 1992. *Excavations at Saraçhane in Istanbul*, vol. II. Princeton: Princeton University Press.

References

Heather, Peter 1991a. *Goths and Romans 332–489*. New York and Oxford: Clarendon Press and Oxford University Press.

1991b. *The Goths in the Fourth Century*. Liverpool: Liverpool University Press.

1996. *The Goths*. Oxford: Blackwell.

Hegel, Georg Wilhelm Friedrich 1902. *Lecture on the Philosophy of History*. London: G. Bell and Sons.

Hegmon, Michelle 1992. "Archaeological research on style." *ARA* 21:517–36.

1994. "Boundary-making strategies in early Pueblo societies: style and architecture in the Kayenta and Mesa Verde regions." In *The Ancient Southwestern Community. Models and Methods for the Study of Prehistoric Social Organization*, pp. 171–90. Ed. W. H. Wills and Robert D. Leonard. Albuquerque: University of New Mexico Press.

Hellenkemper, Hansgerd 1987. "Die byzantinische Stadtmauer von Nikopolis in Epeiros: ein kaiserlicher Bauauftrag des 5. oder 6. Jahrhundert?." In *Nikopolis*, pp. 243–51.

Hendy, Michael F. 1985. *Studies in the Byzantine Monetary Economy c. 300–1450*. Cambridge: Cambridge University Press.

Henning, Joachim 1981. "Ostasiatische Einflüsse auf die landwirtschaftliche Produktion Ost- und Südosteuropas im frühen Mittelalter." In *Pliska*, pp. 66–70. Vol. III.

1986. "Bulgarien zwischen Antike und Mittelalter im Spiegel der Wirtschaftsarchäologie." *Das Altertum* 32, no. 2:100–12.

1987. *Südosteuropa zwischen Antike und Mittelalter. Archäologische Beiträge zur Landwirtschaft des I. Jahrtausends u.Z.* Berlin: Akademie Verlag.

1989. "Vostochnoe po proiskhozhdeniiu oruzhie i snariazhenie vsadnikov v kladakh sel'skokhoziaistvennykh zheleznykh izdelii v iugo-vostochnoi Evrope (VIII–X vv.)." In *Istoriia*, pp. 87–104.

Hensel, Witold 1988. "The cultural unity of the Slavs in the early Middle Ages." *ArchPol* 27:201–8.

1994. "Des méthodes de recherche sur l'ethnogénèse et la topogénèse des Slaves." In *Sbornik*, pp. 162–4.

Herder, Johann Gottfried 1994a. *Sämtliche Werke*, vol. XVII. Hildesheim and New York: Olms-Weidmann.

1994b. *Sämtliche Werke*, vol. XIV. Hildesheim and New York: Olms-Weidmann.

Herrmann, Joachim 1979a. "Die frühmittelalterlichen Siedlungen auf dem Gelände des Kastells Iatrus." In *Iatrus*, pp. 101–17. Vol. I.

1979b. "Stand und Probleme der Ausgrabungen. Die Siedlungsperioden und deren Datierung." In *Iatrus*, pp. 11–21. Vol. I.

1982. "Militärische Demokratie und die Übergangsperiode zur Klassengesellschaft." *EAZ* 23:11–31.

1986a. "Die altbulgarische Siedlung über dem antiken Kastell Iatrus/Krivina bei Ruse, VR Bulgarien. Zum Abschluß der Ausgrabungen." In *Iatrus*, pp. 5–16. Vol. III.

1986b. "Getreidekultur, Backteller und Brot Indizien – frühslawischer Differenzierung." In *Mélange*, pp. 267–72.

1987a. "Arkheologicheskiiat grad Iatrus i rannata istoriia na Bălgariia." In *Dokladi*, pp. 189–99.

References

1987b. "Militärische Demokratie und Allodismus in Mitteleuropa zwischen Antike und Feudalgesellschaft." *EAZ* 28:257–67.

1992. "Karasura 1981–1991. Zu den bisherigen Ergebnissen von Ausgrabungen und Forschungsarbeiten in Südthrakien zwischen Stara Zagora und Plovdiv." *ZfA* 26:153–80.

Hesse, Brian 1990. "Pig lovers and pig haters: patterns of Palestinian pork production." *Journal of Ethnobiology* 10, no. 2:195–225.

Hessen, Otto von 1974. "Byzantinische Schnallen aus Sardinien im Museo Archeologico zu Turin." In *Festschrift*, pp. 545–57. Vol. II.

Hides, Shaun 1996. "The genealogy of material culture and cultural identity." In *Identity*, pp. 25–47.

Higbed, J. P. 1967. "Pepys and a hoard." *Australian Numismatic Journal* 18:190–2.

Hines, John 1984. *The Scandinavian Character of Anglian England in the Pre-Viking Period*. Oxford: BAR.

1994. "The becoming of the English: identity, material culture and language in early Anglo-Saxon England." *ASSAH* 7:49–59.

1997. *A New Corpus of Anglo-Saxon Great Square-Headed Brooches*. Woodbridge and Rochester: Boydell Press and Society of Antiquaries of London.

Hodder, Ian 1982. *Symbols in Action. Ethnoarchaeological Studies of Material Culture*. Cambridge, London, and New York: Cambridge University Press.

1990. "Style as historical quality." In *Uses*, pp. 44– 51.

Hoddinott, Ralph 1963. *Early Byzantine Churches in Macedonia and Southern Serbia: A Study of the Origins and the Initial Development of East Christian Art*. London: Macmillan.

1975. *Bulgaria in Antiquity: An Archaeological Introduction*. New York: St Martin's Press.

Hodges, Richard 1982. *Dark Age Economics: The Origins of Towns and Trade AD 600–1000*. New York: St Martin's Press.

Hodges, Richard, and Gieraj Saraçi 1994–5. "Late-antique and Byzantine Butrint: interim report on the port and its hinterland." *JRA* 10:207–34.

Hodges, Richard, and David Whitehouse 1983. *Mohammed, Charlemagne & the Origins of Europe. Archaeology and the Pirenne Thesis*. Ithaca: Cornell University Press.

Holy, Ladislav 1979. "The segmentary lineage structure and its existential status." *The Queen's University Papers in Social Anthropology* 4:1–22.

Honigman, Ernst 1929. *Die sieben Klimata und die πόλις ἐπίσημοι*. Heidelberg: C. Winter.

Hood, Sinclair 1970. "Isles of refuge in the early Byzantine period." *Annual of the British School at Athens* 65:37–44.

Horedt, Kurt 1957. "Die befestigte Ansiedlung von Moreşti und ihre frühgeschichtliche Bedeutung." *Dacia* 1:298–308.

1958. *Contribuţii la istoria Transilvaniei în secolele IV–XIII*. Bucharest: Editura Academiei RPR.

1964. "Aşezarea fortificată de la Şeica Mică (r. Mediaş)." *SCIV* 15, no. 2:187–204.

1969. "Befestigte Siedlungen des 6. Jhs. u.Z. aus Siebenbürgen." In *Siedlung, Burg und Stadt. Studien zu ihren Anfängen*, pp. 129–38. Ed. Joachim Herrmann. Berlin: Akademie Verlag.

References

1977. "Der östliche Reihengräberkreis in Siebenbürgen." *Dacia* 21:251–68.

1979a. *Moreşti. Grabungen in einer vor- und frühgeschichtlichen Siedlung in Siebenbürgen.* Bucharest: Kriterion.

1979b. "Die Polyederohrringe des 5.–6. Jhs. u. Z. aus der SR Rumänien." *ZfA* 13:241–50.

Hornstein, Franz 1957. "Ἴστρος 'αμαξευόμενος. Zur Geschichte eines literarischen Topos." *Gymnasium* 64:154– 61.

Horowitz, D. L. 1975. "Ethnic identity." In *Ethnicity. Theory and Experience*, pp. 111–40. Ed. Nathan Glazer and Daniel P. Moynihan. Cambridge, Mass., and London: Harvard University Press.

Hösler, Joachim 1995. *Die sowjetische Geschichtswissenschaft 1953 bis 1991. Studien zur Methodologie- und Organisationsgeschichte.* Munich: Otto Sagner.

Howard-Johnston, J. D. 1995. "The siege of Constantinople in 626." In *Constantinople*, pp. 131–42.

Hoxha, Gezim 1993. "Skhodra, chef-lieu de la province Prévalitane." *CCARB* 40:551–67.

Hromada, Jozef 1991. "Včasnoslovanské žiarove pohrebisko v Bratislave-Dubravke." *SlovArch* 39, nos. 1–2:277–85.

Hübener, Wolfgang 1989. "Über merowingerzeitliche Schildbuckel." *Acta Praehistorica et Archaeologica* 21:85– 97.

Hurdubeţiu, I. 1969. "Originea şcheilor şi răspîndirea lor pe teritoriul carpato-dunărean." *Studii şi Articole de Istorie* 14:195–205.

Huszár, László 1955. "Das Münzmaterial in den Funden der Völkerwanderungszeit im mittleren Donaubecken." *ActaArchHung* 5:61–109.

Iakobson, A. L. 1979. *Keramika i keramicheskoe proizvodstvo srednevekovoi Tavriki.* Leningrad: Nauka.

Ibler, Ursula 1992. "Pannonische Gürtelschnallen des späten 6. und 7. Jahrhunderts." *AV* 43:135–48.

Iorga, Nicolae 1937. *Histoire des Roumains et de la romanité orientale.* 2 vols. Bucharest: Imprimerie de l'Etat.

Ippen, Theodor 1907. "Denkmäler verschiedener Altersstufen in Albanien." *Wissenschaftliche Mittheilungen aus Bosnia und Hercegowina* 10:3–70.

Irmscher, Johannes 1969. "Geschichtsschreiber der justinianischen Zeit." *WZRostock* 18:469–74.

1971. "Zur Geschichtstheorie der justinianischen Epoche." In *Acta Conventus XI Eirene, 21–25 oct. 1968*, pp. 337–46. Warsaw: Ossolineum.

1980. "Die Slawen und das Justinianische Reich." In *Rapports*, pp. 157–69. Vol. II.

Isajiw, Wsevolod 1974. "Definitions of ethnicity." *Ethnicity* 1:111–24.

Işfănoni, Doina 1991. "Rolul structurilor plastico-decorative ale ceramicii transilvănene în relevarea identiţăţii etnice a olarilor." In *Nemzetiség-identitás. A IV. Nemzetközi néprajzi nemzetiségkutató konferencia elöadásai*, pp. 223–5. Ed. Zoltán Ujváry, Ernö Eperjessy, and András Krupa. Békécsaba and Debrecen: Ethnica.

Iurukova, Iordanka 1969a. "Imitations barbares de [sic] monnaies de bronze byzantines du VI-e siècle." *Byzantinoslavica* 30:83–7.

1969b. "Les invasions slaves au sud du Danube d'après les trésors monétaires." *Byzantinobulgarica* 3:255–63.

1980. "Un trésor de monnaies d'or byzantines du VII-e siècle découvert à Nessèbre." In *Nessèbre*, pp. 186–90. Ed. V. Velkov. Vol. II. Sofia: BAN.

References

1992a. "Săkrovishteto ot Akalan." *Numizmatika i Sfragistika* 1–2:10–16.

1992b. "Trouvailles monétaires de Sadovetz." In *Uenze* 1992, pp. 279–333.

Ivanov, I. 1993. "Ulpia-Oescus – römische und frühbyzantinische Stadt in Moesia Inferior (Nordbulgarien)." *BHR* 21, nos. 2–3:23–48.

Ivanov, S. A. 1983. "Oborona Vizantii i geografiia 'varvarskikh' vtorzhenii cherez Dunai v pervoi polovine VI v." *VV* 44:27–47.

1984. "Oborona balkanskikh provincii Vizantii i proniknovenie 'varvarov' na Balkany v pervoi polovine VI v." *VV* 45:35–53.

1987. "Poniatiia 'soiuza' i 'podchineniia' u Prokopiia Kesariiskogo." In *Struktura*, pp. 27–32.

1988. "Neispol'zovannoe vizantiiskoe svidetel'stvo VI v. o slavianakh." *VV* 49:181–4.

1991a. "Anty v titulature vizantiiskikh imperatorov." In *Svod*, pp. 260–4. Vol. I.

1991b. "Martin Brakarskii." In *Svod*, pp. 357–60. Vol. I.

1991c. "Otkuda nachinat' etnicheskuiu istoriiu slavian? (Po povodu novogo truda pol'skikh issledovatelei)." *SovS* 5:3–13.

1991d. "Psevdo-Kesarii." In *Svod*, pp. 251–64. Vol. I.

1993. "Slavianskaia etnichnosti kak metodologicheskaia problema." *SovS* 2:23–6.

1995a. "Feodor Sinkell." In *Svod*, pp. 83–90. Vol. II.

1995b. "Feofilakt Simokatta." In *Svod*, pp. 10–64. Vol. II.

1995c. "Georgii Pisida." In *Svod*, pp. 65–74. Vol. II.

1995d. "Paskhal'naia khronika." In *Svod*, pp. 75–82. Vol. II.

1995e. "Prodolzhatel' Moskha." In *Svod*, pp. 511–13. Vol. II.

Ivanov, S. A., L. A. Gindin, and V. L. Cymburskii 1991. "Prokopii Kesariiskii." In *Svod*, pp. 170–249. Vol. I.

Ivanov, Teofil. 1974. "Die letzten Ausgrabungen des römischen und frühbyzantinischen Donau-Limes in der VR Bulgarien." In *Actes IX*, pp. 55–69.

1980. *Abritus, rimski kastel i rannovizantiiski grad v Dolna Miziia.* Sofia: Izdatelstvo na Bălgarskata Akademiia na Naukite.

Ivanov, Teofil, D. Serafimova, and N. Nikolov 1969. "Razkopki v Sandanski prez 1960 g." *IBAI* 31:105–209.

Ivanov, Teofil, and Stoian Stoianov 1985. *Abritus. Its History and Archaeology.* Razgrad: Cultural and Historical Heritage Directorate.

Ivanov, V. V. 1976. "Iazyk kak istochnik pri etnogeneticheskikh issledovaniiakh i problematika slavianskikh drevnostei." In *Voprosy*, pp. 30–47.

Ivanov, V. V., and V. N. Toporov 1980. "O drevnikh slavianskikh etnonimakh (Osnovnye problemy i perspektivy)." In *Kul'tura*, pp. 11–45.

Ivanova, O. V. 1980. "Slaviane i Fessalonika vo vtoroi polovine VII v. po dannym 'Chudes Sv. Dimitriia' (Postanovka voprosa)." In *Kul'tura*, pp. 81–107.

1987. "Formy politicheskoi organizacii slavianskogo obshchestva v central'noi i iuzhnoi chastiakh balkanskogo poluostrova v VII–VIII vv." In *Struktura*, pp. 56–65.

1995a. "Chudesa Sv. Dimitriia Solunskogo." In *Svod*, pp. 91–211. Vol. II.

1995b. "Isidor Sevil'skii." In *Svod*, pp. 353–8. Vol. II.

Ivanova, O. V., and G. G. Litavrin 1985. "Slaviane i Vizantiia." In *Gosudarstva*, pp. 34–98.

Ivison, Eric A. 1996. "Burial and urbanism at Late Antique and Early Byzantine Corinth (c. AD 400–700)." In *Towns in Transition. Urban Evolution in Late*

References

Antiquity and the Early Middle Ages, pp. 99–125. Ed. N. Christie and S. T. Loseby. Aldershot and Brookfield: Scolar Press.

Janković, Đorđe 1980. "Pozdneantichnye fibuly VI–VII vekov i slaviane." In *Rapports*, pp. 171–81. Vol. II.

—— 1981. *Podunavski deo oblasti Akvisa u VI i početkom VII veka*. Belgrade: Arheološki Institut.

Jarnut, Jörg 1985. "Aspekte frühmittelalterlicher Ethnogenese in historischer Sicht." In *Entstehung von Sprachen und Völkern. Glotto- und ethnogenetische Aspekte europäischer Sprachen. Akten des 6. Symposiums über Sprachkontakt in Europa, Mannheim 1984*, pp. 83–91. Ed. P. Sture Ureland. Tübingen: Max Niemeyer.

Jaskanis, Danuta, and Marian Kachinski 1981. *The Balts – the Northern Neighbours of the Slavs*. Warsaw: Ministry of Art and Culture in the Polish People's Republic.

Jaskanis, Jan 1996. *Cecele. Ein Gräberfeld der Wielbark-Kultur in Ostpolen*. Cracow: Wydawnictwo i drukarnia "Secesja".

Jeffreys, Elizabeth 1990a. "Chronological structures in Malalas' chronicle." In *Studies in John Malalas*, pp. 111–66. Ed. Elizabeth Jeffreys, Brian Croke, and Scott Roger. Sydney: Australian Association for Byzantine Studies.

—— 1990b. "Malalas' sources." In *Studies in John Malalas*, pp. 167–216. Ed. Elizabeth Jeffreys, Brian Croke, and Scott Roger. Sydney: Australian Association for Byzantine Studies.

Jelínková, Dagmar 1990. "K chronologii sídlistnich nálezu s keramikou pražského typu na Morave." In *Praveké*, pp. 251–81.

—— 1993. "Pavlov – slavianskoe poselenie 6–8 vv." In *Actes XIIb*, pp. 74–83. Vol. IV.

Jenkins, Richard 1994. "Rethinking ethnicity: identity, categorization and power." *ERS* 17, no. 2:189–223.

Jeremić, Miroslav 1994–5. "The Caričin Grad necropolis." *Starinar* 45–6:181–95.

—— 1995. "Balajnac, agglomération protobyzantine fortifiée." *AT* 3:193–207.

Jeremić, Miroslav, and Mihailo Milinković 1995. "Die byzantinische Festung von Bregovina (Südserbien)." *AT* 3:209–25.

Jireček, Konstantin 1911. *Geschichte der Serben*, vol. I. Gotha: F. A. Perthes.

Johnson, Lesley 1995. "Imagining communities: medieval and modern." In *Concepts of National Identity in the Middle Ages*, pp. 1–15. Ed. Simon Forde, Lesley Johnson, and Alan V. Murray. Leeds: University of Leeds.

Jones, A. H. M. 1964. *The Later Roman Empire, 284–602: A Social, Economic and Administrative Survey*. Oxford: Oxford University Press.

Jones, Siân 1994. "Archaeology and ethnicity. Constructing identities in the past and the present." PhD Dissertation. University of Southampton.

—— 1996. "Discourses of identity in the interpretation of the past." In *Identity*, pp. 62–80.

—— 1997. *The Archaeology of Ethnicity. Constructing Identities in the Past and Present*. London and New York: Routledge.

Jørgensen, Anne Nørgård 1999. "A peaceful discussion of a martial topic: the chronology of Scandinavian weapon graves." In *The Pace of Change. Studies in Early-Medieval Chronology*, pp. 148–59. Ed. John Hines, Karen Høilund Nielsen, and Frank Siegmund. Oxford: Oxbow Books.

Jovanović, Aleksandar 1982–3. "Hajdučka Vodenica, kasnoantičko i ranovizantijsko utvrđenje." *Starinar* 32–3:319–31.

References

1984. "Un petit trésor de monnaies de bronze de la forteresse protobyzantine près de Slatinska reka." *Numizmatičar* 7:31–8.

Kalić, Jovanka 1985. "Neueste Ergebnisse der historischen Forschung zur Landnahme der Slaven auf dem Balkan." *JGO* 33:366–77.

Kalinina, T. M. 1995. "Al-Akhtal." In *Svod*, pp. 508–9. Vol. II.

Kalinowski, Zygmunt 1999. "The Temple complex at the episcopal residence in Novae: a double church or two churches?." In *Limes*, pp. 65–73.

Kalligas, Haris 1990. *Byzantine Monemvasia. The Sources*. Monemvasia: Akroneon.

Kaminskii, V. N. 1986. "Voinskoe snariazhenie rannesrednevekovykh plemen Severo-Zapadnogo Kavkaza (Po materialam mogil'nika Moshchevaia Balka)." *Kul'tura i byt adygov* 6:19–40.

Kampffmeyer, U. et al. 1988. *Untersuchungen zur rechnergestützten Klassifikation der Form von Keramik*. Frankfurt a.M., Bern, and Paris: Peter Lang.

Kaplan, Michel 1992. *Les hommes et la terre à Byzance du VI-e au XI-e siècle. Propriété et exploitation du sol*. Paris: Publications de la Sorbonne.

Karaiskaj, Gjerak 1984. *Butrint. Dhe fortifikimet e tij*. Tirana: Neutori.

1989. "Die albanische Stadt Sarda. Entstehung der mittelalterlichen Stadt in Albanien." In *Actes XI*, pp. 2637–56. Vol. III.

Karaman, Ljubo 1956. "Glossen zu einigen Fragen der slawischen Archäologie." *ArchIug* 2:101–10.

Karayannopoulos, J. 1971. "Zur Frage der Slavenansiedlungen auf dem Peloponnes." *RESEE* 9:443–60.

1989. *Les Slaves en Macédoine. La prétendue interruption des communications entre Constantinople et Thessalonique du 7-e au 9-e siècle*. Athens: Comité national grec des études du Sud-Est européen.

1990. "Τὸ κιβώριο τῆς Ἐκκλησίας τῆς Κορίνθου." *Lakonikai Spoudai* 10:79–85.

Kardulias, Paul Nick 1988. "The Byzantine fortress at Isthmia, Greece and the transition from Late Antiquity to the medieval period in the Aegean." PhD Dissertation. Ohio State University.

1992. "Estimating population at ancient military sites: the use of historical and contemporary analogy." *AAnt* 57, no. 2:276–87.

1993. "Anthropology and population estimates for the Byzantine fortress at Isthmia." In *Corinthia*, pp. 139–48.

Kasapides, Dimitri 1991–2. "Τόπειρος-Χάνθεια." *Vyzantinos Domos* 5–6:85–96.

Kastelić, Jozo 1956. "Les boucles d'oreilles à corbeille en Slovenie." *ArchIug* 2:119–29.

Katić, Lovre 1950–1. "Vjerodostojnost Tome Arcidakona i posljedni dani Solina." *VAHD* 53:99–120.

Kazanski, Michel 1991a. *Les Goths (I–er–VII–e siècle après J.-C.)*. Paris: Errance.

1991b. "Quelques objets baltes trouvés en Gaule, datés entre la fin du IV-e siècle et le VIII-e siècle. A propos des contacts entre l'Occident et le rivage oriental de la mer Baltique. *ArchMéd* 21: 1–20.

1992. "L'influence danubienne dans la steppe pontique pendant la seconde moitié du Ve siècle: le rôle des Angiskires." In *Medieval Europe 1992. Death and Burial*, pp. 139–44. Vol. IV. York: Medieval Europe.

1993. "The sedentary elite in the 'empire' of the Huns and its impact on material civilisation in southern Russia during the early Middle Ages (5th–7th centuries

References

AD)." In *Cultural Transformations and Interactions in Eastern Europe*, pp. 211–35. Ed. John Chapman and Pavel Dolukhanov. Aldershot and Brookfield: Avebury.

1994. "Les plaques-boucles méditérranéennes des V–e–VI–e siècles." *ArchMéd* 24:137–98.

Kazanski, Michel, and J.-P. Sodini 1987. "Byzance et l'art 'nomade'. Remarques à propos de l'essai de J. Werner sur le dépôt de Malaja Pereščepina (Pereščepino)." *Revue Archéologique* 1:71–90.

Keefe, Susan Emley 1992. "Ethnic identity: the domain of perceptions of and attachment to ethnic groups and cultures." *Human Organization* 51, no. 1:35–43.

Kent, J. P. C. 1974. "Interpreting coin-finds." In *Coins and the Archaeologist*, pp. 184–200. Ed. J. Casey and R. Reece. Oxford: British Archaeological Reports.

Kent, John H. 1950. "A Byzantine statue base at Corinth." *Speculum* 25:544–6.

Keramidchiev, Apostol 1981–2. "Eksploatacija na mermerite vo antičko vreme." *MAA* 7–8:109–24.

Kessiakova, Elena 1989. "Une nouvelle basilique à Philippopolis." In *Actes XI*, pp. 2539–59. Vol. III.

Kharalambieva, Anna 1989. "Dva tipa kasnoantichni fibuli văv Varnenskiia muzei." *INMV* 25:29–40.

——— 1991. "Fibuli ot V v. ot Severoiztochna Bălgariia." *Arkheologiia* 23, no. 1:33–8.

——— 1992. "Fibuli ot I–VII v. v Dobrichkiia muzei." *Dobrudzha* 9:127–40.

——— 1993. "Bügelfibeln aus dem 7. Jh. südlich der unteren Donau." In *Actes XIIb*, pp. 25–32. Vol. IV.

Kharalambieva, Anna, and Georgi At. Atanasov 1991. "Fibuli ot V–VI v. v Shumenskiia muzei." *INMV* 27:42–63.

Kharalambieva, Anna, and Dimităr Ivanov 1986. "Kăsnoantichni fibuli ot Muzeia v Ruse." *GMSB* 12:9–20.

Khavliuk, P. I. 1961. "Ranneslavianskie poseleniia v srednei chasti Iuzhnogo Pobuzh'ia." *SA* 3:187–201.

——— 1963. "Ranneslavianskie poseleniia Semenki i Samchincy v srednem techenii Iuzhnogo Buga." In *Obrazovaniia*, pp. 320–50.

——— 1974. "Ranneslavianskie poseleniia v basseine Iuzhnogo Buga." In *Drevnosti*, pp. 181–215.

Khazanov, Anatolii M. 1974. "'Military democracy' and the epoch of class formation." In *Soviet*, pp. 133–46.

——— 1985. "Rank society and rank societies: processes, stages, and types of evolution." In *Development*, pp. 82–96.

Khrushkova, L. G. 1979. "Mramornye izdeliia vizantiiskogo proiskhozhdeniia iz Vostochnogo Prichernomor'ia." *VV* 40:127–34.

Kidd, Dafydd 1992. "The Velestínon (Thessaly) hoard – a footnote." In *Awarenforschungen*, pp. 509–15. Vol. II.

Kidd, Dafydd, and Ludmila Pekarskaya 1995. "New insight into the hoard of 6th–7th century silver from Martynovka." In *Noblesse*, pp. 351–60.

Kilian, Klaus 1980. "Zu einigen früh- und hochmittelalterlichen Funden aus der Burg von Tiryns." *Archäologisches Korrespondenzblatt* 10:281–90.

Kipp, Rita Smith, and Edward M. Schortman 1989. "The political impact of trade in chiefdoms." *AAnth* 91:370–85.

References

Kiss, Attila 1977. *Avar Cemeteries in County Baranya*. Budapest: Akadémiai kiadó.
1983. "Egy Baldenheim típusú sisak a Magyar Nemzeti Múzeum Régészeti Gyüjteményében." *ArchÉrt* 110:274–81.
1984. "Heruler in Nordserbien." In *Interaktionen*, pp. 133–7.
1987a. "Frühmittelalterliche byzantinische Schwerter im Karpatenbecken." *ActaArchHung* 39:193–210.
1987b. "Die Herrscher des Karpatenbeckens im 5./6. Jahrhundert aus archäologischer Sicht." *Anzeiger des Germanischen Nationalmuseums und Berichte aus dem Forschungsinstitut für Realienkunde* 1:57–68.
1989–90. "V–VI. századi Kárpát-medencei uralkodók-régész szemmel." *Agria* 25–6:201–20.
1992. "Germanen im awarenzeitlichen Karpatenbecken." In *Awarenforschungen*, pp. 35–134. Vol. I.
1996. *Das awarenzeitlich-gepidische Gräberfeld von Kölked-Feketekapu A*. Innsbruck: Universitätsverlag Wagner.
Klaić, Nada 1984. "Problemima stare domovine, dolaska i pokrstenja dalmatinskih Hrvata." *ZC* 38:253–70.
1985. "Najnoviji radovi o 29, 30 i 31. poglavju u djelu De administrando imperio cara Konstantin VII. Porfirogeneta." *SP* 15:31–60.
Klanica, Zdenek 1986. *Počatky slovanského osídleni našich zemi*. Prague: Academia.
1993. "Muntenice – slavianskoe poselenie VII–X vv." In *Actes XIIb*, pp. 83–91. Vol. IV.
Klein, L. S. 1993. *Fenomen sovetskoi arkheologii*. St Petersburg: FARN.
Klejn, Leo S. 1974. "Kossinna im Abstand von vierzig Jahren." *JMV* 58:7–55.
1977. "A panorama of theoretical archaeology." *CAnth* 18, no. 1:1–42.
1981. "Die Ethnogenese als Kulturgeschichte, archäologisch betrachtet. Neue Grundlagen." In *Beiträge zur Ur- und Frühgeschichte*, pp. 13–25. Ed. Hans Kaufmann and Klaus Simon. Vol. I. Berlin: VEB Deutscher Verlag der Wissenschaften.
Klenina, Elena 1999. "Table and cooking pottery of the IV–VI AD from the excavation of the episcopal residence at Novae." In *Limes*, pp. 83–8.
Kleppe, Else Johansen 1977. "Archaeological material and ethnic identification. A study of Lappish material from Varanger, Norway." *Norwegian Archaeological Review* 10, nos. 1–2:32–46.
Knific, Timotej 1994. "Vranje near Sevnica: a Late Roman settlement in the light of certain pottery finds." *AV* 45:211–37.
Kobyliński, Zbigniew 1989. "An ethnic change or a socio-economic one? The 5th and 6th centuries AD in the Polish lands." In *Approaches*, pp. 303–12.
1990. "Early medieval hillforts in Polish lands in the 6th to the 8th centuries: problems of origins, function, and spatial organization." In *Baltic*, pp. 147–56.
Koch, Guntram 1988. "Frühchristliche und frühbyzantinische Zeit (4.–8. Jh.)." In *Albanien. Schätze aus dem Land der Skipetaren*, pp. 118–37. Ed. Guntram Koch. Mainz: Philipp von Zabern.
Koch, Ursula 1974. "Mediterrane und fränkische Glasperlen des 6. und 7. Jahrhunderts aus Finnland." In *Festschrift*, pp. 495–520. Vol. II.
Koder, Johannes 1976. "Arethas von Kaisareia und die sogenannte Chronik von Monemvasia." *JÖB* 25:75–80.

References

1978. "Zur Frage der slavischen Siedlungsgebiete im mittelalterlichen Griechenland." *ByzZ* 71:315–31.

1986. "Ammerkungen zu den Miracula Sancti Demetrii." In *Byzance. Hommage à André N. Stratos*, pp. 523–36. Vol. II. Athens: N. A. Stratou.

Kohl, Philip, and Clare Fawcett 1995. "Archaeology in the service of the state: theoretical considerations." In *Nationalism, Politics, and the Practice of Archaeology*, pp. 3–18. Ed. Philip Kohl and Clare Fawcett. Cambridge: Cambridge University Press.

Koicheva, Kina, and Anna Kharalambieva 1993. "Fibuli ot Istoricheskiia Muzeia v Gabrovo (III–VII vek)." *GMSB* 19:57–72.

Koledarov, P. S. 1969. "Settlement structure of the Bulgarian Slavs in their transition from a clan to a territorial community." *Byzantinobulgarica* 3:125–32.

Komata, Damian 1976. "Forteresses hautes-médiévales albanaises." *Iliria* 5:181–203.

Kondić, Vladimir 1974. "Ergebnisse der neuen Forschungen auf dem obermoesischen Donaulimes." In *Actes IX*, pp. 39– 54.

1982–3a. "Bosman, ranovizantijsko utvrđenje." *Starinar* 32–3:137–45.

1982–3b. "Ravna (Campsa), rimsko i ranovizantijsko utvrđenje." *Starinar* 32–3:233–51.

1984a. "Les formes des fortifications protobyzantines dans la région des Portes de Fer." In *Villes*, pp. 131–61.

1984b. "Le trésor de monnaies de bronze de la forteresse protobyzantine de Bosman." *Numizmatičar* 7:51– 6.

Köpstein, Helga 1979. "Zum Bedeutungswandel von Σκλάβος/Sclavus." *ByzF* 7:67–88.

Korkuti, Muzafer, and Karl M. Petruso 1993. "Archaeology in Albania." *AJA* 97, no. 4:707–43.

Koroliuk, V. D. 1970. "Rannefeodal'naia gosudarstvennost' i formirovanie feodal'noi sostvennosti u vostochnykh i zapadnykh slavian (do serediny XI v.)." In *V International Congress of Economic History, Leningrad, 10–14 August 1970*, pp. 27–42. Moscow: Nauka.

Korošec, Josip 1958a. "Istraživanja slovenskie keramike ranog srednieg veka v Jugoslaviji." *RVM* 7:5–12.

1958b. "Ostava brončanih matrica za otiskivanje u Biskupiji kod Knina." *SP* 6:29–44.

Korzukhina, G. F. 1955. "K istorii srednego Podneprov'ia v seredine I tysiacheletiia n.e." *SA* 22:61–82.

Kos, Milko 1931. "K poročilom Pavla Diakona o Slovencih." *Časopis na zgodovino in narodopisje* 26:202–16.

Kos, Peter 1986. *The Monetary Circulation in the Southeastern Alpine Region ca. 300 BC–AD 1000*. Ljubljana: Narodni muzeja.

Kosciushko-Valiuzhinich, K. 1902. "Otchet' o raskopkakh' v' Khersones' v' 1901 godu." *IIAK* 4:51–119.

Kossinna, Gustaf 1911. *Die Herkunft der Germanen. Zur Methode der Siedlungsarchäologie*. Würzburg: C. Kabitzsch.

1936. *Ursprung und Verbreitung der Germanen in vor- und frühgeschichtlicher Zeit*. Leipzig: C. Kabitzsch.

Kostrzewski, Józef 1969. "Über den gegenwärtigen Stand der Erforschung der Ethnogenese der Slaven in archäologischer Sicht." In *Das heidnische und christ-*

References

liche Slaventum. Acta II Congressus internationalis historiae Slavicae Salisburgo-Ratisbonensis anno 1967 celebrati, pp. 11–25. Ed. Franz Zagiba. Vol. 1. Wiesbaden: Otto Harrassowitz.

Kotigoroshko, Viacheslav Grigorievich 1977. "Novye dannye k izucheniu drevnei istorii slavian Zakarpat'ia." *SlovArch* 25, no. 1:81–102.

Kougeas, S. B. 1912. "Ἐπὶ τοῦ καλουμένου χρονικῷ Περὶ τῆς κτίσεως τῆς Μονεμβασίας." *Neos Hellenomnemon* 9:473– 80.

Kousoupov, B. 1984. "L'église 'Sainte Sophie' à Sofia." In *Actes X*, pp. 267–71. Vol. 11.

Kovačević, Jovan 1969. "Arheološki prilog preciziranju hronologije slovenskog naseljavanja Balkana." In *Simpozijum*, pp. 57–83.

Kovács, István 1913. "A mezöbándi ásatások." *Dolgozátok az Erdélyi Nemzéti Múzeum érem- és régiség tárából* 4:265–329.

Kovács, László 1981. "Der landnahmezeitliche Grabfunde von Hajdúböszörmeny-Erdös tanya." *ActaArchHung* 33:81–103.

Kovrig, Ilona 1963. *Das awarenzeitliche Gräberfeld von Alattyán*. Budapest: Akadémiai kiadó.

Kozlov, V. 1974. "On the concept of ethnic community." In *Soviet*, pp. 73–87.

Krader, Lawrence 1968. *Formation of the State*. Englewood Cliffs, N.J.: Prentice-Hall.

Krautheimer, Richard 1986. *Early Christian and Byzantine Architecture*. London and New York: Penguin Books.

Kravchenko, N. M. 1979. "Issledovaniia slavianskikh pamiatnikov na Stugne." In *Slaviane i Rus' (na materialakh vostochnoslavianskikh plemen i drevnei Rusi). Sbornik nauchnykh trudov*, pp. 74–92. Ed. V. D. Baran. Kiev: Naukova Dumka.

Krieger, A. 1944. "The typological concept." *AAnt* 9, no. 3:271–88.

Kristiansen, Kristian 1991. "Chiefdoms, states, and systems of social evolution." In *Chiefdoms: Power, Economy, and Ideology*, pp. 16–43. Ed. Timothy Earle. Cambridge, New York, and Port Chester: Cambridge University Press.

Krivov, M. V. 1995. "Siriiskii 'Smeshannyi khronikon'." In *Svod*, pp. 517–18. Vol. 11.

Krivushin, I. V. 1991. "Stasis po Feofilaktu Simokatte, Evagriu i Feofanu (voennyi miatezh 588–589 gg.)." In *Vizantii*, pp. 47–57.

1994. "Les personnages dans les Histoires de Théophylacte Simocatta. Réalité et fiction." *Byzantinoslavica* 55, no. 1:8–18.

Kropotkin, V. V. 1959. "Mogil'nik Suuk-Su i ego istoriko-arkheologicheskoe znachenie (po dannym pogrebal'nogo obriada)." *SA* 1:181–4.

1962. *Klady vizantiiskikh monet na territorii SSSR*. Moscow: Nauka.

1965. "Novye nakhodki vizantiiskikh monet na territorii SSSR." *VV* 26:166–89.

1970. "Vizantiiskaia chasha iz Krylosskogo klada VII v." *VV* 31:194–5.

1971. "Klad serebriannykh veshchei VII veka iz s. Krylos v Podnestrov'e." *AAC* 12:65–71.

Krüger, Bruno 1988. "Zur militärischen Demokratie bei den germanischen Stämme." In *Familie*, pp. 539–45.

Krumphanzlová, Zdenka 1992. "Amber: its significance in the early Middle Ages." *PA* 83:350–71.

Krusch, Bruno 1882. "Die Chronicae des sogenannten Fredegar." *Neues Archiv* 7:247–351, 421–516.

Kryganov, A. V. 1990. "Aziatskie elementy v vooruzhenii rannesrednevekovykh vostochnoevropeiskikh kochevnikov." In *Voennoe delo drevnego srednevekovogo nase-*

References

leniia Severnoi i Central'noi Azii, pp. 71–80. Ed. Iu. S. Khudiakov and Iu. A. Plotnikov. Novosibirsk: Akademia Nauk SSSR – Sibirskoe otdelenie.

Kuchma, V. V. 1978. "Slaviane kak veroiatnyi protivnik Vizantiiskoi imperii po dannym dvukh voennykh traktatov." In *Khoziaistvo i obshchestvo na Balkanakh v srednie veka*, pp. 4–15. Ed. M. M. Freidenberg. Kalinin: Kalininskii Gosudarstvennyi Universitet.

1982. "'Strategikos' Onasandra i 'Strategikon Mavrikiia': opyt sravnitel'noi kharakteristiki." *VV* 43:35–53.

1991. "'Strategikon' Mavrikiia." In *Svod*, pp. 364–93. Vol. 1.

Kühn, Herbert 1956. "Das Problem der masurgermanischen Fibeln in Ostpreussen." In *Documenta Archaeologica Wolfgang La Baume Dedicata 8.II.1955*, pp. 79–108. Ed. Otto Kleemann. Bonn: L. Rohrscheid.

1965. *Die germanischen Bügelfibeln der Völkerwanderungszeit in der Rheinprovinz*. Graz: Akademische Druck- und Verlagsanstalt.

1974. *Die germanischen Bügelfibeln der Völkerwanderungszeit in Süddeutschland*. Graz: Akademische Druck- und Verlagsanstalt.

1981. *Die germanischen Bügelfibeln der Völkerwanderungszeit im Mitteldeutschland*. Graz: Akademische Druck- und Verlagsanstalt.

Kukharenko, Iu V. 1955. "Slavianskie drevnosti V–IX vekov na territorii Pripiatskogo Poles'ia." *KSIA* 57:33–8.

1960. "Pamiatniki prazhskogo tipa na territorii Pridneprov'ia." *Slavia Antiqua* 7:111–24.

Kulakov, V. I. 1989. "Mogil'niki zapadnoi chasti Mazurskogo poozer'ia konca V-nachala VIII vv. (po materialom raskopok 1878–1938 gg.)." *Barbaricum* 1:148–276.

1990. *Drevnosti prussov VI–XIII vv*. Moscow: Nauka.

Kurz, Karel 1969. "Wirtschaftshistorische Glossen zur Landwirtschaft der römischen Provinzen an der Wende der Antike und des Mittelalters (Zur Situation in der Umgebung von Sirmium)." In *Simpozijum*, pp. 95–103.

Kusternig, Andreas 1982. "Einleitung." In *Quellen zur Geschichte des 7. und 8. Jahrhunderts*, pp. 3–43. Ed. Herwig Wolfram. Darmstadt: Wissenschaftliche Buchgesellschaft.

Kuzmanov, Georgi 1974. "Rannovizantiiski keramichei kompleks ot krepostta Ovech." *INMV* 10:312–16.

1978. "Rannovizantiiska keramika ot kastela na nos Kaliakra." *Arkheologiia* 20, no. 2:20–6.

1985. "Rannovizantiiska keramika ot Trakiia i Dakiia (IV-nachaloto na VII v.)." *RP* 13:1–111.

1987. "Ceramica del primo periodo bizantino a Ratiaria." *Ratiariensia* 3–4:111–18.

1992. "Die lokale Gefässkeramik." In *Uenze 1992*, pp. 201–21.

Labuda, Gerard 1949. *Pierwsze państwo słowiańskie. Państwo Samona*. Poznań: Księgarnia Akademicka.

1950. "Chronologie des guerres de Byzance contre les Avars et les Slaves à la fin du VI-e siècle." *Byzantinoslavica* 11:167–73.

Larick, Roy 1986. "Age grading and ethnicity in the style of Loikop (Samburu) spears." *WA* 18, no. 2:269–83.

References

1991. "Warriors and blacksmiths: mediating ethnicity in East African spears." *JAA* 10:299–331.

Laser, Rudolf 1982. *Die römischen und frühbyzantinischen Fundmünzen auf dem Gebiet der DDR.* Berlin: Akademie Verlag.

Lászlo, Gyula 1955. *Etudes archéologiques sur l'histoire de la société des Avars.* Budapest: Akadémiai kiadó.

Leanza, S. 1971. "Motivi cristiani nelle Storie di Teofilatto Simocatta." In *Umanità e storia. Scritti in onore di Adelchi Attisani,* pp. 1–22. Naples: Giannini.

1972. "Citazioni e reminiscenze di autori classici nelle opere di Teophilatto Simocatta." In *Studi classici in onore di Quintino Cataudella,* pp. 573–90. Vol. II. Catania: Facoltà di Lettere e Filosofia.

Lebedev, G. S. 1989. "Arkheologo-lingvisticheskaia gipoteza slavianskogo etnogeneza." In *Slaviane. Etnogeneza i etnicheskaia istoriia (Mezhdisciplinarnye issledovaniia),* pp. 105–15. Ed. A. S. Gerd and G. S. Lebedev. Leningrad: Izdatel'stvo Leningradskogo universiteta.

1992. *Istoriia otechestvennoi arkheologii, 1700–1917 gg.* St Petersburg: Izdatel'stvo S.-Petersburgskogo Universiteta.

Lederman, Rena 1990. "Big men, large and small? Towards a comparative perspective." *Ethnology* 29:3–15.

Lee, A. D. 1993. *Information and Frontiers. Roman Foreign Relations in Late Antiquity.* Cambridge: Cambridge University Press.

Lee, Everett S. 1966. "A theory of migration." *Demography* 3:47–57.

Lehr-Spławinski, Tadeusz 1946. *O pochodzeniu i praojczynie Słowian.* Poznań: Wydawnictwo Instytutu Zachodniego.

Leigh, David 1991. "Aspects of early brooch design and production." In *Anglo-Saxon Cemeteries. A Reappraisal. Proceedings of a Conference Held at Liverpool Museum 1986,* pp. 107–24. Ed. Edmund Southworth. Wolfeboro Falls: Alan Sutton.

Lemerle, Paul 1953. "La composition et la chronologie des deux premiers livres des Miracula S. Demetrii." *ByzZ* 46:349–61.

1979. *Les plus anciens recueils des Miracles de Saint Démétrius et la pénétration des Slaves dans les Balkans,* vol. I. Paris: Editions du Centre National de la Recherche Scientifique.

1980. "Invasions et migrations dans les Balkans depuis la fin de l'époque romaine jusqu'au VIII-e siècle." In *Essais sur le monde byzantin,* pp. 265–308. London: Variorum.

1981. *Les plus anciens recueils des Miracles de Saint Démétrius et la pénétration des Slaves dans les Balkans. II: Commentaire.* Paris: Editions du Centre National de la Recherche Scientifique.

Levchenko, M. V. 1938. "Vizantiia i slaviane v VI–VII vv." *VDI* 4:23–48.

Levinskaia, I. A., and S. R. Tokhtas'ev 1991a. "Agafii Mirineiskii." In *Svod,* pp. 292–310. Vol. I.

1991b. "Menandr Protektor." In *Svod,* pp. 311–56. Vol. I.

Liapushkin, I. I. 1961. *Dneprovskoe lesostepnoe Levoberezh'e v epokhu zheleza.* Moscow: Nauka.

1965. "Nekotorye voprosy iz predystorii vostochnykh slavian." *KSIA* 100:116–25.

Lilie, R.-J. 1977. "'Thrakien' und 'Thrakesion.' Zur byzantinischen Provinzorganisation am Ende des 7. Jahrhunderts." *JÖB* 26:7–47.

References

1985. "Kaiser Herakleios und die Ansiedlung der Serben. Überlegungen zum Kapitel 32 des De Administrando Imperio." *SF* 44:17–43.

Lindholm, Charles 1985. "Models of segmentary political action: the examples of Swat and Dir, NWFP, Pakistan." In *Anthropology in Pakistan: Recent Socio-Cultural and Archaeological Perspectives*, pp. 21–39. Ed. Stephen Pastner and Louis Flam. Karachi: Indus Publications.

Linka, N. V., and A. M. Shovkoplias 1963. "Ranneslavianskoe poselenie na r. Tiasmine." In *Obrazovaniia*, pp. 234–42.

Lipking, Iu. A. 1974. "Mogil'niki tret'ei chetverty I tys. n.e. v Kurskom Posem''e." In *Drevnosti*, pp. 136–52.

Litavrin, G. G. 1984. "Slavinii VII–IX vv. Social'no-politicheskie organizacii slavian." In *Etnogenez narodov Balkan i severnogo Prichernomor'ia. Lingvistika, istoriia, arkheologiia*, pp. 193–203. Ed. S. B. Bernshtein and L. A. Gindin. Moscow: Nauka.

1985. "Predstavleniia 'varvarov' o Vizantii i vizantiicakh v VI–X vv." *VV* 46:100–8.

1986. "O dvukh Khilbudiakh Prokopiia Kesariiskogo." *VV* 47:24–30.

1987. "Etnosocial'naia struktura slavianskogo obshchestva v epokhu poseleniia na Balkanakh (VI–VII vv.)." In *Struktura*, pp. 33–44.

1991a. "Ioann Malala." In *Svod*, pp. 265–75. Vol. 1.

1991b. "Izvestia Menandra Protiktora ob otnosheniiakh avarov i slavian." In *Vizantiia, Sredizemnomorie, slavianskii mir*, pp. 7–18. Ed. G. G. Litavrin et al. Moscow: Izdatel'stvo Moskovskogo Universiteta.

1995a. "Feofan Ispovednik." In *Svod*, pp. 248–324. Vol. 11.

1995b. "Iz aktov shestogo vselenskogo sobora." In *Svod*, pp. 212. Vol. 11.

1995c. "Monemvasiiskaia khronika." In *Svod*, pp. 325–44. Vol. 11.

1995d. "Patriarkh Nikifor." In *Svod*, pp. 221–47. Vol. 11.

1995e. "Skholiia Arefy." In *Svod*, pp. 345–8. Vol. 11.

1999. "O pokhode avarov v 602 g. protiv antov." In *Vizantiia i slaviane (sbornik statei)*, pp. 568–78. Ed. G. G. Litavrin. St Petersburg: Aleteia.

Liubarskii, Iakov N. 1995. "Concerning the literary technique of Theophanes the Confessor." *Byzantinoslavica* 56:317–22.

Liubenova, Veneciia 1981. "Selishteto ot rimskata i rannovizantiiskata epokha." In *Pernik I. Poselishten zhivot na khǎlma Krakra ot V khil. pr. n.e. do VI v. na n.e.*, pp. 107–203. Ed. Teofil Ivanov. Sofia: BAN.

Ljubinković, M. 1973. "Les Slaves des régions centrales des Balkans et Byzance." In *Berichte*, pp. 173–94. Vol. 11.

Losert, Hans 1991. "Zur Deutung der Brandgräber in einigen merowingerzeitlichen Friedhöfen Mittel- und Unterfrankens." *Welt der Slaven* 36:365–92.

Lowie, Robert 1961. *The Origin of the State*. New York: Russell.

Lucas, Jack A. 1978. "The significance of diffusion in German and Austrian historical ethnology." In *Diffusion and Migration: Their Roles in Cultural Development*, pp. 30–44. Ed. P. G. Duke et al. Calgary: University of Calgary.

Lunt, Horace G. 1985. "Slavs, Common Slavic, and Old Church Slavonic." In *Litterae Slavicae Medii Aevi. Francisco Venceslao Mares Sexagenario Oblatae*, pp. 185–204. Ed. Johannes Reinhart. Munich: Otto Sagner.

1992. "Notes on nationalist attitudes in Slavic studies." *Canadian Slavonic Papers* 34, no. 4:459–70.

References

1997. "Common Slavic, Proto-Slavic, Pan-Slavic: what are we talking about?." *International Journal of Slavic Linguistics and Poetics* 41:7–67.

L'vova, Z. A., and A. I. Semenov 1985. "K proverke osnovanii rekonstrukcii peresh-chepinskogo mecha." *ASGE* 26:77–87.

Lyons, Patricia J. 1987. "Language and style in the Peruvian montana." In *Conference 18*, pp. 101–14.

McCorry, Maureen, and David A. T. Harper 1984. "A preliminary multivariate analysis of everted rim pottery from Ulster." *Journal of Irish Archaeology* 2: 1–5.

MacDonald, William K. 1990. "Investigating style: an explanatory analysis of some Plains burials." In *Uses*, pp. 52–60.

McGuire, Randall H. 1982. "The study of ethnicity in historical archaeology." *JAA* 1:159–78.

Mackensen, Michael 1987. "Mediterrane Sigillata, Lampen und Amphoren." In Bierbrauer 1987, pp. 229–65.

1992. "Amphoren und Spatheia von Golemannovo Kale." In Uenze 1992, pp. 239–54.

McLaughlin, Castle 1987. "Style as a social boundary marker: a Plains Indian example." In *Conference 18*, pp. 55–66.

Macrides, Ruth J. 1990. "Subversion and loyalty in the cult of St. Demetrios." *Byzantinoslavica* 51, no. 2:189–97.

Mączyńska, Magdalena 1998. "Die Endphase der Przeworsk-Kultur." *EAZ* 39, no. 1:65–99.

Madgearu, Alexandru 1992. "The placement of the fortress Turris." *BS* 33:203–8.

1996. "The province of Scythia and the Avaro-Slavic invasions." *BS* 37, no. 1:35–61.

1997. "The downfall of the lower Danubian Late Roman frontier." *RRH* 36, nos. 3–4:315–36.

Madsen, Torsten 1988. *Multivariate Archaeology. Numerical Approaches in Scandinavian Archaeology*. Aarhus: Aarhus University Press.

Madyda-Legutko, Renata, and Krzysztof Tunia 1991. "Die ersten Spuren der früh-slawischen Besiedlung in den West-Beskiden." *Archaeoslavica* 1:83–93.

Madzharov, Mitko 1989. "Diocletianopolis, ville paléochrétienne de Thrace." In *Actes XI*, pp. 2521–37. Vol. III.

Magdalino, Paul 1993. "The history of the future and its uses: prophecy, policy, and propaganda." In *The Making of Byzantine History. Studies Dedicated to Donald M. Nicol*, pp. 3–45. Ed. Roderick Beaton and Charlotte Roueche. Aldershot and Brookfield: Variorum.

Mahmood, Cynthia K., and Sharon L. Armstrong 1992. "Do ethnic groups exist? A cognitive perspective on the concept of cultures." *Ethnology* 31:1–14.

Makhitov, N. A. 1981. "Iuzhnyi Ural v VI–VIII vv." In *Stepi*, pp. 23–8.

Maksimov, E. V., and R. V. Terpilovskii 1993. "Kievskaia kul'tura." In *Slaviane i ikh sosedi v konce I tysiacheletiia do n.e.-pervoi polovine I tysiacheletiia n.e*, pp. 106–22. Ed. I. P. Rusanova and E. A. Symonovich. Moscow: Nauka.

Maksimović, Lubomir 1980. "Severni Ilirik u VI veku." *ZRVI* 19:17–57.

1982. "Struktura 32. glave spisa 'De administrando Imperio'." *ZRVI* 21:25–32.

1984. "L'administration de l'Illyricum septentrional à l'époque de Justinien." In *Philadelphie et autres études*, pp. 143–51. Ed. H. Ahrweiler. Paris: Publications de la Sorbonne.

References

Mal, Josip 1939. *Probleme aus der Frühgeschichte der Slowenen.* Ljubljana: Nova Zalozba.
Malingoudis, Phaidon 1985. "Zur frühslawische Sozialgeschichte im Spiegel der Toponymie." *EB* 21, no. 1:87–91.
1987. "Frühe slawische Elemente im Namengut Griechenlands." In *Völker,* pp. 53–68.
1990. "K voprosu o ranneslavianskom iazychestve: svidetel'stva Psevdo-Kesariia." *VV* 51:86–91.
Mallory, J. 1973. "A short history of the Indo-European problem." *JIES* 1:21–65.
Mańczak, Witold 1988. "Pourquoi la Dacie, au contraire des autres provinces danubiennes, n'a-t-elle pas été slavisée?." *Vox Romanica* 47:21–7.
Maneva, Elica 1981–2. "Rezultati od zaštitnite iskopuvanja extra muros vo Herakleja." *MAA* 7–8:125–42.
1987. "Casque à fermoir d'Heraclée." *ArchIug* 24:101–11.
Mango, Cyril 1990. *Nicephorus, Short History.* Washington: Dumbarton Oaks.
1997. *The Chronicle of Theophanes Confessor. Byzantine and Near Eastern History AD 284–813.* Oxford: Clarendon Press.
Mango, Marlia Mundell 1992. "The purpose and places of Byzantine silver stamping." In *Ecclesiastical Silver Plate. Papers of the Symposium Held May 16–18, 1986 at the Walters Art Gallery, Baltimore and Dumbarton Oaks, Washington D.C.,* pp. 204–15. Ed. Susan A. Boyd and Marlia Mundell Mango. Washington, DC: Dumbarton Oaks.
1995. "Silver plate among the Romans and among the barbarians." In *Noblesse,* pp. 77–88.
Mano-Zisi, Đorđe 1954–5. "Iskopavanja na Caričinom Gradu 1953 i 1954 godine." *Starinar* 5–6:155–80.
1958. "Iskopavanja na Caričinom Gradu 1955 i 1956 godine." *Starinar* 7–8:311–28.
1969. "Terme krai srednie kapija u suburbiumu Caričina grada." *Starinar* 20:205–12.
Margetić, Lujo 1977. "Konstantina Porfirogenet i vrijeme dolaska Hrvata." *Zbornik Historijskog Zavoda Jugoslavenske Akademije Znanosti i Umjetnosti* 8:5–88.
1988. "Note ai 'Miracula S. Demetrii'." *Studi Medievali* 29, no. 2:755–60.
1992. "Neka pitanja boravka langobarda u Sloveniji." *AV* 43:149–73.
Marin, Emilio 1989. "La topographie chrétienne de Salone. Les centres urbains de la pastorale." In *Actes XI,* pp. 1117–31. Vol. II.
Marinescu, Constantin 1996. "Transformations: classical objects and their re-use during Late Antiquity." In *Shifting Frontiers in Late Antiquity,* pp. 285–98. Ed. Ralph W. Mathisen and Hagith S. Sivan. Aldershot and Brookfield: Variorum.
Marović, Ivan 1984. "Reflexions about the year of the destruction of Salona." *VAHD* 77:293–314.
Martin, Max 1987. "Beobachtungen an den frühmittelalterlichen Bügelfibeln von Altenerding (Oberbayern)." *BV* 52:269–80.
Martini, Wolfram, and Cornelius Steckner 1993. *Das Gymnasium von Samos. Das frühbyzantinische Klostergut.* Bonn: Habelt.
Marx, Karl 1965. *Pre-Capitalist Economic Formations.* New York: International Publishers.
Mastny, Vojtech 1971. *The Czechs under Nazi Rule. The Failure of National Resistance, 1939–1942.* New York and London: Columbia University Press.

References

Matei, Mircea D. 1962. "Die slawische Siedlungen von Suceava (Nordmoldau, Rumänien)", *SlovArch* 10:149–74.

Matei, Mircea D., and Alexandru Rădulescu 1973. "Şantierul arheologic Udeşti (jud. Suceava)." *Suceava* 3:265–89.

Mavrodin, V. V. 1945. *Obrazovanie drevnerusskogo gosudarstva.* Leningrad: Izdatel'stvo Leningradskogo Universiteta.

Menghin, Wilfried 1982. *Die Langobarden. Archäologie und Geschichte.* Stuttgart: Konrad Theiss.

Menke, Manfred 1986. "Archäologische Befunde zu Ostgoten des 5. Jahrhunderts in der Zone nordwärts der Alpen." *Archaeologia Baltica* 7:239–81.

1990. "Zu den Fibeln der Awarenzeit aus Keszthely." *Wosinsky Mór Múzeum Évkönyve* 15:187–214.

Meřínský, Zdenek 1993. "Slovanské sídlište u Postorné (okres Břeclav) a struktura časne slovanského a predvelkomorávského osídleni na soutoku Moravy a Dyje." *Jižní Morava* 29:7–30.

Metcalf, D. M. 1962a. "The Aegean coastlands under threat: some coins and coin hoards from the reign of Heraclius." *Annual of the British School at Athens* 57:14–23.

1962b. "The Slavonic threat to Greece circa 580: some evidence from Athens." *Hesperia* 31:134–57.

1976. "Coinage and coin finds associated with a military presence in the medieval Balkans." In *Kovanje i kovnice antičkog i srednjovekovnog novca*, pp. 88–97. Ed. Vladimir Kondič. Belgrade: Arheološki Institut.

1991. "Avar and Slav invasions into the Balkan peninsula (c. 575–625): the nature of the numismatic evidence." *JRA* 4:140–8.

Meyer, Gustav 1894. *Neugriechische Studien.* Vienna: F. Tempsky.

Meyer, Henry Cord 1996. *Drang nach Osten. Fortunes of a Slogan-concept in German–Slavic Relations, 1849–1990.* Bern and Berlin: Peter Lang.

Migotti, Branka 1995. "Vrste i namjene ranokršćanskih zdanja u Dalmaciji." In *Radovi Filozofskog fakulteta u Zadru – Razdio povijesnih znanosti*, pp. 113–14. Ed. Janko Belošević. Zadar: Filozofski fakultet.

Mihăescu, H. 1974. "Einleitung zu meiner Maurikios-Ausgabe." *Vyzantina* 6:193–213.

Mihăilă, Gheorghe 1971. "Criteriile determinării împrumuturilor slave în limba română." *Studii şi Cercetări de Lingvistică* 22, no. 4:349–67.

1973. *Studii de lexicologie şi istorie a lingvisticii româneşti.* Bucharest: Editura Didactică şi Pedagogică.

Mikhailov, Stamen 1977. "Die Bügelfibeln in Bulgarien und ihre historische Interpretation." In *Archäologie als Geschichtswissenschaft: Studien und Untersuchungen*, pp. 317–27. Ed. Joachim Herrmann. Berlin: Akademie Verlag.

Mikić, Živko 1992–3. "Erste Ergebnisse anthropologischer Untersuchung des Germanenfriedhofes von Viminacium (Serbien)." *Starinar* 43–4:191–9.

Mikołajczyk, A. 1982. "Romantic illusions and the economic reality of the 16th and 18th century coin-hoards: some examples from Central Poland." In *Actes du 9ème Congrès international de numismatique, Berne, Septembre 1979*, pp. 968–75. Ed. Tony Hackens and Raymond Weiller. Vol. II. Louvain-la-Neuve and Luxembourg: Association internationale des numismates professionels.

References

Mikulčić, Ivan 1974. "Über die Größe der spätantiken Städte in Makedonien." *Živa Antika* 24:191–212.

1982. "Der Untergang der Paläste im spätantiken Stobi, Nordmakedonien." In *Palast*, pp. 535–44.

1986a. "Frühchristlicher Kirchenbau in der S. R. Makedonien." *CCARB* 33:221–51.

1986b. "Spätantike Fortifikationen in der SR Makedonien." *CCARB* 33:253–77.

Mikulčić, Ivan, and Miloš Bilbija 1981–2. "Markovi Kuli, Vodno, Skopje, 1979 i 1980." *MAA* 7–8:205–20.

Mikulčić, Ivan, and Nada Nikuljska 1978. "Ranovizantiski grad 'Markovi kuli' na Vodno." *MAA* 4:137–50.

1979. "Ranovizantiskiot grad na Markovi kuli na Vodno kaj Skopje – istražuvanja 1977 godina." *MAA* 5:65–74.

Milchev, Atanas 1970. "Zur Frage der materiellen Kultur und Kunst der Slawen und Protobulgaren in den bulgarischen Ländern während des frühen Mittelalters (VI.–X. Jh.)." In *I. Międzynarodowy kongres archeologii słowiańskiej. Warszawa 14–18 IX 1965*, pp. 20–61. Ed. Witold Hensel. Vol. III. Wrocław, Warsaw, and Cracow: Wydawnictwo Polskiej Akademii Nauk.

1975. "Slaviane, protobolgary i Vizantiia v bolgarskikh zemliakh v VI–IX vv." In *Actes XIV*, pp. 387– 95. Vol. II.

1977. "Eine Festung am unterdonauländische Limes bei Nova Cerna (Bezirk Silistra)." In *Studien zu den Militärgrenzen Roms. 2. Vorträge des 10. internationalen Limeskongress in der Germania inferior*, pp. 351–7. Ed. Dorothea Haupt and Günther Horn. Cologne: Rheinland Verlag.

Milchev, Atanas, and Stefka Angelova 1970. "Razkopki i prouchvaniia v m. Kaleto krai s. Nova Cherna." *Arkheologiia* 12, no. 1:26–38.

Milchev, Atanas, and Georgi Draganov 1992. "Arkheologicheski ostanki v raiona na s. Koprivec, Rusensko." *Arkheologiia* 24, no. 1:36–41.

Milchev, Atanas, and Kina Koicheva 1978a. "Arkheologicheski danni za poselishtniia zhivot v dve kreposti v Gabrovski okrăg." *GMSB* 4:52–65.

1978b. "Rannovizantiiska bazilika v m. Gradishte, krai Gabrovo." *Arkheologiia* 20, no. 4:25–33.

Milich, Petar 1995. "Cumulative Slavicity: cultural interaction and language replacement in the North Balkans during the Slavic migration period, AD 500–900." PhD Dissertation. Ohio State University.

Milinković, Mihailo 1982a. "Dobrinja-Litice. Kasnoantičko utvrđenje." *NZ* 6:238–9.

1982b. "Kasnoantička utvrđenja u Ostrovici i Šaronjama kod Tutina." *NZ* 6:131–40.

1985. "Ranovizantijsko utvrđenje na Tupom Kršu i okolna utvrđenja u Tutinskoj oblasti." *NZ* 9:47–54.

1995. "Die Gradina auf dem Jelica-Gebirge und die frühbyzantinischen Befestigungen in der Umgebung von Čačak, Westserbien." *AT* 3:227–50.

1999. "Ranovizantijsko utvrđenje kod Bregovine." In *Prokuplje u praistoriji antici i srednjem veku*, pp. 87–116. Ed. Miloje Vašić and Dragoslav Marinković. Belgrade/Prokuplje: Arkheološki Institut/Narodni Muzej Toplice.

Miller, David Harry 1996. "Frontier societies and the transition between Late

References

Antiquity and the early Middle Ages." In *Shifting Frontiers in Late Antiquity*, pp. 158– 71. Ed. Ralph W. Mathisen and Hagith S. Sivan. Aldershot: Variorum.

Miller, Stella G. 1977. "Excavations at Nemea, 1976." *Hesperia* 46:1–26.

Miloševic, Gordana 1987. "Ranovizantijska arhitektura na Svetinji u Kostolcu." *Starinar* 38:39–57.

Milošević, Petar, and Miroslav Jeremić 1986. "Le castellum à Milutinovac." *DS* 3:245–63.

Minasian, R. S. 1978. "Klassifikaciia ruchnogo zhernovogo postava (po materialam Vostochnoi Evropy I tysiacheletiia n.e.)." *SA* 3:101–12.

———. 1980. "Chetyre gruppy nozhei vostochnoi Evropy epokhi rannego srednevekov'ia (K voprosu o poiavlenii slavianskikh form v lesnoi zone)." *ASGE* 21:68–74.

Minchev, A. 1983. "The late Roman fine ware import to the western Black Sea coast." In *Bulgaria*, pp. 194–201.

Minić, Dušica 1984. "Le trésor de monnaies de bronze protobyzantin de Dobra." *Numizmatičar* 7:12–17.

Miraj, F. 1980. "Per nje interpretim te ri te monogrameve ne tullat e murit rrethues te Durresit." *Monumentet* 20:125–30.

Mirković, Mirjana 1999. "Eine Schiffslände des späten 6. Jahrhunderts bei Viminacium?." In *Limes*, pp. 19–26.

Mirnik, Ivan A. 1981. *Coin Hoards in Yugoslavia*. Oxford: BAR.

———. 1982. "Ostava bizantskog novca s Majsana." *Numizmatičar* 5:141–6.

Mishulin, A. V. 1939. "Drevnie slaviane i sud'by Vostochnorimskoi imperii." *VDI* 1:290–307.

Mitova-Dzhonova, Dimitrina 1968. "Rannovizantiisko zhilishtino stroitelstvo v kastela Iatrus." *Arkheologiia* 10, no. 3:13–23.

———. 1974. "Peribolosăt pri rannokhristianskata bazilika u nas." In *Prouchvaniia i konservaciia na pametnicite na kulturata v Bălgariia*, pp. 53–64. Ed. R. Rachev. Sofia: Nauka i iskustvo.

———. 1984. "Archäologische und schriftliche Angaben über das Asylrecht in der frühchristlichen und mittelalterlichen Kirche auf dem Territorium des heutigen Bulgarien." In *Actes X*, pp. 339–46. Vol. II.

———. 1986. "Stationen und Stützpunkte der römischen Kriegs- und Handelsflotte am Unterdonaulimes." In *Akten 13*, pp. 504–9.

Mitrea, Bucur 1975. "Date noi cu privire la secolul VII. Tezaurul de hexagrame bizantine de la Priseaca (jud. Olt)." *SCN* 6:113–25.

Mitrea, Ioan 1972. "Contribuția cercetărilor arheologice de la Curtea Domnească din Bacău și Davideni-Neamț la cunoașterea epocii sec. VI–VII din Moldova." *Studii și cercetări științifice. Istorie și filologie:* 5–22.

———. 1973. "Cîteva fibule romano-bizantine descoperite în Moldova." *SCIV* 24, no. 4:663–4.

———. 1974–6. "Principalele rezultate ale cercetărilor arheologice din așezarea de la Davideni (sec. V–VII e.n.)." *MemAnt* 6–8:65–92.

———. 1978. "Așezarea prefeudală de la Izvoare-Bahna (II). Contribuții la arheologia epocii de formare a poporului român." *Carpica* 10:205–28.

———. 1980. "Șantierul arheologic Izvoare-Bahna." *MCA* 14:432–49.

———. 1983. "Rezultatele cercetărilor arheologice din așezarea de la Izvoarele-Bahna (sec. VI–IX e.n.)." *MCA* 15:429–34.

References

1992. "Noi descoperiri arheologice în aşezarea din secolele V–VII de la Davideni-Neamţ." *MemAnt* 18:203–32.

1994. "Aşezarea din secolele V–VII de la Davideni, jud. Neamţ. Cercetările arheologice din anii 1988–1991." *MemAnt* 19:279–332.

1994–5. "Deux fibules 'digitées' trouvées sur le site de Davideni, dép. de Neamţ (VIe–VIIe siècles)." *Dacia* 38–9:445–7.

1995. "Fibule descoperite în aşezarea de la Davideni-Neamţ (sec. V–VII d.H.)." *MemAnt* 20:123–31.

Mitrea, Ioan, and Alexandru Artimon 1971. "Descoperiri prefeudale la Curtea Domnească Bacău." *Carpica* 4:225–52.

Mitrea, Ioan, C. Eminovici, and V. Momanu 1986–7. "Aşezarea din secolele V–VII de la Ştefan cel Mare, jud. Bacău." *Carpica* 18–19:215–50.

Mogil'nikov, V. A. 1981. "Sibirskie drevnosti VI–X vv. Tiurki." In *Stepi*, pp. 29–43.

Mokienko, V. M. 1996. "Gde zhili pervye slaviane." In *Raznye grani edinoi nauki: uchenye – molodym slavistam*, pp. 40–57. Ed. P. A. Dimitriev and G. I. Safronov. St Petersburg: Izdatel'stvo S. Petersburgskogo Universiteta.

Mommsen, Theodor (ed.) 1882. *Iordanis Romana et Getica*. Berlin: Weidmann.

(ed.) 1895. *C. Iulii Solini Collectanea rerum memorabilium*. Berlin: Weidmann.

Morgan, Lewis Henry 1877. *Ancient Society, or Researches in the Lines of Human Progress from Savagery through Barbarism to Civilization*. New York: H. Holt & Co.

Moorhead, John 1994. *Justinian*. New York: Longman.

Morintz, Sebastian 1961. "Săpăturile de pe dealul Ciurel." *MCA* 7:658–63.

Morintz, Sebastian, and Petre Roman 1962. "Săpăturile de pe dealul Ciurel." *MCA* 8:761–7.

Morintz, Sebastian, and Dinu V. Rosetti 1959. "Din cele mai vechi timpuri şi pînă la formarea Bucureştilor." In *Bucureşti*, pp. 11–47.

Morrisson, Cécile 1981. "Monnaies en plomb byzantines de la fin du VI-e et du début du VII-e siècle." *Rivista Italiana di Numismatica e Scienze Affini* 83:119–32.

1986. "Alterazioni e svalutazioni." In *La cultura bizantina. Oggetti e messaggio. Moneta ed economia*, pp. 234–61. Ed. André Guillou and Paolo Odorico. Rome: L'Erma di Bretschneider.

1989. "Monnaie et prix à Byzance du V-e au VII-e siècle." In *Hommes*, pp. 239–64. Vol. 1.

Morrisson, Cécile, and Jean-Claude Cheynet 1990. "Lieux de trouvaille et circulation des sceaux." *SBS* 2:105–36.

Mortimer, Catherine 1994. "Lead-alloy models for three early Anglo-Saxon brooches." *ASSAH* 7:27–33.

Moscalu, Emil 1983. *Ceramica traco-getică*. Bucharest: Muzeul Naţional de Istorie.

Moutsopoulos, Nikolaos 1987. "Monasteries outside the walls of Thessaloniki during the period of Slav raids." *Cyrillomethodianum* 11:129–94.

Muçaj, Skënder 1993. "Les basiliques paléochrétiennes de Bylis et leur architecture." *CCARB* 40:569–83.

Müller, Robert 1989. "Vorbericht über die Freilegung des Grabes eines hohen Militärs aus der Mittelawarenzeit in Gyenesdiás." *CAH*:141–64.

Müller-Wiener, Wolfgang 1989. "Bischofsresidenzen des 4.–7. Jhs. im östlichen Mittelmeer-Raum." In *Actes XI*, pp. 651–709. Vol. 1.

References

Munson, Henry Jr 1989. "On the irrelevance of the segmentary lineage model in the Moroccan Rif." *AAnth* 91:386–400.

Mushmov, Nikola A. 1934. "Vizantiiski olovni pechati otă sbiraka na Narodniia Muzei." *IBAI* 8:331–49.

Musset, Lucien 1965. *Les invasions: le second assaut contre l'Europe chrétienne (VII-e–XI-e siècles)*. Paris: Presses universitaires de France.

1983. "Entre deux vagues d'invasions: la progression slave dans l'histoire européenne du Haut Moyen Age." In *Slavi*, pp. 981–1028.

n.a. 1953a. "Şantierul Hlincea-Iaşi." *SCIV* 4, nos. 1–2:312–34.

1953b. "Santierul Sarata-Monteoru." *SCIV* 4, nos. 1–2:83–6.

1954. "Şantierul arheologic Moreşti (r. Tg. Mureş, reg. aut. maghiară)." *SCIV* 5, nos. 1–2:199–232.

1955a. "Şantierul arheologic Moreşti." *SCIV* 6, nos. 3– 4:643–87.

1955b. "Şantierul arheologic Sărata Monteoru." *SCIV* 6, nos. 3–4:510–11.

Nagy, Margit 1988. "Frühawarenzeitliche Grabfunde aus Budapest. Bemerkungen zur awarenzeitlichen Tierornamentik." In *Popoli delle steppe: Unni, Avari, Ungari*, pp. 373–407. Vol. 1. Spoleto: Presso sede del centro.

1995. "L'oreficeria." In *Avari*, pp. 93–101.

Nagy, Sándor 1959. "Nekropola kod Aradca iz ranog srednieg veka." *RVM* 8:45–102.

Nandriş, Grigore 1939. "The earliest contacts between Slavs and Roumanians." *Slavonic and East European Review* 18:142–54.

Neppi Mòdona, A. 1974. "Umbauten am römischen Theatern und Wandlungen der Funktion in Zusammenhang mit ihrer Zeit. Stobi und Salona." *Das Altertum* 20:108–17.

Nestor, Ion 1961. "L'établissement des Slaves en Roumanie à la lumière de quelques découvertes archéologiques récentes." *Dacia* 5:429–48.

1963. "La pénétration des Slaves dans la péninsule balkanique et dans la Grèce continentale. Considérations sur les recherches historiques et archéologiques." *RESEE* 1, nos. 1–2:41–68.

1965. "Cîteva consideraţii cu privire la cea mai veche locuire a slavilor pe teritoriul RPR." In *Omagiu lui P. Constantinescu-Iaşi cu prilejul împlinirii a 70 ani*, pp. 147–51. Bucharest: Editura Academiei RSR.

1969. "Les éléments les plus anciens de la culture slave dans les Balkans." In *Simpozijum*, pp. 141–7.

1970. "Formarea poporului român." In *Istoria poporului român*, pp. 98–114. Ed. A. Oţetea. Bucharest: Editura Academiei RSR.

1973. "Autochtones et Slaves en Roumanie." In *Slavianite*, pp. 29–33.

Nestor, Ion, and Eugenia Zaharia 1959. "Săpăturile de la Sărata Monteoru (r. Buzău, reg. Ploieşti)." *MCA* 5:511–18.

1960. "Săpăturile de la Sărata Monteoru." *MCA* 6:509–14.

1973. "Raport preliminar despre săpăturile de la Bratei, jud. Sibiu (1959–1972)." *MCA* 10:191–201.

Neverett, Margot Susan 1991. "An attribute analysis and seriation of the ceramic materials from the Anderson site (33 Er 75), Erie County, Ohio." MA Thesis. Kent State University.

Nicolas, Guy 1973. "Fait 'ethnique' et usages du concept d' 'ethnie'." *Cahiers Internationaux de Sociologie* 54:95– 126.

References

Niederle, Lubor 1911. *Život starých Slovanů*. Prague: Nákladem Bursíka & Kohouta.
  1923. *Manuel de l'antiquité slave. L'histoire*. Paris: Champion.
  1925. *Slovanské starožitnosti*, vol. 1. Prague: Nákladem Bursíka & Kohouta.
  1926. *Manuel de l'antiquité slave. La civilisation*. Paris: Champion.
Nieke, Margaret R. 1993. "Penannular and related brooches: secular ornament or symbol in action?." In *The Age of Migrating Ideas. Early Medieval Art in Northern Britain and Ireland. Proceedings of the Second International Conference on Insular Art Held in the National Museum of Scotland in Edinburgh, 3–6 January 1991*, pp. 128–134. Ed. Michael Spearman and John Higgitt. Stroud: Alan Sutton.
Nikolajević, Ivanka 1971. "Veliki posed u Dalmaciji u V i VI veku u svetlosti arheoloških nalaza." *ZRVI* 13:277–91.
  1975. "Salona Christiana aux VI-e et VII-e siècles." In *Disputationes Salonitanae 1970*, pp. 91–5. Ed. Željko Rapanić. Split: Musée Archéologique de Split.
  1983. "L'arte bizantina: ricettività e creatività locale." In *Slavi*, pp. 801–29.
Niţu, Anton, Emilia Zaharia, and Dan Teodoru 1960. "Sondajul din 1957 de la Spinoasa-Erbiceni (r. Tg. Frumos, reg. Iaşi)." *MCA* 6:531–9.
Noll, Rudolf 1974. "Zum Silberschatz von Kuczurmare." In *In memoriam Constantini Daicoviciu*, pp. 267–73. Cluj: Dacia.
Novosel'cev, A. P. 1993. "'Mir istorii' ili mif istorii?." *Voprosy Istorii* 1:23–31.
Nubar, Hamparţumian 1964. "Un sigiliu bizantin descoperit la Histria." *SCIV* 15, no. 1:81–3.
Nystazopoulou-Pelekidou, Maria 1970. "Συμβολὴ εἰς τὴν χρονολόγησιν τῶν ἀβαρικῶν καὶ σλαβικῶν ἐπιδρομῶν ἐπὶ Μαυρικίου." *Symmeikta* 2:145–82.
  1986. "Les Slaves dans l'Empire byzantin." In *The 17th International Byzantine Congress. Major Papers. Dumbarton Oaks/Georgetown University, Washington D.C., August 3–8, 1986*, pp. 345–67. New Rochelle, N.Y.: Aristide D. Caratzas.
Ober, J. 1987. "Pottery and miscellaneous artifacts from fortified sites in northern and western Attica." *Hesperia* 56:197–227.
Oberländer-Târnoveanu, Ernest 1980. "Monede bizantine din secolele VII–X descoperite în nordul Dobrogei." *SCN* 7:163–5.
Obolensky, Dimitri 1971. *The Byzantine Commonwealth. Eastern Europe, 500–1453*. New York and Washington: Praeger.
O'Donnell, James J. 1982. "The aims of Jordanes." *Historia* 31, no. 2:223–40.
Oetelaar, Gerald A. 1993. "Identifying site structure in the archaeological record: an Illinois Mississippian example." *AAnt* 58, no. 4:662–87.
Ognenova-Marinova, L. 1969. "Les briques à estampilles de Nessèbre." In *Nessèbre*, pp. 109–20. Ed. T. Ivanov. Vol. 1. Sofia: BAN.
Okamura, Jonathan Y. 1981. "Situational ethnicity." *ERS* 4, no. 4:452–65.
Okamura, L. 1990. "Coin hoards and frontier forts: problems of interpretation." In *Akten 14*, pp. 39–46.
Okey, Robin 1992. "Central Europe/Eastern Europe: behind the definitions." *P&P* 137:102–33.
Okulicz, Jerzy 1973. *Pradzieje ziem pruskich od póznego paleolitu do VII w.n.e.* Wrocław, Warsaw, Gdańsk, and Cracow: Ossolineum.
  1989. "Próba interpretacij archeologicznej ludów bałtyjskich w połowie pierwszego tysiąclecia naszej ery." *Barbaricum* 1:64–100.
Olajos, Thérèse 1981. "Contributions à une analyse de la genèse de l'Histoire universelle de Théophylacte Simocatta." *ActaAntHung* 29:417–24.

References

1981–2. "Données et hypothèses concernant la carrière de Théophylacte Simocatta." *Acta Classica Universitatis Scientiarum Debreceniensis* 17–18:39–47.

1982. "Quelques remarques sur le style de Théophylacte Simocatta." *JÖB* 32, no. 3:157–64.

1985. "Contribution à la chronologie des premières installations des Slaves dans l'Empire byzantin." *Byzantion* 55:506–15.

1988. *Les sources de Théophylacte Simocatta historien.* Leiden: Brill.

1994. "Quelques remarques sur une peuplade slave en Hellade." *VV* 55, no. 2:106–10.

Olster, David Michael 1993. *The Politics of Usurpation in the Seventh Century: Rhetoric and Revolution in Byzantium.* Amsterdam: Adolf M. Hakkert.

Opaiţ, Andrei 1984. "Beobachtungen zur Entwicklung der zwei Amphoratypen." *Peuce* 9:311–27.

1990. "O săpătură de salvare în oraşul antic Ibida." *SCIV* 41:19–54.

1991. "Ceramica din aşezarea şi cetatea de la Independenţa (Murighiol) secolele V î.e.n.–VII e.n." *Peuce* 10:133–82.

1996. *Aspecte ale vieţii economice din provincia Scythia (secolele IV–VI p.Ch.). Producţia ceramicii locale şi de import.* Bucharest: Institutul Român de Tracologie.

Opaiţ, A., and T. Bănică 1992. "Das ländliche Territorium der Stadt Ibida (2.–7. Jh.) und einige Betrachtungen zum Leben auf dem Land an der unteren Donau." In *Schwarzmeerküste*, pp. 103–12.

Opaiţ, Andrei, Cristina Opaiţ, and Teodor Bănică 1992. "Der frühchristliche Komplex von Slava Rusă." In *Schwarzmeerküste*, pp. 113–22.

Opaiţ, Cristina 1991. "Descoperiri monetare în fortificaţia de la Independenţa, judeţul Tulcea." *Peuce* 10:457–83.

Orlov, R. S. 1985. "Kul'tura kochevnikov IV–VIII vv." In *Karta*, pp. 98–105.

Orton, Clive 1993. "How many pots make five? An historical review of pottery quantifications." *Archaeometry* 35, no. 2:169–84.

Ostrogorski, George 1959. "The Byzantine Empire in the world of the seventh century." *DOP* 13:1–17.

Ovcharov, Dimităr 1971. "Dve rannovizantiiski kreposti ot Severoiztochna Bălgariia." *Arkheologiia* 13, no. 4:18–31.

1973. "Proteikhizmata v sistemata na rannovizantiiskite ukrepleniia po nashite zemi." *Arkheologiia* 15, no. 4:11–23.

1977. "Observations sur le système de fortifications de la haute époque byzantine dans les terres bulgares d'aujourd'hui durant les 5–6-es siècles." In *Akten 11*, pp. 467–71.

1982. *Vizantiiski i bălgarski kreposti V–X vek.* Sofia: BAN.

Painter, Kenneth 1988. "Roman silver hoards: ownership and status." In *Argenterie*, pp. 97–112.

Palacký, František 1868. *Die Geschichte des Hussitenthums und Prof. Constantin Höfler kritische Studien.* Prague: F. Tempsky.

Pálko, A. 1972. "Descoperiri din secolul al VII-lea în valea Arieşului." *SCIV* 23, no. 4:677–9.

Pallas, D. 1981. "Données nouvelles sur quelques boucles et fibules considerées comme avares et slaves et sur Corinthe entre le VI-e et le IX-e siècles." *Byzantinobulgarica* 7:295–318.

Pancake, Cherri M. 1991. "Communicative imagery in Guatemala Indian dress." In

References

Textile Traditions of Mesoamerica and the Andes: An Anthology, pp. 45–62. Ed. Margot Blum Schevill, Janet Catherine Berlo, and Edward B. Dwyer. New York and London: Garland.

Papuc, Gheorghe 1977. "Considerații privind perioada de sfîrșit a cetății Tropaeum Traiani." *Pontica* 10:357–60.

Parczewski, Michal 1991. "Origins of early Slav culture in Poland." *Antiquity* 65, no. 248:676–83.

———. 1993. *Die Anfänge der frühslawischen Kultur in Polen*. Vienna: Österreichische Gesellschaft für Ur- und Frühgeschichte.

Parnicki-Pudelko, Stefan 1983. "The early Christian episcopal basilica in Novae." *ArchPol* 21–2:241–70.

———. 1984. "Wczesnochrześciańska bazylika episkopalna w Novae." *Balcanica* 1:271–304.

Parsons, Talcott 1975. "Some theoretical considerations on the nature and trends of change of ethnicity." In *Ethnicity: Theory and Experience*, pp. 53–83. Ed. N. Glazer and D. P. Moynihan. Cambridge, Mass., and London: Harvard University Press.

Pasztory, Esther 1989. "Identity and difference: the uses and meanings of ethnic styles." *Studies in the History of Art* 27:15–38.

Patoura, Sophie 1985. "Les invasions barbares en Illyrie et en Thrace (IV–e–VI–e s.): conséquences démographiques et économiques." In *Communications grecques présentées au V-e Congrès international des études du Sud-Est européen. Belgrade: 11–17 septembre 1984*, pp. 191–210. Ed. T. P. Giochalas. Athens: Hellenike Epitrope Spoudon Notioanatolikis Europis.

———. 1997. "Une nouvelle considération de la politique de Justinien envers les peuples du Danube." *Byzantinoslavica* 58:78–86.

Pătruț, Ioan 1968. "Otnositel'no drevnosti slavianskogo vliianiia na rumynskii iazyk." *Romanoslavica* 16:23–9.

———. 1971. "Latin et slave dans le lexique du roumain." *Revue Roumaine de Linguistique* 16:299–309.

———. 1974. *Studii de limba română și slavistică*. Cluj: Dacia.

———. 1976. "Despre durata și structura dialectală a limbii slave comune." *Cercetări de Lingvistică* 21:183–7.

Pech, Stanley Z. 1969. *The Czech Revolution of 1848*. Chapell Hill: University of North Carolina Press.

Peisker, Jan 1905. "Die älteren Beziehungen der Slawen zu Turkotataren und Germanen und ihre sozialgeschichtliche Bedeutung." *Vierteljahresschrift zur Sozial- und Wirtschaftsgeschichte* 3:187–360.

———. 1926. "The expansion of the Slavs." In *The Cambridge Medieval History*, pp. 418–58. Ed. H. M. Gwatkin and J. P. Whitney. New York and Cambridge: Macmillan and Cambridge University Press.

Pekarskaja, Ljudmila V., and Dafydd Kidd 1994. *Der Silberschatz von Martynovka (Ukraine) aus dem 6. und 7. Jahrhundert*. Innsbruck: Universitätsverlag Wagner.

Pekkanen, Tuomo 1971. "L'origine degli Slavi e il loro nome nella letteratura greco-latina." *Quaderni Urbinati di Cultura Classica* 11:51–64.

Peniak, S. I. 1980. *Rann'oslov'ians'ke i davn'orus'ke naselennia Zakarpattia VI–XIII st.* Kiev: Naukova Dumka.

References

Peršic, Abram I. 1988. "Das Problem der militärischen Demokratie." In *Familie*, pp. 78–86.

Petersen, Charles C. 1992. "The Strategikon. A forgotten classic." *Military Review* 72, no. 8:70–9.

Petersmann, Hubert 1992. "Vulgärlateinisches aus Byzanz." In *Zum Umgang mit fremden Sprachen in der griechisch-römischen Antike: Kolloquium der Fachrichtungen Klassische Philologie der Universitäten Leipzig und Saarbrücken am 21. und 22. November 1989 in Saarbrücken*, pp. 219–31. Ed. Carl Werner von Müller. Stuttgart: Steiner.

Petre, Aurelian 1966. "Contribuţia atelierelor romano-bizantine la geneza unor tipuri de fibule 'digitate' din sec. VI–VII e.n." *SCIV* 17, no. 2:255–76.

—— 1987. *La romanité en Scythie Mineure (IIe–VIIe siècles de notre ère)*. *Recherches archéologiques*. Bucharest: Institut des Etudes Sud-Est-Européennes.

Pétrequin, P. et al. 1987. "L'importation d'ambre balte: un échantillonnage chronologique de l'est de la France." *Revue Archéologique de l'Est et du Centre-Est* 38:273–84.

Petrikovits, H. v 1966. "Frühchristliche Silberlöffel." In *Corolla memoriae Erich Swoboda dedicata*, pp. 173–82. Graz and Cologne: Böhlau.

Petrov, V. P. 1963a. "Pamiatniki Korchaskogo tipa (po materialam raskopok S. S. Gamchenko)." In *Obrazovaniia*, pp. 16–38.

—— 1963b. "Stecovka, poselenie tret'ei chetverti I tysiacheletiia n.e. (po materialam raskopok 1956–1958 v Potiasmine)", in *Obrazovaniia*, pp. 209–33.

Petrović, Petar 1982–3. "Saldum, rimsko i ranovizantisjko utvrðenje na ustju potoka Kožica." *Starinar* 33–4:129–34.

—— 1994–5. "Les forteresses de la basse antiquité dans la région du Haut Timok." *Starinar* 45–6:55–66.

Petrovics, I. 1987. "Bulgarians of southern Transylvania in the Middle Ages." In *Dokladi*, pp. 273–8.

Petru, Peter 1978. "Kontinuiteta in diskontinuiteta neselitve v prehodnem obdobju iz kasne antike v zgodnij srednji veh." *ZC* 32, no. 3:221–32.

Petrucci, Peter R. 1995. "The historical development of the Rumanian /î/." In *Contemporary Research in Romance Linguistics. Papers from the 22nd Linguistic Symposium on Romance Languages El Paso/Cd. Juárez, February 1992*, pp. 167–76. Ed. Jon Amastae et al. Amsterdam and Philadelphia: John Benjamins.

—— 1999. *Slavic Features in the History of Rumanian*. Munich and Newcastle: LINCOM Europa.

Petsas, Ph. 1969. "Ἀρχαιοτήτης καὶ μνημεία Κεντρικῆς Μακεδονίας." *Archaiologikon Deltion* 24:302–11.

Pieta, Karol 1987. "Die Slowakei im 5. Jahrhundert." In *Germanen*, pp. 385–97.

Pigulevskaia, Nina 1970. "Une chronique syrienne du VI-e siècle sur les tribus slaves." *Folia Orientalia* 12:211– 14.

Pilarić, Georgina 1975. "Anthropologische Untersuchungen über künstlich deformierte Schädel aus dem frühmittelalterlichen Gräberfeld in Rakovčani bei Prijedor." *WMBHL* 5:245–70.

Pillinger, Renate 1985. "Monumenti paleocristiani in Bulgaria." *Rivista di Archeologia Cristiana* 61, nos. 3–4:275–310.

—— 1992. "Ein frühchristliches Grab mit Psalmzitaten in Mangalia/Kallatis (Rumänien)." In *Schwarzmeerküste*, pp. 97–102.

References

Pippidi, Dionisie M., Gabriela Bordenache, and V. Eftimie 1961. "Şantierul arheo-logic Histria." *MCA* 7:229–64.

Pisarev, Atanas 1990. "Le système de fortification entre le Danube et les versants nord des Balkans pendant l'antiquité tardive." In *Akten 14*, pp. 875–82.

Pizarro, Joaquín Martínez 1989. *A Rhetoric of the Scene. Dramatic Narrative in the Early Middle Ages*. Toronto: University of Toronto Press.

Pleiner, Radomir 1988. "Brannversuche in einem nachgebildeten slawischen Töpferofen." *SlovArch* 36, no. 2:299–308.

Pleinerová, Ivana 1979. "Zu den frühslawischen Grubenhäusern." In *Rapports*, pp. 629–37. Vol. I.

  1980. "O kharaktere ranneslavianskikh poselenii prazhskogo i korchaskogo tipov." *SA* 2:51–5.

  1986. "Březno: experiments with building Old Slavic houses and living in them." *PA* 77:104–76.

Pleinerová, Ivana, and Evžen Neustupny 1987. "K otazce stravy ve staroslovanském období (Experiment v Březne)." *ArchRoz* 39:90–101, 117–19.

Pletneva, Svetlana 1980. "Drevnite bălgari v iztochna Evropa." *IBID* 37:23–39.

Pliakov, Z. 1973. "Die Stadt Sandanski und das Gebiet von Melnik und Sandanski im Mittelalter." *Byzantinobulgarica* 4:175–201.

Plog, Stephen, and Jeffrey L. Hantman 1986. "Multiple regression analysis as a dating method in the American Southwest." In *Spatial Organization and Exchange. Archaeological Survey of Northern Black Mesa*, pp. 86–113. Ed. Stephen Plog. Carbondale and Edwardsville: Southern Illinois University Press.

Podgórska-Czopek, Joanna 1991. "Materialy z wczesnosłowiańskiej osady w Grodzisku Dolnym, stan 3, woj. Rzeszów." *Archaeoslavica* 1:9–60.

Poenaru-Bordea, Gheorghe 1976. "Monnaies byzantines des VI–e–VII–e siècles en Dobroudja." In *Actes XIV*, pp. 203– 13. Vol. III.

Poenaru-Bordea, Gheorghe, and Radu Ocheşanu 1980. "Probleme istorice dobro-gene (sec. VI–VII) în lumina monedelor bizantine din colecţia Muzeului de istorie naţională şi arheologie din Constanţa." *SCIV* 31, no. 3:377–96.

  1983–5. "Tezaurul de monede bizantine de aur descoperit în săpăturile arheolo-gice din anul 1899 de la Axiopolis." *BSNR* 77–9, nos. 131–3:177–97.

Pogodin, A. L. 1901. *Iz istorii slavianskikh peredvizhenii*. St Petersburg: A. P. Lopukhina.

Pohl, Walter 1980. "Die Gepiden und die Gentes an der mittleren Donau nach dem Zerfall des Attillareiches." In *Donau*, pp. 239–305.

  1988. *Die Awaren. Ein Steppenvolk im Mitteleuropa 567–822 n. Chr*. Munich: C. H. Beck.

  1991a. "Conceptions of ethnicity in early medieval studies." *ArchPol* 29:39–49.

  1991b. "Zur Dynamik barbarischer Gesellschaften: das Beispiel der Awaren." *Klio* 73:595–600.

  1992. "Herrschaft und Subsistenz. Zum Wandel der byzantinischen Randkulturen an der Donau vom 6.–8. Jahrhundert." In *Awarenforschungen*, pp. 13–24. Vol. I.

  1994. "Tradition, Ethnographie und literarische Gestaltung: eine Zwischenbilanz." In *Ethnogenese und Überlieferung. Ausgewandte Methode der Frühmittelalterforschung*, pp. 9–26. Ed. Karl Brunner and Brigitte Merta. Vienna and Munich: R. Oldenbourg.

References

1996. "Die Langobarden in Pannonien und Justinians Gotenkrieg." In *Verhältnisse*, pp. 27–36.

1997. "The Empire and the Lombards: treaties and negotiations in the sixth century." In *Kingdoms of the Empire. The Integration of Barbarians in Late Antiquity*, pp. 75–133. Ed. Walter Pohl. Leiden, New York, and Cologne: Brill.

Popescu, Dorin 1941–4. "Fibeln aus dem Nationalmuseum für Altertümer in Bucureşti." *Dacia* 9–10:485–505.

Popescu, Emilian 1967. "Die spätgriechische Inschriften aus Klein-Skythien." *Dacia* 11:163–76.

1976. *Inscripţiile greceşti şi latine din secolele IV-XIII descoperite în România*. Bucharest: Editura Academiei RSR.

Popović, I. 1959. "Die Einwanderung der Slaven in das Oströmische Reich im Lichte der Sprachforschung." *ZfS* 4:707–21.

Popović, Ivana 1994–5. "Les particularités de l'outillage protobyzantin dans les Balkans du Nord." *Starinar* 45–6:67–75.

Popović, Lj., and E. Čerškov 1956. "Ulpiana. Prethodni izveštaj o arheološkim istraživanjima od 1954 do 1956 god." *Glasnik Muzeja Kosovo i Metohije* 1:319–26.

Popović, Marko 1987. "Svetinja, novi podaci o ranovizantijskom Viminacijumu." *Starinar* 38:1–37.

1991. *The Fortress of Belgrade*. Belgrade: Institute for the Protection of Cultural Monuments of Serbia.

Popović, Vladislav 1975. "Les témoins archéologiques des invasions avaro-slaves dans l'Illyricum byzantin." *MEFRA* 87, no. 1:445–504.

1978. "La descente des Koutigoures, des Slaves et des Avares vers la Mer Egée: le témoignage de l'archéologie." *CRAI* 6:597–649.

1980. "Aux origines de la slavisation des Balkans: la constitution des premières sklavinies macédoniennes vers la fin du VI-e siècle." *CRAI* 8:230–57.

1981. "Une invasion slave sous Justin II inconnue des sources écrites." *Numizmatičar* 4:111–26.

1982. "Desintegration und Ruralisation der Stadt im Ost-Illyricum vom 5. bis 7. Jahrhundert n. Chr." In *Palast*, pp. 545–66.

1984a. "Un étui de peigne en os de type 'mérovingien' et les objets d'origine ethnique étrangère à Caričin Grad." In *Caričin Grad*, pp. 160–78. Ed. N. Duval and V. Popovič. Belgrade and Rome: Arheološki Institut and Ecole Française de Rome.

1984b. "Petits trésors et trésors démembrés de monnaie de bronze protobyzantines de Serbie." *Numizmatičar* 7:57–90.

1989–90. "Trois inscriptions protobyzantines de Bregovina." *Starinar* 40–1:279–90.

Postică, Gheorghe 1994. *Românii din codrii Moldovei în Evul Mediu timpuriu (Studiu arheologic pe baza ceramicii din aşezarea Hansca)*. Chişinău: Universitas.

Pottier, Henri 1983. *Analyse d'un trésor de monnaies en bronze enfoui au VI-e siècle en Syrie byzantine. Contribution à la méthodologie numismatique*. Brussels: Cercle d'études numismatiques.

Poulík, Josef 1948. *Staroslovanská Morava*. Prague: Nákladem Statního archeologického ustavu.

Poulter, Andrew G. 1983. "Town and country in Moesia inferior." In *Bulgaria*, pp. 74–118.

References

1988. "Nicopolis ad Istrum, Bulgaria: an interim report on the excavations 1985–7." *Antiquaries Journal* 68:69–89.

1992. "The use and abuse of urbanism in the Danubian provinces during the Later Roman Empire." In *The City in Late Antiquity*, pp. 99–135. Ed. John Rich. New York: Routledge.

1995. *Nicopolis ad Istrum: A Roman, Late Roman, and Early Byzantine City*. London: Society for the Promotion of Roman Studies.

Poutiers, Jean-Cristian 1975. "A propos des forteresses antiques et médiévales de la Plaine danubienne. Essai de reconstitution du réseau routier entre Iskăr et Ogosta." *EB* 2:60–73.

Praetzellis, Adrian 1993. "The limits of arbitrary excavation." In *Practices of Archaeological Stratigraphy*, pp. 68–86. Ed. E. C. Harris. London and San Diego: Academic Press.

Pralong, Annie 1988. "Remarques sur les fortifications byzantines de Thrace orientale." In *Géographie historique du monde méditerrannéen*, pp. 179–200. Ed. Hélène Ahrweiler. Paris: Publications de la Sorbonne.

Preda, Constantin 1967. "Tipar pentru bijuterii din sec. VI e.n. descoperit la Olteni (r. Videle, reg. Bucureşti)." *SCIV* 18, no. 3:513–14.

Preda, Constantin, and Hamparţumian Nubar 1973. *Histria III. Descoperirile monetare 1914–1970*. Bucharest: Editura Academiei RSR.

Preidel, Helmut 1954. *Die Anfänge der slawischen Bevölkerung Böhmens und Mährens*, vol. I. Gräfelfing: Edmund Gaus.

Prendi, Frano 1979–80. "Një varrezë e kulturës arbërore ne Lezhë." *Iliria* 9–10:123–70.

Press, Ludwika, and Tadeusz Sarnowski 1990. "Novae. Römisches Legionslager und frühbyzantinische Stadt an der unteren Donau." *Antike Welt* 21, no. 4:225–43.

Press, Ludwika et al. 1973. "Novae – sector zachodni, 1971. Sprawozdanie tymczasowe z wykopalisk ekspedycji archeologicznej Universitetu Warszawskiego." *Archeologia* 24:101–46.

Prikhodniuk, Oleg M. 1975. *Slov'iani na Podilli (VI–VII st. n.e.)*. Kiev: Naukova Dumka.

1980. *Arkheologychny pam'iatki seredn'ogo Pridnyprov'ia VI–IX st. n.e.* Kiev: Naukova Dumka.

1983. "K voprosu o prisutstvii antov v Karpato-Dunaiskikh zemliakh." In *Dnestr*, pp. 180–91.

1988. "Obshchestvenno-khoziaistvennaia struktura slavianskikh poselenii (po materialam pen'kovskoi kul'tury)." In *Trudy*, pp. 189–94. Vol. IV.

1989. "Anty i Pen'kovskaia kul'tura." In *Drevnie slaviane i Kievskaia Rus'*, pp. 58–69. Ed. P. P. Tolochko. Kiev: Naukova Dumka.

1994. "Tekhnologiia virobnictva ta vitoki iuvelirnogo stiliu metalevikh prikras Pastirs'kogo gorodishcha." *Arkheolohiia* 3, no. 2:61–77.

Prikhodniuk, O. M. et al. 1991. "Martynovskii klad." *MAIET* 2:72–92.

Pringle, Denys 1981. *The Defense of Byzantine Africa from Justinian to the Arab Conquest: An Account of the Military History and Archaeology of the African Provinces in the Sixth and Seventh Centuries*. Oxford: BAR.

Pritsak, Omeljan 1983. "The Slavs and the Avars." In *Slavi*, pp. 353–435.

Proudfoot, A. S. 1974. "The sources of Theophanes for the Heraclian dynasty." *Byzantion* 44:367–437.

References

Przyluski, Jean 1940. "Les confrèries des loups-garous dans les sociétés indo-européennes." *Revue de l'Histoire des Réligions* 121:128–45.

Radomerský, P. 1953. "Byzantské mince z pokladu v Zemianském Vrbovku." *PA* 44:109–22.

Rafalovich, I. A. 1968. "Poselenia VI–VII vv. u s. Hanska." *KSIA* 113:75–103.

1969. "Zemledelie u rannykh slavian v Moldavii (VI–IX vv.)." In *Dalekoe proshloe Moldavii*, pp. 75–90. Ed. N. A. Ketraru et al. Kishinew: Redakcionno-izdatel'skii otdel Akademii Nauk Moldavskoi SSR.

1972a. "Moldaviia i puti rasseleniia slavian v iugo-vostochnoi Evrope." In *Iugo-vostochnaia Evropa v srednie veka*, pp. 7–31. Ed. Ia. S. Grosul. Vol. 1. Kishinew: Shtiinca.

1972b. "Raskopki ranneslavianskogo poseleniia VI–VII vv. n.e. u sela Selishte." In *Arkheologicheskie issledovaniia v Moldavii v 1968–1969 gg.*, pp. 122–42. Ed. I. A. Rafalovich. Kishinew: Shtiinca.

1972c. *Slaviane VI–IX vekov v Moldavii.* Kishinew: Shtiinca.

1973. "Issledovaniia ranneslavianskikh poselenii v Moldavii." In *Arkheologicheskie issledovaniia v Moldavii v 1970–1971 g.*, pp. 134–54. Ed. G. F. Chebotarenko. Kishinew: Shtiinca.

1974. "Kul'tura slavian Moldavii." In *Drevniaia kul'tura Moldavii*, pp. 81–108. Ed. V. S. Zelenchuk. Kishinew: Shtiinca.

Rafalovich, I. A., and N. V. Golceva 1981. "Ranneslavianskoe poselenie V–VII vv. Dancheni I." In *Arkheologicheskie issledovaniia Moldavii v 1974–1976 gg.*, pp. 125–40. Kishinew: Shtiinca.

Rafalovich, I. A., and V. L. Lapushnian 1971. "Raboty Reutskoi ekspedicii." In *Arkehologicheskie otkrytiia 1970 g.*, pp. 361–2. Ed. B. A. Rybakov. Moscow: Nauka.

1973. "Raboty Reutskoi arkheologicheskoi ekspedicii." In *Arkheologicheskie issledovaniia v Moldavii v 1972 g.*, pp. 110–30. Kishinew: Shtiinca.

1974. "Mogil'niki i ranneslavianskoe gorodishche u s. Selishte." In *Arkheologicheskie issledovaniia v Moldavii (1973 g.)*, pp. 104–39. Ed. V. I. Markevich. Kishinew: Shtiinca.

Rappoport, P. A. 1972. "Die ostslavischen Wohnbauten des 6.-13. Jh." *ZfA* 6: 228–39.

1975. "Drevnerusskoe zhilishche." In *Drevnee zhilishche narodov vostochnoi Evropy*, pp. 104–55. Ed. M. G. Rabinovich. Moscow: Nauka.

Räsänen, Matti 1994. "The concepts and contents of everyday life." In *Everyday Life and Ethnicity. Urban Families in Loviisa and Võru 1888–1991*, pp. 17–18. Ed. Anna Kirveennummi, Matti Räsänen, and Timo J. Virtanen. Helsinki: Suomalaisen Kirjallisuuden Seura.

Rauhutowa, Jadwiga 1981. "Debrešte (Makedonien, Jugoslawien), eine frühbyzan-tinische Stätte." In *Symposium italo-polacco. Le origini di Venezia. Problemi, espe-rienze, proposte, Venezia, 28–29 febbraio – 1–2 marzo 1980*, pp. 33–48. Venice: Marsilio.

Rautman, Marcus 1998. "Handmade pottery and social change: the view from Late Roman Cyprus." *Journal of Mediterranean Archaeology* 11, no. 1:81–104.

Rejholcová, Maria 1990. "Včasnoslovanské pohrebisko v Čakajovciach okres Nitra." *SlovArch* 38, no. 2:357–417.

Repnikov, N. 1906. "N'ekotorye mogil'niki oblasti krymskikh gotov'." *IIAK* 19:1–80.

References

Rice, Prudence M. 1987. *Pottery Analysis. A Sourcebook.* Chicago and London: University of Chicago Press.

1989. "Ceramic diversity, production, and use." In *Quantifying Diversity in Archaeology*, pp. 109–17. Ed. Robert D. Leonard and George T. Jones. Cambridge and London: Cambridge University Press.

Richards, J. D. 1982. "Anglo-Saxon pot shapes: cognitive investigations." *Science and Archaeology* 24:33–46.

Richards, John W. 1986. "The Slavic zadruga and other archaic Indo-European elements in traditional Slavic society." *Mankind Quarterly* 26, nos. 3–4:321–37.

Riedinger, Rudolf 1969. *Pseudo-Kaisarios. Überlieferungsgeschichte und Verfasserfrage.* Munich: C. H. Beck.

Riemer, E. 1992. "Byzantinische Körbchen- und Halbmondohrringe im Römisch-Germanischen Museum Köln (Sammlung Diergardt)." *Kölner Jahrbuch für Vor- und Frühgeschichte* 25:121–36.

Rigby, P. 1985. *Persistent Pastoralists: Nomadic Societies in Transition.* London: Zed Press.

Ringrose, T. J. 1992. "Bootstrapping and Correspondence Analysis in archaeology." *Journal of Archaeological Science* 19:615–29.

Roe, Peter G. 1995. "Style, society, myth, and structure." In *Style, Society, and Person: Archaeological and Ethnological Perspectives*, pp. 27–76. Ed. Christopher Carr and Jill E. Neitzel. New York and London: Plenum Press.

Roesler, Robert 1873. "Über den Zeitpunkt der slavischen Ansiedlung an der unteren Donau." *Sitzungsberichte* 73:77– 126.

Roman, Petre, and Suzana Ferche 1978. "Cercetările de la Ipoteşti (jud. Olt)." *SCIV* 29, no. 1:73–93.

Romanchuk, A. I. 1985. "Raskopki vo vtorom kvartale Khersonesa." In *Arkheologicheskie otkrytiia 1983 goda*, pp. 348–9. Ed. B. A. Rybakov. Moscow: Nauka.

Romanova, G. A. 1983. "O rabote Dneprovskoi levoberezhnoi ekspedicii." In *Arkheologicheskie otkrytiia 1981 goda*, pp. 310–11. Ed. B. A. Rybakov. Moscow: Nauka.

Romashov, S. A. 1992–4. "Bolgarskie plemena Severnogo Prichernomor'ia v V–VII vv." *AEMA* 8:207–52.

Ronin, V. K. 1995a. "Pis'ma papy Grigoriia I." In *Svod*, pp. 350–2. Vol. II.

1995b. "'Zhitie Sv. abbata Kolumbana i ego uchenikov' Iony iz Bobb'o." In *Svod*, pp. 359–63. Vol. II.

Roosens, Eugeen E. 1989. *Creating Ethnicity. The Process of Ethnogenesis.* Newbury Park and London: Sage Publications.

Rose, Valentin 1887. *Leben des heiligen David von Thessalonike.* Berlin: A. Asher.

Rosetti, Alexandru 1954. *Influenţa limbilor slave meridionale asupra limbii române (sec. VI–XII).* Bucharest: Editura Academiei RPR.

Rosetti, Dinu V. 1934. "Siedlungen der Kaiserzeit und der Völkerwanderungszeit bei Bukarest." *Germania* 18:206–13.

Roska, Martin 1934. "Das gepidische Gräberfeld von Veresmart." *Germania* 18:123–30.

Rosser, John 1985. "The role of the great Isthmus corridor in the Slavonic invasions of Greece." *ByzF* 9:245–53.

References

Rostafiński, J. 1908. *O pierwotnych siedzibach i gospodarstwie słowian w przedhistorycznych czasach.* Cracow: Nakladem M. Arcta.

Roth, Helmut 1986. *Kunst und Handwerk im frühen Mittelalter. Archäologische Zeugnisse von Childerich I. bis zu Karl dem Grossen.* Stuttgart: Konrad Theiss.

Roth, Helmut, and Claudia Theune 1988. *SW I–V: Zur Chronologie merowingerzeitlicher Frauengräber in Südwestdeutschland.* Stuttgart: Landesdenkmalamt Baden-Württemberg.

Rouse, Irving 1986. *Migrations in Prehistory. Inferring Population Movement from Cultural Remains.* New Haven and London: Yale University Press.

Rousseau, Jérôme 1985. "The ideological prerequisites of inequality." In *Development*, pp. 36–45.

Rousseau, Philip 1998. "Procopius's 'Buildings' and Justinian's pride." *Byzantion* 68:121–30.

Rubin, Berthold 1954. *Prokopius von Kaisareia.* Stuttgart and Waldsee: Alfred Druckenmüller.

Rudolph, Wolf W. 1979. "Excavations at Porto Cheli and vicinity. Preliminary report V: the early Byzantine remains." *Hesperia* 48:294–320.

Rusanova, I. P. 1958. "Arkheologicheskie pamiatniki vtoroi poloviny I tysiacheletii n.e. na territorii drevlian." *SA* 4:33–46.

1963. "Poselenie u s. Korchaka na r. Tetereve." In *Obrazovaniia*, pp. 39–50.

1968. "Keramika ranneslavianskikh poselenii Zhitomirshchiny." *ArchRoz* 20:576–82.

1970. "Karta rasprostraneniia pamiatnikov tipa Korchak (VI–VII vv. n. e.)." In *Sosedi*, pp. 93–6.

1973a. "Pogrebal'nye pamiatniki vtoroi poloviny I tysiacheletiia n. e. na territorii Severo-Zapadnoi Ukrainy." *KSIA* 135:3–9.

1973b. *Slavianskie drevnosti VI–IX vv. mezhdu Dneprom i zapadnym Bugom.* Moscow: Nauka.

1976. *Slavianskie drevnosti VI–VII vv. Kultura prazhskogo tipa.* Moscow: Nauka.

1978. "O rannei date pamiatnikov prazhskogo tipa." In *Rus'*, pp. 138–43.

1993. "Vvedenie." In *Slaviane i ikh sosedi v konce I tysiacheletiia do n.e.-pervoi polovine I tysiacheletiia n.e*, pp. 5–18. Ed. I. P. Rusanova and E. A. Symonovich. Moscow: Nauka.

Rusanova, Irina P., and B. O. Timoshchuk 1984. *Kodyn, slavianskie poseleniia V–VIII vv. na r. Prut.* Moscow: Nauka.

Russell, James 1982. "Byzantine 'instrumenta domestica' from Anemurium: the significance of the context." In *City*, pp. 133–62.

Rusu, Mircea 1959. "Pontische Gürtelschnallen mit Adlerkopf (VI.–VII. Jh. u.Z.)." *Dacia* 3:485–523.

1978. "Populaţiile turce, slavii şi autohtonii din bazinul carpato-dunărean în veacurile VI–XI." *Anuarul Institutului de Istorie şi Arheologie "A. D. Xenopol"* 21:121–34.

1981. "Les populations du groupe turc, les Slaves et les autochtones du bassin carpatho-danubien au VI–IX-e siècles." *RRH* 20:19–31.

Rybakov, Boris A. 1939. "Anty i Kievskaia Rus'." *VDI* 1:319–37.

1943. "Ranniaia kul'tura vostochnykh slavian." *IZ* 11–12:73–80.

1948. *Remeslo drevnei Rusi.* Moscow: Izdatel'stvo Akademii Nauk SSSR.

References

1949. "Novyi Sudzhanskii klad antskogo vremeni." *Kratkie soobshcheniia o dokladakh i polevykh issledovaniiakh Instituta Istorii Material' noi Kul' tury* 27:75–84.

1953. "Drevnie rusi. K voprosu ob obrazovanii iadra drevnerusskoi narodnosti v svete trudov I. V. Stalina." *SA* 17:23–104.

Sackett, James R. 1985. "Style and ethnicity in the Kalahari: a reply to Wiessner." *AAnt* 50, no. 1:154–9.

1986. "Isochrestism and style: a clarification." *JAA* 5:266–77.

1990. "Style and ethnicity in archaeology: the case for isochrestism." In *Uses*, pp. 32–43.

Sági, K. 1964. "Das langobardische Gräberfeld von Vörs." *ActaArchHung* 16:409–42.

Sahlins, Marshall D. 1961. "The segmentary lineage: an organization of predatory expansion." *AAnth* 63:322–45.

1963. "Poor man, rich man, big-man, chief: political types in Melanesia and Polynesia." *CSSH* 5:283–303.

Salamon, Agnés, and István Erdelyi 1971. *Das völkerwanderungszeitliche Gräberfeld von Környe*. Budapest: Akademiai kiadó.

Šalkovský, Peter 1988. "K vyvoju a strukturé osídlenia v dobe slovanskej na Slovensku." *SlovArch* 36, no. 2:379– 414.

1993. "Frühmittelalterliche Hausbaukultur in der Slowakei." In *Actes XIIb*, pp. 65–74. Vol. IV.

Sâmpetru, Mihai 1994. *Oraşe şi cetăţi romane târzii la Dunărea de Jos*. Bucharest: Institutul Român de Tracologie.

Sandu, Vasilica 1992. "Cercetări arheologice în zona Lunca-Bîrzeşti." *CAB* 4:163–94.

Sarvas, P. 1981. "Schätze und Schatzfunde." In *LAGOM. Festschrift für Peter Berghaus zum 60. Geburtstag am 20. November 1979*, pp. 7–12. Ed. Thomas Fischer and Peter Ilisch. Münster: Numismatischer Verlag der Münzenhandlung Dombrowski.

Šašel, Jaroslav 1979. "Antiqui Barbari. Zur Besiedlungsgeschichte Ostnoricums und Pannoniens im 5. und 6. Jahrhundert nach den Schriftquellen." In *Von der Spätantike zum frühen Mittelalter: aktuelle Probleme in historischer und archäologischer Sicht*, pp. 125–39. Ed. J. Werner and E. Ewig. Sigmaringen: Thorbecke.

Sasse, Barbara 1990. "Frauengräber im frühmittelalterlichen Alamannien." In *Frauen in Spätantike und Frühmittelalter (Lebensbedingungen-Lebensnormen-Lebensformen). Beiträge zu einer internationalen Tagung am Fachbereich Geschichtswissenschaften der Freien Universität Berlin 18. bis 21. Februar 1987*, pp. 45–64. Ed. Werner Affeldt. Sigmaringen: Jan Thorbecke.

Schafarik, Paul Joseph 1844. *Slawische Alterthümer*, 2 vols. Leipzig: Wilhelm Engelmann.

Schelesniker, Herbert 1973. *Der Name der Slaven. Herkunft, Bildungsweise und Bedeutung*. Innsbruck: Institut für Sprachwissenschaft der Leopold-Franzens Universität Innsbruck.

Schneider, Reinhard 1993. "Zur Problematik eines undifferenzierten Landnahmenbegriffs." In *Probleme*, pp. 11–57. Vol. I.

Schöneburg, P. 1991. "Eine frühchristliche Basilika bei der antiken Straßenstation Karasura." *Das Altertum* 37:228–34.

Schrader, Otto 1901. *Reallexikon der indogermanischen Altertumskunde. Grundzüge einer Kultur- und Völkergeschichte Alteuropas*. Strasbourg: K. J. Trubner.

References

Schramm, Gottfried 1981. *Eroberer und Eingesessene. Geographische Lehnnahmen als Zeugen der Geschichte Südosteuropas im ersten Jahrtausend n.Chr.* Stuttgart: Anton Hirsemann.

1995. "Venedi, Antes, Sclaveni, Sclavi. Frühe Sammelbezeichnungen für slawische Stämme und ihr geschichtlicher Hintergrund." *JGO* 43:161–200.

Schreiner, Peter 1985. "Städte und Wegenetz in Mösien, Dakien und Thrakien nach dem Zeugnis des Theophylaktos Simokates." *Schriften der Balkankommission. Antiqu. Abt.* 16:25–35.

Schultz, S. 1978. "Streufunde aus Isaccea (Noviodunum)." *Pontica* 11:97–104.

Schulze-Dörrlamm, Mechthild 1986. "Romanisch oder germanisch? Untersuchungen zu den Armbrust- und Bügelknopffibel des 5. und 6. Jhs. n. Chr. aus den Gebieten westlich des Rheins und südlich der Donau." *JRGZ* 33:593–720.

1987a. "Berichte über die Neuerwerbung von 48 byzantinischen Gürtelschnallen des 5.-7. Jhs. und von 7 byzantinischen Schnallen des 7.-10. Jhs." *JRGZ* 34:801–4.

1987b. "Review of 'Der Grabfund von Malaja Pereščepina und Kuvrat, Kagan der Bulgaren', by Joachim Werner." *BJ* 187:852–4.

Schürtz, Heinrich 1902. *Altersklassen und Männerbünde. Eine Darstellung der Grundformen der Gesellschaft.* Berlin: Georg Reimer.

Schuster-Šewc, H. 1985. "Zur Geschichte und Etymologie des ethnischen Namens Sorb/Serb/Sarb/Srb." *ZfS* 6:851–6.

Schütz, Joseph 1991. "Zwei germanische Rechtstermini des 7. Jahrhunderts. Fredegari: 'befulci' – Edictus Rothari: 'fulcfree'." In *Festschrift für Erwin Wedel zum 65. Geburtstag*, pp. 409–14. Munich: Hieronymus.

Schwarcz, Andreas 1992. "Die Erhebung des Vitalianus, die Protobulgaren und das Konzil von Heraclea 515." *BHR* 4:3– 10.

Scorpan, Constantin 1968. "O nouă problemă pentru secolele VI–VII e.n." *Pontica* 1:364–6.

1974. "Sacidava – a new Roman fortress on the map of the Danube limes." In *Actes IX*, pp. 109–16.

1977. "Contribution à la connaissance de certains types céramiques romano-byzantins (IVe–VIIe siècles) dans l'espace istro-pontique." *Dacia* 21:269–97.

1978. "Descoperiri arheologice diverse de la Sacidava." *Pontica* 11:155–80.

Scott, Roger 1987. "Justinian coinage and Easter reforms and the date of the 'Secret History'." *BMGS* 11:215–22.

1990a. "The Byzantine chronicle after Malalas." In *Studies in John Malalas*, pp. 38–54. Ed. Elizabeth Jeffreys, Brian Croke, and Scott Roger. Sydney: Australian Association for Byzantine Studies.

1990b. "Malalas and his contemporaries." In *Studies in John Malalas*, pp. 67–85. Ed. Elizabeth Jeffreys, Brian Croke, and Scott Roger. Sydney: Australian Association for Byzantine Studies.

Sedin, Anatolii A. 1995. "Gorodishche Nikodimovo (Nikadzimava)." *SlA* 36:159–64.

Sedov, V. V. 1972. "Formirovanie slavianskogo naseleniia srednego Podneprov'ia." *SA* 4:116–30.

1976. "Rannii period slavianskogo etnogeneza." In *Voprosy*, pp. 68–108.

References

1978. "Etnografiia Vostochnoi Evropy serediny I tysiacheletiia n.e. po dannym arkheologii i Iordana." In *Vostochnaia Evropa v drevnosti i srednevekov'e*, pp. 9–15. Ed. M. A. Korostovcev. Moscow: Nauka.

1979. *Proiskhozhdenie i ranniaia istoriia slavian.* Moscow: Nauka.

1982. *Vostochnye slaviane v VI–XIII vv.* Moscow: Nauka.

1994. *Slaviane v drevnosti.* Moscow: Institut Arkheologii Rossiiskoi Akademii Nauk.

1996. "Sovremennoe sostaianie problemy etnogeneza slavian." *SlA* 37:21–40.

Sekeres, Lászlo 1957. "Jedan interesantan nalaz iz ranog srednieg veka iz Nose." *RVM* 6:231–6.

Sellnow, Irmgard 1990. "Das Problem der 'Völkerschaft' – eine völkerkundliche Kontroverse." *EAZ* 31:199–214.

Senior, Louise M., and Dunbar P. Birnie 1995. "Accurately estimating vessel volume from profile illustrations." *AAnt* 60, no. 2:319–34.

Serikov, N. I. 1991. "Ioann Efesskii." In *Svod*, pp. 276– 91. Vol. I.

Service, Elman 1971. *Primitive Social Organization.* New York: Random House.

Setton, Kenneth M. 1950. "The Bulgars in the Balkans and the occupation of Corinth in the 7th century." *Speculum* 25:502–43.

1952. "The emperor Constans II and the capture of Corinth by the Onogur Bulgars." *Speculum* 27:351–62.

Sgibea-Turcu, Mioara 1963. "Fibule din sec. III şi VI e.n. descoperite în săpăturile arheologice de la Militari." *CAB* 1:373–84.

Shanin, Teodor 1989. "Ethnicity in the Soviet Union: analytical perceptions and political strategies." *CSSH* 31:409–24.

Shapiro, Gary 1984. "Ceramic vessels, site permanence, and group size: a Mississippian example." *AAnt* 49, no. 4:696–712.

Shapovalov, G. I. 1990. "Iakyr V–VII st. z Dnypra bylia ostrova Khorticia." *Arkheolohiia* 1:120–1.

Shchukin, Mark B. 1980. "Nekotorye problemy khronologii cherniakhovskoi kul'tury i istorii slavian." In *Rapports*, pp. 399–411. Vol. II.

Shear, T. Leslie 1973. "The Athenian Agora: excavations of 1972." *Hesperia* 42:359–407.

Shennan, Stephen 1989. "Introduction: archaeological approaches to cultural identity." In *Approaches*, pp. 1– 32.

1990. *Quantifying Archaeology.* Edinburgh: Edinburgh University Press and Academic Press.

Shnirel'man, Viktor. A. 1993. "Zlokliucheniia odnoi nauki: etnogeneticheskie issledovaniia i stalinskaia nacional'naia politika." *Etnograficheskoe Obozrenie* 3:52–68.

1995. "From internationalism to nationalism: forgotten pages of Soviet archaeology in the 1930s and 1940s." In *Nationalism, Politics, and the Practice of Archaeology*, pp. 120–38. Ed. Philip Kohl and Clare Fawcett. Cambridge: Cambridge University Press.

Shovkoplias, A. M. 1957. "Keramicheskie kompleksy s gory Kiselevki v Kieve." *KSIA* 7:100–3.

1963. "Ranneslavianskaia keramika s gory Kiselevki v Kieve." In *Obrazovaniia*, pp. 138–44.

References

Shovkoplias, A. M., and I. O. Gavritukhin 1993. "Kompleksy Prazhskoi kul'tury s Oboloni i nekotorye problemy izucheniia pamiatnikov tipa Korchak." *KSIA* 208:52–62.

Shuvalov, P. V. 1989. "Etnokulturnye processy na territorii Dnestro-Dunaiskogo mezhdurech'ia v seredine I tys. n.e." PhD Dissertation. Institute of Archaeology, Leningrad.

1991. "Severo-vostok Balkanskogo poluostrova v epokhu pozdnei antichnosti (social'no-demograficheskie aspekty politicheskoi istorii)." In *Vizantii*, pp. 39–47.

Sigrist, Christian 1967. *Regulierte Anarchie. Untersuchungen zum Fehlen und zur Entstehung politischer Herrschaft in segmentären Gesellschaften Afrikas.* Olten and Freiburg im Breisgau: Walter Verlag.

Šimák, J. V. 1933. *Jan Peisker.* Prague: Nákladem České Akademie Ved a Umení.

Šimek, Emanuel 1923. *Čechy a Morava za doby římské. Kritická studie.* Prague: Nákladem Filosofické fakulty University Karlovy.

Simon, László 1991. "Korai avar kardok." *Studia Comitatensia* 22:263–346.

1991–2. "A tápéi korai avar kard." *Móra Ferenc Múzeum Évkönyve* 1:31–5.

1995. "Le armi." In *Avari*, pp. 113–23.

Simoni, Katica 1977–8. "Dva priloga istraživanju germanskih nalaza seobe naroda u Jugoslaviji." *VAMZ* 10– 11:209–33.

1988. "Srebrna zlica iz Siska." *VAMZ* 21:79–86.

1989. "Funde aus der Völkerwanderungszeit in den Sammlungen des Archäologischen Museums in Zagreb." *VAMZ* 22:107–34.

Simonova, E. N. 1970. "Pal'chataia fibula Vengerskogo Nacional'nogo Muzeia." In *Sosedi*, pp. 75–9.

Simonyi, Dezsö 1964. "Pannoniai bolgarok és a kuturgur-bolgarok." *ArchÉrt* 91:194–200.

Skedros, James Constantine 1996. "St. Demetrios of Thessaloniki: civic patron and divine protector (4th–7th c. CE)." PhD Dissertation. Harvard University, Cambridge.

Skibo, James M., Michael B. Schiffer, and Nancy Kowalski 1989. "Ceramic style analysis in archaeology and ethnoarchaeology: bridging the analytical gap." *JAA* 8:388–409.

Sklenář, Karel 1983. *Archaeology in Central Europe: The First 500 Years.* Leicester and New York: Leicester University Press and St Martin's Press.

Skružný, Ludvík 1964. "Pekáče – jejich výskyt, funkce a datovaní." *PA* 55, no. 2:370–91.

Skrzhinskaia, E. Ch. 1957. "O sklavenakh i antakh, o Mursianskom ozere i gorode Novietune (Iz kommentariia k Iordanu)." *VV* 12:3–30.

Slabe, Marijan 1978. "Künstlich deformierte Schädel der Völkerwanderungszeit in Jugoslawien im Lichte ihrer Aussagekraft." In *Problemi*, pp. 67–73.

1986. "O nakitu in okrasu iz časa preseljevanja ljudstev na slovenskem." In *Mélange*, pp. 199–204.

Slezkine, Yuri 1996. "N. Ia. Marr and the national origins of Soviet ethnogenetics." *Slavic Review* 55, no. 4:826–62.

Smedley, John 1988. "Seventh-century Byzantine coins in southern Russia and the problem of light weight solidi." In *Studies in Early Byzantine Gold Coinage*, pp.

References

111–30. Ed. Wolfgang Hahn and William E. Metcalf. New York: American Numismatic Society.

Smilenko, Alla Trofimovna 1965. *Glodos'ki skarbi*. Kiev: Naukova Dumka.

1968. "Nakhodka 1928 g. u g. Novye Senzhary (Po materialam obsledovaniia A. K. Takhtaia)." In *Slaviane i Rus.' Sbornik*, pp. 158–66. Ed. E. I. Krupnov et al. Moscow: Nauka.

1980. "O kharakternykh chertakh kul'tury vostochnykh slavian VI–IX vekov." In *Rapports*, pp. 757–65. Vol. II.

Smith, Anthony D. 1984. "National identity and myths of ethnic descent." *Research in Social Movements, Conflict and Change* 7:95–130.

1986. *The Ethnic Origins of the Nations*. Oxford and Cambridge: Blackwell.

1995. "National identities: modern and medieval?." In *Concepts of National Identity in the Middle Ages*, pp. 21– 46. Ed. Simon Forde, Lesley Johnson, and Alan V. Murray. Leeds: University of Leeds.

Smith, Carol A. 1976. "Exchange systems and the spatial distribution of elites: the organization of stratification in agrarian societies." In *Regional Analysis*, pp. 309–81. Ed. Carol A. Smith. Vol. II. New York: Academic Press.

Smith, Marion F. 1988. "Function form whole vessel shape: a method and an application to Anasazi Black Mesa, Arizona." *AAnth* 90:912–23.

Smolla, Günter 1979–80. "Das Kossinna-Syndrom." *Fundberichte aus Hessen* 19–20:1–9.

Snively, Carolyn S. 1984. "Cemetery churches of the early Byzantine period in Eastern Illyricum: location and martyrs." *GOTR* 29:117–24.

Sodini, Jean-Pierre 1984a. "L'habitat urbain en Grèce à la veille des invasions." In *Villes*, pp. 341–97.

1984b. "La sculpture architecturale à l'époque paléochrétienne en Illyricum." In *Actes X*, pp. 207–98. Vol. I.

1993. "La contribution de l'archéologie à la connaissance du monde byzantin (IV–e–VII–e siècles)." *DOP* 47:139–84.

Sokolova, I. V. 1991. "Vizantiiskie pechati VI-pervoi poloviny IX v. iz Khersonesa." *VV* 52:201–13.

Somogyi, Péter 1987. "Typologie, Chronologie und Herkunft der Maskenbeschläge: zu den archäologischen Hinterlassenschaften osteuropäischer Reiterhirten aus der pontischen Steppe im 6. Jahrhundert." *Archaeologia Austriaca* 71:121–54.

1997. *Byzantinische Fundmünzen der Awarenzeit*. Innsbruck: Universitätsverlag Wagner.

Šonje, Ante 1976. "Ranovizantinska bazilika sv. Agneze u Muntajani Poreština u Istri." *Starinar* 27:53–69.

1976–8. "Ranobizantska bazilika Sv. Agneze u Muntajani kod Poreča." *Jadranski zbornik* 10:189– 236.

Sós, Agnés Cs 1961. "Ujabb avarkori leletek Csepel szigetröl." *ArchÉrt* 88:32–51.

1963. "Bemerkungen zur Frage des archäologischen Nachlasses der awarenzeitlichen Slawen in Ungarn." *SlA* 10:301–29.

1973. "Zur Problematik der Awarenzeit in der neueren ungarischen archäologischen Forschung." In *Berichte*, pp. 85–102. Vol. II.

Sós, Agnés Cs., and Agnés Salamon 1995. *Cemeteries of the Early Middle Ages (6th–9th Centuries AD) at Pókaszepetk*. Budapest: Akadémiai kiadó.

References

Sotiroff, G. 1972. "Did Justinian do it?." *Anthropological Journal of Canada* 10, no. 4:2–7.

Soustal, Peter 1991. *Tabula Imperii Byzantini 6: Thrakien (Thrake, Rodope und Haimimontus)*. Vienna: Verlag der Österreichischen Akademie der Wissenschaften.

Spahiu, Hëna 1976. "La ville haute-médiévale albanaise de Shurdhah (Sarda)." *Iliria* 5:151–67.

Spasovska-Dimitrioska, Gordana 1981–2. "Arkheološki istražuvanja na gradišteto 'Venec' kaj s. Miokazi, Kičevsko." *MAA* 7–8:165–75.

Spaulding, Albert C. 1953. "Statistical techniques for the discovery of artifact types." *AAnt* 18, no. 4:305–13.

———. 1982. "Structure in archeological data: nominal variables." In *Typology*, pp. 1–20.

Speck, Paul 1993. "De miraculis Sancti Demetrii qui Thessalonicam profugus venit." In *Varia IV: Beiträge*, pp. 255–532. Ed. Sofia Kotzabassi and Paul Speck. Bonn: Rudolf Habelt.

Sperber, Daniel 1982. *Essays on Greek and Latin in the Mishna, Talmud and Midrashic Literature*. Jerusalem: Makor.

Spicyn, A. A. 1928. "Drevnosti antov." In *Sbornik statei v chest' akademika Alekseia Ivanovicha Sobolevskogo*, pp. 492–5. Ed. V. N. Peretca. Leningrad: Izdatel'stvo Akademii Nauk SSSR.

Spieser, Jean-Michel 1984a. "La ville en Grèce du III-e au VII-e siècle." In *Villes*, pp. 315–40.

———. 1984b. *Thessalonique et ses monuments du IV-e au VI-e siècle. Contribution à l'étude d'une ville paléochrétienne*. Athens and Paris: Ecole Française d'Athènes and Boccard.

Spiru, I. 1970. "Fibule descoperite în judeţul Teleorman." *RM* 7, no. 6:531.

Srejović, Dragoslav 1986. "Felix Romuliana: carska palata ili? . . . ." *Starinar* 37:87–102.

Srejović, Dragoslav, Anka Lalović, and Đorđe Janković 1980. "Gamzigrad." *Starinar* 31:65–80.

Stahl, Henri H. 1980. *Traditional Romanian Village Communities. The Transition from the Communal to the Capitalist Mode of Production in the Danube Region*. Cambridge and Paris: Cambridge University Press and Editions de la Maison des Sciences de l'Homme.

Staňa, Čenek. 1985. "Mährische Burgwälle im 9. Jahrhundert." In *Die Bayern und ihre Nachbarn. Berichte des Symposiums der Kommission für Frühmittelalterforschung 25. bis 28. Oktober 1982, Stift Zwettl, Niederösterreich*, pp. 157–200. Ed. Herwig Friesinger and Falko Daim. Vol. II. Vienna: Verlag der Österreichischen Akademie der Wissenschaften.

Stancheva, M. 1978. "Sofia au Moyen Age à la lumière de nouvelles études archéologiques." *Byzantinobulgarica* 5:211–28.

Stange-Zhirovova, Nadezhda 1980–1. "Le culte du loup chez les Slaves orientaux d'après les sources folkloriques et ethnographiques." *Slavica Gandensia* 7–8:181–7.

Stark, Miriam T., Jeffery J. Clark, and Mark D. Elson 1995. "Causes and consequences of migration in the 13th century Tonto Basin." *JAA* 14:212–46.

Stavridou-Zafraka, A. 1992. "Slav invasions and the theme organization in the Balkan peninsula." *Vyzantiaka* 12:165–79.

References

Ştefan, Alexandru-Simion 1977. "Nouvelles recherches de photo-interpretation archéologique concernant la défense de la Scythie Mineure." In *Akten 11*, pp. 451–65.

Ştefan, Gheorghe 1967. "Tomis et Toméa. A propos des luttes entre Byzantins et Avares à la fin du VI-e siècle de notre ère." *Dacia* 11:253–8.

1968, "Le problème de la continuité sur le territoire de la Dacie." *Dacia* 12:347–54.

Ştefan, Gheorghe, Ioan Barnea, and Bucur Mitrea 1962. "Şantierul arheologic Garvăn (Dinogetia)(r. Măcin, reg. Galaţi)." *MCA* 8:675–92.

Stefanov, Stefan 1974. "Novgrad. Starinni selishta." *IBAI* 34:250–311.

Stehli, Petar, and Andreas Zimmermann 1980. "Zur Analyse neolithischer Gefäßformen." *Archäo-Physika* 7:147–77.

Stein, Ernest 1968. *Histoire du Bas-Empire*, vol. II. Amsterdam: Adolf M. Hakkert.

Steinberger, L. 1920. "Wandalen=Wenden." *Archiv für Slavische Philologie* 37:116–22.

Steindorff, Ludwig 1985. "Wölfisches Heulen. Ein Motiv in mittelalterlichen slavischen Quellen." *Byzantinoslavica* 46, no. 1:40–9.

Stevović, Ivan 1991. "New cognizance on early Byzantine Dubrovnik in the 6th century." *Starinar* 42:141–51.

Stoliarik, E. S. 1992. *Essays on Monetary Circulation in the North-Western Black Sea Region in the Late Roman and Byzantine Periods (Late 3rd Century–Early 13th Century AD)*. Odessa: Polis.

Strauß, Ernst-Günther 1992. *Studien zur Fibeltracht der Merowingerzeit*. Bonn: Rudolf Habelt.

Strumins'kyj, Bohdan 1979–80. "Were the Antes Eastern Slavs?." *Harvard Ukrainian Studies* 3–4:786–96.

Šturms, Eduard 1950. "Zur ethnischen Deutung der 'masurgermanischen' Kultur." *Archaeologia Geographica* 1:20–2.

Sukhobokov, O. V. 1975. *Slaviane Dneprovskogo Levoberezh'ia (Romenskaia kul'tura i ee predshestvenniki)*. Kiev: Naukova Dumka.

Sukhobokov, O. V., and S. P. Iurenko 1978. "Etnokul'turnye processy na territorii levoberezhnoi Ukraine v I tysiacheletiia n.e." In *Problemy*, pp. 124–42.

Sulimirski, Tadeusz 1973. "Die Veneti-Venedae und deren Verhältnis zu den Slawen." In *Berichte*, pp. 381–7. Vol. II.

Surowiecki, Wawrzyniec 1964. *Śledzenie początku narodów słowiańskich*. Wrocław: Zaklad narodowy im. Ossolińskich.

Susini, Giancarlo 1982. "Ratiaria capitale." In *Miscellanea Agostino Pertusi*, pp. 235–9. Vol. II. Bologna: Patron.

Sverdlov, M. B. 1977. "Obshchestvennyi stroi slavian v VI-nachale VII veka." *SovS* 3:46–59.

Svoboda, Bedřich 1953. "Poklad byzantského kovotepce v Zemianskem Vrbovku." *PA* 44:33–108.

Swietosławski, Witold 1993. "Die Elemente der fernöstlichen Bewaffnung im früh-mittelalterlichen West-und Mitteleuropa." In *Actes XIIb*, pp. 282–4. Vol. IV.

Swoboda, Roksanda M. 1986. "Zu spätantiken Bronzeschnallen mit festem, dreieck-igem Beschlag." *Germania* 64:91–103.

Swoboda, Wincenty 1970. "O wiarygodności przekazu powieści dorocznej o Obrach." *SlA* 17:73–91.

Symonovich, E. O. 1969. "Dva rann'oseredn'ovichnikh poselennia na Chernigivshchini." In *Starozhitnosti*, pp. 87–92.

References

1975. "Rannesrednevekovaia kul'tura lesnoi polosy Podneprov'ia (tipa Kolochin-Akatovo) i ee mesto v slavianskom etnogeneze." *SlA* 22:17–28.

Szábo, János Gyözö 1965. "Az Egri múzeum avarkori emlékanyaga I. Kora-avarkori sírleletek tarnaméráról." *Agria* 3:29–71.

Szábo, József J., and Istvan Vörös 1979. "Gepida lelöhelyek Battonya határában." *ArchErt* 106:218–30.

Szádeczky-Kardoss, Samuel 1985. "Bemerkungen über den 'Quaestor Iustinianus exercitus'. Zur Frage der Vorstufen der Themenverfassung." In *Eirene*, pp. 61–4.

1986a. *Avarica. Über die Awarengeschichte und ihre Quellen*. Szeged: University of Szeged Press.

1986b. "Die Nachricht des Isidorus Hispalensis und des spanischen Fortsetzers seiner 'Historia' über einen Slaweneinfall in Griechenland." In *Szlávok, Protobolgárok, Bizánc*, pp. 51–61. Ed. Nino Nikolov, Samu Szádeczky-Kardoss, and Terézia Olajos. Szeged: József Attila University Press.

1991. "Vernachlässigte Quellenangaben zur Geschichte des ersten awarischen Khaganates." In *Varia Eurasiatica. Festschrift für Professor András Róna-Tas*, pp. 171–82. Szeged: Department of Altaic Studies.

Szafran-Szadkowska, Lucyna 1983. *Zagadnienie etnogenezy słowian w historiografii polskiej w okresie od sredniowiecza do konca XIX stulecia*. Opole: Wyzsza Szkola Pedagogiczna im. Powstancóv Śląskich.

Szatmári, S. 1980. "Das Gräberfeld von Oroszlány und seine Stelle in der frühawarenzeitlichen Metallkunst." *ActaArchHung* 32:97–116.

Székely, Zoltán 1974–6. "Aşezări din secolele VI–IX e. n. în sud-estul Transilvaniei." *Aluta* 6–7:35–78.

1975. "Aşezarea prefeudală de la Sălaşuri (com. Veţca, jud. Mureş)." *Marisia* 5:71–80.

1992. "Aşezări din secolele VI–XI p. Ch. în bazinul Oltului superior." *SCIV* 43, no. 2:245–306.

Szentpéteri, J. 1993a. "Archäologische Studien zur Schicht der Waffenträger des Awarentums im Karpatenbecken I." *ActaArchHung* 45:165–246.

1993b. "Die oberste Führungsschicht des awarenzeitlichen Heeres im Spiegel der archäologischen Quellen." In *Actes XIIb*, pp. 261–70. Vol. IV.

Szőke, Béla Miklós 1995. "Avari e Slavi." In *Avari*, pp. 49–55.

Szydłowski, Jerzy 1980. "Zur Anwesenheit der Westslawen an der mittleren Donau im ausgehenden 5. und 6. Jahrhundert." In *Donau*, pp. 233–7.

Szynkiewicz, Slawoj 1990. "Mythologized representations in Soviet thinking on the nationalities problem." *Anthropology Today* 6, no. 2:2–5.

Tăpkova-Zaimova, Vasilka 1964. "Sur quelques aspects de la colonisation slave en Macédoine et en Grèce." *EB* 1:111–23.

1974. "Slavianskite zaselvaniia na Balkanskiia poluostrov v ramkite na 'varvarskite' nashestviia prez VI i VII v." *IBID* 29:199–207.

Tăpkova-Zaimova, Vasilka, and Mikhail Voinov 1965. "La politique de Byzance dans ses rapports avec les 'Barbares'." *EH* 2:32–46.

Taylor, Timothy 1993. "Conversations with Leo Klejn." *CAnth* 34, no. 5:723–35.

Teall, John L. 1965. "The barbarians in Justinian's armies." *Speculum* 40:294–322.

Tebbetts, Diane 1984. "Food as an ethnic marker." *Pioneer America Society Transactions* 7:81–8.

References

Tejral, Jaroslav 1975. "K langobardském odkazu v archeologických pramenech na území Československa." *SlovArch* 23:379–446.

1990. "K chronologii spon z langobardských pohřebišt v Podunají." In *Praveké*, pp. 231–50.

Tel'nov, N. P. 1985. "Ranneslavianskie poseleniia Gordineshti I i Corpachi." In *Issledovaniia*, pp. 91–105.

1991. "Slavianskie zhilishcha VI–X vv. Dnestrovsko-Prutskogo mezdurech'ia." In *Drevnosti Iugo-Zapada SSSR*, pp. 145–66. Ed. P. P. Byrnia. Kishinew: Shtiinca.

Tel''nov, N. P., and T. F. Riaboi 1985. "Novye dannye o ranneslavianskom poselenii u s. Gansk." In *Issledovaniia*, pp. 105–17.

Teodor, Dan Gh 1970. "Şantierul arheologic Suceava." *MCA* 9:375–82.

1971. "Descoperiri din sec. VI–VII e.n. de la Iaşi-Crucea lui Ferenţ." *Cercetări istorice* 2:119–28.

1972. "La pénétration des Slaves dans les régions du sud-est de l'Europe d'après les données archéologiques des régions orientales de la Roumanie." *Balcanoslavica* 1:29–42.

1980. *The East-Carpathian Area of Romania in the V–XI Centuries AD.* Oxford: BAR.

1984a. *Civilizaţia romanică la est de Carpaţi în secolele V–VII (aşezarea de la Botoşana-Suceava).* Bucharest: Editura Academiei RSR.

1984b. *Continuitatea populaţiei autohtone la est de Carpaţi. Aşezările din secolele VI–XI e.n. de la Dodeşti- Vaslui.* Iaşi: Junimea.

1991. *Creştinismul la est de Carpaţi de la origini şi pînă în secolul al XVI-lea.* Iaşi: Junimea.

1992. "Fibule 'digitate' din secolele VI–VII în spaţiul carpato-dunăreano-pontic." *AM* 15:119–52.

Teodor, Eugen S. 1996. *Sistemul Compas. Studiu de morfologie analitică numerică, aplicat ceramicii uzuale din perioada de migraţie a slavilor.* Bucharest: Muzeul Naţional de Istorie a României.

Teodor, Silvia 1975. "Săpăturile de la Cucorăni (jud. Botoşani)." *AM* 8: 148–209.

1978. "Săpăturile arheologice de la Budeni, com. Dolhasca (jud. Suceava)." *Suceava* 5:141–59.

Teodorescu, Victor 1971. "O nouă cultură arheologică recent precizată în ţara noastră, cultura Ipoteşti-Cîndeşti (sec. V–VII)." In *Sesiunea de Comunicări ştiinţifice a muzeelor de istorie, dec. 1964*, pp. 104–30. Vol. 2. Bucharest.

1972. "Centre meşteşugăreşti din sec. V/VI–VII în Bucureşti." *BMIM* 9:73–99.

Terpilovskii, R. V. 1984. *Rannie slaviane Podesen'ia III–V vv.* Kiev: Naukova Dumka.

1992. "The Slavs of the Dnieper Basin in the migration period." In *Medieval Europe 1992. Death and Burial*, pp. 161–6. Vol. IV. York: Medieval Europe 1992.

1994. "Praslov'ians'ky starozhitnosty skhidnoi Evropi. Perspektivi poshuku." In *Zbirnyk*, pp. 73–9.

Tettamanti, S. 1980. "Der awarische Grabfund von Dany." *ActaArchHung* 32:153–60.

Theodorescu, Dinu 1963. "L'édifice romano-byzantin de Callatis." *Dacia* 7:257–300.

Thomas, Edith B. 1988. "Spätantike und frühbyzantinische Silbergegenstände im mittleren Donaugebiet, innerhalb und außerhalb der Grenzen des Römerreiches." In *Argenterie*, pp. 135–51.

Timoshchuk, B. A. 1978. "Slavianskie poseleniia VI–VII vv. v severnoi Bukovine." In *Rus'*, pp. 186–91.

References

1985. "Social'naia tipologiia selishch VI–X vv." In *Issledovaniia*, pp. 3–24.

1990a. "Ob issledovanii vostochnoslavianskikh poselenii VI–IX vv." In *Problemy izucheniia drevnikh poselenii v arkheologii (sociologicheskii aspekt)*, pp. 128–49. Ed. V. I. Guliaev and G. F. Afanas'ev. Moscow: Institut Arkheologii Akademii Nauk SSSR.

1990b. *Vostochnoslavianskaia obshchina VI–X vv. n.e.* Moscow: Nauka.

Timoshchuk, B. A., I. P. Rusanova, and L. P. Mikhailina 1981. "Itogi izucheniia slavianskikh pamiatnikov Severnoi Bukoviny V–X vv." *SA* 2:80–93.

Timoshchuk, B. O., and O. M. Prikhodniuk 1969. "Rann'oslov'ians'ky pam'iatki VI–VII st. v seredn'omu Podnystrov'i." In *Starozhitnosti*, pp. 71–9.

Tirpaková, Anna, and Ivona Vlkolinská 1992. "The application of some mathematical-statistical methods for the analysis of Slavic pottery." In *Computer Applications and Quantitative Methods in Archaeology 1991*, pp. 183–6. Ed. Gary Lock and John Moffett. Oxford: BAR.

Tishkov, Valery A. 1994. "Inventions and manifestations of ethno-nationalism in Soviet academic and public discourse." In *Assessing Cultural Anthropology*, pp. 443–53. Ed. Robert Borofsky, B. Dobson, and M. Jarrett. New York: McGraw-Hill.

Todorova, Maria 1993. *Balkan Family Structure and the European Pattern: Demographic Developments in Ottoman Bulgaria*. Washington and Lanham: American University Press.

Tolstov, S. P. 1935. "Voiennaia demokratiia i problema 'geneticheskoi revolucii'." In *Lenin i osnovnye problemy doklassovogo obshchestva*, pp. 203–15. Ed. S. N. Bykovskii. Moscow: Izdatel'stvo Akademii Nauk SSSR.

Tomás, Vojtech 1984. *Česká historiografie a pozitivismus. Svetonázorové a metodologické aspekty*. Prague: Academia.

Tomičić, Željko 1986–7. "Novija ranosrednjovjekovna istraživanja odjela za arheologiju." *Prilozi* 3–4:141–73.

1988–9. "Arheološka svejdočanstva o ranobizantskom vojnom graditeljstvu na sjevernojadranskim otočima." *Prilozi* 5–6:29–53.

Tomka, Péter 1980. "Das germanische Gräberfeld aus dem 6. Jahrhundert in Fertöszentmiklós." *ActaArchHung* 32:5–30.

1995. "Il costume." In *Avari*, pp. 81–91.

Torbatov, Sergei 1997. "Quaestura exercitus: Moesia Secunda and Scythia under Justinian." *ArchBulg* 1, no. 3:78–87.

Toropu, Octavian 1976. *Romanitatea tîrzie şi străromânii în Dacia traiană subcarpatică*. Craiova: Scrisul Românesc.

Tóth, Elvira H., and Attila Horváth 1992. *Kunbábony. Das Grab eines Awarenkhagans*. Kécskemét: Museumdirektion der Selbstverwaltung des Komitats Bács-Kiskun.

Tóth, T. 1967. "Észak-dunántul avarkori népességének embertani problémái." *Arrabona* 9:55–65.

Townsend, Joan B. 1985. "The autonomous village and the development of chiefdoms." In *Development*, pp. 141–55.

Travlos, J., and A. Frantz 1965. "The church of St. Dionysios the Areopagite and the palace of the archbishop of Athens in the 16th century." *Hesperia* 34, no. 3:157–202.

Třeštík, Dušan 1996. "Příchod prvních slovanů do českých zemí v letech 510–535." *Český Časopis Historický* 94:241–62.

441

References

Tret'iakov, P. N. 1971. "Chto takoe 'Pastyrskaia kul'tura'?." *SA* 4:102–13.

———. 1974. "Drevnosti vtoroi i tret'ei chetvertei I tys. n.e. v verkhnem i srednem Podesen'e." In *Drevnosti*, pp. 40–118.

Trigger, Bruce G. 1970. "Settlement patterns in archaeology." In *Introductory Readings in Archaeology*, pp. 237–262. Ed. Brian M. Fagan. Boston: Little, Brown & Co.

———. 1989. *A History of Archaeological Thought*. Cambridge: Cambridge University Press.

Trombley, Frank R. 1985. "Monastic foundations in sixth-century Anatolia and their role in the social and economic life of the countryside." *GOTR* 30, no. 1:45–59.

Trubachev, O. N. 1985. "Linguistics and ethnogenesis of the Slavs: the ancient Slavs as evidenced by etymology and onomastics." *JIES* 13, nos. 1–2:203–56.

———. 1991. *Etnogenez i kul'tura drevneishikh slavian. Lingvisticheskie issledovaniia*. Moscow: Nauka.

Tschauner, Hartmut W. W. 1985. "La tipología: herramienta u obstáculo? La clasificación de artefactos en arqueología." *Boletín de Antropología Americana* 12:39–74.

Tudor, D. 1965. *Sucidava. Une cité daco-romaine et byzantine en Dacie*. Brussels: Latomus.

Tudor, Dumitru, Octavian Toropu, Constantin Tătulea, and Marin Nica 1980. "Şantierul arheologic Sucidava-Corabia." *MCA* 14:357–63.

Tudor, Ersilia, and Ion Chicideanu 1977. "Săpăturile arheologice de la Brăteştii de Sus, judeţul Dîmboviţa." *Valachica* 9:119–51.

Tuleshkov, Nikola 1988. *Arkhitektura na bălgarskite manastiri*. Sofia: BAN.

Turcu, Mioara 1992a. "Descoperiri arheologice la Militari-Cîmpul Boja (Bucureşti), secolele II–III şi VI." *CAB* 4:37–55.

———. 1992b. "Şantierul arheologic la Mihăileşti. Sondaj arheologic în situl Poşta-Buturugeni." *CAB* 4:229–40.

Turcu, Mioara, and Radu Ciuceanu 1992. "Săpături arheologice pe Dealul Văcăreşti." *CAB* 4:196–204.

Turcu, Mioara, and C. Marinescu 1968. "Consideraţii privind 'Foişorul Mavrocordaţilor'." *BMIM* 6:119–29.

Turlej, Stanislaw 1997. "Was Monemvasia founded in the times of Justinian I?." *Byzantinoslavica* 58:405–12.

———. 1998. "The so-called Chronicle of Monemvasia. A historical analysis." *Byzantion* 68:446–68.

Tvengsberg, Per Martin 1991. "Slash-and-burn cultivation as a supposition for migratory subsistence: Finnish agriculture and ethnicity in Scandinavia and the Delaware valley." *New Jersey Folklife* 16:14–18.

Tyszkiewicz, Lech A. 1989. "Problem zależności Słowian od Awarów w VI–VII wieku." *Balcanica* 4:95–108.

Udolph, Jürgen 1979. *Studien zu slavischen Gewässernamen und Gewässerbezeichnungen. Ein Beitrag zur Frage der Urheimat der Slaven*. Heidelberg: C. Winter.

Uenze, Syna 1966. "Die Schnallen mit Riemenschlaufe aus dem 6. und 7. Jahrhundert." *BV* 31:142–81.

———. 1974. "Gegossene Fibeln mit Scheinumwicklung des Bügels in den östlichen Balkanprovinzen." In *Festschrift*, pp. 483–94. Vol. II.

References

1992. *Die spätantiken Befestigungen von Sadovec. Ergebnisse der deutsch-bulgarisch-österreichischen Ausgrabungen 1934–1937*. Munich: C. H. Beck.

Ugrin, E. 1987. *Le trésor de Zalésie*. Louvain-la-Neuve: Département d'archéologie et d'histoire de l'art.

Urbańczyk, Przemysław 1977. "Geneza wczesnośredniowiecznych metalowych pochew broni białej ze stanowisk kultury pruskiej." *Przeglad Archeologiczny* 25:107–45.

Urciuoli, Bonnie 1995. "Language and borders." *ARA* 24:525–46.

Vagalinski, Ljudmil F. 1994. "Zur Frage der ethnischen Herkunft der späten Strahlenfibeln (Finger- oder Bügelfibeln) aus dem Donau-Karpaten-Becken (M. 6.-7. Jh.)." *ZfA* 28:261–305.

Vaklinova, Margarita 1984. "Ateliers de décoration architecturale au Ve et VIe siècle dans la région de Nicopolis ad Nestum (Bulgarie)." In *Actes X*, pp. 61–649. Vol. II.

1989. "Pogrebeniia ot perioda na velikoto preselenie pri Pleven." In *Istoriia*, pp. 129–42.

Vakulenko, L. V. 1983. "Poselenie pozdnerimskogo vremeni u s. Sokol i nekotorye voprosy slavianskogo etnogeneza." In *Dnestr*, pp. 155–80.

Vakulenko, L. V., and O. M. Prikhodniuk 1984. *Slavianskie poseleniia I tys. n.e. u s. Sokol na Srednem Dnestre*. Kiev: Naukova Dumka.

1985. "Problema preemstvennosti cherniakhovskikh i rannesrednevekovykh drevnostei v svete novykh issledovanii na srednem Dnestre." *SlovArch* 33, no. 1:71–136.

Vallet, Françoise 1995. "Une tombe de riche cavalier lombard découverte à Castel Trosino." In *Noblesse*, pp. 335–49.

Váňa, Zdenek 1983. *The World of the Ancient Slavs*. Detroit: Wayne State University Press.

Van Der Leeuw, S. E. 1994. "Cognitive aspects of 'technique'." In *The Ancient Mind. Elements of Cognitive Archaeology*, pp. 135–42. Ed. Colin Renfrew and Ezra B. W. Zubrow. Cambridge: Cambridge University Press.

Van Doorninck, F. H. Jr 1989. "The cargo amphoras on the 7-th century Yassi Ada and 11-th century Serçe Liman shipwrecks: two examples of a reuse of Byzantine amphoras as transport jars." In *Recherches*, pp. 247–57.

Várady, L. 1976. "Jordanes-Studien. Jordanes und das Chronicon des Marcellinus Comes. Die Selbständigkeit des Jordanes." *Chiron* 6:441–87.

Vareka, Pavel 1994. "Customs and rites connected with the building process of a rural house and its importance for the study of archaic notions of space and landscape." In *Mediaevalia Archaeologica Bohemica 1993*, pp. 139–44. Ed. Jan Fridrich, Jan Klápště, and Pavel Vareka. Prague: Institute of Archaeology.

Varsik, Vladimír 1992. "Byzantinische Gürtelschnallen im mittleren und unteren Donauraum im 6. und 7. Jahrhundert." *SlovArch* 40, no. 1:77–103.

Vašić, Miloje 1982-3. "Čezava – Castrum Novae." *Starinar* 32-3:91–122.

1990. "Čezava-Castrum Novae. La stratigraphie, la chronologie et les phases architectoniques." In *Akten 14*, pp. 897–911.

1994-5. "Le limes protobyzantin dans la province de Mésie Première." *Starinar* 45-6:41–53.

1999. "Transdrobeta (Pontes) in the Late Antiquity." In *Limes*, pp. 33–7.

References

Vašić, Miloje, and Vladimir Kondić 1986. "Le limes romain et paléobyzantin des Portes de Fer." In *Akten 13*, pp. 542–60.

Vasil'ev, A. 1898. "Slaviane v' Grecii." *VV* 5:404–38, 626–70.

Vasil'ev, M. A. 1992. "Sleduet li nachinat' ethnicheskuiu istoriiu slavian s 512 goda?." *SovS* 1:3–20.

Vasilev, Radoslav 1979. "Prouchvaniiata na slavianskite arkheologicheski pametnici ot Severna Bălgariia ot kraia na VI do kraia na X v." *Arkheologiia* 21, no. 3:12–22.

Văzharova, Zhivka 1964. "Slavianite na iug ot Dunava (po arkheologicheski danni)." *Arkheologiia* 6, no. 2:23–33.

1968. "Pamiatniki Bolgarii konca VI–XI v. i ikh etnicheskaia prinadlezhnosti." *SA* 3:148–59.

1971. "Slaviani i prabălgari (tiurko-bălgari) v svetlinata na arkheologicheskite danni." *Arkheologiia* 13, no. 1:1–23.

1973. "Slaviane i prabolgary v sviazi s voprosom sredizemnomorskoi kul'tury." In *Slavianite*, pp. 239–66.

1986. *Srednovekovnoto selishte s. Garvăn, Silistrenski okrăg (VI–XV v.)*. Sofia: BAN.

Veh, Otto 1951. *Zur Geschichtsschreibung und Weltauffassung des Prokop von Caesarea*. Bayreuth: Gymnasium.

Veimarn, E. V. 1958. "Oboronitel'nye sooruzheniia Eski-Kermena." In *Istoriia i arkheologiia srednevekovogo Kryma*, pp. 7–54. Ed. A. P. Smirnov. Moscow: Izdatel'stvo Akademii Nauk SSSR.

Veimarn, E. V., and A. I. Aibabin 1993. *Skalistinskii mogil'nik*. Kiev: Naukova Dumka.

Veit, Ulrich 1989. "Ethnic concepts of German prehistory: a case study on the relationship between cultural identity and archaeological objectivity." In *Approaches*, pp. 35–56.

Vékony, Gábor 1973. "A koraavarkori keramikatípusok történeti topográfiájához." *ArchÉrt* 100:211–34.

Velkov, Velizar 1962. "Les campagnes et la population rurale en Thrace au IV–e–VI–e siècles." *Byzantinobulgarica* 1:31–60.

1977. *Cities in Thrace and Dacia in Late Antiquity*. Amsterdam: Adolf M. Hakkert.

1983. "La Thrace et la Mésie inférieure pendant l'époque de la Basse Antiquité (IV–VI ss.)." In *Bulgaria*, pp. 177–93.

1985. "Frühbyzantinische Inschriften aus Dacia Ripensis." *Vyzantina* 13:886–91.

1987. "Der Donaulimes in Bulgarien und das Vordringen der Slawen." In *Völker* pp. 141–69.

1991. "Sofia zwischen Antike und Mittelalter." In *Frühgeschichte der europäischen Stadt. Voraussetzungen und Grundlagen*, pp. 92–6. Ed. H. Brachmann and J. Herrmann. Berlin: Akademie Verlag.

1992. "Mesembria zwischen dem 4. und dem 8. Jahrhundert." In *Schwarzmeerküste*, pp. 19–22.

Velkov, Velizar, and Stefan Lisikov 1994. "An early Byzantine and mediaeval fort in the Haemus with an inscription and grafitti of emperor Anastasius." In *Sbornik*, pp. 257–65.

Velychenko, Stephen 1992. "The origins of the official Soviet interpretation of Eastern Slavic history: a case study of policy formulation." In *Beiträge zur 6. internationalen Konferenz zur altrussischen Geschichte*, pp. 221–53. Wiesbaden: Otto Harrassowitz.

References

1993. *Shaping Identity in Eastern Europe and Russia. Soviet-Russian and Polish Accounts of Ukrainian History 1914–1991*. New York: St Martin's Press.

Verdery, Katherine 1994. "Ethnicity, nationalism, and state-making. 'Ethnic groups and boundaries': past and future." In *Anthropology*, pp. 33–58.

Vergote, J. 1972. "Folterwerkzeuge." In *Reallexikon für Antike und Christentum. Sachwörterbuch zur Auseinandersetzung des Christentums mit der antiken Welt*, pp. 112–41. Ed. Theodor Klauser. Vol. VII. Stuttgart: Anton Hiersemann.

Verlinden, Charles 1937. "L'origine de *sclavus*=esclave." *Bulletin Du Cange* 17:97–128.

Vickers, Michael 1971. "The stadium at Thessaloniki." *Byzantion* 41:339–48.

1974. "The late Roman walls of Thessalonica", in *Congress 8*, pp. 249–55.

Vida, Tivadar 1990–1. "Chronologie und Verbreitung einiger awarenzeitlichen Keramiktypen." *Antaeus* 20–1:131–44.

1992. "Zu einigen handgeformten frühawarischen Keramiktypen und ihre östlichen Beziehungen." In *Awarenforschungen*, pp. 517–77. Vol. II.

1993. "Zur Frage der byzantinischen Traditionen der awarenzeitlichen Keramik." In *Actes XIIb*, pp. 279–82. Vol. IV.

1995. "La ceramica." In *Avari*, pp. 103–11.

1999. *Die awarenzeitliche Keramik I. (6.–7. Jh.)*. Berlin and Budapest: Balassi Kiadó.

Vîlceanu, D., and Alexandru Barnea 1975. "Ceramica lucrată cu mîna din aşezarea romano-bizantină de la Piatra Frecăţei (sec. VI e.n.)." *SCIV* 26, no. 2:209–18.

Vinokur, Ion Srulevich 1980. "Cherniakhovskie tradicii i pamiatnikakh prediny i tret'ei chetverti I tysiacheletiia n.e. lesostepnogo Dnestro-Dneprovskogo mezhdurech'ia." In *Rapports*, pp. 867–77. Vol. II.

1994. "Persha livarna forma dlia pal'chastikh fibul." In *Zbirnyk* pp. 23–7.

Vinokur, I. S., and O. M. Prikhodniuk 1974. "Ranneslavianskoe poselenie na r. Smotrich." In *Drevnosti*, pp. 227–41.

Vinski, Zdenko 1957. "Arheološki spomenici velike seobe naroda u Srijemu." *Situla* 2:1–54.

1967. "Kasnoantički starosjedioci u Salonitanskoj regiji prema arheološkoj ostavštini predslavenskog supstrata." *VAHD* 69:5–98.

1968. "Krstoliki nakit epohe seobe naroda u Jugoslaviji." *VAMZ* 3:103–66.

1970. "Zur Datierung einiger Kleinfunde aus späten salonitanischen Gräber", in *Adriatica praehistorica et antiqua. Zbornik radova posvećen Grgi Novak*, pp. 699–703. Ed. Vladimir Mirosavljević, Duje Rendić-Miočević, and Mate Suić. Zagreb: Arheološki Institut.

1971. "Haut Moyen Age." In *Epoque préhistorique et protohistorique en Yougoslavie – Recherches et résultats*, pp. 375–97. Ed. Grga Novak et al. Belgrade: Société archéologique de Yougoslavie.

1982. "Sljem epohe seobe naroda naden u Sinju." *SP* 12:7–34.

Vladimirova, Dochka 1985. "Ekzagii ot Dolna Miziia." *Numizmatika* 9, no. 1:22–31.

Vlasenko, I. G. 1985. "Raskopki poselenii Ivancha II i Braneshti III." In *Issledovaniia*, pp. 141–52.

Vlassa, Nicolae et al. 1966. "Săpăturile arheologice de la Iernut." *AMN* 3:399–410.

Voinov, Mikhail. 1956. "Za prviia dopir na Asparukhovite bălgari i slavianite i za datata na osnovanieto na bălgarska dărzhava." *IIBI* 6:453–8.

Vojtěchovská, Ivana, and Ivana Pleinerová 1997. "Polozemnice z období stěhování národů z Libčic n.Vlt-Chýnova, okr. Praha-západ." *ArchRoz* 49, no. 1:28–32.

References

Voronov, Iu N., and O. Kh. Bgazhba 1987. "Krepost' Cibilium odin iz uzlov Kavkazskogo limesa Iustinianovskoi epokhi." VV 48:116–32.

Vryonis, Speros 1981. "The evolution of Slavic society and the Slavic invasions in Greece. The first major Slavic attack on Thessaloniki, AD 597." *Hesperia* 50:378–90.

1992. "The Slavic pottery (jars) from Olympia, Greece." In *Byzantine Studies. Essays on the Slavic World and the Eleventh Century*, pp. 15–42. Ed. Speros Jr Vryonis. New Rochelle, N.Y.: Aristide D. Caratzas.

Vuga, Davorin 1980. "A study of burying methods in the period of the Great Migration (5th to 6th Century) in the South-Eastern Alpine and Cisalpine world." *Balcanoslavica* 9:17–25.

Wachtel, K. 1974. "Zum gegenwärtigen Forschungsstand der Kastellgrabung Iatrus." In *Actes IX*, pp. 137–41.

Wagner, Norbert 1967. *Getica. Untersuchungen zum Leben des Jordanes und zur frühen Geschichte der Goten*. Berlin: Walter de Gruyter.

Wahle, Ernest 1941. *Zur ethnischen Deutung frühgeschichtlicher Kulturprovinzen. Grenzen der frühgeschichtlichen Erkenntnis*, vol. I. Heidelberg: C. Winter.

Waldbaum, Jane C. 1983. *Metalwork from Sardis: The Finds through 1974*. Cambridge and London: Harvard University Press.

Waldmüller, Lothar 1976. *Die ersten Begegnungen der Slawen mit dem Christentum und den christlichen Völkern vom VI. bis VIII. Jahrhundert*. Amsterdam: Adolf M. Hakkert.

Wason, Paul K. 1994. *The Archaeology of Rank*. Cambridge: Cambridge University Press.

Watson, George R. 1969. *The Roman Soldier*. Ithaca: Cornell University Press.

Watson, Patty Jo 1995. "Archaeology, anthropology, and the culture concept." *AJA* 97, no. 4:683–94.

Webster, David 1975. "Warfare and the evolution of the state: a reconsideration." *AAnt* 40, no. 4:464–70.

Weiser, Wolfram 1985. "Neue byzantinische Kleimünzen aus Blei." *Schweizerische Münzblätter* 35, no. 140:13–16.

Weiss, Günther, and Anastasios Katsanakis 1988. *Das Ethnikon Sklabenoi, Sklaboi in den griechischen Quellen bis 1025*. Stuttgart: Franz Steiner Verlag.

Weithmann, Michael W. 1978. *Die slavische Bevölkerung auf der griechischen Halbinsel. Ein Beitrag zur historischen Ethnographie Südosteuropas*. Munich: Rudolf Trofenil.

Wendel, Michael 1986. "Die mittelalterliche Siedlungen." In *Iatrus*, pp. 27–207. Vol. III.

1987. "Razkopki na obekt 'Karasura' do s. Rupkite, Starozagorski okrǎg." In *Dokladi*, pp. 200–4.

1992. "Die Gemarkung Kaleto des Dorfes Rupkite bei Čirpan (Bulgarien) im Mittelalter." *ZfA* 26:279–99.

Wenskus, Richard 1961. *Stammesbildung und Verfassung. Das Werden der frühmittelalterlichen Gentes*. Cologne: Böhlau.

Werner, Joachim 1935. *Münzdatierte austrasische Grabfunde*. Berlin: Walter de Gruyter.

1950. "Slawische Bügelfibeln des 7. Jahrhunderts." In *Reinecke Festschrift zum 75. Geburtstag von Paul Reinecke am 25. September 1947*, pp. 150–72. Ed. G. Behrens. Mainz: E. Schneider.

References

1953. *Slawische Bronzefiguren aus Nordgriechenland*. Berlin: Akademie Verlag.

1955. "Byzantinische Gürtelschnallen des 6. und 7. Jahrhunderts aus der Sammlung Diergardt." *KJVF* 1:36–48.

1956. *Beiträge zur Archäologie des Attila-Reiches*. Munich: Verlag der Bayerischen Akademie der Wissenschaften.

1960. "Neues zur Frage der slawischen Bügelfibeln aus süd-osteuropäischen Ländern." *Germania* 38:114–20.

1962. *Die Langobarden in Pannonien. Beiträge zur Kenntnis der langobardischen Bodenfunde vor 568*. Munich: Verlag der Bayerischen Akademie der Wissenschaften.

1970. "Zur Verbreitung frühgeschichtlicher Metallarbeiten (Werkstatt-Wanderhandwerk-Handel-Familienverbindung)." *Antikvariskt Arkiv* 38:65–81.

1974. "Nomadische Gürtel bei Persern, Byzantinern und Langobarden." In *Atti del convegno internazionale sul tema: La civiltà dei Langobardi in Europa (Roma, 24–26 maggio 1971)(Cividale del Friuli, 27–28 maggio 1971)*, pp. 109–39. Rome: Accademia Nazionale dei Lincei.

1977. "Der Grabfund von Taurapilis, Rayon Utna (Litauen) und die Verbindung der Balten zum Reich Theoderichs." In *Archäologische Beiträge zur Chronologie der Völkerwanderungszeit*, pp. 87–92. Ed. G. Kossack and J. Reichstein. Bonn: Rudolf Habelt.

1984a. *Der Grabfund von Malaja Pereščepina und Kuvrat, Kagan der Bulgaren*. Munich: Verlag der Bayerischen Akademie der Wissenschaften.

1984b. "Zu den Bügelfibeln aus den völkerwanderungszeitlichen Brandgräberfeldern Masuriens." *Germania* 62, no. 1:74–7.

1988. *Adelsgräber von Niederstotzingen bei Ulm und von Bokchondong in Südkorea: Jenseitsvorstellungen vor Rezeption von Christentum und Buddhismus im Lichte vergleichender Archäologie*. Munich: C. H. Beck.

1991. "Expertise zu dem Bronzearmring mit verdickten Enden und Perlleisten von Bratislava-Dubravka." *SlovArch* 39, no. 1–2:287–8.

1992. "Golemanovo Kale und Sadovsko Kale: Kritische Zusammenfassung der Grabungsergebnisse." In Uenze 1992, pp. 391–417.

Werner, Michael 1986. "The Moesian limes and the imperial mining districts." In *Akten 13*, pp. 561–4.

Werner, Robert 1980. "Zur Herkunft der Anten. Ein ethnisches und soziales Problem der Spätantike." *Kölner Historische Abhandlungen* 28:573–95.

Wessely, C. 1889. "Die Pariser Papyri des Fundes von El-Faijum." *Denkschriften der kaiserlichen Akademie der Wissenschaften. Philosophisch-historische Classe* 37:97–256.

Westerink, L. G. 1972. "Marginalia by Arethas in Moskow Greek Ms. 231." *Byzantion* 42:241–2.

Whallon, Robert 1982. "Variables and dimensions: the critical step in quantitative typology." In *Typology*, pp. 127–61.

Whitby, L. M. 1982a. "The Great Chronographer and Theophanes." *BMGS* 8:1–20.

1982b. "Theophylact's knowledge of languages." *Byzantion* 52:425–8.

1983. "Theophanes' chronicle source for the reigns of Justin II, Tiberius and Maurice (AD 565–602)." *Byzantion* 53:312–45.

1985a. "Justinian's bridge over the Sangarius and the date of Procopius' 'De aedificiis'." *Journal of Hellenic Studies* 105:129–48.

References

1985b. "The Long Walls of Constantinople." *Byzantion* 55:560–83.

1988. *The Emperor Maurice and his Historian: Theophylact Simocatta on Persian and Balkan Warfare*. Oxford: Clarendon Press.

Whitby, Michael, and Mary Whitby 1986. *The History of Theophylact Simocatta. An English Translation with Introduction and Notes*. Oxford: Clarendon Press.

Whitehouse, Harvey 1992. "Leaders and logics, persons and polities." *History and Anthropology* 6, no. 1:103–24.

Whittaker, C. R. 1994. *Frontiers of the Roman Empire. A Social and Economic Study*. Baltimore: Johns Hopkins University Press.

Whitting, P. D. 1973. *Byzantine Coins*. New York: Putnam.

Whittow, Mark 1990. "Ruling the late Roman and early Byzantine city: a continuous history." *P&P* 129:3–29.

1996. *The Making of Byzantium, 600–1025*. Berkeley and Los Angeles: University of California Press.

Wielowiejski, Jerzy 1987. "Depositi dell'ambra sul territorio tra la parte media del Danubio e il mar Baltico dal I secolo a.C. al V secolo d.C." *ArchPol* 25–6:75–84.

Wiessner, Polly 1983. "Style and social information in Kalahari San projectile points." *AAnt* 48, no. 2:253–76.

1985. "Style or isochrestic variation? A reply to Sackett." *AAnt* 50, no. 1:160–6.

1990. "Is there a unity to style?." In *Uses*, pp. 105–12.

Wiita, John Earl 1977. "The Ethnika in Byzantine military treatises." PhD Dissertation. University of Minnesota (Minneapolis).

Willems, Willem J. H. 1989. "Rome and its frontier in the north: the role of the periphery." In *The Birth of Europe. Archaeology and Social Development in the First Millennium AD.*, pp. 33–45. Ed. Klavs Randsborg. Rome: L'Erma di Bretschneider.

Willey, Gordon R. 1953. *Prehistoric Settlement Patterns in the Virú Valley, Peru*. Washington: Bureau of American Ethnology.

1989. "Settlement pattern studies and evidences for intensive agriculture in the Maya Lowlands." In *Archaeological Thought in America*, pp. 167–82. Ed. C. C. Lamberg-Karlovsky. Cambridge and New York: Cambridge University Press.

Williams, Brackette F. 1992. "Of straightening combs, sodium hydroxide, and potassium hydroxide in archaeological and cultural-anthropological analyses of ethnogenesis." *AAnt* 57, no. 4:608–12.

Wiseman, James R. 1984. "The city in Macedonia Secunda." In *Villes*, pp. 289–314.

Wobst, H. M. 1977. "Stylistic behavior and information exchange." In *For the Director: Research Essays in Honor of James B. Griffin*, pp. 317–42. Ed. C. E. Cleland. Ann Arbor: University of Michigan Museum of Anthropology.

Wojciechowski, Tadeusz 1873. *Chrobacja. Rozbiór starożytności słowiańskich*. Cracow: Akademia Umiejetnosci.

Wołagiewicz, Ryszard 1993. *Ceramika kultury wielbarskiej miedzy Baltykiem a Morzem Czarnym*. Szczecin: Muzeum Narodowe w Szczecinie.

Wolff, Larry 1994. *Inventing Eastern Europe. The Map of Civilization on the Mind of the Enlightenment*. Stanford: Stanford University Press.

Wolfram, Herwig 1981. "Gothic history and historical ethnography." *Journal of Medieval History* 7:309–19.

1987. *Die Geburt Mitteleuropas. Geschichte Österreichs vor seiner Entstehung 378–907*. Vienna: Siedler Verlag.

References

1988. *History of the Goths*. Berkeley, Los Angeles, and London: University of California Press.

1990. "Le genre de l'origo gentis." *RBPH* 68, no. 4:789–801.

Wood, Ian 1994a. "Fredegar's fables." In *Historiographie*, pp. 359–66.

1994b. *The Merovingian Kingdoms 450–751*. London and New York: Longman.

1995. "Defining the Franks: Frankish origins in early medieval historiography." In *Concepts of National Identity in the Middle Ages*, pp. 47–57. Ed. Simon Forde, Lesley Johnson, and Alan V. Murray. Leeds: University of Leeds.

Wozniak, Frank E. 1979. "Byzantine diplomacy and the Lombard-Gepidic wars." *BS* 20:139–58.

1982. "The Justinianic fortification of interior Illyricum." In *City*, pp. 199–209.

1987. "Nikopolis and the Roman defense of Epirus." In *Nikopolis*, pp. 263–7.

Yannopoulos, Panayotis 1978. *L'hexagramme, un monayage byzantin en argent du VII-e siècle*. Louvain-la-Neuve: Institut Supérieur d'Archéologie et d'Histoire.

1980. "La pénétration slave en Argolide." In *Etudes argiennes*, pp. 323–71. Athens: Ecole Française d'Athènes.

1993. "Métropoles du Péloponnèse mésobyzantin: un souvenir des invasions avaro-slaves." *Byzantion* 63:388–400.

Yelvington, Kevin A. 1991. "Ethnicity as practice? A comment on Bentley." *CSSH* 33, no. 1:158–75.

Ylli, Xhelal 1997. *Das slavische Lehngut im Albanischen*. Munich: Otto Sagner.

Yoffee, Norman 1993. "Too many chiefs (or, Safe texts for the '90s)." In *Archaeological Theory: Who Sets the Agenda?* pp. 60–78. Ed. Norman Yoffee and Andrew Sherratt. Cambridge: Cambridge University Press, 1993.

Young, Bailey K. 1992. "Text aided or text misled? Reflections on the uses of archaeology in medieval history." In *Text-Aided Archaeology*, pp. 135–47. Ed. Barbara J. Little. Boca Raton, Ann Arbor, and London: CRC Press.

Zábojník, Jozef 1988. "On the problems of settlements of the Avar Khaganate period in Slovakia." *ArchRoz* 40:401–37.

Zacek, Joseph Frederick 1970. *Palacky. The Historian as Scholar and Nationalist*. The Hague and Paris: Mouton.

Zaharia, Eugenia 1994–5. "La station no. 2 de Bratei, dép. de Sibiu (VIe–VIIIe siècle)." *Dacia* 38–9:297–356.

Zahariade, Mihail, and Andrei Opaiţ. 1986. "A new Late Roman fortification on the territory of Romania: the burgus at Topraichioi, Tulcea county." In *Akten 13*, pp. 565–72.

Zakythinos, Dionysios A. 1945. Οἱ Σλάβοι ἐν Ἑλλάδι. Συμβολαὶ εἰς τὴν ἱστορίαν τοῦ μεσαιωνικοῦ Ἑλληνισμοῦ. Athens: Aetos.

Zanini, E. 1988. "Confine e frontiera: il limes danubiano nel VI secolo." In *MILION. Studi e ricerche d'arte bizantina*, pp. 257–71. Rome: Biblioteca di Storia Patria.

Zasterová, Bohumila 1964. "Zu den Quellen zur Geschichte Wolhyniens und der Duleben im 6. Jahrhundert." In *Byzantinische Beiträge*, pp. 231–8. Ed. Johannes Irmscher. Berlin: Akademie Verlag.

1966. "Les débuts de l'établissement définitif des Slaves en Europe méridionale. Confrontation de la conception de L. Niederle avec l'état actuel des recherches." *VPS* 6:33–52.

1967. "Lubor Niederle historik." *ArchRoz* 18:153–65.

1971. *Les Avares et les Slaves dans la Tactique de Maurice*. Prague: Academia.

References

1976. "Zu einigen Fragen aus der Geschichte der slawischen Kolonisation auf dem Balkan." In *Studien*, pp. 59–72.

Zedeño, María Nieves 1985. "La relación forma-contenido en la clasificación cerámica." *Boletín de Antropología Americana* 11:19–26.

Zeiller, Jacques 1918. *Les origines chrétiennes dans les provinces danubiennes de l'Empire romain*. Paris: De Boccard.

Zeman, Jiří 1966. "Zu den chronologischen Fragen der ältesten slawischen Besiedlung im Bereich der Tschekoslowakei." *ArchRoz* 18:157–85.

1968. "Zu den Fragen der Interpretation der ältesten slawischen Denkmäler in Böhmen." *ArchRoz* 20:667–73.

1979. "K problematice časne slovanske kultury ve středni Evrope." *PA* 70, no. 1:113–30.

1987. "Böhmen im 5. und 6. Jahrhundert." In *Germanen*, pp. 515–27.

Zeuss, Kaspar 1837. *Die Deutschen und die Nachbarstämme*. Munich: Ignaz Joseph Lentner.

Zhekov, Gospodin 1987. "Dve imitacii na vizantiiski medni moneti ot VI vek." *Numizmatika* 21, no. 1:22–5.

Zheku, K. 1972. "Zbulime epigrafike në muret rrethuese të Kalasë së Durrësit." *Monumentet* 3:35–46.

Zirra, Vlad, and Gheorghe Cazimir 1963. "Unele rezultate ale săpăturilor arheologice de pe Cîmpul lui Boja din cartierul Militari." *CAB* 1:56–71.

Zoll-Adamikowa, Helena. 1980. "Die Verwendbarkeit der Grabfunde aus dem 6.–10. Jh. für die Aussonderung der Stammesgruppen bei den Westslawen." In *Rapports*, pp. 941–52. Vol. II.

1983. "Die oberirdischen Brandbestattungen bei den Slawen im Lichte der schriftlichen und archäologischen Quellen." *ArchPol* 21–2: 223–32.

Zubar', V. M., and Iu V. Pavlenko 1988. *Khersones Tavricheskii i raspostranenie khristianstva na Rusi*. Kiev: Naukova Dumka.

INDEX

Index

Index

Index

Index

Index

Index

Index

Index

Index

Index

Cambridge Studies in Medieval Life and Thought
Fourth series

Titles in series

★ *Also published as a paperback*